Eighth Edition

Principles of California Real Estate

Kathryn J. Haupt
David L. Rockwell

Rockwell Publishing Company

Copyright© 1996
By Rockwell Publishing Company
13218 N.E. 20th
Bellevue, WA 98005
(206)747-7272 / 1-800-221-9347

ISBN: 1-887051-02-3

PRINTED IN CANADA

Cover design: Kathy Bain

Table of Contents

Chapter 1

The Nature of Real Property and Estates in Land

 Outline

 Chapter Overview

Real estate agents are concerned not just with the sale of land and houses, but with the sale of real property. Real property includes the land and improvements, and it also encompasses the rights that go along with ownership of land. Furthermore, while an owner typically has full title to and possession of the property, there are many different kinds of ownership. An owner may have a more limited interest instead of full title, or may allow someone else (a tenant) to take possession of the property without taking title. The first portion of this chapter describes all of the components of real property and explains the distinction between real and personal property. The second part of this chapter explains the various types of ownership interests.

The Bundle of Rights

There are two types of property: **real property** (realty) and **personal property** (personalty). Real property is commonly described as land, anything affixed to the land, and anything incidental or appurtenant to the land. Sometimes it is referred to as "that which is immovable." Personal property, on the other hand, is usually movable. A car, a sofa, and a hat are simple examples of personal property.

The distinction between real and personal property is very important in real estate transactions. When a piece of land is sold, anything that is considered part of the real property is transferred to the buyer along with the land, unless otherwise agreed. But if an item is considered personal property, the sellers can take it with them when they leave.

Of course, the principal component of real property is land. But real property is more than just the surface of the earth. It also includes everything beneath the surface down to the center of the earth, and everything above the surface, to the upper reaches of the sky.

A parcel of real property can be imagined as an inverted pyramid, with its tip at the center of the globe and its base above the earth's surface. The landowner owns not only the earth's surface within the boundaries of the parcel, but also everything under or over the surface.

The rights and privileges associated with land ownership are also considered part of the real property. Think of real property as the land, plus a bundle of rights. The owner's bundle of rights includes the rights to use, lease, enjoy, encumber, will, sell, or do nothing at all with the land.

Appurtenances

In addition to the basic bundle of ownership rights, a landowner has appurtenant rights. An **appurtenance** is a right or interest that goes along with or pertains to a piece of land. A landowner may have any or all of these appurtenances:

- air rights,
- water rights,
- solid mineral rights,
- oil and gas rights, and
- support rights.

Appurtenances are ordinarily transferred along with the land, but the landowner can sell certain

appurtenant rights separately from the land. For example, the owner may keep the land but sell his or her mineral rights to a mining company.

Air Rights

In theory, a landowner's rights extend to the upper limits of the sky. In practice, however, this is no longer true. Congress, through the Air Commerce Act of 1926 and the Civil Aeronautics Act of 1938, gave the federal government complete control over our nation's airspace. A landowner still has the exclusive right to use the lower reaches of airspace over his or her property, but may do nothing that would interfere with normal air traffic.

On the other hand, sometimes air traffic interferes with a property owner's right to the normal use of his or her land. If aircraft overflights cause substantial damage to a property, the owner may sue the government for some form of reimbursement. The classic example is an airport built next door to a chicken farm. The noise and vibrations

Fig.1.1 The inverted pyramid

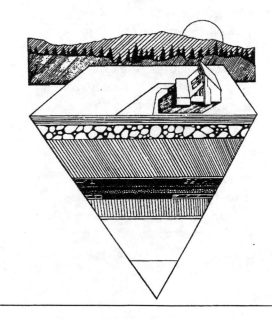

from overflights are so severe that the chickens no longer lay eggs. If the land cannot be used for any other reasonable purpose, the value of the land is significantly diminished. The landowner may be able to force the government to condemn the property and compensate him or her for its fair market value.

Water Rights

Water is found both on the surface of the earth and beneath the surface. Surface water may be confined to a channel or basin, or it may be unconfined water, such as run-off or flood water. The water beneath the surface may also be "confined" in the sense that it runs in recognizable underground streams, or it may collect in porous ground layers called aquifers.

There are two types of property rights that may apply to confined surface waters:

1. riparian rights, and
2. prior appropriation.

Riparian Rights. Riparian rights are the water rights of a landowner with respect to water that flows through or adjacent to his or her property. Such a landowner, called a riparian landowner, has a right to make reasonable use of the stream's natural flow. Riparian landowners generally have the right to use stream water for domestic uses, which include drinking, bathing, and irrigating a personal-use produce garden. Upstream landowners are prevented from substantially diminishing the flow in quantity, quality, or velocity.

Whether a riparian owner also owns the land under the stream depends on whether the stream or river is considered navigable. If the stream or river is navigable (used in commerce), the government owns the land under the stream, and the riparian landowner only owns the land to the mean high water mark of the streambed. If the stream or river is not navigable, the riparian owner owns the land

under the stream to the midpoint of the stream. When property borders on the ocean (or on a bay connected to it), the property owner only owns the land above the mean high water mark.

If a landowner's property is bordered by a lake rather than a river or stream, he or she is called a **littoral** owner. A littoral owner is entitled to have the natural purity of the lake's waters maintained, to have the lake maintained at its natural level, and to use the lake for fishing or recreation. A littoral owner does not own the lake bed—unless, of course, the lake is entirely within the boundaries of his or her property.

There is one important restriction on a riparian or littoral owner's water rights. A riparian or littoral owner may never divert water from a stream or lake for use on non-riparian land—that is, land that does not adjoin the lake or stream from which the water is taken.

> **Example:** Brown is a riparian landowner. She owns Lot C, a parcel of property that borders Swiftwater River. She also owns Lot D, a parcel of property that is about 300 feet inland. She cannot divert water from Swiftwater River to feed the livestock that graze on her non-riparian property, Lot D.

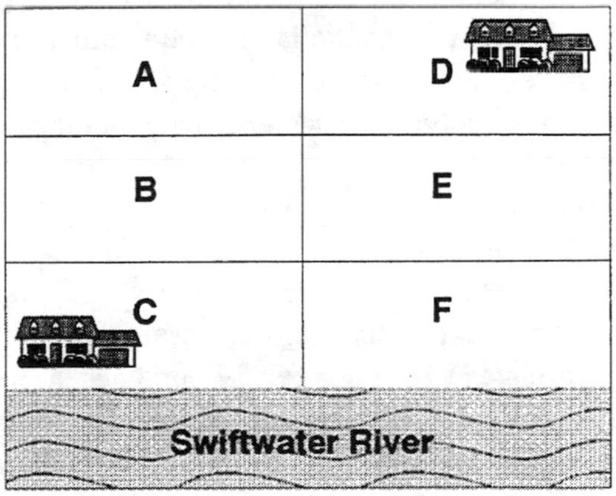

Fig.1.2 Riparian and non-riparian property

Appropriative Rights. Riparian and littoral rights are tied to the ownership of land bordering a body of water. The second major type of water rights, appropriative rights, do not depend on land ownership. Instead, appropriative rights are based on a permit system called the prior appropriation system.

To establish an appropriative right, someone who wants to use water from a particular lake or stream applies to the state government for a permit. It is not necessary for the applicant to own land beside the body of water. Water taken by a permit holder does not have to be used on property adjacent to the water source.

Water Rights in California. The appropriation system is primarily used in the western United States, where water resources are scarce and are therefore carefully controlled. This is certainly true of California. As a result of years of legislation and litigation, California has an extremely complex body of law that regulates the use of water in the state. The basis of this body of law is the system of prior appropriation, the most common method of obtaining water rights in California. California also recognizes a limited form of riparian rights.

Navigible Waterways. All navigable waterways in the United States are owned and controlled by the federal or state government. As mentioned earlier, the government owns the land underneath a navigable waterway. In addition, there is a public right of way on all navigable waters; the general public has the right to use the waterways for transportation and other reasonable purposes.

Ground Water. There are also different types of water rights that apply to ground water; the type of right correlates with the type of ground water. Ground water that runs in underground streams is governed by the same riparian rights rules as surface streams. On the other hand, percolating or diffused ground water found in aquifers is considered part of the land, and landowners have **overlying rights** to the ground water under their property. These overlying rights may be absolute, or they may be limited to reasonable use. Reasonable use means that the water may not be used on land outside of the ground water basin from which it is removed.

The appropriation system may also be applied to ground water. (A water table shows the depth at which ground water may be found.)

Solid Mineral Rights

A landowner owns all the solid minerals within the "inverted pyramid" under the surface of his or her property. These minerals are considered to be real property until they are extracted from the earth, at which point they become personal property.

Remember that a landowner can sell his or her mineral rights separately from the rest of the property. When rights to a particular mineral are sold, the purchaser automatically acquires an implied easement—the right to enter the land in order to extract the minerals.

Oil and Gas Rights

Ownership of oil and gas is not as straightforward as ownership of solid minerals. In their natural state, oil and gas lie trapped beneath the surface in porous layers of earth. However, once an oil or gas reservoir has been tapped, the oil and gas begin to flow toward the point where the reservoir has been pierced by the well. This is because oil and gas deposits are under great pressure and, when a well is drilled, the oil and gas migrate to the area of lower pressure around the well. A well on one parcel of land can attract all the oil and gas from the surrounding properties. Thus, a landowner could theoretically remove all the oil and gas from beneath adjoining properties without ever trespassing.

Ownership of oil and gas is governed by the "rule of capture." That is, a landowner owns all of the oil and gas produced from wells on his or her property. The oil and gas become the personal property of the landowner once they are brought to the surface. The rule of capture has the effect of stimulating oil and gas production, since the only way for a landowner to protect his or her interest in the underlying gas and oil is to drill an offset well to keep the oil and gas from migrating to the neighbor's wells.

Other Appurtenant Rights

In addition to rights concerning air, water, minerals, and oil and gas, there are some other important appurtenant rights.

A piece of land is supported by the other land that surrounds it. A landowner has **support rights**—the right to the natural support provided by the land beside and beneath his or her property. **Lateral support** is support from adjacent land, which may be disturbed by construction or excavations on the adjacent property. **Subjacent support**—support from the underlying earth—may become an issue when a landowner sells his or her mineral rights.

Easements and restrictive covenants create appurtenant rights. These are discussed in detail in Chapter 2.

Stock in a mutual water company is also considered appurtenant to real property. A mutual water company is a company that is created to secure adequate water supplies at reasonable rates for water users in a particular area. The company's stock is issued to the water users.

Attachments

You have seen that the land and appurtenances are considered part of the real property. The third element of real property is attachments. There are two types of attachments:

1. natural, and
2. man-made.

Natural Attachments

Natural attachments are plants attached to the earth by roots, such as trees, shrubs, and crops. Natural attachments that grow spontaneously, without the help of humans, are called fructus naturales; this includes all naturally occurring trees and plants. They are almost always classified as real property. Plantings cultivated by people are called **emblements**, or fructus industriales, and they are also a part of the real property. However, crops from emblements are treated as personal property. Thus, a cultivated apple orchard would be realty, but the apples themselves would be personalty.

A special rule, called the **doctrine of emblements**, applies to crops planted by a tenant farmer. If the tenancy is for an indefinite period of time and the tenancy is terminated through no fault of the tenant before the crops are ready for harvest, he or she has the right to re-enter the land and harvest the crops. If the crops are an annual product of perennial plants, such as pears or apples, the right to re-enter and harvest the fruit applies only to the first crop that matures after the tenancy is terminated.

Man-made Attachments: Fixtures

Articles attached to the land by people are called **fixtures**. Houses, fences, and cement patios are all examples of fixtures. Fixtures are considered part of the real property.

Fixtures always start out as personal property—for example, lumber is personal property, but it becomes a fixture when it is used to build a fence. So it is sometimes difficult to determine whether a particular item has become a fixture or is still personal property. If the item remains personal property, the owner can remove it from the property after selling the land. But if the item is a fixture, it is transferred to the buyer along with the land unless otherwise agreed.

Distinguishing Fixtures from Personal Property

Buyers and sellers often disagree as to exactly what has been purchased and sold. For instance, is the heirloom chandelier installed by the seller real property that is automatically transferred to the buyer, or can the seller take it with him when he moves out?

The easiest way to avoid such a controversy is to put the intentions of the parties in writing. If there is a **written agreement** between the landlord and tenant, buyer and seller, or lender and borrower stipulating how a particular item shall be treated—as part of the real estate or as personal property—a court will respect and enforce that agreement. The stipulation between a buyer and seller would normally be found in the purchase and sale agreement. For example, if a seller planned to take certain shrubs from the property before the transaction closed, he or she would need to include a statement to that effect in the sales agreement, since shrubs are usually considered part of the realty.

In the absence of a written agreement, courts apply a series of tests to classify the item in dispute. These tests include:

- the method of attachment,
- the intention of the annexor,
- adaptation of the item to the realty, and
- the relationship of the parties.

Method of Attachment. As a general rule, any item a person permanently attaches to the land becomes a part of the real estate. A permanent attachment occurs when the item is:

- annexed to the land by roots, as with trees and shrubs;
- embedded in the earth, like sewer lines or septic tanks;
- permanently resting on the land, as in the case of certain types of buildings; or

- attached by any other enduring method, such as by cement, plaster, nails, bolts, or screws.

It isn't absolutely necessary for an item to be physically attached to the real property in order to be considered a fixture. Often there is physical annexation even without actual attachment. The force of gravity alone may be sufficient, as in the case of a building with no foundation. Also, an article enclosed within a building may be considered annexed to the real property if it cannot be removed without dismantling it or tearing down part of the building.

Even easily movable articles may be considered "attached" to the real property, if they are essential parts of other fixtures. This rule is known as the doctrine of constructive annexation: an essential accessory is considered constructively annexed to the real property, even though it is not physically attached. For example, the key to the front door of a house is a fixture. The doctrine of constructive annexation also applies to fixtures that have been temporarily removed for servicing or repair. For example, a built-in dishwasher that has been sent to the repair shop is still constructively annexed to the house it is ordinarily attached to.

Intention of the Annexor. Over time, the courts decided that the "method of attachment" test was too rigid. It didn't allow for special situations where something permanently affixed would be classified more justly as personal property. Now, the "intention of the annexor" test is considered a more important criterion. Courts try to determine what the person who annexed the item to the property intended. Did he or she intend the item to become part of the realty or to remain personal property? Each of the other tests (including method of attachment) is viewed as objective evidence of this intent. For instance, permanently imbedding a birdbath in concrete indicates an intent to make the item a permanent fixture, while just setting it out in the yard does not.

Adaptation of the Item to the Realty. If an unattached article was designed or adapted specifically for use on a particular property, it is probably a fixture. Examples include pews in a church, or storm windows built for a particular building.

Relationship of the Parties. Intent is also indicated by the relationship between the parties: landlord/tenant, buyer/seller, borrower/lender. For example, it is generally held that a tenant who installs an item, such as new lighting, probably does so with the intention of removing it at the expiration of the lease. On the other hand, it's assumed that an owner making the same alteration is trying to improve the property and does not intend to remove the item. So an item that would be considered personal property if installed by a tenant might be considered a fixture if installed by an owner.

Items installed by a tenant so he or she can carry on a trade or business are called **trade fixtures**. Trade fixtures may be removed unless there is a contrary provision in the lease, or the fixtures have become an integral part of the land or improvement. In the latter case, if the tenant still wants to remove the fixtures, it is his or her responsibility to either restore the property to its original condition, or compensate the landlord for any physical damage resulting from the removal. Trade fixtures that are not removed by the tenant become the property of the landlord.

Fig.1.3 Fixture tests

Fixture Tests

- Written agreement
- Method of attachment
- Intention of the annexor
- Adaptation to the property
- Relationship of the parties

Mobile Homes as Fixtures

The distinction between fixtures and personal property has special significance in connection with mobile homes. Mobile homes have matured from trailers in parks to modern manufactured homes: roomy structures that can be set permanently on a full-sized lot. The efficient methods used in building manufactured homes make them significantly less expensive than traditional site-built homes—making home ownership a reality for more people.

A manufactured home is personal property until it is permanently attached to land by removing any wheels and mounting the unit on a concrete pad or other foundation. When they are still personal property, manufactured homes can be sold by a dealer without a real estate license, and the sales are subject to sales tax.

Once a manufactured home is permanently attached to the land, it will be taxed as real property, and its sale is no different from the sale of a site-built home. Many lenders offer financing programs for this type of property, with terms nearly identical to those offered for site-built homes. In cases where a lot is purchased with the intention of placing a new manufactured home on the site, the lender will finance the land purchase, the site improvements, the purchase of the home (from the dealer), and the labor costs to set up the home on the site.

The regulation of mobile homes is discussed in Chapter 4.

Estates

People can have many different types of interests in real property. The word "estate" refers to an interest in real property that is or may become possessory. In other words, someone has now, or may have in the future, the right to exclusively occupy and use the property.

Different types of estates are distinguished by two features: their duration (how long the estate holder has the right of possession); and time of possession (whether the holder has the right to possess the property right now, or not until sometime in the future). There are different names for each type of estate.

It is important to note that while all estates are interests in land, not every interest in land is an estate. Interests that are not estates are called nonpossessory interests or encumbrances; they are covered in Chapter 2.

> **Example:** A mortgage gives a lender a financial interest in the property—a lien—but this interest is not an estate, because it is not a possessory interest.

Estates fall into two categories:

1. freehold estates, and
2. leasehold (less-than-freehold) estates.

A **freehold estate** is an interest in real property that has an indeterminable (not fixed or certain) duration. The holder of such an estate is usually referred to as an owner. All other possessory interests are leasehold (less-than-freehold) estates. A **leasehold estate** has a limited duration (a one-year lease is an example). The holder of a leasehold estate is referred to as a tenant; a tenant has possession of the property but not title.

Freehold Estates

The freehold estate got its name back in the Middle Ages—it originally referred to the holdings of a freeman under the English feudal system. Freehold estates can be subdivided into fee simple estates and life estates.

Fee Simple Estates. The fee simple estate (also called the "fee," the "fee simple," or the "fee simple absolute") is the largest estate that can exist in land, the highest and most complete form of ownership. It is of potentially infinite duration and represents the whole "bundle of rights."

A fee simple estate is freely transferable and inheritable, so it is sometimes referred to as the **estate of inheritance**. A fee simple estate has no set termination point, and theoretically can be owned forever by the titleholder and his or her heirs. When a fee simple owner transfers title by deed, it is presumed that the grantee (the new owner) receives a fee simple absolute estate, unless the deed includes language that indicates an intent to confer a lesser estate (such as a life estate, described below).

Fee Simple Defeasible Estates. A fee simple estate may be qualified when it is transferred from one owner to another. For example, in a deed, the grantor may specify that the grantee's estate will continue only as long as a certain condition is met ("on the condition that the property is used as low-cost housing"), or until a certain event occurs ("until Aunt Jolene has a daughter"). If the requirement is not met, or if the event occurs, the new owner could forfeit title to the property. These types of estates are referred to as fee simple defeasible estates.

Fig.1.4 Characteristics of estates

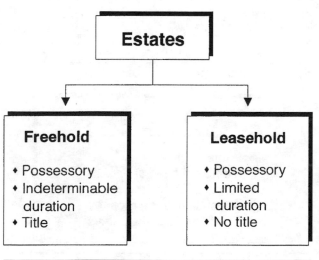

Until the 1980s, certain types of fee simple defeasible estates terminated automatically if the condition stated in the deed was not met. These types of estates were abolished by the California legislature. Now, the only type of defeasible estate recognized in California is called a **fee simple subject to a condition subsequent** (sometimes called a **conditional fee**). This estate does not end automatically when the condition is breached. Instead, the grantor must file a lawsuit to get the property back.

Life Estates. An estate for life is a freehold estate whose duration is limited to the lifetime of a specified person or persons.

> **Example:** Noel gives a parcel of property to Beatrice for her lifetime, calling for a reversion of title to Noel upon Beatrice's death. Beatrice is the **life tenant** (holder of the life estate), and the duration of the life estate is measured by her lifetime.

The measuring life may be that of the life tenant (as in the example above, where Beatrice's life is the measuring life), or it may be the life of another person. Suppose, for example, Angie gives a parcel of property to Howard for the life of Charlie. Howard has a life estate which will end when Charlie dies.

The fee simple estate is a perpetual estate; the life estate is a lesser estate because it is limited in duration. In granting a life estate, a fee simple owner transfers only part of what he or she owns, so there must be something left over after the life estate terminates. What remains is either an estate in reversion or an estate in remainder.

Estate in Reversion. If the grantor stipulates that the property will revert back to the grantor at the end of the measuring life, the grantor holds an estate in reversion. The grantor has a future possessory interest in the property. Upon the death of the person whose life the estate is measured by, the property will revert to the grantor or his or her heirs.

Estate in Remainder. If the grantor stipulates that the property should go to a person other than the grantor at the end of the life estate, that other person has an estate in remainder and is called the **remainderman**. The only difference between reversion and remainder estates is that the former is held by the grantor and the latter by a third party. The interest that will pass to the designated party at the end of the life estate is a fee simple estate. (If the grantor doesn't name a remainderman, an estate in reversion is created.)

Rights and Duties of Life Tenants. The life tenant has the same rights as the fee simple absolute owner, including the right to profits or rents, and the right to lease or mortgage the property. Similarly, the life tenant has the same duties as the fee simple owner: to pay taxes, assessments, and liens. But the life tenant also has certain additional duties because there is someone with a future possessory interest in the property:

- The life tenant must not commit **waste**, which means that the life tenant must not engage in acts that will permanently damage the property and harm the interests of the reversionary or remainder estate.
- The life tenant must also allow for the reasonable inspection of the property by the remainderman or grantor, who is permitted to check the property for possible waste.

The life tenant may transfer or lease his or her interest in the property. But it should be noted that the life tenant can only give, sell, or lease that which he or she has. In other words, a lease given by a life tenant will terminate upon the death of the person designated as the measuring life. The lease need not be honored by a remainderman. Similarly, a mortgage on a life estate loses its status as a valid lien upon the death of the person named as the measuring life.

Leasehold Estates

Less-than-freehold estates are more commonly known as **leasehold estates**. (They may also be called "chattels real.") The holder of a leasehold estate is the tenant, who does not own the property, but rather has a right to exclusive possession of the property for a specified period of time.

The leasehold is created with a **lease**. The parties to a lease are the **landlord** (**lessor**), who is the owner of the property, and the **tenant** (**lessee**), the party with the right of possession. The lease creates the relationship of landlord and tenant. It grants the tenant the right of exclusive possession, with a reversion of the possessory rights to the landlord at the end of the rental period. The lease is a contract and its provisions are interpreted under contract law.

Types of Leasehold Estates. The four most important leasehold estates are:

1. tenancy for a specific term (estate for years),
2. periodic tenancy,
3. tenancy at will, and
4. tenancy at sufferance.

Term Tenancy. A term tenancy, or estate for years, is a tenancy for a fixed term. The name "estate for years" is misleading in the sense that the duration need not be for a year or a period of years; it must only be for some fixed term.

> **Example:** Bob rents a cabin in the mountains from Clark for a period from June 1 through September 15. Bob has an estate for years (term tenancy) because the rental term is fixed.

A term tenancy terminates automatically when the term expires. Neither party is required to give notice to terminate the lease agreement. As with most contracts, a lease is assignable by the tenant unless the lease includes a no-assignment clause. (Assignment is discussed in Chapter 7.) If either party wants to terminate the lease before the end of the lease period, he or she may do so only if the other party consents. The termination of a lease by mutual consent is called **surrender**.

Fig.1.5 Types of estates

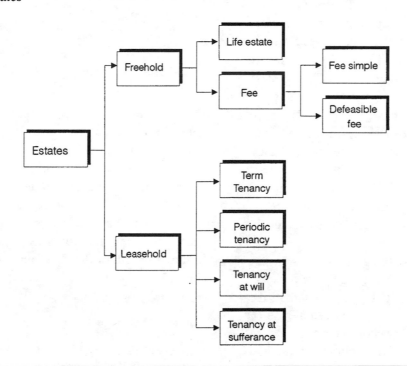

Periodic Tenancy. A periodic tenancy does not have a fixed termination date. A periodic tenancy lasts for a specific period (for example, one year, one month, or one week) and continues for successive similar periods (another year, month, or week) until either party gives proper notice of termination. Unlike a term tenancy, which terminates automatically, a periodic tenancy automatically renews itself at the end of each period, unless one of the parties gives notice. Failure to give proper notice results in the automatic extension of the lease for an additional period.

Like a term tenancy, a periodic tenancy is assignable unless assignment is prohibited by the terms of the lease agreement.

Tenancy at Will. A tenancy at will is usually created after a periodic tenancy or term tenancy has terminated. This estate is created with the agreement of both parties and can be terminated at the will of either. A tenancy at will often arises when a lease has expired and the parties are in the process of negotiating the terms of a new lease. The term of the tenancy is indefinite; it will continue until either party gives proper notice to terminate. The required notice period is usually prescribed by state statute. Note, however, that unlike the term tenancy or periodic tenancy, which are not affected by the death of the landlord or tenant, the tenancy at will automatically expires upon the death of either the landlord or the tenant. Also, the tenancy at will is not assignable.

Tenancy at Sufferance. The tenancy at sufferance is the lowest type of estate; in fact, though it is sometimes called an "estate at sufferance," technically it isn't an estate at all. In a tenancy at sufferance, a tenant who came into possession of the property lawfully, under a valid lease, holds over after the lease has expired. The tenant continues in possession of the premises, but without the consent of the landlord.

Example: Joe has a one-year lease with Landlord Sam. At the end of the term, Joe refuses to move out. Joe initially obtained possession of the property legally (under a valid lease), but he is remaining on the property without Sam's consent.

Tenancy at sufferance is simply a way to distinguish between someone who entered into possession of the property legally but no longer has a right to possession, and a trespasser, who never had permission to enter the property in the first place. Because a tenant at sufferance does not hold an estate (a possessory interest in the property), the landlord is not required to give the tenant notice of termination. Even so, the tenant cannot be forced off the property; the landlord must follow proper legal procedures for eviction (see Chapter 8).

Chapter Summary

1. There are two types of property: real property and personal property. Real property is the land, anything affixed to the land, and anything appurtenant to the land. Movable items, such as furniture, are usually personal property.

2. Appurtenances to land include air rights, water rights, mineral rights, oil and gas rights, and support rights.

3. Attachments may be natural (growing plants) or man-made (fixtures). The tests used to distinguish fixtures from personal property include provisions in a written agreement, the method of attachment, the intention of the annexor, the adaptation of the item to the realty, and the relationship of the parties.

4. An estate is a possessory interest in real property. Someone who has a freehold estate has title to the property and is considered an owner. Someone who has a leasehold (less-than-freehold) estate has possession of the property, but does not have title.

5. Freehold estates include the fee simple absolute, the qualified fee, and the life estate. A life estate lasts only as long as a specified person is alive; then the property either reverts to the grantor or else passes to the remainderman. Leasehold estates include the term tenancy, the periodic tenancy, and the tenancy at will. (The tenancy at sufferance, which arises when a tenant holds over without the landlord's permission, is not really an estate.)

Key Terms

Real property—Land, attachments, and appurtenances.

Personal property—Anything that is not real property; its main characteristic is movability.

Appurtenance—A right incidental to the land that is transferred with it.

Emblements—Crops, such as wheat, produced annually through the labor of the cultivator.

Trade fixtures—Personal property attached to real property by a tenant for use in his or her trade or business. Trade fixtures are removable by the tenant.

Riparian—The water rights of a landowner who owns land bordering on a stream or other surface water. Riparian water rights only allow reasonable use of the water.

Littoral land—Land bordered by a stationary body of water, such as a lake.

Lateral support—Support of a piece of land provided by the surrounding land.

Subjacent support—Support of a piece of land provided by the underlying earth.

Estate—An interest in land that is or may become possessory.

Freehold estate—A possessory interest that has an indeterminable duration.

Less-than-freehold (leasehold) estate—A possessory interest that has a limited duration.

Fee simple absolute—The highest and most complete form of ownership, which is of potentially infinite duration.

Fee simple subject to a condition subsequent—A fee simple estate that is subject to termination if a certain condition is not met or if a specified event occurs. Also called a conditional fee or qualified fee.

Life estate—A freehold estate whose duration is measured by the lifetime of one or more persons.

Remainder—A future interest that becomes possessory when a life estate terminates, and that is held by someone other than the grantor of the life estate (or the grantor's heirs).

Reversion—A future interest that becomes possessory when a life estate terminates, and that is held by the grantor (or his or her heirs).

Waste—Destruction, damage, or material alteration of property by someone in possession who holds less than a fee estate (such as a life tenant), or by a co-owner.

Lessor—One who leases property to another; a landlord.

Lessee—One who leases property from another; a tenant.

Term tenancy—A leasehold estate with a fixed term; also called an estate for years.

Periodic tenancy—A leasehold estate that renews itself at the end of each period unless one party gives the other notice of termination.

Tenancy at will—A tenancy that may arise after a periodic tenancy or a term tenancy terminates. It can be terminated by either party.

Tenancy at sufferance—A situation in which a tenant (who entered into possession of the property lawfully) stays on after the lease ends without the landlord's consent.

Chapter 1—Quiz
The Nature of Real Property and Estates in Land

1. Real property is equivalent to:

   a) land
   b) personal property
   c) land, attachments, and appurtenances
   d) land and water

2. The most important consideration in determining whether an article is a fixture is:

   a) physical attachment
   b) the annexor's intent
   c) adaptation of the article to the realty
   d) intended use of the article

3. Articles installed in or on realty by tenants for use in a business are called:

   a) fructus industriales
   b) trade fixtures
   c) emblements
   d) easements

4. A right that goes with or pertains to real property is called:

   a) an attachment
   b) an appurtenance
   c) personal property
   d) a fixture

5. A landowner's rights regarding water in a stream flowing through his or her land are called:

   a) riparian rights
   b) littoral rights
   c) appropriative rights
   d) easement rights

6. Minerals become personal property when they are:

   a) surveyed
   b) extracted from the land
   c) taken to a refinery
   d) claimed

7. Rights to oil and gas are determined by:

   a) the rule of capture
   b) the inverted pyramid
   c) the Bureau of Land Management
   d) the Department of the Interior

8. Whether land borders on a lake or stream is irrelevant under the system of:

   a) riparian rights
   b) capture rights
   c) littoral rights
   d) appropriative rights

9. A fee simple title in real estate is of indefinite duration, and can be:

   a) freely transferred
   b) encumbered
   c) inherited
   d) All of the above

10. A conveyance of title with the condition that the land shall not be used for the sale of intoxicating beverages creates:

    a) a less-than-freehold estate
    b) a defeasible fee
    c) a life estate
    d) a reservation

11. Mr. Lewis was given real property for the term of his natural life. Which of the following statements is incorrect?

    a) Lewis has a freehold estate
    b) Lewis has a fee simple estate
    c) Lewis is the life tenant
    d) If Lewis leases the property to someone else, the lease will terminate if Lewis dies during its term

12. Baker sold a property to Lane, but reserved a life estate for himself and remained in possession. Later Baker sells his life estate to Clark and surrenders possession to Clark. Lane then demands immediate possession as fee owner.

    a) Lane is entitled to possession
    b) Clark should sue Baker for return of the purchase price
    c) Baker is liable for damages
    d) Clark can retain possession during Baker's lifetime

13. Jacob deeds a property to Smith for the life of Jones. Which of the following is true?

    a) Jones holds a life estate; Smith holds an estate in reversion
    b) Smith holds a life estate; Jacob holds an estate in remainder
    c) Smith holds a fee simple estate; Jones holds a life estate
    d) Smith holds a life estate; Jacob holds an estate in reversion

14. Johnston, a life tenant, decides to cut down all the trees on the ten-acre property and sell them for timber. Mendez, the remainderman, can stop Johnston's actions on the principle that:

    a) a life tenant can never cut down any trees on the property for any reason
    b) a life tenant cannot commit waste
    c) Mendez's interest is superior to Johnston's because it is a possessory estate
    d) Mendez has no grounds on which to protest Johnston's actions

15. Ms. Jones and Ms. Adams signed an agreement for the use and possession of real estate, for a period of 120 days. This is a:

    a) term tenancy
    b) tenancy at sufferance
    c) periodic tenancy
    d) tenancy at will

Answer Key

1. c) Real property is made up of land, everything that is attached to the land (e.g., fixtures), and everything that is appurtenant to the land (e.g., water rights).

2. b) The intention of the party who annexed the item is the primary consideration in determining whether it is a fixture. The other tests provide evidence of the annexor's intention.

3. b) An article installed by a tenant for use in a business is called a trade fixture, and it remains the tenant's personal property.

4. b) An appurtenance is a right or interest that goes with the property. Riparian rights are an example.

5. a) Riparian rights include the right to reasonable use of the water that flows through a property owner's land.

6. b) When minerals are extracted from the land, they become personal property.

7. a) The rule of capture determines ownership of oil and gas. This rule provides that the landowner owns all the oil and gas removed from a well on his or her property, even if the oil or gas was originally beneath someone else's property.

8. d) To obtain a water appropriation permit, it is not necessary to own riparian or littoral land.

9. d) The fee simple owner has the full bundle of rights.

10. b) A defeasible fee is an estate that will fail if a certain event occurs or a certain condition is not met.

11. b) Although a life estate is a freehold estate, it is not a fee simple estate.

12. d) Baker was entitled to sell his life estate to Clark. Clark can retain possession during Baker's lifetime.

13. d) Smith has possession of the property for the duration of Jones's life, so Smith has a life estate. Because no remainderman was named, Jacob has an estate in reversion, and the property will revert to Jacob after Jones's death.

14. b) A life tenant cannot commit waste. In other words, the life tenant cannot damage the property or harm the interests of the remainderman.

15. a) A lease with a set termination date is a term tenancy (or estate for years).

Chapter 2

Methods of Holding Title and Encumbrances on Land

 Outline

I. Methods of Holding Title
   A. In severalty
   B. Concurrently
   C. Ownership by syndicates
   D. Condominiums and cooperatives
II. Financial Encumbrances (Liens)
   A. Types of liens
      1. mortgages
      2. deeds of trust
      3. construction liens
      4. judgment liens
      5. attachment liens
      6. property tax liens
      7. special assessments
      8. other tax liens
   B. Lien priority
   C. Homestead law
III. Non-Financial Encumbrances
   A. Easements
      1. types of easements
      2. creating an easement
      3. terminating an easement
   B. Profits
   C. Private restrictions
   D. Licenses
   E. Encroachments

 Chapter Overview

A property may be owned by more than one person at the same time. And an interest in real property may be held by someone other than the property owner; these interests are called encumbrances. No matter how many people own a single parcel of property, it almost always carries some encumbrances.

The first portion of this chapter explains the various ways co-owners can hold title. The second portion of this chapter describes types of encumbrances and the effects they have on ownership and transfer of property.

Methods of Holding Title

Title to real property may be held by one person, which is ownership in severalty, or it may be held by two or more persons at the same time, which is concurrent ownership.

Ownership in Severalty

When one person holds title to property individually, the property is owned in severalty. The term is derived from the word "sever," which means to keep separate or apart. A sole owner is free to dispose of the property at will. Real property may be owned in severalty by a natural person (a human being) or an artificial person (such as a corporation, a city, or a state).

Concurrent Ownership

Concurrent ownership (also called co-ownership) exists where two or more people simultaneously share title to a piece of property. There are several forms of concurrent ownership, each with distinctive legal characteristics. In California, there are four forms of concurrent ownership:

- joint tenancy,
- tenancy in common,
- community property, and
- tenancy in partnership.

Joint Tenancy. A joint tenancy exists where two or more persons are joint and equal owners of certain real property. Only one title exists and it is vested in two or more persons. The key distinguishing feature of this form of ownership is the **right of survivorship**: on the death of one of the joint tenants, his or her interest automatically passes by operation of law to the other joint tenant(s).

To create a joint tenancy, the "four unities of title" must exist. These unities are:

- unity of interest,
- unity of title,
- unity of time, and
- unity of possession.

These four unities signify that each joint tenant has an equal interest in the property (unity of interest), that each received title through the same deed or will (unity of title), which was executed and delivered at one time (unity of time), and that each holds undivided possession of the property (unity of possession). If any one of these unities does not exist when the tenancy is created, a joint tenancy is not established.

Each joint tenant has an equal interest in the property and an equal right to possess (occupy) the entire property. Therefore, use by a particular joint tenant cannot be confined to any specific part of the property.

Example: Two joint tenants own the property fifty-fifty; each has the right to possess and use the whole property at any time. One joint tenant cannot exclude the other from any part of the property.

Fig.2.1 Joint tenancy and the right of survivorship

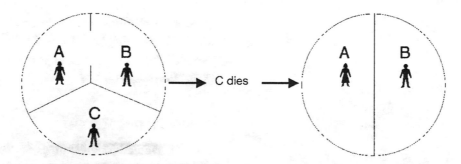

A, B, and C owned property as joint tenants, each with a ¹/₃ interest. Then C died. Now, by the right of survivorship, A and B own the property as joint tenants, each with a ½ interest.

Since title passes directly to the other joint tenant(s) upon the death of one joint tenant (because of the right of survivorship), property held in joint tenancy can't be willed. The heirs of a deceased joint tenant hold no interest in the joint tenancy property.

Example: Jones, Smith, and Brown own property as joint tenants. Jones dies. Smith and Brown now own the entire property fifty-fifty. Neither the heirs nor the creditors of Jones can make any legal claim to the property. On her death, it ceased to be a part of her estate. Accordingly, the property is not subject to probate and could not have been willed by Jones.

Termination of Joint Tenancy. A joint tenancy is terminated when any one of the four unities is destroyed. A joint tenant is not prevented from conveying his or her interest in the joint tenancy and may freely do so. However, the conveyance will destroy the unities of time and title. This terminates the joint tenancy with respect to the ownership of the conveying joint tenant.

Example: Aaron, Bob, and Caroline own a piece of property as joint tenants. If Aaron conveys his interest to Alice, that terminates the joint tenancy with respect to that one-third interest. Since Alice did not receive title through the same deed or at the same time as Bob and Caroline, Alice can't be a joint tenant. Bob and Caroline are still joint tenants in relation to one another, but Alice holds title as a tenant in common.

The advantage to holding property in joint tenancy is that the title passes directly to the other joint tenant(s) upon the death of one joint tenant. In this way, the normal delays and costs caused by probate proceedings are avoided. Also, the survivors hold the property free from the debts of the deceased tenant and also from the liens against his or her interest. However, there are disadvantages, such as the fact that a joint tenant gives up the right to dispose of his or her property by will.

Tenancy in Common. In contrast to joint tenancy, a tenancy in common involves only one unity: unity of possession. Tenants in common may have unequal interests in the property, but their interests are always undivided. That is, there could be a 60/40 division of ownership between two tenants in common, but each would have an equal right to possess the whole property. Regardless of the percentage of ownership, a tenant in common cannot be confined to any specific portion of the property. A tenant in

Fig.2.2 Tenancy in common

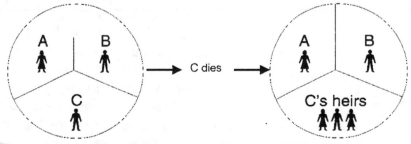

A, B, and C owned property as tenants in common. Then C died, and his heirs inherited his share of the property. Now the property is owned by A, B, and C's heirs as tenants in common.

common cannot be charged rent for the use of the land while in possession.

No right of survivorship attaches to the tenancy in common. Each tenant in common may transfer his or her title by will or deed. He or she may also mortgage his or her interest without the consent of the other owners. Such a transfer does not terminate the tenancy in common.

Termination of Tenancy in Common. A tenancy in common may be terminated by a **partition suit**, a legal action that divides the interests in the property and destroys the unity of possession. If possible, a court will actually divide the land into separate parcels. Often the property cannot be divided fairly, so the court orders the property sold and the proceeds divided among the tenants in accordance with their fractional interests.

Community Property. The community property system of ownership is of Spanish origin; for historical reasons, it is used in several western states, including California. In those states, all the property owned by a married couple is classified either as the separate property of one spouse or the community property of husband and wife.

A spouse's separate property is the property he or she owned before the marriage, and any property he or she acquires during the marriage by inheritance, will, or gift. All other property the husband or wife acquires during the marriage is community property. For example, property purchased with wages earned by either spouse during the marriage is community property.

A spouse's separate property remains his or her separate property even if it is used to purchase another type of property during the marriage.

Example: Susan accumulated $15,000 before her marriage. She left the money in a savings account and, after her marriage, did not deposit any additional funds into the account. The $15,000 plus accumulated interest remains her separate property. If she takes $10,000 out of the account and uses it to purchase some stock, that stock is her separate property as well.

The separate property of either spouse is free from the interests and claims of the other spouse; it may be transferred or encumbered without the approval or interference of the other spouse. Any conveyance or encumbrance of community property, however, requires the approval of both spouses.

In some states that do not have a community property system, married couples may hold title to property as tenants by the entireties. A **tenancy by the entireties** is quite similar to a joint tenancy, but there are some differences. A tenancy by the entireties can only be created by a married couple, and (unlike a joint tenant) a tenant by the entireties cannot convey his or her interest without the other tenant's consent. Tenancy by the entireties is not recognized in community property states such as California, and it has been abolished in a number of other states as well.

Tenancy in Partnership. The fourth form of concurrent ownership recognized in California is tenancy in partnership. Ownership takes this form when a busi-

Fig.2.3 Comparison of joint tenancy and tenancy in common

	Joint Tenancy	Tenancy in Common
Creation Presumed	No	Yes
Equal Possession	Yes	Yes
Equal Interests	Yes	No
Right of Survivorship	Yes	No
Ability to Convey Interest	Yes	Yes

ness organized as a partnership owns property. Partnerships are described in the next section of this chapter.

Forms of Business Ownership

The discussion so far has focused on ownership by individuals, whether in severalty or concurrently. Real property can also be owned by business entities.

A **syndicate** is a group of individuals who come together and pool their resources to carry out an enterprise. The syndicate, as such, is not a recognized legal entity. A syndicate may be a business association or a non-profit organization, and it may be organized in any one of these forms:

- as a partnership,
- as a corporation,
- as a limited liability company,
- as a joint venture, or
- as a trust.

The parties who create a syndicate usually decide which form of organization to use based on tax consequences and other considerations, such as the members' personal liability for the syndicate's debts. The form of organization affects how a syndicate holds title to real property.

Partnerships. A partnership is generally defined as an association of two or more persons, to carry on, as co-owners, a business for profit. There are two types of partnerships:

- general, and
- limited.

A **general partnership** is formed by a contract. Although the agreement need not be in writing, it is wise to spell out all the terms in a written agreement. If the agreement is not in writing, the partnership will be governed by the terms of California's Uniform Partnership Act. If the agreement is in writing, the terms of the written agreement will govern, instead of the terms of the Uniform Act.

The partners in a general partnership all share in the profits and management of the partnership. Unless otherwise agreed, each partner has an equal share of the profits and losses, and each has an equal voice in management and control of the business. Each partner can be held personally liable for the debts of the partnership.

Also, each partner is both a principal for and an agent of the general partnership for business purposes. Thus, the authorized acts of one partner (including the execution of legal documents) are binding on the partnership. Needless to say, a partnership is a fiduciary relationship; all the partners have a duty to act with utmost good faith toward one another. (See Chapter 5 for a discussion of agency.)

In general, all property acquired for the partnership's business is **partnership property**, owned by the partners as **tenants in partnership**. This is true whether title to the property is held in the partnership's name, or in the name of one or more of the partners. Unless otherwise agreed, each partner has an equal right to possess all partnership property for partnership purposes. Partnership property is not subject to the claims of creditors of individual partners; it can only be reached by creditors of the partnership.

When title to partnership property is held in the partnership's name, it must also be conveyed in the partnership's name. Since each partner is an agent for the partnership, any authorized partner can sign the deed.

A **limited partnership** is a partnership with one or more general partners, who have unlimited partnership liability and an exclusive right to manage the partnership, and one or more limited partners. Limited partnerships must strictly conform to the statutory requirements of the California Uniform Limited Partnership Act, and there must be a written limited partnership agreement.

A limited partner's personal liability is limited to the amount of his or her capital contribution to the business. A limited partner has no voice in management. In fact, if a limited partner does take part in the day-to-day control of the business, he or she may be held liable to the same extent as a general partner. Thus, a limited partner should be cautious about his or her participation in the business.

Corporations. A corporation is owned by its shareholders, individuals who purchase shares in the company as an investment. But the corporation is legally a separate entity from its shareholders. In the eyes of the law, a corporation is an "artificial person." It can enter into contracts, own property, and incur debts and liabilities, just like a natural person (a human individual).

A corporation is capable of perpetual existence; the death of a shareholder does not affect its operation. Corporate property is owned by the corporation in severalty, not by the shareholders. The shareholders own only a right to share in the profits of the business.

The main advantage to the corporate form of organization is that the liability of the shareholders is limited to the amount of their investment in the corporation. The main drawback to the corporate form of organization is double taxation. First the corporation must pay income taxes on any profits it generates. Then if the profits are distributed to the shareholders as dividends, the same money is taxed again as the personal income of the shareholders. Business investors can avoid double taxation by choosing a different form of organization, such as a partnership or a limited liability company.

A corporation formed under the laws of California is a called a **domestic corporation**. All other corporations, incorporated in other states or foreign countries, are called **foreign corporations**. Foreign corporations may conduct business in California, but they must obtain a certificate of qualification from the Secretary of State and must abide by any conditions and limitations that are imposed.

Limited Liability Companies. In the eyes of many business experts, a limited liability company (LLC) is the "best of both worlds." It combines many of

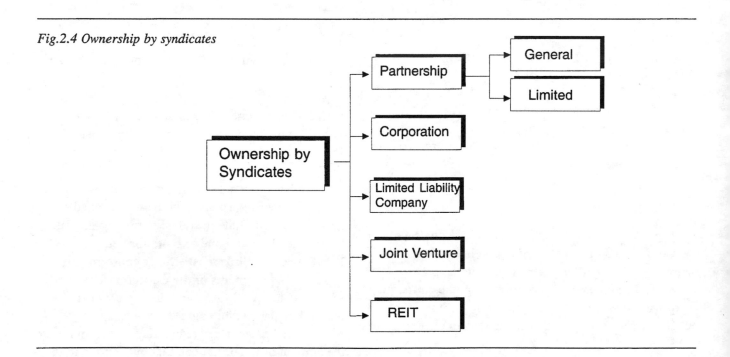

Fig.2.4 Ownership by syndicates

the advantages of a corporation with many of the advantages of a partnership.

An LLC is easily created. Two or more business owners (called members) draw up an LLC operating agreement and file articles of organization with the Secretary of State. LLC agreements can be quite flexible: members can choose virtually any manner of allocating income, losses, or appreciation among themselves. Once the LLC is created, annual statements must be filed with the state and an annual fee must be paid.

LLC members have the flexibility of a general partnership when it comes to managing the business. Certain members may be appointed to manage the company, or all of the members may manage the company. All managing members can bind the LLC with their actions. However, unlike the general partnership, all managing members are not personally liable for the company's contractual liabilities. LLC members have the same type of limited liability enjoyed by corporate stockholders or limited partners. Regardless of their level of participation in the company, LLC members risk only their initial investment in the company.

As noted earlier, a major disadvantage to the corporate form of ownership is the double taxation imposed on corporations and their stockholders. Income earned by an LLC, on the other hand, is taxed at only one level—the member level. LLC income is taxed as the personal income of each member, in the same manner as partnership income.

Joint Ventures. A joint venture is similar to a partnership, except that it is created for a single business transaction or for a series of individual transactions. It is not intended to be an ongoing business of indefinite duration. Joint ventures are generally governed by the same rules as partnerships. An example of a joint venture would be a property owner, an architect, and a building contractor joining together to design and construct a particular building.

Real Estate Investment Trusts. In a trust, one or more trustees manage property for the benefit of others (the **beneficiaries**). A trust instrument vests title to the property in the trustees, who have only the powers expressly granted in the instrument.

The Internal Revenue Code offers tax benefits to real estate investors who organize their syndicate as a real estate investment trust (REIT). An REIT must have at least 100 investors, and must invest exclusively in real estate and real estate mortgages.

Because an REIT is unincorporated, it avoids double taxation. As long as at least 95% of its income is distributed to the shareholders, the trust pays taxes only on the earnings it retains. Yet the investors, like corporate shareholders, are shielded from liability for the REIT's debts.

Condominiums and Cooperatives

Condominiums and cooperatives provide alternatives to ownership of a traditional single-family home. In a sense, they combine aspects of individual ownership with aspects of concurrent ownership.

Condominiums. Someone who buys a unit in a condominium owns the unit itself in severalty, but shares ownership of the common areas with other unit owners as tenants in common. Each unit owner obtains separate financing to buy his or her unit, receives an individual property tax bill, and may acquire a title insurance policy for the unit. A lien can attach to a single unit, so that the unit can be foreclosed on separately, without affecting the other units in the condominium.

An elected governing board usually manages the condominium, and monthly assessments are made to cover maintenance costs for the common areas. The sale of a condominium unit ordinarily does not require the approval of the other unit owners, and the seller's interest in the common areas passes to the buyer.

A condominium usually involves one or more multi-family residential buildings, but commercial and industrial properties can also be developed as condominiums. To establish a condominium, a condominium plan and declaration must be recorded. Condominiums are generally regulated as subdivisions (see Chapter 4).

Cooperatives. In a cooperative, ownership of the property is vested in a single entity—usually a corporation. The residents of the cooperative building own shares in the corporation, rather than owning the property itself. They are tenants with long-term proprietary leases on their units; they do not hold title to their units.

To establish a cooperative, the corporation gets a mortgage loan to buy or construct the building, and other funds are raised by selling shares in the corporation to prospective tenants. The rent that each tenant pays to the corporation is a pro rata share of the mortgage, taxes, operating expenses, and other debts for the whole property. The cooperative corporation is managed by an elected board of directors.

In many cooperatives, a tenant cannot transfer stock or assign his or her proprietary lease without the consent of the governing board or a majority of the members. This approval process is used to screen out undesirable tenants; however, discrimination in violation of fair housing laws is not allowed (see Chapter 15). Like condominiums, cooperatives are generally regulated as subdivisions.

Differences Between Condominiums and Cooperatives. In a condominium, each unit is owned individually. In a cooperative, a corporation owns the whole project; the tenants own shares in the corporation and have proprietary leases on their units.

In a condominium, each unit owner secures individual financing to buy the unit. In a cooperative, the corporation takes out one blanket loan for the entire project. One advantage of condominiums over cooperatives is that a condominium owner is not re- sponsible for any default on another unit owner's loan. In a cooperative, if one tenant defaults on his or her share of the mortgage payments, the other tenants must cure the default or risk having the mortgage on the entire project foreclosed. This is also true for tax assessments and other liens.

A condominium owner can usually sell his or her unit to anyone who can pay for it. In a cooperative, the corporation usually must approve of the proposed tenant.

Encumbrances

An encumbrance is a right or interest in real property held by someone other than the property owner. The interest can be financial or non-financial in nature. A financial encumbrance only affects title; a non-financial encumbrance also affects the use or physical condition of the property.

Financial Encumbrances (Liens)

Financial encumbrances are more commonly called liens. A **lien** is a security interest in property. A creditor obtains a security interest in the debtor's property; if the debt isn't paid off, the security interest allows the creditor to force the property to be sold, so that the creditor can collect the debt out of the sale proceeds. This is called **foreclosure.** The most familiar example of a lien is a mortgage.

A creditor who has a lien against (a security interest in) the debtor's property is called a **secured creditor.** The lien does not prevent the debtor from transferring the property, but the new owner takes title subject to the lien. The creditor can still foreclose if the debt is not repaid.

Liens may be voluntary or involuntary. A **voluntary lien** is one the debtor voluntarily gives to the creditor, usually as security for a loan. The two

Fig.2.5 Liens

	Voluntary	Involuntary
Specific	Mortgages Deeds of trust	Property taxes Special assessments Construction liens
General		Judgments IRS liens

types of voluntary liens are mortgages and deeds of trust. **Involuntary liens** (sometimes called statutory liens) are given to creditors without the property owner's consent, by operation of law. Examples of involuntary liens are property tax liens and judgment liens.

> **Example:** Mayer sues Bronson for $125,000 for injuries sustained in a car crash. Mayer wins the suit. The $125,000 judgment against Bronson can become a lien on his property.

Liens may also be general or specific. A **general lien** attaches to all of the debtor's property. An example would be the judgment lien discussed above. Any property owed by Bronson could be encumbered by the judgment. On the other hand, a **specific lien** attaches only to a particular piece of property. A mortgage is an example of a specific lien. It is a lien only against the particular piece of property offered as security for the loan.

Types of Liens

Here are brief descriptions of the most common types of liens against real estate.

Mortgages. A mortgage is a specific, voluntary lien created by a contract between the landowner (the **mortgagor**) and the creditor (the **mortgagee**). The mortgagee is usually a lender, who will not loan money unless the borrower gives a lien as security for repayment.

Deeds of Trust. A deed of trust (also called a trust deed) is used for the same purpose as a mortgage. However, there are three parties to a trust deed rather than the two found in a mortgage transaction. The borrower is called a **trustor** or **grantor**; the lender or creditor is called the **beneficiary**; and there is an independent third party (often an attorney or title insurance company) called the **trustee**. The most significant difference between mortgages and deeds of trust is in the foreclosure process. Mortgages and deeds of trust are discussed in more detail in Chapter 9.

Construction Liens. A person who provides labor, materials, or professional services for the improvement of real property may be entitled to claim a construction lien against the property. For example, if a plumber who is involved in remodeling a bathroom isn't paid, he or she can claim a lien against the property for the amount owed. Eventually, if necessary, the plumber could foreclose on the lien, forcing the property to be sold to pay the debt.

A construction lien is a specific, involuntary lien, attaching only to the property where work was performed or materials were supplied. Construction liens are often called **mechanics' liens**, and a construction lien claimed by someone who provides materials (as opposed to labor) is sometimes called a **materialman's lien**.

Many construction projects involve a complicated hierarchy of contractors, subcontractors, laborers, and materials suppliers, all of whom may be entitled to claim construction liens. However, before a construction lien can be successfully created, the lien claimant must comply with numerous statutory requirements.

Preliminary Notice. California law requires a lien claimant to give the property owner a preliminary notice of his or her right to claim a lien within 20 days after he or she begins providing services or materials. However, this notice is not necessary if the claimant has a contract directly with the owner. (The general contractor probably has a contract directly with the owner; the electrician, for example, probably does not.)

Claim of Lien. The period of time during which a claim of lien can be filed and recorded varies, depending on whether a notice of completion or notice of cessation has been filed by the property owner.

When a project has been completed, the property owner has ten days in which to file a **notice of completion** at the recorder's office. A project is considered completed:

- if the project is subject to acceptance by any public entity, on the date of that acceptance; or
- 30 days after all labor on the project has ceased.

A property owner is allowed to file a **notice of cessation** after all work on the project has been stopped for a continuous period of 30 days, regardless of whether the project is actually completed.

When the property owner files a notice of completion or notice of cessation, all construction liens must be filed and recorded within 30 days. The only exception to this rule is that the original or general contractor may file and record a lien within 60 days after the notice is filed. If the property owner fails to file a notice of completion or a notice of cessation, all construction liens may be filed and recorded up to 90 days after the work on the project has ceased.

Foreclosure. To foreclose a construction lien, the lienholder must file a court action within 90 days after the lien was filed and recorded. Otherwise, the lien automatically becomes null and void, and has no further force or effect.

Judgment Liens. Judgment liens are involuntary, general liens. If a lawsuit results in a money judgment against the loser, the winner (the judgment creditor) may obtain a lien against the loser's (the judgment debtor's) property. The lien attaches to all the property owned by the debtor in the county where the judgment was entered, and also attaches to any property acquired by the debtor during the lien period (the length of time the judgment creditor has to take action on the lien). The judgment lien may also be recorded in other counties in the state, if the debtor owns property in other counties.

Once a judgment lien has attached, the debtor must pay the judgment to free the property from the lien. If it's not paid, the property can be sold by a designated official to satisfy the judgment. To do this, the court issues a **writ of execution**.

Attachment Liens. When someone files a lawsuit, there is a very real danger that by the time a judgment is entered, the **defendant** (the party sued) will have sold his or her property and disappeared, leaving the other party with little more than a piece of paper. To prevent this, the **plaintiff** (the person who started the lawsuit) can ask the court to issue a writ of attachment. A **writ of attachment** directs the sheriff to seize enough of the defendant's property to satisfy the judgment the plaintiff is seeking. The writ of attachment is recorded and creates a lien on the defendant's real property pending resolution of the lawsuit.

Property Tax Liens. Property is assessed (appraised for tax purposes) and taxed according to its value (ad valorem). When property taxes are levied, a lien attaches to the property until they are paid. Property tax liens are involuntary, specific liens. (Property taxation is discussed in more detail in Chapter 4.)

Special Assessments. Special assessments result from local improvements, such as road paving or sewer lines, that benefit some, but not all, property owners within the county. The properties that have benefited from the improvement are assessed for their share of the cost of the improvement. The assessment creates an involuntary, specific lien against the property. (Special assessments are also discussed in Chapter 4.)

Other Tax Liens. Many other taxes, such as federal income taxes, estate or inheritance taxes, and gift taxes can result in liens against property.

Lien Priority

It is not unusual for a piece of property to have more than one lien against it. In fact, the dollar amount of all the liens may add up to more than the property will bring at a forced sale. When this happens, someone has to decide how to distribute the proceeds of the sale. Rather than allocating the money among all the lienholders in a pro rata fashion (proportionate distribution), the liens are paid according to their priority. This means that the lien with the highest priority is paid first. If any money is left over, the lien with the second highest priority is paid, and so forth.

The most common way to determine lien priority is by the date the lien was recorded. The lien that was recorded first will be paid first, even though another lien may have been created first.

> **Example:** Suppose Bakerman borrows money from two banks—$5,000 from National Bank on March 17, and $5,000 from State Bank on May 5 of the same year. Bakerman gives mortgages to both banks when the loan funds are received. If National Bank does not record its mortgage until July 14, but State Bank promptly records its mortgage on May 5, State Bank's lien will be paid before National Bank's in the event of foreclosure.

While the general rule is "first in time (to record), first in right," there are some exceptions to the rule; some types of liens are given special priority. In California, special priority is given to property tax and special assessment liens (they have priority over all other liens) and to construction liens (their priority is determined by the date the claimant began working on the project, even though the claim of lien was recorded later on).

The Homestead Law

Homestead laws are state laws that give homeowners limited protection against lien foreclosure. In California, the homestead law offers protection only against judgment liens. It does not apply to construction liens, tax liens, or liens for child support, or to voluntary liens—mortgages or deeds of trust.

A **homestead** is an owner-occupied dwelling, together with any appurtenant buildings and land. Homestead protection may be claimed by filing a **declaration of homestead** at the county recorder's office, or by claiming the exemption after the property has become subject to a judgment lien foreclosure proceeding. A declaration of homestead may be filed by the owner, the owner's spouse, or by a guardian, attorney-in-fact, or other person authorized to act on behalf of the owner.

Exemption. When a homestead declaration has been filed, the homestead property is exempt from judgment liens to the extent of the homestead exemption. Currently, the standard exemption is $50,000. The exemption for a member of a family unit is $75,000. The exemption is $100,000 if the debtor is over 65, over 55 and low income, married and low income, or unable to work because of a disability.

A judgment creditor cannot foreclose on a homestead unless the net value of the property is greater than the amount of the exemption. When a judgment lien is foreclosed and homestead property is sold, the sale proceeds are applied in the following manner:

1. to pay all liens and encumbrances not subject to the homestead exemption (a deed of trust, for example);
2. to the homestead claimant in the amount of the exemption ($50,000, $75,000, or $100,000);
3. to pay the costs of sale;
4. to the judgment creditor to satisfy the debt; and
5. any surplus to the homestead claimant.

Money paid to the former owner as a result of the homestead exemption is protected from judgment creditors after the foreclosure sale for up to six months, during which time the funds may be reinvested in another homestead property.

Termination. Homestead protection is terminated when the property is sold, when the homesteader files a declaration of abandonment, or when the homesteader files a declaration of homestead on another property. Funds from the voluntary sale of the homestead property (up to the amount of the homestead exemption) are protected from judgment creditors just as the proceeds of a forced sale are protected—for up to six months, to allow the homesteader to purchase another home.

Homestead protection does not terminate automatically on the death of the claimant. It continues for the benefit of the spouse, children, or other family members living on the property.

Non-Financial Encumbrances

While financial encumbrances only affect title to property, non-financial encumbrances affect the physical use or condition of the property itself. Thus, a property owner can find the use of his or her land limited by a right or interest held by someone else. Non-financial encumbrances include easements, profits, and private restrictions. We will also discuss licenses and encroachments in this section. While they are not actually interests in real property, they do have certain features in common with non-financial encumbrances.

Easements

An easement is a right to use another person's land for a particular purpose. It is a non-possessory interest in land. That means that the easement holder has a right to use the land, but has no title or right of possession. An easement is not an estate.

Example: A landowner has an easement across her neighbor's lot for access to the public road.

Fig.2.6 Types of encumbrances

Encumbrances

Financial
- mortgages
- deeds of trust
- construction liens
- judgment liens
- attachment liens
- property tax liens
- other tax liens

Non-Financial
- easements
- private restrictions
- profits

Fig.2.7 Easement appurtenant

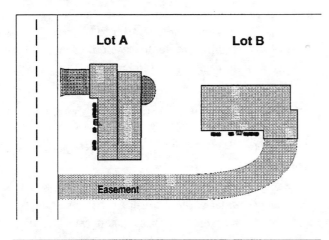

She has a right to make reasonable use of that easement to get to and from her property. However, she does not have the right to build a shed on the easement, or to use the easement in any way other than as a driveway.

Types of Easements. There are two main types of easements: easements appurtenant and easements in gross.

Easements Appurtenant. An easement appurtenant burdens one parcel of land for the benefit of another parcel of land. The parcel with the benefit is called the **dominant tenement**; the one with the burden is called the **servient tenement**. The owner of the dominant tenement is called the **dominant tenant**; the owner of the servient tenement is known as the **servient tenant**. Do not confuse the terms "tenement," which is the land, and "tenant," which is the landowner.

Probably the most common example of an easement appurtenant is a driveway easement providing access across one parcel of land to another. (This type of easement is sometimes referred to as an easement for ingress and egress. Ingress means a way into property and egress means a way out of property.) In Figure 2.7, Lot B has an easement appurtenant crossing Lot A. The easement provides access to a public road. Lot B is the dominant tenement. Lot A is the servient tenement.

An easement appurtenant passes with or "runs" with the land. This means that if either the dominant or servient tenement is transferred to a new owner, the new owner also acquires the benefit or the burden of the easement. Refer to Figure 2.7 again. If Lot B were sold, the new owner would still have an easement across Lot A. If Lot A were sold, the new owner would still bear the burden of allowing the owner of Lot B to use the easement.

Easements in Gross. An easement in gross benefits a person (a dominant tenant) rather than a parcel of land. Where there is an easement in gross there is no dominant tenement, only a servient tenement.

Example: Wilson (who owns no property) has the right to enter Able's land and fish in Able's stream. Wilson is a dominant tenant with an easement in gross over Able's land (the servient tenement). The easement serves Wilson and not a parcel of land.

Since an easement in gross belongs to an individual, and not a parcel of land, it is a personal right that is extinguished on the death of the dominant tenant. In the example above, when Wilson dies, the easement will disappear. A personal easement in gross may not be assigned by its owner to a third party.

Most easements in gross are commercial easements. The most common example is the easement held by a utility company, which allows company employees to enter property to install and service the lines. Because commercial easements in gross are considered more substantial interests than personal easements, they can be assigned from one utility company to another.

Creating an Easement. Easements can be created by any of these methods:

- express grant,
- express reservation,
- implication,

- prescription,
- reference to a recorded plat,
- dedication, or
- condemnation.

Express Grant. An easement is created by express grant when a property owner grants someone else the right to use the property. The grant must be put into writing and comply with all the other requirements for conveyance of an interest in land (see Chapter 3).

When granting an easement, the grantor does not have to specify the location of the easement. For example, a grant of an easement "across Lot A for purposes of ingress and egress" would be valid (assuming that all the other requirements for a proper conveyance are met).

Express Reservation. When a landowner conveys a portion of his or her property, he or she may reserve an easement in that parcel to benefit the parcel of land that is retained. Like an express grant, an express reservation must be in writing.

> **Example:** Carmichael owns 100 acres bordering a state highway. She sells 50 acres—including all the highway frontage. In the deed, she reserves to herself an easement across the conveyed land so that she will have access to the remaining 50 acres.

Implication. An easement by implication can be either an implied grant or an implied reservation. This type of easement can only arise when a property is divided into more than one lot, and the grantor neglects to grant or reserve an easement on one lot for the benefit of the other. There are two requirements for an easement to be created by implication:

1. it must be reasonably necessary for the enjoyment of the property, and
2. there must have been apparent prior use.

The second requirement is fulfilled if the use was established before the property was divided, and would have been apparent from an inspection of the property.

Prescription. An easement by prescription is created through long and continued use of land without the permission of the landowner. Acquiring an easement by prescription is similar to acquiring ownership through adverse possession. (See Chapter 3.) Here are the necessary elements of an easement by prescription:

- the use is **open and notorious** (apparent to the landowner);
- the use is **hostile** (without the permission of the landowner);
- the use is **reasonably continuous** for five years;
- the use is under some **claim of right**; and
- if **property taxes** are assessed separately against the easement, they are paid by the easement claimant for the five-year period.

Reference to a Recorded Plat. When a landowner subdivides and sells his or her land under a recorded plat, the lot purchasers acquire easements to use the roads and alleys shown on the plat.

Dedication. A private landowner may grant an easement to the public to use some portion of his or her property for a public purpose, such as a sidewalk. The dedication may be expressly stated or implied.

Condemnation. The government may exercise its power of eminent domain and condemn private property to gain an easement for a public purpose, such as a road. This power may also be exercised by private companies that serve the public, such as railroad and power companies.

Terminating an Easement. An easement can be terminated by:

- release,
- merger,
- failure of purpose,
- abandonment, or
- prescription.

Release. The holder of the easement (the dominant tenant) may release his or her rights in the servient tenement. This would be done by a written document, usually a quitclaim deed to the owner of the servient tenement.

Merger. Since an easement is, by definition, the right to make some use of another person's land, if the easement holder acquires ownership of the servient tenement, the easement is terminated through merger.

Failure of Purpose. If the purpose for which the easement was created ceases, then the easement terminates. For example, if an easement were created for a railroad and the railroad company removed the rails and discontinued its use, the easement would be terminated through failure of purpose.

Abandonment. An easement is also terminated if the easement holder abandons it. This requires acts by the holder indicating an intent to abandon the easement. Mere non-use is not abandonment.

Example: If the dominant tenant were to build a fence that blocked any further use of an easement that had been used for ingress and egress, it would be reasonable for the servient tenant to conclude that the easement had been abandoned.

Note that a servient tenant can bring a suit to have an easement terminated because of abandonment after 20 years of non-use. If the court finds abandonment, the easement will be terminated.

Prescription. An easement is extinguished if the owner of the servient tenement prevents the dominant tenant from using the easement for the statutory period of time (five years).

Example: The servient tenant builds a brick wall around his property. The dominant tenant can no longer use his easement for ingress and egress. If the wall remains undisturbed for five years, the easement will be terminated.

Profits

A profit is the right to take something from the land, such as timber, peat, or gravel. It must be created in writing or by prescription to be effective. The difference between a profit and an easement is that the easement is just a right to use another's land, but a profit allows the removal of something from the land.

Private Restrictions

Private restrictions (also known as deed restrictions) are restrictions on the use of a property that were imposed by some previous owner. For example, when selling a house long ago, a previous owner might have stated in the deed that the poplar trees in the front yard must not be cut down. Like easements, private restrictions can "run with the land," binding all subsequent owners of the property.

As long as a private restriction isn't unconstitutional, in violation of a law, or contrary to a judicial determination of public policy, it can be enforced in court. (An example of an unenforceable restriction is one prohibiting the sale or lease of property to non-white buyers—see Chapter 15.) If a deed restriction is found invalid—for example, because it is discriminatory—the deed will still be valid, but the restriction will be unenforceable.

Most subdivision developers impose a list of restrictions on all lots within the subdivision, before they begin selling individual lots. This is called a declaration of restrictions, or **CC&Rs** (covenants, conditions, and restrictions). The CC&Rs typically include rules limiting all the lots to single-family residential use, requiring property maintenance, and preventing activities that would bother the neighbors. The rules are intended to ensure that the subdivision will remain a desirable place to live.

It is up to the property owners within a subdivision to enforce the CC&Rs. If the residents have failed to enforce a particular restriction in the past, they may no longer be able to enforce it.

Example: The subdivision's CC&Rs state that recreational vehicles may not be parked within

Fig.2.8 Encroachments

TOOL SHED
ENCROACHMENT

OVERHANGING TREE LIMBS

PATIO BUILT OVER PROPERTY LINE

view of the street. Over the years, however, many homeowners have broken this rule and their neighbors haven't complained. If someone tries to start enforcing the parking restriction now, a court might rule that it has been abandoned and is no longer enforceable.

Covenants vs. Conditions. A private restriction is either a covenant or a condition. A **covenant** is a promise to do or not do something, as in a contract. A property owner who violates a covenant may be sued, leading to an injunction (a court order directing the owner to comply with the covenant) or payment of damages for failure to comply. Violation of a **condition** can have more serious consequences. A condition in a deed makes the grantee's title conditional, so that he or she owns a defeasible fee (rather than a fee simple absolute—see Chapter 1). Breach of the condition could result in forfeiture of title.

Whether a particular restriction is a covenant or a condition depends on the wording in the deed. Courts try to avoid forfeitures, so they will usually interpret a restriction as a covenant rather than a condition, if there is any ambiguity. (CC&Rs are virtually always covenants, even though the term includes the word "conditions.")

Licenses

Like an easement, a license gives someone the right to make some use of another person's land. However, easements and licenses are different in many ways. An easement must be created in writing or through action of law. Ordinarily, a license is just oral permission to cross, hunt, fish on, or make some other use of a landowner's property. An easement is irrevocable. A license can be revoked at the will of the landowner. In general, easements are permanent, and licenses are temporary. A license is a personal right that does not run with or pass with the land. It cannot be assigned. Since the license is revocable at the will of the landowner, it is not actually considered an encumbrance or an interest in the property.

Encroachments

An encroachment is a physical object that is wholly or partially on someone else's property, such as a fence or garage built partially over the property line onto the neighbor's land. Most encroachments are unintentional—the result of miscalculation or poor planning.

An encroachment may be a **trespass** if it violates the neighboring owner's right to possession. A court can order an encroachment to be removed, or if the cost of the removal would be too high, it could order the encroacher to pay damages to the neighbor. There is a three year statute of limitations on bringing a court action for trespass on real property. That means that the property owner must bring suit within three years of the time he or she discovered (or should have discovered) the encroachment, or the right to sue for damages or the removal of the encroachment will be lost.

Chapter Summary

1. Title to real property can be held in severalty or concurrently. In California, the methods of concurrent ownership are joint tenancy, tenancy in common, community property, and tenancy in partnership. The distinguishing feature of joint tenancy is the right of survivorship.

2. Real property can be owned by a syndicate, which may be organized as a general or limited partnership, a corporation, a limited liability company, a joint venture, or a real estate investment trust.

3. In a condominium, each unit is separately owned, and all the unit owners own the common areas as tenants in common. A cooperative is owned by a corporation; a resident owns shares in the corporation, and has a proprietary lease for a particular unit.

4. An encumbrance is a right or interest in real property held by someone other than the property owner. Encumbrances may be financial (liens) or non-financial (easements, profits, private restrictions).

5. A financial encumbrance (lien) affects the title to the property. It gives a creditor the right to sell the property and use the proceeds to pay off a debt if the debtor fails to repay it. A lien may be voluntary or involuntary, general or specific. The most common types of liens include mortgages, deeds of trust, construction liens, tax liens, and judgment liens.

6. A non-financial encumbrance affects the use or possession of the property. For example, an easement gives the easement holder the right to use portions of someone else's property for certain purposes. Private restrictions affect how an owner may use his or her own property.

7. An encroachment is a physical object that is wholly or partially on someone else's property.

O—🔑 Key Terms

Ownership in severalty—Sole ownership of property.

Joint tenancy—Joint ownership with right of survivorship.

Tenancy in common—Joint ownership where there is no right of survivorship.

Community property—Property owned jointly by husband and wife (in California and other community property states).

Partnership—An association of two or more persons to carry on a business for profit.

Corporation—An artificial person; a legal entity separate from its shareholders.

Limited liability company—A form of business entity that offers its members tax benefits and limited liability.

Real estate investment trust—A trust that invests exclusively in real estate and real estate mortgages.

Encumbrance—A right or interest in real property held by someone other than the property owner.

Voluntary lien—A security interest given to a creditor voluntarily.

Involuntary lien—A security interest given to a creditor through operation of law.

General lien—A lien that attaches to all of a debtor's property.

Specific lien—A lien that attaches only to one particular piece of property.

Construction lien—A lien on property in favor of someone who provided labor or materials to improve it; also called a mechanic's lien or materialman's lien.

Easement—The right to use another's land for a particular purpose.

Easement appurtenant—An easement that benefits and runs with a parcel of land, the dominant tenement.

Easement in gross—An easement that benefits an individual rather than a parcel of land.

Easement by implication—An easement created automatically because it is necessary for the enjoyment of the benefited land.

Prescriptive easement—An easement created by continuous use for the statutory period, without the landowner's permission.

Merger—When both the dominant and servient tenements are acquired by one owner, resulting in termination of the easement.

Abandonment—A method of terminating an easement; it requires action by the easement holder, not simply non-use.

License—Revocable permission to enter another's land, which does not create an interest in the property.

Profit—The right to take something (such as minerals) from another's land.

CC&Rs—Covenants, conditions, and restrictions; private restrictions imposed by a subdivision developer.

Condition—A restriction on the use of land, the violation of which may result in forfeiture of title.

Covenant—A promise by a landowner to refrain from using his or her land in a particular manner.

Encroachment—A physical object that intrudes onto another's property, such as a tree branch or a fence.

Chapter 2—Quiz
Methods of Holding Title and Encumbrances on Land

1. The four unities of title, time, interest, and possession are necessary for a:

   a) tenancy in common
   b) partnership
   c) mortgage
   d) joint tenancy

2. Which of the following is wrong or doesn't make sense? Joint tenants always have:

   a) equal rights to possession of the property
   b) the right to will good title to heirs
   c) the right of survivorship
   d) equal interests in the property

3. A, B, and C own property as joint tenants. C dies and B sells her interest in the property to D. The property is now owned:

   a) as joint tenants by A, D, and C's widow E, his sole heir
   b) by A and D as joint tenants
   c) by A and D as tenants in common
   d) None of the above

4. Real estate property taxes are:

   a) general, involuntary liens
   b) general, voluntary liens
   c) specific, voluntary liens
   d) specific, involuntary liens

5. A lawsuit against Mr. Thatcher is pending. The court rules that a lien should be placed on his farm, holding it as security in case of a negative judgment. This is:

   a) adverse possession
   b) prescription
   c) attachment
   d) appurtenance

6. Which of the following has priority over a mortgage that has already been recorded?

   a) A deed of trust
   b) A judgment lien
   c) A property tax lien
   d) None of the above

7. If there were two trust deeds against the same property and you wished to find out which one had higher priority, you could find this information at the county recorder's office. The priority is usually established by:

   a) the printed trust deed forms, which have the words "first trust deed" and "second trust deed" on their face
   b) the date and time of recording
   c) the county auditor's stamp, which says "first trust deed" or "second trust deed"
   d) the execution date of each document

8. When there's an easement appurtenant, the dominant tenement:

   a) can only be used for purposes of ingress and egress
   b) is burdened by the easement
   c) receives the benefit of the easement
   d) cannot be sold

9. You have the right to cross another's land to get to your house. You probably own:

   a) a dominant tenement
   b) a servient tenement
   c) Both of the above
   d) Neither of the above

10. An easement in gross benefits:

    a) a dominant tenement
    b) a servient tenement
    c) Both of the above
    d) Neither of the above

11. One difference between a commercial easement in gross and a personal easement in gross is that the commercial easement in gross:

    a) is not an encumbrance
    b) is considered a possessory interest in real property
    c) can be assigned to another party
    d) can be revoked by the owner of the servient tenement

12. Which of the following is not a method of creating an easement?

    a) Implication
    b) Express grant in a deed
    c) Dedication
    d) Spoken grant

13. The creation of an easement by prescription is similar to acquiring ownership of property by:

    a) adverse possession
    b) escheat
    c) alluvium
    d) intestate succession

14. A has an easement over B's property. If A buys B's property, the easement:

    a) goes with the land
    b) is terminated
    c) is unaffected
    d) None of the above

15. A porch or balcony that hangs over the established boundary line of a parcel of land is called:

    a) an easement in gross
    b) an encroachment
    c) an easement appurtenant
    d) a license

Answer Key

1. d) A valid joint tenancy requires all four unities: title, time, interest, possession.

2. b) A joint tenant cannot will his or her interest in the property. The right of survivorship means the surviving joint tenants acquire the deceased tenant's title.

3. c) When C dies, his interest in the property goes to A and B. When B sells her interest to D, the joint tenancy is terminated and a tenancy in common is created between A and D.

4. d) Property tax liens are specific (they attach only to the taxed property) and involuntary.

5. c) In an attachment, a lien is created against the defendant's property, pending the outcome of the lawsuit.

6. c) Property tax liens always have priority over other liens.

7. b) The time of recording governs lien priority, rather than the time of the execution of the documents.

8. c) The dominant tenement is benefited by the easement; the servient tenement is burdened by the easement.

9. a) Since you have the right to use another's property to reach your own, you probably own a dominant tenement.

10. d) An easement in gross benefits an individual—the dominant tenant—rather than any parcel of land. There is no dominant tenement.

11. c) A commercial easement in gross can be assigned to another party, but a personal easement in gross cannot be.

12. d) Like any other interest in land, an easement must be granted in writing unless it is created by operation of law.

13. a) You obtain an easement by prescription in much the same way as you obtain ownership by adverse possession: the use must be open and notorious, hostile, and continuous for five years.

14. b) The principle of merger means that when one person acquires ownership of both the dominant tenement and the servient tenement, the easement is terminated.

15. b) An overhanging porch or balcony is an encroachment.

Chapter 3

How to Transfer Real Property

 Outline

 Chapter Overview

A property owner may transfer property to someone else by choice, as when an owner deeds property to a buyer or wills it to a friend. Property may also be transferred involuntarily, as in a foreclosure sale or a condemnation. This chapter describes the various types of transfers, voluntary and involuntary. It also discusses how and why deeds and other documents are recorded, and how title insurance works. The final section of the chapter explains methods of legal description—how a parcel of land is identified in a deed.

Introduction

The process of transferring ownership of real property from one party to another is called **alienation**. Alienation may be either voluntary or involuntary. Voluntary alienation includes transferring property by deed or will. Involuntary alienation (a transfer of property without any action by the owner) can be the result of rules of law, accession, or occupancy (the process of adverse possession).

Voluntary Alienation

Patents

Title to all real property originates with the sovereign government. The government holds absolute title to all the land within its boundaries, except what it grants to various other entities or persons. Title to land passes from the government to a private party by a document known as a **patent**. The patent is the ultimate source of title for all the land under private ownership.

Deeds

The most common form of voluntary alienation is transfer by deed. With a deed, the owner of real property, called the **grantor**, conveys all or part of his or her interest in the property to another party, called the **grantee**. The process of transferring real property by deed is known as **conveyance**. A grantor conveys real property to a grantee by means of a deed.

Types of Deeds. There are many different types of deeds, but the ones used most often in California are the grant deed, the quitclaim deed, the trustee's deed, and the court-ordered deed.

Grant Deed. The grant deed is the most commonly used deed in California. A grant deed uses the term "grant" in its words of conveyance and carries two warranties:

1. the grantor has not previously conveyed title to anyone else, and
2. the grantor has not caused any encumbrances to attach to the property other than those already disclosed.

These two basic warranties apply even if they are not expressly stated in the grant deed. Additional warranties and covenants (promises) may be stated in the deed if the parties so desire. The grant deed also conveys to the grantee all **after-acquired** title of the grantor. This means that if the grantor's title was defective at the time of transfer, but the grantor later acquires a more perfect title, the additional interest passes automatically to the grantee under the original deed.

Quitclaim Deed. The quitclaim deed contains no warranties of any sort and does not convey after-acquired title. It conveys only the interest the grantor has when the deed is delivered. It may convey nothing at all, if the grantor has no interest at that time. But if the grantor does have an interest in the property, the quitclaim deed will convey that interest equally as well as any other type of deed.

The usual reason for using a quitclaim deed is to cure "clouds" on the title. A cloud is a title defect, often the result of a technical flaw in an earlier conveyance. Perhaps the name of one of the parties was misspelled, or the land was inaccurately described. A quitclaim deed is also used when the grantor is unsure of the validity of his or her title and wishes to avoid any warranties in that regard

> **Example:** Smith holds title by virtue of an inheritance that is being challenged in probate court. If Smith wants to transfer the property, she will probably use a quitclaim deed, because she is not sure that her title is valid.

In a quitclaim deed, words such as "grant" or "convey" should be avoided. The use of these words may imply that the grantor is warranting the title. A quitclaim deed should use only terms such as "release," "remise," or "quitclaim" to describe the transfer of the estate.

Trustee's Deed. When a property is foreclosed under a deed of trust, the trustee conveys the property to the buyer at the foreclosure sale with a trustee's deed. The trustee's deed states that the conveyance is in accordance with the trustee's powers and responsibilities under the deed of trust. (Deeds of trust are discussed in Chapter 9.)

Deeds Executed by Court Order. Court-ordered deeds are used after a court-ordered sale of property.

Fig.3.1 Grant deed

RECORDING REQUESTED BY

AND WHEN RECORDED MAIL THIS DEED AND, UNLESS
OTHERWISE SHOWN BELOW, MAIL TAX STATEMENTS TO:

NAME

STREET
ADDRESS

CITY,
STATE
ZIP

Title Order No.............. Escrow No.................

This space for Recorder's use

GRANT DEED

THE UNDERSIGNED GRANTOR(s) DECLARE(s)
DOCUMENTARY TRANSFER TAX is $_____

☐ computed on full value of property conveyed, or
☐ computed on full value less value of liens or encumbrances remaining at time of sale, and

FOR A VALUABLE CONSIDERATION, receipt of which is hereby acknowledged,

hereby GRANT(S) to

the following described real property in the
County of _____ , State of California:

Dated _____

_____

_____

_____

_____

STATE OF CALIFORNIA
COUNTY OF _____ } SS.
On _____ before me, the under-
signed, a Notary Public in and for the said State, personally appeared

known to me to be the person(s) whose name(s) is (are) subscribed
to the within instrument and acknowledged that..................................
executed the same. Witness my hand and official seal.
Signature _____

(Space above for official notarial seal)

MAIL TAX STATEMENTS TO PARTY SHOWN ON FOLLOWING LINE; IF NO PARTY SHOWN, MAIL AS DIRECTED ABOVE

| Name | Street Address | City & State |

A common example is the sheriff's deed used to transfer property to the highest bidder at a court-ordered foreclosure sale (see Chapter 9). Court-ordered deeds usually state the exact amount of the purchase price approved by the court, and carry no warranties of title.

Other Deeds. Two other types of deeds, the **warranty deed** and the **special warranty deed**, are rarely used in California. The warranty deed gives the greatest protection to a real estate buyer. Under a warranty deed, the grantor makes five basic promises, or covenants, to the grantee. These covenants warrant against defects in the title that arose either before or during the grantor's period of ownership (tenure).

The special warranty deed contains the same covenants found in the general warranty deed, but the scope of the covenants is limited to defects that arose during the grantor's tenure. The grantor makes no assurances regarding defects that may have existed before he or she obtained title. This type of deed may be used by entities such as corporations, which may not have the authority to make further warranties.

Requisites of a Valid Deed. To be valid, a deed must:

- be in writing,
- identify the parties,
- be signed by a competent grantor,
- have a living grantee,
- contain words of conveyance (the granting clause), and
- include an adequate description of the property.

In Writing. The statute of frauds is a state law that requires certain contracts and other legal transactions to be in writing. With only a few minor exceptions, the statute of frauds applies to any transfer of an interest in real property. An unwritten deed cannot transfer title; it has no legal effect.

Identification of the Parties. Both the grantor and the grantee must be identified in the deed. The name of the grantee is not required, as long as an adequate description is given; for example, "John Smith's only sister."

Signed by a Competent Grantor. The grantor must sign the deed. In addition to requiring a deed to be in writing, the statute of frauds also requires the deed to be signed by the party to be bound by the transfer.

If the grantor can't sign his or her full name (because of disability or illiteracy), he or she may sign by making a mark. But a signature by mark must be accompanied by the signatures of witnesses who can attest to the grantor's execution of the deed.

Deeds from corporations are usually signed by an authorized officer of the corporation, and the signature must be accompanied by the corporate seal.

If there is more than one grantor, all of the grantors must sign the deed. If a prior deed named several grantees, all of them must sign as grantors of a new deed. The signatures of both the husband and the wife are required to convey community property (see Chapter 2). For this reason, it is a good idea (although not required) to state the grantor's marital status in the deed and to obtain the spouse's signature if the grantor is married, even if the property is not community property.

A grantor must be legally competent when he or she signs the deed. This means that the grantor must be an adult (at least 18 years old) and sane. If the grantor is not competent, the deed is not valid.

Living Grantee. The grantee does not have to be competent in order for the deed to be valid. It is only necessary for the grantee to be alive (or, if the grantee is a corporation, legally in existence) and identifiable when the deed is executed.

Words of Conveyance. The requirement of words of conveyance, the granting clause, is easily satisfied. One word—"grant"—or a similar word is sufficient. Additional technical language usually does more harm than good, and should be avoided since it adds nothing to the validity of the deed.

Description of the Property. A valid deed must contain an adequate description of the property to

Fig.3.2 Deed requirements

A Valid Deed (in writing)	
I hereby grant	. . . words of conveyance
Green Farm	. . . adequate description of property
to Harry Tucker.	. . . identifiable, living grantee
(signed) Sam Smith	. . . signature of competent grantor

be conveyed. A legal description of the property should always be included. Land description is discussed in depth later in this chapter.

Acknowledgment, Delivery, and Acceptance. To successfully convey property, more than a valid deed is necessary; a proper conveyance also requires acknowledgment,* delivery, and acceptance.

Acknowledgment occurs when the grantor swears before a witness (usually a notary public) that his or her signature is genuine and made voluntarily. The witness cannot be a person who has an interest in the transfer. For example, if Grandma deeds her property to Granddaughter, who is a notary public, Granddaughter cannot acknowledge the deed.

A valid deed becomes effective, so that title is transferred, when the deed is **delivered** to the grantee. Delivery must occur while the grantor is alive.

> **Example:** When Sam Wiggins died, a deed was found in his safety deposit box. The deed transferred his property to his nephew, Frank Wiggins. The deed was void because it was not delivered during Sam's lifetime.

Delivery is more than the mere physical transfer of the document; the grantor's intent is a key element of delivery. The grantor must have the intention of immediately transferring title to the grantee. The conveyance is completed when the grantee accepts delivery of the deed. The grantee may accept delivery of the deed through an agent.

> **Example:** Clark deeds his property to Martinez. Clark hands the deed to Martinez's attorney, intending to immediately transfer ownership to Martinez. This is considered delivery to an agent of the grantee, and the transfer is effective.

Because this area involves some complicated legal issues, a real estate lawyer should always be consulted when there is a question concerning delivery.

Nonessential Terms. There are some elements that should be included in a deed, even though they aren't required. A deed should include a **habendum clause**, which states the nature of the interest the grantor is conveying. Is the grantor conveying a fee simple absolute or a life estate? Unless otherwise specified, the grantor's entire interest is presumed to pass to the grantee. If there is more than one grantee, the deed should say how they will hold title: is this a tenancy in common or a joint tenancy?

---

* While not strictly required, acknowledgment is a practical necessity, since it is often the only way to prove the validity of the grantor's signature.

A recital of the consideration is helpful because it shows that the transfer is a purchase instead of a gift. If the transfer is a gift, the grantee may be vulnerable to the claims of the grantor's creditors. Rather than stating the actual purchase price, the recital of consideration usually says something like, "for $1.00 and other valuable consideration."

Other non-essential items include the date of conveyance, the grantee's signature, the grantor's seal, warranties, and technical terminology. "I hereby grant Green Farm to Harry Tucker. (signed) Sam Smith" is a valid deed, assuming that Sam Smith is legally competent.

Wills

The will (or testament) is another method of voluntary alienation. In general, a will must be:

1. in writing,
2. signed by the person making it (the testator), and
3. attested to by two or more competent witnesses.

A will must be signed by the testator in the presence of at least two witnesses. The witnesses must also sign an acknowledgment that the maker declared the document to be his or her will.

California also recognizes a type of unwitnessed will, called a **holographic will**. A holographic will is one that is completely handwritten, signed, and dated by the testator. Holographic wills do not need to be signed in the presence of witnesses. If a portion of a holographic will is typewritten or preprinted, those provisions will be disregarded by the probate court.

Terminology. The person making the will is called the **testator** (male) or **testatrix** (female). A testator **bequeaths** personal property to **legatees** and **devises** real property to **devisees**. An amendment to a will is called a **codicil**. The directions contained in the will are carried out by an **executor** (or **executrix**) who is named in the will, under the supervision of the probate court. **Probate** is the procedure by which a will is proved valid and the testator's directions are carried out.

Probate Procedures. Probate procedures vary considerably from state to state. However, a few points of general application should be noted. A will does not convey any interest until the testator has died and the will has been probated. The probate court (in California, the superior court) must approve all conveyances of real property under the will, unless the estate is probated under the nonintervention method. The court also must approve any brokerage commissions pertaining to such conveyances.

Fig.3.3 Will terminology

Will Terminology

Testator/Testatrix: one who makes a will

Bequeath: to transfer personal property by will

Devise: to transfer real property by will

Executor/Executrix: carries out directions in a will

Probate: procedure to prove a will's validity

Involuntary Alienation

The patent, the deed, and the will are the three most common methods of transferring property voluntarily. We will now look at the ways interests in real property can be conveyed without any voluntary action on the part of the owner.

Involuntary alienation can be the result of rule of law, adverse possession, or accession. Alienation by rule of law includes dedication, intestate succession and escheat, condemnation, and decisions of the courts regarding real property.

Dedication

When a private owner gives real property to the public, it is called dedication. While dedication may be voluntary, most often it is required in exchange for a benefit from a public entity.

Example: The county requires a land developer to dedicate land within a new subdivision for public streets, in exchange for permission to subdivide.

This type of dedication is called **statutory dedication** because it involves compliance with relevant statutory procedures. In the example above, the subdivision statutes require that land for streets and utilities must be dedicated before a parcel can be subdivided.

A second type of dedication is called **common law dedication**. The usual requirement for common law dedication is the owner's acquiescence in the public's use of his or her property for a prolonged period of time. If property has been used by the public for long enough, a government entity can pass an ordinance accepting a common law dedication. The dedication may be treated as a transfer of ownership, or it may only establish a public easement, depending on the circumstances.

Example: Barker owns some lakefront property. For many years, people from town have walked across a corner of his lot to gain access to the lake, and Barker has done nothing to prevent this. Barker's acquiescence to this public use could be considered a common law dedication.

Intestate Succession and Escheat

When a person dies without leaving a will, he or she is said to have died intestate. The law provides for the distribution of his or her property by a process called **intestate succession**. The procedure varies from state to state, but in general the property passes first to the surviving spouse, then to any surviving children, then to various other relatives.

Persons who take property by intestate succession are called heirs. Intestate succession is supervised by the probate court. The court appoints an administrator, who is responsible for distributing the property in the manner required by the intestate succession statutes.

If a person dies intestate and the probate court is unable to locate any heirs, then the intestate person's property will pass back to the state according to the law of **escheat**. Since the state is the ultimate source of title to property, it is also the ultimate heir when there are no intervening interested parties.

Condemnation

The government has the constitutional power to take private property for public use, as long as it pays just compensation to the owner of the condemned property. The government's power to condemn (or "take") property is called the power of **eminent domain**. Before the power of eminent domain can be exercised, the following requirements must be met:

- The use must be a **public use**—that is, it must benefit the public. The government cannot take one person's land for the sole purpose of turning it over to another person. Taking property for a public park would qualify as a public use.
- The condemning entity must pay **just compensation** to the owner. Generally, just compensation is the fair market value of the property.

The power of eminent domain may be exercised by any government entity, and also by some semi-public entities, such as utility companies.

Inverse Condemnation. If a property owner feels that his or her property has been taken or damaged by a public entity, he or she may bring a suit called an **inverse condemnation action** to force the government to pay the fair market value of the taken or damaged property.

Court Decisions

Title to property can also be conveyed by court order in accordance with state statutes and the precedents of the common law. The most common forms of court action affecting title to property are the quiet title action, the suit for partition, and foreclosure.

Quiet Title. The quiet title action is used to remove a cloud on the title when the title cannot be cleared by the more peaceful means of an agreement and a quitclaim deed. In a quiet title action, the court decides questions of property ownership. The result is a binding determination of the various parties' interests in a particular piece of real estate.

> **Example:** A seller has found a potential buyer for his property. However, a title search shows a gap in the title; the public record doesn't indicate who owned the property for a certain time period.
>
> The seller brings a quiet title action. The defendants are all those who have a potential interest in the land. (This includes whoever the mystery person was who held title during the gap, even though his or her name is unknown.)
>
> The seller asks the court to declare his title valid, thereby "quieting title" to the land. If no defendants appear to challenge the seller's title, the court will grant the seller's request. The buyer can safely rely on the court's decision and consummate the sale.

Suit for Partition. A suit for partition is a means of dividing property held by more than one person when the co-owners cannot agree on how to divide it. For example, joint tenants may wish to end their joint tenancy but be unable to decide among themselves who gets what portion of the property. The court divides the property for them, and the owners are then bound by the court's decision. In many cases, the court will order the property sold and the proceeds divided among the co-owners.

> **Example:** White and Black are joint tenants. The joint tenancy property is a vacation home in the mountains. White and Black have a big argument and decide they want to terminate their joint tenancy. However, because they are so angry with each other, they cannot agree on how to divide the property. White wants to sell the property to a third party and split the proceeds. Black wants to buy out White's interest and keep the vacation home for himself. Finally, White files a suit for partition. The court orders the vacation home sold and divides the proceeds between White and Black. Black must abide by the court's decision, even though he doesn't like it.

Foreclosure Actions. Persons holding liens against real property may force the sale of the property if the debts secured by their liens are not paid. Foreclosure is available for any type of lien that attaches to real property, including mortgages, deeds of trust, construction liens, and judgment liens.

Adverse Possession

Adverse possession is another type of involuntary alienation. **Adverse possession** is the process by which the possession and use of property mature into title. The law of adverse possession encourages the fullest and most productive use of land. It provides that someone who actually uses property may eventually attain a greater interest in that property than the owner who does not use it. The precise requirements for obtaining title by adverse possession vary from state to state. These requirements are often highly technical, and they must be followed exactly in order to obtain title. Legal counsel should be obtained in transactions where title may be affected by adverse possession.

Requirements. In California, there are five basic requirements for adverse possession. Possession of the land must be:

1. actual, open, and notorious;
2. hostile to the owner's interest;
3. under claim of right or color of title;

4. continuous and uninterrupted for a specific period of time; and
5. the adverse possessor must have paid the property taxes during the required period of possession.

Actual, Open, and Notorious. Actual possession means occupation and use of the property in a manner appropriate to the type of property. It does not require residence on the property unless residence is an appropriate use. Thus, actual possession of farmland may be achieved by fencing the land and planting crops, while actual possession of urban property would require a residential or commercial use of the property.

The requirement of "open and notorious" possession means that the possession must put the true owner on notice that his or her interest in the property is being threatened. "Open and notorious" and "actual" possession overlap. Actual possession generally constitutes reasonable notice to the world that the adverse possessor is occupying the property.

Hostile. The adverse possessor must intend to claim ownership of the property and defend that claim against all parties. Hostile intent is proven by the adverse possessor's actions. If the adverse possessor uses the property in the same fashion as an owner would use it, then hostile intent exists. Note that the hostility requirement cannot be satisfied if the possession is with the permission of the actual owner.

Claim of Right or Color of Title. Hostile intent is also proven by "claim of right" or "color of title," which refers to the adverse possessor's good faith but mistaken belief that he or she is the owner of the land. An example of an adverse possessor with color of title is one who takes possession under an invalid deed. Under those circumstances, the adverse possessor may acquire title to all the property described in the defective instrument, even if he or she occupies only part of the property.

Continuous and Uninterrupted. An adverse possessor must have continuous and uninterrupted possession of the property for the length of time

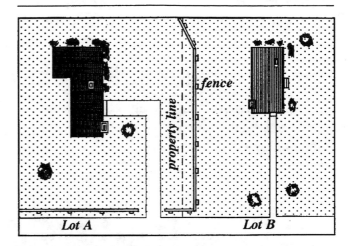

Fig.3.4 Adverse possession
Use of property—here the strip between Lot A's fence and the true property line—can mature into title by the process of adverse possession. If all the requirements of adverse possession are met, Lot A will include all the property to the fence line.

prescribed by state statute. In California, the possession must be continuous and uninterrupted for five years, and the adverse possessor must pay the taxes on the property during that period.

In some cases, intermittent use of the property may be enough to fulfill the continuity requirement. This is true if the property is a type that an owner would ordinarily use only at certain times of year, such as seasonal farmland or summer resort property. However, the continuity requirement is not met if the adverse possessor fails to use the property for a significant period when it would ordinarily be used, or if the true owner interrupts the period of possession.

Successive adverse possessors can add together their periods of possession to equal the statutory time period; this is called **tacking**. For example, if Brown adversely possesses property for four years and then transfers possession to Green, who possesses the property for three years, Green can claim title because the total period of adverse possession is more than five years.

Note that title to government property can never be acquired by adverse possession.

Perfecting Title. Since the adverse possessor's interest in the property is not recorded, he or she must take additional steps to acquire marketable title. Unless the true owner is willing to provide a quitclaim deed, the adverse possessor has to file a quiet title action.

Accession

Accession is any addition to real property from natural or artificial causes. It can result in involuntary alienation. Accession includes:

- accretion,
- reliction,
- avulsion, and
- the addition of fixtures.

Accretion. When riparian or littoral land is slowly enlarged by waterborne soil deposits (called alluvion or alluvium), the riparian or littoral owner acquires title to the new land. A key feature of accretion is that the build-up of soil must be so gradual that the process is virtually imperceptible.

Reliction. When riparian or littoral land is enlarged by the gradual retreat of the body of water, the riparian or littoral owner acquires title to the newly exposed land. Like accretion, reliction must be very gradual. Reliction is also called dereliction.

Avulsion. Accretion and reliction, both gradual processes, are contrasted with avulsion. Avulsion occurs when land is violently torn away by flowing water or waves and deposited somewhere else, or when land is exposed by a sudden change in a watercourse. Unlike accretion and reliction, avulsion does not necessarily result in involuntary alienation of

Fig.3.5 Involuntary alienation

Involuntary Alienation		
Type	**Property taken by**	**Action**
Dedication	Public	Given in exchange for a benefit from a public entity
Escheat	State	Person dies without heirs or will
Condemnation	Government entity	Entity files condemnation suit and pays just compensation
Court decisions	Private or public parties	Party files court action, such as quiet title, partition, foreclosure
Adverse possession	Adverse possessor	Actual, open, notorious, hostile, continuous possession of land for statutory period
Accession	Private landowner	By accretion, reliction, avulsion, or addition of fixtures

the land that has been moved or exposed. The original owner still has title to that land, if there is some way to claim it. If unclaimed, it eventually becomes part of the property it is now attached to.

Fixtures. Personal property may be converted to real property if it meets the fixture tests discussed in Chapter 1. Generally, it must be clear that the personal property was intended to become a part of the realty. An exception is the case of an improvement made in error. If a person makes an improvement on someone else's land in the mistaken but good faith belief that he or she owns the land, then he or she may remove the improvement upon payment of damages to the true owner.

Recording

Once an interest in property has been transferred (voluntarily or involuntarily), the new owner protects his or her interest by recording the document of conveyance with the county clerk. Recording is a way to provide convenient access to information regarding ownership of a piece of property to anyone who is interested.

The Recording Process

Recording is accomplished by filing a copy of the deed or other document at the county clerk's office in the county where the property is located. The recorder catalogs, or **indexes**, the document twice, once under the grantor's last name and once under the grantee's last name. Sometimes a document will also be indexed according to tract, so that all documents affecting a particular property are listed together.

These indexes serve as the basis for **title searches**. A purchaser can search the grantor index to determine if the seller has already conveyed the interest to another party. The purchaser can also search the grantee index to discover the source of the seller's title, and trace the title back through a **chain of title** (successive grantors and grantees) that is long enough to ensure the validity of the seller's title.

Almost any document affecting title to land may be recorded—a deed, a mortgage, an abstract of judgment, a lis pendens (a notice of pending legal proceedings that may affect property), and so on. A deed or other document of conveyance must be acknowledged before it can be recorded, primarily to protect against forgeries. Also, the Federal Fair Housing Act prohibits the recording of any deed that contains a racially restrictive covenant (see Chapter 15).

The Effect of Recording

Recording has two significant consequences. Most importantly, it gives **constructive notice** of recorded interests to "the world." In other words, anyone who later acquires an interest in the property is held to know about all the other recorded interests, even if he or she does not check the record.

> **Example:** Jones owns Haystack Farm. She sells the farm to Chin, who immediately records his deed. One week later, Jones sells Haystack Farm to Brown. Jones pretends she still owns the farm, and Brown simply takes her word for it; he doesn't do a title search. When Brown tries to record his deed, he discovers that Jones did not have title to Haystack Farm when she sold it to him.
>
> Although Brown didn't actually know about the conveyance from Jones to Chin, he had constructive notice of that conveyance. He could have found out about it by checking the public record. As a result, he has no claim to the property. Chin owns Haystack Farm. Brown could sue Jones to get his money back, but she has probably left town by now.

A grantee who fails to record his or her deed can lose title to a subsequent good faith purchaser who did not have notice of the earlier conveyance. In a conflict between two purchasers, the one who records his or her deed first has good title to the property—even if the other purchaser's deed was executed first.

> **Example:** Jones sells Haystack Farm to Chin, but Chin does not record his deed. One week later, Jones sells the same property to Brown. No one tells Brown about the previous conveyance to Chin.
>
> Since Chin's deed isn't recorded, Brown doesn't have constructive notice of Chin's interest in the property. Even if Brown does a title search, there's nothing in the public record to indicate that Jones no longer owns the property.
>
> Brown qualifies as a subsequent good faith purchaser without notice. If he records his deed before Chin records his, Brown has good title to the property.

In addition to providing constructive notice, recording also creates a presumption that the recorded instrument is valid and effective. Recording will not serve to validate an otherwise invalid deed, nor will it protect against interests that arise by operation of law, such as adverse possession.

Wild Deeds

Because of the grantor/grantee system of indexing, it is possible for a deed to be recorded in such a way that a title search would not discover it.

> **Example:** Suppose Smith sells property to Montgomery, who does not record her deed. Montgomery then conveys the property to Juarez, who promptly records his deed. If Smith then makes another conveyance of the same property to Walker, Walker will not be able to discover Juarez's interest because Juarez is not in Smith's chain of title. There is a break in the chain of title between Smith and Juarez because the connecting deed was not recorded.

The general rule in these situations is that the subsequent purchaser (in the example above, Walker) is not charged with constructive notice of a deed that is not in the chain of title. A deed outside the chain of title is called a **wild deed**.

Title Insurance

Given the complexity of real property law and the high cost of real estate, it's natural that a prospective buyer will want to do everything possible to protect his or her interest. One means of accomplishing this is to obtain warranties of title from the seller, but warranties aren't very valuable if the seller is financially unable to back them up.

The buyer could also obtain a complete history of all the recorded interests in the property (called a **chain of title**) or a condensed history of those interests (called an **abstract of title**), and then have the history examined by an attorney who could render an opinion on the condition of the title. But the buyer would still have no protection against latent or undiscovered defects in the title. Therefore, most buyers will protect their interests with a title insurance policy.

In a title insurance policy, the title insurance company agrees to indemnify the policy holder against any loss caused by defects in the title, except for any defects specifically excluded from coverage. In other words, the company will reimburse the policy holder for any covered loss. The title company will also handle the legal defense against any claims covered by the policy.

Obtaining Title Insurance

There are two steps to getting a title insurance policy. First, the buyer (or the seller) pays a fee to the title company to cover the cost of a title search. Most title companies have their own microfilmed sets of records (called title plants), so they do not have to search the files in the recorder's office.

Fig.3.6 Title insurance

Title Insurance Coverage	
Standard Coverage	**Extended Coverage**
Marketable title	Marketable title
Latent defects in title	Latent defects in title
forged deed	forged deed
incompetent grantor	incompetent grantor
Right of access	Right of access
	Parties in possession
	tenants
	adverse possessors
	Matters discovered by survey
	boundary lines
	encroachments
	area
	Unrecorded construction liens
	Tax liens

After the title search is completed, the title company issues a report (a preliminary title report) on the condition of the title. The report lists all defects and encumbrances of record; these items will be excluded from the policy coverage. If the buyer is satisfied with the report, he or she purchases an insurance policy by paying the required premium; one payment covers the entire life of the policy.

Limits on Coverage

Title insurance policies may be limited in a number of ways. As mentioned above, all defects and encumbrances of record are listed in the policy and excluded from coverage. In addition, the liability of the title

company cannot exceed the face value of the policy. The extent of protection also varies according to the nature of the policy. The two most common types of policies are the standard coverage policy and the extended coverage policy.

The **standard coverage** policy is used to insure the owner against defects in title, including hidden risks such as forgery. It does not insure against the interests of a person in actual possession of the property (such as an adverse possessor), nor against interests that would be discovered only by an inspection of the premises (such as an encroachment).

The **extended coverage** policy insures against all matters covered by the standard policy, plus matters not of public record, such as the rights of parties in possession of the property, unrecorded construction liens, and encroachments. Extended coverage is most often purchased by the buyer to insure his or her lender's lien position; this is known as a mortgagee's policy.

A buyer may want to obtain coverage for a specific problem not included in the standard policy. He or she can do so by purchasing an endorsement to cover the particular problem.

Title insurance never protects a landowner from losses due to governmental action, such as condemnation or zoning changes.

Title insurance coverage is also limited to losses resulting from defects in the particular interest covered. Thus, an owner's policy covers only defects in title, a mortgagee's policy only insures the lender's lien priority, and a leaseholder's policy only insures the validity of a lease.

Methods of Land Description

When land is transferred from one party to another, it is essential to accurately describe the property being conveyed. An ambiguous or uncertain description could make a contract or a deed invalid, and confusion over exactly what was transferred can cause problems not only for the parties involved in the current transaction, but also for the parties in future transactions.

There are three major methods of describing land:

- metes and bounds,
- government survey, and
- platting.

Metes and Bounds

The metes and bounds method describes a parcel by establishing its boundaries. The boundaries are described by reference to three things:

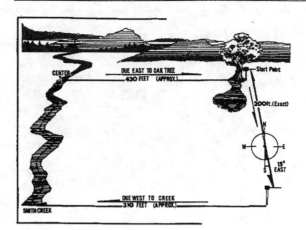

Fig.3.7 Metes and bounds description
A tract of land, located in Smith County and described as follows: beginning at the old oak tree, thence south 15° east, 200 feet, thence north 90° west, 310 feet more or less to the centerline of Smith Creek, thence northwesterly along the centerline of Smith Creek to a point directly west of the old oak tree, thence north 90° east, 430 feet more or less to the point of beginning.

- monuments, which may be natural objects such as rivers or trees, or man-made objects such as roads or survey markers;
- directions or courses, in the form of compass readings; and
- distances, measured in any convenient units of length.

Point of Beginning. A metes and bounds description begins at a convenient and well-defined point along the boundary of a tract of land (called the point of beginning). It then sets out directions that would allow a surveyor to trace the boundaries of the tract all the way back to the point of beginning. The point of beginning will always be described by reference to a monument, such as "the SW corner of the intersection of Front and Cherry," or "200 feet north of the old oak tree."

Note that the point of beginning does not have to be a monument itself, but can be described by referring to a monument, such as the old oak tree in the example above.

Tracing Boundaries by Course and Distance.
The point of beginning is established, then courses and distances are given. For example, "north, 100 feet" is a course and distance. Both the course and the distance may be described in terms of a monument; for example, "northerly along the eastern edge of Front Street 100 feet" or "north, 100 feet more or less, to the centerline of Smith Creek."

If there is a discrepancy between a monument and a course or distance, the monument will take precedence. In the examples above, the first boundary would be along the edge of Front Street, even if that edge does not run due north, and the second boundary would extend to the center of Smith Creek even if the actual distance to that point is not 100 feet.

A metes and bounds description continues with a series of courses and distances, until the parcel's boundaries have been described all the way around back to the point of beginning. A metes and bounds description must end at the point of beginning, or else it does not describe a totally enclosed tract. Figure 3.7 illustrates a simple metes and bounds description.

Metes and bounds descriptions tend to be quite lengthy, and they are often confusing. Furthermore, monuments and reference points do not always maintain their exact locations over the years. An actual survey of the property is usually necessary when dealing with a metes and bounds description.

Conflicting Directions. As noted above, discrepancies sometimes occur between the various elements of a metes and bounds description. In resolving such discrepancies, the order of priority is as follows:

1. natural monuments,
2. then man-made monuments,
3. then courses,

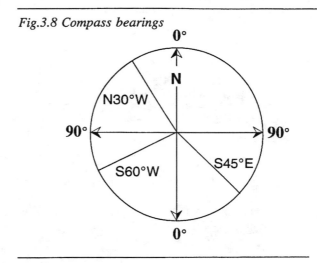

Fig.3.8 Compass bearings

4. then distances,
5. then names (e.g., "Smith Farm"),
6. then areas (e.g., "40 acres").

In a conflict between any two of these elements, the one with higher priority will prevail.

Compass Bearings. Directions or courses in metes and bounds descriptions are given in a peculiar fashion. A direction is described by reference to its deviation from either north or south, whichever is closer. Thus, northwest or 315° is written as north 45° west, since it is a deviation of 45° to the west of north. Similarly, south southeast or 157½° is written south 22½° east, since it is a deviation of 22½° to the east of south. East and west are both written relative to north: north 90° east, north 90° west, respectively.

Government Survey

The government survey system, also called the rectangular survey system, describes land by reference to a series of grids. This system of land description was adopted after many of the northeastern states were already surveyed. Thus, this method of land description is mainly used west of the Mississippi River.

Fig.3.9 Principal meridians and baselines

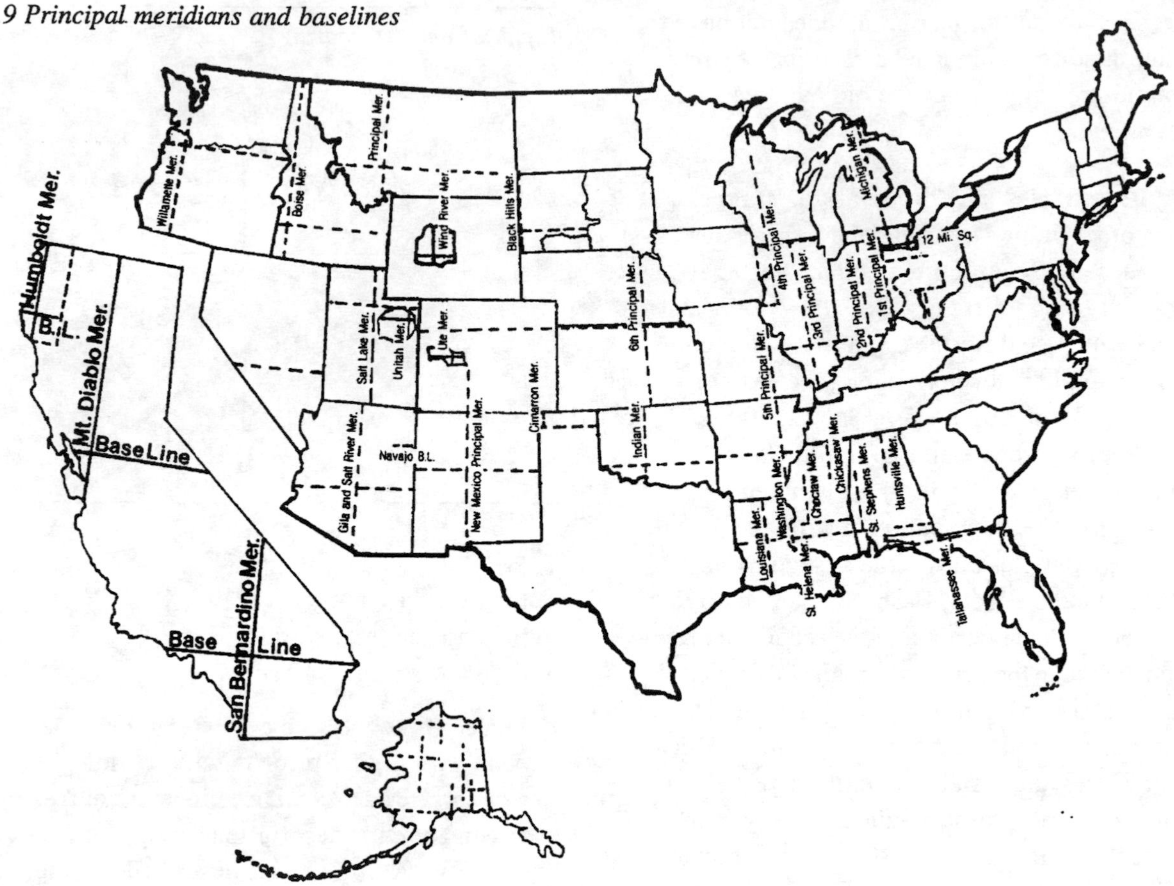

Fig.3.10 Units of land measurement

UNITS OF MEASUREMENT FOR LAND	
UNITS OF AREA	1 Tract = 24 mi. × 24 mi. (576 sq. mi.) = 16 townships 1 Township = 6 mi. × 6 mi. (36 sq. mi.) = 36 sections 1 Section* = 1 mi. × 1 mi. (1 sq. mi.) = 640 acres 1 Acre = 43,560 sq. ft. = 160 sq. rods 1 Square Acre = 208.71 ft × 208.71 ft.
UNITS OF LENGTH	1 Mile = 5,280 ft. = 320 rods = 80 chains 1 Rod = 16½ ft. 1 Chain = 66 ft. = 4 rods

* Note: To determine the area of partial sections, simply multiply the fraction of the section by 640. For example,

    1 half-section = ½ × 640 = 320 acres
    1 quarter-section = ¼ × 640 = 160 acres
    1 quarter-quarter section = ¼ × ¼ × 640 = 40 acres

Fig.3.11 Township lines and range lines

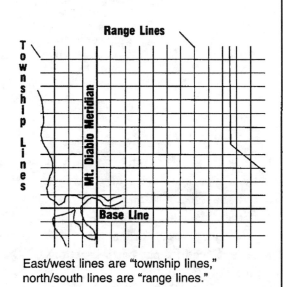

East/west lines are "township lines,"
north/south lines are "range lines."

Fig.3.12 Township

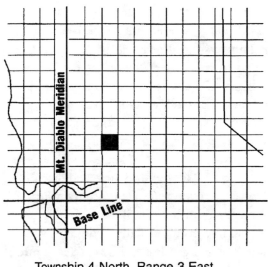

Township 4 North, Range 3 East

Fig.3.13 Section numbers

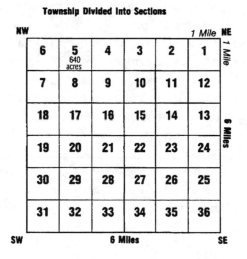

A township contains 36 sections.

Fig.3.14 Sections and partial sections

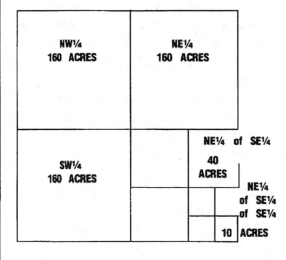

A section can be divided up into smaller
parcels.

The grids used in the government survey system may seem confusing at first, and we recommend that you study the accompanying diagrams closely.

The grids are composed of two sets of lines, one set running north/south, the other east/west. Each grid is identified by a **principal meridian**, which is the original north/south line established in that grid, and by a **base line**, which is the original east/west line. In California, there are three principal meridians: Humboldt, Mt. Diablo, and San Bernardino. Each has its own base line. (See Figure 3.9.)

Grid lines run parallel to the principal meridian and the base line at intervals of six miles. The east/west lines are called **township lines**, and they divide the land into rows or tiers called **township tiers**. The north/south lines, called **range lines**, divide the land into columns called **ranges**. Every fourth range line is a **guide meridian**. (See Figure 3.11.)

A particular area of land that is located at the intersection of a range and a township tier is called a **township**, and it is identified by its position relative to the principal meridian and base line. For example, the township that is located in the fourth tier north of the base line and the third range east of the principal meridian is called "Township 4 North, Range 3 East." (See Figure 3.12.) This is often abbreviated "T4N, R3E."

Grid systems are identical across the country, so it is necessary to include in the description the name of the principal meridian that is being used as a reference. (Since each principal meridian has its own base line, it is not necessary to specify the base line.) It is also a good practice to mention the county and state where the land is situated, so as to avoid any possible confusion. Thus, a complete description of a township would be T4N, R3E of the _____ Meridian, _____ County, State of California.

Each township measures 36 square miles and contains 36 sections. Each section is one square mile, or 640 acres. (See Figure 3.13.) These sec-

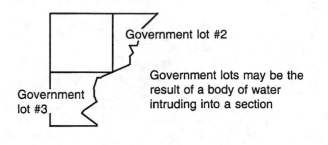

Fig.3.15 Government lots

Government lot #2

Government lots may be the result of a body of water intruding into a section

Government lot #3

tions are numbered in a special way, starting with the northeast corner, and working across and down in a snakelike fashion, ending with the southeast corner.

Smaller parcels of land can be identified by reference to sections and partial sections, as illustrated in Figure 3.14.

Government Lots. A government lot is a section of land of irregular shape or size that is referred to by a lot number. Because of the curvature of the earth, range lines converge, so it is impossible to keep all sections exactly one mile square. As a result, the sections along the north and west boundaries of each township are irregular in size. The quarter sections along the north and west boundaries of these sections are used to take up the excess or shortage. The quarter-quarter sections, then, along the north and west boundaries of a township are given government lot numbers.

Another situation in which government lots occur is when a body of water or some other obstacle makes it impossible to survey a square-mile section.

Platting

The platting method of land description is sometimes referred to as the lot and block method, or the maps and plats system. When land is subdivided, lots

Fig.3.16 Plat map

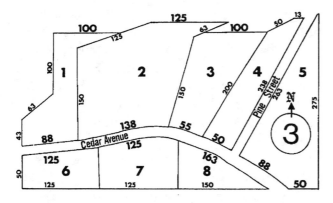

and blocks (groups of lots surrounded by streets) are mapped out by a surveyor on a subdivision plat (map). The plat is then recorded in the county where the land is located.

After the plat is recorded, a reference to one of the lot numbers on the specified plat is a sufficient legal description of the lot. Since a detailed description of the lot is already on file in the recorder's office, that description may be incorporated into any legal document simply by reference to the lot number and subdivision plat.

To find the precise location and dimensions of the parcel, you would look in the map book at the county recorder's office. Here is an example of a lot and block description:

> Lot 2, Block 4 of Tract number 455, in the City of Fresno, County of Fresno, State of California, as per map recorded in Book 25, page 92, of maps, in the office of the recorder of said county.

Plat maps frequently contain a considerable amount of useful information beyond a detailed description of lot boundaries. For example, they may include area measurements, the locations of various ease-ments, right-of-way dimensions, the location of survey markers, and a list of use restrictions apply-ing to the land. (However, studying a plat map is not a substitute for a thorough title search.)

Other Methods of Land Description

There are other methods of describing land be-sides the three major systems discussed above. When an adequate description of property is al-ready a matter of public record—contained in a recorded document—then a simple reference to that earlier document serves as an adequate property description in a new document. (For example, "All that land described in the grant deed recorded under recording number 92122401503 in Orange County, California.") Also, generalized descriptions such as "all my lands" or "Smith Farm" can be adequate, as long as they make it possible to determine exactly what property is being described. But it's always best to use the least ambiguous description possible, to prevent future problems. It should be noted that street addresses are not acceptable descriptions in many states.

Air Lots. Not all real property can be described simply in terms of its position on the face of the earth. Some forms of real property (e.g., condomini-ums) require description in terms of elevation above the ground as well. These descriptions are made by reference to an established plane of elevation, called a **datum**. Most large cities have their own official datum, and frequently subsidiary reference points, called bench marks, are also established. A **bench mark** is a point whose position relative to a datum has been accurately measured. Thereafter, surveyors can use the bench mark as a reference when it is more convenient than the datum.

Chapter Summary

1. A transfer of ownership of property from one person to another is called alienation. Alienation may be either voluntary or involuntary.

2. Property may be transferred voluntarily by patent, deed, or will. The deed is the most common way of voluntarily transferring property. To be valid, a deed must be in writing, identify the parties, be signed by a competent grantor, have a living grantee, contain words of conveyance, and include an adequate description of the property. For property to be successfully conveyed, there must be delivery and acceptance as well as a valid deed. Once the deed is delivered and accepted, it should be recorded to protect the new owner's interest.

3. When a person dies, his or her real property is transferred to devisees under a will or to heirs by the rules of intestate succession. A person who dies without a will is said to have died intestate. Property from an estate is distributed under the jurisdiction of the probate court. If a person dies without a valid will and without heirs, the property escheats to the state.

4. In addition to intestate succession and escheat, there are several other methods of involuntary alienation, including dedication, condemnation, court decisions, and adverse possession. When someone uses property openly and continuously without the owner's permission for five years, he or she may acquire title by adverse possession.

5. Ownership of property may be transferred by accession. Accession refers to an addition to real property by various natural means, including accretion, reliction, and avulsion. The addition of fixtures is also a form of accession.

6. Documents affecting real property are recorded to provide constructive notice of their contents to anyone interested in the property. Recording also creates a presumption that the document is valid.

7. To protect a newly acquired interest in real property, the owner usually obtains a title insurance policy. The title insurance company will reimburse the owner for any loss caused by defects in title, and will defend the title against the legal claims of others.

8. Before property can be transferred, it must be adequately described. There are three major methods of land description: metes and bounds, government survey, and platting.

O—⚷ Key Terms

Alienation—The transfer of title, ownership, or an interest in property from one person to another. Alienation may be voluntary or involuntary.

Deed—A written instrument that, when properly executed, delivered, and accepted, conveys title or ownership of real property from the grantor to the grantee.

Grant deed—The deed most commonly used in California. It carries two warranties: the covenant of the right to convey, and the covenant against encumbrances caused by the grantor.

Quitclaim deed—A deed that conveys and releases any interest in a piece of real property that the grantor may have. It contains no warranties of any kind, but does transfer any right, title, or interest the grantor has at the time the deed is executed.

Acknowledgment—A formal declaration made before an authorized official, such as a notary public or county clerk, by a person who has signed a document; he or she states that the signature is genuine and voluntary.

Will—The written declaration of an individual that designates how his or her estate will be disposed of after death.

Intestate—When a person dies without leaving a valid will, he or she dies intestate.

Escheat—The reversion of property to the state when a person dies without leaving a will and without heirs entitled to the property.

Adverse possession—A means by which a person may acquire title to property by using it openly and continuously without the owner's permission for the required statutory period.

Dedication—When a private owner voluntarily or involuntarily gives real property to the public.

Eminent domain—The power of the government to take (condemn) private property for public use, upon payment of just compensation to the owner.

Condemnation—The act of taking private property for public use under the power of eminent domain.

Accession—The acquisition of title to additional property by its annexation to existing property. This can be caused by human beings, as when fixtures are attached to the land, or by nature, as when silt is deposited on the banks of a river.

Constructive notice—Notice of a fact imputed to a person by law (as opposed to actual notice); he or she had the opportunity to discover the fact in question by searching the public record.

Title search—An inspection of the public record to determine all rights to a piece of property.

Chain of title—A complete history of all the recorded interests in a piece of real property.

Abstract of title—A condensed history of the recorded interests in a piece of real property.

Preliminary title report—A report issued after a title search by a title insurance company, listing all defects and encumbrances of record.

Wild deed—A recorded deed that cannot be located under the grantor-grantee system of indexing.

Metes and bounds—A system of land description in which the boundaries of a parcel of land are described by reference to monuments, courses, and distances.

Monument—A visible marker (natural or artificial) used in a survey or a metes and bounds description to establish the boundaries of a piece of property.

Point of beginning—The starting point in a metes and bounds description; a monument or a point described by reference to a monument.

Course—In a metes and bounds description, a direction, stated in terms of a compass bearing.

Distance—In a metes and bounds description, the length of a boundary measured in any convenient unit of length.

Government survey—A system of land description in which the land is divided into squares called townships, and each township is, in turn, divided up into 36 sections, each one square mile.

Principal meridian—In the government survey system, the main north-south line in a particular grid, used as the starting point in numbering the ranges and township tiers.

Range—In the government survey system, a strip of land six miles wide, running north and south.

Township tier—In the government survey system, a strip of land six miles wide, running east and west.

Township—The intersection of a range and a township tier in the government survey system. It is parcel of land that is six miles square and contains 36 sections.

Section—One square mile of land, containing 640 acres. There are 36 sections in a township.

Government lot—In the government survey system, a parcel of land that is not a regular section.

Platting—The system of description used for subdivided (platted) land. The properties within a subdivision are assigned lot numbers on a plat map, which is then recorded; the location and dimensions of a particular lot can be determined by consulting the recorded map.

Air lot—A parcel of property above the surface of the earth, not containing any land: for example, a condominium unit on the third floor.

Chapter 3—Quiz
How to Transfer Real Property

1. The process of transferring real property is called:

    a) avulsion
    b) quitclaim
    c) alienation
    d) dereliction

2. The government transfers title to private parties by means of a:

    a) patent
    b) deed
    c) quitclaim
    d) escheat

3. A grant deed warrants that:

    a) no one has adversely possessed the property
    b) the grantor has not previously conveyed title to anyone else
    c) the purchase price was fair and equitable
    d) title has been duly recorded

4. Clouds on title are usually cleared by:

    a) a suit for partition
    b) title insurance
    c) adverse possession
    d) a quitclaim deed

5. A valid deed must refer to a grantee who is:

    a) competent
    b) over 21 years old
    c) identifiable
    d) intestate

6. Conveyance requires a valid deed, plus:

    a) recording
    b) delivery
    c) acceptance
    d) Both b) and c)

7. A person who makes a will is called:

    a) a grantor
    b) an executor
    c) a testator
    d) an escheat

8. An unwitnessed, handwritten will is called:

    a) a formal will
    b) a holographic will
    c) a nuncupative will
    d) None of the above

9. The process by which possession of property can result in ownership of the property is called:

    a) fee simple
    b) succession
    c) adverse possession
    d) reliction

10. A quitclaim deed conveys:

    a) whatever interest the grantor has
    b) only a portion of the interest held by the grantor
    c) only property acquired by adverse possession
    d) None of the above

11. The main reason why a grantee should make sure the deed gets recorded is:

    a) to give constructive notice of his or her interest in the property
    b) to show acceptance of the conveyance
    c) to make the transfer of title effective
    d) to prevent adverse possession

12. A section of a township contains the following number of acres:

    a) 360
    b) 580
    c) 640
    d) 760

13. A parcel that measures ¼ of a mile by ¼ of a mile is:

    a) $\frac{1}{4}$ of a section
    b) $\frac{1}{8}$ of a section
    c) $\frac{1}{16}$ of a section
    d) $\frac{1}{36}$ of a section

14. The distance between the east and west boundary lines of a township is:

    a) six miles
    b) sixty-six miles
    c) one mile
    d) two miles

15. A township contains 36 sections that are numbered consecutively 1 through 36. The last section in the township is located in the:

    a) southeast corner
    b) southwest corner
    c) northeast corner
    d) northwest corner

Answer Key

1. c) The general term for the process of transferring real property is alienation.

2. a) The government transfers title to property with a patent.

3. b) A grant deed warrants that the grantor actually owns the interest that is being conveyed.

4. d) A quitclaim deed is commonly used to clear clouds on title. It only conveys whatever interest the grantor has at the time of delivery, and includes no warranties.

5. c) The grantee is only required to be alive and identifiable. He or she need not be competent.

6. d) To successfully convey property, the deed must be delivered and accepted.

7. c) A testator (or testatrix) is the person who makes a will.

8. b) A holographic will is one that is handwritten by the testator, and not witnessed.

9. c) Adverse possession encourages the full use of land by providing a means by which a user may acquire ownership rights.

10. a) A quitclaim deed transfers whatever interest the grantor has. If the grantor has good title, it conveys good title. If the grantor has no interest in the property, it conveys nothing at all.

11. a) Recording a deed gives constructive notice of the grantee's interest.

12. c) One section contains 640 acres.

13. c) A section is one mile on each side, a quarter section is ½ mile on each side, and a quarter of a quarter section is ¼ mile on each side.

14. a) A township measures 6 miles by 6 miles.

15. a) Section 36 is always in the southeast corner of the township.

Government Restrictions on Property Rights

Outline

Chapter Overview

Although a property owner has many rights in regard to his or her property, those rights are limited by certain powers of the federal, state, and local governments. This chapter examines the ways in which governmental powers affect property ownership most directly. The first part of the chapter explains planning, zoning, and other public restrictions on land use, and the second section discusses the government's power to tax property.

Land Use Controls

In the United States, the powers of government are determined by the federal and state constitutions. Thus, efforts by the federal, state, and local governments to control the use of private property raise constitutional issues. When a property owner objects to a land use law, the central question is often whether the law is constitutional—whether the Constitution gives the government the power to interfere with private property rights in this way.

The constitutional basis for land use control laws is the **police power**. The police power is the power vested in a state to adopt and enforce laws and regulations necessary for the protection of the public's health, safety, morals, and general welfare. A state may delegate its police power to local governmental bodies.

It is the police power that allows state and local governments to regulate a private individual's use of his or her property. The Constitution does not give the federal government a general power to regulate for the public health, safety, morals, and welfare. But the federal government does have authority to use its other powers (such as the power to regulate interstate commerce) to advance police power objectives.

Exercises of the police power must meet constitutional limitations. As a general rule, a land use law or regulation will be considered constitutional if it meets these four criteria:

1. it is reasonably related to the protection of the public health, safety, morals, or general welfare;
2. it applies in the same manner to all property owners who are similarly situated (it is not discriminatory);
3. it does not reduce a property's value so much that the regulation amounts to a confiscation; and
4. it benefits the public by preventing harm that would be caused by the prohibited use of the property.

Government land use controls take a variety of forms: comprehensive plans, zoning ordinances, building codes, subdivision regulations, and environmental laws. All of these are intended to protect the public from problems that unrestricted use of private property can cause.

Comprehensive Planning

To alleviate the problems caused by haphazard, unplanned growth, California require cities and counties to have a planning agency, usually called a **planning commission**.

The planning commission is responsible for designing and adopting a comprehensive, long-term plan for all the development within the city or county. This is often called the "master plan" or "general plan." The purpose of the general plan is to outline the community's development goals and design an overall physical layout to achieve those goals. Once the general plan has been adopted, all development and all land use regulations (such as zoning laws) must conform to it.

The government uses both its police power and its power of eminent domain (discussed later) to implement the comprehensive plans developed by planning commissions.

Zoning

Zoning ordinances divide a community into areas (or zones) that are set aside for specific uses, such as agricultural, residential, commercial, or industrial use. Each of these basic classifications may be

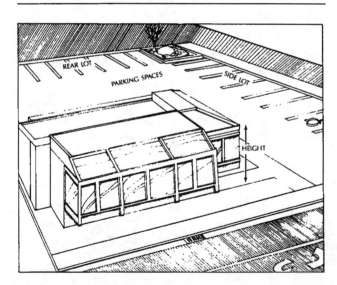

Fig.4.1 Zoning
A zoning ordinance may regulate a building's use, height, setback requirements, and off-street parking.

further divided. For instance, an industrial district may be divided into a light industrial zone and a heavy industrial zone. Keeping certain uses in certain zones helps ensure that only compatible uses are located in the same area.

Zoning ordinances regulate the height, size, and shape of buildings, as well as use. They also usually include setback and side yard requirements, prescribing the minimum distance between a building and the property lines. These regulations control population density, provide some aesthetic guidelines, and preserve adequate open spaces and access to air and daylight.

Instead of prescribing specific height, setback, and side yard requirements for buildings, some communities have ordinances that allow the **floor area ratio** (FAR) method to be used in certain circumstances. FAR controls the ratio between the area of the building's floor space and the area of the lot it occupies.

Example: A floor area ratio of two would permit 100% of the lot to be covered by a two-story building or 50% of the lot to be covered by a four-story building. Thus, the FAR method allows greater flexibility in the shape and height of a building.

Zoning Exceptions and Amendments. Complications inevitably arise when zoning regulations are administered and enforced. So zoning ordinances provide for certain exceptions and changes to their rules, including:

- nonconforming uses,
- variances,
- conditional uses, and
- rezones.

Nonconforming Uses. A **nonconforming use** can arise when an area is zoned for the first time, or when a zoning ordinance is amended. Certain established uses that were lawful before may not conform to the rules laid down in the new ordinance. These nonconforming uses will be permitted to continue.

Example: Smith has been lawfully operating a bakery for seven months when his property is rezoned for single-family residential use. Smith's bakery will be allowed to continue as a nonconforming use.

Even though nonconforming uses are allowed to remain, the local government wants all uses to con-

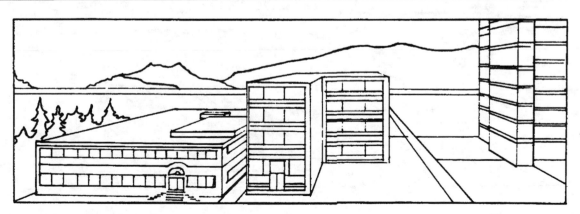

Fig.4.2 Floor area ratio (FAR)
A two-story, a four-story, and an eight-story building, all with a floor area ratio of two.

form to the current zoning laws at some point. Consequently, the owners of a nonconforming use property are often prohibited from enlarging the use, rebuilding if the property is destroyed, or resuming the use after abandoning it.

Example: Smith's bakery burns to the ground in a terrible fire. The zoning authority will not allow him to rebuild the bakery in this residential zone. He will have to sell the property and use the insurance proceeds to buy a bakery located in a commercial zone.

Variances. In some cases, if a zoning law were strictly enforced, the property owner's injury would far outweigh the benefit of enforcing the zoning requirement. Under these circumstances, a variance may be available. A **variance** is authorization to build or maintain a structure or use that is prohibited by the zoning ordinance. For example, a variance might authorize construction of a house even though the topography of the lot makes it virtually impossible to comply with normal setback requirements. In most communities, the property owner applies to the local zoning authority for a variance.

A variance usually will not be granted unless the property owner faces severe practical difficulties or undue hardship (not created by the property owner him or herself) as a result of the zoning. The owner is generally required to prove that the zoning prevents any reasonable use of the land, not merely the most profitable use.

Example: Corelli owns a piece of property that would make a perfect site for a convenience store, but it is in a residential zone. Corelli will not be able to get a variance by claiming that she could make much more money by building a convenience store than she could by building a single-family home.

Most variances authorize only minor deviations from the zoning law. A variance should not change the essential character of the neighborhood or conflict with the community's general plan.

In California, local authorities may not grant use variances—variances that authorize a land use not otherwise permitted in a zone. For instance, a variance allowing a commercial or retail use in a single-family residential zone would not be permitted.

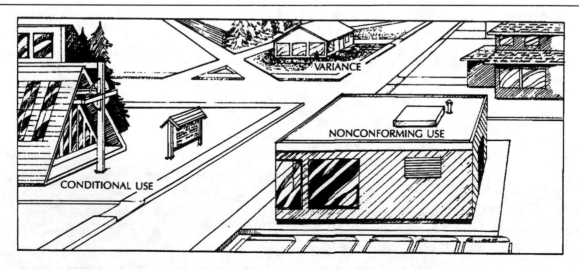

Fig.4.3 Zoning exceptions
A conditional use, a variance, and a nonconforming use.

Example: Corelli owns a piece of property in a residential zone. Unfortunately, the land does not drain properly, so she is not permitted to construct a single-family home on the lot. However, the lot would make a perfect site for storage lockers. Corelli requests a variance. Whether or not Corelli is suffering undue hardship because of the zoning law is immaterial; the local authority does not have the power to grant a variance that would allow a commercial use in a residential zone.

Conditional Uses. Various special uses, such as schools, hospitals, and churches, don't fit into the ordinary zoning categories. These uses are necessary to the community, yet they may have adverse effects on neighboring properties. So in most communities the zoning authority can issue **conditional use permits** (also called special exception permits), allowing a limited number of these uses to operate in compliance with specified conditions. For example, a property owner might be given a conditional use permit to build a private school in a residential neighborhood, as long as the school meets certain requirements for parking, security, and so on.

Rezones. If a property owner believes that his or her property has been zoned improperly, he or she may petition the local appeals board for a **rezone** (sometimes called a zoning amendment). Usually, notice must be given to surrounding landowners and a hearing must be held before any decision is made on a petition.

Building Codes

The enactment of building codes is another exercise of the police power. Building codes protect the public from unsafe or unworkmanlike construction. They are generally divided into specialized areas, such as a fire code, an electrical code, and a plumbing code. Codes specify construction standards as well as requirements for the materials used in the construction. A structure built before a new, stricter standard is enacted may still be required to meet the new standard.

Enforcement of building codes is usually accomplished through the building permit system. A property owner must obtain a permit from the city or county before constructing a new building or repairing, improving, or altering an existing building. For example, it is usually necessary to have a building permit in order to add on to a home, to convert a carport into a garage, or even to build a fence. The permit requirement allows officials to inspect the building plans to verify that building codes and zoning ordinances have been satisfied. Once the completed building has been inspected and found satisfactory, a **certificate of occupancy** is issued.

Subdivision Regulations

Another way in which state and local governments control land use is by regulating subdivisions. A subdivision is generally considered to be the division of one parcel of land into two or more parcels.

Types of Subdivisions. There are several types of subdivisions in California. Subdivisions are usually residential, but may be commercial, industrial, or recreational.

Standard Subdivisions. The typical housing development—where each individual owner owns his or her own parcel of land—is considered to be a standard subdivision. A standard subdivision is technically defined as one with no common rights of either ownership or use among the various owners of the individual parcels created by the division.

Standard subdivisions usually consist of five or more lots that have been improved with utilities. Individuals may purchase a lot on which to build their own home, or developers may purchase several or all of the lots, build houses on the lots, and then sell the homes to individual homeowners.

Common Interest Subdivisions. These are subdivisions where individual owners own or lease a separate lot or unit along with an undivided interest in the common areas of the project. Condominium and cooperative projects are examples of common interest subdivisions. For example, a condominium owner owns the residential unit in severalty, and has an undivided interest in the common areas of the condominium project, such as the lobby, elevators, parking lot, and recreational areas. (See Chapter 2.)

Undivided Interest Subdivisions. In an undivided interest subdivision, individual owners own undivided interests in a parcel of land and have a nonexclusive right to use and occupy the property. The undivided interests are typically tenancies in common. An example of an undivided interest subdivision is a recreational vehicle park.

Land Projects. A land project is a subdivision in a remote area that consists of 50 or more lots without on-site improvements, with less than 1,500 registered voters residing within a certain distance of the subdivision.

Before land projects were regulated, many lots were sold on the basis of misleading promotional activities. For example, lots were sold to buyers who were unaware of the extremely speculative nature of their purchases. State laws were passed allowing the Commissioner to require that reasonable arrangements be made to assure the completion and maintenance of the improvements. The Commissioner may also determine whether the financial burden of completing the construction bears a reasonable relationship to the value of the lots. A public report must be given to prospects before they purchase a lot, and purchasers have the right to rescind the sales agreement within a limited time period.

Planned Unit Developments. Some communities use planned unit developments (PUDs) to provide flexibility in zoning requirements. A PUD is often larger than a traditional subdivision. In most PUDs the houses are clustered close together on undersized lots, to provide larger open spaces that are shared by all of the residents.

A PUD developer may be allowed to mix residential and retail uses, single- and multi-family homes, or some other combination that wouldn't ordinarily be permitted in the district. In return, the developer usually must provide more open space, dedicate more land for public use, or take other actions that would benefit the public.

To qualify for a PUD, a developer submits detailed plans of the proposed development to the planning authority for approval. The planning authority may require additional concessions to the community before granting approval for the project. Some communities designate specific areas as PUD zones. More often, a floating-zone system is used: a PUD could be put in any area if the developer's proposal is approved.

Mobile Homes and Mobile Home Parks. Mobile homes (manufactured homes) and mobile home parks are regulated by the California Mobile Home Code, which is administered by the Department of Housing and Community Development. The code regulates mobile home sales practices, determines when mobile homes become real property, and defines certain mobile home park lots as subdivisions, subject to the requirements of the Subdivided Lands Act (discussed below).

Laws that Regulate Subdivisions. There are various laws that regulate the subdivision of land in California: the Subdivision Map Act, the Subdivided Lands Act, and the Interstate Land Sales Full Disclosure Act. The **Subdivision Map Act** is a "procedural" law—a law that sets forth the procedures that must be followed in order to subdivide land. The **Subdivided Lands Act** is a "consumer protection" law—a law that requires the subdivider to disclose certain information to those who purchase subdivision lots. The Interstate Land Sales Full Disclosure Act is a federal consumer protection law that applies to subdivision lots sold in interstate commerce.

The Subdivision Map Act. The Subdivision Map Act is a set of procedures that must be followed before a subdivision can be created. It gives cities and counties the power to control the formation of subdivisions, and sets out rules for the exercise of that power. The purpose of the Subdivision Map Act is to ensure that new subdivisions comply with the local general plan. It also ensures that adequate public utilities are provided for each new subdivision. The act applies to all subdivisions of land with two or more parcels, but its most important provisions affect only subdivisions with five or more parcels.

When land is subdivided into five or more parcels, the subdivider must file a **tentative subdivision map** with the local planning agency. The tentative map shows the proposed lot boundaries, the location of utility easements and access roads, and the provisions for the control of flooding and geologic hazards. The planning agency sends copies of the map to other government entities for their recommendations. These government entities include transportation, health, and parks departments, school districts, city or county surveyors, and public utilities. Once these entities report back to the planning agency, the planning agency can approve or reject the tentative map, or approve it on the condition that the subdivider take certain actions. For example, the agency may require the subdivider to dedicate some of the subdivision property for public streets.

When the planning agency approves a tentative map, the subdivider has 24 months to file a **final map**, showing the subdivision in its final form. The final map must bear the signatures of the owners and each public utility or other entity that considered the tentative map. No sale, lease, or contract for the sale or lease of any subdivided property is valid until a final map is filed.

Instead of tentative and final maps, a **parcel map** can be filed for subdivisions with two to four lots, and for condominiums and cooperatives. Parcel maps can also be used for subdivisions with lots that are 40 acres or larger, certain subdivisions with access to existing streets, and some subdivisions zoned for commercial or industrial use. A parcel map does not have to be as detailed as a tentative subdivision map or final map.

The Subdivided Lands Act. The Subdivided Lands Act requires a subdivider to disclose certain information to lot buyers. It applies to most subdivisions with five or more parcels. The five lots need not be contiguous if they are part of the same project. And the act applies to any sale that takes place in California, whether or not the property is in the state.

The Subdivided Lands Act also applies to mobile home parks and planned unit developments with five or more lots; to condominiums, community apartment projects, and cooperatives with five or more units; to some residential timeshare projects; and to land projects. Leases of apartments, offices, and stores within a building are exempt from the law. Subdivisions that are entirely within the limits of an incorporated city may also be exempt if the developer complies with certain rules.

Lots in a subdivision covered by the act cannot be sold, leased, or financed until the Real Estate Commissioner investigates the subdivision and issues a **final subdivision public report**. A public report is issued only if the subdivision meets the requirements set forth in the Subdivided Lands Act. A report will be denied:

1. if there is any evidence that the subdivision is unsuitable for the use proposed by the subdivider;
2. unless there is assurance that the purchaser will get what he or she pays for.

For example, to obtain a final public report for a residential subdivision, the subdivider must be able to show that streets and other improvements will be completed and that there will be adequate drinking water and other utilities. The subdivider also must be able to demonstrate that any deposit money will be made secure, that there are satisfactory arrangements to clear any construction liens or blanket mortgage liens, and that when the transaction is completed, title will be conveyed to the purchaser.

When the Commissioner has determined that a subdivision has met all legal requirements, a final subdivision public report will be issued. A public report includes the following information:

- the subdivision location and size;
- the subdivider's name and the project name;
- the legal interest to be acquired by the purchaser;
- the procedure for handling the purchase money;
- the amount of any taxes and assessments;
- any private restrictions;
- any unusual costs the purchaser will have to bear;
- any hazards or adverse environmental factors; and
- any unusual or potentially harmful financial or conveyancing arrangements.

All prospective purchasers must receive a copy of the final report before entering into a sales agreement. They must also sign a receipt proving that they received a copy of the report. That receipt must be kept by the subdivider for at least three years.

A final public report is valid for five years, unless a material change occurs in the subdivision. A material change includes physical changes to the subdivision itself (such as new street or lot lines), changes in the documents used to transfer or finance the lots, and any new conditions that affect the value or use of the lots.

Often, the Commissioner will issue a **preliminary report** before he or she issues the final report. If the developer gives a prospective buyer a copy of a preliminary report, the buyer can reserve a lot in the subdivision. However, until the buyer receives the final report, he or she has the right to back out and have any deposit refunded in full.

If a final public report is used for advertising purposes, it must be used in its entirety. A subdivider cannot, in an advertisement, refer to any improvements or facilities that do not actually exist, unless their completion is provided for with a bond. And an artist's rendering of the subdivision cannot be used in any advertisement unless it is described as such.

If the Commissioner discovers that a subdivider is violating any provisions of the Subdivided Lands Act, the Commissioner can stop the violations or sales of the lots with a Desist and Refrain order.

ILSFDA. The **Interstate Land Sales Full Disclosure Act** (ILSFDA) is a federal law designed to inform consumers about subdivisions offered for sale or lease in interstate commerce. The law generally applies to subdivisions containing 25 or more vacant lots. It is, however, a very complex statute and there are numerous exemptions based on considerations such as the number of lots, the size of the lots, whether the subdivision is subject to state or local registration and disclosure requirements, whether the purchaser has actually seen the lot, and many other factors.

For subdivisions that are not exempt:

1. Subdividers must file a Statement of Record with the Office of Interstate Land Sales Registration (OILSR, a division of HUD); the statement becomes effective if not rejected within 30 days.
2. Subdividers must give each prospective buyer or lessee, before signing any contract, a printed Property Report setting forth all necessary facts regarding the property that would enable the buyer to make an informed decision (e.g., description of the subdivision and lot, condition of title, liens or other encumbrances, condition of access, availability of utilities).
3. If the developers make any representations (express or implied) to the effect that they will provide roads, sewers, water, gas or electric services, or recreational amenities, then the contract with the purchaser must specifically bind the developers to do so; this is known as the "anti-fraud" provision.

Environmental Laws

The federal and state governments have enacted a number of laws aimed at preserving and protecting the physical environment, and many local governments have additional environmental regulations.

These laws can have a substantial impact on the ways in which a property owner is allowed to use his or her land.

National Environmental Policy Act (NEPA). NEPA is a federal law that requires federal agencies to prepare an **environmental impact statement** (EIS) for any governmental action that would have a significant impact on the environment. NEPA also applies to private uses or developments that require the approval of a federal agency.

CERCLA. The Comprehensive Environmental Response, Compensation, and Liability Act, a federal law, concerns liability for environmental cleanup costs. In some cases, the current owners of contaminated property may be required to pay for cleanup, even if they did not cause the contamination.

Air and Water Pollution Control Laws. Federal legislation sets national standards for air and water quality and requires the states to implement these objectives. Permits are required for the discharge of pollutants into the air or water.

California Environmental Quality Act (EQA). This California law is similar to the National Environmental Policy Act. EQA requires state or local agencies to prepare an **environmental impact report** (EIR) for any project (public or private) that may have a significant impact on the environment. A development can only be excepted from this requirement if the public agency overseeing the project rules that it will not have significant adverse effects.

A public hearing is held for each EIR. Alternatives to the proposed action must be considered, and a developer may be required to make changes in the project to reduce its impact.

California Coastal Act. The Coastal Act established the Coastal Commission, which researches ways to protect the California coastline and controls development along the coast. It has several regional divisions, and no development is permitted in the coastal zone without a permit from the appropriate regional board.

Alquist-Priolo Act. Under the Alquist-Priolo Special Studies Zone Act, any application for new residential development or construction in certain areas of the state must include a geologic report. The report considers the earthquake risks for the property.

Eminent Domain

As you've seen, the government can regulate the use of private property with a variety of laws—zoning ordinances, building codes, and so on. These laws are based on the police power, the government's power to regulate for the public health, safety, morals, and general welfare. Another governmental power that can be used to control land use is the power of **eminent domain**.

The power of eminent domain is the federal or state government's power to take private property for a public purpose upon payment of **just compensation** to the owner. A state government may delegate the power of eminent domain to local governments, and to private entities that serve the public, such as utility companies and railroads.

Condemnation is the process by which the government exercises its power of eminent domain. When a particular property is needed for a public purpose, the government first offers to buy it from the owner. If the owner refuses to sell for the price offered, the government files a condemnation lawsuit. The court will order the property to be transferred to the government. The owner's only grounds for objection are that the intended use of the property is not a public use, or that the price offered is not just compensation. (Just compensation is usually defined as the fair market value of the property.)

A local government can use the power of eminent domain to implement its general plan. For example, to fulfill the plan's open space goals, several pieces of private property might be condemned for use as public parks.

It is important to understand the distinction between eminent domain and the police power. Eminent domain involves taking property away from the private owner, and the Constitution requires the government to pay the owner compensation. In an exercise of the police power, private property is regulated, but not taken away from the owner. The government is not required to compensate the owner for a proper exercise of the police power, even though the action (such as a zoning change) may significantly reduce the value of the property.

Taxation

Real property taxes affect a property owner's title. The taxes create liens, and if the property owner fails to pay the taxes, the government can sell the property to collect them. Real property taxation has always been a popular method of raising revenues because land has a fixed location, is relatively indestructible, and is essentially impos-

sible to conceal. Thus, there is a high degree of certainty that the taxes will be collected.

In this section, we will discuss these three types of taxes on real property:

- general real estate taxes (also called ad valorem taxes),
- special assessments (also called improvement taxes), and
- the real estate excise tax (also called the documentary transfer tax).

General Real Estate Taxes

General real estate taxes are levied to support the general operation and services of government. Public schools and police and fire protection are examples of government services paid for with general real estate tax revenues. These taxes are levied by a number of governmental agencies, such as cities, counties, school districts, and water districts. Thus, a single property can be situated in five or six taxing districts.

Assessment. General real estate taxes are **ad valorem** taxes. That means the amount of tax owed depends on the value of the property. The valuation of

Fig.4.4 Comparison of police power and eminent domain

	Police Power	**Eminent Domain**
Public purpose	*Yes*	*Yes*
Taking of property	*No*	*Yes*
Compensation required	*No*	*Yes*

Fig.4.5 *Property tax dates*

```
          Real Property Taxes
       (Tax Year = July 1 – June 30)

Taxes become lien                    March 1
Taxes levied                    by September 1
Tax bill mailed                  by November 1
First installment due             November 1
First installment delinquent      December 10
Second installment due            February 1
Second installment delinquent        April 10
```

property for purposes of taxation is called **assessment**. In California, property must be assessed at its **full cash value**, and as a general rule, the tax rate may not exceed **one percent** of the property's full cash value. (Proposition 13 governs property assessment and taxation in California.)

Protection from drastic tax increases is given to those who own the same houses for a long period of time. The purchase price of a home becomes its **base value**. (If a home was last purchased prior to 1975, the property's 1975 value is its base value.) As long as the same person owns the property and no improvements are made, its assessed value cannot increase more than 2% per year. If the owner improves the property (by building a deck, for example), the assessed value may be increased by the amount the improvements add to the actual value.

The property's assessment is increased to the current full cash value only if there is a new owner or new construction on the property. When the property is sold or otherwise transferred, the new owner must file a **change in ownership statement** with the county recorder or assessor within 45 days of the transfer. Unless the transaction is exempt from reassessment on a change in ownership, the assessed value may be stepped up to the price paid or to the

fair market value at the time of the transfer. That becomes the new base value.

Reassessment Exceptions. To avoid the harsh result of an increased assessment following a transfer of title when the property hasn't been sold or traded for profit, the law exempts several types of transfers from reassessment. These include:

- transfers where the method of holding title is changed but the ownership isn't;
- certain transfers between parents and children; and
- transfers between spouses to create or terminate a community property or joint tenancy interest.

Also, when a senior citizen (over the age of 55) or a severely and permanently disabled homeowner sells his or her home and replaces it with another home in the same county, the assessed value of the old home can be used as the assessed value of the new home. The market value of the new home must be equal to or less than the market value of the old home, and the new home must be purchased within two years after the sale of the old one. A seller who purchases a replacement home in a different county may or may not be able to transfer the assessed value of the old home to the new home. That will depend on the laws of the county where the new home is located.

Property owners who are dissatisfied with the assessment of their property may appeal to the county board of equalization. The board of equalization has the power to adjust the assessed value of property.

Collection of Taxes. General real estate taxes are levied annually, on or before September 1 for each tax year. The tax year runs from July 1 through June 30 of the next calendar year. The tax lien attaches to the property on the previous March 1. So the lien for the July 1995–June 1996 tax year attached on March 1, 1995. Since the taxes are not levied until September, the specific amount of the tax lien isn't known when the lien attaches.

A tax bill is mailed to each property owner on or before November 1 of each year. The tax bill reflects the assessor's appraised value, less any exemptions to which the property owner is entitled. The assessed value is multiplied by the tax rate (no more than 1%), and the result is the amount of tax the property owner must pay.

An owner may pay his or her taxes in two installments, or may pay the total amount when the first installment is due. The first installment is due on November 1, covers the period from July through December, and is delinquent if not paid by 5:00 PM on December 10. The second installment is due February 1, covers the period from January through June, and is delinquent if not paid by 5:00 PM on April 10. A 10% penalty is added to any delinquent payment.

If the property taxes are not paid, the tax collector can foreclose on the tax lien. First a notice of impending default is published, and the property owner is informed of his or her opportunity to pay the taxes by June 30. If the taxes remain delinquent after June 30, the property is considered "in default" and a five-year redemption period begins to run. During this five-year period, the owner can redeem the property by paying the back taxes, interest, costs, and other penalties. If, after five years, the property has not been redeemed, it is deeded to the state. The tax collector can then sell the property at a tax sale, and apply the proceeds to the tax debt. Any surplus from the sale is paid to the former owner or other parties who had an interest in the property.

Tax Exemptions. While the general rule is that all property is taxed at full cash value, there are numerous total or partial exemptions. Property owned by the federal, state, or local government is totally exempt from taxation; so is most property that is used for religious, educational, charitable, or welfare purposes. There are also partial exemptions for owner-occupied homes and homes owned by veterans, senior citizens, and the disabled.

Special Assessments

Special assessments, also called local improvement taxes, are levied to pay for improvements that benefit particular properties, such as the installation of street lights or the widening of a street. Only the properties that benefit from the improvement are taxed, on the theory that the value of those properties is increased by the improvement. A special assessment is usually a one-time tax, although the property owners may be allowed to pay it off in installments.

Like general real estate taxes, special assessments create liens against the taxed properties. If an owner fails to pay the assessment, the government can foreclose on the property.

Here is a summary of the distinctions between general real estate taxes and special assessments:

1. General real estate taxes are levied to pay for ongoing government services, such as police protection. A special assessment is levied to pay for a specific improvement, such as adding sidewalks to a section of street.
2. General real estate taxes are levied against all taxable real property within a taxing district, for the benefit of the entire community. A special assessment, on the other hand, is levied against only those properties that benefit from the improvement in question.
3. General real estate taxes are levied every year. A special assessment is a one-time tax, levied only when a property is benefited by a public improvement.

Real Estate Excise Tax

An excise tax is levied on each sale of real property in California; it is called the documentary transfer tax. The tax is based on the property's selling price. The rate is currently fifty-five cents per $500 of value, or fraction thereof.

Example: A house is sold for $202,000.

$$\$202,200 \div \$500 = \$404.40$$
$$\$405 \times \$0.55 = \$222.75$$

The seller is required to pay $222.75 for the documentary transfer tax.

The transfer tax does not apply to the amount of any loan the buyer is assuming or taking subject to. If the buyer in the example above had assumed the seller's existing $125,200 trust deed, the tax would only be due on the $77,000 difference between the sales price and the assumed loan. The tax would then be only $84.70.

Chapter Summary

1. The police power—the government's power to adopt and enforce laws for the protection of the public health, safety, morals, and general welfare—is the constitutional basis for land use controls, including planning, zoning, building codes, and subdivision regulations.

2. Many communities have a general plan: a comprehensive, long-term plan for development. (Certain counties and cities are required by law to adopt a general plan.) The plan is implemented with zoning ordinances and other laws.

3. Zoning ordinances provide for certain exceptions to their rules (including nonconforming uses, variances, and conditional uses), and also have procedures for rezones.

4. Someone who subdivides land must comply with both the California Subdivision Map Act and the Subdivided Lands Act. In certain cases, a developer may also be required to comply with the Interstate Land Sales Full Disclosure Act.

5. A number of important federal and state environmental laws affect land use, including NEPA, CERCLA, EQA, the California Coastal Act, and the Alquist-Priolo Act.

6. A government entity can use the power of eminent domain to implement its general plan. When property is taken under the power of eminent domain, the government must pay just compensation to the owner. (Compensation is not required when property is merely regulated under the police power.)

7. The government's power to tax also affects property ownership. General real estate taxes are levied each year to pay for ongoing government services. Special assessments are levied to pay for improvements that benefit specific properties. The real estate excise tax must be paid on every sale of real property in California.

O━┳ Key Terms

Police power—The power of state governments to regulate for the protection of the public health, safety, morals, and general welfare.

General plan—A comprehensive, long-term plan of development for a community, which is implemented by zoning and other laws.

Zoning—A method of controlling land use by dividing a community into zones for different types of uses.

Nonconforming use—A use that was previously legal, and which is allowed to continue although it does not conform to a new zoning ordinance.

Variance—An authorization to deviate from the rules in a zoning ordinance, granted because strict enforcement would cause undue hardship for the property owner.

Conditional use permit—A permit that allows a special use, such as a school or hospital, to operate in a neighborhood where it would otherwise be prohibited by the zoning.

Rezone—An amendment to a zoning ordinance; a property owner who feels his or her property has been zoned improperly may apply for a rezone.

Building codes—Regulations that set minimum standards for construction methods and materials.

Eminent domain—The government's power to take private property for public use, upon payment of just compensation to the owner.

Condemnation—The process of taking property pursuant to the power of eminent domain.

Certificate of occupancy—A statement issued by a local government agency (such as a building department) verifying that a newly constructed building is in compliance with all codes and may be occupied.

Subdivision—A piece of land divided into two or more parcels.

Land project—A subdivision that consists of 50 or more unimproved lots in a remote area with less than 1,500 registered voters residing within a certain distance.

General real estate taxes—Taxes levied against real property annually to pay for general government services; based on the value of the property taxed (ad valorem).

Special assessment—A tax levied against property that benefits from a local improvement project, to pay for the project.

Documentary transfer tax—A state tax levied on each sale of real estate, based on the selling price of the property.

Chapter 4—Quiz
Government Restrictions on
Property Rights

1. The police power is the government's power to:

   a) take private property for public use
   b) enact laws for the protection of the public health, safety, morals, and general welfare
   c) tax property to pay for police protection
   d) None of the above

2. Which of the following is likely to be controlled by a zoning ordinance?

   a) Use of the property
   b) Building height
   c) Placement of a building on a lot
   d) All of the above

3. Which of the following is NOT likely to be one of the goals of a land use control law?

   a) Ensuring that properties are put to their most profitable use
   b) Controlling growth and population density
   c) Ensuring that neighboring uses are compatible
   d) Preserving access to light and air

4. As a general rule, when a new zoning ordinance goes into effect, nonconforming uses:

   a) must comply with the new law within 90 days
   b) must shut down within 90 days
   c) will be granted conditional use permits
   d) are allowed to continue, but not to expand

5. An owner who feels that his or her property was improperly zoned should apply for a:

   a) conditional use permit
   b) variance
   c) rezone
   d) nonconforming use permit

6. A property owner is generally required to show undue hardship in order to obtain a:

   a) nonconforming use permit
   b) special exception permit
   c) rezone
   d) variance

7. Which of these is an example of a variance?

   a) Authorizing a hospital to be built in a residential zone
   b) Authorizing a structure to be built only 12 feet from the lot's boundary, although the zoning ordinance requires 15-foot setbacks
   c) Allowing a grocery store to continue in operation after the neighborhood is zoned residential
   d) Approving the subdivision of a parcel of land into two or more lots

8. Which of these is NOT an exercise of the police power?

   a) Condemnation
   b) Building codes
   c) Zoning ordinances
   d) Subdivision regulations

9. Eminent domain differs from the police power in that:

   a) the government is required to compensate the property owner
   b) it can be exercised only by the state government, not a city or county government
   c) it affects only the use of the property, not the title
   d) the property must be unimproved

10. The Hancocks are planning to add a room onto their house. Before construction begins, they are probably required to:

    a) request a zoning inspection
    b) submit a proposal to the planning commission
    c) obtain a building permit
    d) All of the above

11. A special assessment is the same thing as:

    a) a general real estate tax
    b) an improvement tax
    c) a real estate excise tax
    d) an ad valorem tax

12. General real estate taxes are:

    a) used to support the general operation and services of government
    b) levied annually
    c) based on the value of the taxed property
    d) All of the above

13. A subdivision in a remote area with 50 or more lots is called:

    a) an undivided interest subdivision
    b) a land project
    c) a common interest subdivision
    d) a standard subdivision

14. Lots in a subdivision cannot be sold until:

    a) a final map is filed with the local planning agency
    b) a parcel map is filed with the Office of Interstate Land Sales
    c) a preliminary public report is issued by the Commissioner
    d) All of the above

15. Which of these is a state law that requires an environmental impact statement to be prepared in certain circumstances?

    a) ILSFDA
    b) CERCLA
    c) EQA
    d) None of the above

Answer Key

1.b) The police power is the government's power to pass laws (such as zoning ordinances) for the protection of the public health, safety, morals, and general welfare.

2.d) Zoning ordinances typically control the height and placement of buildings as well as type of use.

3.a) Land use controls are not aimed at encouraging the most profitable use of particular properties. In some cases they prohibit more profitable uses that would be detrimental to the public health, safety, or welfare.

4.d) A nonconforming use (a use established before new zoning rules go into effect, which does not comply with those rules) is ordinarily allowed to continue, but the use cannot be expanded, rebuilt after destruction, or resumed after abandonment.

5.c) A rezone is an amendment to the zoning ordinance, giving a particular area a new zoning designation.

6.d) A variance is granted when the property owner shows that strict enforcement of the zoning law would result in undue hardship.

7.b) A variance authorizes the improvement of property in a manner not ordinarily allowed by the zoning ordinance.

8.a) Condemnation is an exercise of the power of eminent domain, not the police power.

9.a) When a government body takes property under the power of eminent domain, it is required to pay compensation to the owner. Compensation is not required if a property loses value due to regulation under the police power.

10.c) A building permit is generally required before an addition or remodeling project is begun, to ensure that the structure will comply with the building codes and zoning.

11.b) A special assessment is also called an improvement tax; it is levied to pay for a particular public improvement.

12.d) All of these statements concerning general real estate taxes are true.

13.b) A land project is a rural subdivision of more than 50 lots. Special disclosure and rescission rights apply to the sale of lots in land projects.

14.a) A final map must be filed with the local planning agency before a subdivision lot can be sold.

15.c) EQA is the California Environmental Quality Act. (CERCLA is a federal environmental law, and ILSFDA is a federal subdivision law.)

Chapter 5

Agency Law

Outline

Chapter Overview

In a typical real estate transaction, a seller hires a real estate broker to find and negotiate with potential buyers on the seller's behalf. The broker is the seller's agent. Agency is a special legal relationship, involving certain duties and liabilities. The law of agency governs many aspects of a real estate agent's relationships with clients and customers. This chapter explains what an agency relationship is and how one is created, then discusses agency duties and liabilities.

Introduction to Agency

An agency relationship arises when one person authorizes another to represent him or her, subject to his or her control, in dealings with third parties. The parties in an agency relationship are the **agent**, the person authorized to represent another, and the **principal**, the party who authorizes and controls the actions of the agent. Persons outside the agency relationship who seek to deal with the principal through the agent are called **third parties**.

Real Estate Agency

In a typical real estate transaction, there is an agency relationship between the property owner and the real estate broker that the owner has listed the property with. The property owner is the principal, who employs the broker to act as his or her agent. The broker/agent represents the seller/principal's interests in negotiations with potential buyers/third parties. The seller/principal is referred to as the listing broker's client.

Although real estate brokers usually represent sellers, in some cases a buyer hires a real estate broker to locate a particular kind of property and negotiate a purchase. That broker is the buyer's agent, and the buyer is that broker's principal. A broker's principal is whoever has hired the broker to act on his or her behalf. See Chapter 6 for a full discussion of the various types of real estate agency relationships.

An agency relationship has significant legal implications. For a third party, dealing with the agent can be the legal equivalent of dealing with the principal.

When an agent who is authorized to do so signs a document or makes a promise, it's as if the principal signed or promised. When a third party provides information to an agent, the principal may be held to have received the information—even if the agent never actually relayed it to the principal. And if the agent does something wrong, the principal may be held liable to third parties for harm resulting from the agent's actions.

Salesperson as Broker's Agent. Under the terms of the California Real Estate Law (discussed in Chapter 18), a real estate salesperson cannot act directly as the agent of a principal in a real estate transaction. Rather, the salesperson acts as the agent of his or her broker, and it is the broker who acts as the principal's agent. This does not mean the principal cannot be held liable for the salesperson's acts, however. Unless an agent has no authority to employ other people in carrying out the agency, the principal may be legally responsible for the acts of the agent's agent. And a real estate broker is presumed to have the authority to employ a salesperson, because that's the standard practice in the industry.

So the seller/principal can be held liable for a real estate salesperson's acts.

At the same time, the broker/agent is always liable for the salesperson's acts. Under certain circumstances, when an agent delegates authority to another person, that person becomes the principal's **subagent** (as opposed to merely the agent of the agent). The principal may be held liable for the acts of the subagent, while the original agent is not held liable for them. However, California statutes expressly state that a real estate salesperson is never a subagent of his or her broker's principal. Thus, the broker is never legally excused from responsibility for the salesperson; the broker/agent, as well as the seller/principal, can be held liable for the salesperson's acts.

Types of Agents

The extent to which the principal can be bound by the agent's actions depends first of all on the scope of authority granted to the agent. There are three basic types of agents:

- universal agents,
- general agents, and
- special agents.

A **universal agent** is authorized to do anything that can be lawfully delegated to a representative. This type of agent has the greatest degree of authority.

A **general agent** is authorized to handle all of the principal's affairs in one or more specified areas. He or she has the authority to conduct a wide range of activities on an ongoing basis on behalf of the principal. For example, a business manager who has the authority to handle personnel matters, enter into contracts, and manage the day-to-day operations of the business is a general agent.

A **special agent** has limited authority to do a specific thing or conduct a specific transaction. An attorney who is hired to litigate a specific legal matter, such as a person's divorce, is a special agent.

In most cases, a real estate broker is a special agent, because he or she has only limited authority.

For example, a seller hires a broker to find a buyer for a particular piece of property. And the broker is only authorized to negotiate with third parties, not to sign a contract on the seller's behalf. A real estate broker can be granted broader powers, but usually is not.

Employee vs. Independent Contractor

A real estate agent may occupy one of two roles as he or she earns a living: **employee** or **independent contractor**. An independent contractor is hired to perform a particular job, and uses his or her own judgment as to how the job will be completed. In contrast, an employee is hired to perform whatever jobs the employer requires, and is given instructions on how to accomplish each task. An employee is supervised and controlled much more closely than an independent contractor. Various employment and tax laws apply only when someone is hired as an employee, and not when someone is hired as an independent contractor.

In many cases, a real estate agent clearly fits into one category or the other; for example, a broker is virtually always an independent contractor in relation to his or her principal (the buyer or the seller). When it comes to the relationship between a broker and a salesperson, however, the distinction between employee and independent contractor may be an issue.

Whether a salesperson is his or her broker's employee or an independent contractor depends on the degree of control the broker exercises over the salesperson. If the broker closely directs the activities of the salesperson and controls how the salesperson carries out his or her work, the salesperson may be considered an employee. For example, if the broker requires the salesperson to work on a set schedule, tells the salesperson when to go where, and decides what steps the salesperson should take in marketing each property, the salesperson is probably the broker's employee.

Most brokers exercise much less control over their salespersons' work than that. They generally focus on the end results—listings, closings, and satisfied clients—and not on the details of how the salesperson accomplishes those results. A broker usually isn't concerned with where the salesperson is or what he or she is doing at any given time. The salesperson is paid on the basis of results (by commission) rather than hours spent on the job. Thus, in most cases, a real estate salesperson is an independent contractor, not the broker's employee.

Fig.5.1 Comparison of employee and independent contractor

Employee
- Broker withholds taxes, social security
- Broker controls activities

Independent Contractor
- Pays own taxes, social security
- Controls own activities

If a salesperson were an employee, the broker would be required to withhold money from the salesperson's compensation to pay certain federal and state taxes (income tax, social security, unemployment insurance, and industrial accident insurance). An independent contractor, on the other hand, is responsible for paying his or her own social security and income taxes.

The Internal Revenue Code provides that a real estate salesperson will be considered an independent contractor for federal income tax purposes if three conditions are met:

1. the individual is a licensed real estate salesperson;
2. substantially all of his or her compensation is based on commission rather than hours worked; and,
3. the services are performed under a written contract providing that the individual will not be treated as an employee for federal tax purposes.

Even when a salesperson is considered an independent contractor for federal income tax purposes, he or she may be treated as an employee under other laws. For example, the state real estate license law makes the broker responsible for supervising the salesperson's actions, and the broker may be held liable for the salesperson's misconduct. (See Chapter 18.)

Creating an Agency Relationship

No particular formalities are required to create an agency relationship; the only requirement is the consent of both parties. An agency may be formed by express agreement, by ratification, or by estoppel.

Express Agreement

Most agencies are created by express agreement: the principal appoints someone to act as an agent, and the agent accepts the appointment. The agreement does not need to be in writing in order to create a valid agency.

The agency agreement also does not have to be supported by consideration. Agency rights, responsibilities, and liabilities arise even when the principal has not promised to compensate the agent for the services rendered.

A real estate agency between a seller and a broker is established by a written listing agreement.

Fig.5.2 Types of agency authority

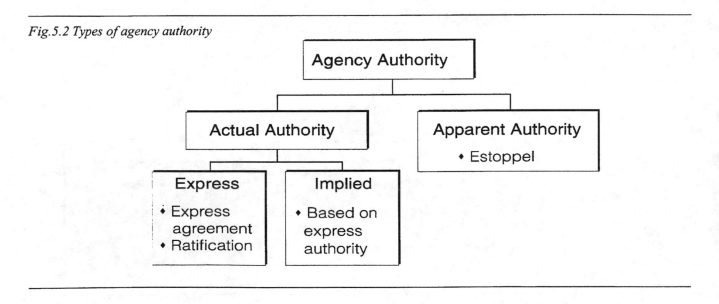

Because of the statute of frauds (see Chapter 7), if the agreement isn't in writing, the broker cannot sue the seller for compensation. Yet even without a written agreement, the broker still may be the seller's agent, with all of the duties and liabilities that agency entails.

Ratification

An agency is created by ratification when the principal gives approval after the fact to acts performed by:

- a person who is without authority to act for the principal, or
- an agent whose actions exceed the scope of authority granted by the principal.

The principal may ratify unauthorized acts expressly, or by accepting the benefits of the acts. For example, if the principal accepts a contract offer negotiated by someone who wasn't authorized to negotiate on his or her behalf, the principal ratifies the agency.

Estoppel

The legal doctrine of estoppel bars someone from using as a defense (in a lawsuit) an argument that contradicts a previously held position. An agency can be created by estoppel when it would be unfair to a third party to deny the agent's authority, because the principal has allowed the third party to believe there was an agency relationship.

> **Example:** In the past, Son has frequently been known to handle business affairs for Father; he appears to be Father's general agent, but actually is not.
> With Father's knowledge, Son gives Broker an exclusive listing for one of Father's properties. Father does nothing to dissuade Broker from believing that the listing is valid; he doesn't protest when Broker places a "For Sale" sign on the property or shows it to prospective buyers.

Broker negotiates a sale, but at closing Father refuses to pay Broker's commission, claiming Son never had the authority to commit him to paying a commission. Broker sues Father for the commission. The court will probably estop (prohibit) Father from denying that Son was his agent, since he negligently or deliberately allowed Broker to believe that Son was authorized to list the property.

The Agent's Authority

Once an agency relationship has been established, the principal is bound by and liable for acts of the agent that are within the scope of the agent's actual or apparent authority.

Actual Authority

Actual authority is authority granted to the agent by the principal—either expressly or by implication. **Express actual authority** is communicated to the agent in express terms, either orally or in writing. **Implied actual authority** is the authority to do what is necessary to carry out acts that were expressly authorized.

> **Example:** When a seller lists property with a broker, the broker is given express actual authority to find a buyer for the property. Based on custom in the real estate industry, the broker also has the implied actual authority to delegate certain tasks to a licensed salesperson. In contrast, the authority granted to the broker does not imply the power to enter into a contract or execute a deed on the seller's behalf.

Apparent Authority

A person has apparent authority when he or she has no actual authority to act, but the principal negligently or deliberately allows it to appear that the person's actions are authorized. In other words, the principal's words or conduct lead a third party to believe that this person (the apparent agent or ostensible agent) has authority to act on behalf of the principal. This corresponds to an agency created by estoppel, explained above.

A principal is bound by acts performed within the scope of an ostensible agent's apparent authority. However, declarations of the agent alone cannot establish apparent authority; the principal must be aware of the declarations or acts and make no effort to deny that they are authorized.

A third party has a duty, when dealing with an agent, to make a reasonable effort to discover the scope of the agent's authority. The third party will not be able to hold the principal liable when an agent acts beyond the scope of his or her actual authority and the principal's conduct does not indicate approval of those acts. Especially when a contract with a third party limits the agent's authority to make representations, the third party is on notice that any representations made by the agent beyond the written terms of the agreement are unauthorized and not binding on the principal.

Duties of the Parties in an Agency Relationship

Each of the parties in an agency relationship owes certain duties to the other party, and also has certain responsibilities to third parties.

The Agent's Duties to the Principal

An agency relationship is a **fiduciary** relationship. A fiduciary is a person who stands in a special position of trust and confidence in relation to someone else. The other party has a legal right to rely on the fiduciary, and the law holds the fiduciary to high standards of conduct.

As a fiduciary, an agent must serve the best interests of the principal. The agent owes the principal these fiduciary duties:

- reasonable care and skill,
- obedience and utmost good faith,
- accounting,
- loyalty, and
- disclosure of material facts.

Reasonable Care and Skill. An agent has a duty to use reasonable care and skill in the performance of his or her duties. If an agent claims to possess certain skills or abilities, the agent must act as a competent person having those skills and abilities would act. For example, a person who holds him or herself out as a real estate broker must exercise the care and skill that a competent broker would bring to the agency. If the broker causes the principal harm due to carelessness or incompetence, the broker will be liable to the principal.

Obedience and Utmost Good Faith. The agent must obey the instructions of the principal and carry them out in good faith. The agent's acts must be in conformity with the purpose and intent of the instructions. A broker can be held liable for any loss caused by failure to obey the principal's instructions.

Accounting. The agent must account for any funds or other valuable items he or she receives on behalf of the principal. The agent is required to report to the principal on the status of those funds (called **trust funds**) and avoid mixing (**commingling**) them with his or her own money. In California, a real estate broker is required to deposit all trust funds in a special trust or escrow account, to prevent improper use of the funds. California's trust fund requirements are discussed in Chapter 18.

Loyalty. The agency relationship is based on confidence, so loyalty is essential. The agent must place the principal's interests above the interests of a third party by refusing to reveal **confidential information**.

Example: In negotiations with a prospective buyer, a seller's real estate agent should not reveal the seller's financial condition or willingness to accept less than the listing price, unless the seller has authorized such disclosure.

Loyalty to the principal also means that the agent must not make any **secret profits** from the agency. For example, it is a breach of fiduciary duty for a broker to list a property for less than it is worth, secretly buy it through an intermediary, and then sell it for a profit. In California and most other states, the license law prohibits a real estate agent from buying an interest in property from the principal (through a relative or friend, for example) without the full knowledge and consent of the principal.

In summary, the agent must not personally profit from the agency relationship through the use of confidential information, and must not have any personal interest in the transaction unless it is with the principal's knowledge and consent.

Disclosure of Material Facts. The agent must inform the principal of any material facts that come to the agent's attention. Any fact that could influence the principal's judgment in the transaction must be revealed. For instance, if a seller's real estate agent discovers that a potential buyer is in a shaky financial situation, the agent must inform the seller, even if it means losing a sale and the subsequent commission.

It's important for an agent to remember that communication to the agent is deemed to be communication to the principal. If a third party provides information to the agent, in the eyes of the law the information has been provided to the principal, regardless of whether the agent actually told the principal. Thus, the principal may be held liable for failure to perform some required task the agent knew about but never communicated to the principal. However, the agent will in turn be liable to the principal for any loss caused by the failure to communicate information or disclose material facts.

A real estate agent representing a seller must be especially careful to avoid these disclosure problems:

- failure to present all offers,
- failure to inform the seller of the property's true value,
- failure to disclose any relationship between the agent and the buyer, and
- failure to reveal a dual agency.

A real estate agent must **present all offers** to the seller, regardless of how unacceptable a particular offer may appear to be. The principal, not the agent, decides whether or not to accept a particular offer. The agent should never hesitate to inform the principal of an offer, even if its acceptance would mean a smaller commission for the agent; the agent's first loyalty must be to the principal.

A seller's agent is also required to inform the principal of the **property's true value**. It is not improper for a real estate agent to buy the principal's property with the principal's knowledge and consent, and then resell the property for a profit. But the agent must provide the principal with his or her estimate of the real value of the property before the property is sold.

The seller's agent must inform the principal if the agent has any **relationship with a buyer**—before the principal decides whether to accept the buyer's offer. If the buyer is a friend, relative, or business associate of the agent, or a company in which the agent has an interest, there may be a conflict of interest. The principal has a right to have this information when making his or her decision.

The agent is also required to reveal a dual agency. There is a **dual agency** when a real estate broker is employed by both the seller and the buyer in the same transaction. In most states, including California, dual agency is legal as long as the broker has fully informed and obtained the consent of both parties. However, a conflict of interest is inherent in a dual agency. A seller wants to get the highest possible price for the property, while the buyer wants to pay the lowest price. It is difficult, if not impossible, to adequately represent these two opposing interests simultaneously. Thus, a dual agency should be entered into with great caution, if at all.

An agent should also be careful to avoid situations where it appears to each party that the agent is working on that party's behalf. For instance, a salesperson working for the listing broker is the seller's agent, but the buyer may believe that the salesperson (who is showing the buyer various properties) is representing him in negotiations with the seller. A seller's agent should carefully explain to each potential buyer that the agent is acting for the seller and owes the seller loyalty.

To avoid some of the confusion regarding who is representing whom, many states are requiring real estate brokers to provide sellers and prospective buyers with an agency disclosure statement at some point before a binding purchase and sale agreement is in entered into. California's agency disclosure rules are discussed in Chapter 6.

The Agent's Duties to Third Parties

While agents owe utmost good faith and loyalty to their principals, this doesn't mean they can treat third parties with reckless disregard. In recent years, courts have held agents to increasingly higher standards of honesty and fair dealing in their transactions with third parties.

Real estate brokers must avoid inaccuracies in their statements to prospective buyers. Any intentional material misrepresentation may constitute actual fraud, and even an unintentional misrepresentation may be considered constructive fraud or negligence. In either case, the buyer has the right to rescind the transaction and/or sue for damages. (See Chapter 7.)

Misrepresentations, which may be grounds for a lawsuit, should not be confused with mere opinions, predictions, or puffing. These are nonfactual or exaggerated statements that a buyer should realize he or she can't rely on. Since it isn't reasonable

to rely on them, opinions, predictions, and puffing generally can't be the basis of a lawsuit.

Examples:

Opinion: "*I think this is the best buy on the market.*"

Prediction: "*The properties in this neighborhood could double in value over the next ten years.*"

Puffing: "*This is a dream house; it has a fabulous view.*"

It should be noted, however, that in California there is a growing tendency to treat these types of statements as representations of material facts. Unsophisticated buyers may rely on such statements and purchase property as a result of this reliance. All real estate agents should be wary of idle sales talk that could be construed as a statement of fact, such as the "prediction" given above of a property's dramatic increase in value.

There are some facts a real estate agent need not disclose to a third party. State statutes provide that agents do not have to disclose that a house was occupied by someone with AIDS, or that someone died on the premises more than year earlier, no matter what the cause. Naturally, if a prospective buyer asks about AIDS or deaths on the property, the agent can be held liable for answering falsely.

Duty to Inspect. Aside from avoiding misrepresentation, the seller and the seller's agent have a duty to disclose any known **latent defects** in the property to the buyer. A latent defect is one that is not discoverable by ordinary inspection.

A decade ago, a seller's agent could merely pass on the seller's information about the property to the prospective buyer. If the seller didn't tell the agent about the property's problems, the agent didn't have to go looking for them. Today, however, California law specifically imposes a duty of inspection on any agent who represents the seller of a one- to four-unit residential property, unless that property is a new home in a subdivision offered for sale for the first time.

The agent must conduct a reasonably competent and diligent visual inspection of the property, and disclose to prospective buyers any material information the inspection reveals. The agent is not required to inspect areas of the property that aren't reasonably accessible to visual inspection. In the case of a condominium or cooperative unit, the agent is only required to inspect the unit being sold. It should be noted that the agent's duty to inspect the property does not relieve buyers of the duty to use reasonable care to protect themselves.

Transfer Disclosure Statement. The disclosures required by the agent's duty to inspect the property are most often made in the appropriate section of the Real Estate Transfer Disclosure Statement, which the seller must present to the buyer in any transaction involving one- to four-unit residential property. The Transfer Disclosure Statement is used to list:

- the seller's disclosure of what is included in the sale;
- the seller's disclosure of any known defects in the property;
- the seller's disclosure of any other types of problems with the property, such as environmental hazards, structural changes made without appropriate permits, neighborhood nuisances, etc.; and
- the agent's disclosure of any material facts about the condition of the property that came from the seller or the agent's visual inspection of the property.

A sample Real Estate Transfer Disclosure Statement is shown in Figure 5.3.

The Agent's Liabilities

Tort Liability. A **tort** is broadly defined as a civil wrong that is not a breach of contract. More specifically, it is a negligent or intentional wrongful act involving breach of a duty imposed by law. The most common tort lawsuits are those involving personal injuries, such as a lawsuit filed against a negligent driver by someone injured in a car accident.

A real estate broker's duties to the principal (the seller) and to third parties (prospective buyers) give rise to tort liability. If the broker breaches fiduciary duties owed to the seller, the seller can sue the broker in tort. The court can order the broker to pay damages that will put the seller as nearly as possible in the position he or she would have been in if the broker hadn't breached his or her duties.

If the broker misrepresents the property to a buyer, the buyer can sue the broker in tort. In addition, the buyer can sue the broker's principal, the seller. That's because a principal is liable for torts committed by the agent within the scope of his or her agency. So the seller can be held liable to the buyer even if the seller wasn't aware of the broker's misrepresentations. An innocent seller who has been held liable for the broker's misconduct can, in turn, sue the broker.

Liability for Seller's Statements. The principal is liable for torts the agent commits within the scope of the agency, but the agent generally isn't liable for the principal's torts. Thus, a real estate agent isn't liable for passing on to the buyer false statements made by the seller, as long as the agent had no reason to believe the statements were untrue.

Note that the agent may be held liable for passing on false information if he or she suspected—or should have suspected—that it was false. The agent could also be held liable for the false information if the agent's visual inspection of the property should have brought the true information to light.

Warranty of Authority. The agent's liability is further limited by the "warranty of authority" rule. In dealing with third parties, the agent claims only to represent the principal; he or she does not guarantee the ability of the principal to perform as promised. Thus, if the seller lacks the ability to transfer the title to the property, the buyer could sue the seller, but not the seller's broker.

Fig.5.3 Transfer disclosure statement

REAL ESTATE TRANSFER DISCLOSURE STATEMENT
(CALIFORNIA CIVIL CODE 1102, ET SEQ.)
CALIFORNIA ASSOCIATION OF REALTORS® (C.A.R.) STANDARD FORM

THIS DISCLOSURE STATEMENT CONCERNS THE REAL PROPERTY SITUATED IN THE CITY OF_____
_____, COUNTY OF_____, STATE OF CALIFORNIA,
DESCRIBED AS _____
THIS STATEMENT IS A DISCLOSURE OF THE CONDITION OF THE ABOVE DESCRIBED PROPERTY IN COMPLIANCE
WITH SECTION 1102 OF THE CIVIL CODE AS OF _____, 19____. IT IS NOT A WARRANTY
OF ANY KIND BY THE SELLER(S) OR ANY AGENT(S) REPRESENTING ANY PRINCIPAL(S) IN THIS TRANSACTION,
AND IS NOT A SUBSTITUTE FOR ANY INSPECTIONS OR WARRANTIES THE PRINCIPAL(S) MAY WISH TO OBTAIN.

I
COORDINATION WITH OTHER DISCLOSURE FORMS

This Real Estate Transfer Disclosure Statement is made pursuant to Section 1102 of the Civil Code. Other statutes require disclosures, depending upon the details of the particular real estate transaction (for example: special study zone and purchase-money liens on residential property).

Substituted Disclosures: The following disclosures have or will be made in connection with this real estate transfer, and are intended to satisfy the disclosure obligations on this form, where the subject matter is the same:

☐ Inspection reports completed pursuant to the contract of sale or receipt for deposit.
☐ Additional inspection reports or disclosures: _____
_____
_____
(LIST ALL SUBSTITUTED DISCLOSURE FORMS TO BE USED IN CONNECTION WITH THIS TRANSACTION)

II
SELLER'S INFORMATION

The Seller discloses the following information with the knowledge that even though this is not a warranty, prospective Buyers may rely on this information in deciding whether and on what terms to purchase the subject property. Seller hereby authorizes any agent(s) representing any principal(s) in this transaction to provide a copy of this statement to any person or entity in connection with any actual or anticipated sale of the property.

THE FOLLOWING ARE REPRESENTATIONS MADE BY THE SELLER(S) AND ARE NOT THE REPRESENTATIONS OF THE AGENT(S), IF ANY. THIS INFORMATION IS A DISCLOSURE AND IS NOT INTENDED TO BE PART OF ANY CONTRACT BETWEEN THE BUYER AND SELLER.

Seller ☐ is ☐ is not occupying the property.

A. The subject property has the items checked below (read across):

☐ Range	☐ Oven	☐ Microwave
☐ Dishwasher	☐ Trash Compactor	☐ Garbage Disposal
☐ Washer/Dryer Hookups	☐ Window Screens	☐ Rain Gutters
☐ Burglar Alarms	☐ Smoke Detector(s)	☐ Fire Alarm
☐ T.V. Antenna	☐ Satellite Dish	☐ Intercom
☐ Central Heating	☐ Central Air Conditioning	☐ Evaporator Cooler(s)
☐ Wall/Window Air Conditioning	☐ Sprinklers	☐ Public Sewer System
☐ Septic Tank	☐ Sump Pump	☐ Water Softener
☐ Patio/Decking	☐ Built-in Barbeque	☐ Gazebo
☐ Sauna	☐ Pool	☐ Spa ☐ Hot Tub
☐ Security Gate(s)	☐ Automatic Garage Door Opener(s)*	☐ Number of Remote Controls_____
Garage: ☐ Attached	☐ Not Attached	☐ Carport
Pool/Spa Heater: ☐ Gas	☐ Solar	☐ Electric
Water Heater: ☐ Gas	☐ Solar	☐ Electric
Water Supply: ☐ City	☐ Well	☐ Private Utility ☐ Other_____
Gas Supply: ☐ Utility	☐ Bottled	

Exhaust Fan(s) in_____ 220 Volt Wiring in_____
Fireplace(s) in_____ ☐ Gas Starter_____
☐ Roof(s): Type:_____ Age:_____(approx.)
☐ Other:_____
Are there, to the best of your (Seller's) knowledge, any of the above that are not in operating condition? ☐ Yes ☐ No If yes, then describe. (Attach additional sheets if necessary.): _____
_____
_____

B. Are you (Seller) aware of any significant defects/malfunctions in any of the following? ☐ Yes ☐ No If yes, check appropriate space(s) below.
☐ Interior Walls ☐ Ceilings ☐ Floors ☐ Exterior Walls ☐ Insulation ☐ Roof(s) ☐ Windows ☐ Doors ☐ Foundation ☐ Slab(s)
☐ Driveways ☐ Sidewalks ☐ Walls/Fences ☐ Electrical Systems ☐ Plumbing/Sewers/Septics ☐ Other Structural Components
(Describe: _____
_____)
If any of the above is checked, explain. (Attach additional sheets if necessary):_____
_____
_____

*This garage door opener may not be in compliance with the safety standards relating to automatic reversing devices as set forth in Chapter 12.5 (commencing with Section 19890) of Part 3 of Division 13 of the Health and Safety Code.

Buyer and Seller acknowledge receipt of copy of this page, which constitutes Page 1 of 2 Pages.
Buyer's Initials (_____) (_____) Seller's Initials (_____) (_____)

OFFICE USE ONLY
Reviewed by Broker or Designee _____
Date _____

TDS-14 FEB 95

Reprinted with permission, California Association of REALTORS®. Endorsement not implied.

Subject Property Address: _____ , 19 _____

C. Are you (Seller) aware of any of the following:

1. Substances, materials, or products which may be an environmental hazard such as, but not limited to, asbestos, formaldehyde, radon gas, lead-based paint, fuel or chemical storage tanks, and contaminated soil or water on the subject property .... ☐ Yes ☐ No
2. Features of the property shared in common with adjoining landowners, such as walls, fences, and driveways, whose use or responsibility for maintenance may have an effect on the subject property .... ☐ Yes ☐ No
3. Any encroachments, easements or similar matters that may affect your interest in the subject property .... ☐ Yes ☐ No
4. Room additions, structural modifications, or other alterations or repairs made without necessary permits .... ☐ Yes ☐ No
5. Room additions, structural modifications, or other alterations or repairs not in compliance with building codes .... ☐ Yes ☐ No
6. Fill (compacted or otherwise) on the property or any portion thereof .... ☐ Yes ☐ No
7. Any settling from any cause, or slippage, sliding, or other soil problems .... ☐ Yes ☐ No
8. Flooding, drainage or grading problems .... ☐ Yes ☐ No
9. Major damage to the property or any of the structures from fire, earthquake, floods, or landslides .... ☐ Yes ☐ No
10. Any zoning violations, nonconforming uses, violations of "setback" requirements .... ☐ Yes ☐ No
11. Neighborhood noise problems or other nuisances .... ☐ Yes ☐ No
12. CC&R's or other deed restrictions or obligations .... ☐ Yes ☐ No
13. Homeowners' Association which has any authority over the subject property .... ☐ Yes ☐ No
14. Any "common area" (facilities such as pools, tennis courts, walkways, or other areas co-owned in undivided interest with others) .... ☐ Yes ☐ No
15. Any notices of abatement or citations against the property .... ☐ Yes ☐ No
16. Any lawsuits by or against the seller threatening to or affecting this real property, including any lawsuits alleging a defect or deficiency in this real property or "common areas" (facilities such as pools, tennis courts, walkways, or the property, or owned in undivided interest with others) .... ☐ Yes ☐ No

If the answer to any of these is yes, explain. (Attach additional sheets if necessary.): _____
_____
_____

Seller certifies that the information herein is true and correct to the best of the Seller's knowledge as of the date signed by the Seller.

Seller_____ Date_____
Seller_____ Date_____

III
AGENT'S INSPECTION DISCLOSURE

(To be completed only if the seller is represented by an agent in this transaction.)
THE UNDERSIGNED, BASED ON THE ABOVE INQUIRY OF THE SELLER(S) AS TO THE CONDITION OF THE PROPERTY AND BASED ON A REASONABLY COMPETENT AND DILIGENT VISUAL INSPECTION OF THE ACCESSIBLE AREAS OF THE PROPERTY IN CONJUNCTION WITH THAT INQUIRY, STATES THE FOLLOWING:

☐ Agent notes no items for disclosure.
☐ Agent notes the following items: _____
_____
_____

Agent (Broker
Representing Seller) _____ By_____ Date_____
    (PLEASE PRINT)   (ASSOCIATE LICENSEE OR BROKER-SIGNATURE)

IV
AGENT'S INSPECTION DISCLOSURE

(To be completed only if the agent who has obtained the offer is other than the agent above.)
THE UNDERSIGNED, BASED ON A REASONABLY COMPETENT AND DILIGENT VISUAL INSPECTION OF THE ACCESSIBLE AREAS OF THE PROPERTY, STATES THE FOLLOWING:

☐ Agent notes no items for disclosure.
☐ Agent notes the following items: _____
_____
_____

Agent (Broker
obtaining the Offer) _____ By_____ Date_____
    (PLEASE PRINT)   (ASSOCIATE LICENSEE OR BROKER-SIGNATURE)

V

BUYER(S) AND SELLER(S) MAY WISH TO OBTAIN PROFESSIONAL ADVICE AND/OR INSPECTIONS OF THE PROPERTY AND TO PROVIDE FOR APPROPRIATE PROVISIONS IN A CONTRACT BETWEEN BUYER AND SELLER(S) WITH RESPECT TO ANY ADVICE/INSPECTIONS/DEFECTS.
I/WE ACKNOWLEDGE RECEIPT OF A COPY OF THIS STATEMENT.

Seller_____ Date_____ Buyer_____ Date_____
Seller_____ Date_____ Buyer_____ Date_____
Agent (Broker
Representing Seller) _____ By_____ Date_____
  (PLEASE PRINT) (ASSOCIATE LICENSEE OR BROKER-SIGNATURE)
Agent (Broker
obtaining the Offer) _____ By_____ Date_____
  (PLEASE PRINT) (ASSOCIATE LICENSEE OR BROKER-SIGNATURE)

SECTION 1102.2 OF THE CIVIL CODE PROVIDES A BUYER WITH THE RIGHT TO RESCIND A PURCHASE CONTRACT FOR AT LEAST THREE DAYS AFTER THE DELIVERY OF THIS DISCLOSURE IF DELIVERY OCCURS AFTER THE SIGNING OF AN OFFER TO PURCHASE. IF YOU WISH TO RESCIND THE CONTRACT, YOU MUST ACT WITHIN THE PRESCRIBED PERIOD.
A REAL ESTATE BROKER IS QUALIFIED TO ADVISE ON REAL ESTATE. IF YOU DESIRE LEGAL ADVICE, CONSULT YOUR ATTORNEY.

This form is available for use by the entire real estate industry. The use of this form is not intended to identify the user as a REALTOR. REALTOR is a registered collective membership mark which may be used only by real estate licensees who are members of the NATIONAL ASSOCIATION OF REALTORS and who subscribe to its Code of Ethics.

Copyright 1990, 1994, CALIFORNIA ASSOCIATION OF REALTORS
525 South Virgil Avenue, Los Angeles, California 90020

    — OFFICE USE ONLY —
Reviewed by Broker or Designee _____
Date _____

Page 2 of 2 Pages.

REAL ESTATE TRANSFER DISCLOSURE STATEMENT (TDS-14 PAGE 2 OF 2)

Example: A broker lists Ackerman's property and negotiates a sale to Martinez. At closing, Martinez discovers that there are several judgment liens against the property and that Ackerman cannot convey marketable title. Martinez could sue Ackerman for any damages this may have caused her, but the broker is immune because he did not guarantee his client's capacity to perform.

The Principal's Duties to the Agent

An agency agreement is often an enforceable contract, obligating each party—principal and agent—to do specified things in fulfillment of the contract. If either one fails to do what he or she agreed to, the other can sue for breach of contract.

However, an agent's fiduciary duties to the principal are a matter of law, not contract. Similarly, the principal has some duties to the agent even in the absence of an express contract.

Under certain circumstances, the principal may have a duty to indemnify the agent for losses suffered because of the agency. More generally, the principal has a duty to reimburse the agent for expenses incurred in carrying out the agency. But in real estate it's the custom (sometimes reflected in the express terms of the listing agreement) for a broker to pay expenses out of his or her commission. It would be quite unusual for a broker to present a seller with a bill for gas and mileage, for example.

Perhaps the principal's most important duty is the duty to compensate the agent for his or her services. Even if there is no specific provision for compensation in the agency agreement, there is a presumption that the principal will pay for services rendered.

That presumption doesn't really apply in the real estate field, however. To be legally entitled to compensation for services rendered to a seller, a real estate broker must:

- have a valid, written employment contract,
- be properly licensed while representing the seller, and
- fulfill the terms of the employment agreement.

Unless all three of these requirements are met, the seller is not obligated to pay the broker a commission. As you'll see in Chapter 18, it would be illegal for the seller to pay the broker if he or she was not properly licensed. The different types of listing agreements, and what a broker has to do to earn a commission under each type, are discussed in Chapter 8.

Terminating an Agency

Once an agency relationship is terminated, the agent is no longer authorized to represent the principal. An agency may be terminated either by acts of the parties or by operation of law.

Termination by the Acts of the Parties

There are several ways the parties can terminate an agency agreement. These include:

- mutual agreement,
- revocation by the principal, and
- renunciation by the agent.

Mutual Agreement. The parties may, of course, terminate the agency by mutual agreement at any time.

Principal Revokes. The principal may revoke the agency by firing the agent whenever he or she wishes. (Remember that an agency relationship requires the consent of both parties.) However, in some cases revoking an agency breaches a contractual agreement, and the principal may be liable for any damages suffered by the agent because of the breach. For example, in some cases a seller who revokes a real estate broker's agency can be held liable for the broker's commission.

Agent Renounces. The agent can renounce the agency at any time. Like revocation, renunciation may be a breach of contract, in which case the agent

Fig.5.4 Termination of agency

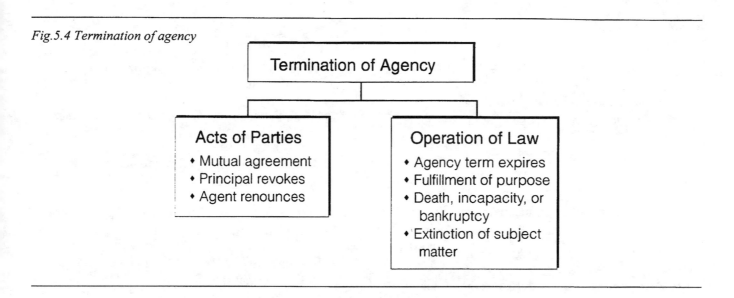

could be liable for the principal's damages resulting from the breach. But since an agency contract is a personal services contract (the agent has agreed to provide personal services to the principal), the principal could not demand specific performance as a remedy. The courts will not force a person to perform personal services, because that would violate the constitutional prohibition against involuntary servitude.

Termination by Operation of Law

Several events terminate an agency relationship automatically; neither party has to take any action. These events include:

- expiration of the agency term,
- fulfillment of the purpose of the agency,
- death, incapacity, or bankruptcy of either party, and
- extinction of the subject matter.

Expiration of Agency Term. An agency terminates automatically when its term expires. If the agency agreement did not include an expiration date, it is deemed to expire within a reasonable time (which would vary, depending on the type of agency in question). If there is no expiration date, either party may terminate the agency without liability for damages, although the other party might be able to demand reimbursement for expenses incurred before the termination. In California, an exclusive listing agreement must specify a termination date. (See Chapter 8.)

Fulfillment of Purpose. An agency relationship terminates when its purpose has been fulfilled. For example, if a broker is hired to sell the principal's property and the broker does so, the agency is terminated by fulfillment.

Death, Incapacity, or Bankruptcy. The agency is terminated before it expires if the agent or the principal dies. Most states provide that the agency also terminates when either party becomes incompetent. Generally, the agent has no authority to act after the death or incompetency of the principal, even if the agent is unaware of the principal's death or incompetency. An agency is also terminated by the bankruptcy of either party.

Extinction of Subject Matter. The subject matter of a real estate agency is the property in question. If the property is in any way extinguished (e.g., sold or destroyed), the agency automatically terminates.

Chapter Summary

1. In an agency relationship, the agent represents the principal in dealings with third parties. An agent may be a universal, general, or special agent, depending on the scope of authority granted.

2. Most agency relationships are created by express agreement (oral or written), but they can also be created by ratification or estoppel. Acts performed by an agent or an ostensible agent are binding on the principal if they fall within the scope of the agent's actual or apparent authority.

3. An agent owes fiduciary duties to the principal, including the duties of reasonable care and skill, obedience and utmost good faith, accounting, loyalty, and disclosure of material facts. The agent must inform the principal of all offers, the property's true value, any relationship between the agent and the buyer, and a dual agency.

4. An agent owes third parties a duty of good faith and fair dealing. Neither the seller nor the seller's agent may misrepresent the property, and they must reveal any known latent defects to prospective buyers. An agent has the duty to visually inspect the property and reveal the results of that inspection to prospective buyers. An agent generally won't be held liable for innocently passing false statements from the seller on to a buyer, unless the agent knew or should have suspected that the statements were inaccurate.

5. An agency relationship can be terminated by: mutual agreement; revocation; renunciation; expiration; fulfillment of purpose; the death, incapacity, or bankruptcy of either party; or extinction of the subject matter.

Key Terms

Principal—The person who authorizes an agent to act on his or her behalf.

Agent—A person authorized to represent another in dealings with third parties.

Third party—A person seeking to deal with the principal through the agent.

Fiduciary—Someone who holds a special position of trust and confidence in relation to another.

Ratification—When the principal gives approval to unauthorized actions after they are performed, creating an agency relationship after the fact.

Estoppel—When the principal allows a third party to believe an agency relationship exists, so that the principal is legally precluded (estopped) from denying the agency.

Actual authority—Authority the principal grants to the agent either expressly or by implication.

Apparent authority—Where no actual authority has been granted, but the principal allows it to appear that the agent is authorized, and therefore is estopped from denying the agency. Also called ostensible authority.

Dual agent—An agent who is acting on behalf of both parties to a transaction at the same time.

Secret profit—Any profit an agent receives as a result of the agency relationship and does not disclose to the principal.

Chapter 5—Quiz
Agency Law

1. An agency relationship can be created by each of the following except:

   a) written agreement
   b) oral agreement
   c) ratification
   d) warranty of authority

2. An agency relationship requires:

   a) consideration
   b) the consent of both parties
   c) an enforceable contract
   d) None of the above

3. Hanson owns a tract of commercial property that Ashworth wants to buy. During negotiations, Hanson allows Ashworth to assume that Broker Timmons is his agent. Ashworth probably can rely on the representations Timmons makes concerning the property because:

   a) an express agency has been created
   b) Timmons is Hanson's general agent
   c) an agency has been created by estoppel
   d) prospective buyers may rely on any information obtained from a licensed broker

4. Garcia acted on behalf of Hilton without her authorization. At a later date, Hilton gave her approval to Garcia's actions. This is an example of:

   a) express agreement
   b) ratification
   c) estoppel
   d) assumption of authority

5. An agency relationship can be terminated by:

   a) renunciation without the principal's consent
   b) incapacity of either party
   c) extinction of the subject matter
   d) All of the above

6. An agent warrants:

   a) his or her authority to act on the principal's behalf
   b) the principal's capacity to perform
   c) all the information the principal provides concerning the property
   d) None of the above

7. A seller lists his home with a broker at $130,000; he asks for a quick sale. When the broker shows the house to a buyer, he says the seller is financially insolvent and will take $110,000. The buyer offers $110,000 and the seller accepts. In regard to the broker's conduct, which of the following is true?

   a) He did not violate his fiduciary duties to the seller because the seller accepted the offer
   b) He did not violate his fiduciary duties to the seller because he fulfilled the purpose of his agency
   c) He violated his fiduciary duties to the seller by disclosing confidential information to the buyer
   d) He was unethical, but there was no violation of fiduciary duties, since the broker did not receive a secret profit

8. Stark lists his property with Billings, a licensed broker. Billings shows the property to her cousin, who decides he would like to buy it. Which of the following is true?

    a) Billings can present her cousin's offer to Stark, as long as she tells Stark that the prospective buyer is one of her relatives

    b) Billings violated her fiduciary duties to Stark by showing the property to one of her relatives

    c) It was not unethical for Billings to show the property to a relative, but it would be a violation of her fiduciary duties if she presented her cousin's offer to Stark

    d) It is not necessary for Billings to tell Stark that the buyer is related to her, as long as he is offering the full listing price for the property

9. A seller listed her property with a broker for $75,000. The seller wanted a $9,000 downpayment. A buyer made an offer of $70,000 with a $10,000 downpayment, which the broker submitted to the seller. The seller said she would think it over and let the broker know. In the meantime, another buyer made an offer of $72,000 with a $6,000 downpayment. The broker refused to present this offer to the seller until the seller had advised him whether she was accepting the first offer. The broker was:

    a) right, because the first offer had priority

    b) right, because the second offer had a smaller downpayment

    c) wrong, because the second offer was for more money

    d) wrong, because the agent must submit all offers promptly

10. Both the seller and his real estate agent know the plumbing is leaking. Which of the following is true?

    a) The agent does not have to mention this to prospective buyers if the seller gave her written instructions not to

    b) It would be a breach of the agent's fiduciary duties if she disclosed this information to prospective buyers

    c) The agent is required to discuss the leak with prospective buyers only if they ask about the plumbing

    d) The agent is required to disclose this information to all prospective buyers

11. A principal cannot be held liable for any acts performed by the agent that were not:

    a) expressly authorized by the principal

    b) within the scope of the agent's actual authority

    c) within the scope of the agent's actual or apparent authority

    d) ratified after the fact

12. A real estate agent tells potential buyers: "This is a great old house. They just don't make them like they used to." This statement would be considered:

    a) a misrepresentation

    b) actual fraud

    c) self-dealing

    d) puffing

13. In most cases, a listing broker:

    a) is authorized to enter into contracts on
        behalf of the seller
    b) is considered a special agent
    c) Both of the above
    d) Neither of the above

14. There can be no agency relationship between a
    seller and a real estate broker unless:

    a) the seller agrees to pay the broker a com-
        mission
    b) they have a written listing agreement
    c) the seller records a power of attorney
    d) None of the above

15. Dual agency is:

    a) no longer legal in California
    b) legal as long as both principals consent to
        the arrangement
    c) legal as long as the agent receives equal
        compensation from both principals
    d) encouraged by many professional associa-
        tions as the best way of representing a
        client's interests

Answer Key

1.d) An agency relationship may be created by express agreement (written or oral), ratification, or estoppel.

2.b) The consent of both parties is necessary to the creation of an agency relationship, but consideration is not. There does not have to be an enforceable contract between the principal and the agent.

3.c) When a principal allows a third party to believe that someone is acting as his or her agent, an agency relationship has been created by estoppel.

4.b) An agency relationship is created by ratification when the principal approves of unauthorized actions after the fact.

5.d) Any of the choices listed can terminate an agency relationship.

6.a) An agent typically only warrants that he or she is authorized to act on the principal's behalf.

7.c) The broker was disloyal to his principal and violated his fiduciary duties by disclosing confidential information to a third party.

8.a) A seller's real estate agent is required to tell the seller if the prospective buyer is related to the agent.

9.d) An agent must submit all offers to the principal, whether or not another offer (better or worse) is outstanding.

10.d) The leaky plumbing is a known latent defect, and the agent must disclose it to all prospective buyers; failure to reveal it is a violation of the duty of good faith and fair dealing that an agent owes to third parties.

11.c) The principal can be held liable for acts that were not expressly authorized, but cannot be held liable for acts that were not within the scope of the agent's actual or apparent authority.

12.d) This is an example of puffing, an exaggerated statement that the buyers should realize they can't depend on.

13.b) A listing broker is usually a special agent, with limited authority to represent the principal in a particular transaction; it is rare for a listing broker to be authorized to sign contracts on behalf of the principal.

14.d) An agency relationship is established between a seller and a real estate broker when the seller appoints the broker as his or her agent (orally or in writing) and the broker consents to the agency. A broker can't sue a seller for a commission without a written listing agreement, but agency duties and liabilities arise even without a written agreement and even without a promise of compensation.

15.b) Dual agency is legal, but only if both the seller and the buyer are informed that the agent is representing both of them, and they both give their consent to the arrangement.

Chapter 6

Types of Agency Relationships

 Outline

 Chapter Overview

In today's real estate market, there is a great deal of confusion about agency representation. Does the real estate agent represent the buyer, the seller, or both in any given real estate transaction? Does it matter? The first part of this chapter discusses the various types of agency relationships that are possible, and explains some of the reasons why it matters very much which party the agent represents. The second part of the chapter discusses California's agency disclosure requirements, and the final section explores the impact of antitrust laws on real estate licensees.

Introduction

In the 1980s various organizations (including the Federal Trade Commission, the National Association of Realtors, and the Association of Real Estate License Law Officials) conducted studies on the question of agency representation. Those organizations concluded that many real estate buyers and sellers were confused about whom the real estate agent actually represented. Buyers, in particular, .

appeared bewildered by the rules of agency. They often thought that the real estate agent represented them, when in fact the agent typically represented the sellers.

Novice buyers and sellers—as well as novice real estate agents—may genuinely wonder why it matters whom the real estate agent represents. As long as the agent does the job—finding a buyer for a listed property—does it matter which party he or she is representing? The answer is yes, it matters a great deal, for two important reasons:

1. **The complexity of real estate transactions.** Today's real estate transactions are increasingly complex. In the 1990s, buyers and sellers have to do more than decide on a purchase price and closing date. They must learn about issues concerning property values, land use and the environment, home and pest inspections, financing, property condition disclosures, fair housing, and contract preparation. Can "their" real estate agent be relied on to give them sound advice and help them make decisions about those matters?

   An agent is retained by a *principal* for his or her expertise, and is expected to give reliable advice. On the other hand, an agent must give a *third party* accurate information, but is not required (or even allowed, in some cases) to give that third party advice or recommend a course of action.

2. **Fear of lawsuits.** Our legal climate encourages litigation, and increasing numbers of lawsuits are filed against brokers each year. Confusion about agency representation is the basis for many a lawsuit.

   If a buyer and seller are confused about whom the real estate agent represents, they are both apt to expect advice from that agent. However, an agent only gives advice to his or her principal. An agent can, and usually does, give information to a customer, but he or she does not give advice to a customer. If the customer erroneously believes that the real estate agent is acting on his or

her behalf, the customer may treat information—or even a sales pitch—as advice and act on it to his or her detriment. If that customer becomes dissatisfied with his or her decision, a lawsuit may be the result.

In the last several years, many states began passing agency disclosure laws—laws that require real estate agents to disclose to both the buyer and the seller, in writing, the identity of the party they represent. While the provisions of these laws vary from state to state, their purpose remains the same. Disclosure laws help prevent confusion over who is representing whom, and enable the parties to make more informed choices about representation. (California's disclosure laws are discussed later in this chapter.) But disclosure laws are only half the battle. Real estate agents must understand the consequences of the different types of agency relationships, and must learn to avoid problems that may arise because of those relationships.

Definitions

Before addressing the different types of agency relationships and the impact they have on the parties, we need to briefly review the definitions of some of the terms we'll be using:

- **Agent**—As explained in Chapter 5, an agent is someone who is authorized to represent another in dealings with third parties. In lay terms, an agent is usually someone who has expertise in a certain area, and who will use that expertise to the advantage of his or her client.
- **Real estate agent**—Real estate agent is the generic term given to real estate licensees. Real estate brokers are the only real estate agents who are authorized to act directly for a buyer or seller; real estate salespeople act on behalf of their real estate brokers.
- **Client**—A client is the person who has engaged the services of an agent. A client may be a real estate seller, buyer, landlord, or tenant.

- **Customer**—In transactions where the agent is representing a seller or a landlord, third parties are generally referred to as customers. A customer may be a buyer or a tenant. As discussed in Chapter 5, while an agent owes fiduciary duties to a client, an agent's only responsibilities to the customer are honesty and fair dealing.
- **Listing salesperson**—The salesperson that takes the listing on a home. This salesperson may or may not be the one who procures the buyer.
- **Listing broker**—The broker for whom the listing salesperson works.
- **Selling salesperson**—The salesperson who procures a buyer for a property. This salesperson may or may not have taken the listing for the property sold.
- **Selling broker**—The broker for whom the selling salesperson works.
- **Cooperating broker**—A broker who did not take the listing on the property and who attempts to find a buyer. (The cooperating broker who succeeds in procuring a buyer is the selling broker.)

Once you grasp the roles played by real estate agents, as they were just defined, you can understand the different types of real estate sales. Real estate transactions can be roughly divided into **in-house** sales and **cooperative** sales.

- **In-house sale**—A sale in which the buyer and the seller are brought together by salespeople working for the same broker.

Example: Salesperson Morgenstern works for Broker Opstad. She obtains a listing on a home. Morgenstern and all of Opstad's other agents try to find a buyer for the home. Bailey, another salesperson who works for Opstad, finds a buyer. Morgenstern is the listing salesperson; Bailey is the selling salesperson. Because they both work for the same broker, this is called an in-house sale.

- **Cooperative transaction**—A sale in which the listing agent and the selling agent work for different brokers. A selling broker is often referred to as a cooperating broker.

Example: In the previous example, both Morgenstern and Bailey work for the same broker. Now suppose that Morgenstern works for Broker Opstad and Bailey works for Broker Nyhart. When Bailey finds a buyer for Morgenstern's listing, it is a cooperative transaction. Morgenstern is the listing agent; Opstad is the listing broker. Bailey is the selling agent; Nyhart is the selling broker. Nyhart is also called a cooperating broker. The commission earned on the transaction is split four ways: Opstad, Morgenstern, Nyhart, and Bailey each get a portion of the commission. (The commission earned on an in-house transaction is split only three ways: between the broker and the listing salesperson and the selling salesperson.)

In-house sales are generally preferred by the listing broker and both the listing and the selling salesperson because each agent's share of the commission is larger than when the sale is a cooperative transaction.

Types of Agency Relationships

There are few restrictions on which party a real estate agent may represent. Generally, the types of agency relationships can be divided into the following categories:

- seller agency,
- buyer agency, and
- dual agency.

Seller Agency

Traditionally, real estate agents nearly always represented the seller. While other types of agency relationships are gaining popularity, seller agency is still the most common type of agency relationship.

Fig.6.1 Types of agency relationships

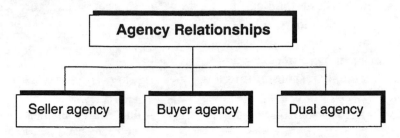

Creation of Seller Agency. Most seller agency relationships are created with a written listing agreement (discussed in Chapter 8). In a typical listing agreement, the seller hires a broker to find a buyer who is ready, willing, and able to purchase the property on the seller's terms. In return for his or her services, the broker receives a commission (usually a percentage of the sales price).

A seller agency relationship can also be created by the words or conduct of the parties, although the broker will be prevented from suing for a commission if there is no written listing agreement. (See the discussion of implied agency in Chapter 5.)

As the agent of the seller, a real estate broker must use his or her best efforts to promote the interests of the seller. However, a seller's agent can (and is expected to) provide services to the buyer as well, such as filling out a purchase offer, presenting the offer to the seller, and helping to secure financing. These services help close a transaction, and are thus considered to be in the best interests of the seller. They do not violate the agent's fiduciary duties to the seller.

Many buyers are content with the traditional seller agency relationship, as long as it is fully disclosed. They use the services of a real estate agent because they want access to multiple listing inventory; they want to receive complete, honest information about a property; and they want someone to present their offers to the seller. The seller agency relationship often satisfies those requirements nicely, and the buyers do not have to commit to a buyer agency relationship to get the help they need.

Seller Agency Situations. In both in-house and cooperative transactions, a seller's agent must be very careful to treat the buyer fairly. However, that agent must not act as if he or she is representing the buyer. In other words, the agent must fully disclose all the material facts and answer the buyer's questions honestly; but the agent should not give the buyer advice, such as suggesting how much to offer for the listed property.

> **Example:** Harrison works for Yates, the listing broker. Harrison shows the listed house to Tsui. The listing price is $115,000, but Harrison knows the owner will accept an offer of $108,000. Tsui asks Harrison, "How low do you think the seller will go?" Harrison should make it clear to Tsui that he represents the seller, and cannot divulge that kind of information. If he does so, or gives Tsui any other advice, Tsui may reasonably believe that Harrison represents him (Tsui) instead of the seller. A court could find that an agency relationship between Harrison and Tsui had arisen by implication. Also, the seller could sue both Harrison and his broker (Yates) for breach of fiduciary duties.

Sometimes the buyer has had a previous relationship with the seller's agent.

Example: Suppose Tsui listed his home with Harrison and liked him so well that he wanted Harrison to help him find another home. Harrison shows Tsui a home listed by another salesperson working for Yates.

Under the circumstances, it would be easy for Tsui to think that Harrison is acting as his agent. However, unless otherwise agreed, Harrison is the seller's agent, and should emphasize this fact to Tsui. Tsui should be reminded that Harrison is obligated to disclose any material information Tsui tells him to the seller, and that in all negotiations Harrison will be representing the seller's best interests.

When a transaction is a cooperative sale—a sale that involves two brokers—there are special dangers for the selling agent. While it is usually obvious that the listing broker represents the seller, it is by no means obvious which party the selling broker represents.

Example: A listing is obtained by Broker Yates. A salesperson working for Broker Chase finds a buyer. The salesperson has never met the seller, and has never even met Broker Yates. Does that salesperson represent the buyer or the seller?

Until recently, many listing agreements provided that any member of the multiple listing service who found a buyer for a listed property automatically represented the seller. Today, however, many listing agreements state that other members of the MLS act as cooperating agents only (a cooperating agent is simply any member of the MLS who attempts to find a buyer); no agency relationship between the seller and the other MLS members is implied by the terms of the listing agreement. It is up to each individual cooperating agent to decide whether he or she will represent the seller or the buyer.

If the cooperating agent decides to act as the seller's agent, disclosure is the key to a smooth transaction. The buyer must understand that the agent he or she has been working with face-to-face is, in fact, the seller's agent. In cooperative transactions, it is quite easy for the buyer to mistakenly be-

lieve that the selling agent is working on his or her behalf. Thus, buyers often tell selling agents confidential information. However, it is a seller's agent's responsibility to pass along that confidential information to the seller. And that agent must be sure that his or her natural desire to help the buyer does not interfere with the agent's fiduciary obligations to the seller.

Example: Martinson works for Baker as a salesperson. She has shown the Greens many houses in the course of several weeks. Martinson enjoys the Greens and has worked very hard to find them a house they like. Martinson does not have an agency agreement with the Greens, and is acting in the capacity of a seller's agent.

Finally, the Greens decide to make an offer on a house listed by Broker Rush. The Greens are very excited about the house, and tell Martinson that they are willing to pay full price for it. Nevertheless, they decide to start out with an offer that is $5,000 less than the listing price.

Since Martinson is acting as the seller's agent, she is obligated to tell the seller that the Greens are willing to pay the full listing price. She should have made it very clear to the Greens that she was not acting as their agent (no matter how much she liked them), and that she was obligated to act in the seller's best interests.

Of course, as discussed previously, just because the selling agent represents the seller does not mean that he or she cannot provide the buyer with valuable services. The selling agent can still explain the fundamentals of purchasing a home, prequalify the buyers to determine the price range they can afford, screen the available properties and show the buyers the ones that most suit their needs, present offers to the seller, help find financing, and estimate closing costs. This fairly lengthy list of services is enough to satisfy most buyers' needs.

Buyer Agency

There are times when a buyer wants more than the services a seller's real estate agent can provide to a customer. Some buyers want advice on property values and help in determining how much to offer for a particular house. They want someone to help them negotiate the terms of the sale and give them advice on confidential matters. For those buyers, a buyer agency relationship is usually the answer.

Advantages of Buyer Agency. A buyer agency relationship can be beneficial for the buyer in many respects.

Access to More Properties. Generally, a buyer's agent is compensated when the buyer purchases a home—any home. So a buyer's agent will often pursue less traditional means of searching for properties. A seller's agent is generally limited to showing a buyer properties listed by his or her own office or those published by the multiple listing service. Otherwise, the agent could not be sure of getting paid for his or her efforts. A buyer's agent, on the other hand, is free to spend time searching out properties that have not been submitted to the multiple listing service—for instance, properties that are for sale by owner, properties with open listings, properties listed exclusively with other brokers, and properties in foreclosure or probate proceedings.

Expert Advice. Seller's agents are, by definition, trying to find a buyer for the seller's home. They develop expert sales techniques designed to convince the buyer to sign on the dotted line. Buyer's agents, on the other hand, are free to advise the buyer on the pros and cons of purchasing any given home. They can educate the buyer on various issues he or she should be aware of, such as energy costs and property value trends.

Help with Negotiating. Buyers often feel uncomfortable negotiating for a property, especially one they really want to buy. They may be afraid to make a mistake through ignorance, or they may feel pressured to make a high offer quickly before someone else snaps up the property. A buyer's broker can use his or her intimate knowledge of the real estate market to help the buyer get the property on the best possible terms.

Fiduciary Duties. A buyer's agent owes all of his or her fiduciary duties to the buyer rather than the seller. This means that the agent owes the buyer the duties of loyalty, obedience and good faith, reasonable care and skill, accounting, and disclosure of material facts. For many buyers, loyalty is the most important characteristic of buyer agency. The duty of loyalty means that the agent must put the buyer's interests ahead of his or her own, and any information disclosed to the agent by the buyer must be kept confidential.

> **Example:** Johnson is looking for a house. She is a first-time home buyer and decides to engage Broker Mendez to represent her. Mendez shows her many houses, and there are two that interest her. One is a large fixer-upper that is selling for $145,000. The other is a small, newer house in mint condition that is selling for $136,000. Because Mendez must put Johnson's interests before his own, he advises her to purchase the smaller, $136,000 house because it suits her needs better. He does so even though he would make a bigger commission if she purchased the $145,000 house.
>
> Mendez advises Johnson to offer $129,900 for the $136,000 house. Johnson agrees to do so, but tells Mendez that she is willing to pay the full listing price. Because Mendez is Johnson's agent, he is obligated to keep this information confidential. If he had been the seller's agent, he would have been required to disclose this information to the seller.

Buyer agency relationships also offer advantages to the broker. When a buyer signs an agency agreement, the broker can be assured of greater client loyalty. Seller's agents often find themselves spending many hours showing houses to a buyer, only to have that buyer purchase a house through another agent. This does not happen nearly so often to a buyer's agent. A buyer's agent may also be able to avoid conflicts of interest better. Some seller's agents become so attached to their buyers that they violate their duties to their sellers as they try to get a good price for their buyers.

Creation of Buyer Agency. Most buyer agency relationships are created with a written **representation agreement**. While the terms of representation agreements vary, they generally provide for the following:

- term of the agreement;
- general characteristics of the property the buyer wants;
- price range;
- conditions under which a fee will be earned;
- who will pay the fee; and
- some description of the broker's duties.

An example of a representation agreement is shown in Figure 6.2.

Buyer's Agent's Compensation. There are several different ways to compensate a buyer's agent. The three most common ways are:

- a retainer,
- a seller-paid fee, and
- a buyer-paid fee.

Some agents insist on a **retainer**—a fee paid upfront—before agreeing to a buyer agency relationship. The fee is usually nonrefundable, but will be credited against any hourly fee or commission that the broker becomes entitled to.

Many buyer agency agreements provide that the agent will be paid by the seller. (Note that the source of the commission does not determine which party the agent is representing.) Typically, the seller pays the buyer's agent through a **commission split**. The commission split is based on a provision found in many listing agreements whereby any cooperating broker who procures a buyer will be entitled to the selling broker's portion of the commission, regardless of who that cooperating broker represents.

Example: Helms lists his property with Broker Thurston. He agrees to pay Thurston 6% of the sales price as a commission. The listing agreement includes a clause that entitles any cooperating broker who procures a buyer to the selling broker's portion of the commission.

Broker Adams has a buyer agency agreement with Green. Green offers $100,000 for Helms's house and Helms accepts the offer.

When the transaction closes, Helms pays a $6,000 commission; $3,000 goes to Broker Thurston and $3,000 goes to Broker Adams.

Most sellers are willing to pay the buyer's agent's commission because the sales commission is virtually always split between the listing broker and the selling broker. The fact that the seller pays the buyer's agent's fee does not mean that the seller pays a bigger commission. It merely means that a portion of the commission is going to someone who has represented the buyer.

Some buyer's agents prefer to have the buyer pay the fee directly. When the buyer pays the fee, there is less confusion about the possibility of seller agency or dual agency. Furthermore, the buyer's agent may help the buyer purchase a property that is for sale by owner. In that case, the seller has not agreed to pay a commission to anyone, so there is nothing to split.

A buyer-paid fee may be based on an hourly rate, which essentially makes the agent a consultant. Alternatively, a buyer's agent may charge a percentage fee, where the commission is based on a percentage of the sales price. A third possibility is a flat fee—a specified sum that is payable if the buyer purchases a property found by the broker.

Some buyer agency agreements provide that the buyer's agent will accept a commission split if one is available, but the buyer will pay the fee if the purchased property was unlisted (for example, if the property was for sale by owner).

Buyer Agency Situations. As with seller agency, buyer agency relationships can arise in in-house transactions or cooperative sales. Cooperative sales

Fig.6.2 Buyer representation agreement

**EXCLUSIVE AUTHORIZATION TO LOCATE PROPERTY
(BUYER–BROKER AGREEMENT)**
THIS IS INTENDED TO BE A LEGALLY BINDING AGREEMENT — READ IT CAREFULLY.
CALIFORNIA ASSOCIATION OF REALTORS" (C.A.R.) STANDARD FORM

EXCLUSIVE RIGHT TO LOCATE PROPERTY: I, hereinafter called "Buyer," employ and grant to _____,
hereinafter called "Broker," the exclusive and irrevocable right, commencing on _____, 19____ and expiring
at 11:59 P.M. on _____, 19____, to locate property and negotiate terms and conditions acceptable to Buyer for
purchase, exchange, option, or lease as follows:

1. **PROPERTY:** The property to be located by Broker shall substantially meet the following requirements, or as subsequently modified by, or acceptable
   to Buyer:
   Type: ☐ Residential   ☐ Residential income   ☐ Commercial
   ☐ Industrial   ☐ Vacant land   ☐ Other _____
   General description: _____
   _____
   _____
   Approximate price range: $_____ to $_____
   General location: _____
   _____
   Preferred terms: _____
   _____
   Other: _____
   _____

2. **BROKER'S AUTHORITY:** Broker is authorized to locate and present properties to Buyer, to present offers authorized by Buyer, and to negotiate
   for acceptance of such offers.

3. **COMPENSATION TO BROKER:**
   **NOTICE: The amount or rate of real estate commissions is not fixed by law. They are set by each broker individually
   and may be negotiable between the Buyer and Broker.**
   Buyer agrees to compensate Broker, irrespective of agency relationship(s), as follows:
   (a) **Property listed with Broker:**
   No compensation shall be payable by Buyer if the property purchased by Buyer is listed with Broker and purchased by Buyer directly through
   Broker.
   (b) **Property listed with another broker:**
   _____ percent of the purchase price, or $_____.
   (c) **Property not listed with any broker:**
   _____ percent of the purchase price, or $_____.
   (d) The applicable compensation provided in subparagraphs (b), (c) and (e) if Buyer or any person acting in Buyer's behalf enters into an agreement
   to purchase, exchange for, or obtain an option on any property of the type described, or any other property located for Buyer by Broker, during
   the term of this Agreement or any extension, on the terms shown herein or any other terms acceptable to Buyer or any person acting in Buyer's
   behalf.
   (e) _____ percent of the gross rental or $_____ if Buyer or anyone acting in Buyer's behalf enters into a lease of such
   property, during the term of this Agreement or any extension.
   (f) If anyone other than Buyer compensates Broker for services covered by this Agreement, that amount shall be credited against Buyer's obligation.
   If that amount exceeds Buyer's obligation to Broker, the excess shall be disclosed to principals and ☐ paid to Broker, ☐ credited to Buyer,
   or ☐ Other _____
   (g) The applicable compensation provided in subparagraphs (b) and (c) if Buyer, or any person acting in Buyer's behalf, within _____ calendar
   days after the termination of this Agreement or any extension, enters into an agreement to purchase, exchange for, obtain an option on, or
   lease any property located for Buyer by Broker, or on which Broker negotiates in Buyer's behalf during the term of this Agreement, provided
   Buyer has received notice in writing of the addresses of such property, before or upon termination of this Agreement or any extension hereof.
   (h) Broker is authorized to divide compensation with other brokers in any manner acceptable to Broker. Permission is hereby given Broker to
   collect compensation from anyone other than Buyer in connection with any transaction resulting from this Agreement. Broker shall disclose
   to Buyer the amount and source of such compensation.
   (i) If requested by Broker, Buyer shall execute and deliver an instruction to the escrow holder in any resulting transaction irrevocably assigning
   Broker's compensation as above, payable from any funds deposited by Buyer or from proceeds of any loan obtained by Buyer.
   (j) Other: _____
   _____
   _____

4. **AGENCY RELATIONSHIPS:** Broker agrees to act as the agent of Buyer in any resulting transaction. Depending upon the circumstances, it may
   be necessary or appropriate for Broker to act as agent of both Buyer and Seller, exchange party, or one or more additional parties in any resulting
   transaction. In such event, Broker will seek Buyer's consent to Broker's representation of additional parties as soon as practicable. However,
   if Broker is the listing Broker on any property in which Buyer is interested, Buyer understands that Broker will act as agent of only the Seller with
   respect to a transaction involving that property, unless Buyer and Seller consent to Broker acting for both as a dual agent. If a property selected
   by Buyer is a one to four family residential property, Broker will provide agency relationships disclosure as required by law.

5. **OTHER POTENTIAL BUYERS:** Buyer understands that other potential buyers may consider, make offers on, or purchase through Broker the
   same or similar properties as Buyer is seeking to acquire. Buyer consents to Broker's representation of such other potential buyers before, during,
   and after the expiration of this Agreement.

Buyer hereby acknowledges receipt of copy of this page, which constitutes Page 1 of _____ Pages.
Buyer's Initials (_____) (_____)

THIS STANDARDIZED DOCUMENT HAS BEEN APPROVED BY THE CALIFORNIA ASSOCIATION OF REALTORS" (C.A.R.) IN FORM ONLY NO REPRESENTATION IS MADE AS TO THE
APPROVAL OF THE FORM OF ANY SUPPLEMENTS NOT CURRENTLY PUBLISHED BY C.A.R. OR THE LEGAL VALIDITY OR ADEQUACY OF ANY PROVISION IN ANY SPECIFIC
TRANSACTION. IT SHOULD NOT BE USED WITH EXTENSIVE RIDERS OR ADDITIONS.

△ REAL ESTATE BROKER IS THE PERSON QUALIFIED TO ADVISE ON REAL ESTATE TRANSACTIONS. IF YOU DESIRE LEGAL OR TAX ADVICE, CONSULT AN APPROPRIATE PROFESSIONAL.

The copyright laws of the United States (17 U.S. Code) forbid the unauthorized
reproduction of this form by any means including facsimile or computerized formats.
Copyright © 1988, CALIFORNIA ASSOCIATION OF REALTORS"
525 South Virgil Avenue, Los Angeles, California 90020
REVISED 11/93

OFFICE USE ONLY
Reviewed by Broker or Designee _____
Date _____

Reprinted with permission, California Association of REALTORS®. Endorsement not implied.

6. **BROKER'S AND BUYER'S DUTIES:** Broker agrees to exercise reasonable effort and due diligence to achieve the purpose of this Agreement. Buyer agrees to provide to Broker, upon request, relevant personal and financial information to assure Buyer's ability to acquire property as above. Buyer further agrees to view or consider property of the general type set forth in this Agreement, and to negotiate in good faith to acquire such property if satisfactory to Buyer. In the event completion of any resulting transaction is prevented by Buyer's default, Buyer shall pay to Broker the compensation provided above upon such default.

7. **MEDIATION OF DISPUTES:** BROKER AND BUYER AGREE TO MEDIATE ANY DISPUTE OR CLAIM BETWEEN THEM ARISING OUT OF THIS CONTRACT OR ANY RESULTING TRANSACTION BEFORE RESORTING TO ARBITRATION OR COURT ACTION. Mediation is a process in which parties attempt to resolve a dispute by submitting it to an impartial, neutral mediator who is authorized to facilitate the resolution of the dispute but who is not empowered to impose a settlement on the parties. Mediation fee, if any, shall be divided equally among the parties involved. Before the mediation begins, the parties agree to sign a document limiting the admissibility in arbitration or any civil action of anything said, any admission made, and any documents prepared, in the course of the mediation, consistent with Evidence Code §1152.5. IF ANY PARTY COMMENCES AN ARBITRATION OR COURT ACTION BASED ON A DISPUTE OR CLAIM TO WHICH THIS PARAGRAPH APPLIES WITHOUT FIRST ATTEMPTING TO RESOLVE THE MATTER THROUGH MEDIATION, THEN IN THE DISCRETION OF THE ARBITRATOR(S) OR JUDGE, THAT PARTY SHALL NOT BE ENTITLED TO RECOVER ATTORNEY'S FEES EVEN IF THEY WOULD OTHERWISE BE AVAILABLE TO THAT PARTY IN ANY SUCH ARBITRATION OR COURT ACTION. However, the filing of a judicial action to enable the recording of a notice of pending action, for order of attachment, receivership, injunction, or other provisional remedies, shall not in itself constitute a loss of the right to recover attorney's fees under this provision. The following matters are excluded from the requirement of mediation hereunder: (a) a judicial or non-judicial foreclosure or other action or proceeding to enforce a deed of trust, mortgage, or installment land sale contract as defined in Civil Code §2985, (b) an unlawful detainer action, (c) the filing or enforcement of a mechanic's lien, and (d) any matter which is within the jurisdiction of a probate court.

8. **ARBITRATION OF DISPUTES:** Any dispute or claim in law or equity between Buyer and Broker arising out of this contract or any resulting transaction which is not settled through mediation shall be decided by neutral, binding arbitration and not by court action, except as provided by California law for judicial review of arbitration proceedings.

   The arbitration shall be conducted in accordance with the rules of either the American Arbitration Association (AAA) or Judicial Arbitration and Mediation Services, Inc. (JAMS). The selection between AAA and JAMS shall be made by the claimant first filing for the arbitration. The parties to an arbitration may agree in writing to use different rules and/or arbitrator(s). In all other respects, the arbitration shall be conducted in accordance with Part III, Title 9 of the California Code of Civil Procedure. Judgment upon the award rendered by the arbitrator(s) may be entered in any court having jurisdiction thereof. The parties shall have the right to discovery in accordance with Code of Civil Procedure §1283.05. The following matters are excluded from arbitration hereunder: (a) a judicial or non-judicial foreclosure or other action or proceeding to enforce a deed of trust, mortgage, or installment land sale contract as defined in Civil Code §2985, (b) an unlawful detainer action, (c) the filing or enforcement of a mechanic's lien, (d) any matter which is within the jurisdiction of a probate or small claims court, and (e) an action for bodily injury or wrongful death, or for latent or patent defects, to which Code of Civil Procedure §337.1 or §337.15 applies. The filing of a judicial action to enable the recording of a notice of pending action, for order of attachment, receivership, injunction, or other provisional remedies, shall not constitute a waiver of the right to arbitrate under this provision.

   "NOTICE: BY INITIALLING IN THE SPACE BELOW YOU ARE AGREEING TO HAVE ANY DISPUTE ARISING OUT OF THE MATTERS INCLUDED IN THE 'ARBITRATION OF DISPUTES' PROVISION DECIDED BY NEUTRAL ARBITRATION AS PROVIDED BY CALIFORNIA LAW AND YOU ARE GIVING UP ANY RIGHTS YOU MIGHT POSSESS TO HAVE THE DISPUTE LITIGATED IN A COURT OR JURY TRIAL. BY INITIALLING IN THE SPACE BELOW YOU ARE GIVING UP YOUR JUDICIAL RIGHTS TO DISCOVERY AND APPEAL, UNLESS THOSE RIGHTS ARE SPECIFICALLY INCLUDED IN THE 'ARBITRATION OF DISPUTES' PROVISION. IF YOU REFUSE TO SUBMIT TO ARBITRATION AFTER AGREEING TO THIS PROVISION, YOU MAY BE COMPELLED TO ARBITRATE UNDER THE AUTHORITY OF THE CALIFORNIA CODE OF CIVIL PROCEDURE. YOUR AGREEMENT TO THIS ARBITRATION PROVISION IS VOLUNTARY."

   "WE HAVE READ AND UNDERSTAND THE FOREGOING AND AGREE TO SUBMIT DISPUTES ARISING OUT OF THE MATTERS INCLUDED IN THE 'ARBITRATION OF DISPUTES' PROVISION TO NEUTRAL ARBITRATION."

   Buyer's Initials _____   Broker's Initials _____

9. **EQUAL HOUSING OPPORTUNITY:** Properties will be presented in compliance with federal, state and local anti-discrimination laws.

10. **ATTORNEY'S FEES:** In any action, proceeding, or arbitration arising out of this Agreement, the prevailing party shall be entitled to reasonable attorney's fees and costs.

11. **ADDITIONAL TERMS:** _____

    _____
    _____
    _____
    _____
    _____
    _____
    _____

12. **CAPTIONS:** The captions in this Agreement are for convenience of reference only and are not intended as part of this Agreement.

13. **AMENDMENTS:** This Agreement may not be amended, modified, altered or changed in any respect whatsoever except by a further agreement in writing executed by Buyer and Broker.

14. **ENTIRE CONTRACT:** Time is of the essence. All prior agreements between the parties are incorporated in this Agreement which constitutes the entire contract. Its terms are intended by the parties as a final expression of their agreement with respect to such terms as are included herein and may not be contradicted by evidence of any prior agreement or contemporaneous oral agreement. The parties further intend that this Agreement constitutes the complete and exclusive statement of its terms and that no extrinsic evidence whatsoever may be introduced in any judicial or arbitration proceeding, if any, involving this Agreement.

I acknowledge that I have read and understand this Agreement, and have received a copy of this page which constitutes page 2 of 2 pages.

Date _____   Date _____
Broker _____   Buyer _____
By _____   Buyer _____
Address _____   Address _____

Telephone _____   Telephone _____

REFER TO REVERSE SIDE FOR IMPORTANT INFORMATION

This form is available for use by the entire real estate industry. The use of this form is not intended to identify the user as a REALTOR®. REALTOR® is a registered collective membership mark which may be used only by real estate licensees who are members of the NATIONAL ASSOCIATION OF ...

Page 2 of ____ Pages

OFFICE USE ONLY
Reviewed by Broker or Designee _____
Date _____

8. ARBITRATION: Arbitration is the referral of a dispute to one or more impartial persons for final and binding determination. It is private and informal, designed for quick, practical, and inexpensive settlements. Arbitration is an orderly proceeding, governed by rules of procedure and standards of conduct prescribed by law.

ENFORCEMENT OF ARBITRATION AGREEMENTS
UNDER CALIFORNIA CODE OF CIVIL PROCEDURE SECTIONS 1281, 1282.4, 1283.1, 1283.05, 1287.4 & 1287.6

§ 1281: A written agreement to submit to arbitration an existing controversy or a controversy thereafter arising is valid, enforceable and irreversible, save upon such grounds as exist for the revocation of any contract.

§ 1282.4. A party to the arbitration has the right to be represented by an attorney at any proceeding or hearing in arbitration under this title. A waiver of this right may be revoked; but if a party revokes such waiver, the other party is entitled to a reasonable continuance for the purpose of procuring an attorney.

§ 1283.1 (a) All of the provisions of Section 1283.05 shall be conclusively deemed to be incorporated into, made a part of, and shall be applicable to, every agreement to arbitrate any dispute, controversy, or issue arising out of or resulting from any injury to, or death of, a person caused by the wrongful act or neglect of another.

(b) Only if the parties by their agreement so provide, may the provisions of Section 1283.05 be incorporated into, made a part of, or made applicable to, any other arbitration agreement.

§ 1283.05. To the extent provided in Section 1283.1 depositions may be taken and discovery obtained in arbitration proceedings as follows:

(a) After the appointment of the arbitrator or arbitrators, the parties to the arbitration shall have the right to take depositions and to obtain discovery regarding the subject matter of the arbitration, and, to that end, to use and exercise all of the same rights, remedies, and procedures, and be subject to all of the same duties, liabilities, and obligations in the arbitration with respect to the subject matter thereof, as provided in Chapter 2 (commencing with Section 1985) of, and Article 3 (commencing with Section 2016) of Chapter 3 of, Title 3 of Part 4 of this code, as if the subject matter of the arbitration were pending in a civil action before a superior court of this state, subject to the limitations as to depositions set forth in subdivision (e) of this section.

(b) The arbitrator or arbitrators themselves shall have power, in addition to the power of determining the merits of the arbitration, to enforce the rights, remedies, procedures, duties, liabilities, and obligations of discovery by the imposition of the same terms, conditions, consequences, liabilities, sanctions, and penalties as can be or may be imposed in like circumstances in a civil action by a superior court of this state under the provisions of this code, except the power to order the arrest or imprisonment of a person.

(c) The arbitrator or arbitrators may consider, determine, and make such orders imposing such terms, conditions, consequences, liabilities, sanctions, and penalties, whenever necessary or appropriate at any time or stage in the course of the arbitration, and such orders shall be as conclusive, final, and enforceable as an arbitration award on the merits, if the making of any such order that is equivalent to an award or correction of an award is subject to the same conditions, if any, as are applicable to the making of an award or correction of an award.

(d) For the purpose of enforcing the duty to make discovery, to produce evidence or information, including books and records, and to produce persons to testify at a deposition or at a hearing, and to impose terms, conditions, consequences, liabilities, sanctions, and penalties upon a party for violation of any such duty, such party shall be deemed to include every affiliate of such party as defined in this section. For such purpose:

(1) The personnel of every such affiliate shall be deemed to be the officers, directors, managing agents, agents, and employees of such party to the same degree as each of them, respectively, bears such status to such affiliate; and

(2) The files, books, and records of every such affiliate shall be deemed to be in the possession and control of, and capable of production by, such party. As used in this section, "affiliate" of the party to the arbitration means and includes any party or person for whose immediate benefit the action or proceeding is prosecuted or defended, or an officer, director, superintendent, member, agent, employee, or managing agent of such party or persons.

(e) Depositions for discovery shall not be taken unless leave to do so is first granted by the arbitrator or arbitrators.

§ 1287.4. If an award is confirmed, judgment shall be entered in conformity therewith. The judgment so entered has the same force and effect as, and is subject to all the provisions of law relating to, a judgment in a civil action; and it may be enforced like any other judgment of the court in which it is entered.

§ 1287.6. An award that has not been confirmed or vacated has the same force and effect as a contract in writing between the parties to the arbitration.

are probably the most common type of buyer agency situations. The buyer engages the broker's services; the broker then finds a home for the buyer, typically listed by another brokerage firm. These are the least complicated types of transactions.

If a buyer's agent shows the buyer a home listed by his or her own brokerage, complications can arise. As the agent of the listing broker, a salesperson is automatically assumed to be the seller's agent. When that same agent chooses to represent the buyer, a dual agency situation may be the result.

Dual Agency

A dual agency relationship exists when an agent represents both the seller and the buyer in the same transaction. A dual agent owes fiduciary duties to both principals. Because the interests of the buyer and the seller usually conflict, it is difficult to represent them both without being disloyal to one or both. For this reason, dual agency is strongly disfavored.

> **Example:** Broker Davis represents both the buyer and the seller in a real estate transaction. The seller informs Davis that she is in a big hurry to sell and will accept any reasonable offer. The buyer tells Davis that he is very interested in the house, and is willing to pay the full listing price. Should Davis tell the buyer of the seller's eagerness to sell? Should Davis tell the seller about the buyer's willingness to pay full price?

There is virtually always a conflict between representing the best interests of the buyer and representing the best interests of the seller. In fact, it is really impossible for a dual agent to fully represent both parties. Thus, a more accurate name for dual agency is **limited dual agency**.

Each party to a dual agency should be informed that he or she will not receive full representation—certain facts must necessarily be withheld from each party. For example, both the buyer and the seller usually agree that each party's negotiating

position will be kept confidential. The dual agent will not tell the buyer the seller's bottom line, nor will the dual agent tell the seller how much the buyer is willing to pay.

Creation of Dual Agency. A dual agency can be created expressly, with full disclosure to both parties. Sometimes, dual agency is created unintentionally and without full disclosure.

Disclosed Dual Agency. Dual agency is legal in California, even though it is universally discouraged. However, before acting as a dual agent, a broker must have the informed consent of both parties to the transaction. Acting as a dual agent without full disclosure is a violation of the Real Estate Law, and will lead to disciplinary action. (See Chapter 18.)

Dual agency disclosure should be comprehensive. Buyers and sellers, eager to get on with the business of buying and selling a home, may agree to a dual agency without really understanding what it means. They may accept the agent's explanation at face value and sign a boilerplate disclosure form without question. Later, one party may feel that his or her interests were neglected and that fiduciary duties were breached. These kinds of disappointments often lead to legal action. (Statutory agency disclosure requirements are discussed later in this chapter.)

Disclosure should occur as early as possible in the transaction. A broker contemplating dual agency should carefully explain what dual agency means to both parties. The industry's concerns about dual representation should be fully aired and the parties should be encouraged to ask any questions they might have. If the parties do not understand the extent of the potential for conflicts of interest, they cannot give their informed consent.

Inadvertent Dual Agency. A dual agency may be created unintentionally.

> **Example:** Randall lists her property with Broker Mancini. Salesperson Ostergard works for Mancini, and is considered Randall's agent. Ostergard

shows Randall's house to Ostergard's good friend Susan, who immediately makes on offer on the property. Throughout the negotiation process, Ostergard discusses the transaction in detail with Susan; Susan naturally listens carefully to Ostergard and acts on what she considers to be Ostergard's advice. Both Ostergard and Susan are acting as if Ostergard is Susan's agent.

After the sale closes, Randall discovers that Susan is Ostergard's friend and claims there was an undisclosed dual agency. Even though Ostergard did not intend to create a dual agency, he may be subject to a lawsuit by Randall and disciplinary action by the Department of Licensing.

Many dual agency lawsuits involve an accidental or unintended dual agency in which the conduct of the seller's agent, or the personal relationship between the agent and the buyer, is such that an implied agency is created with the buyer.

Whenever a real estate agent has a close relationship with the buyer, a dual agency may be created inadvertently. For this reason, an agent would be wise to enter into a buyer agency agreement before working with a:

- relative,
- close friend,
- close business associate,
- former client, or
- former customer.

Dual Agency Situations. Dual agency can arise in both in-house and cooperative transactions.

In-house Sales. In-house sales often give rise to a dual agency situation.

Example: Salesperson Yaeger works for Broker Ogden. Buyer Plunkett discusses her housing needs with Yaeger and decides she wants to enter into a buyer agency relationship with Yaeger.

Fig.6.3 Agency relationships

Type of Agency	Method of Creation	Duties
Seller agency	Listing agreement	Fiduciary duties to seller; honesty and fair dealing to buyer
Buyer agency	Representation agreement	Fiduciary duties to buyer; honesty and fair dealing to seller
Dual agency	Express agreement/full disclosure Inadvertent creation/no disclosure	Fiduciary duties to both parties; typically agrees to keep some information confidential for both parties

Yaeger (on behalf of Broker Ogden) and Plunkett enter into a buyer agency agreement.

Yaeger shows Plunkett a house listed by one of Ogden's other salespeople. Since Yaeger is Ogden's agent, he is also considered the seller's agent, along with Ogden. In showing the seller's house to Plunkett, Ogden is now in the position of a dual agent and must make the appropriate disclosures.

Cooperative Transactions. Dual agency can occur in cooperative transactions, when a seller's subagent (via a multiple listing association) also agrees to represent the buyer. This type of dual agency occurs less frequently today, because many multiple listing services no longer require their members to act as subagents of the seller. Instead, many MLS listing forms give cooperating agents the option of working as a buyer's agent rather than as a subagent of the seller.

Agency Disclosure Requirements

To avoid some of the confusion about who is representing whom, California law requires real estate agents to give buyers two disclosure forms before the purchase and sale agreement is signed. The first form is called an **agency disclosure form** (see Figure 6.4). It clearly explains the duties of a seller's agent, a buyer's agent, and a dual agent. The agent must ask the buyer to sign this disclosure form, and to sign a receipt acknowledging that he or she received a copy of it.

The second form is called an **agency confirmation statement**. The agent checks a box on the confirmation statement to show which party or parties he or she is representing. The buyer must sign the statement, indicating that he or she understands the agent's role and accepts it.

Both forms must also be presented to the seller. The seller should receive and sign the agency disclosure form and receipt before signing a listing agreement. He or she should sign the agency confirmation statement before signing the purchase and sale agreement.

The agency confirmation statement does not need to be a separate document; most agency confirmation statements are included in the purchase and sale agreement. (See Chapter 8.) If that is the case, the parties should sign the agency confirmation statement before or at the same time that they sign the purchase and sale agreement.

If the selling agent is not the same person as the listing agent, the selling agent is also required to give these two forms to each of the parties.

Antitrust Laws and Their Effect on Licensees

Our discussion of agency relationships illustrates how important it is to treat both clients and customers fairly and honestly, and fully disclose any conflicts of interest. It is also important that real estate agents treat other real estate agents fairly and honestly, no matter whom they are representing. In addition to agency law, federal antitrust laws impose certain restrictions on a real estate agent's behavior towards clients and customers, and towards other agents.

Federal antitrust laws are not new: the **Sherman Act** was passed in 1890, over 100 years ago. The Sherman Act prohibits any agreement that has the effect of restraining trade, including conspiracies. The act defines a **conspiracy** as two or more business entities participating in a common scheme that has the effect of restraining trade.

At the foundation of antitrust laws is the notion that free enterprise is a part of our democratic society, and that competition is good for both the economy and society as a whole. While many people associate antitrust laws with big steel mills and telephone companies, in 1950 antitrust laws were held to apply to the real estate industry. In a landmark case,

Fig.6.4 Agency disclosure statement

DISCLOSURE REGARDING
REAL ESTATE AGENCY RELATIONSHIPS
(As required by the Civil Code)
CALIFORNIA ASSOCIATION OF REALTORS® (C.A.R.) STANDARD FORM

When you enter into a discussion with a real estate agent regarding a real estate transaction, you should from the outset understand what type of agency relationship or representation you wish to have with the agent in the transaction.

SELLER'S AGENT

A Seller's agent under a listing agreement with the Seller acts as the agent for the Seller only. A Seller's agent or a subagent of that agent has the following affirmative obligations:

To the Seller:
A Fiduciary duty of utmost care, integrity, honesty, and loyalty in dealings with the Seller.

To the Buyer and the Seller:
(a) Diligent exercise of reasonable skill and care in performance of the agent's duties.
(b) A duty of honest and fair dealing and good faith.
(c) A duty to disclose all facts known to the agent materially affecting the value or desirability of the property that are not known to, or within the diligent attention and observation of, the parties.

An agent is not obligated to reveal to either party any confidential information obtained from the other party that does not involve the affirmative duties set forth above.

BUYER'S AGENT

A selling agent can, with a Buyer's consent, agree to act as agent for the Buyer only. In these situations, the agent is not the Seller's agent, even if by agreement the agent may receive compensation for services rendered, either in full or in part from the Seller. An agent acting only for a Buyer has the following affirmative obligations:

To the Buyer:
A fiduciary duty of utmost care, integrity, honesty, and loyalty in dealings with the Buyer.

To the Buyer and the Seller:
(a) Diligent exercise of reasonable skill and care in performance of the agent's duties.
(b) A duty of honest and fair dealing and good faith.
(c) A duty to disclose all facts known to the agent materially affecting the value or desirability of the property that are not known to, or within the diligent attention and observation of, the parties.

An agent is not obligated to reveal to either party any confidential information obtained from the other party that does not involve the affirmative duties set forth above.

AGENT REPRESENTING BOTH SELLER & BUYER

A real estate agent, either acting directly or through one or more associate licensees, can legally be the agent of both the Seller and the Buyer in a transaction, but only with the knowledge and consent of both the Seller and the Buyer.

In a dual agency situation, the agent has the following affirmative obligations to both the Seller and the Buyer:
(a) A fiduciary duty of utmost care, integrity, honesty and loyalty in the dealings with either Seller or the Buyer.
(b) Other duties to the Seller and the Buyer as stated above in their respective sections.

In representing both Seller and Buyer, the agent may not, without the express permission of the respective party, disclose to the other party that the Seller will accept a price less than the listing price or that the Buyer will pay a price greater than the price offered.

The above duties of the agent in a real estate transaction do not relieve a Seller or Buyer from the responsibility to protect his or her own interests. You should carefully read all agreements to assure that they adequately express your understanding of the transaction. A real estate agent is a person qualified to advise about real estate. If legal or tax advice is desired, consult a competent professional.

Throughout your real property transaction you may receive more than one disclosure form, depending upon the number of agents assisting in the transaction. The law requires each agent with whom you have more than a casual relationship to present you with this disclosure form. You should read its contents each time it is presented to you, considering the relationship between you and the real estate agent in your specific transaction.

This disclosure form includes the provisions of Sections 2079.13 to 2079.24, inclusive, of the Civil Code set forth on the reverse hereof. Read it carefully.

I/WE ACKNOWLEDGE RECEIPT OF A COPY OF THIS DISCLOSURE.

BUYER/SELLER _____ Date _____ Time _____ AM/PM

BUYER/SELLER _____ Date _____ Time _____ AM/PM

AGENT _____ By _____ Date_____
(Please Print)   (Associate Licensee or Broker-Signature)

This Disclosure form must be provided in a listing, sale, exchange, installment land contract, or lease over one year, if the transaction involves one-to-four dwelling residential property, including a mobile home, as follows:
(a) From a Listing Agent to a Seller: Prior to entering into the listing.
(b) From an Agent selling a property he/she has listed to a Buyer: Prior to the Buyer's execution of the offer.
(c) From a Selling Agent to a Buyer: Prior to the Buyer's execution of the offer.
(d) From a Selling Agent (in a cooperating real estate firm) to a Seller: Prior to presentation of the offer to the Seller.

It is not necessary or required to confirm an agency relationship using a separate Confirmation form if the agency confirmation portion of the Real Estate Purchase Contract is properly completed in full. However, it is still necessary to use this Disclosure form..

THIS STANDARDIZED DOCUMENT HAS BEEN APPROVED BY THE CALIFORNIA ASSOCIATION OF REALTORS® (C.A.R.) IN FORM ONLY. NO REPRESENTATION IS MADE AS TO THE APPROVAL OF THE FORM OF ANY SUPPLEMENTS NOT CURRENTLY PUBLISHED BY C.A.R. OR THE LEGAL VALIDITY OR ADEQUACY OF ANY PROVISION IN ANY SPECIFIC TRANSACTION. IT SHOULD NOT BE USED WITH EXTENSIVE RIDERS OR ADDITIONS.

A REAL ESTATE BROKER IS THE PERSON QUALIFIED TO ADVISE ON REAL ESTATE TRANSACTIONS. IF YOU DESIRE LEGAL OR TAX ADVICE, CONSULT AN APPROPRIATE PROFESSIONAL.

This form is available for use by the entire real estate industry. The use of this form is not intended to identify the user as a REALTOR®. REALTOR® is a registered collective membership mark which may be used only by members of the NATIONAL ASSOCIATION OF REALTORS® who subscribe to its Code of Ethics.

The copyright laws of the United States (17 U.S. Code) forbid the unauthorized reproduction of this form by any means including facsimile or computerized formats.
Copyright © 1987-1995, CALIFORNIA ASSOCIATION OF REALTORS®
525 South Virgil Avenue, Los Angeles, California 90020

OFFICE USE ONLY
Reviewed by Broker or Designee _____
Date _____

FORM AD-14

Reprinted with permission, California Association of REALTORS®. Endorsement not implied.

the United States Supreme Court held that mandatory fee schedules, established and enforced by a real estate board, violated the Sherman Act (*United States v. National Association of Real Estate Boards*).

If a real estate agent violates antitrust laws, he or she may be subject to civil and criminal actions. If an individual is found guilty of violating the Sherman Act, he or she can be fined up to $100,000 and/or sentenced to three years' imprisonment. If a corporation is found guilty of violating the Sherman Act, it can be fined up to one million dollars.

Activities prohibited by antitrust laws can be grouped into three main categories:

- price fixing (fixing commission rates),
- group boycotts, and
- tie-in arrangements.

Price Fixing

Price fixing is defined as the cooperative setting of prices or price ranges by competing firms. To avoid the appearance of price fixing, two agents from different brokerages should never discuss their commission rates. It is a discussion between competing agents that is dangerous—a broker can discuss commission rates with his or her own salespeople. One exception to this general prohibition is that two competing brokers may discuss a commission split in a cooperative sale (the split between the listing broker and the selling broker).

Even a casual announcement that a broker is planning on raising his or her commission rates could lead to problems.

Example: Broker Wiseman goes to a dinner given by his local MLS. He is called on to discuss current market conditions, and in the middle of his speech, he announces that he is going to raise his commission rate, no matter what anyone else does. This statement could be viewed as an invitation to conspire to fix prices. If any other MLS members raise their rates in response to his announcement, they can be held to have accepted Wiseman's invitation to conspire.

Brokers must understand that they do not have to actually consult with each other to be charged with conspiring to fix commission rates. The kind of scenario described in the previous example is enough to lead to an antitrust lawsuit.

Publications that appear to fix prices are prohibited as well. Any association that tries to publish "recommended" or "going" commission rates could be sued.

Group Boycotts

A **group boycott** is an agreement between two or more real estate brokers to exclude other brokers from fair participation in real estate activities. The purpose of group boycotts is to hurt or destroy a competitor, and they are automatically unlawful under antitrust laws.

Example: Becker and Jordan are both brokers. They have lunch together and begin discussing the business practices of a third broker, Harley. Becker says that Harley is just a "discount broker" and is dishonest and lazy. Becker states that he will never do business with him. Jordan laughs and agrees. She says that she never returns any of Harley's calls when he is inquiring about a listed property. She suggests that Becker do the same. Becker and Jordan could be found guilty of a conspiracy to boycott.

If a broker feels another broker is dishonest or unethical, that broker may choose not to do business with him or her. However, that broker cannot tell other brokers to do the same.

Tie-in Arrangements

A **tie-in arrangement** is defined as an agreement to sell one product, only on the condition that the buyer also purchases a different (or "tied") product.

Example: Brown is a subdivision developer. Tyson, a builder, wants to buy a lot. Brown tells Tyson that he will sell him a lot only if Tyson agrees that after Tyson builds a house on the lot, he will list the improved property with Brown. (This is called a "list-back" agreement.)

Tie-in arrangements are automatically violations of the antitrust laws.

Avoiding Antitrust Violations

There are several ways to prevent possible antitrust violations. Brokers should:

- always establish their fees and other listing policies independently, without consulting competing firms;

- never use listing forms that contain preprinted commission rates;
- never imply to a client that the commission rate is fixed or non-negotiable, or refer to a competitor's commission policies when discussing commission rates;
- never discuss their business plans with competitors;
- never tell clients or competitors not to work with a competing firm because of doubts about that competing firm's competency or integrity, or because that broker won't do business with that other firm;
- train their licensees to be aware of what may constitute an antitrust law violation.

Chapter Summary

1. A real estate agent can represent the buyer, the seller, or both parties to a real estate transaction. Whom the agent represents has important consequences in terms of fiduciary duties and liabilities.

2. A seller agency is usually created with the listing agreement. A seller's agent owes the seller fiduciary duties, and owes the buyer fairness and honest dealing. A salesperson who works for the seller's broker also works for the seller. Both in-house transactions and cooperative sales are appropriate situations for seller agency. If a cooperating agent is acting on the seller's behalf, he or she must be careful to avoid any actions that might give rise to an agency relationship with the buyer.

3. Buyer's agents can provide special services to buyers, including access to more properties, expert advice, help with negotiating, and loyalty. Buyer agency relationships are generally created with a representation agreement. A buyer's agent may be paid by the buyer or the seller. If the agent is paid by the buyer, the fee may be in the form of a retainer, a commission, an hourly fee, or a flat rate.

4. Dual agency occurs when an agent represents both the seller and the buyer in the same transaction. Dual agencies are unlawful without the full, informed consent of both parties. Dual agencies often arise inadvertently, through the agent's actions.

5. California law requires agents to disclose to the parties whom they represent. Two disclosure forms, the agency disclosure form and an agency confirmation statement, must be given to both the buyer and the seller before the purchase and sale agreement is signed.

6. Antitrust laws prohibit price fixing, group boycotts, and tie-in arrangements. Real estate brokers must be especially careful to avoid discussing commission rates with competing brokers.

Key Terms

Agent—Someone who is authorized to represent another in dealings with third parties; usually someone who has expertise in a certain area, and who will use that expertise to the advantage of his or her client.

Client—A client is the person who has engaged the services of an agent. A client may be a real estate seller, buyer, landlord, or tenant.

Customer—In transactions where the agent is representing a seller or a landlord, third parties are generally referred to as customers. A customer may be a buyer or a tenant. An agent's primary responsibilities to the customer are honesty and fair dealing.

Listing agent—The agent that takes the listing on a home. This agent may or may not be the agent who procures a buyer.

Selling agent—The agent who procures a buyer for a property. The selling agent may or may not have taken the listing for the property sold.

In-house sale—A sale in which the buyer and the seller are brought together by salespeople working for the same broker.

Cooperative sale—A sale in which the buyer and the seller are brought together by salespeople working for different brokers.

Group boycott—An agreement between two or more real estate brokers to exclude other brokers from equal participation in real estate activities.

Tie-in arrangement—An agreement to sell one product, only on the condition that the buyer also purchases a different product.

Chapter 6—Quiz
Agency Relationships

1. Burns listed her property with Callahan. Callahan is a salesperson for Broker Tierny. Carter is also a salesperson for Tierny. In the absence of any other agreement, Carter will be automatically considered:

   a) the seller's agent
   b) a principal
   c) a dual agent
   d) the buyer's agent

2. Able listed Green's property. Able:

   a) cannot give a buyer any information about Green's property without being considered a dual agent
   b) can safely give a buyer information about Green's property
   c) must sign a disclaimer of liability if he presents a buyer's offer to purchase to Green
   d) is a buyer's agent

3. A principal is held liable for:

   a) the actions of his or her broker
   b) the actions of his or her broker's salesperson
   c) his or her own actions
   d) All of the above

4. Harrison agrees to act as Buyer Brown's agent. They sign a representation agreement in which Brown agrees to pay Harrison an hourly fee.

   a) This fee arrangement is illegal because it turns Harrison into a consultant rather than an agent
   b) This is a valid fee arrangement
   c) Brown and Harrison need to agree on a maximum total fee for an hourly fee to be legal
   d) Hourly fees are valid only in seller agency situations

5. Kelley works for Broker Sharpe. Kelley's good friend wants Kelley to try to find a house for her. Kelley shows her friend a house listed by another one of Sharpe's salespeople. Kelley:

   a) is in danger of becoming a dual agent because the buyer is a personal friend
   b) is automatically acting as a buyer's agent in this situation
   c) should request special approval of the sale from the Real Estate Commission
   d) is only the seller's agent, no matter what she says to or how she acts towards her friend

6. Which one of the following is not a benefit of buyer agency?

   a) The buyer has access to more properties
   b) The buyer gets the benefit of expert advice
   c) Since the agent represents both parties, the buyer has access to information about the seller's bottom-line sales price
   d) The buyer gets help with negotiating the sales price

7. A real estate agent is more assured of buyer loyalty when acting as a:

   a) seller's agent
   b) buyer's agent
   c) undisclosed dual agent
   d) party to the transaction

8. Disclosure of a dual agency:

   a) does not need to be in writing
   b) should only meet the bare legal requirements
   c) should come as early in the transaction as possible
   d) must be given to the buyer only after presenting the written offer to purchase

9. In a typical disclosed dual agency situation, both parties agree that the agent will:

   a) keep each party's negotiating position confidential
   b) disclose all material facts to both parties, no matter how confidential
   c) act only as a facilitator, and owe loyalty to neither party
   d) refer all conflicts of interest to the Board of Equalization

10. According to California law, a real estate agent must disclose his or her agency status:

    a) only if he or she is the listing agent
    b) only if he or she is the selling agent
    c) to the seller before signing a listing agreement
    d) to the buyer before signing a listing agreement

11. Federal antitrust laws apply:

    a) only to franchised firms, because of their ability to conspire to restrain trade
    b) only to large real estate firms that could actually affect the real estate market
    c) only to individual agents, not to real estate companies
    d) to all members of the real estate industry

12. Great County MLS publishes a monthly list of the commission rates charged by all member firms. The multiple listing association:

    a) could be found guilty of price fixing
    b) is not guilty of price fixing, because it is simply reporting newsworthy information
    c) is not guilty of price fixing because no two competing firms are discussing rates
    d) is not guilty of price fixing because only real estate brokers can be guilty of price fixing, not multiple listing associations

13. An agreement to sell one product only on the condition that the buyer also purchases a different product is called:

    a) price fixing
    b) a group boycott
    c) a tie-in arrangement
    d) None of the above

14. Several members of an MLS decide to refuse to do business with a broker because of his race. They know that they can put him out of business in a matter of months. Those MLS members:

    a) are guilty of participating in a group boycott
    b) are guilty of racial discrimination only, not participating in a group boycott
    c) are conspiring to create a tie-in arrangement
    d) are within their rights as members of an MLS

15. A broker conducts a sales meeting once a week for her salespeople. At one meeting, she discusses commission rates at length. She is:

    a) guilty of price fixing
    b) guilty of a tie-in arrangement
    c) guilty of a group boycott
    d) not guilty of any antitrust violation

Answer Key

1.a) A salesperson is generally considered to act for the same party as his or her broker (for the seller, in this case).

2.b) A seller's agent can give a buyer information about the seller's property without violating his or her fiduciary duties. In fact, this is vital part of the duties a seller's agent agrees to assume.

3.d) A principal is liable for his or her own actions and the actions of his or her broker and that broker's salespersons.

4.b) An hourly fee is a valid fee arrangement for a buyer's agent.

5.a) When an agent's customer is also a good friend, there is always a danger of a dual agency arising by implication.

6.c) A buyer who retains his or her own agent does not get information about the seller's negotiating position.

7.b) A buyer's agent has more assurance of buyer loyalty because of the representation agreement signed by the buyer.

8.c) Disclosure of a dual agency should come as early in the transaction as possible. (California's agency disclosure laws require written disclosure of agency status.)

9.a) The parties in a dual agency situation generally agree that the dual agent will keep information on each party's negotiating position confidential.

10.c) An agency disclosure must be made to the seller prior to signing a listing agreement.

11.d) Federal antitrust laws were extended to the real estate industry in 1950.

12.a) Even publishing a list of the "going rates" for commissions may be considered price fixing.

13.c) This is the definition of a tie-in arrangement. Tie-in arrangements are automatically violations of antitrust laws.

14.a) The actions of the brokers would qualify as a group boycott. (They would also be considered guilty of discrimination.)

15.d) A broker may discuss commission rates with his or her own affiliated salespeople.

Chapter 7

Contract Law

 Outline

 Chapter Overview

Contracts are a significant part of the real estate business. Almost everyone has a basic understanding of what a contract is, but real estate agents need more than that. This chapter explains the requirements that must be met in order for a contract to be valid and binding, how a contract can be terminated, what is considered a breach of contract, and what remedies are available when a breach occurs. The various types of contracts that a real estate agent should be familiar with are discussed in the following chapter.

Introduction

A real estate agent deals with contracts on a daily basis: listing agreements, purchase and sale agreements, option agreements, and leases are all contracts. Thus, it is essential for an agent to understand the legal requirements and effects of contracts.

Simply stated, a contract is "an agreement between two or more competent persons to do or not do certain things in exchange for consideration." An agreement to sell a car, deliver lumber, or rent an apartment is a contract. And if it meets minimum legal requirements, it can be enforced in court.

Fig.7.1 Contract classifications

Express *Written or oral*	OR	**Implied** *Acts of the parties*
Unilateral *One promise*	OR	**Bilateral** *Two promises*
Executory *Not yet fully performed*	OR	**Executed** *Fully performed*

Legal Classifications of Contracts

There are certain basic classifications that apply to any contract, no matter what type it is. Every contract is either express or implied, either unilateral or bilateral, and either executory or executed.

Express vs. Implied

An **express** contract is one that has been put into words. It may be written or oral. Each party to the contract has stated what he or she is willing to do and has been told what to expect from the other party. Most contracts are express. On the other hand, an **implied** contract, or contract by implication, is created by the acts of the parties, not by express agreement.

> **Example:** A written lease agreement expires, but the tenant continues to make payments and the landlord continues to accept them. Both parties have implied their consent to a new lease contract.

Unilateral vs. Bilateral

A contract is **unilateral** if only one of the contracting parties is legally obligated to perform. That party has promised to do a particular thing if the other party does something else; but the other party has not promised to do anything, and is not legally obligated to do anything.

> **Example:** In an open listing agreement, a seller promises to pay a real estate broker a commission if the broker finds a buyer for the property. The broker does not promise to try to find a buyer, but if he or she does, the seller is obligated to pay. An open listing agreement is a unilateral contract.

A **bilateral** contract is formed when each party promises to do something, so that both parties are legally obligated to perform. Most contracts are bilateral.

> **Example:** In an exclusive listing agreement, a seller promises to pay a real estate broker a commission if the broker finds a buyer for the property. The broker promises to try to find a buyer. An exclusive listing agreement is a bilateral contract.

Executory vs. Executed

An **executory** contract is one that has not yet been performed, or is in the process of being performed. An **executed** contract has been fully performed. With respect to contracts, the terms "executed" and "performed" mean the same thing.

Elements of a Valid Contract

Four elements are needed for a valid and binding contract:

1. legal capacity to contract,
2. mutual consent,
3. a lawful objective, and
4. consideration.

Capacity

The first requirement for a valid contract is that the parties have the legal capacity to enter into a contract. A person must be at least 18 years old to enter into a valid contract, and he or she must also be mentally competent.

Age Eighteen. Eighteen years of age is sometimes referred to as the **age of majority**. When a minor makes an agreement concerning real property, the agreement is "void." Neither the minor nor the other party can sue to enforce the agreement.

> **Example:** Bret, a 16-year-old, signs a purchase and sale agreement, agreeing to buy Melody's house. If either Bret or Melody breaches the agreement, the other could not enforce it, because it is void.

Most other types of contracts entered into by a minor are "voidable" by the minor. This means that the contract cannot be enforced against the minor. The minor is free to decide whether he or she wants to go through with the transaction. But if the minor does want to go through with it, the other party is bound. (Void and voidable contracts are discussed in more detail later in this chapter.)

The purpose of this rule is to prevent the enforcement of contracts against those who may be too young to understand their significance.

Competent. A person must also be mentally competent in order to have capacity to contract. If a person has been declared incompetent by a court, any contract he or she signs is void. If a court declares someone incompetent after a contract is signed, but the party was probably incompetent when the contract was signed, the contract is voidable at the discretion of the court-appointed guardian.

Contracts entered into by a person who is temporarily incompetent (for example, under the influence of alcohol or drugs) may be voidable if he or she takes legal action within a reasonable time after regaining mental competency.

Representing Another. Often, one person has the capacity to represent another person or entity in a contract negotiation. For instance, the affairs of minors and incompetents are handled by parents or court-appointed guardians; corporations are represented by properly authorized officers; partnerships are represented by individual partners; deceased persons are represented by executors or administrators; and a competent adult can appoint another competent adult to act on his or her behalf through a power of attorney. In each of these cases, the authorized representative can enter into a contract on behalf of the person represented. (Note that a minor does not have the ability to appoint an agent, so a minor cannot enter into a listing agreement with a real estate agent.)

Mutual Consent

Mutual consent is the second requirement for a valid contract. Each party must consent to the agreement. When someone signs an agreement, consent is presumed, so no contract should be signed until its contents are fully understood. A person can't use failure or inability to read an agreement as an excuse for nonperformance. An illiterate person should have a contract explained thoroughly by someone who is concerned with his or her welfare.

Mutual consent is sometimes called mutual assent, mutuality, or "a meeting of the minds." But no matter what it's called, it is achieved through the process of **offer and acceptance**.

Offer. A contract offer shows the willingness of the person making it (the **offeror**) to enter into a contract under the stated terms. To be valid, an offer must:

1. Express a willingness to contract. Whatever words make up the offer, they must clearly indicate that the offeror intends to enter into a contract.
2. Be definite and certain in its terms. An offer that does not clearly state what the offeror is proposing is said to be illusory—vague—and any agreement reached as a result is unenforceable.

Terminating an Offer. Sometimes circumstances change after an offer has been made, or perhaps the offeror has had a change of heart. If an offer terminates before it is accepted, no contract is formed. There are many things that can terminate an offer before it is accepted, including:

• revocation by the offeror,
• lapse of time,
• death or incompetency of the offeror,
• rejection of the offer, or
• a counteroffer.

The offeror can **revoke** the offer at any time until he or she is notified that the offer has been accepted. To effect a proper "offer and acceptance," the accepting party must not only accept the offer, but must also communicate that acceptance to the offeror before the offer is revoked (see the discussion of acceptance below).

Many offers include a deadline for acceptance. If a deadline is set and acceptance is not communicated within the time allotted, the offer terminates automatically. If a time limit is not stated in the offer, a reasonable amount of time is allowed. What is reasonable is determined by the court if a dispute arises.

If the offeror dies or is declared incompetent before the offer is accepted, the offer is terminated.

A **rejection** also terminates an offer. Once the **offeree** (the person to whom the offer was made) rejects the offer, he or she cannot go back later and create a contract by accepting the offer.

Example: Howard offers to purchase Maria's house for $195,000. Maria rejects the offer the next day. The following week, Maria changes her

Fig.7.2 Mutual consent is achieved through the process of offer and acceptance

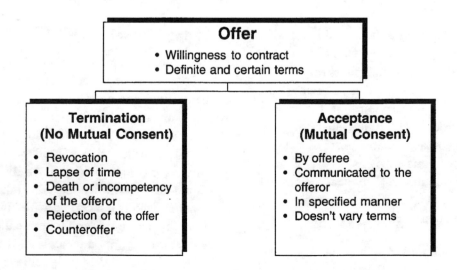

mind and decides to accept Howard's offer. But it's too late to do this, because the offer terminated with her rejection.

A **counteroffer** (also called a qualified acceptance) is actually a rejection of the offer and a tender of a new offer. Instead of either accepting or rejecting the offer outright, the offeree "accepts" with certain modifications. This happens when some, but not all, of the original terms are unacceptable to the offeree. When there is a counteroffer, the roles of the parties are reversed: the original offeror becomes the offeree and can accept or reject the revised offer. If he or she chooses to accept the counteroffer, there is a binding contract. If the counteroffer is rejected, the party making the counteroffer cannot go back and accept the original offer. The original offer was terminated by rejection.

> **Example:** Pavek offers to buy Harrison's property under the following conditions: the purchase price is $150,000, the closing date is January 15, and the downpayment is $15,000. Harrison agrees to all the terms but the closing date, which she wants to be February 15. By changing one of the terms, Harrison has rejected Pavek's initial offer and made a counteroffer. Now it is up to Pavek to either accept or reject Harrison's counteroffer.

Acceptance. An offer can be revoked at any time until acceptance has been communicated to the offeror. To create a binding contract, the offeree must communicate acceptance to the offeror in the manner and within the time limit stated in the offer (or before the offer is revoked). If no time or manner of acceptance is stated in the offer, a reasonable time and manner is implied. The offeree's acceptance must also be free of any negative influences, such as fraud, undue influence, or duress. If an offer or acceptance is influenced by any of these negative forces, the contract is voidable by the damaged party.

Fraud is misrepresentation of a material fact to another person who relies on the misrepresentation as the truth in deciding to enter into a transaction.

- **Actual fraud** occurs when the person making the statement either knows the statement is false and makes it with an intent to deceive, or doesn't know whether or not the statement is true but makes it anyway. For example, a seller who paints over cracks in the basement and then tells the buyer that the foundation is completely sound is committing actual fraud.
- **Constructive fraud** occurs when a person who occupies a position of confidence and trust, or who has superior knowledge of the subject matter, makes a false statement with no intent to deceive. For example, if a seller innocently points out incorrect lot boundaries, it may be constructive fraud.

Undue influence is using one's influence to pressure a person into making a contract, or taking advantage of another's distress or weakness of mind to induce him or her to enter into a contract.

Duress is compelling someone to do something—such as enter into a contract—against his or her will, with the use of force or constraint.

Menace is the threat of force or constraint.

Lawful Objective

The third requirement for a valid contract is a lawful objective. Both the purpose of the contract and the consideration for the contract (discussed below) must be lawful. Examples of contracts with unlawful objectives are contracts to pay interest rates in excess of the state's usury limit, or contracts relating to unlawful gambling. If a contract does not have a lawful objective, it is void.

Sometimes contracts contain some lawful provisions and some unlawful provisions. In these situations, it may be possible to sever the unlawful portions of the contract and enforce the lawful portions.

> **Example:** Callahan and Baker enter into a contract to buy and sell an apartment house. A clause in the contract prohibits the buyer from renting

any of the apartments to persons of a certain race. The contract to buy and sell the property would probably be enforceable, but the clause prohibiting rentals to members of a certain race would be void because it is unlawful.

Consideration

The fourth element of a valid contract is **consideration**. Consideration is something of value—money, goods, services, or promises to provide money, goods, or services—exchanged by the contracting parties. It must be either a benefit to the party receiving it or a detriment to the party offering it. The typical real estate purchase and sale contract involves a promise by the purchaser to pay a certain amount of money to the seller at a certain time, and a promise by the seller to convey title to the purchaser when the price has been paid. Both parties have given and received consideration.

While consideration is usually the promise to do a particular act, it can also be a promise to not do a particular act. For example, Aunt Martha may promise to pay her nephew Charles $1,000 if he promises to stop smoking.

As a general rule, a contract is enforceable as long as the consideration has value, even though the value of the consideration exchanged is unequal. A contract to sell a piece of property worth $120,000 for $105,000 is enforceable. However, in cases where the disparity in value is quite large (such as a contract to sell a piece of property worth $185,000 for $55,000), a court may refuse to enforce the contract. This is particularly likely to happen if the parties have unequal bargaining power (for example, when the buyer is a well-informed real estate developer and the seller is elderly, uneducated, and inexperienced in business).

The Writing Requirement

For most contracts used in real estate transactions, there is a fifth requirement: they must be put into writing, as required by the statute of frauds.

Fig.7.3 Elements of a contract

A Valid Real Estate Contract
- Capacity
- Mutual consent
- Lawful objective
- Consideration
- In writing

The **statute of frauds** is a state law that requires certain types of contracts to be in writing and signed. Only the types of contracts covered by the statute of frauds have to be in writing; other contracts may be oral. (An oral contract is sometimes called a parol contract.)

Each state has its own statute of frauds, and the requirements vary slightly from state to state. In virtually every state, however, almost all of the contracts typically used in a real estate transaction are covered by the statute. In California, the statute of frauds applies to:

1. any agreement for the sale or exchange of real property or an interest in real property;
2. a lease of real property that will expire more than one year after it was agreed to;
3. an agency agreement authorizing an agent to purchase or sell real property, or lease it for more than one year;
4. an agency agreement authorizing an agent to find a buyer or seller for real property, if the agent will receive compensation (a listing agreement); and
5. an assumption of a mortgage or deed of trust.

The "writing" required by the statute of frauds does not have to be in any particular form, nor does it have to be contained entirely in one document. A note or memorandum about the agreement or a series of letters will suffice, as long as the writing:

1. identifies the subject matter of the contract,
2. indicates an agreement between the parties and its essential terms, and
3. is signed by the parties to be bound.

If the parties fail to put a contract that is covered by the statute of frauds in writing, the contract is usually unenforceable. However, a court will enforce such an oral agreement under certain circumstances. This might occur if there is both evidence that the contract exists and evidence of its terms, and if one party has completely or substantially performed his or her obligations under the contract. This is a relatively rare occurrence; the safest course is to put the contract in writing.

Legal Status of Contracts

Four terms are used to describe the legal status of a contract: a contract is void, voidable, unenforceable, or valid. These terms have already been used throughout our discussion, and now we'll look more closely at what each one means.

Void

A void contract is no contract at all; it has no legal effect. This most often occurs because one of the essential elements, such as mutual consent or consideration, is completely lacking.

> **Example:** Talbot signed a contract promising to deed some property to Wetherall, but Wetherall did not offer any consideration in exchange for Talbot's promise. Since the contract is not supported by consideration, it is void.

A void contract may be disregarded. Neither party is required to take legal action to withdraw from the agreement.

Voidable

A voidable contract is a contract which on its face appears to be valid, but which has some defect giving one or both of the parties the power to withdraw from the agreement. For example, contracts entered into as a result of fraud are normally voidable by the injured party (the one defrauded).

It is important to note that action must be taken to rescind a voidable contract. Unlike a contract that is void from the outset, a voidable contract cannot simply be ignored. Failure to take action within a reasonable time may result in a court declaring that the contract was ratified. Alternatively, the injured party may decide that he or she would rather continue with the agreement; in that case, he or she may expressly ratify it.

Unenforceable

An unenforceable contract is one that cannot be enforced in court for one of the following reasons:

1. its contents cannot be proved,
2. the other party has a voidable contract, or
3. the statute of limitations has expired.

Contents Cannot Be Proved. This is most often a problem associated with oral agreements. Even if the law does not require a certain kind of contract to be written, it is a good idea to put it in writing because it avoids confusion and misunderstanding. Furthermore, even if a contract is in writing, the written agreement must clearly state all the contract terms. Vaguely worded contracts are considered illusory and unenforceable.

One Party Has a Voidable Contract. If one party has a voidable contract, the other is left with an unenforceable contract. (Note that the party who has the voidable contract can enforce the contract against the other party.)

Statute of Limitations Expired. A statute of limitations is a type of law that sets a deadline for filing a lawsuit. Unless an injured party files suit before the deadline set by the applicable statute of limitations, his or her legal claim is lost forever. The purpose of a statute of limitations is to prevent one person from suing another too many years after an event, when memories have faded and evidence has been lost.

Every state has a statute of limitations for contracts. If one of the parties to a contract fails to perform his or her obligations (breaches the contract), the other party has to sue within a certain number of years after the breach. Otherwise, the statute of limitations will run out and the contract will become unenforceable.

In California, the statute of limitations generally requires lawsuits concerning written contracts to be filed within four years after their breach, and lawsuits concerning many oral contracts to be filed within two years after their breach.

Valid

If the contract contains all the essential elements, the contents can be proved in court, and it is free of any negative influences, it is a valid agreement and can be enforced in a court of law.

Discharging a Contract

Once there is a valid, enforceable contract, it may be discharged by:

1. full performance, or
2. agreement between the parties.

Full Performance

Full performance means that the parties have performed all their obligations—the contract is executed. For example, once the deed to the property has been transferred to the buyer and the seller

Fig.7.4 Legal status of contracts

Type of Contract	Legal Effect	Example
Void	No contract at all	An agreement for which there is no consideration
Voidable	Valid until rescinded by one party	A contract based on fraud
Unenforceable	Party may not sue for performance	A contract after the limitations period has expired
Valid	Binding and enforceable	An agreement with all the requirements for a valid contract

has received the purchase price, the purchase and sale agreement has been discharged by full performance.

Agreement Between the Parties

The parties to a contract can agree to discharge the contract by one of several methods:

- rescission,
- cancellation,
- assignment,
- novation, or
- accord and satisfaction.

Rescission. Sometimes the parties to a contract agree that they would be better off if the contract had never been signed. In such a case, they may decide to rescind the contract. A rescission is occasionally referred to as a "contract to destroy a contract."

The buyer and seller sign an agreement that terminates their previous agreement and puts them as nearly as possible back in the positions they were in before entering into the agreement. If any money or other consideration has changed hands, it will be returned.

In certain circumstances, a contract can be rescinded by court order (rather than by agreement between the parties). Court-ordered rescission is discussed later in this chapter.

Cancellation. A cancellation does not go as far as a rescission. The parties agree to terminate the contract, but previous acts are unaffected. For example, money that was paid prior to the cancellation is not returned.

When contracting to purchase real property, a buyer generally gives the seller a deposit to show that he or she is acting in good faith and intends to fulfill the terms of their agreement. This is called an **earnest money deposit**, and the seller is entitled to keep it if the buyer defaults on the contract. If the

buyer and seller agree to terminate the contract and the seller refunds the earnest money deposit to the buyer, the contract has been rescinded. If the seller keeps the deposit, the contract has been cancelled.

Assignment. Sometimes one of the parties to a contract wants to withdraw by assigning his or her interest in the contract to another person. As a general rule, a contract can be assigned from one person to another unless a clause in the contract prohibits assignment. Technically, assignment does not discharge the contract. The new party (the assignee) assumes primary liability for the contractual obligations, but the withdrawing party (the assignor) is still secondarily liable.

> **Example:** A buyer is purchasing a home on a land contract over a 15-year period. In the absence of any prohibitive language, she can sell the home, accept a cash downpayment, and assign her contract rights and liabilities to the new buyer. The new buyer would assume primary liability for the contract debt, but the original buyer would retain secondary liability.

One exception to the rule that a contract can be assigned unless otherwise agreed: a personal services contract can't be assigned without the other party's consent.

> **Example:** A nightclub has a contract with a singer for several performances. The singer cannot assign her contract to another singer—it is a personal services contract. The nightclub management has a right to choose who will be singing in their establishment.

Novation. The term "novation" has two generally accepted meanings. One type of novation is the substitution of a new party into an existing obligation. If a buyer under a land contract is released by the seller in favor of a new buyer under the same contract, there has been a novation. The first buyer is relieved of all liability connected with the contract.

Novation may also be the substitution of a new obligation for an old one. If a landlord and tenant agree to tear up a three-year lease in favor of a new ten-year lease, it is a novation.

Assignment vs. Novation. The difference between assignment and novation concerns the withdrawing party's liability. When a contract is assigned, there is continuing liability for the assignor. In a novation, on the other hand, the withdrawing party is released from liability, because he or she was replaced with an individual who was approved by the other party. Novation, unlike assignment, always requires the other party's consent.

Accord and Satisfaction. An accord and satisfaction occurs when someone with a contractual right against another accepts something different (usually less) than what was called for in the original agreement.

> **Example:** Able is obligated to pay Baker $1,000 on July 4. He offers to pay $750 on June 20 instead, explaining that he simply does not have and will not be able to get any more money than that. If Baker agrees to accept $750 on June 20 as satisfaction of the $1,000 owed on July 4, Able pays it, and Baker accepts it, there has been an accord (the agreement) and satisfaction (performance of the agreement). This relieves Able of the original obligation.

Breach of Contract

A breach of contract occurs when a party fails, without legal excuse, to perform any of the promises contained in the agreement. Before the damaged party can seek a remedy in court for the failure to perform, the breach must be a **material breach**. A breach is material when the promise that has not been fulfilled is an important part of the contract.

Many standard contract forms state that **"time is of the essence** of this contract." That phrase is used to warn the parties that timely performance is crucial and that the failure to meet a deadline is a material breach. But the phrase often doesn't have any real effect. Unless the parties actually insist on timely performance, a court is likely to hold that the "time is of the essence" clause has been waived.

When a breach occurs, there are four possible remedies available to the damaged party:

- rescission,
- liquidated damages,
- damages, or
- specific performance.

Rescission

As previously explained, a rescission is a termination of the contract in which the parties are returned to their original positions. The seller refunds the buyer's earnest money deposit and the buyer gives up his or her equitable interest in the property. The rescission can be by agreement, or it can be ordered by a court at the request of one party when the other party has breached the contract.

Liquidated Damages

The parties to a contract sometimes agree in advance to an amount that will serve as full compensation to be paid in the event that one of the parties defaults. This sum is called liquidated damages.

> **Example:** Able agrees to buy 25,000 hinges from Baker. They agree that if Baker cannot deliver the hinges to Able on time, Baker will pay Able $3,000 as full compensation. If Baker fails to deliver the hinges on time, Able will only receive $3,000 from Baker; she could not sue for any additional amount, even if her actual damages were greater than $3,000.

In a real estate transaction, the buyer's earnest money deposit is often treated as liquidated damages. If the seller keeps the deposit and releases the buyer from the contract, the agreement is canceled. (Note that California has special rules that govern liquidated damages clauses in purchase and sale agreements. See Chapter 8.)

Damages

This is the amount of money that can be recovered through a court action by a person who has been damaged by the default of another. A damages award is generally intended to put the nonbreaching party in the financial position he or she would have been in if the other party had fulfilled the terms of the contract.

> **Example:** Suppose Able and Baker (from the example above) did not agree to any liquidated damages. Baker fails to deliver the hinges on time, and Able suffers $7,000 in damages because she must quickly purchase the hinges from another supplier at a much higher price. Able can sue Baker for the $7,000 in damages.

Suppose a home seller breaches a purchase and sale agreement. Of course, the buyer has no good faith deposit to keep as liquidated damages, so he or she may choose to sue the seller for monetary compensation for the harm that was caused by the breach.

Specific Performance

Specific performance is a legal action designed to compel a defaulting party to perform under the terms of the contract. For example, a court can order a seller to sign and deliver a deed to a buyer to complete a purchase.

Specific performance is usually only available as a remedy when monetary damages are not sufficient compensation. For example, when the purchase of real property is involved, the court may order specific performance because there is no other property that is just like the one the seller agreed to sell. Payment of damages would not enable the buyer to purchase another property just like it.

Fig.7.5 When a contract is breached

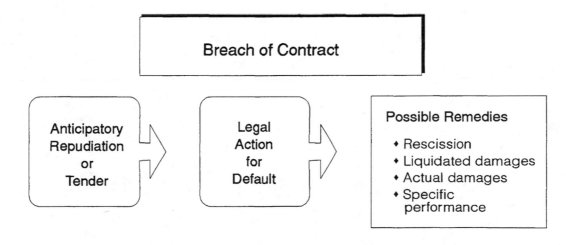

Tender

A tender is an unconditional offer by one of the contract parties to perform his or her part of the agreement. It is frequently referred to as "an offer to make an offer good." A tender is usually made when it appears that the other party is going to default; it is necessary before legal action can be taken on the breach.

Example: A seller suspects the buyer does not plan to complete the purchase (and he intends to sue the buyer if this happens). The seller must attempt to deliver the deed to the buyer as promised in the purchase and sale agreement. When the tender is made, if the buyer refuses to pay the agreed price and accept the deed, the buyer is placed in default and the seller may then file a lawsuit.

Of course, if a buyer has reason to believe the seller does not plan to complete the sale, he or she tenders by attempting to deliver the full amount promised in the purchase and sale agreement to the seller. When the seller refuses to accept the money and deliver the deed, he or she is in default.

Sometimes there is an **anticipatory repudiation** by one of the parties. An anticipatory repudiation is a positive statement by the defaulting party indicating that he or she will not or cannot perform according to the terms of the agreement. When this happens, no tender is necessary as a basis for a legal action.

Chapter Summary

1. A contract is "an agreement between two or more competent persons to do or not do certain things for consideration." Every contract is either express or implied, either unilateral or bilateral, and either executory or executed.

2. For a contract to be valid and binding, the parties must have the legal capacity to contract, and there must be mutual consent (offer and acceptance), a lawful objective, and consideration. The statute of frauds requires real estate contracts to be in writing.

3. A contract may be void, voidable, unenforceable, or valid.

4. An existing contract can be discharged by full performance or by agreement between the parties. The parties can agree to terminate the contract by rescission or cancellation, or they can arrange an assignment, a novation, or an accord and satisfaction.

5. A breach of contract occurs when a party fails, without legal excuse, to perform any material promise contained in the agreement. When a breach occurs, the four possible remedies are rescission, liquidated damages, damages, or specific performance.

Key Terms

Contract—An agreement between two or more competent persons to do or not do certain things for consideration.

Capacity—A person must be mentally competent and at least 18 years of age to have the capacity to contract.

Mutual consent—The agreement of both parties to the terms of the contract, effected by offer and acceptance.

Offer—A communication that shows the willingness of the person making it (the offeror) to enter into a contract.

Acceptance—A communication showing the willingness of the offeree to be bound by the terms of the offer.

Counteroffer—A qualified acceptance; technically a rejection of the offer, with a new offer made on slightly different terms.

Fraud—The misrepresentation of a material fact to someone who relies on the misrepresentation as the truth in deciding whether to enter into a contract.

Undue influence—Using one's influence to pressure someone into entering into a contract, or taking advantage of another's distress to induce him or her to enter into a contract.

Duress—Compelling someone to enter into a contract with the use of force or constraint.

Menace—Compelling someone to enter into a contract with the threat of force or constraint.

Consideration—Something of value exchanged by the parties to a contract; either a benefit to the party receiving it or a detriment to the party offering it.

Statute of frauds—A state law that requires certain contracts to be in writing and signed, including most contracts related to real estate transactions.

Valid—When a contract contains all the necessary elements and is enforceable in court.

Void—When a contract lacks an essential element, so that it has no legal force or effect.

Voidable—When one of the parties can choose to rescind the contract, because of lack of capacity, fraud, etc.

Unenforceable—When a contract cannot be enforced in a court of law because its contents cannot be proved, or it is voidable by the other party, or the statute of limitations has expired.

Rescission—When a contract is terminated and any consideration given is returned, putting the parties as nearly as possible back into the position they were in prior to entering into the contract.

Cancellation—When a contract is terminated but previous contractual acts are unaffected.

Assignment—When one party transfers his or her rights and obligations under the contract to another party, but remains secondarily liable.

Novation—When one party is completely replaced with another, or one contract is completely replaced with another, and all liability under the original contract ends.

Liquidated damages—An amount that the parties agree in advance will serve as full compensation if one of the parties defaults.

Specific performance—A remedy for breach of contract in which the court orders the defaulting party to perform as agreed in the contract.

Tender—An unconditional offer by one of the parties to perform his or her part of the agreement, made when it appears that the other party is going to default.

Chapter 7—Quiz
Contract Law

1. A contract can be valid and binding even though:

   a) it is not supported by consideration
   b) it does not have a lawful objective
   c) it is not put into writing
   d) there was no offer and acceptance

2. To have capacity to contract, a person must have:

   a) reached the age of majority
   b) been declared competent by a court
   c) a high school diploma or general equivalency certificate
   d) All of the above

3. An offer to purchase property would be terminated by any of the following, EXCEPT:

   a) failure to communicate acceptance of the offer within the prescribed period
   b) revocation after acceptance has been communicated
   c) a qualified acceptance of the offer by the offeree
   d) death or insanity of the offeror

4. A counteroffer:

   a) terminates the original offer
   b) will result in a valid contract if accepted by the other party
   c) Both of the above
   d) None of the above

5. Tucker sends Jonson a letter offering to buy his property for $20,000 in cash, with the transaction to close in 60 days. Jonson sends Tucker a letter that says, "I accept your offer; however, the closing will take place in 90 days." Which of the following is true?

   a) Jonson's statement is not a valid acceptance
   b) Jonson's statement is a counteroffer
   c) There is no contract unless Tucker accepts the counteroffer
   d) All of the above

6. Which of these could be consideration for a contract?

   a) $63,000
   b) A promise to convey title
   c) A promise to not sell property during the next 30 days
   d) All of the above

7. An executory contract is one which:

   a) is made by the executor of an estate for the sale of probate property
   b) has not yet been performed
   c) has been completely performed
   d) has been proposed but not accepted by either party

8. A void contract is one that:

   a) lacks an essential contract element
   b) needs to be rescinded by the injured party
   c) can be rescinded by agreement
   d) can no longer be enforced because the deadline set by the statute of limitations has passed

9. A voidable contract is:

   a) not enforceable by either party
   b) enforceable unless action is taken to rescind it
   c) void unless action is taken to rescind it
   d) None of the above

10. The statute of frauds is a law that requires:

   a) all contracts to be supported by consideration
   b) unlawful provisions to be severed from a contract
   c) certain contracts to be unilateral
   d) certain contracts to be in writing and signed

11. A contract can be discharged by all of the following except:

   a) novation
   b) performance
   c) cancellation
   d) breach

12. Bronowski and Murdock have a five-year contract. After two years, they agree to tear up that contract and replace it with a new ten-year contract. This is an example of:

   a) novation
   b) rescission
   c) duress
   d) specific performance

13. Graves and Chung are parties to a contract that doesn't prohibit assignment. If Chung assigns his interest in the contract to Stewart:

   a) Graves is not required to fulfill the contract
   b) Graves can sue for anticipatory repudiation
   c) Chung remains secondarily liable to Graves
   d) Chung is relieved of all further liability under the contract

14. A clause in the contract provides that if one party breaches, the other party will be entitled to $3,500 and cannot sue for more than that. This is a:

   a) just compensation provision
   b) compensation cap
   c) satisfaction clause
   d) liquidated damages provision

15. The McClures agreed to sell their house to Jacobsen, but then they breached the contract by refusing to go through with the sale. If Jacobsen wants a court order requiring the McClures to convey the house to her as agreed, she should sue for:

   a) damages
   b) specific performance
   c) liquidated damages
   d) rescission

Answer Key

1.c) Only certain types of contracts are required to be in writing, but all contracts require consideration, a lawful objective, and offer and acceptance.

2.a) A person has capacity to contract if he or she has reached the age of majority (in California, age 18) and is mentally competent. (It isn't necessary to be declared competent by a court, however.)

3.b) If the offeree accepts the offer before the offeror revokes it, a binding contract is formed.

4.c) A counteroffer terminates the original offer (operating as a rejection), but if the counteroffer is then accepted, a valid contract is formed.

5.d) All of the options are true statements.

6.d) Consideration is almost anything of value: money, goods, services, or a promise to do or not do something.

7.b) An executory contract has not yet been performed; an executed contract is one that has been fully performed.

8.a) A contract that lacks an essential element (consent, consideration, etc.) is void; it has no legal force or effect, so there is nothing to rescind.

9.b) A voidable contract can be rescinded by the injured party, but unless it is rescinded it will be enforceable.

10.d) The statute of frauds requires certain contracts to be in writing and signed by the party or parties to be bound.

11.d) Performance, rescission, cancellation, novation, and accord and satisfaction are all ways of discharging a contract. Breach does not discharge the contract; the breaching party is liable to the other party.

12.a) Novation is the replacement of an existing contract with a new contract, or the replacement of a party to a contract with a new party.

13.c) A contract can be assigned unless otherwise agreed, but the assignor remains secondarily liable to the other party.

14.d) Liquidated damages is an amount the contracting parties agree in advance will be paid as damages if one of them breaches the contract.

15.b) If the court granted Jacobsen specific performance, the McClures would be ordered to convey the house as agreed in the contract (not merely to pay Jacobsen damages as compensation).

Chapter 8

Types of Real Estate Contracts

 Outline

 Chapter Overview

Real estate agents must be familiar with the specific types of real estate contracts, as well as understanding the basic principles of contract law. This chapter describes several types of contracts related to real estate, including broker/salesperson agreements, listing agreements, deposit receipts, land contracts, options, and leases.

Broker/Salesperson Agreements

The type of contract a new licensee is likely to encounter first is a broker/salesperson agreement. California law requires a broker to have a written employment agreement with each licensee who works for him or her. The agreement must be signed by both parties. It should include all the basic terms of the employment relationship, such as the duties of the parties, the amount and type of supervision to be exercised by the broker, the basis for the licensee's compensation, and the grounds for terminating the relationship. A copy of the CAR Broker/Associate Licensee Contract form is shown below.

Fig.8.1 Broker/salesperson agreement

BROKER-ASSOCIATE LICENSEE CONTRACT
(Independent Contractor)
THIS IS INTENDED TO BE A LEGALLY BINDING CONTRACT — READ IT CAREFULLY.
CALIFORNIA ASSOCIATION OF REALTORS® (C.A.R.) STANDARD FORM

THIS AGREEMENT, made this _____ day of _____, 19____, by and between
_____
_____ (hereinafter "Broker") and
_____ (hereinafter "Associate Licensee").

IN CONSIDERATION of the respective representations and covenants herein, Broker and Associate Licensee agree and contract as follows:

1. **BROKER:** Broker represents that he/she/it is duly licensed as a real estate broker by the State of California. ☐ doing business as _____ (Firm name), ☐ a sole proprietorship, ☐ a partnership, ☐ a corporation. Broker is a member of the _____ Board(s)/Association(s) of REALTORS®, and a Participant in the _____ multiple listing service(s).

2. **ASSOCIATE LICENSEE:** Associate Licensee represents that, (a) he/she is duly licensed by the State of California as a ☐ real estate broker, ☐ real estate salesperson, and (b) he/she has not used any other names within the past five years except _____ _____. Broker shall keep his/her/its license current during the term of this agreement. Associate Licensee shall keep his/her license current during the term of this agreement, including satisfying all applicable continuing education and provisional license requirements.

3. **LISTING AND SALES ACTIVITIES:** Broker shall make available to Associate Licensee, equally with other licensees associated with Broker, all current listings in Broker's office, except any listing which Broker may choose to place in the exclusive servicing of Associate Licensee or one or more other specific licensees associated with Broker. Associate Licensee shall not be required to accept or service any particular listing or prospective listing offered by Broker, or to see or service particular parties. Broker shall not restrict Associate Licensee's activities to particular geographical areas. Broker shall not, except to the extent required by law, direct or limit Associate Licensee's activities as to hours, leads, open houses, opportunity or floor time, production, prospects, sales meetings, schedule, inventory, time off, vacation, or similar activities. In compliance with Commissioner's Regulation 2780, et seq. (Title 10, California Code of Regulations, §2780, et seq.), Broker and Associate Licensee shall at all times be familiar with, and act in compliance with, all applicable federal, California and local anti-discrimination laws.

4. **BROKER SUPERVISION:**
   (a) Associate Licensee shall submit for Broker's review:
   i. All documents which may have a material effect upon the rights and duties of principals in a transaction, within 24 hours after preparing, signing, or receiving same. Broker may exercise this review responsibility through another licensee provided the Broker and the designated licensee have complied with Commissioner's Regulation 2725 (Title 10, California Code of Regulations, §2725).
   ii. Any documents or other items connected with a transaction pursuant to this agreement, in the possession of or available to Associate Licensee, (i) immediately upon request by Broker or Broker's designated licensee, and/or (ii) as provided in Broker's Office Policy Manual, if any.
   iii. All documents associated with any real estate transaction in which Associate Licensee is a principal.
   (b) In addition, without affecting Associate Licensee's status, Broker shall have the right to direct Associate Licensee's actions to the extent required by law, and Associate Licensee shall comply with such directions. All trust funds shall be handled in compliance with Business and Professions Code §10145, and other applicable laws.

5. **OFFICE FACILITIES:** Broker shall make available for Associate Licensee's use, along with other licensees associated with Broker, the facilities of the real estate office operated by Broker at _____ and the facilities of any other office locations made available by Broker pursuant to this agreement.

6. **ASSOCIATE LICENSEE'S EFFORTS:** Associate Licensee shall work diligently and with his/her best efforts, (a) to sell, exchange, lease, or rent properties listed with Broker or other cooperating Brokers, (b) to solicit additional listings, clients, and customers, and (c) to otherwise promote the business of serving the public in real estate transactions to the end that Broker and Associate Licensee may derive the greatest benefit possible, in accordance with law.

7. **UNLAWFUL ACTS:** Associate Licensee shall not commit any act for which the Real Estate Commissioner of the State of California is authorized to restrict, suspend, or revoke Associate Licensee's license or impose other discipline, under California Business and Professions Code Sections 10176 or 10177 or other provisions of law.

8. **LISTING COMMISSIONS:** Commissions shall be charged to parties who desire to enter into listing agreements and other contracts for services requiring a real estate license, with Broker,
   ☐ as shown in "Exhibit A" attached which is incorporated as a part of this agreement by reference, or
   ☐ as follows: _____
   _____
   Any proposed deviation from that schedule must be reviewed and approved in advance by Broker. Any permanent change in commission schedule shall be disseminated by Broker to Associate Licensee.

9. **COMPENSATION TO ASSOCIATE LICENSEE:** Associate Licensee shall receive a share of commissions which are actually collected by Broker, on listings and other contracts for services requiring a real estate license which are solicited and obtained by Associate Licensee, and on transactions of which Associate Licensee's activities are the procuring cause,
   ☐ as shown in "Exhibit B" attached which is incorporated as a part of this agreement by reference, or
   ☐ as follows: _____
   _____
   _____
   The above commissions may be varied by written agreement between Broker and Associate Licensee before completion of any particular transaction. Expenses which must be paid from commissions, or are incurred in the attempt to collect commissions, shall be paid by Broker and Associate Licensee in the same proportion as set forth for the division of commissions.

10. **DIVIDING COMPENSATION WITH OTHER LICENSEES IN OFFICE:** If Associate Licensee and one or more other licensees associated with Broker both participate on the same side (either listing or selling) of a transaction, the commission allocated to their combined activities shall be divided by Broker and paid to them according to the written agreement between them which shall be furnished in advance to Broker.

11. **COMMISSIONS PAID TO BROKER:** All commissions will be received by Broker. Associate Licensee's share of commissions shall be paid to him/her, after deduction of offsets, immediately upon collection by Broker or as soon thereafter as practicable, except as otherwise provided in (a) Paragraph 9, above, (b) Broker's Office Policy Manual, or (c) a separate written agreement between Broker and Associate Licensee. Broker may impound in Broker's account Associate Licensee's share of commissions on transactions in which there is a known or pending claim against Broker and/or Associate Licensee, until such claim is resolved.

12. **UNCOLLECTED COMMISSIONS:** Neither Broker nor Associate Licensee shall be liable to the other for any portion of commissions not collected. Associate Licensee shall not be entitled to any advance payment from Broker upon future commissions.

The copyright laws of the United States (17 U.S. Code) forbid the unauthorized reproduction of this form by any means including facsimile or computerized formats.
Copyright 1990, CALIFORNIA ASSOCIATION OF REALTORS®
525 South Virgil Avenue, Los Angeles, California 90020

MO-JAN-91

FORM I-14

Reprinted with permission, California Association of REALTORS®. Endorsement not implied.

13. **ASSOCIATE LICENSEE EXPENSES; OFFSETS:** Associate Licensee shall provide and pay for all professional licenses, supplies, services, and other items required in connection with Associate Licensee's activities under this agreement, or any listing or transaction, without reimbursement from Broker except as required by law. If Broker elects to advance funds to pay expenses or liabilities of Associate Licensee, Associate Licensee shall repay to Broker the full amount advanced on demand, or Broker may deduct the full amount advanced from commissions payable to Associate Licensee on any transaction without notice.

14. **INDEPENDENT CONTRACTOR RELATIONSHIP:** Broker and Associate Licensee intend that, to the maximum extent permissible by law, (a) this agreement does not constitute a hiring or employment agreement by either party, (b) Broker and Associate Licensee are independent contracting parties with respect to all services rendered under this agreement or in any resulting transactions, (c) Associate Licensee's only remuneration shall be his/her proportional share, if any, of commissions collected by Broker, (d) Associate Licensee retains sole and absolute discretion and judgment in the methods, techniques, and procedures to be used in soliciting and obtaining listings, sales, exchanges, leases, rentals, or other transactions, and in carrying out Associate Licensee's selling and soliciting activities, except as required by law or in Broker's Office Policy Manual, (e) Associate Licensee is under the control of Broker as to the results of Associate Licensee's work only, and not as to the means by which those results are accomplished except as required by law, or in Broker's Office Policy Manual, if any, (f) this agreement shall not be construed as a partnership, (g) Associate Licensee has no authority to bind Broker by any promise or representation unless specifically authorized by Broker in writing, (h) Broker shall not be liable for any obligation or liability incurred by Associate Licensee, (i) Associate Licensee shall not be treated as an employee with respect to services performed as a real estate agent, for state and federal tax purposes, and (j) the fact the Broker may carry worker compensation insurance for his/her/its own benefit and for the mutual benefit of Broker and licensees associated with Broker, including Associate Licensee, shall not create an inference of employment.

15. **LISTINGS AND OTHER AGREEMENTS PROPERTY OF BROKER:** All listings of property, and all agreements for performance of licensed acts, and all acts or actions requiring a real estate license which are taken or performed in connection with this agreement, shall be taken and performed in the name of Broker. All listings shall be submitted to Broker within 24 hours after receipt by Associate Licensee. Associate Licensee agrees to and does hereby contribute all right and title to such listings to Broker for the benefit and use of Broker, Associate Licensee, and other licensees associated with Broker.

16. **TERMINATION OF RELATIONSHIP:** Broker or Associate Licensee may terminate their relationship under this agreement at any time, on 24 hours written notice, with or without cause. Even after termination, this agreement shall govern all disputes and claims between Broker and Associate Licensee connected with their relationship under this agreement, including obligations and liabilities arising from existing and completed listings, transactions, and services.

17. **COMMISSIONS AFTER TERMINATION AND OFFSET:** If this agreement is terminated while Associate Licensee has listings or pending transactions that require further work normally rendered by Associate Licensee, Broker shall make arrangements with another licensee associated with Broker to perform the required work, or shall perform the work him/herself. The licensee performing the work shall be reasonably compensated for completing work on those listings or transactions, and such reasonable compensation shall be deducted from Associate Licensee's share of commissions. Except for such offset, Associate Licensee shall receive his/her regular share of commissions on such sales or other transactions, if actually collected by Broker, after deduction of any other amounts or offsets provided in this agreement.

18. **ARBITRATION OF DISPUTES:** All disputes or claims between Associate Licensee and other licensee(s) associated with Broker, or between Associate Licensee and Broker, arising from or connected in any way with this agreement, which cannot be adjusted between the parties involved, shall be submitted to the Board of REALTORS' of which all such disputing parties are members for arbitration pursuant to the provisions of its Bylaws, as may be amended from time to time, which are incorporated as a part of this agreement by reference. If the Bylaws of the Board do not cover arbitration of the dispute, or if the Board declines jurisdiction over the dispute, then arbitration shall be pursuant to the rules of the American Arbitration Association as may be amended from time to time, which are incorporated as a part of this agreement by reference. The Federal Arbitration Act, Title 9, U.S. Code, Section 1, et seq., shall govern this agreement.

19. **PROPRIETARY INFORMATION AND FILES:** Associate Licensee shall not use to his/her own advantage, or the advantage of any other person, business or entity, except as specifically provided in this agreement, either during Associate Licensee's association with Broker or thereafter, any information gained for or from the business or files of Broker. All files and documents pertaining to listings and transactions are the property of Broker and shall be delivered to Broker by Associate Licensee immediately upon request or upon termination of their relationship under this agreement.

20. **INDEMNITY AND HOLD HARMLESS:** All claims, demands, liabilities, judgments, and arbitration awards, including costs and attorney's fees, to which Broker is subjected by reason of any action taken or omitted by Associate Licensee in connection with services rendered or to be rendered pursuant to this agreement shall be:

☐ Paid in full by Associate Licensee, who hereby agrees to indemnify and hold harmless Broker for all such sums, or

☐ Other: _____
_____
_____

Associate Licensee shall pay to Broker the full amount due by him/her on demand, or Broker may deduct the full amount due by Associate Licensee from commissions due on any transaction without notice.

21. **ADDITIONAL PROVISIONS:** _____
_____
_____

22. **DEFINITIONS:** As used in this agreement, the following terms have the meanings indicated:

(a) "Listing" means an agreement with a property owner or other party to locate a buyer, exchange party, lessee, or other party to a transaction involving real property, a mobile home, or other property or transaction which may be brokered by a real estate licensee, or an agreement with a party to locate or negotiate for any such property or transaction.

(b) "Commission" means compensation for acts requiring a real estate license, regardless of whether calculated as a percentage of transaction price, flat fee, hourly rate, or in any other manner.

(c) "Transaction" means a sale, exchange, lease, or rental of real property, a business opportunity, or a mobile home which may lawfully be brokered by a real estate licensee, or a loan secured by any property of those types.

(d) "Associate Licensee" means the real estate broker or real estate salesperson licensed by the State of California and rendering the services set forth herein for Associate Licensee.

23. **NOTICES:** All notices under this agreement shall be in writing. Notices may be delivered personally, or by certified U.S. mail, postage prepaid, or by facsimile, to the parties at the addresses noted below. Either party may designate a new address for purposes of this agreement by giving notice to the other party. Notices mailed shall be deemed received as of 5:00 P.M. on the second business day following the date of mailing.

24. **ATTORNEY FEES:**
In any action, proceeding, or arbitration between Broker and Associate Licensee arising from or related to this agreement, the prevailing party shall, in the discretion of the court or arbitrator, be entitled to reasonable attorney fees in addition to other appropriate relief.

25. **ENTIRE AGREEMENT; MODIFICATION:** All prior agreements between the parties concerning their relationship as Broker and Associate Licensee are incorporated in this agreement, which constitutes the entire contract. Its terms are intended by the parties as a final and complete expression of their agreement with respect to its subject matter, and may not be contradicted by evidence of any prior agreement or contemporaneous oral agreement. This agreement may not be amended, modified, altered, or changed in any respect whatsoever except by a further agreement in writing duly executed by Broker and Associate Licensee.

BROKER: **ASSOCIATE LICENSEE:**

_____   _____
(Signature)   (Signature)

_____   _____
(Name Printed)   (Name Printed)

_____   _____
(Address)   (Address)

_____   _____
(City, State, Zip)   (City, State, Zip)

_____   _____
(Telephone)   (Fax)   (Telephone)   (Fax)

NOTE: (1) Broker and Associate Licensee should each receive an executed copy of this agreement.
        (2) Attach commission schedules Exhibits A and B if applicable.

This form is available for use by the entire real estate industry. The use of this form is not intended to identify the user as a REALTOR'. REALTOR' is a registered collective membership mark which may be used only by real estate licensees who are members of the NATIONAL ASSOCIATION OF REALTORS' and who subscribe to its Code of Ethics.

MO-JAN-95

Listing Agreements

A listing agreement is a written employment agreement between a property owner and a real estate broker. The property owner employs the broker to find a buyer who is ready, willing, and able to buy the owner's property on the owner's terms. A listing agreement does not give the agent the authority to accept offers on behalf of the seller, or to transfer title to the seller's property.

In California, a broker cannot sue to collect a commission unless he or she has a written listing agreement with the property owner. What the broker must do in order to earn the commission depends on what type of listing the broker has, and on the specific terms of the listing agreement.

Types of Listing Agreements

There are three types of listing agreements:

- exclusive agency listings,
- exclusive right to sell listings, and
- open listings.

Exclusive Agency Listing. With an exclusive agency listing, the seller hires one broker to find a buyer. The listing broker is the only agent who is authorized

Fig.8.2 Listing agreements

Type of Listing	Legal Effect
Exclusive agency listing	Broker gets commission unless owner sells the property
Exclusive right to sell listing	Broker gets commission no matter who sells the property
Open listing	Broker gets commission only if procuring cause of the sale

to find a buyer (thus the name "exclusive agency"). The seller must pay the listing broker a commission if the property is sold by anyone other than the seller. However, if the seller finds a buyer for the property without anyone else's help, the broker is not entitled to a commission.

An exclusive agency listing must have a definite termination date; otherwise, the broker may be subject to disciplinary action (see Chapter 18).

Exclusive Right to Sell Listing. With an exclusive right to sell listing, the seller hires one broker to find a buyer, and must pay that broker a commission if the property is sold during the listing term, regardless of who finds the buyer—even if the seller finds the buyer without anyone's help.

As with an exclusive agency listing, an exclusive right to sell listing requires a definite termination date.

Open Listing. With an open listing (also called a non-exclusive listing), the seller has the freedom to employ many brokers to find a ready, willing, and able buyer. The first broker to find a buyer is the only broker who is entitled to the commission; all the other brokers are out of luck. And as with an exclusive agency listing, if the seller finds a buyer on his or her own, no broker is entitled to a commission.

There is another way of explaining the commission arrangement under an open listing: a broker is entitled to a commission under an open listing only if he or she is the **procuring cause** of the sale. To be the procuring cause, the broker must be primarily responsible for bringing the buyer and the seller together. Generally, the broker who negotiates the purchase and sale agreement between the buyer and the seller is the procuring cause of the sale.

With open listings, several brokers may be showing the property and negotiating offers at the same time. Thus, confusion and arguments may arise as to who was the procuring cause of the sale.

Example: Tse gives five open listings to five different brokers. Broker A and Broker B show Tse's property to the same buyer; Broker B successfully negotiates the sales contract between Tse and that buyer. Broker A claims at least part of the commission, because he showed the buyer the property first. However, because Broker B negotiated the sale, she is the procuring cause, and she is the only broker who is entitled to the commission.

Open Listings vs. Exclusive Listings. Brokers prefer not to use open listings, because their prospects of actually earning a commission under an open listing are not very good. Since another broker may find a buyer at any moment, a broker with an open listing may hesitate to spend much time or money looking for a buyer. Also, brokers are reluctant to risk potential disagreements with other brokers over who is entitled to the commission.

Exclusive listings (exclusive agency and exclusive right to sell listings) avoid these problems because only one broker is authorized to find the buyer. This is why the Code of Ethics of the National Association of Realtors® encourages the use of exclusive listings whenever possible. In theory, exclusive listings result in better service to the seller. Since a broker has a more secure claim for a commission if the property is sold under an exclusive listing, the broker is likely to work harder to sell the property.

Remember that the only type of listing that guarantees the broker a commission no matter who sells the property is the exclusive right to sell listing. Under an open listing or an exclusive agency listing, the seller is free to sell the property on his or her own without incurring any obligation to pay the broker a commission. The exclusive right to sell listing eliminates the potential for disputes between the seller and broker over who was the procuring cause of the sale. The exclusive right to sell listing is the type of listing used most often.

Elements of a Valid Listing Agreement

A listing agreement must have all the essential elements of a valid contract that were discussed in the previous chapter, including competent parties, offer and acceptance, consideration, and a lawful purpose. Also, under the statute of frauds, a listing agreement must be in writing and must be signed by the seller. If there is no written listing agreement, the broker cannot sue the seller for a commission, even though an oral agreement may have established an agency relationship between the broker and the seller (see Chapter 5).

Property Description. A listing agreement must identify the seller's property. The street address is useful, but it may not be enough to identify the property with certainty. It's a good idea to attach a legal description of the property to the listing agreement as an exhibit. Any pages attached to a contract should be dated and initialed by the parties, to show that the attachments are intended to be part of the agreement.

Terms of Sale. A listing agreement should specify what the seller wants in the way of an offer, including the sales price and the amount of the downpayment. The seller can reject any offer that doesn't meet the sales terms described in the listing agreement, without becoming liable for a commission. However, if an offer is made that does meet those terms, and the seller rejects the offer, the broker may be entitled to a commission. Thus, it is very important that all the essential terms of sale be set forth clearly and fully in the listing agreement.

Commission Amount. A provision stating the amount (or rate) of the broker's commission is another key part of every listing agreement. The commission is usually computed as a percentage of the sales price. The commission rate or amount must be negotiable between the seller and the broker. In fact, it is a violation of state and federal antitrust laws for brokers to set uniform commission rates. Any discussion of commission rates among members of competing firms could give rise to a charge of price-fixing. (See Chapter 6.)

Fig.8.3 Exclusive right to sell listing agreement

EXCLUSIVE AUTHORIZATION AND RIGHT TO SELL
MULTIPLE LISTING AUTHORIZATION
THIS IS INTENDED TO BE A LEGALLY BINDING CONTRACT — READ IT CAREFULLY.
CALIFORNIA ASSOCIATION OF REALTORS® (C.A.R.) STANDARD FORM

1. **EXCLUSIVE RIGHT TO SELL:** I, the undersigned ("Seller") hereby employ and grant _____ ("Broker") the exclusive and irrevocable right commencing on _____ 19_____, and expiring at 11:59 PM on _____ 19_____ to sell or exchange the real property situated in the City of _____ County of _____, California described as follows: _____ ("Property")

2. **TERMS OF SALE:** The selling price shall be _____ _____ ($_____), to be paid as follows: _____ _____

    The following items of personal property are included in the above price: _____ _____

3. **MULTIPLE LISTING SERVICE (MLS):** Broker is a Participant of _____ Multiple Listing Service (MLS) and this listing information will be provided to the MLS to be published and disseminated to its Participants and Subscribers in accordance with its Rules and Regulations. Broker is authorized to cooperate with other real estate brokers, and to report the sale, its price, terms and financing for the publication, dissemination, information and use by authorized Association/Board members, MLS Participants and Subscribers.

4. **TITLE INSURANCE:** Evidence of title shall be a California Land Title Association policy of title insurance in the amount of the selling price. Upon request, a title insurance company can provide information about other types of title insurance coverage.

5. **COMPENSATION TO BROKER:**
    Notice: The amount or rate of real estate commissions is not fixed by law. They are set by each Broker individually and may be negotiable between the Seller and Broker.
    Seller agrees to pay to _____ Broker(s), irrespective of agency relationship(s), as compensation for services _____ percent of the sales price, or $_____ as follows:
    (a) if the Property is sold by Broker, or through any other person including Seller, on the above terms or any other price and terms acceptable to Seller during the above time period or any extension of said time period;
    (b) if the Property is withdrawn from sale, transferred, conveyed, leased, rented, or made unmarketable by a voluntary act of Seller, without the consent of Broker, during the above time period or any extension of said time period;
    (c) if within _____ calendar days of the final termination, including extensions, of this Exclusive Authorization and Right to Sell, the Property is sold, conveyed, or otherwise transferred to anyone with whom Broker(s) have had negotiations prior to final termination provided that Broker has given to Seller, prior to or upon termination, a written notice including the names of the prospective purchaser(s). This section (c) shall not apply if Seller enters into a valid listing agreement with another licensed real estate broker after the final termination of this Exclusive Authorization and Right to Sell;
    (d) in the event of an exchange, permission is hereby given Broker to represent all parties and collect compensation from them provided that there is full disclosure to all parties of such agency;
    (e) if completion of the sale is prevented by default of Seller, then upon such default;
    (f) if completion of the sale is prevented by a party to the transaction other than Seller, then only if and when Seller collects damages by suit or otherwise and then in an amount not less than one-half of the damages recovered, but not to exceed the above compensation, after first deducting title and escrow expenses and the expenses of collection, if any;
    (g) Broker(s) is authorized to cooperate with other brokers, and divide with other brokers such compensation in any manner acceptable to Broker(s);
    (h) Seller hereby irrevocably assigns to Broker(s) the funds and proceeds of Seller in escrow equal to the above compensation.

6. **AGENCY RELATIONSHIPS:** Broker shall act as the agent for Seller in any resulting transaction. Depending upon the circumstances, it may be necessary or appropriate for Broker to act as agent of both Seller and Buyer, exchange party, or one or more additional parties. If applicable, Broker shall, as soon as practicable, disclose to Seller any election to act as a dual agent representing both Seller and Buyer. If the Property is a residential dwelling with one to four units, Broker shall provide agency relationships disclosure as required by law. Seller understands that Broker may have or obtain listings on other properties and that potential buyers may consider, make offers on, or purchase through Broker property the same as or similar to Seller's Property. Seller consents to Broker's representation of sellers and buyers of other properties before, during, and after the expiration of this agreement.

7. **DEPOSIT:** Broker is authorized to accept and hold on Seller's behalf a deposit to be applied toward the purchase price.

8. **HOME WARRANTY PLAN:** Seller is informed that home warranty plans are available. Such plans may provide additional protection and benefit to Seller and potential buyers. Cost and coverage may vary.

* 9. **KEYBOX:** Seller authorizes Broker to install a KEYBOX: (Initial) YES (____/____) NO (____/____)

10. **SIGN:** Seller authorizes Broker to install a FOR SALE/SOLD sign on the property: (Initial) YES (____/____) NO (____/____)

11. **PEST CONTROL:** Seller shall furnish a current Wood Destroying Pests and Organisms Inspection Report of the main building and all structures of the Property, except _____   (Initial) YES (____/____) NO (____/____)

12. **DISCLOSURE:** Unless exempt, Seller shall complete and sign a Real Estate Transfer Disclosure Statement concerning the condition of the Property. Seller agrees to save and hold Broker harmless from all claims, disputes, litigation, and/or judgments arising from any incorrect information supplied by Seller, or from any material facts which Seller knows but fails to disclose.

* 13. **EARTHQUAKE SAFETY:** If the Property is a residential dwelling with one to four units, Seller acknowledges receipt of a copy of the *Homeowner's Guide to Earthquake Safety* from Broker.   (Initial) (____/____)

* 14. **TAX WITHHOLDING:** Seller agrees to perform any act reasonably necessary to carry out the provisions of FIRPTA (Internal Revenue Code §1445) and California Revenue and Taxation Code §18662, and regulations thereunder.

15. **EQUAL HOUSING OPPORTUNITY:** The Property is offered in compliance with federal, state, and local anti-discrimination laws.

16. **ATTORNEY'S FEES:** In any action, proceeding, or arbitration arising out of this agreement, involving the Seller and/or Broker(s), the prevailing party shall be entitled to reasonable attorney's fees and costs except as provided in paragraph 17.

Broker and Seller acknowledge receipt of copy of this page, which constitutes Page 1 of _____ Pages.
Seller's Initials (_____) (_____)   Broker's Initials (_____) (_____)

*READ REVERSE SIDE OF PAGE 2 OF THIS AGREEMENT FOR ADDITIONAL INFORMATION

THIS STANDARDIZED DOCUMENT HAS BEEN APPROVED BY THE CALIFORNIA ASSOCIATION OF REALTORS® (C.A.R.) IN FORM ONLY. NO REPRESENTATION IS MADE AS TO THE APPROVAL OF THE FORM OF ANY SUPPLEMENTS NOT CURRENTLY PUBLISHED BY C.A.R. OR THE LEGAL VALIDITY OR ADEQUACY OF ANY PROVISION IN ANY SPECIFIC TRANSACTION. IT SHOULD NOT BE USED WITH EXTENSIVE RIDERS OR ADDITIONS.
A REAL ESTATE BROKER IS THE PERSON QUALIFIED TO ADVISE ON REAL ESTATE TRANSACTIONS. IF YOU DESIRE LEGAL OR TAX ADVICE, CONSULT AN APPROPRIATE PROFESSIONAL.

The copyright laws of the United States (17 U.S. Code) forbid the unauthorized reproduction of this form by any means including facsimile or computerized formats.
Copyright © 1993, CALIFORNIA ASSOCIATION OF REALTORS®
525 South Virgil Avenue, Los Angeles, California 90020

OFFICE USE ONLY
Reviewed by Broker or Designee _____
Date _____

Reprinted with permission, California Association of REALTORS®. Endorsement not implied.

Property Address: _____

17. **MEDIATION OF DISPUTES:** BROKER AND SELLER AGREE TO MEDIATE ANY DISPUTE OR CLAIM BETWEEN THEM ARISING OUT OF THIS CONTRACT OR ANY RESULTING TRANSACTION BEFORE RESORTING TO ARBITRATION OR COURT ACTION. Mediation is a process in which parties attempt to resolve a dispute by submitting it to an impartial, neutral mediator who is authorized to facilitate the resolution of the dispute but who is not empowered to impose a settlement on the parties. Mediation fee, if any, shall be divided equally among the parties involved. Before the mediation begins, the parties agree to sign a document limiting the admissibility in arbitration or any civil action of anything said, any admission made, and any documents prepared, in the course of the mediation, consistent with Evidence Code §1152.5. IF ANY PARTY COMMENCES AN ARBITRATION OR COURT ACTION BASED ON A DISPUTE OR CLAIM TO WHICH THIS PARAGRAPH APPLIES WITHOUT FIRST ATTEMPTING TO RESOLVE THE MATTER THROUGH MEDIATION, THEN IN THE DISCRETION OF THE ARBITRATOR(S) OR JUDGE, THAT PARTY SHALL NOT BE ENTITLED TO RECOVER ATTORNEY'S FEES EVEN IF THEY WOULD OTHERWISE BE AVAILABLE TO THAT PARTY IN ANY SUCH ARBITRATION OR COURT ACTION. However, the filing of a judicial action to enable the recording of a notice of pending action, for order of attachment, receivership, injunction, or other provisional remedies, shall not in itself constitute a loss of the right to recover attorney's fees under this provision. The following matters are excluded from the requirement of mediation hereunder: (a) a judicial or non-judicial foreclosure or other action or proceeding to enforce a deed of trust, mortgage, or installment land sale contract as defined in Civil Code §2985. (b) an unlawful detainer action, (c) the filing or enforcement of a mechanic's lien, and (d) any matter which is within the jurisdiction of a probate court.

18. **ARBITRATION OF DISPUTES:** Any dispute or claim in law or equity between Seller and Broker arising out of this contract or any resulting transaction which is not settled through mediation shall be decided by neutral, binding arbitration and not by court action, except as provided by California law for judicial review of arbitration proceedings.

   The arbitration shall be conducted in accordance with the rules of either the American Arbitration Association (AAA) or Judicial Arbitration and Mediation Services, Inc. (JAMS). The selection between AAA and JAMS rules shall be made by the claimant first filing for the arbitration. The parties to an arbitration may agree in writing to use different rules and/or arbitrator(s). In all other respects, the arbitration shall be conducted in accordance with Part III, Title 9 of the California Code of Civil Procedure. Judgment upon the award rendered by the arbitrator(s) may be entered in any court having jurisdiction thereof. The parties shall have the right to discovery in accordance with Code of Civil Procedure §1283.05. The following matters are excluded from arbitration hereunder: (a) a judicial or non-judicial foreclosure or other action or proceeding to enforce a deed of trust, mortgage, or installment land sale contract as defined in Civil Code §2985, (b) an unlawful detainer action, (c) the filing or enforcement of a mechanic's lien, (d) any matter which is within the jurisdiction of a probate or small claims court, and (e) an action for bodily injury or wrongful death, or for latent or patent defects, to which Code of Civil Procedure §337.1 or §337.15 applies. The filing of a judicial action to enable the recording of a notice of pending action, for order of attachment, receivership, injunction, or other provisional remedies, shall not constitute a waiver of the right to arbitrate under this provision.

   "NOTICE: BY INITIALLING IN THE SPACE BELOW YOU ARE AGREEING TO HAVE ANY DISPUTE ARISING OUT OF THE MATTERS INCLUDED IN THE 'ARBITRATION OF DISPUTES' PROVISION DECIDED BY NEUTRAL ARBITRATION AS PROVIDED BY CALIFORNIA LAW AND YOU ARE GIVING UP ANY RIGHTS YOU MIGHT POSSESS TO HAVE THE DISPUTE LITIGATED IN A COURT OR JURY TRIAL. BY INITIALLING IN THE SPACE BELOW YOU ARE GIVING UP YOUR JUDICIAL RIGHTS TO DISCOVERY AND APPEAL, UNLESS THOSE RIGHTS ARE SPECIFICALLY INCLUDED IN THE 'ARBITRATION OF DISPUTES' PROVISION. IF YOU REFUSE TO SUBMIT TO ARBITRATION AFTER AGREEING TO THIS PROVISION, YOU MAY BE COMPELLED TO ARBITRATE UNDER THE AUTHORITY OF THE CALIFORNIA CODE OF CIVIL PROCEDURE. YOUR AGREEMENT TO THIS ARBITRATION PROVISION IS VOLUNTARY."

   "WE HAVE READ AND UNDERSTAND THE FOREGOING AND AGREE TO SUBMIT DISPUTES ARISING OUT OF THE MATTERS INCLUDED IN THE 'ARBITRATION OF DISPUTES' PROVISION TO NEUTRAL ARBITRATION."

   Seller's Initials ___/___   Broker's Initials ___/___

19. **ADDITIONAL TERMS:** _____
   _____
   _____
   _____
   _____
   _____
   _____
   _____
   _____
   _____
   _____
   _____
   _____
   _____

20. **ENTIRE CONTRACT:** All prior agreements between the parties are incorporated in this agreement, which constitutes the entire contract. Its terms are intended by the parties as a final, complete, and exclusive expression of their agreement with respect to its subject matter and may not be contradicted by evidence of any prior agreement or contemporaneous oral agreement. This agreement and any supplement, addendum, or modification, including any photocopy or facsimile, may be executed in two or more counterparts, all of which shall constitute one and the same writing.

21. **CAPTIONS:** The Captions in this contract are for convenience of reference only and are not intended as part of this contract.

I, the Seller, warrant that I am the owner of the Property or have the authority to execute this contract. I acknowledge that I have read and understand this contract, including the information on the reverse side, and have received a copy.

Date _____ 19____, _____, California   Telephone _____ Fax _____
Seller _____   Address _____
Seller _____   City _____ State _____ Zip _____

In consideration of the above, Broker agrees to use diligence in procuring a purchaser.
Date _____ , 19____   Telephone _____ Fax _____
Real Estate Broker _____   Address _____
By _____   City _____ State _____ Zip _____

OFFICE USE ONLY
Reviewed by Broker or Designee _____
Date _____

Page 2 of _____ Pages.

WA AUG 95

A special law applies to listing agreements for one- to four-unit residential properties and mobile homes. If the broker uses a preprinted form for the listing agreement, it must state in boldface type that the amount or rate of the commission is not fixed by law and may be negotiated. The commission rate or amount cannot be printed in the form—it must be filled in for each transaction.

Sometimes the amount of the broker's commission is determined in a special way. Under a **net listing**, the seller stipulates the net amount of money he or she requires from the sale of the property. The broker then tries to sell the property for more than that net amount. When the property is sold, the seller receives the required net and the broker keeps any money in excess of that amount as the commission.

> **Example**: The seller insists on getting $145,000 from the sale of her property. The broker sells the property for $158,000. $158,000 less the required $145,000 net equals $13,000. Thus, the broker's commission is $13,000. If the broker had sold the property for more, his commission would have been more. Likewise, if the broker had sold the property for less, his commission would have been less.

Net listings are seldom used because of the potential for abuse; an unscrupulous broker could easily take advantage of the seller under a net listing. In California, a broker who uses a net listing must reveal the amount of his or her commission to the seller before the seller becomes committed to the transaction. Failure to do so may result in disciplinary action.

Net listings can be open, exclusive agency, or exclusive right to sell listings.

Earning the Commission

A listing agreement can make the payment of the broker's commission dependent on any lawful condition. For instance, the parties may include a "no sale, no commission" provision in the listing agreement. This condition makes the commission contingent upon the transaction closing and the seller receiving the full purchase price. If this condition is not met (for example, because the buyer could not get financing), the commission need not be paid. However, if the condition is not met because of the bad faith or fraud of the seller, the broker may still collect his or her commission.

In the absence of such a provision, it is usually not necessary for the sale to actually close for the broker to be entitled to a commission. Once the broker has procured a ready, willing, and able buyer, the commission is earned, even if the sales agreement is never consummated. Many factors may prevent the sale from closing, but they will not prevent the broker from earning the commission. Some of those factors include:

- the seller changing his or her mind about selling,
- defects in the seller's title,
- the inability of the seller to deliver possession, or
- the mutual agreement of the seller and the buyer to cancel the sales agreement.

Furthermore, there is no need for the buyer and seller to actually sign a purchase and sale agreement before the broker is entitled to a commission. It is enough if the parties agree on the essential terms of the sales transaction. These essential terms include:

- price,
- amount of cash downpayment,
- mortgage term,
- interest rate, and
- amortization.

Also, as described above, if the broker presents the seller with an offer that complies with all the terms of sale specified in the listing agreement, but the seller rejects the offer, the broker may be entitled to the commission.

Sometimes a transaction fails to close and the broker and seller get into a dispute over whether the commission was in fact earned. For example, the seller may claim that the buyer found by the broker was not a ready, willing, and able buyer at all. A ready, willing, and able buyer is defined as one who is not only willing to enter into a binding contract on the seller's terms and conditions, but is also financially and contractually able to do so.

In California, if the parties signed a purchase and sale agreement, courts will automatically assume that the buyer was ready, willing, and able. This is based on the theory that the seller accepted the buyer when he or she signed the written agreement, thereby waiving his or her right to claim that the buyer was unacceptable. This is true even if the buyer immediately defaults because of a financial inability to perform.

If no written agreement was signed, the broker has to prove that the prospective buyer was financially able to perform the contract.

It should be noted that a salesperson may only receive a commission from the broker he or she is licensed under. The salesperson cannot accept any compensation from any other broker or agent, or directly from the seller. If the seller fails to pay the broker his or her commission, it is the broker who must sue the seller. The broker's salesperson cannot sue the seller, even though the salesperson is entitled to a portion of the broker's commission.

Safety Clauses. Safety clauses are found in most listing agreements. Under this type of provision, the broker is entitled to a commission if the seller sells the property after the listing term expires to any person the broker negotiated with during the listing term. This protects the broker from parties who conspire to deprive the broker of a commission by waiting until the listing has expired before they sign a purchase and sale agreement. The broker usually has to provide the seller with a list of the parties he or she negotiated with, and the list must be delivered to the seller on or before the expiration of the listing. This way the seller knows whom he or she can sell the property to without becoming liable for a commission.

Deposit Receipts

When a seller accepts a buyer's offer, they enter into a purchase and sale agreement. A purchase and sale agreement is a written contract between the buyer and seller that describes all the terms of the sale. In California, purchase and sale agreements are usually referred to as **deposit receipts**.

In most transactions, the buyer presents a written, signed offer to the seller along with a good faith deposit. The standard form used by the buyer to make the offer also serves as the buyer's receipt for the deposit. If the seller chooses to accept the offer, he or she signs the form, and the form then becomes the binding contract of sale.

Agreements to buy and sell property must be in writing under the statute of frauds. A copy of the CAR Real Estate Purchase Contract and Receipt for Deposit is reprinted below.

The basic provisions of the deposit receipt are fairly simple. The deposit receipt:

- identifies the parties,
- describes the property,
- sets forth the price and method of payment, and
- states the date for closing the transaction (when title and possession are transferred).

However, most deposit receipts are quite detailed. It's important for the deposit receipt to state all the terms of the parties' agreement clearly and accurately. Who is required to do what and when depends on the terms of the deposit receipt.

Fig.8.4 Commissions

Earning a Commission

- Agent is properly licensed
- Valid, written listing agreement
- Ready, willing, and able buyer
- Parties agree on essential terms of sale

Fig.8.5 Deposit receipt

REAL ESTATE PURCHASE CONTRACT AND RECEIPT FOR DEPOSIT
THIS IS MORE THAN A RECEIPT FOR MONEY. IT IS INTENDED TO BE A LEGALLY BINDING CONTRACT. READ IT CAREFULLY.
CALIFORNIA ASSOCIATION OF REALTORS® (C.A.R.) STANDARD FORM
(FOR USE WITH ONE-TO-FOUR FAMILY RESIDENTIAL PROPERTY)

DATE: _____ 19____ at _____, California.
RECEIVED FROM _____
_____ ("Buyer")
A DEPOSIT OF _____ Dollars $_____
TOWARD THE PURCHASE PRICE OF _____ Dollars $_____
FOR PURCHASE OF PROPERTY SITUATED IN _____, COUNTY OF _____, California,
DESCRIBED AS _____ ("Property").

1. **FINANCING: THE OBTAINING OF THE LOANS BELOW IS A CONTINGENCY OF THIS AGREEMENT.** Buyer shall act diligently and in good faith to obtain the designated loans.

    A. **LOAN CONTINGENCY** shall remain in effect until: (Check only ONE of the following:)

    ☐ (1) The designated loans are funded and/or the assumption of existing financing is approved by lender and completed.

    OR ☐ (2) ____ days from acceptance of the offer, by which time Buyer shall give to Seller written notice of Buyer's election to cancel this Agreement because of Buyer's inability to obtain the designated loans, or obtain approval of assumption of existing financing. If Buyer does not give Seller such notice, the contingency of obtaining the designated loans shall be removed by the method specified in paragraph 28.

    B. **BUYER'S DEPOSIT** .... $ _____

    PAYABLE TO _____

    shall be deposited ☐ with Escrow Holder, ☐ into Broker's trust account, or ☐ _____

    by Personal Check, (or, if checked:) ☐ Cashier's Check, ☐ Cash, or ☐ _____

    TO BE HELD UNCASHED UNTIL the next business day after acceptance of the offer, or ☐ _____

    C. **INCREASED DEPOSIT** .... $ _____

    within ____ days from acceptance of the offer, shall be deposited

    ☐ with Escrow Holder, ☐ into Broker's trust account, or ☐ _____

    D. **BALANCE OF DOWN PAYMENT** .... $ _____

    to be deposited with Escrow Holder within sufficient time to close escrow.

    E. **FIRST LOAN IN THE AMOUNT OF** .... $ _____

    ☐ NEW First Deed of Trust in favor of ☐ LENDER, ☐ SELLER; or

    ☐ ASSUMPTION of Existing First Deed of Trust:

    encumbering the Property, securing a note payable at approximately $_____ per month, at maximum interest of ____%

    fixed rate, or ____% initial adjustable rate with a maximum lifetime interest rate cap of ____%, balance due in _____ years.

    Buyer shall pay loan fees/points not to exceed _____

    F. **SECOND LOAN IN THE AMOUNT OF** .... $ _____

    ☐ NEW Second Deed of Trust in favor of ☐ LENDER, ☐ SELLER; or

    ☐ ASSUMPTION of Existing Second Deed of Trust:

    encumbering the Property, securing a note payable at approximately $_____ per month, at maximum interest of ____%

    fixed rate, or ____% initial adjustable rate with a maximum lifetime interest rate cap of ____%, balance due in _____ years.

    Buyer shall pay loan fees/points not to exceed _____

    G. **ADDITIONAL FINANCING TERMS:** _____

    H. **TOTAL PURCHASE PRICE,** not including costs of obtaining loans and other closing costs .... $ _____

    I. **OBTAINING DEPOSIT, DOWN PAYMENT, and OTHER CLOSING COSTS** by Buyer is NOT a contingency, unless otherwise agreed in writing.

    J. **FHA/VA FINANCING:** ☐ (If checked)

    (1) Seller shall pay _____% of loan as discount points.

    (2) Seller shall pay other fees which Buyer is not permitted to pay, not to exceed $ _____

    (3) Seller shall pay the cost of repairs required by lender, not otherwise provided for in this Agreement, not to exceed $ _____

    (4) All other charges to obtain financing shall be paid by Buyer unless otherwise agreed in writing.

    (5) OTHER: _____

    K. **IF THIS IS AN ALL CASH OFFER,** Buyer shall, within 5 (or ☐ ____) days from acceptance, provide to Seller written verification of sufficient funds to close this transaction. Seller may cancel this Agreement in writing within 5 (or ☐ ____) days (1) after receipt of the verification, if Seller disapproves it, or (2) after the time to provide the verification expires, if Buyer fails to provide it.

    L. **LOAN APPLICATIONS; PREQUALIFICATION:**

    (1) For **NEW** and **ASSUMED** lender financing: Within 10 (or ☐ ____) days from acceptance, Buyer shall provide to Seller a letter from lender stating that, based on a review of Buyer's written application and credit report, Buyer is prequalified for the NEW and/or ASSUMED loans indicated above. If Buyer fails to provide such letter within that time, Seller may cancel this Agreement in writing.

    (2) For **SELLER** financing: Within 5 (or ☐ ____) days after acceptance: (a) Buyer shall submit to Seller a completed loan application on FNMA/FHLMC Uniform Residential Loan Application; (b) Buyer authorizes Seller and/or Brokers to obtain, at Buyer's expense, a copy of Buyer's credit report; (c) Buyer shall provide any supporting documentation reasonably requested by Seller. Seller may cancel this Agreement in writing if Buyer fails to provide such documents within that time, or if Seller disapproves the application, credit report, or supporting documentation, within 5 (or ☐ ____) days from receipt of those documents.

    Buyer and Seller acknowledge receipt of copy of this page, which constitutes Page 1 of ____ Pages.

    Buyer's Initials (_____) (_____)   Seller's Initials (_____) (_____)

THIS STANDARDIZED DOCUMENT HAS BEEN APPROVED BY THE CALIFORNIA ASSOCIATION OF REALTORS® (C.A.R.) IN FORM ONLY. NO REPRESENTATION IS MADE AS TO THE APPROVAL OF THE FORM OF ANY SUPPLEMENTS NOT CURRENTLY PUBLISHED BY C.A.R. OR THE LEGAL VALIDITY OR ADEQUACY OF ANY PROVISION IN ANY SPECIFIC TRANSACTION. IT SHOULD NOT BE USED WITH EXTENSIVE RIDERS OR ADDITIONS.

A REAL ESTATE BROKER IS THE PERSON QUALIFIED TO ADVISE ON REAL ESTATE TRANSACTIONS. IF YOU DESIRE LEGAL OR TAX ADVICE, CONSULT AN APPROPRIATE PROFESSIONAL.

The copyright laws of the United States (17 U.S. Code) forbid the unauthorized reproduction of this form by any means including facsimile or computerized formats.
Copyright © 1993-1995, CALIFORNIA ASSOCIATION OF REALTORS®
525 South Virgil Avenue, Los Angeles, California 90020
REVISED 9/95

— OFFICE USE ONLY —
Reviewed by Broker or Designee _____
Date _____

BROKER'S COPY

Reprinted with permission, California Association of REALTORS®. Endorsement not implied.

Property Address: _____ , 19____

M. EXISTING LOANS: For existing loans to be taken over by Buyer, Seller shall, within the time specified in paragraph 28A(4), request and provide to Buyer copies of all applicable notes and deeds of trust, loan balances, and current interest rates. Buyer shall, within the time specified in paragraph 28A(2), provide written notice to Seller of any items reasonably disapproved. Differences between estimated and actual loan balances shall be adjusted at close of escrow by ☐ cash down payment, ☐ seller financing, or _____ Impound accounts, if any, shall be assigned and charged to Buyer and credited to Seller, (or, if checked:) _____ IF THIS IS AN ASSUMPTION OF A VA LOAN, THE SALE IS CONTINGENT UPON SELLER BEING PROVIDED A RELEASE OF LIABILITY AND SUBSTITUTION OF ELIGIBILITY, UNLESS OTHERWISE AGREED IN WRITING

N. LOAN FEATURES: LOAN DOCUMENTS CONTAIN A NUMBER OF IMPORTANT FEATURES AFFECTING THE RIGHTS OF THE BORROWER AND LENDER READ ALL LOAN DOCUMENTS CAREFULLY.

O. ADDITIONAL SELLER FINANCING TERMS: The following terms apply ONLY to financing extended by Seller under this Agreement. The maximum interest rate specified in paragraphs 1E and/or 1F above, as applicable, shall be the actual fixed interest rate for Seller financing. Buyer's promissory note, deed of trust, and other documents, as appropriate, shall incorporate and implement the following additional terms:

(1) Deed of trust shall contain a REQUEST FOR NOTICE OF DEFAULT on senior loans.

(2) Buyer shall sign and pay for a REQUEST FOR NOTICE OF DELINQUENCY prior to close of escrow and at any future time if requested by Seller.

(3) Note and deed of trust shall contain an acceleration clause making the loan due, when permitted by law, at Seller's option, upon the sale or transfer of the Property or any interest in it.

(4) Note shall contain a late charge of 6% of the installment due, or $5.00, whichever is greater, if the installment is not received within 10 days of the date it is due

(5) Title insurance coverage in the form of a joint protection policy shall be provided insuring Seller's deed of trust interest in the Property. Any increased cost over owner's policy shall be paid by Buyer.

(6) Tax Service shall be obtained and paid for by Buyer to notify Seller if property taxes have not been paid.

(7) Buyer shall provide and maintain fire and extended coverage insurance, during the period of the seller financing, in an amount sufficient to replace all improvements on the Property, or equal to the total encumbrances against the Property, whichever is less, with a loss payable endorsement in favor of Seller. BUYER AND SELLER ARE ADVISED THAT (a) INSURANCE POLICIES VARY IN THE TYPES OF RISKS COVERED, (b) EARTHQUAKE, FLOOD, AND OTHER OPTIONAL TYPES OF COVERAGE ARE AVAILABLE, and (c) BUYER AND SELLER SHOULD DISCUSS THESE SUBJECTS WITH AN INSURANCE AGENT OR INSURANCE BROKER.

(8) The addition, deletion, or substitution of any person or entity under this Agreement, or to title, prior to close of escrow, shall require Seller's written consent. Seller may grant or withhold consent in Seller's sole discretion. Any additional or substituted person or entity shall, if requested by Seller, submit to Seller the same documentation as required for the original named Buyer. Seller and/or Brokers may obtain a credit report, at Buyer's expense, on any such person or entity.

(9) Buyer and Seller shall each provide to the other, through escrow, their Social Security Numbers or Taxpayer Identification Numbers.

NOTE: If the Property contains 1 to 4 dwelling units, Buyer and Seller shall execute a Seller Financing Disclosure Statement (C.A.R. Form SFD-14) (Civil Code §§2956-2967), if applicable, as provided by arranger of credit, as soon as practicable prior to execution of security documents. ESCROW HOLDER SHALL BE INSTRUCTED BY BUYER AND SELLER TO PERFORM, ARRANGE, OR VERIFY ITEMS 1-9 ABOVE, AS APPLICABLE, PRIOR TO CLOSE OF ESCROW.

2. ESCROW: Escrow shall close ☐ within _____ days from acceptance of the offer, or ☐ on _____ , 19____ . This Agreement shall, to the extent feasible, constitute escrow instructions of Buyer and Seller. Escrow instructions consistent with this Agreement shall be signed by Buyer and Seller and delivered to _____ , the designated Escrow Holder. ☐ within _____ days after acceptance of the offer, ☐ at least _____ days before close of escrow, ☐ or _____ . Escrow fee to be paid as follows: _____ . Escrow instructions may include matters required to close this transaction which are not covered by this Agreement. The omission from escrow instructions of any provision in this Agreement shall not constitute a waiver of the provision or the contractual rights or obligations of any party. Any change in terms or provisions of this Agreement requires the mutual, written consent of the Buyer and Seller. Buyer and Seller hereby jointly instruct Escrow Holder and Brokers (a) that Buyer's deposits placed into escrow or into Broker's trust account shall be held as a good faith deposit toward the completion of this transaction, and (b) to pay compensation due Brokers under this Agreement. Release of Buyer's funds will require mutual, signed release instructions from both Buyer and Seller, judicial decision, or arbitration award.

3. TITLE AND VESTING: Buyer shall be provided a current preliminary (title) report covering the Property. Buyer shall, within the time specified in paragraph 28A(2), provide written notice to Seller of any items reasonably disapproved. At close of escrow:

A. Title to the Property shall be transferred by grant deed (or, for stock cooperative, by assignment of stock certificate), and shall include OIL, MINERAL, and WATER rights, if currently owned by Seller, unless otherwise agreed in writing.

B. Title shall be free of liens, except as provided in this Agreement.

C. Title shall be subject to all other encumbrances, easements, covenants, conditions, restrictions, rights, and other matters, which are either:

(1) Of record and shown in the preliminary (title) report, unless disapproved in writing by Buyer within the time specified in paragraph 28A(2); or

(2) Disclosed to or discovered by Buyer prior to the close of escrow, unless disapproved in writing by Buyer within the time specified in paragraph 28A(1) or 28A(2), whichever is later.

D. Buyer shall be provided a California Land Title Association (CLTA) owner's policy issued by _____ at _____ Company, at _____ expense.

NOTE: (1) A preliminary (title) report is only an offer by the title insurer to issue a policy of title insurance and may not contain every item affecting title. (2) An American Land Title Association (ALTA-R) policy may provide greater protection for Buyer and may be available at the same or slightly higher cost than a CLTA policy. (3) The designated title company can provide information, at Buyer's request, about availability and desirability of various title insurance coverages. (4) If Buyer desires an ALTA-R owner's policy or other title coverage, Buyer shall so instruct Escrow Holder and pay the increased cost, if any, over a CLTA policy. (5) ALTA LENDER'S title insurance policy, if required, shall be paid by Buyer. (6) For Seller financing, paragraph 1O(5) provides for a joint protection policy. (7) Title shall vest as designated in Buyer's escrow instructions. **(THE MANNER OF TAKING TITLE MAY HAVE SIGNIFICANT LEGAL AND TAX CONSEQUENCES. BUYER SHOULD GIVE THIS MATTER SERIOUS CONSIDERATION.)**

4. PRORATIONS:

A. Real property taxes and assessments, interest, rents, Homeowners' Association regular dues and regular assessments, premiums on insurance assumed by Buyer, and payments on bonds and assessments assumed by Buyer, shall be PAID CURRENT and prorated between Buyer and Seller, as of the date of close of escrow, (or if checked:) ☐ _____

B. Payments on Mello-Roos and other Special Assessment District bonds and assessments which are now a lien, and payments on Homeowners' Association special assessments which are now a lien, shall be PAID CURRENT and prorated between Buyer and Seller as of the date of close of escrow, with payments that are not yet due to be assumed by Buyer WITHOUT CREDIT toward the purchase price, (or if checked:) ☐ _____

C. County transfer tax or transfer fee shall be paid by _____
City transfer tax or transfer fee shall be paid by _____
Homeowners' Association transfer fee shall be paid by _____

D. THE PROPERTY WILL BE REASSESSED UPON CHANGE OF OWNERSHIP. THIS WILL AFFECT THE TAXES TO BE PAID. Any supplemental tax bills shall be paid as follows: (1) for periods after close of escrow, by Buyer (or by final acquiring party, if part of an exchange), and (2) for periods prior to close of escrow, by Seller. TAX BILLS ISSUED AFTER CLOSE OF ESCROW SHALL BE HANDLED DIRECTLY BETWEEN BUYER AND SELLER.

Buyer and Seller acknowledge receipt of copy of this page, which constitutes Page 2 of _____ Pages.

Buyer's Initials (_____) (_____)   Seller's Initials (_____) (_____)

OFFICE USE ONLY
Reviewed by Broker or Designee _____
Date _____

Property Address: _____ , 19 _____

5. **OCCUPANCY:** Buyer ☐ does, ☐ does not, intend to occupy Property as Buyer's primary residence.

6. **POSSESSION AND KEYS:** Seller shall deliver possession and occupancy of the Property to Buyer ☐ on the date of close of escrow at _____ AM/PM, or ☐ no later than _____ days after date of close of escrow at _____ AM/PM, or ☐ _____ Property shall be vacant unless otherwise agreed in writing. If applicable, Seller and Buyer shall execute Interim Occupancy Agreement (C.A.R. Form IOA-14) or Residential Lease Agreement After Sale (C.A.R. Form RLAS-14). Seller shall provide keys and/or means to operate all Property locks, mailboxes, security systems, alarms, and garage door openers. If applicable, Buyer may be required to pay a deposit to a Homeowners' Association (HOA) to obtain keys to accessible HOA facilities.

7. **BUYER'S INVESTIGATION OF PROPERTY CONDITION:** Buyer's acceptance of the condition of the Property is a contingency of this Agreement. Buyer shall have the right to conduct inspections, investigations, tests, surveys, and other studies ("Inspections") at Buyer's expense. Buyer shall, within the time specified in paragraph 28A(1), complete these inspections and notify Seller in writing of any items disapproved. Buyer is strongly advised to exercise these rights and to make Buyer's own selection of professionals with appropriate qualifications to conduct inspections of the entire Property. **IF BUYER DOES NOT EXERCISE THESE RIGHTS, BUYER IS ACTING AGAINST THE ADVICE OF BROKERS. BUYER UNDERSTANDS THAT ALTHOUGH CONDITIONS AND DEFECTS ARE OFTEN DIFFICULT TO LOCATE AND DISCOVER. ALL REAL PROPERTY AND IMPROVEMENTS CONTAIN DEFECTS AND CONDITIONS WHICH ARE NOT READILY APPARENT AND WHICH MAY AFFECT THE VALUE OR DESIRABILITY OF THE PROPERTY. BUYER AND SELLER ARE AWARE THAT BROKERS DO NOT GUARANTEE, AND IN NO WAY ASSUME RESPONSIBILITY FOR, THE CONDITION OF THE PROPERTY. BUYER IS ALSO AWARE OF BUYER'S OWN AFFIRMATIVE DUTY TO EXERCISE REASONABLE CARE TO PROTECT HIMSELF OR HERSELF, INCLUDING THOSE FACTS WHICH ARE KNOWN TO OR WITHIN THE DILIGENT ATTENTION AND OBSERVATION OF THE BUYER** (Civil Code §2079.5).

Seller shall make the Property available for all Inspections. Buyer shall keep the Property free and clear of liens; indemnify and hold Seller harmless from all liability, claims, demands, damages, and costs; and repair all damages arising from the Inspections. No Inspections may be made by any governmental building or zoning inspector or government employee without the prior written consent of Seller, unless required by local law. Buyer shall provide to Seller, at no cost, upon request of Seller, complete copies of all Inspection reports obtained by Buyer concerning the Property.

BUYER IS STRONGLY ADVISED TO INVESTIGATE THE CONDITION AND SUITABILITY OF ALL ASPECTS OF THE PROPERTY AND ALL MATTERS AFFECTING THE VALUE OR DESIRABILITY OF THE PROPERTY, INCLUDING, BUT NOT LIMITED TO, THE FOLLOWING:

   A. CONDITION OF SYSTEMS AND COMPONENTS: Built-in appliances, foundation, roof, plumbing, heating, air conditioning, electrical, mechanical, security, pool/spa, and other structural and non-structural systems and components, any personal property included in the sale, and energy efficiency of the Property.

   B. SIZE AND AGE: Square footage, room dimensions, lot size, and age of Property improvements. (Any numerical statements regarding these items are APPROXIMATIONS ONLY, have not been and will not be verified, and should not be relied upon by Buyer.)

   C. LINES AND BOUNDARIES: Property lines and boundaries. (Fences, hedges, walls, and other natural or constructed barriers or markers do not necessarily identify true Property boundaries. Property lines may be verified by survey.)

   D. WASTE DISPOSAL: Type, size, adequacy, capacity, and condition of sewer and septic systems and components should be checked. (Property may not be connected to sewer, and applicable fees may not have been paid. Septic tank may need to be pumped and leach field may need to be inspected.)

   E. GOVERNMENTAL REQUIREMENTS AND LIMITATIONS: Possible absence of required governmental permits, inspections, certificates, or other determinations affecting the Property; limitations, restrictions, and requirements affecting the use of the Property, future development, zoning, building, size, governmental permits, and inspections.

   F. RENT AND OCCUPANCY CONTROL: Some cities and counties impose restrictions which may limit the amount of rent that can lawfully be charged, and/or the maximum number of persons who can lawfully occupy the Property.

   G. WATER AND UTILITIES; WELL SYSTEMS AND COMPONENTS: Water and utility availability and use restrictions. Adequacy, condition, and performance of well systems and components.

   H. ENVIRONMENTAL HAZARDS: Potential environmental hazards including asbestos, formaldehyde, radon, methane, other gases, lead-based paint, other lead contamination, fuel or chemical storage tanks, contaminated soil or water, hazardous waste, waste disposal sites, electromagnetic fields, nuclear sources, and other substances, materials, products, or conditions.

   I. GEOLOGIC CONDITIONS: Geologic/seismic conditions, soil and terrain stability, suitability, and drainage.

   J. NEIGHBORHOOD, AREA, AND SUBDIVISION CONDITIONS: Neighborhood or area conditions including schools, proximity and adequacy of law enforcement, proximity to commercial, industrial, or agricultural activities, crime statistics, fire protection, other governmental services, existing and proposed transportation, construction, and development which may affect noise, view, or traffic, airport noise, noise or odor from any source, wild and domestic animals, other nuisances, hazards, or circumstances, facilities and condition of common areas of common interest subdivisions, and possible lack of compliance with any Homeowners' Association requirements.

   K. PERSONAL FACTORS: Conditions and influences of significance to certain cultures and/or religions, and personal needs, requirements, and preferences of Buyer.

   L. VERIFICATION: Brokers have not and will not verify any of the items above, unless otherwise agreed in writing.

BUYER SHOULD MAKE FURTHER INQUIRIES: Buyer is advised to make further inquiries and to consult government agencies, lenders, insurance agents, architects, and other appropriate persons and entities concerning the use of the Property under applicable building, zoning, fire, health, and safety codes, and for evaluation of potential hazards.

8. **CONDITION OF PROPERTY:** No warranties or representations are made regarding the adequacy, condition, performance, or suitability of the Property, or any of its systems or components, except as specifically agreed in writing.
   (Check ONLY paragraph A or B; do NOT check both.)

   ☐ **A. SELLER WARRANTY:** (If A is checked, do NOT also check B.)
   Seller warrants that at the time possession is made available to Buyer:
   (1) Roof shall be free of leaks KNOWN to Seller or DISCOVERED during escrow.
   (2) Built-in appliances (including free-standing oven and range, if included in sale), plumbing, heating, air conditioning, electrical, water, sewer, and pool/spa systems, if any, shall be operative. (Septic/Well systems are not covered in this paragraph. Read paragraph 19.)
   (3) Plumbing systems, shower pans, and shower enclosures shall be free of leaks KNOWN to Seller or DISCOVERED during escrow.
   (4) All fire, safety, and structural defects in chimneys and fireplaces KNOWN to Seller or DISCOVERED during escrow shall be repaired by Seller.
   (5) All broken or cracked glass, and torn existing window and door screens, shall be replaced.
   (6) Property, including pool/spa, landscaping, and grounds, shall be maintained in substantially the same condition as on the date of acceptance of the offer.
   (7) SELLER SHALL HAVE WATER, GAS, AND ELECTRICAL UTILITIES ON FOR BUYER'S INSPECTIONS AND THROUGH THE DATE POSSESSION IS MADE AVAILABLE TO BUYER.
   (8) All debris and all personal property not included in the sale shall be removed.
   (9) _____
   NOTE TO BUYER: This warranty is limited to items specified in this paragraph 8A. Items discovered in Buyer's Inspections which are not covered by this paragraph shall be governed by the procedure in paragraphs 7 and 28.
   NOTE TO SELLER: Disclosures in the Real Estate Transfer Disclosure Statement (C.A.R. Form TDS-14), and items discovered in Buyer's Inspections, do NOT eliminate Seller's obligations under this warranty unless specifically agreed in writing.

OR ☐ **B. "AS-IS" CONDITION:** (If B is checked, do NOT also check A.)
   Property is sold "AS IS," in its present condition, as of the time of acceptance of the offer, without warranty. Seller shall not be responsible for making corrections or repairs of any nature EXCEPT:
   (1) Property, including pool/spa, landscaping, and grounds, shall be maintained in substantially the same condition as on the date of acceptance of the offer.
   (2) SELLER SHALL HAVE WATER, GAS, AND ELECTRICAL UTILITIES ON FOR BUYER'S INSPECTIONS AND THROUGH THE DATE POSSESSION IS MADE AVAILABLE TO BUYER.
   (3) This paragraph does not relieve Seller of contractual obligations, if any, under paragraph 13 (Smoke Detector(s) and Water Heater Bracing), paragraph 14 (Retrofit), paragraph 19 (Septic/Sewer/Well System(s)), paragraph 20 (Pest Control), and elsewhere in this Agreement.
   (4) _____

   NOTE TO BUYER AND SELLER: Buyer retains the right to disapprove the condition of the Property based upon items discovered in Buyer's Inspections under paragraph 7. SELLER REMAINS OBLIGATED TO DISCLOSE KNOWN MATERIAL DEFECTS AND TO MAKE OTHER DISCLOSURES REQUIRED BY LAW.

Buyer and Seller acknowledge receipt of copy of this page, which constitutes Page 3 of _____ Pages.

Buyer's Initials (_____)   Seller's Initials (_____) (_____)

OFFICE USE ONLY
Reviewed by Broker or Designee _____
Date _____

EQUAL HOUSING OPPORTUNITY

MR SEP 95

Property Address: _____ _____ , 19____

9. TRANSFER DISCLOSURE STATEMENT; MELLO-ROOS NOTICE: Unless exempt:

A. A Real Estate Transfer Disclosure Statement (TDS) (C.A.R. Form TDS-14) shall be completed by Seller and delivered to Buyer (Civil Code §§1102-1102.15). Buyer shall sign and return a copy of the TDS to Seller or Seller's agent. Buyer shall be provided a TDS within 5 (or ☐ _____) days from acceptance of the offer, unless previously provided to Buyer.

B. Seller shall make a good faith effort to obtain a disclosure notice from any local agencies which levy on the Property a special tax pursuant to the Mello-Roos Community Facilities Act, and shall promptly deliver to Buyer any such notice made available by those agencies.

C. If the TDS or the Mello-Roos disclosure notice, or a supplemental or amended disclosure under paragraph 10, is delivered to Buyer after the offer is signed, Buyer shall have the right to terminate this Agreement within three (3) days after delivery in person, or five (5) days after delivery by deposit in the mail, by giving written notice of termination to Seller or Seller's agent.

D. Disclosure in the TDS, or exemptions from providing it, do not eliminate Seller's obligation to disclose known material defects, or to meet Seller's other obligations under this Agreement.

10. SUBSEQUENT DISCLOSURES: In the event Seller, prior to close of escrow, becomes aware of adverse conditions materially affecting the Property, or any material inaccuracy in disclosures, information, or representations previously provided to Buyer (including those made in a Real Estate Transfer Disclosure Statement (TDS) pursuant to Civil Code §1102, et seq.), Seller shall promptly provide a supplemental or amended disclosure, in writing, covering those items. If Buyer disapproves of any conditions so disclosed, Buyer may terminate this Agreement under the procedure in paragraph 9C.

11. PROPERTY DISCLOSURES: When applicable to the Property and required by law, Seller shall provide to Buyer, at Seller's expense, the following disclosures and information. Buyer shall then, within the time specified in paragraph 28A(2), investigate the disclosures and information, and provide written notice to Seller of any item disapproved pursuant to paragraphs 11A-11D(2) below.

A. **GEOLOGIC, EARTHQUAKE AND SEISMIC HAZARD ZONES DISCLOSURE:** If the Property is located in an Earthquake Fault Zone (Special Studies Zone) (EFZ), (Public Resources Code §§2621-2625), Seismic Hazard Zone (SHZ) (Public Resources Code §§2690-2699.6), or in a locally designated geologic, seismic, or other hazard zone or area where disclosure is required by law, Seller shall, within the time specified in paragraph 28A(3), disclose to Buyer in writing these facts and any other information required by law. (GEOLOGIC, SEISMIC AND FLOOD HAZARD DISCLOSURE (C.A.R. Form GFD-14) SHALL SATISFY THIS REQUIREMENT.) Construction or development of any structure may be restricted in such zones. Disclosure of EFZs and SHZs is required only if maps, or information contained in such maps, are "reasonably available" (Public Resources Code §§2621.9(c)(1) and 2694(c)(1)).

B. **SPECIAL FLOOD HAZARD AREAS:** If the Property is located in a Special Flood Hazard Area designated by the Federal Emergency Management Agency (FEMA), Seller shall, within the time specified in paragraph 28A(3), disclose this fact to Buyer in writing. (GEOLOGIC, SEISMIC AND FLOOD HAZARD DISCLOSURE (C.A.R. Form GFD-14) SHALL SATISFY THIS REQUIREMENT.) Government regulations may impose building restrictions and requirements which may substantially impact and limit construction and remodeling of improvements in such areas. Flood insurance may be required by lender. In addition, Seller will notify Buyer if Seller has received federal flood disaster assistance on the Property, in which case, Buyer will be required to maintain flood insurance.

C. **STATE FIRE RESPONSIBILITY AREAS:** If the Property is located in a State Fire Responsibility Area, Seller shall, within the time specified in paragraph 28A(3), disclose this fact to Buyer in writing (Public Resources Code §4136). Disclosure may be made in the Real Estate Transfer Disclosure Statement (C.A.R. Form TDS-14). Government regulations may impose building restrictions and requirements which may substantially impact and limit construction and remodeling of improvements in such areas. Disclosure of these areas is required only if the Seller has actual knowledge that the Property is located in such an area or if maps of such areas have been provided to the county assessor's office.

D. **EARTHQUAKE SAFETY:**

(1) **PRE-1960 PROPERTIES:** If the Property was built prior to 1960 and contains ONE TO FOUR DWELLING UNITS of conventional light frame construction, Seller shall, unless exempt, within the time specified in paragraph 28A(3), provide to Buyer: (a) a copy of "The Homeowner's Guide to Earthquake Safety," and (b) written disclosure of known seismic deficiencies (Government Code §§8897-8897.5).

(2) **PRE-1975 PROPERTIES:** If the Property was built prior to 1975 and contains RESIDENTIAL, COMMERCIAL, OR OTHER STRUCTURES constructed of masonry or pre-cast concrete, with wood frame floors or roofs, Seller shall, unless exempt, within the time specified in paragraph 28A(3), provide to Buyer a copy of "The Commercial Property Owner's Guide to Earthquake Safety" (Government Code §§8893-8893.5).

(3) **ALL PROPERTIES:** If the booklets described in paragraphs 11D(1) and 11D(2) are not required, Buyer is advised that they are available and contain important information that may be useful for ALL TYPES OF PROPERTY.

E. **ENVIRONMENTAL HAZARDS AND ENERGY EFFICIENCY BOOKLETS:** "Environmental Hazards: Guide for Homeowners and Buyers" booklet, and a home energy rating booklet, when available, contain useful information for ALL TYPES OF PROPERTY.

F. **LEAD-BASED PAINT:** For residential property constructed prior to 1978, when effective, Buyer and Seller are required to sign a lead-based paint disclosure form(s). (DISCLOSURE AND ACKNOWLEDGMENT OF LEAD-BASED PAINT BEFORE SALE (C.A.R. Form FLS-14), when applicable, and/or NOTICE TO PURCHASERS OF HOUSING CONSTRUCTED BEFORE 1978 (C.A.R. Form LPD-14) for FHA-financed property, shall satisfy this requirement.) In addition, when effective, Buyer shall be furnished a copy of "Protect Your Family From Lead in Your Home" booklet.

12. CONDOMINIUM/COMMON INTEREST SUBDIVISION: If the Property is a unit in a condominium, planned development, or other common interest subdivision:

A. The Property has _____ parking spaces assigned to it.

B. The current regular Homeowners' Association (HOA) dues/assessments are $_____ ☐ Monthly, ☐ _____.

C. Seller shall, within the time specified in paragraph 28A(4), request and provide to Buyer any known pending special assessments, claims, or litigation; copies of covenants, conditions, and restrictions; articles of incorporation; by-laws; other governing documents; most current financial statement distributed (Civil Code §1365); statement regarding limited enforceability of age restrictions, if applicable; current HOA statement showing any unpaid assessments (Civil Code §1368); any other documents required by law; and the most recent 12 months of HOA minutes, if available. Buyer shall, within the time specified in paragraph 28A(2), provide written notice to Seller of any items disapproved. Cost of obtaining those items shall be paid by Seller.

D. No warranty is made regarding the Property's compliance with any governing document or HOA requirements, unless agreed in writing.

13. SMOKE DETECTOR(S) AND WATER HEATER BRACING: State law requires that residences be equipped with operable smoke detector(s), and that all water heaters must be braced, anchored, or strapped to resist falling or horizontal displacement due to earthquake. Local law may impose additional requirements. Unless exempt, Seller shall, prior to close of escrow, provide to Buyer a written statement of compliance and any other documents required, in accordance with applicable state and local laws. (SMOKE DETECTOR AND WATER HEATER STATEMENT OF COMPLIANCE (C.A.R. Form SDC-14) SHALL SATISFY THE STATE PORTION OF THIS REQUIREMENT.) Additional smoke detector(s) and water heater bracing, anchoring, or strapping, if required, shall be installed at Seller's expense prior to close of escrow.

14. RETROFIT: ☐ Buyer, ☐ Seller, shall pay the cost of compliance with any minimum mandatory government retrofit standards and inspections required as a condition of closing escrow under local, state, or federal law, including, but not limited to, repairs required for mandatory compliance with building and safety requirements, and energy and utility efficiency requirements, EXCEPT: _____, and except as otherwise agreed in writing.

15. GOVERNMENTAL COMPLIANCE:

A. Seller represents that Seller has no knowledge of any notice, filed or issued against the Property, of violations of city, county, state, or federal building, zoning, fire, or health laws, codes, statutes, ordinances, regulations, or rules, EXCEPT: _____.

B. Seller shall promptly disclose to Buyer any improvements, additions, alterations, or repairs ("Repairs") made by Seller or known to Seller to have been made without required governmental permits, final inspections, and approvals.

C. If Seller receives notice or is made aware of any of the above violations prior to close of escrow, Seller shall immediately notify Buyer in writing. Buyer shall, within the time specified in paragraph 28A(2), provide written notice to Seller of any items disapproved.

D. Nothing in this paragraph relieves Seller of any other obligations in this Agreement. Neither Buyer nor Seller shall be required to make Repairs to the Property for any purpose, unless agreed in writing between Buyer and Seller, or required by law as a condition of closing escrow. No warranty is made concerning the presence or absence of building permits or inspections, or compliance or lack of compliance with building codes, unless agreed in writing.

Buyer and Seller acknowledge receipt of copy of this page, which constitutes Page 4 of _____ Pages.

Buyer's Initials (_____) (_____)   Seller's Initials (_____) (_____)

OFFICE USE ONLY
Reviewed by Broker or Designee _____
Date _____

BROKER'S COPY

MR SEP 95

Property Address: _____ _____, 19____

16. **FIXTURES:** All EXISTING fixtures and fittings that are attached to the Property, or for which special openings have been made, are INCLUDED IN THE PURCHASE PRICE (unless excluded below), and shall be transferred free of liens. These include, but are not limited to, existing electrical, lighting, plumbing and heating fixtures, fireplace inserts, solar systems, built-in appliances, screens, awnings, shutters, window coverings, attached floor coverings, television antennas, satellite dishes and related equipment, private integrated telephone systems, air coolers/conditioners, pool/spa equipment, water softeners (if owned by Seller), security systems/alarms (if owned by Seller), garage door openers/remote controls, attached fireplace equipment, mailbox, in-ground landscaping including trees/shrubs, and _____

ITEMS EXCLUDED: _____

17. **PERSONAL PROPERTY:** The following items of personal property, free of liens and without warranty of condition (unless provided in paragraph 8A) or fitness for use, are included: _____

18. **HOME WARRANTY PLANS:** Buyer and Seller are informed that home warranty plans are available to provide additional protection and benefit to Buyer and Seller.
☐ (If checked:) Buyer and Seller elect to purchase a one-year home warranty plan with the following optional coverage: _____
_____, at a cost not to exceed $_____,
to be paid by _____, and to be issued by _____ Company.

19. **SEPTIC/SEWER/WELL SYSTEMS:** Prior to close of escrow:
   A. (If checked:) ☐ Buyer, ☐ Seller, shall pay to have septic system inspected and certified as operative.
   B. (If checked:) ☐ Buyer, ☐ Seller, shall pay to have septic system pumped if required by inspector for certification.
   C. (If checked:) ☐ Buyer, ☐ Seller, shall pay for sewer connection, if required by local law in effect prior to close of escrow.
   D. (If checked:) ☐ Buyer, ☐ Seller, shall pay to have wells tested for potability.
   E. (If checked:) ☐ Buyer, ☐ Seller, shall pay to have wells tested for productivity to produce a minimum of _____ gallons per minute (GPM).
   F. All testing shall comply with any local laws pertaining to testing. Buyer shall, within the time specified in paragraph 28, provide written notice to Seller of any items disapproved under paragraph 19D or 19E.
   NO WARRANTY is made as to the appropriate type, size, adequacy, or capacity of the septic, sewer, or well systems, unless agreed in writing.

20. **PEST CONTROL:**
☐ (If checked, the following PEST CONTROL terms apply:)
   A. Seller shall, within the time specified in paragraph 28A(3), provide to Buyer a current written Wood Destroying Pests and Organisms Inspection Report ("Report") covering the main building and attached structures (and, if checked: ☐ detached garages or carports, ☐ decks, ☐ the following other structures on the Property: _____).
   If the Property is a unit in a condominium, planned development, or residential stock cooperative, the Report shall cover only the separate interest and any exclusive-use areas being transferred, and shall NOT cover common areas.
   B. ☐ Buyer, ☐ Seller, shall pay for the Report, which shall be prepared by _____
   a registered structural pest control company.
   C. If no infestation or infection by wood destroying pests or organisms is found, the Report shall include a written Certification.
   D. If requested by Buyer or Seller, the Report shall separately identify each recommendation for corrective work as follows:
   "Section 1" — Infestation or infection which is evident.
   "Section 2" — Conditions which are present and deemed likely to lead to infestation or infection.
   E. ☐ Buyer, ☐ Seller, shall pay for work recommended to correct conditions described in "Section 1."
   F. ☐ Buyer, ☐ Seller, shall pay for work recommended to correct conditions described in "Section 2," if requested by Buyer.
   G. Nothing in this paragraph 20 shall relieve Seller of the obligation, if any, to repair or replace shower pans and shower enclosures, if required by paragraph 8. A WATER TEST OF SHOWER PANS MAY NOT BE PERFORMED ON UNITS ON AN UPPER LEVEL WITHOUT THE CONSENT OF THE OWNERS OF PROPERTY BELOW THE SHOWER.
   H. Work to be performed at Seller's expense may be performed by Seller or through others, provided that:
   (1) All required permits and final inspections are obtained; and
   (2) Upon completion of repairs a Certification is provided to Buyer.
   I. If inspection of inaccessible areas is recommended in the Report, Buyer has the option to accept and approve the Report, or request in writing, within 5 (or ☐ _____) days of receipt of the Report, that further inspection be made. BUYER'S FAILURE TO NOTIFY SELLER IN WRITING OF SUCH REQUEST SHALL CONCLUSIVELY BE CONSIDERED APPROVAL OF THE REPORT. If further inspection recommends "Section 1" and/or "Section 2" corrective work, such work, and the inspection, entry, and closing of the inaccessible areas, shall be paid for by the party designated in paragraphs 20B, 20E, and/or 20F. If no infestation or infection is found, the inspection, entry, and closing of the inaccessible areas shall be paid for by Buyer.
   J. Inspections, corrective work, and Certification under this paragraph shall not include roof coverings. Read paragraph 7A concerning inspection of roof coverings.
   K. Certification shall be issued prior to close of escrow. However, if Buyer and Seller agree in writing that work to be performed at Seller's expense will be done after close of escrow, funds equal to one and one-half times the amount of the approved estimate shall be held in escrow unless otherwise agreed in writing. Such funds shall be disbursed upon Buyer's receipt of Certification. Any remaining balance shall be returned to Seller.
   L. "Certification" means a written statement by a registered structural pest control company, that on the date of inspection or re-inspection, the Property is "free" or is "now free" of "evidence of active infestation in the visible and accessible areas." (Business and Professions Code §§8519(a) and 8519(b).)

21. **RENTAL PROPERTY:** ☐ (If checked:) Buyer shall take the Property subject to the rights of existing tenants. Seller shall, within the time specified in paragraph 28A(3), deliver to Buyer copies of all leases, rental agreements, outstanding notices sent to tenants, and current income and expense statements ("Rental Documents"). Seller shall, within the time specified in paragraph 28A(4), request from tenants and provide to Buyer any tenant estoppel certificates. Buyer shall, within the time specified in paragraph 28A(2), provide written notice to Seller of any items disapproved. Seller shall make no changes in leases and tenancies, and shall enter into no new leases or rental agreements, during the pendency of this transaction, without Buyer's prior written consent. Seller shall transfer to Buyer, through escrow, all unused tenant deposits. No warranty is made concerning compliance with governmental restrictions, if any, limiting the amount of rent that can lawfully be charged, and/or the maximum number of persons who can lawfully occupy the Property, unless otherwise agreed in writing.

22. **SELECTION OF SERVICE PROVIDERS:** If Brokers give Buyer or Seller referrals to professional persons, service or product providers, or vendors of any type, including, but not limited to, lending institutions, loan brokers, title insurers, escrow companies, inspectors, structural pest control companies, contractors, and home warranty companies ("Providers"), the referrals are given based on the following disclosures:
   A. Brokers do not guarantee the performance of any Providers.
   B. Buyer and Seller are free to select Providers other than those referred or recommended by Brokers.

23. **REPAIRS:** Repairs under this Agreement shall be completed prior to close of escrow, unless otherwise agreed in writing, and shall be performed in compliance with applicable governmental permit, inspection, and approval requirements. It is understood that exact restoration of appearance or cosmetic items following all such Repairs may not be possible. Repairs shall be performed in a skillful manner with materials of quality comparable to that of existing materials.

24. **FINAL VERIFICATION OF CONDITION:** Buyer shall have the right to make a final inspection of the Property approximately 5 (or ☐ _____) days prior to close of escrow, NOT AS A CONTINGENCY OF THE SALE, but solely to confirm that: (a) Repairs have been completed as agreed in writing by Buyer and Seller, (b) Seller has complied with Seller's other obligations, and (c) the Property is otherwise in substantially the same condition as on the date of acceptance of the offer, unless otherwise agreed in writing.

Buyer and Seller acknowledge receipt of copy of this page, which constitutes Page 5 of _____ Pages.
Buyer's Initials (_____) (_____) Seller's Initials (_____) (_____)

OFFICE USE ONLY
Reviewed by Broker or Designee _____
Date _____

BROKER'S COPY

Property Address: _____ _____, 19____

25. SALE OF BUYER'S PROPERTY:

☐ (If checked:) This Agreement is CONTINGENT ON THE CLOSE OF ESCROW OF BUYER'S PROPERTY described as _____
_____ ("Buyer's Property") which is listed for sale
with _____ Company and/or in Escrow No. _____
with _____ Company, scheduled to close escrow on _____, 19____

A. (Check ONLY 1 or 2; do NOT check both.) After acceptance of this offer:

☐ (1) Seller SHALL have the right to continue to offer the Property for sale. If Seller accepts another written offer, Seller shall give Buyer written notice to (a) remove this contingency in writing, (b) provide written verification of sufficient funds to close escrow on this transaction, without the sale of Buyer's Property, and (c) comply with the following additional requirements: _____
_____
If Buyer fails to complete those actions within _____ hours or _____ days after receipt of such notice, Seller may cancel this Agreement in writing.

OR ☐ (2) Seller shall NOT have the right to continue to offer the Property for sale, EXCEPT for back-up offers.

B. If Buyer's Property does not close escrow by the date specified in paragraph 2 (Escrow) for close of escrow on this transaction, then either Seller or Buyer may cancel this Agreement in writing.

26. CANCELLATION OF PRIOR SALE; BACK-UP OFFER:

☐ (If checked:) Buyer understands that Seller has entered into one or more contracts to sell the Property to other buyers. This Agreement is in back-up position number _____ and is contingent upon written cancellation of the prior contracts and any related escrows between Seller and the other buyers. Seller and the other buyers may mutually agree to modify or amend the terms of the prior contracts. Buyer may cancel this Agreement in writing at any time before Seller provides to Buyer copies of written cancellations of the prior contracts signed by the parties to those contracts. If Seller is unable to provide such written cancellations signed by Seller and the other buyers, by _____, 19____, then either Buyer or Seller may cancel this Agreement in writing.

A. BUYER'S DEPOSIT CHECK SHALL BE: (Check ONLY 1 or 2; do NOT check both.)

☐ (1) HELD UNCASHED until copies of the written cancellations signed by all parties to the prior contracts are provided to Buyer, OR

☐ (2) IMMEDIATELY handled as provided in paragraph 1B.

B. TIME PERIODS IN THIS AGREEMENT for INSPECTIONS, CONTINGENCIES, COVENANTS, and other obligations, shall begin: (Check ONLY 1 or 2; do NOT check both.)

☐ (1) On the day after acceptance of the offer; OR

☐ (2) On the day after Seller provides to Buyer copies of signed cancellations of prior contracts. However, if the date for close of escrow in paragraph 2 is a specific calendar date, that date shall NOT be extended unless agreed by Buyer and Seller in writing.

27. COURT CONFIRMATION:

☐ (If checked:) This Agreement is CONTINGENT upon court confirmation on or before _____, 19____. The court may allow open, competitive bidding, resulting in the Property being sold to the highest bidder. Buyer is advised to be in court when the offer is considered for confirmation. Court confirmation may be required in probate, conservatorship, guardianship, receivership, bankruptcy, or other proceedings. Buyer understands that the Property may continue to be marketed by Brokers and others, and that Brokers may represent other competitive bidders prior to and at the court confirmation. If court confirmation is not obtained by the date shown above, Buyer may cancel this Agreement in writing.

28. TIME PERIODS; SATISFACTION/REMOVAL OF CONTINGENCIES; DISAPPROVAL/CANCELLATION RIGHTS:

A. TIME PERIODS: Buyer and Seller agree to be bound by the following time periods, which can be changed only by mutual written agreement:

BUYER HAS:

(1) _____ days from acceptance of the offer to complete all inspections, investigations (including inspections for lead-based paint under federal law if applicable), and review of documents and other applicable information, and either to disapprove in writing any items which are unacceptable to Buyer, or to remove the contingency associated with such disapproval right, by the method specified in paragraph 28B or 28C, EXCEPT that, for GEOLOGIC INSPECTIONS under paragraph 7, Buyer shall have an additional 7 days to complete those actions.

(2) _____ days from receipt of each of the following items either to disapprove in writing any items unacceptable to Buyer, or to remove the contingency associated with such disapproval right, by the method specified in paragraph 28B or 28C: Existing Loan Documents (paragraph 1M), Preliminary (Title) Report (paragraph 3), Geologic/Earthquake/Seismic/Flood/State Fire Responsibility Zones/Areas Disclosures (paragraphs 11A, 11B, and 11C), Known Seismic Deficiency and Disclosures (paragraph 11D(1)(b)), Condominium/Common Interest Subdivision Documents (paragraph 12), Governmental Compliance Disclosures (paragraph 15), Well System Reports furnished by Seller (paragraphs 19D and 19E), Rental Documents and Tenant Estoppel Certificates (paragraph 21).

SELLER HAS:

(3) _____ days from acceptance of the offer to provide to Buyer, if applicable, the following items: Pest Control Report (paragraph 20), Geologic/Earthquake/Seismic/Flood/State Fire Responsibility Zones/Areas Disclosures (paragraphs 11A, 11B, and 11C), Earthquake Guide and Disclosures (paragraphs 11D(1) and 11D(2)), Rental Documents (paragraph 21).

(4) _____ days from acceptance of the offer to request, and 2 days after receipt thereof to provide to Buyer, the following items: Existing Loan Documents (paragraph 1M), Preliminary (Title) Report (paragraph 3), Condominium/Common Interest Subdivision Documents (paragraph 12), Tenant Estoppel Certificates (paragraph 21).

B. PASSIVE REMOVAL (Unless paragraph 28C is checked, the Passive method shall apply):

(1) If Buyer does not give to Seller written notice of items reasonably disapproved, or of cancellation (based on inability to obtain loans, if applicable, or based on any other cancellation right of Buyer), within the strict time periods specified, Buyer shall conclusively be deemed to have: (a) completed all inspections, investigations, review of applicable documents and disclosures and removed the contingency of obtaining loans, if applicable; (b) elected to proceed with the transaction; and (c) assumed all liability, responsibility, and expense for repairs or corrections other than for items which Seller has otherwise agreed in writing to repair or correct.

(2) If Buyer does give to Seller written notice of items reasonably disapproved, within the strict time periods specified, Seller shall have _____ days in which to respond in writing.

(3) If Seller's response indicates that Seller is unwilling or unable to repair or correct any items reasonably disapproved by Buyer, or if Seller does not respond within the strict time period specified, Buyer shall have _____ days (after receipt of Seller's response, or after the expiration of the time for Seller to respond, whichever occurs first) to cancel this Agreement in writing.

(4) If Buyer does not give such written notice of cancellation pursuant to paragraph 28B(3) within the strict time period specified, Buyer shall conclusively be deemed to have elected to proceed with the transaction without repair or correction of any items which Seller has not otherwise agreed in writing to repair or correct.

C. ☐ ACTIVE REMOVAL (If this paragraph is checked, then paragraph 28B shall NOT apply):

(1) If Buyer does not give to Seller written notice of removal of all contingencies (including the contingency of obtaining loans, if applicable), or of items reasonably disapproved, or of cancellation (based on inability to obtain loans, if applicable, or based on any other cancellation right of Buyer), within the strict time periods specified, Seller shall have the right to cancel this Agreement in writing.

(2) If Buyer does give to Seller written notice of items reasonably disapproved, within the strict time periods specified, Seller shall have _____ days in which to respond in writing.

(3) If Seller's response indicates that Seller is unwilling or unable to repair or correct any items reasonably disapproved by Buyer, or if Seller does not respond within the strict time period specified, Buyer shall have _____ days (after receipt of Seller's response, or after the expiration of the time for Seller to respond, whichever occurs first) to either cancel this Agreement, or elect to proceed, in writing.

(4) If Buyer does not give such written notice of cancellation or of election to proceed pursuant to paragraph 28C(3) within the strict time period specified, Seller shall have the right to cancel this Agreement by giving written notice to Buyer.

Buyer and Seller acknowledge receipt of copy of this page, which constitutes Page 6 of _____ Pages.

Buyer's Initials (_____) (_____)   Seller's Initials (_____) (_____)

┌─ OFFICE USE ONLY ─┐
Reviewed by Broker or Designee _____
Date _____

BROKER'S COPY

Property Address: _____ , 19____

D. **CANCELLATION OF SALE/ESCROW: RETURN OF DEPOSITS:** If Buyer or Seller provides written notice of cancellation pursuant to rights duly exercised under paragraphs 1A, 1L, 3, 7, 9, 11, 12, 15, 21, 25, 26, 27, or 30, the deposits, less costs and fees, as applicable, shall be returned to Buyer. Buyer and Seller understand that, in such event: (1) Buyer and Seller are each required to sign mutual instructions to cancel the transaction and escrow, and release deposits, as provided by law; (2) A party may be subject to a civil penalty of up to $1,000 for refusal to sign such instructions (Civil Code §1057.3) if no good faith dispute exists as to who is entitled to the deposited funds; (3) Fees and costs may be payable to service providers and vendors for services and products provided during escrow.

29. **TAX WITHHOLDING:**

A. Under the Foreign Investment in Real Property Tax Act (FIRPTA), IRC §1445, every Buyer must, unless an exemption applies, deduct and withhold 10% of the gross sales price from Seller's proceeds and send it to the Internal Revenue Service, if the Seller is a "foreign person" under that statute.

B. In addition, under California Revenue and Taxation Code §18662, every Buyer must, unless an exemption applies, deduct and withhold 3½% of the gross sales price from Seller's proceeds and send it to the Franchise Tax Board if the Seller has a last known address outside of California or if the Seller's proceeds will be paid to a financial intermediary of the Seller.

C. Penalties may be imposed on a responsible party for non-compliance with the requirements of these statutes and related regulations. Seller and Buyer agree to execute and deliver any instrument, affidavit, statement, or instruction reasonably necessary to carry out these requirements, and to withholding of tax under those statutes if required. (SELLER'S AFFIDAVIT OF NON-FOREIGN STATUS AND/OR CALIFORNIA RESIDENCY (C.A.R. Form AS-14), OR BUYER'S AFFIDAVIT (C.A.R. Form AB-11), IF APPLICABLE, SHALL SATISFY THESE REQUIREMENTS.)

30. **PROPERTY DESTRUCTION OR DAMAGE:** This paragraph applies only to destruction or damage that occurs after acceptance of the offer.

A. In the event of destruction or damage through no fault of Buyer or Seller, before Buyer receives either title or possession:

(1) If such destruction or damage totals 1% or less of the purchase price, Seller shall repair such destruction or damage and the transaction shall go forward.

(2) If such destruction or damage exceeds 1% of the purchase price, Buyer shall have the right only to elect to either (a) terminate this Agreement by giving written notice of cancellation to Seller, or (b) purchase the Property in its then-present condition. If Buyer elects to purchase the property in its then-present condition, Seller shall credit Buyer 1% of the purchase price, and shall assign to Buyer all rights to any insurance claims and proceeds covering the destruction or damage.

B. In the event of destruction or damage through no fault of Buyer or Seller, after Buyer receives possession but before title has transferred to Buyer:

(1) If such destruction or damage totals 1% or less of the purchase price (a) Seller shall be under no obligation to repair such destruction or damage, (b) the transaction shall go forward, and (c) Seller shall assign to Buyer all rights to any insurance claims and proceeds covering the destruction or damage.

(2) If such destruction or damage exceeds 1% of the purchase price, Buyer shall have the right only to elect to either (a) terminate this Agreement by giving written notice of cancellation to Seller, or (b) purchase the Property in its then-present condition. If Buyer elects to purchase the property in its then-present condition, Seller shall assign to Buyer all rights to any insurance claims and proceeds covering the destruction or damage.

C. Destruction or damage after title has transferred to Buyer shall be borne by Buyer.

D. In the event the transaction is terminated under this paragraph, any expenses paid by Buyer or Seller for credit reports, appraisals, title examination, inspections of any kind, or other items, shall remain that party's responsibility.

IF TRANSFER OF TITLE AND POSSESSION DO NOT OCCUR AT THE SAME TIME, BUYER AND SELLER ARE ADVISED TO SEEK ADVICE OF THEIR INSURANCE ADVISORS AS TO THE INSURANCE CONSEQUENCE THEREOF.

31. **MULTIPLE LISTING SERVICE (MLS):** Brokers are authorized to report the terms of this transaction to any MLS, to be published and disseminated to persons authorized to use the information on terms approved by the MLS.

32. **EQUAL HOUSING OPPORTUNITY:** The Property is sold in compliance with federal, state, and local anti-discrimination laws.

33. **MEDIATION OF DISPUTES:** BUYER AND SELLER AGREE TO MEDIATE ANY DISPUTE OR CLAIM ARISING BETWEEN THEM OUT OF THIS CONTRACT OR ANY RESULTING TRANSACTION BEFORE RESORTING TO ARBITRATION OR COURT ACTION. Mediation is a process by which parties attempt to resolve a dispute or claim by submitting it to an impartial, neutral mediator, who is authorized to facilitate the resolution of the dispute, but who is not empowered to impose a settlement on the parties. Mediation fees, if any, shall be divided equally among the parties involved. In addition, Buyer and Seller agree to mediate disputes or claims involving either or both Brokers, consistent with this provision, provided either or both Brokers shall have agreed to such mediation prior to or within a reasonable time after the dispute or claim is presented to Brokers. Any election by either or both Brokers to participate in mediation shall not result in Brokers being deemed parties to the purchase and sale Agreement. IF ANY PARTY COMMENCES AN ARBITRATION OR COURT ACTION BASED ON A DISPUTE OR CLAIM TO WHICH THIS PARAGRAPH APPLIES WITHOUT FIRST ATTEMPTING TO RESOLVE THE MATTER THROUGH MEDIATION, THEN IN THE DISCRETION OF THE ARBITRATOR(S) OR JUDGE, THAT PARTY SHALL NOT BE ENTITLED TO RECOVER ATTORNEY'S FEES, EVEN IF THEY WOULD OTHERWISE BE AVAILABLE TO THAT PARTY IN ANY SUCH ARBITRATION OR COURT ACTION. This mediation provision applies whether or not the Arbitration of Disputes provision is initialed. Exclusions are listed in paragraph 35.

34. **ARBITRATION OF DISPUTES:** (If initialed by all parties:) **Buyer and Seller agree that any dispute or claim in law or equity arising between Buyer and Seller out of this contract or any resulting transaction, which is not settled through mediation, shall be decided by neutral, binding arbitration and not by court action, except as provided by California law for judicial review of arbitration proceedings. In addition, Buyer and Seller agree to arbitrate disputes or claims involving either or both Brokers, consistent with this provision, provided either or both Brokers shall have agreed to such arbitration prior to or within a reasonable time after the dispute or claim is presented to Brokers. Any election by either or both Brokers to participate in arbitration shall not result in Brokers being deemed parties to the purchase and sale Agreement.**

The arbitration shall be conducted in accordance with the rules of either the American Arbitration Association (AAA) or Judicial Arbitration and Mediation Services, Inc./Endispute (JAMS/Endispute). The selection between AAA and JAMS/Endispute rules shall be made by the claimant first filing for arbitration. The parties to an arbitration may agree in writing to use different rules and/or arbitrator(s). In all other respects, the arbitration shall be conducted in accordance with Part III, Title 9 of the California Code of Civil Procedure. Judgment upon the award rendered by the arbitrator(s) may be entered in any court having jurisdiction thereof. The parties shall have the right to discovery in accordance with Code of Civil Procedure §1283.05. Exclusions are listed in paragraph 35.

"NOTICE: BY INITIALLING IN THE SPACE BELOW YOU ARE AGREEING TO HAVE ANY DISPUTE ARISING OUT OF THE MATTERS INCLUDED IN THE 'ARBITRATION OF DISPUTES' PROVISION DECIDED BY NEUTRAL ARBITRATION AS PROVIDED BY CALIFORNIA LAW AND YOU ARE GIVING UP ANY RIGHTS YOU MIGHT POSSESS TO HAVE THE DISPUTE LITIGATED IN A COURT OR JURY TRIAL. BY INITIALLING IN THE SPACE BELOW YOU ARE GIVING UP YOUR JUDICIAL RIGHTS TO DISCOVERY AND APPEAL, UNLESS THOSE RIGHTS ARE SPECIFICALLY INCLUDED IN THE 'ARBITRATION OF DISPUTES' PROVISION. IF YOU REFUSE TO SUBMIT TO ARBITRATION AFTER AGREEING TO THIS PROVISION, YOU MAY BE COMPELLED TO ARBITRATE UNDER THE AUTHORITY OF THE CALIFORNIA CODE OF CIVIL PROCEDURE. YOUR AGREEMENT TO THIS ARBITRATION PROVISION IS VOLUNTARY."

"WE HAVE READ AND UNDERSTAND THE FOREGOING AND AGREE TO SUBMIT DISPUTES ARISING OUT OF THE MATTERS INCLUDED IN THE 'ARBITRATION OF DISPUTES' PROVISION TO NEUTRAL ARBITRATION."

Buyer's Initials / _____ Seller's Initials / _____

35. **EXCLUSIONS FROM MEDIATION AND ARBITRATION:** The following matters are excluded from mediation and arbitration hereunder: (a) a judicial or non-judicial foreclosure or other action or proceeding to enforce a deed of trust, mortgage, or installment land sale contract as defined in Civil Code §2985, (b) an unlawful detainer action, (c) the filing or enforcement of a mechanic's lien, (d) any matter which is within the jurisdiction of a probate or small claims court, and (e) an action for bodily injury or wrongful death, or for latent or patent defects to which Code of Civil Procedure §337.1 or §337.15 applies. The filing of a court action to enable the recording of a notice of pending action, for order of attachment, receivership, injunction, or other provisional remedies, shall not constitute a violation of the Mediation of Disputes and Arbitration of Disputes provisions.

Buyer and Seller acknowledge receipt of copy of this page, which constitutes Page 7 of _____ Pages.

Buyer's Initials (_____) (_____)   Seller's Initials (_____) (_____)

┌─────────────────────────────────────┐
│ ──── OFFICE USE ONLY ────   │
│ Reviewed by Broker or Designee ____ │
│ Date ____   │
└─────────────────────────────────────┘

EQUAL HOUSING OPPORTUNITY

MR SEP 95

BROKER'S COPY

Property Address: _____ _____ . 19____

36. LIQUIDATED DAMAGES: (If initialled by all parties:)

Buyer's Initials _____   Seller's Initials _____

Buyer and Seller agree that if Buyer fails to complete this purchase by reason of any default of Buyer:
- A. Seller shall be released from the obligation to sell the Property to Buyer.
- B. Seller shall retain, as liquidated damages for breach of contract, the deposit actually paid. However, the amount retained shall be no more than 3% of the purchase price if the Property is a dwelling with no more than four units, one of which Buyer intends to occupy as Buyer's residence. Any excess shall promptly be returned to Buyer.
- C. Buyer and Seller shall sign RECEIPT FOR INCREASED DEPOSIT/LIQUIDATED DAMAGES (C.A.R. Form RID-11) for any increased deposit.
- D. In the event of a dispute, funds deposited in trust accounts or escrow are not released automatically and require mutual, signed release instructions from both Buyer and Seller, judicial decision, or arbitration award.

37. ATTORNEY'S FEES: In any action, proceeding, or arbitration between Buyer and Seller arising out of this Agreement, the prevailing party between Buyer and Seller shall be entitled to reasonable attorney's fees and costs from the non-prevailing Buyer or Seller, except as provided in paragraph 33.

38. DEFINITIONS: As used in this Agreement:
- A. "DAYS" means calendar days, unless otherwise required by law.
- B. "DAYS FROM ACCEPTANCE" means the specified number of calendar days after acceptance of the offer or final counter offer is communicated to the other party as specified in paragraph 42, not counting the calendar date on which acceptance is communicated.
- C. "CLOSE OF ESCROW" means the date the grant deed or other evidence of transfer of title is recorded.
- D. "LOCAL LAW" means any law, code, statute, ordinance, regulation, or rule, adopted by a city or county.
- E. "REPAIRS" means alterations, repairs, replacements, or modifications of the Property.
- F. SINGULAR and PLURAL terms each include the others, when appropriate.

39. TIME OF ESSENCE; ENTIRE CONTRACT; CHANGES: Time is of the essence. All agreements between the parties are incorporated in this Agreement which constitutes the entire contract. Its terms are intended by the parties as a final, complete, and exclusive expression of their agreement with respect to its subject matter and may not be contradicted by evidence of any prior agreement or contemporaneous oral agreement. The captions in this Agreement are for convenience of reference only and are not intended as part of this Agreement. This Agreement may not be extended, amended, modified, altered, or changed in any respect whatsoever except in writing signed by Buyer and Seller.

40. OTHER TERMS AND CONDITIONS; ATTACHED SUPPLEMENTS:
- A. _____
  _____
- B. The following ATTACHED supplements are incorporated in this Agreement:
  ☐ _____   ☐ _____

41. AGENCY CONFIRMATION: The following agency relationships are hereby confirmed for this transaction:

Listing Agent: _____ is the agent of (check one):
(Print Firm Name)

☐ the Seller exclusively; or ☐ both the Buyer and Seller.

Selling Agent: _____ (if not same as Listing Agent) is the agent of (check one):
(Print Firm Name)

☐ the Buyer exclusively; or ☐ the Seller exclusively; or ☐ both the Buyer and Seller. Real Estate Brokers are not parties to the purchase and sale Agreement between Buyer and Seller. (IF THE PROPERTY CONTAINS 1–4 RESIDENTIAL DWELLING UNITS, BUYER AND SELLER MUST ALSO BE GIVEN ONE OR MORE DISCLOSURES REGARDING REAL ESTATE AGENCY RELATIONSHIPS FORMS (C.A.R. Form AD-14).)

42. OFFER: This is an offer to purchase the Property. All paragraphs with spaces for initials by Buyer and Seller are incorporated in this Agreement only if initialled by all parties. If at least one, but not all parties initial, a counter offer is required until agreement is reached. Unless acceptance is signed by Seller and a signed copy delivered in person, by mail, or facsimile, and personally received by Buyer or by _____, who is authorized to receive it, by _____, 19___ at _____ AM/PM, the offer shall be deemed revoked and the deposit shall be returned. Buyer and Seller acknowledge that Brokers are not parties to the purchase and sale Agreement. Buyer has read and acknowledges receipt of a copy of the offer and agrees to the above confirmation of agency relationships. If this offer is accepted and Buyer subsequently defaults, Buyer may be responsible for payment of Brokers' compensation. This Agreement and any supplement, addendum, or modification, including any photocopy or facsimile, may be signed in two or more counterparts, all of which shall constitute one and the same writing.

BUYER _____

BUYER _____

Receipt for deposit is acknowledged, and agency relationships are confirmed as above. Real Estate Brokers are not parties to the purchase and sale Agreement between Buyer and Seller.

Real Estate Broker (Selling) _____   Date _____
(Print Firm Name)

By _____

Address _____

Telephone _____   Fax _____

ACCEPTANCE

The undersigned Seller accepts the above offer, agrees to sell the Property on the above terms and conditions (if checked: ☐ SUBJECT TO ATTACHED COUNTER OFFER), and agrees to the above confirmation of agency relationships. Seller agrees to pay compensation for services as follows:
_____, to _____, Broker, and
_____, to _____, Broker, payable (a) on recordation of the deed or other evidence of title, or (b) if completion of sale is prevented by default of Seller, upon Seller's default, or (c) if completion of sale is prevented by default of Buyer, only if and when Seller collects damages from Buyer, by suit or otherwise, and then in an amount equal to one-half of the damages recovered, but not to exceed the above compensation, after first deducting title and escrow expenses and the expenses of collection, if any. Seller hereby irrevocably assigns to Brokers such compensation from Seller's proceeds and irrevocably instructs Escrow Holder to disburse those funds to Brokers at close of escrow. Commission instructions can be amended or revoked only with the consent of the Brokers. In any action, proceeding, or arbitration relating to the payment of such compensation, the prevailing party shall be entitled to reasonable attorney's fees and costs, except as provided in paragraph 33. The undersigned Seller has read and acknowledges receipt of a copy of this Agreement, and authorizes Brokers to deliver a signed copy to Buyer.

SELLER _____   Date _____

SELLER _____   Time _____

Agency relationships are confirmed as above. Real Estate Brokers are not parties to the purchase and sale Agreement between Buyer and Seller.

Real Estate Broker (Listing) _____   Date _____
(Print Firm Name)

By _____

Address _____

Telephone _____   Fax _____

(____/____) **ACKNOWLEDGMENT OF RECEIPT:** Buyer, or the person authorized in paragraph 42, acknowledges receipt of signed acceptance on
(Initials)   (date) _____, at _____ AM/PM.

This form is available for use by the entire real estate industry. The use of this form is not intended to identify the user as a REALTOR®. REALTOR® is a registered collective membership mark which may be used only by real estate licensees who are members of the NATIONAL ASSOCIATION OF REALTORS® and who subscribe to its Code of Ethics.

Page 8 of _____ Pages.
BROKER'S COPY

OFFICE USE ONLY
Reviewed by Broker or Designee _____
Date _____

Typical Provisions

A typical deposit receipt includes the following provisions.

Identification of the Parties. Of course, the parties must be properly identified in the agreement. Everyone who has an ownership interest in the property must sign the contract, and each party must have the capacity to enter into a contract.

Description of the Property. The deposit receipt must describe the property with certainty. As with the listing agreement, a full legal description of the property is not required. However, it is always a good idea to include the legal description, to be on the safe side. The full legal description should be initialed by the parties and attached as an exhibit to the deposit receipt.

Terms of Sale. The deposit receipt should set forth as clearly as possible all the terms of the sale, such as what is included in or excluded from the sale, the amount of the downpayment, the total sales price, and the method of payment.

Many deposit receipt forms include a preprinted checklist of the most common types of financing arrangements. But regardless of the form used, all the financing arrangements should be fully described, including the type of loan, the principal amount, the interest rate, how the loan is amortized, the term of the loan, and the monthly payments. (Types of financing programs are discussed in Chapter 11.)

Conditions of Sale. Most deposit receipts are conditional. For example, it is common to condition a sale on the buyer's ability to obtain the necessary financing. If the buyer is unable to obtain the financing after making a good faith effort to do so, he or she does not have to go through with the sale, and does not have to forfeit the deposit.

Any and all conditions must be clearly stated in the deposit receipt. A provision that describes such a condition is called a **contingency clause**. The contingency clause should state exactly what must occur to fulfill the condition, and it should explain how one party is to notify the other when the condition has been fulfilled or waived. There should also be a time limit placed on the condition (for example, if the condition is not fulfilled by January 15, the contract is void). Finally, the contingency clause should explain the parties' rights in the event that the condition is not met or waived.

If a real estate licensee believes that a condition imposed in a deposit receipt may affect the date of closing or the date the buyer can take possession of the property, the licensee is required to explain that to the parties. Failure to do so is a violation of the California Real Estate Law, and may lead to disciplinary action (see Chapter 18).

Condition of the Property. The buyer's right to inspect the property and receive the Transfer Disclosure Statement is often discussed in the deposit receipt. (The Transfer Disclosure Statement is discussed in Chapter 5.)

The buyer may be encouraged to thoroughly inspect the property, and a list of elements that should be inspected may be included. Typically, such a list might include:

- the structural components of the home,
- the size and age of the home and lot,
- the property lines and boundaries,
- the waste disposal system,
- water and utilities,
- environmental hazards,
- geologic conditions, and
- neighborhood conditions.

The seller may warrant the condition of certain elements (such as the roof, plumbing, or appliances) in the deposit receipt, or the seller may sell the property "as is." Note that even if the seller sells the property "as is," the seller is legally obligated to disclose all known material defects to the buyer.

Encumbrances and Condition of Title. The seller usually states in the deposit receipt that the title to the property is free of liens and other encumbrances, except for current taxes and other recorded encumbrances.

Escrow and Closing. It's a good idea for a deposit receipt to include the arrangements for the escrow. At the very least, the agreement should set the closing date for the transaction.

Date of Possession. Possession of the property is usually transferred to the buyer on the closing date, but other arrangements can be made in the deposit receipt.

Good Faith Deposit. The deposit receipt should not only acknowledge receipt of the good faith deposit, it should also explain the circumstances in which the deposit will be refunded to the buyer or forfeited to the seller. In many cases, the deposit is treated as liquidated damages (see Chapter 7). In a residential transaction, a liquidated damages provision in a deposit receipt must be in boldface type and must be initialed by the parties. The amount of the liquidated damages may not exceed 3% of the purchase price.

Broker's Compensation. Many deposit receipts also provide for the payment of the broker's commission. In most cases, this provision is merely a reaffirmation of the commission agreement set forth in the listing agreement. But if the broker has risked working under an oral or implied listing agreement thus far, such a provision in the deposit receipt will satisfy the requirement for a written listing agreement, should the broker need to sue the seller for the commission.

Land Contracts

Under a land contract (also called a real estate contract, installment sales contract, or contract for deed), a buyer purchases property on an installment basis. The parties to the contract are the **vendor** (seller) and the **vendee** (buyer). Periodic payments towards the purchase price are made over a period of years, and during that time the vendor (seller) retains legal title to the property. The deed is not delivered to the vendee (buyer) until the full purchase price is paid. In the meantime, the vendee has equitable title to the property, which is the right to possess and enjoy the property while paying off the purchase price.

> **Example:** Bendermann agrees to buy Jones's farm for $250,000, to be paid at the rate of $25,000 per year, plus 9% interest, for ten years. Jones allows Bendermann to take possession of the farm, and she promises to convey legal title to the farm to Bendermann when he has paid her the full purchase price. Bendermann and Jones have entered into a land contract.

Rights and Responsibilities of the Parties

Both the vendee and the vendor have various rights and responsibilities under a land contract. The vendor retains legal title to the property, and has the right to transfer or encumber the property without the vendee's consent. However, if legal title is transferred, the new owner takes title subject to the rights of the vendee under the land contract. And if the vendor creates any liens against the property, he or she must pay them off before delivering the deed to the vendee: the vendor is required to deliver clear, marketable title when the vendee pays off the contract.

If the vendor does create liens against the property, he or she must apply the vendee's contract payments to any amounts due on the liens. For example, if the vendor owes a $400 monthly payment on a deed of trust, he or she must apply the first $400 of the vendee's $450 payment against this expense, rather than using the money for any other purpose. This protects the vendee from the possibility that the vendor will default on the lien and lose the property through foreclosure.

There are also statutory restrictions on the vendor's right to create liens if the land contract is unrecorded. (Note that the vendor cannot prohibit the vendee from recording the contract.) The vendor cannot encumber the property with liens that add up to more than the unpaid contract balance, unless the vendee consents to the liens. The vendor also cannot create liens without the vendee's consent if the monthly payments on those liens total more than the vendee's monthly payment on the land contract.

The vendee also has the right to encumber the property. However, few lenders are willing to make loans with a vendee's equitable interest as the only security.

The vendee's main responsibility is to make the required installment payments to the vendor, as called for in the land contract. Generally, the vendee is also responsible for keeping the property insured and paying the property taxes.

If the vendee pays the purchase price in full, but the vendor fails to transfer legal title to the property, the vendee can sue for specific performance of the contract (see Chapter 7).

If the vendee defaults under the contract (for example, by failing to make the installment payments), the vendor can terminate the contract by sending the vendee the proper notice. The vendor must reimburse the vendee for the amount he or she paid to the vendor under the contract. However, the vendee's reimbursement can be reduced by any damages that the vendor incurred, and by the fair market rental value of the property for the period the vendee was in possession.

Example: Porter paid Rollins $8,800 over a ten-month period under a land contract. The rental value of the property for that period of time was $750 a month, or $7,500. Porter would only be entitled to a reimbursement of $1,300. ($8,800 – $7,500 = $1,300).

The vendee has the right to cure the default and reinstate the contract. And once the vendee has paid a substantial portion of the contract price, he or she gains a right of redemption.

Remedies on Default

Fig.8.6 Rights and responsibilities of parties to a land contract

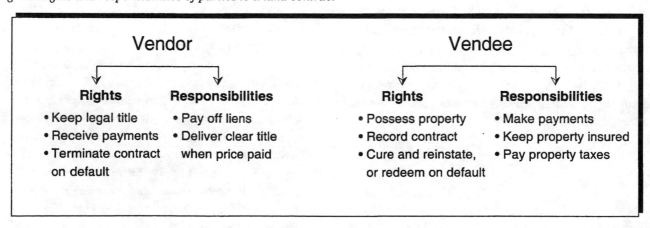

Vendor		Vendee	
Rights	**Responsibilities**	**Rights**	**Responsibilities**
• Keep legal title	• Pay off liens	• Possess property	• Make payments
• Receive payments	• Deliver clear title when price paid	• Record contract	• Keep property insured
• Terminate contract on default		• Cure and reinstate, or redeem on default	• Pay property taxes

Reasons for Using a Land Contract

A land contract is essentially a security instrument that is used in conjunction with seller financing: the seller extends credit to the buyer and holds title to the property as security for the repayment of the debt. (See Chapter 9 for a detailed discussion of security instruments.) However, because of the vendee's rights of reinstatement, reimbursement, and redemption under a land contract, most people prefer to use deeds of trust in conjunction with seller-financed transactions (see Chapter 9). One exception is the Cal-Vet program, which regularly uses land contracts to finance home purchases by veterans (see Chapter 11).

Option Agreements

An option agreement is essentially a contract to make a contract; it is an agreement that creates a right to buy or lease property for a fixed price within a set period of time. The parties to an option agreement are the **optionor** (the one who grants the option) and the **optionee** (the one who has the option right). In an option to purchase, the optionor is the seller and the optionee is the buyer.

> **Example:** Alvarez is offering to sell his property for $120,000. Conners isn't yet sure that he wants to buy the property, but he doesn't want to lose the opportunity to do so. He asks Alvarez to give him a three-week option to purchase, and Alvarez agrees. They execute a written option agreement, and Conners pays Alvarez $750 as consideration for the option. The option gives Conners the right to buy the property at the stated price ($120,000) during the next three weeks, but does not obligate him to buy it at all.

The optionor is bound to keep the offer open for the period specified in the option agreement. He or she is not allowed to sell or lease the property to anyone other than the optionee until the option expires.

If the optionee decides to exercise the option (that is, to buy or lease the property on the stated terms), he or she must give written notice of acceptance to the optionor. If the optionee fails to exercise the option within the specified time, the option expires automatically.

Requirements for an Option

Because an option is a contract, it must have all the necessary elements of a contract, including consideration. The consideration may be a nominal amount—there's no set minimum. But some consideration must, in fact, pass from the optionee to the optionor; a mere statement of consideration in the agreement is not sufficient. (There is an exception to this rule for lease/option agreements, where the provisions of the lease are treated as sufficient consideration to support the option.)

The option contract must be in writing; oral options are unenforceable. Furthermore, since an option to purchase anticipates that a sale may take place, the underlying terms of the sale (price, financing, etc.) should be spelled out in the option agreement.

Option Rights

The executed option gives the optionee a contract right, but does not create an interest in real property. An option is not a lien, and also cannot be used as security for a mortgage or a deed of trust.

If the optionor dies during the option period, that will not affect the rights of the optionee, who may still exercise the right to purchase or lease. The option contract is binding on the heirs and assignees of the optionor.

An option can be assigned, unless the agreement includes a provision prohibiting assignment. One exception is when the consideration paid by the optionee is in the form of an unsecured promissory note. In that case, the optionee must obtain the optionor's written permission before the option may be assigned.

Recording an Option

An option agreement may be recorded to give third parties constructive notice of the option. In that case, if the optionee exercises the option, his or her interest in the property will relate back to the date the option was recorded, taking priority over the rights of intervening third parties.

A recorded option that is not exercised creates a cloud on the optionor's title. The optionor should obtain a release from the optionee, and record the release to remove the cloud.

Leases

A lease is both a method of conveyance and a contract. A lease conveys a less-than-freehold (leasehold) estate from the owner (the **landlord**) to the **tenant**. As we discussed in Chapter 2, the holder of a leasehold estate does not own the property, but rather has a right to exclusive possession of the property for a specified period of time.

The lease is also a contract, sometimes called a **rental agreement**. It sets out the rights and responsibilities of the two contracting parties, the landlord and the tenant. It should be noted, however, that certain covenants and terms are implied by law in all leases, whether or not they are written in the agreement. These implied covenants (found in the California Landlord-Tenant Law) are discussed below.

Validity

As with any contract, the parties to a lease must be competent. There must be an offer and accep-

tance, and the lease agreement must be supported by consideration, which is typically the rental payment. Both the amount of the rental payment and when it is due should be stated in the lease. Most leases require the rent to be paid at the beginning of the rental period. However, if the lease does not specify when the rent is to be paid, it is not due until the end of the rental period.

Under the statute of frauds, a lease must be in writing if it is for longer than one year, or if it won't be fully performed within one year after the contract is made. Any lease that should be in writing but is not creates a periodic tenancy.

A written lease must be signed by the landlord. The tenant usually signs the lease as well, but the tenant's signature isn't required. A tenant who takes possession of the property and pays rent is considered to have accepted the terms of the lease. However, it is wise to have both parties sign the lease. Also, since a lease is a contract pertaining to real property, an accurate legal description of the property should be included.

Basic Provisions

The following are some common provisions found in most lease agreements.

Use of the Premises. A tenant's use of the leased property is restricted by law to legal uses. Many landlords place additional restrictions on the use of the property, such as restricting commercial space to retail use. The restricting language must be clear, or the restrictions will be unenforceable. At a minimum, the lease should state that the premises are to be used only for the specified purpose and for no other. If there is no limitation in the lease, or if the language is not clearly restrictive, the tenant may use the premises for any legal purpose.

Security Deposit. In California, a security deposit is defined as any payment, fee, deposit, or charge (including advance rental payments) paid by the tenant to secure the performance of the lease agreement. These payments are considered security depos-

Fig. 8.7 Residential lease

RESIDENTIAL LEASE OR MONTH-TO-MONTH RENTAL AGREEMENT
THIS IS INTENDED TO BE A LEGALLY BINDING CONTRACT — READ IT CAREFULLY.
CALIFORNIA ASSOCIATION OF REALTORS® (C.A.R.) STANDARD FORM

_____, California _____, 19____
_____, Landlord and
_____, Tenant, agree as follows:

1. PROPERTY: Landlord rents to Tenant and Tenant rents from Landlord the real property and improvements described as:
_____
(Street address or other description)
_____ ("Premises"). The following personal property
(City, County, State)
is included: _____

2. RENT; TERM: Tenant agrees to pay rent monthly, at the rate of $_____, in advance, on the _____ day
of each calendar month. The term begins on _____, 19____, ("Commencement Date"), as a:
☐ A. month-to-month tenancy, which may be terminated by either party, by giving written notice to the other at least 30 days prior to the intended
termination date; or,
☐ B. lease ending _____, 19____, with a total rent of $_____, monthly
installments as above; or,
☐ C.

3. LATE CHARGE: Tenant acknowledges that late payment of rent may cause Landlord to incur costs and expenses, the exact amount of which
are extremely difficult and impractical to determine. These costs may include, but are not limited to, processing and accounting expenses, late
charges that may be imposed on Landlord by terms of any loan secured by the Premises, costs for additional attempts to collect rent, and preparation
of notices. Therefore, if any installment of rent due from Tenant is not received by Landlord within _____ calendar days after date due, Tenant
shall pay to Landlord an additional sum of $_____ as a late charge which shall be deemed additional rent. Landlord and
Tenant agree that this late charge represents a fair and reasonable estimate of the costs that Landlord may incur by reason of Tenant's late payments.
Any late charge due shall be paid with the current installment of rent. Landlord's acceptance of any late charge shall not constitute a waiver
as to any default of Tenant, or prevent Landlord from exercising any other rights and remedies under this Agreement, and as provided by law.

4. PAYMENT: The rent shall be paid to _____, at
(Name)
_____, or
(Address, City, State, Zip Code)
at any other location specified by Landlord.

5. SECURITY DEPOSIT: $_____ shall be given by Tenant as a security deposit. Landlord may use all or any portion of the
security deposit reasonably necessary to: (a) cure Tenant's default in payment of rent, late charges or other sums due; (b) repair damages caused
by Tenant, or by a guest or a licensee of Tenant; (c) clean the Premises, if necessary, upon termination of tenancy; and (d) replace or return personal
property or appurtenances, excluding ordinary wear and tear. If used during the tenancy, Tenant agrees to reinstate the total security deposit
within five days after written notice delivered to Tenant in person or by mail. No later than three weeks after Tenant vacates the Premises, Landlord
shall furnish to Tenant an itemized written statement of the basis for, and the amount of, any security received and the disposition of the security,
and shall return any remaining portion of the security to Tenant. The return of the security deposit at the end of the tenancy, if otherwise due,
will be handled directly between Landlord and Tenant and will not involve any broker who releases the security deposit to Landlord. Landlord
and Tenant each indemnify and release any broker from any liability relating to return of the security deposit.

6. UTILITIES: Tenant agrees to pay for all utilities and services based upon occupancy of the Premises, and the following charges:
_____, except
_____ which shall be paid for by Landlord. If any utilities
(Specify exceptions or write "none")
are not separately metered, Tenant shall pay Tenant's proportional share thereof as reasonably determined by Landlord.

7. CONDITION: Tenant has examined the Premises, all furniture, furnishings, and appliances, if any, and fixtures, including smoke detector(s).
Tenant acknowledges that those items are clean and in operative condition, with the following exceptions: _____
_____

8. OCCUPANTS: The Premises are for the sole use as a personal residence by the following named persons only: _____
_____

9. PETS: No animal or pet shall be kept on or about the Premises without Landlord's prior written consent, except_____

10. LIQUID-FILLED FURNITURE: Tenant shall not use or have liquid-filled furniture on the Premises unless Tenant first gives proof of compliance
to Landlord's reasonable satisfaction, including increased security deposit, under Civil Code section 1940.5.

11. RULES/REGULATIONS: Tenant agrees to comply with all covenants, conditions and restrictions, bylaws, rules, regulations, and decisions
of owners' association, or Landlord, which are at any time posted on the Premises or delivered to Tenant. Tenant shall pay any fines or charges
imposed by owners' association, or other authorities, due to any violation by Tenant, or the guests or licensees of Tenant. Tenant shall not, and
shall ensure that guests and licensees of Tenant shall not, disturb, annoy, endanger, or interfere with other tenants of the building or neighbors,
or use the Premises for any unlawful purposes, including, but not limited to, using, manufacturing, selling, storing, or transporting illicit drugs
or other contraband, or violate any law or ordinance, or commit waste or a nuisance upon or about the Premises.

Landlord and Tenant acknowledge receipt of copy of this page, which constitutes Page 1 of _____ Pages.
Landlord's Initials (_____) (_____)   Tenant's Initials (_____) (_____)

Subject Property Address: _____ Date: _____, 19____

12. **MAINTENANCE/DAMAGE/INSURANCE:** Tenant shall properly use, operate, and safeguard the Premises, all furniture, furnishings, and appliances, and all electrical, gas, and plumbing fixtures, and shall keep them as clean and sanitary as their condition permits. Tenant shall immediately notify Landlord of any damage, and shall pay for all repairs or replacements caused by Tenant, or the guests or invitees of Tenant, excluding ordinary wear and tear. **Tenant's personal property is not insured by Landlord.**

13. **ALTERATIONS:** Tenant shall not paint, wallpaper, add or change locks, or make any other alterations to the Premises without Landlord's prior written consent. Tenant acknowledges receipt of:

- _____ key(s) to Premises.   _____
- _____ key(s) to mailbox.   _____
- _____ key(s) to common area(s).   _____
- _____ remote control device(s) for garage door opener(s).

Tenant may not re-key existing locks or opening devices unless Tenant immediately delivers copies of all keys to Landlord. Tenant shall pay all costs related to loss of any keys or devices, including charges imposed by any owners' association.

14. **ENTRY:** Tenant shall make the Premises available to Landlord, authorized agent, or representative, for the purpose of entering to make necessary or agreed repairs, decorations, alterations, or improvements, or to supply necessary or agreed services, or to show the Premises to prospective or actual purchasers, tenants, mortgagees, lenders, appraisers, or contractors. **Landlord and Tenant agree that four hours notice (oral or written) shall be reasonable and sufficient notice.** In an emergency, Landlord, authorized agent, or representative may enter the Premises, at any time, without prior notice.

15. **ASSIGNMENT/SUBLETTING:** Tenant shall not let or sublet all or any part of the Premises, or assign this Agreement or any interest in it. Any assignment, letting, or subletting that violates this paragraph shall be void. Landlord's acceptance of rent from a person other than the named Tenant shall not be a waiver of this paragraph.

16. **POSSESSION:** If Tenant abandons or vacates the Premises, Landlord may terminate this Agreement and regain lawful possession. If Landlord is unable to deliver possession of the Premises on the Commencement Date, the Commencement Date shall be extended to the date on which possession is made available to Tenant. If Landlord is unable to deliver possession within 10 (or ☐ _____) calendar days after the agreed Commencement Date, Tenant may terminate this Agreement by giving written notice to Landlord, and shall receive a refund of all rent and security deposit paid.

17. **HOLDING OVER:** Any holding over after the term of this Agreement expires, with Landlord's consent, shall create a month-to-month tenancy, which may be terminated by either party, by giving written notice to the other, at least 30 days prior to the intended termination date. Rent shall be at a rate equal to the rent for the immediately preceding month, payable in advance. All other terms and conditions of this Agreement shall remain in full force and effect.

18. **ATTORNEY'S FEES:** In any action or proceeding arising out of this Agreement, the prevailing party shall be entitled to reasonable attorney's fees and costs.

19. **WAIVER:** The waiver of any breach shall not be construed as a continuing waiver of the same or any subsequent breach.

20. **NOTICE:** Notices to Landlord or Manager may be served at _____.
Notices to Tenant may be served at _____

21. **TENANCY STATEMENT (ESTOPPEL CERTIFICATE):** Tenant shall execute and deliver a tenancy statement (estoppel certificate) submitted by Landlord, within 24 hours after receipt, acknowledging that this Agreement is unmodified and in full force, or in full force as modified, and stating the modifications. Failure to comply shall be deemed Tenant's acknowledgement that the certificate submitted by Landlord is true and correct and may be relied upon by a lender or purchaser. (C.A.R. Form TS-14 SHALL SATISFY THIS REQUIREMENT.)

22. **JOINT AND INDIVIDUAL OBLIGATIONS:** If there is more than one Tenant, each one shall be individually and completely responsible for the performance of all obligations of Tenant under this Agreement, jointly with every other Tenant, and individually.

23. **SUPPLEMENTS/OTHER TERMS AND CONDITIONS:** _____
_____
_____
_____
_____
_____
_____

The following ATTACHED supplements are incorporated in this Agreement: _____
_____

24. **TENANT REPRESENTATIONS: CREDIT:** Tenant warrants that all statements in Tenant's rental application are accurate. Tenant authorizes Landlord and Broker(s) to obtain Tenant's credit report at the time of the application and periodically during the tenancy, in connection with approval, modification, or enforcement of this Agreement. Landlord may cancel this Agreement, (a) before occupancy begins, upon disapproval of the credit report(s), or (b) at any time, upon discovering that information in Tenant's application is false. A negative credit report reflecting on Tenant's record may be submitted to a credit reporting agency if Tenant fails to fulfill the terms of payment and other obligations under this Agreement.

25. **ENTIRE CONTRACT:** Time is of the essence. All prior agreements between Landlord and Tenant are incorporated in this Agreement which constitutes the entire contract. It is intended as a final expression of the parties' agreement with respect to the general subject matter covered, and may not be contradicted by evidence of any prior agreement or contemporaneous oral agreement. The parties further intend that this Agreement constitutes the complete and exclusive statement of its terms and that no extrinsic evidence whatsoever may be introduced in any judicial or other proceeding, if any, involving this Agreement.

26. **AGENCY CONFIRMATION:** The following agency relationship(s) are hereby confirmed for this transaction:
Listing Agent: _____ is the agent of (check one):
(Print Firm Name)

☐ the Landlord exclusively; or ☐ both the Tenant and Landlord.
Leasing Agent: _____ (if not same as Listing Agent) is the agent of (check one):
(Print Firm Name)

☐ the Tenant exclusively; or ☐ the Landlord exclusively; or ☐ both the Tenant and Landlord.

27. **ACKNOWLEDGEMENT:** The undersigned have read the foregoing prior to execution and acknowledge receipt of a copy.

Landlord _____ Date _____   Tenant _____ Date _____
(or authorized agent)

Landlord _____ Date _____   Tenant _____ Date _____
(or authorized agent)

This form is available for use by the entire real estate industry. The use of this form is not intended to identify the user as a REALTOR®. REALTOR® is a registered collective membership mark which may be used only by real estate licensees who are members of the NATIONAL ASSOCIATION OF REALTORS® and who subscribe to its Code of Ethics.

OFFICE USE ONLY
Reviewed by Broker or Designee _____
Date _____

Page 2 of _____ Pages.

its regardless of what they are called by the landlord and tenant.

The total security deposit in a residential lease cannot exceed twice the monthly rental payment for unfurnished units, or three times the monthly rental payment for furnished units. However, the landlord can demand a security deposit equal to six months' rent or more if the term of the lease is six months or longer.

Within three weeks after the termination of the lease, the landlord must return the deposit to the tenant, or send a letter explaining the reason for not returning any portion of the deposit. If the deposit or a written explanation is not given to the tenant within the three-week period, the landlord is liable for $600 in statutory damages, in addition to actual damages. The fact that a deposit is labeled "nonrefundable" (for example, "nonrefundable cleaning deposit") has no bearing on this requirement; the landlord must still return the payment or give a written explanation within two weeks.

Inspection and Entry. Most leases give the landlord the right to enter and inspect the leased premises during the lease term. California law provides that a residential landlord may enter the premises to make necessary repairs or improvements, but only on 24 hours' notice to the tenant, unless such notice is impractical (i.e., in an emergency). The tenant may not unreasonably refuse the landlord's legitimate requests to enter the premises for inspection purposes, for necessary repairs or services, or to show the premises to prospective buyers or tenants.

Option to Purchase or Renew. A lease may contain a provision which gives the tenant an option to renew the lease or purchase the property. Most options require the tenant to give notice of his or her intention to exercise the option on or before a specific date.

Manager's Name and Address. If a residential property contains more than two rental units, the name and address of the manager of the rental units must be stated in the lease. (The same information must also be posted in at least two locations on the premises, including all elevators.)

Repairs and Improvements. A tenant is not ordinarily required to make any repairs to the leased property. However, the tenant must return the property to the landlord in the same condition as it was in at the beginning of the lease term (though allowances are made for normal wear and tear). The landlord is typically responsible for making any necessary repairs to the common areas, such as stairs, hallways, or elevators. A residential landlord is required to maintain the property in habitable condition (see below).

Neither the tenant nor the landlord is obligated to improve the property. The tenant may make improvements, which often can be removed by the tenant when the lease expires. (See Chapter 1 for a discussion of fixtures.)

Transferring Leased Property

A landlord can sell the leased property during the term of the lease, but the buyer takes title subject to the lease. This means the buyer must honor the lease for the remainder of its term.

The tenant can also transfer his or her leasehold estate to another party, through assignment, subleasing, or novation. The tenant has the right to assign or sublease without the landlord's consent, unless the lease provides otherwise. A novation always requires the landlord's consent.

In an **assignment**, the tenant transfers the entire unexpired term of the lease.

Example: Landlord leases the premises to Tenant for a period starting January 1, 1992 and ending June 30, 1996. On July 1, 1992, Tenant leases the

Fig.8.8 Methods of transferring a leasehold estate

Transferring Leased Property	
Assignment	Tenant transfers the entire unexpired term of the lease
Sublease	Tenant transfers less than the unexpired term of the lease
Novation	The lease is replaced with a new agreement, or one party is replaced by another party; previously existing liability is extinguished

premises to XYZ Corp. for a term starting July 1, 1992 and ending June 30, 1996. The agreement between Tenant and XYZ is an assignment, because the transfer is for the balance of the unexpired term.

The assignee becomes liable for paying the rent to the landlord (the original lessor) and the assignor (the original tenant) becomes secondarily liable for the rent. This means that the assignee has the primary responsibility for paying the rent, but the original tenant is not fully released from the duty to pay.

A **sublease** is a transfer of the leasehold estate for a period shorter than the unexpired term. The original tenant retains part of the leasehold estate.

Example: Landlord leases the premises to Tenant for a period starting January 1, 1992 and ending June 30, 1996. Tenant, on July 1, 1992, leases the premises to a subtenant for a period starting July 1, 1992, through June 30, 1995, reserving the last year for himself. This agreement is a sublease because the tenant has transferred less than the balance of term.

The sublessee is liable for rent to the sublessor (the original tenant), rather than to the landlord.

The tenant/sublessor remains liable for the rent to the landlord.

A **novation** occurs when a new contract is created and the old contract is extinguished. When an existing lease is replaced with a new lease between the same parties, or a new lease between different parties, it has been novated. The purpose of a novation is to terminate the liability of the tenant under the terms of the original lease.

Termination of a Lease

A lease may be terminated before the end of its term in a variety of ways.

Surrender. A landlord and tenant may mutually agree to terminate a lease. This is called surrender.

Breach of the Implied Covenant of Quiet Enjoyment. In every lease there is an implied covenant of quiet enjoyment. This is the landlord's implied promise to refrain from unlawfully interfering with the tenant's possession of the leased property, and that no third party will lawfully claim a right to possess the property. The tenant is guaranteed the exclusive possession and quiet enjoyment of the property.

The covenant of quiet enjoyment is breached when the tenant is wrongfully evicted from the leased property. There are two types of eviction: actual and constructive.

Actual eviction occurs when the landlord actually expels the tenant from the property. **Constructive eviction** occurs when the landlord causes or permits a substantial interference with the tenant's possession of the property. For example, failure to provide heat in the wintertime has been found to result in constructive eviction.

Breach of the Implied Warranty of Habitability. In all residential leases, the landlord impliedly guarantees that the premises meet all building and housing code regulations which affect health and safety on the premises. If the premises do not meet these criteria, then the tenant must notify the landlord of the defective condition, and the landlord must correct the defect within certain time limits prescribed by statute. If the landlord fails to make the required repairs, the tenant can terminate the lease. Or if the landlord takes legal action to evict the tenant for nonpayment of rent, the tenant can use the uninhabitable condition of the premises as a defense.

Failure to Pay Rent. The tenant has a duty to pay rent as required by the terms of the lease. If, however, the tenant fails to pay the rent, the leasehold estate is not automatically terminated. The landlord is required by statute to give notice of nonpayment to the tenant. After receiving notice, if the tenant still fails to pay, the landlord may bring a court action for **unlawful detainer** to evict the tenant.

If the court finds the tenant in default, it may issue a **writ of possession**, which requires the tenant to move out peaceably or else be forcibly removed by the sheriff.

Although unlawful detainer actions are given priority on the court's docket, the process of legal eviction is often slow. However, landlords should be warned against taking matters into their own hands. A landlord who tries a "self-help" eviction (forcing the tenant out with threats, or by cutting off the utilities) instead of the legal process may end up defending a costly lawsuit.

Illegal or Unauthorized Use. If the tenant uses the premises in an illegal manner, such as in violation of the zoning code, the landlord may demand that the tenant cease the illegal activity or leave the premises. Also, if the tenant uses the premises in a manner not authorized by the lease, the tenant has violated the agreement and the landlord may terminate the lease.

Destruction of the Premises. Unless there is a provision to the contrary, if the lease is for the use of the land and any improvements (buildings) on the land, or for the use of an entire building, the destruction of the building will not terminate the lease. The destruction of a building does not prevent the use and enjoyment of the land, and therefore the purpose of the lease is not frustrated. The tenant is not relieved from the duty to pay the rent to the end of the rental period. If, however, the lease is only for a part of a building, such as an office, apartment, or commercial space, the destruction of the building frustrates the entire purpose of the lease, so the tenant will be released from the duty to pay rent.

Condemnation. Condemnation of property can also result in premature termination of a lease. (See Chapter 4 for a discussion of condemnation.)

Types of Leases

There are five major types of leases: the fixed lease, the graduated lease, the percentage lease, the net lease, and the ground lease.

Sometimes called a "flat," "straight," or "gross" lease, a **fixed lease** provides for a fixed rental amount. The tenant is obligated to pay a fixed sum of money, and the landlord is obligated to pay all of the property's operating expenses: utilities, maintenance costs, taxes, and insurance. This type of lease is most commonly found in residential apartment rentals.

A **net lease** requires the tenant to pay the landlord a fixed rent, plus some or all of the operating expenses.

A **graduated lease** is similar to a fixed lease, but it provides for periodic increases in the rent, usually set at specific future dates and often based on the cost-of-living index. These increases are made possible by the inclusion of an **escalation clause**. This type of lease is also called a "step-up lease."

A **percentage lease** is common in the commercial setting, especially for properties located in shopping centers. The rent is based on a percentage of the or net income from the tenant's business. Typically, the lease provides for a minimum rent plus a percentage of the tenant's business income above a stated minimum.

When a tenant leases land and agrees to construct a building on that land, it is called a **ground lease**. Ground leases are common in metropolitan areas; they are usually long-term, in order to make the construction of buildings worth the tenant's while.

Chapter Summary

1. Brokers and their licensees must have written employment agreements (broker/salesperson agreements) that cover all the basic terms of their relationship.

2. A property owner uses a listing agreement to hire a broker to find a buyer who is ready, willing, and able to buy the owner's property on the owner's terms. There are three different types of listing agreements: exclusive right to sell listings, exclusive agency listings, and open listings. The exclusive right to sell listing is the type most commonly used.

3. Listing agreements must include a property description, the terms of sale the property owner is willing to accept, the amount or rate of the commission, and the conditions under which the commission is earned. Most listing agreements also include a safety clause, which entitles the broker to a commission if the property is sold after the listing expires to anyone the broker negotiated with during the listing term.

4. A deposit receipt form serves as the buyer's offer to purchase, as the receipt for the buyer's good faith deposit, and, when it is signed by the seller, as the binding purchase and sale agreement between the buyer and the seller. It may also be the only written agreement to pay compensation to the broker. The deposit receipt must identify the parties, describe the property, and set forth the price, the method of payment, and the closing date.

5. Under a land contract, the buyer (vendee) purchases the property on an installment basis. The seller (vendor) retains legal title to the property while the contract is being paid off, but the vendee has the right to possess the property during that period. When the vendee has paid the full purchase price, the vendor delivers the deed to the vendee.

6. In an option to purchase, the optionee has a right to buy the property at a specified price (but is under no obligation to buy), and the optionor is not allowed to sell the property to anyone other than the optionee during the option period.

7. A landlord-tenant relationship is created with a lease. A lease must be in writing if it will not be fully performed within a year after the contract is made. A valid lease also requires consideration (usually the rental payment), the signature of the lessor, and a description of the property. Most leases include a security deposit requirement, a limitation on the use of the premises, and a clause allowing entry and inspection by the landlord.

Key Terms

Broker/salesperson agreement—The written employment agreement between a broker and a salesperson licensed to work under the broker.

Listing agreement—A written employment agreement between a property owner and a real estate broker, in which the owner hires the broker to find a buyer who is ready, willing, and able to buy the owner's property on the owner's terms.

Exclusive agency listing—A type of listing that requires the property owner to pay the broker a commission when the property is sold during the listing term by anyone other than the seller. If the seller finds the buyer, the broker is not entitled to a commission.

Exclusive right to sell listing—A type of listing that requires the property owner to pay the broker a commission if the property is sold during the listing term, no matter who sells the property.

Open listing—A type of listing that requires the property owner to pay a commission to the broker only if the broker is the one who actually negotiates an agreement with the ready, willing, and able buyer.

Procuring cause—The person who is primarily responsible for bringing about a sale.

Net listing—A type of listing in which the commission is any amount received from the sale over and above the "net" required by the seller.

Safety clause—A provision in a listing agreement that obligates the seller to pay a commission if the property is sold within a certain period after the listing expires to someone the broker negotiated with during the listing period. Also called an extender clause.

Deposit receipt—A binding contract between a buyer and a seller of real property, and also the receipt for the buyer's good faith deposit.

Contingency clause—A contract clause which provides that unless some specified event occurs, the contract is null and void.

Land contract—A contract for the sale of real property in which the buyer pays the purchase price in installments; the buyer (vendee) takes possession of the property immediately, but the seller

(Vendor) retains legal title until the full price has been paid.

Option agreement—An agreement that gives one party the right to buy or lease the other party's property at a set price for a certain period of time.

Lease—A contract in which one party (the tenant or lessee) pays the other (the landlord or lessor) rent in exchange for the possession of real estate. Also called a rental agreement.

Unlawful detainer—A court action brought by a landlord to evict a defaulting tenant.

Quiz: Chapter 8
Types of Real Estate Contracts

1. The type of listing that provides for payment of a commission to the listing broker regardless of who sells the property is:

   a) an open listing
   b) an exclusive agency listing
   c) an exclusive right to sell listing
   d) a net listing

2. The type of listing that provides for the payment of a commission to the listing broker only if he or she was the procuring cause of the sale is:

   a) an open listing
   b) an exclusive agency listing
   c) an exclusive right to sell listing
   d) a net listing

3. The type of listing that provides for the payment of a commission that consists of any proceeds from the sale over a specified amount is:

   a) an open listing
   b) an exclusive agency listing
   c) an exclusive right to sell listing
   d) a net listing

4. The type of listing that provides for the payment of a commission to the listing broker if anyone other than the seller finds the buyer is:

   a) an open listing
   b) an exclusive agency listing
   c) an exclusive right to sell listing
   d) a net listing

5. The listing broker has negotiated an offer from a ready, willing, and able buyer that matches the seller's terms of sale set forth in the listing agreement. Which of the following is true?

   a) The seller is required to accept the offer and pay the listing broker a commission
   b) The seller is required to accept the offer, but not required to pay the listing broker a commission
   c) The listing broker has earned the commission, whether or not the seller accepts the offer
   d) The listing broker has not earned the commission unless this is an exclusive agency listing

6. A safety clause provides that:

   a) the broker is entitled to a commission whether or not he or she is the procuring cause

b) the buyer must share the cost of the broker's commission

c) the seller warrants the safety of the premises

d) the broker is entitled to a commission if the property is sold after the listing expires to someone the broker previously showed the property to

7. A deposit receipt serves as:

a) the buyer's receipt for the good faith deposit

b) the buyer's offer to purchase

c) a binding contract between the buyer and the seller

d) All of the above

8. A deposit receipt should state:

a) only the purchase price, leaving the other terms to be worked out in the final contract

b) the listing price as well as the purchase price

c) the total purchase price, the method of payment, and the basic financing terms

d) the seller's reasons for selling the property

9. A provision in the deposit receipt states that it will not be a binding contract unless the buyer can obtain financing. This provision is called:

a) a contingency clause

b) a defeasibility clause

c) a bump clause

d) an escrow clause

10. Under a land contract, the vendee initially gets:

a) possession but not title

b) title but not possession

c) possession and title, but not the right to transfer ownership

d) the right to novate the contract without the seller's permission

11. To be binding, a lease must be signed by the:

a) broker

b) beneficiary

c) landlord

d) tenant

12. When leased property is sold, the lease:

a) automatically terminates

b) is breached by constructive eviction

c) must be renegotiated by the tenant and the new owner

d) remains binding on the new owner

13. An oral lease may be valid if it is for less than:

a) one year

b) two years

c) three years

d) four years

14. You have a three-year lease on some commercial

operty. In the first year, your rental payment is $2,000 per month. In the second year, you must pay $2,400 a month, and in the third year, you must pay $2,800 a month. You have a:

a) gross lease
b) graduated lease
c) triple lease
d) straight lease

15. When a tenant assigns a lease, the assignee (new tenant) becomes:

a) secondarily responsible for payment of the rent
b) the subtenant
c) primarily responsible for payment of the rent
d) None of the above

Answer Key

1.c) The exclusive right to sell listing obligates the seller to pay the listing broker a commission if the property sells during the listing period, regardless of who brings about the sale.

2.a) Open listings only obligate the seller to pay a commission to the listing broker if he or she was the actual procuring cause of the sale.

3.d) A net listing is a way of determining the amount of the commission, rather than the circumstances under which a commission is owed.

4.b) An exclusive agency listing obligates the seller to pay the listing broker a commission if any agent (anyone other than the seller) sells the property.

5.c) When the broker presents an offer from a ready, willing, and able buyer that matches the seller's terms of sale, the broker has earned the commission, whether or not the seller accepts the offer. The seller is under no obligation to accept the offer.

6.d) A safety clause entitles the broker to a commission if the property is sold within a certain time after the listing expires to someone he or she introduced to the property or negotiated with during the listing period.

7.d) The deposit receipt is used to set forth the buyer's offer, and also serves as the receipt for the good faith deposit. If the seller signs the form, it becomes a binding contract.

8.c) A deposit receipt should state all the terms of sale, including the total purchase price, the method of payment, and the terms on which the buyer will finance the purchase. It is the parties' final contract, not a preliminary agreement.

9.a) A provision that makes a deposit receipt contingent on the occurrence of a certain event is called a contingency clause.

10.a) Under a land contract, the vendee (buyer) gets possession of the land right away, but does not acquire title until the purchase price is paid in full.

11.c) Though it is wise to have both the landlord and the tenant sign the lease, only the landlord needs to sign in order for it to be valid. By taking possession of the leased property and paying the rent, a tenant is presumed to have accepted the lease.

Chapter 9

Real Estate Finance: Principles

 Outline

I. The Government's Role in Real Estate Finance
   A. U.S. Treasury
   B. Federal Reserve System
   C. Other government agencies
II. Finance Markets and Supply and Demand
   A. Primary market
   B. Secondary market
III. Lenders in the Primary Market
   A. Savings and loan associations
   B. Commercial banks
   C. Savings banks
   D. Mortgage companies
   E. Credit unions
   F. Private lenders
IV. Real Estate Finance Documents
   A. Promissory notes
   B. Security instruments
      1. mortgages
      2. deeds of trust
   C. Security instrument provisions
   D. Foreclosure procedures
   E. Types of mortgage loans
   F. Land contracts
V. Finance Disclosure Requirements
   A. Truth in Lending Act
   B. Purchase Money Loan Disclosure Law
   C. Mortgage Loan Broker Law

 Chapter Overview

Finance— lending and borrowing money— is considered by many to be the core of the real estate industry. If financing were not available, buyers would have to pay cash for their homes, and very few people could afford to do so. Thus, once a purchase and sale agreement has been signed, in most cases the next step is to arrange financing for the transaction. Real estate agents often help their customers with this process, so they need a thorough understanding of real estate finance. This chapter provides background information about how the government influences real estate finance, who lends money to finance home purchases, and how mortgages and other financing instruments work. Chapter 10 explains the loan underwriting process, and Chapter 11 explains the major loan programs (conventional, FHA, VA, and Cal-Vet).

The Government's Role in Real Estate Finance

The government influences real estate finance through its **monetary policy** and its **fiscal policy**: the control it exerts over the supply and cost of money, and the way in which the national debt is financed.

Economic stability is directly tied to the supply of and demand for money. If money is plentiful and can be borrowed cheaply (that is, interest rates are low), increased economic activity is usually the result. On the other hand, if funds are scarce or expensive to borrow, an economic slowdown will result.

Thus, manipulation of the availability and cost of money can do much to achieve economic balance, and certain federal agencies are given the power to exercise this kind of control. The two most prominent agencies are the United States Treasury and the Federal Reserve System.

United States Treasury

The United States Treasury is the nation's fiscal manager; it is responsible for managing the federal government's finances, including the national debt. Treasury funds come from a number of sources, but the largest source is personal and business income taxes.

When the federal government spends more money than it takes in, a shortfall called the **federal deficit** results. It is the Treasury's responsibility to borrow enough money to cover the deficit. It does this by issuing interest-bearing securities that are backed by the U.S. government. The securities can be issued for less than one year (Treasury bills), from one to five years (Treasury notes), or from five to ten years (Treasury certificates). Private investors often prefer to invest in these government securities instead of other investments because of their low risk.

Economic theory maintains that when the United States government borrows money, it competes with private industry for available investment funds. Heavy government borrowing puts a drain on the number of dollars in circulation, which leads to an economic slowdown. The greater the federal deficit, the more money the government has to borrow and the greater the effect on the economy. On the other hand, a small federal deficit translates into limited government borrowing and a more substantial supply of investment funds for private industry.

The government's taxation policies also affect the supply of and demand for money. When taxes are low, taxpayers have more money to lend and invest. When taxes are high, taxpayers not only have less money to lend or invest, they are also more likely to invest what money they do have in tax-exempt securities instead of taxable investments. Since real estate and real estate mortgages are taxable investments, this has a significant impact on the residential finance industry.

The Federal Reserve System

The Federal Reserve System was established in 1913 under the Federal Reserve Act. Frequently referred to as "the Fed," it is the nation's central banking system. The Fed is responsible for regulating commercial banks, and it also oversees implementation of the Truth in Lending Act (discussed later in this chapter). Another function of the Fed—perhaps its most important one—is setting and implementing the government's monetary policy.

The major objectives of monetary policy are high employment, economic growth, price stability, interest rate stability, and stability in financial and foreign exchange markets. Although these goals are interrelated, we are most concerned with the Federal Reserve policies that affect the availability and cost of borrowed money (interest rates), since those have the most direct impact on the real estate industry.

The Federal Reserve System consists of 12 Federal Reserve Banks and their 24 branches, which are situated throughout the United States in 12 Federal Reserve districts. Over 5,000 commercial banks are members of the Federal Reserve. The entire system is regulated by a seven-member Board of Governors in Washington, D.C.; the governors are appointed by the President of the United States and approved by the Senate.

Fig.9.1 Federal Reserve districts

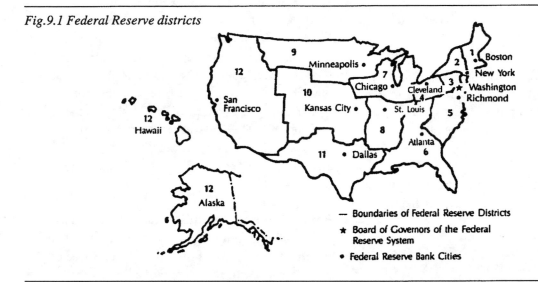

The Fed uses three tools to implement its monetary policy and influence the economy:

- reserve requirements,
- the federal discount rate, and
- open market operations.

Reserve Requirements. A commercial bank's reserve requirements are the percentages of deposits the bank is required to maintain on deposit at the Federal Reserve Bank. Reserve requirements help prevent financial panics (a "run on the bank") by assuring depositors that their funds are safe and accessible; the bank will always have enough money available to meet unusual customer demand.

Reserve requirements also give the Fed some control over the growth of credit. By increasing reserve requirements, the Fed can reduce the amount of money banks have available to lend. On the other hand, a reduction in reserve requirements frees more money for investment or lending. An increase in reserve requirements, then, tends to decrease available loan funds and increase interest rates. Conversely, a decrease in reserve requirements tends to increase available loan funds and decrease interest rates.

Discount Rate. A member of the Federal Reserve System can borrow money from one of the Federal Reserve Banks. As with most loans, the member bank has to pay interest on the money it borrows. The federal discount rate is the interest rate a bank is charged when it borrows from the Fed. When the Fed increases the discount rate, banks usually start charging higher interest rates to their loan customers. They have to charge more interest on the money they lend if they have to pay more interest on the money they borrow. On the other hand, if the Fed lowers the discount rate, banks are likely to lower the interest rates they charge, too.

Open Market Operations. The Fed also buys and sells government securities. These transactions are called open market operations. Open market operations are the Fed's chief method of controlling the money supply, and with the money supply, inflation and interest rates. Only money in circulation is considered part of the money supply, so actions by the Fed that put money into circulation increase the money supply, and actions that take money out of circulation decrease the money supply.

When the Fed buys government securities, it increases the money supply. The Fed may pay for the securities by cash, check, or (if it is buying them from a member bank) simply by crediting the bank's reserves with the Fed. Any of these actions puts more money in circulation. When the Fed sells government securities, the money the buyer uses to pay for the securities is taken out of circulation, decreasing the money supply.

Other things being equal (which they seldom are), interest rates tend to fall with increases in the money supply, and to rise with decreases in the money supply.

Other Government Agencies

There are several other government agencies that influence real estate finance.

Federal Home Loan Bank System. The Federal Home Loan Bank System serves many of the same functions in regard to savings and loan associations that the Federal Reserve System serves in regard to banks. It has much less impact on the national economy than the Federal Reserve, however, since commercial banks control a much greater volume of deposits than savings and loans. The Federal Home Loan Bank System is headed by the Federal Housing Finance Board.

Federal Deposit Insurance Corporation. The FDIC was created through the Bank Act of 1933 to insure bank deposits against bank insolvency. The Federal Savings and Loan Insurance Corporation (FSLIC) was created to fulfill a similar function for savings and loan deposits. In 1989, FSLIC was eliminated and the FDIC was reorganized (see the discussion of the savings and loan crisis and FIRREA later in this chapter). The FDIC now controls two separate insurance funds: the Bank Insurance Fund (BIF), which insures deposits in commercial banks and savings banks, and the Savings Association Insurance Fund (SAIF), which insures deposits in savings and loans.

Department of Housing and Urban Development (HUD). HUD is a federal cabinet department, and its responsibilities are enormous. Urban renewal and rehabilitation projects, public housing, and FHA-insured loans are just some of the programs managed by HUD. It is also responsible for enforcement of the Federal Fair Housing Act (see Chapter 19). The Federal Housing Administration (discussed in Chapter 11) and Ginnie Mae (discussed in the next section of this chapter) are both part of HUD.

Farmers Home Administration. The Farmers Home Administration (FmHA) is a federal agency within the Department of Agriculture; it was established in 1946. In some cases the FmHA makes loans to ranchers and farmers who are unable to obtain financing from private sources. In other cases the agency insures loans made by private lenders—loans the lenders would consider too risky without the FmHA's insurance. FmHA loans may be used to purchase or develop farms, build or rehabilitate farm homes and other farm buildings, or develop rural housing for the elderly.

Cooperative Farm Credit System. Originated in 1916 as part of the Federal Farm Loan Act, the Farm Credit System is a cooperative that works to provide financial assistance to ranchers, farmers, and others in rural areas.

The Finance Markets and Supply and Demand

The real estate market is cyclical: it goes through active periods followed by slumps. These changes may be dramatic, like those that occurred in 1979–1980 and again in recent years, or they may be more moderate. These periodic shifts in the level of activity in the real estate market are called **real estate cycles**. They can be local or regional.

These cycles occur in reaction to the forces of supply and demand. When demand for a product exceeds the supply, the price for the product tends to rise, and the price increase stimulates more production. As production increases, more of the demand is satisfied, until eventually the supply outstrips demand and a buyer's market is created. At that point, prices fall and production tapers off until demand catches up with supply, and the cycle begins again.

In a healthy economy, supply and demand are more or less in balance. This is the ideal; in reality, the forces affecting supply and demand are constantly changing, and so is the balance between them. But as long as supply and demand are reasonably close, the economy functions well. When supply far exceeds demand, or vice versa, the economy suffers.

Because real estate cycles are economically disruptive, the federal government has tried to moderate their severity and duration. This has been done primarily through the creation of a national secondary market that limits the adverse effects of local economic circumstances on real estate markets.

The Primary Market

There are two "markets" that supply the funds available for real estate loans: the primary market and the secondary market. The **primary market** is the most familiar one; it is the local finance market, made up of the various lending institutions in a community. For example, if the Browns want to borrow money to finance the purchase of a home, they will seek a loan in the primary market—perhaps from a mutual savings bank or a savings and loan association.

The original source of funds for the primary market is the savings of individuals and businesses in the local area. For instance, a community savings and loan association is a typical lender in the primary market. It gets its funds from the savings deposits of members of the community. It will use the savings to make real estate loans to members of that same community.

The local economy has a significant effect on the amount of funds a local lender has available. For example, when employment is high, consumers are more likely to borrow money for cars, televisions, vacations, or homes. Businesses expand and borrow to finance their growth. Banks and other lending institutions increase their lending activities to meet the demand, but at the same time, fewer people are saving. This decrease in deposits and corresponding increase in loan demand steadily depletes the funds available for lending. If local lenders could not attract money from other parts of the country to help meet the demand, their funds would be exhausted and the community's economy severely disrupted. Of course, the reverse is also true. When an area is in an economic slump, consumers are more inclined to save than to borrow. Businesses suspend plans for growth. The result is a drop in the demand for money, and the lending institutions' deposits grow.

From a lender's point of view, either too little or too much money on deposit is cause for concern. In the first case, with little money to lend, a lender's primary source of income is affected. In the second case, the lender is paying interest to its depositors, and if it is unable to reinvest the deposited funds quickly, it will lose money.

To get additional funds for real estate lending, a lender may sell the mortgage loans it has already made. For instance, a local savings and loan may decide to sell its mortgages on the secondary market. This is a national market, in which mortgages secured by real estate in all parts of the United States are bought and sold.

The Secondary Market

The availability of funds in the primary market (the ability of a particular lender to lend money to prospective borrowers) depends a great deal on the existence of the national secondary market. As explained above, a particular lender may have either too much or too little money to lend, depending on conditions in the local economy. It is the secondary market that provides balance by transferring funds from areas where there is an excess to areas where there is a shortage.

The secondary market consists of private investors and government agencies that buy and sell real estate mortgage loans. A real estate loan is essentially an investment, just like stocks or bonds. The lender commits its funds to making a loan in the expectation of a return on its investment in the form of interest payments. Real estate loans can be bought and sold just like other investments. The value of the loan is influenced by the rate of return on the loan compared to the market rate of return, as well as the degree of risk associated with the loan (the likelihood of default).

Investors are willing to buy mortgage loans on the secondary market (without ever meeting the borrowers or seeing the properties) because uniform underwriting standards have been established. Underwriting standards are the criteria lenders use to evaluate a loan applicant and the property offered as security, to determine if the loan would be a good investment or would involve too great a risk of default. (This is discussed in more detail in Chapter 10.) A lender generally cannot sell a mortgage on the secondary market unless the loan conforms to the secondary market's underwriting standards. The uniform standards impose a kind of quality control, assuring investors that the loans they're buying are reasonably safe investments.

The secondary market has a stabilizing effect on local mortgage markets. Lenders are willing to commit themselves to long-term real estate loans even when local funds are scarce, because they can raise more funds by liquidating their loans on the secondary market.

The major players in the secondary market are three government-sponsored agencies:

- the Federal National Mortgage Association (FNMA or "Fannie Mae"),
- the Government National Mortgage Association (GNMA or "Ginnie Mae"), and
- the Federal Home Loan Mortgage Corporation (FHLMC or "Freddie Mac").

Federal National Mortgage Association. The Federal National Mortgage Association, often referred to as "Fannie Mae," started out as a federal agency in 1938. Its original purpose was to provide a secondary market for FHA-insured and VA-guaranteed loans; today it buys conventional loans as well.

In 1968, Congress reorganized Fannie Mae as a private corporation, and Fannie Mae common stock was offered over-the-counter to the general public. At the same time, Congress created a new federal agency, the Government National Mortgage Association (Ginnie Mae), to assume Fannie Mae's governmental responsibilities.

Government National Mortgage Association. Ginnie Mae is one of many federal agencies that make up the Department of Housing and Urban Development (HUD). Ginnie Mae was given the responsibility of managing and eventually liquidating the remaining Fannie Mae loans. Today, Ginnie Mae provides government guarantees for securities based on pools of FHA and VA mortgages. The agency also purchases certain types of loans that are socially beneficial but not especially attractive to private investors, such as loans for urban renewal projects and housing for the elderly.

Federal Home Loan Mortgage Corporation. The Federal Home Loan Mortgage Corporation, called "Freddie Mac," was created by the Emergency Home Finance Act of 1970. Its original purpose was to assist savings and loan associations (which were hit particularly hard by the recession of 1969-70) by buying their conventional loans. Freddie Mac is now authorized to buy conventional, FHA, and VA loans from any type of lender.

Fig.9.2 Relationship between the primary and secondary markets. By selling mortgage loans on the secondary market, lenders obtain funds to make more loans.

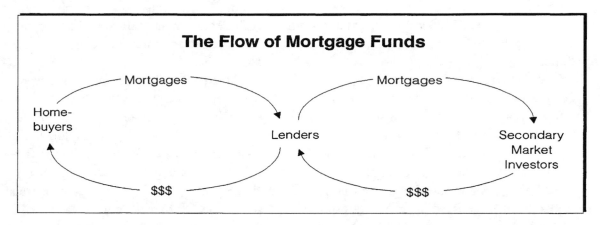

The Flow of Mortgage Funds

Lenders in the Primary Market

There are several major sources of residential financing in the primary market. Most home purchase loans are made by one of these four types of lenders:

- savings and loan associations,
- commercial banks,
- savings banks, and
- mortgage companies.

There are other types of lenders that make residential loans either on a smaller scale or in a different way. But prospective homebuyers ordinarily apply to one of these four major lenders for financing, and it is their lending practices that have the greatest impact on real estate transactions.

Savings and Loan Associations

Savings and loan associations (S&Ls) are sometimes called "thrift institutions" or simply "thrifts." An S&L is chartered (authorized to do business) by either the federal government or a state government.

Savings and loans started out in the nineteenth century strictly as residential real estate lenders. Over the years they carried on their original function, investing the majority of their assets in purchase loans for single-family homes. By the mid-1950s, they dominated local residential mortgage markets, becoming the nation's largest single source of funds for financing homes.

Many factors contributed to the dominance of savings and loans; one of the most important was that home purchase loans had become long-term loans, usually having a 30-year term. Since most of the funds held by S&Ls were long-term deposits, S&Ls felt comfortable making many long-term home loans.

In the late 1970s and early 1980s, things changed. Deregulation made it difficult for S&Ls to compete with other investments. Some S&Ls tried new types of investments that were much more risky than local single-family home loans, and sometimes the risks did not pay off. With economic slumps and management mistakes (and occasionally even fraud), there was a dramatic increase in the failure rate of S&Ls. Hundreds of institutions became insolvent. To protect S&L depositors, the federal government had to appropriate money in its budget (that is, tax dollars) to bail out the savings and loan industry. The ultimate cost is expected to be well over a hundred billion dollars.

In 1989, at the height of the savings and loan crisis, Congress passed the Financial Institutions Reform, Recovery, and Enforcement Act (FIRREA) to reorganize the financial system. The act established new agencies to oversee the industry (the Federal Housing Finance Board, the Office of Thrift Supervision, and the Savings Association Insurance Fund). FIRREA also formed the Resolution Trust Corporation (RTC), which managed insolvent thrifts, selling them or closing them and disposing of their assets. Some of the act's provisions encouraged S&Ls to return to their traditional emphasis on residential lending.

Although FIRREA encourages savings and loans to focus on home mortgages, the total effect of regulatory changes over the years has been to reduce the number of distinctions between S&Ls and banks. From an ordinary customer's point of view, the institutions are now quite similar.

Because of insolvencies and mergers, there are fewer savings and loan associations now than there were before the S&L crisis. S&Ls no longer dominate the residential finance market as they once did; both commercial banks and mortgage companies have increased their market share significantly over the past few years. However, it is not yet clear whether this is a permanent change. There are many financially sound savings and loans, and they are expected to continue to play an important role in residential finance.

Commercial Banks

A commercial bank is either a national bank, chartered by the federal government, or a state bank, chartered by a state government. Commercial banks are the largest source of investment funds in the United States. As their name implies, they were traditionally oriented toward commercial lending activities, supplying capital for business ventures and construction activities on a comparatively short-term basis.

In the past, residential mortgages were not a major part of commercial banks' business. That was partly because most of their deposits were demand deposits (checking accounts), and the government limited the amount of long-term investments the banks could make. It was also a business decision; since regulations allowed commercial banks (unlike S&Ls) to make a wide variety of other types of loans, the banks were not especially interested in residential mortgages.

Although they haven't changed as much as savings and loans, commercial banks have changed significantly in the past two decades. Starting in the 1970s, banks began accepting more and more long-term deposits; demand deposits now represent a much smaller share of banks' total deposits than they once did.

While banks have continued to emphasize commercial loans, they have also diversified their lending, with a substantial increase in personal loans and residential mortgages. Today a commercial bank might have as much as one-fifth of its assets invested in mortgages. That may not sound like a great deal in comparison to savings and loans, which often have almost three-quarters of their assets invested in mortgages. Yet because commercial banks have many more assets than savings and loans, their share of the residential mortgage market has been as large as or larger than the S&Ls' share in recent years.

Mortgage Companies

Mortgage companies have been a rapidly growing force in residential lending. Unlike banks and S&Ls, mortgage companies are not depository institutions. They function more in the role of intermediaries than as sources of lending capital.

Mortgage companies often act on behalf of large investors such as life insurance companies and pension funds. These investors control vast amounts of capital in the form of insurance premiums and employer contributions to employee pensions. This money is generally not subject to sudden withdrawal, which makes it well suited to investment in long-term mortgages. Since these large investors often operate on a national scale, they have neither the time nor the resources to understand the particular risks of local real estate markets or to deal with the day-to-day management of their loans. So they hire local **loan correspondents**. A loan correspondent lends an investor's money to homebuyers and then services the loans in exchange for servicing fees. In some cases a bank or an S&L will act as a loan correspondent, but mortgage companies have specialized in this role.

Mortgage companies also borrow money from banks, use it to originate mortgages, then package the mortgages and sell them to the secondary market and other private investors. In many cases, insurance companies, pensions funds, and other large investors now simply buy loans from mortgage companies instead of using them as loan correspondents.

Unlike banks and S&Ls, mortgage companies do not keep any of the loans they make. The loans are either made on behalf of an investor or else immediately sold to an investor.

Mortgage companies are sometimes called mortgage bankers. The term "mortgage banker" is often confused with "mortgage broker," but there is a distinction between them. A **mortgage broker** simply negotiates loans, bringing borrowers together with lenders in exchange for a commission. Once the loan has been arranged, the mortgage broker's involvement ends. **Mortgage bankers**, on the other hand, originate loans on behalf of an investor and then service the loans to the end of their terms, in exchange for servicing fees. Although mortgage companies may act as mortgage brokers, for the most part they are mortgage bankers.

Credit Unions

Credit unions are depository institutions, like banks and S&Ls. But unlike banks and S&Ls, credit unions usually serve only members of a particular group; for example, the members of a union or a professional association, or the employees of a large company.

In the United States, the first credit unions were established at the beginning of the twentieth century. They specialized in small, personal loans (often unsecured). Since this type of loan was generally not available from banks or savings and loans, small borrowers had previously turned to pawn shops and underworld loan sharks. Credit unions provided an alternative.

In recent years, many credit unions have emphasized home equity loans. A **home equity loan** is a mortgage on the borrower's equity in the home he or she already owns. These are generally short-term loans. The deregulation of financial institutions in the early 1980s allowed credit unions to begin making long-term home purchase loans for the first time. Although they are expected to expand their role as a source of residential financing, it is unlikely that they will take a significant share of the market anytime soon.

Mutual Savings Banks

Traditionally, mutual savings banks (MSBs) were similar to savings and loans. They served their local communities, their customers were individuals rather than businesses, and most of their deposits were savings deposits. Although MSBs made many residential loans, they did not concentrate on them to the extent that savings and loans did.

Today savings banks offer consumers essentially the same services as commercial banks and savings and loans. Residential loans are an important part of their business.

Private Lenders

Real estate limited partnerships, real estate investment trusts (see Chapter 2), and other types of private investment groups put a great deal of money into real estate. They often finance large residential developments and commercial ventures, such as shopping centers and office buildings. They do not offer loans to individual homebuyers, however.

From the homebuyer's point of view, the most important type of private lender is the home seller. Sometimes sellers provide all the financing for the purchase of their homes, and it's even more common for sellers to supplement the financing their buyers obtain from an institutional lender. Sellers are an especially important source of financing when institutional loans are hard to come by or market interest rates are high.

Comparing Types of Lenders

At one time, financial institutions in the United States were quite specialized. It was almost as if each type of institution had its own function—its own types of deposits, its own types of services, and its own types of loans. That is no longer true. To a great extent, all of the major depository institutions can now be regarded as "financial supermarkets," offering a wide range of services and loans.

There still are differences between the types of institutions, in terms of habits and government regulations, but these generally will not affect a loan applicant who wants to finance the purchase of a home.

Real Estate Finance Documents

Once a buyer has found a lender willing to finance the transaction on acceptable terms, the buyer is required to sign the finance documents. The documents used in conjunction with most real estate loans are the promissory note and a security instru-

ment, which will either be a mortgage or a deed of trust.

In this section of the chapter, we'll look first at promissory notes, then at security instruments and foreclosure procedures, and then at some of the many types of mortgage loans. This section closes with a discussion of the land contract, a document used in some seller-financed transactions.

Promissory Notes

A promissory note is a written promise to repay a debt. One person loans another money, and the other signs a promissory note, promising to repay the loan (plus interest, in most cases). The borrower who signs the note is called the **maker**, and the lender is called the **payee**.

Basic Provisions. A promissory note states the loan amount (the **principal**), the amount of the payments, when and how the payments are to be made, and the maturity date—when the loan is to be paid in full. The note also states the interest rate, and whether it is fixed or variable.

The note usually explains the consequences of a failure to repay the loan as agreed. Real estate lenders often protect themselves with late charges, acceleration clauses, and similar provisions; these will be discussed later in this chapter.

Types of Notes. There are various types of promissory notes, classified according to the way the principal and interest is paid off. With a **straight note**, the periodic payments are interest only, and the full amount of the principal is due in a lump sum (called a balloon payment) when the loan term ends. With an **installment note**, the periodic payments include part of the principal as well as interest. If the installment note is **fully amortized**, the periodic payments are enough to pay off the entire loan, both principal and interest, by the end of the term. (Amortization is discussed in Chapter 11.)

Signing and Endorsing the Note. Though many copies of the note may be prepared, the borrower signs only one copy. This is for the borrower's protection. A promissory note is usually a **negotiable instrument**, which means the lender has the option of assigning the debt to someone else by endorsing the note. (A note is endorsed to transfer the right to payment to another party in the same way that a check is endorsed. A check is another example of a negotiable instrument.) Having only one copy of the note signed by the borrower ensures that the lender can assign the note to only one other party. If there were two or three signed copies, it would be possible to assign the note to two or three different parties, so that more than one could demand payment of the same debt from the borrower. When the debt is paid off, the signed copy is returned to the borrower marked "Paid."

To be negotiable, the note must state that it is payable either "to the order of" someone or "to bearer." To sell the note (at the secondary market level), the lender endorses it to a third party purchaser, who is called a **holder in due course**. If the endorsement names a specific holder in due course, it is called a "special endorsement." If no holder in due course is specified, the endorsement is said to be "in blank." The lender may also state that the endorsement is "without recourse." This means that the issue of future payments is strictly between the borrower and the holder in due course; the original lender will not be liable to the holder in due course if the borrower fails to pay as agreed.

Relationship between Note and Security Instrument. It is important to understand the relationship between a promissory note and a security instrument. When a person borrows money to buy real estate, in addition to signing a promissory note in favor of the lender, the borrower also signs a security instrument (either a mortgage or deed of trust). The security instrument is a contract that makes the real property collateral for the loan; it

secures the loan by creating a lien on the property. If the borrower doesn't repay the loan as agreed, the security instrument gives the lender the right to foreclose on the property.

A promissory note can be enforced even if it is not accompanied by a security instrument. If the borrower does not repay as agreed, the payee/lender can file a lawsuit and obtain a judgment against the defaulting borrower. But without a security instrument, the lender may have no way of collecting the judgment. For example, the borrower may have already sold all of his or her property, leaving nothing for the lender (now the judgment creditor) to obtain a lien against.

Security Instruments

As explained above, a security instrument is either a mortgage or a deed of trust. Before going on to discuss the differences between these documents, we should provide some historical background.

Long ago, real estate lenders actually took possession of the land used to secure their loans. In a very literal sense, lenders "held" the property that was used as collateral for a loan until the debt was repaid. During the period of indebtedness, the lender owned the land. When the debt was repaid, title and possession were returned to the borrower.

As the real estate lending business expanded, it became impractical for lenders to take physical possession of all the properties used as collateral for their loans. Gradually, borrowers were permitted to retain possession of their properties, though they still transferred the title to the lender for the term of the loan. The lender had title to the collateral until the debt was repaid, while the borrower kept the full complement of possessory rights—the right to use, lease, sell, enjoy, etc. When title to property is offered as collateral, but the borrower retains possession, it is called **hypothecation**. When title is transferred only as collateral, unaccompanied by possessory rights, it is called **legal title**, bare title, or naked title. The property rights the borrower retains (without legal title) are referred to as equitable rights or **equitable title**.

In the United States today, the execution of a mortgage or a deed of trust is still regarded as a transfer of legal title to the lender in a handful of states. Those states are called "title theory" states. However, most states (including California) now follow "lien theory." According to lien theory, execution of a mortgage or a deed of trust only creates a lien against the property; it does not transfer title. The borrower retains full title to the property throughout the term of the loan, and the lender simply has the right to foreclose the lien if the borrower defaults.

There are actually not many differences between lending and foreclosure procedures in title theory and lien theory states now; the distinction is more theoretical than practical. But when considering the rights of modern real estate lenders and borrowers, it can be useful to remember how hypothecation has evolved.

Mortgages. A mortgage is a legal document in which a property owner (called the **mortgagor**) gives another party (called the **mortgagee**) a security interest in the property. As explained above, a mortgage is usually given to provide collateral for a loan; the mortgagor is the borrower, and the mortgagee is the lender. If the borrower defaults under any of the terms of the mortgage agreement, the lender can demand repayment of the entire debt at once (see the discussion of acceleration clauses below). If the debt is not repaid, the lender can begin foreclosure proceedings.

Any interest in real estate can be mortgaged. In most cases it is the owner's fee simple estate, but lesser interests (such as mineral rights, water rights, or leasehold rights) can be mortgaged if a lender considers them of sufficient value to secure the debt.

The lender should always record the note and the mortgage document immediately after the loan is made. The mortgage does not have to be recorded to create a valid lien on the property, but without recording only the lender and borrower would know the lien exists. Other parties who acquired an interest in the property without notice of the mortgage would not be subject to it, and subsequent liens would have priority over the mortgage.

Deeds of Trust. A popular alternative to the mortgage is the deed of trust, also known as the trust deed. Though its purpose is the same as that of the mortgage—to secure the promissory note—it is different in certain respects, the most significant being the method of foreclosure. In California, the deed of trust is now the preferred security instrument because it makes foreclosure easier. Like a mortgage, a deed of trust should be recorded promptly.

There are three parties to a deed of trust: the **trustor** or **grantor** (the borrower), the **beneficiary** (the lender), and the **trustee** (a neutral third party). The terminology used in a deed of trust has its roots in title theory: the document is a "deed" conveying naked title to a trustee, who acts as a fiduciary for both borrower and lender and holds the deed "in trust" pending repayment of the debt. When the loan has been repaid, the trustee "reconveys" title to the trustor.

In spite of this terminology, in a lien theory state the deed of trust does not actually transfer title to the trustee; it simply creates a lien, and the trustor retains full title during the term of the loan. The trustee's primary role is to handle the foreclosure, if necessary (see below).

Security Instrument Provisions

There is no standard mortgage or deed of trust form, but any security instrument must contain certain provisions and should contain certain others. Most of the following provisions will be found in nearly every mortgage or deed of trust; some of them may also appear in the promissory note. In a few cases (noted below), there is a distinction between the type of provision found in a mortgage and the type found in a deed of trust.

Clause Pledging the Property. Every security instrument must include a statement expressing what the instrument is designed to do, indicating that the property is being pledged as security for the loan. This is sometimes called the mortgaging clause or the granting clause. It may include the words "grant, bargain, sell, and convey," much like a deed, even if the transaction takes place in a lien theory state, where no transfer of title occurs.

Property Description. Like a deed or any other document that transfers an interest in real estate, the security instrument must contain a complete and unambiguous description of the collateral property.

Taxes and Insurance. Security instruments invariably require the borrower to pay general real estate taxes, special assessments, and hazard insurance premiums when due. If the borrower were to allow the taxes to become delinquent or the insurance to lapse, the value of the lender's security interest could be severely diminished—by tax lien foreclosure or a fire, for example.

Property Maintenance. A security instrument also includes a provision requiring the borrower to maintain the property adequately in order to preserve its value. Obviously, the lender's security interest would be jeopardized if the borrower deliberately or carelessly caused the property to lose value.

Acceleration Clause. An acceleration clause states that if the borrower defaults, the lender has the option of declaring the entire loan balance (all the principal still owed) due and payable immediately. Sometimes this is referred to as "calling the note." If the borrower fails to pay the balance, as demanded, the lender can sue on the note or foreclose the lien.

An acceleration clause is likely to appear in both the promissory note and in the security instrument.

Fig.9.3 Promissory note

Promissory Note

FOR VALUE RECEIVED, Maker promises to pay to the order of _____, or to Bearer,

THE SUM OF $_____
PAID AS FOLLOWS: $_____ OR MORE per month starting _____, including interest at _____% per annum.

ACCELERATION: In the event of default, Payee or Bearer can declare all sums due and payable at once.

_____
Maker/Borrower

Date:_____

Acceleration can be triggered by failure to make loan payments as agreed in the note, or by breach of a provision in the security instrument, such as failure to keep the property insured.

Alienation Clause. An alienation clause is also called a **due-on-sale clause**. This provision gives the lender the right to accelerate the loan—demanding immediate payment of the entire loan balance, as described above—if the borrower sells the property or otherwise alienates any interest in it. (Alienation refers to any transfer of an interest in real estate. See Chapter 3.) An alienation clause does not prohibit the sale of the property, but it allows the lender to force the borrower to pay off the loan when the property is sold, which prevents the purchaser from assuming the loan without the lender's approval.

In an **assumption**, the borrower sells the security property to a purchaser who agrees to "assume and pay the mortgage [or deed of trust] according to its terms." The purchaser becomes primarily liable to the lender for repayment of the loan, but the original borrower retains secondary liability in case the purchaser defaults.

Even though the original borrower is secondarily liable after an assumption, lenders prefer to have the opportunity to approve or reject the prospective purchaser. Assumption by a purchaser who is a poor credit risk significantly increases the likelihood of default. An alienation clause allows the lender to evaluate the purchaser. If the purchaser is creditworthy, the lender may agree to an assumption. The lender will usually charge an assumption fee in this situation, and may also raise the interest rate on the loan; in most cases, the lender will release the original borrower from any further liability.

Currently, most real estate finance documents include an alienation clause. But when there isn't an alienation clause, the loan can be assumed without the lender's approval. Alternatively, the borrower can sell the property "subject to" the loan. In

that case, the loan remains a lien against the property but the purchaser does not assume it. The purchaser has no personal liability to the lender, but the property remains "subject to" the lien securing the seller's original loan. Thus, the purchaser runs the risk of losing the property to foreclosure if the seller defaults on the loan.

Late Payment Penalty. If the lender wants to impose a penalty for late payments, the charges must be clearly defined in the finance documents. In California, a late charge cannot exceed: 1) 6% of the principal and interest installment due, or 2) five dollars, whichever is greater. A payment cannot be considered late unless it is paid at least 10 days after the installment due date.

Prepayment Penalty. In California, residential loan documents cannot contain **lock-in clauses**, provisions that prohibit the borrower from prepaying the loan (paying it off early). However, residential lenders can impose penalties on borrowers for prepayment, although these penalties are also limited by law. California law prohibits conventional lenders from imposing prepayment penalties after five years from the date of the security instrument, and also limits the amount of the prepayment penalties that may be charged during those first five years. (All FHA and VA loans can be prepaid without penalty.)

Subordination Clause. Occasionally a security instrument includes a subordination clause, which states that the instrument will have lower lien priority than another mortgage or deed of trust to be executed in the future. The clause makes it possible for a later security instrument to assume a higher priority position—usually first lien position—even though this earlier security instrument was executed and recorded first.

Subordination clauses are common in mortgages and deeds of trust that secure purchase loans for unimproved land, when the borrower is planning to

Fig.9.4 Security instruments

Mortgage or Deed of Trust

- Makes borrower's property collateral for the loan
- Gives lender the power to foreclose if the debt is not paid

get a construction loan later on. The construction lender will demand first lien position for its loan. Lien priority is ordinarily determined by recording date ("first in time is first in right"), but the subordination clause in the earlier land loan allows the later construction loan to have first lien position.

Defeasance Clause. A defeasance clause states that the security instrument will be canceled when the debt has been paid. When a deed of trust debt has been repaid, it is canceled with the signing and recording of a **deed of reconveyance**. If the trustee fails to sign and record the deed of reconveyance within the statutory time limits, the borrower can get a title insurance company to do so after proper notice to the trustee and lender. In that case, the trustee or lender will be liable for any damages caused by the failure to sign and record the deed of reconveyance, and will be subject to a statutory penalty of $300.

When a mortgage debt has been paid in full, a document called a **certificate of discharge** is used to release the mortgage lien. The lender must record the certificate of discharge within the statutory time frame, or be subject to the penalties listed above.

Along with filing the reconveyance deed or certificate of discharge, the lender must also return the original note and deed of trust or mortgage to the borrower.

Foreclosure Procedures

If the borrower does not repay the loan as agreed, the lender may foreclose and collect the debt from the proceeds of a forced sale. Establishing the lender's right to foreclose is the basic purpose of a security instrument. There are different foreclosure procedures for mortgages and deeds of trust; in fact, that is the essential difference between the two types of security instruments.

Mortgage Foreclosure. Mortgage foreclosures are sometimes called judicial foreclosures, because they are carried out through the court system. Upon default, the lender files a lawsuit against the borrower in the county where the collateral property is located. Any junior lienholders (who have liens with lower priority than the mortgage) are notified of the foreclosure action, so that they can take steps to protect their interests.

The lender's attorney will also record a **lis pendens**, which is a notice of a pending legal action (in this case, the foreclosure action). A lis pendens makes the final court judgment binding on anyone who might acquire an interest in the property while the foreclosure action is pending.

When the complaint is heard in court, in the absence of unusual circumstances, the judge will issue a **decree of foreclosure**, ordering the property to be sold to satisfy the debt. The judge appoints a receiver to conduct the sale. The sale, which takes the form of a public auction, is sometimes referred to as a **sheriff's sale**.

Reinstatement. While the foreclosure action is pending, the borrower can cure the loan default by paying all the past due amounts, plus the costs and fees of the lawsuit. This is called **reinstatement**. When the loan is reinstated, all foreclosure proceedings are terminated, and the mortgage continues in full force and effect. Once the decree of foreclosure is issued, this right of reinstatement no longer exists.

Redemption. The borrower may have a second opportunity to reclaim his or her property. After the sheriff's sale, the borrower may, in some cases, **redeem** the property by paying off the entire debt, including interest, costs, and fees. The time period during which this **statutory right of redemption** exists varies. The redemption period continues for three months after the sale if the sale proceeds were enough to pay off the debt, plus interest, costs, and fees. The redemption period continues for one year after the sale date if the proceeds were not enough to pay off the complete debt. However, if the lender waives its right to a deficiency judgment (discussed below) or is prohibited from obtaining a deficiency judgment, there is no right of redemption at all.

Certificate of Sale. When the property is sold subject to the statutory right of redemption, the successful bidder at the sheriff's sale receives a **certificate of sale** instead of a deed. The borrower is entitled to keep possession of the property during the redemption period, provided he or she pays reasonable rent to the holder of the certificate of sale. Only at the end of the redemption period is the certificate holder given a **sheriff's deed**, which transfers title and the right of possession of the property to the new owner.

The redemption period makes bidding at a mortgage foreclosure unappealing to many investors; understandably, they do not want to wait to gain title to the property. For this reason, there are often no outside bidders at a judicial foreclosure sale, and the lender acquires the property by bidding the amount the borrower owes.

If there are outside bidders at the auction and the proceeds from the sale exceed the amount necessary to satisfy all valid liens against the property, the surplus belongs to the borrower.

Deficiency Judgments. If the proceeds of the foreclosure sale are insufficient to satisfy the debt, the lender can get a **deficiency judgment** against the borrower, unless the transaction is exempted by the anti-deficiency rules. A deficiency judgment is a personal judgment against the borrower for the dif-

ference between the amount owing on the debt and the net proceeds from the foreclosure sale.

The anti-deficiency rules prohibit deficiency judgments under the following circumstances:

1. when the foreclosure is by a trustee's sale (a nonjudicial foreclosure);
2. when the security instrument is a purchase money mortgage given to the seller for all or part of the purchase price;
3. when the security instrument is a mortgage given to a third-party lender to finance the purchase of an owner-occupied residential dwelling with four or fewer units; or
4. when the fair market value of the property exceeds the amount of the debt.

As you can see, a deficiency judgment would be prohibited after foreclosure of a typical home purchase loan.

Deed of Trust Foreclosure. A deed of trust foreclosure differs significantly from a mortgage foreclosure. Every deed of trust has a **power of sale** clause. This provision authorizes the trustee to sell the property if the borrower defaults, through a process known as nonjudicial foreclosure. The trustee does not have to file a foreclosure lawsuit or get a judicial decree of foreclosure. Instead, the trustee can sell the property at an auction called a **trustee's sale**, and use the sale proceeds to pay off the debt owed to the lender (beneficiary). As with a sheriff's sale, if the trustee's sale results in a surplus, the excess amount belongs to the borrower.

A nonjudicial foreclosure must be conducted in accordance with the procedures prescribed by statute. These procedures are designed to give the borrower an opportunity to cure the default and reinstate the loan.

Notices of Default and Sale. First, the trustee must give the borrower and all lienholders a notice of default. Three months after the notice of default is issued, the trustee publishes a notice of sale of the property in a newspaper of general circulation. The notice of sale also must be posted on the security property and sent to everyone who received a notice of default. The trustee's sale cannot take place until at least 20 days after the first date of publication of the notice of sale.

Reinstatement and Redemption. As with a mortgage foreclosure, the borrower under a deed of trust has a period in which he or she can reinstate the loan and stop the foreclosure proceedings. The borrower may reinstate the loan at any time from the notice of default up until five business days before the sale. This means the reinstatement period is at least three months and 15 days. The loan is reinstated by paying all past-due installments and penalties. If the loan is reinstated, the trustee cannot sell the property.

The borrower can also redeem the property by paying off the full balance of the loan plus costs at any time prior to the actual sale.

Trustee's Deed. The successful bidder at the trustee's sale receives a trustee's deed, which terminates all of the borrower's rights in the property. There is no post-sale redemption period or right of possession for the borrower, as there may be in a mortgage foreclosure.

The lender may bid at the sale, and is entitled to apply the amount due on the loan towards the bid (which is called credit bidding).

Deficiency Judgments. If a lender forecloses on a deed of trust by means of a trustee's sale, its recovery is limited to the proceeds of the sale. The lender cannot bring any further action against the borrower, even if the sale proceeds do not cover the amount owing on the loan. A suit to recover such a deficiency is barred by the anti-deficiency rules discussed above.

Protection of Junior Lienholders. A trustee's sale under a deed of trust destroys not only the borrower's interest in the property, but also the interests of any junior lienholders (those with subordinate liens). To protect junior lienholders, the senior lienholder must send notices of default and sale to all junior lienholders who have recorded interests in the property.

If the notices are not sent to a lienholder of record, that lienholder is not bound by the sale.

A junior lienholder can protect his or her interest by paying the delinquencies on the senior lien (curing the default) and adding the amount of these payments to the balance due under the junior lien. The junior lienholder may then foreclose his or her own lien. A purchaser at a junior lienholder's sale takes title to the property subject to any senior liens that may exist.

Mortgages vs. Deeds of Trust. Many lenders prefer a deed of trust to a mortgage because it enables them to bypass the court, which often moves slowly due to an overcrowded docket. Also, the trustee's sale is final; there is no statutory redemption period after the sale. The successful bidder at a trustee's sale is given a trustee's deed and takes title immediately. The disadvantage of a deed of trust from the lender's point of view is that after nonjudicial foreclosure there is no right to a deficiency judgment. If the proceeds of the trustee's sale are insufficient to satisfy the debt, the lender takes a loss; the lender is not allowed to sue the borrower to make up the deficiency.

It should be noted that a lender can choose to foreclose a trust deed judicially, by "converting" the trust deed to a mortgage. Though lenders seldom convert trust deeds to mortgages, it is done occasionally when a substantial deficiency is inevitable and the successful enforcement of a deficiency judgment is likely (e.g., the borrower owns other real estate or assets that can be reached). It is also possible for a mortgage to be foreclosed nonjudicially, if the mortgage includes a power of sale clause.

Types of Mortgage Loans

You will often hear "mortgage" or "deed of trust" coupled with an adjective that serves to describe the particular function of the security instrument or the circumstances in which it is used. For example, a "construction mortgage" is a mortgage used to se-

Fig.9.5 Comparison of mortgages and deeds of trust

Security Instruments

Mortgage	Deed of Trust
• Mortgagor and mortgagee • Judicial foreclosure only, unless a power of sale clause is included • Reinstatement before decree of foreclosure • Redemption after the sheriff's sale • Deficiency judgment allowed (subject to limitations)	• Trustor, beneficiary, and trustee • Nonjudicial foreclosure allowed • Reinstatement before the trustee's sale • No post-sale redemption • No deficiency judgment

cure a construction loan; a "blanket mortgage" is one that secures a loan with two or more parcels of property as collateral. Below are explanations of some of the most common of these terms. For the most part, we will use the term "mortgage" here, rather than the more cumbersome phrase "mortgage or deed of trust." In each case, however, a deed of trust could be (and today often would be) used instead of a mortgage.

First Mortgage. This is simply any security instrument that holds first lien position; it has the highest lien priority. A second mortgage is one that holds second lien position, and so on.

Senior and Junior Mortgages. Any mortgage that has a higher lien position than another is called a senior mortgage in relation to that other one, which is called a junior mortgage. A first mortgage is senior to a second mortgage; a second mortgage is junior to a first mortgage, but senior to a third.

As was explained in Chapter 2, lien priority is important in the event of a foreclosure, because the sale proceeds are used to pay off the first lien first. If any money remains, the second lien is paid; then the third is paid, and so on, until the money is exhausted. Obviously, it is much better to be in first lien position than in third.

Purchase Money Mortgage. This term is used in two ways. Sometimes it means any mortgage loan used to finance the purchase of the property that is the collateral for the loan: a buyer borrows money to buy property and gives the lender a mortgage on that same property to secure the loan.

In other cases, "purchase money mortgage" is used more narrowly, to mean a mortgage that a buyer gives to a seller, in a seller-financed transaction. Instead of paying the full price in cash at closing, the buyer gives the seller a mortgage on the property and pays the price off in installments.

Example: The sales price is $80,000. The buyer makes a $20,000 downpayment and signs a note and purchase money mortgage in favor of the seller for the remaining $60,000. The buyer will pay the seller in monthly installments at 10% interest over the next 15 years.

In this narrower sense, a purchase money mortgage is sometimes called a **soft money mortgage**, because the borrower receives credit instead of actual cash. If a borrower gives a lender a mortgage and receives cash in return (as with a bank loan), it is called a **hard money mortgage**.

Budget Mortgage. The monthly payment on a budget mortgage includes not just principal and interest on the loan, but one-twelfth of the year's property taxes and hazard insurance premiums as well. Most residential loans are secured by budget mortgages. This is the safest and most practical way for lenders to make sure the property taxes and insurance premiums are paid on time.

Blanket Mortgage. Sometimes a borrower mortgages several pieces of property as security for one loan. For example, a ten-acre parcel subdivided into 20 lots might be used to secure one loan made to the subdivider. Blanket mortgages usually have a **partial release clause** (also called a partial satisfaction clause, or in a blanket trust deed, a partial reconveyance clause). This provision requires the lender to release certain parcels from the blanket lien when specified portions of the overall debt have been paid off.

> **Example:** A ten-acre parcel subdivided into 20 lots secures a $500,000 loan. The subdivider sells one lot for $50,000. The subdivider pays the lender $45,000 and receives a release for the lot that is being sold. The blanket mortgage is no longer a lien against that lot, so the subdivider can convey clear title to the lot buyer.

Package Mortgage. When personal property is included in the sale of real estate and financed along with the real estate with one loan, the security instrument is called a package mortgage. For example, if a buyer bought ovens, freezers, and other equipment along with a restaurant building, the purchase might be financed with a package mortgage.

Open-end Mortgage. This is a mortgage that sets a borrowing limit, but allows the mortgagor to reborrow, when needed, any part of the debt that has been repaid without having to negotiate a new mortgage. The interest rate on the loan is usually a variable rate that rises and falls with market interest rates. The open-end mortgage is most often used as a business tool by builders and farmers.

Participation Mortgage. This is a loan in which the lender participates in the earnings generated by the mortgaged property, usually in addition to collecting interest payments on the principal. In some cases the lender participates by becoming a part-owner of the property. Participation loans are most common on large commercial projects where the lender is an insurance company or other large investor.

Conventional Mortgage. A conventional mortgage is any loan not insured or guaranteed by a government agency, such as the FHA or the VA. Conventional loans can be made by private individuals, but the term is ordinarily used to refer to loans made by institutional lenders (such as banks or savings and loans).

Wraparound Mortgage. A wraparound mortgage is a new mortgage that includes or "wraps around" an existing first mortgage on the property. Wraparounds are generally used only in seller-financed transactions.

> **Example:** A home is being sold for $100,000; there is an existing $40,000 mortgage on the property. Instead of assuming that mortgage, the buyer merely takes title subject to it. The buyer gives the seller a $20,000 downpayment and a second mortgage for the remaining $80,000 of the purchase price. The $80,000 second mortgage is a wraparound mortgage. Each month, the buyer

makes a payment on the wraparound to the seller, and the seller uses part of that payment to make the monthly payment on the underlying $40,000 mortgage.

Wraparound financing works only if the underlying loan does not contain an alienation clause (see the discussion earlier in this chapter). Otherwise the lender would require the seller to pay off the underlying loan at the time of sale. (If the security instrument is a deed of trust, this type of financing arrangement is called an **all-inclusive trust deed**.)

Construction Mortgage. A construction mortgage is simply a mortgage that secures a construction loan. A construction loan (sometimes called an **interim loan**) is a temporary loan used to finance the construction of improvements on the land. When the construction is completed, the construction loan is replaced by permanent financing, which is called a **take-out loan**.

Construction loans can be profitable, but they are considered quite risky. Accordingly, lenders charge high interest rates and loan fees on construction loans, and they supervise the progress of the construction. There is always a danger that the borrower will overspend on a construction project and exhaust the loan proceeds before construction is completed. If the borrower cannot afford to finish, the lender is left with a security interest in a partially completed project.

Lenders have devised plans for disbursement of construction loan proceeds that guard against overspending by the borrower. There are three common disbursement plans: the fixed disbursement plan, the voucher system, and the warrant system.

Fixed Disbursement Plan. This plan calls for a series of predetermined disbursements, clled obligatory advances, at various stages of construction.

> **Example:** The construction loan agreement stipulates that the lender will release 10% of the proceeds when the project is 20% complete, and thereafter 20% draws will be available whenever construction has progressed another 20% toward completion.

The lender will often hold back 10% or more of the loan proceeds until the period for claiming construction liens has expired, to protect against unpaid liens that could affect the marketability of the property. The construction loan agreement usually

Fig.9.6 Three methods of disbursing construction funds

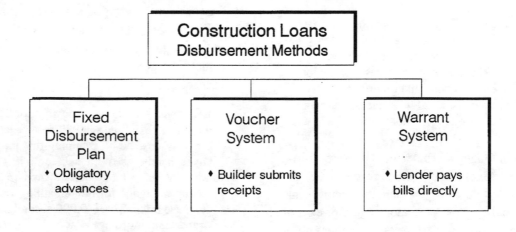

states that if a valid construction lien is recorded, the lender may use the undisbursed portion of the loan to pay it off.

Voucher System. Under the voucher system, the contractor/borrower pays his or her own ills and then submits the receipts to the lender for reimbursement.

Warrant System. A third method of disbursement is the warrant system, in which bills are presented to the lender for direct payment to the supplier or laborer.

Land Contracts

In a seller-financed transaction, the seller may ask the buyer to execute a mortgage or a deed of trust, just like an institutional lender. Sellers also have the option of using a third type of security instrument: the land contract (also called an installment sale contract, real estate contract, contract for deed, or contract of sale).

The rights and responsibilities of the buyer and seller under a land contract are discussed in detail in Chapter 8.

Finance Disclosure Requirements

The typical homebuyer is considerably less knowledgeable about residential financing than the typical lender. And without all the necessary information, the buyer may not be able to make the best financial choices. This is why both the state and federal governments have passed laws that make sure homebuyers get the information they need to make an informed decision about financing. These laws include the Truth in Lending Act, the Residential Purchase Money Loan Disclosure Law, and the Mortgage Loan Broker Law.

The Truth in Lending Act

The Truth in Lending Act (TILA) is a federal consumer protection law that was passed in 1969. The act requires lenders to disclose the complete cost of credit to consumer loan applicants, and also regulates the advertisement of consumer loans. The Truth in Lending Act is implemented by **Regulation Z**, a regulation adopted by the Federal Reserve Board.

Loans Covered by TILA

A loan is a **consumer loan** if it is used for personal, family, or household purposes. A consumer loan is covered by the Truth in Lending Act if it is to be repaid in more than four installments, or is subject to finance charges, and is either:

* for $25,000 or less, or
* secured by real property.

Thus, any mortgage loan is covered by the Truth in Lending Act as long as the proceeds are used for personal, family, or household purposes (such as buying a home or sending children to college).

Lenders and persons who arrange credit in the ordinary course of their business (such as mortgage brokers) must comply with the requirements of the Truth in Lending Act and Regulation Z if they make or arrange for the types of loans described above.

Loans Exempt from TILA

The Truth in Lending Act applies only to loans made to natural persons, so loans made to corporations or organizations are not covered. Loans made for business, commercial, or agricultural purposes are also exempt. So are loans in excess of $25,000, unless the loan is secured by real property. (Real estate loans for personal, family, or household purposes are covered regardless of the loan amount.) Most instances of seller financing are exempt, because extending credit is not in the seller's ordinary course of business.

Fig.9.7 Truth in Lending disclosure statement

FEDERAL REAL ESTATE LOAN DISCLOSURE STATEMENT
CALIFORNIA ASSOCIATION OF REALTORS® (CAR) STANDARD FORM

Broker:

_____
(name)

_____
(address)

Creditor:

_____
(name)

_____
(address)

YOUR LOAN IN THE AMOUNT OF $ _____ IS TO BE SECURED BY A DEED OF TRUST IN FAVOR OF CREDITOR
ON REAL PROPERTY LOCATED AT _____

ANNUAL PERCENTAGE RATE The cost of your credit as a yearly rate.	FINANCE CHARGE The dollar amount the credit will cost you.	AMOUNT FINANCED The amount of credit provided to you or on your behalf.	TOTAL OF PAYMENTS The amount you will have paid after you have made all payments as scheduled.
_____ %	$	$	$

YOUR PAYMENT SCHEDULE WILL BE:

Number of Payments	Amount of Payments	When Payments Are Due

ITEMIZATION OF THE AMOUNT FINANCED OF $ _____

Amount given to you .... $ _____
Amount paid on your account .... $ _____
Amount paid to others on your behalf:
1. Appraisal .... $ _____
2. Credit report .... $ _____
3. Notary............................... $ _____
4. Recording .... $ _____
5. Title insurance .... $ _____
6. Document preparation .... $ _____
7. Property insurance .... $ _____
8. Other _____ (DESCRIBE) $ _____
9. Other _____ (DESCRIBE) $ _____

<u>Insurance</u>:

Property insurance may be obtained by Borrower through any person of his choice. If it is to be purchased through Broker or Creditor, you will pay
$ _____.

Credit life and disability insurance are not required to obtain this loan.

<u>Late Charge</u>: If any payment is not made within _____ days after it is due, a late charge must be paid by Borrower as follows:
_____

<u>Prepayment</u>: If you pay off early, you ☐ MAY ☐ WILL NOT have to pay a penalty.

<u>Acceleration</u>: If the property securing this loan is sold or otherwise transferred, the Creditor ☐ HAS ☐ DOES NOT have the option to require immediate payment of the entire loan amount.

SEE YOUR CONTRACT DOCUMENTS FOR ANY ADDITIONAL INFORMATION ABOUT NONPAYMENT, DEFAULT, ANY REQUIRED REPAYMENT IN FULL BEFORE THE SCHEDULED DATE, AND PREPAYMENT REFUNDS AND PENALTIES.

I HAVE READ AND RECEIVED A COMPLETED COPY OF THIS STATEMENT.

Date_____ , 19 _____.

Borrower _____

*IMPORTANT NOTE:
Asterisk denotes an estimate

Borrower _____

FORM LD-11

Reprinted with permission, California Association of REALTORS®. Endorsement not implied.

Disclosure Requirements

The primary disclosures that the Truth in Lending Act requires a lender or credit arranger to make to a loan applicant are the total finance charge and the annual percentage rate.

The **total finance charge** is the sum of all fees and charges the borrower pays in connection with the loan. In addition to the interest on the loan, all of the following would be included in the total finance charge:

- origination fee,
- discount points paid by the borrower,
- finder's fees,
- service fees, and
- mortgage insurance premiums.

In real estate loan transactions, appraisal fees, credit report charges, and points paid by the seller are not included in the total finance charge. (Points and mortgage insurance are both explained in Chapter 11.)

The **annual percentage rate** (APR) is the relationship of the total finance charge to the amount of the loan, expressed as an annual percentage. The lender is required to compute the APR accurately; the stated figure must be within one-eighth of one percent of the exact calculation.

In a residential mortgage transaction, the lender or credit arranger must give the loan applicant a **disclosure statement** listing good faith estimates of the finance charges within three days after receiving the written application. Most lenders give the disclosure statement to the applicant at the time of application. If any of the estimated figures change over the course of the transaction, new disclosures must be made before closing.

The disclosure statement does not have to be on a particular form, but it must be clear and understandable and include all the disclosures required by Regulation Z. In addition to the total finance charge and annual percentage rate, the form must disclose the total amount financed, the payment schedule, the total number of payments, the total amount that will be paid, and information regarding any balloon payment, late fees, or prepayment charges. It must also state whether the loan may be assumed by someone who buys the security property from the borrower. An example of a TILA disclosure statement form is shown in Figure 9.7.

The Truth in Lending Act has some special rules for home equity loans. When the security property is the borrower's existing principal residence, the act gives the borrower a right of rescission. The home equity borrower has a right to rescind the loan agreement up until three days after signing the agreement, receiving the disclosure statement, or receiving notice of the right of rescission, whichever comes latest. If the borrower never receives the statement or the notice, the right of rescission does not expire for three years. (Remember that this right applies only to home equity loans. There is no right of rescission for a loan financing the purchase or construction of the borrower's principal residence.)

Advertising Under TILA

The Truth in Lending Act strictly controls advertising of credit terms. Its advertising rules apply to anyone who advertises consumer credit, not just lenders and credit arrangers. For example, a real estate broker advertising financing terms for a listed home has to comply with TILA and Regulation Z.

It is always legal to state the cash price or the annual percentage rate in an ad. But if any other particular loan terms (such as the downpayment or the interest rate) are stated in the ad, then all the terms must also be included. For example, if an ad says, "Assume VA loan at 9% interest," it will violate the Truth in Lending Act if it does not go on to reveal the APR, the downpayment, and all the terms of repayment. However, general statements such as "low downpayment," "easy terms," or "affordable interest rate" do not trigger the full disclosure requirement.

Purchase Money Loan Disclosure Law

When a seller carries back a purchase money loan on residential property, California law requires certain disclosures to be made to both the buyer and the seller if an "arranger of credit" is involved. An arranger of credit, for the purposes of this law, is anyone (other than the buyer or seller) who:

- is involved in negotiating the credit agreement,
- participates in preparing the documents, or
- is directly or indirectly compensated for arranging for the financing or the property sale that is facilitated by the financing.

There is an exception for escrow agents and for attorneys representing either party—these are not considered arrangers of credit. But if an attorney or a real estate agent is a party to the transaction, he or she is considered an arranger of credit if neither party is represented by a real estate agent.

Coverage of the Law. The disclosure law applies when the seller gives the buyer credit for all or part of the purchase price, if:

1. the property is residential with one to four units,
2. the credit arrangements involve a finance charge or provide for four or more payments (not including the downpayment), and
3. an arranger of credit is involved.

A transaction is exempt if it is already covered by other disclosure laws, such as the Truth in Lending Act, the Real Estate Settlement Procedures Act, or the Mortgage Loan Broker Law.

Disclosure Requirements. When this disclosure law applies to a transaction, the required disclosures must be made before the buyer signs the note or security instrument. The seller must make disclosures to the buyer, and the buyer must make disclosures to the seller. The arranger of credit is responsible for ensuring that each party discloses all required information to the other.

The statute contains a long list of required disclosures. Here are some of them:

1. the terms of the note and security instrument;
2. a description of the terms and conditions of senior encumbrances (such as a first trust deed the buyer will be assuming);
3. whether the financing will result in a balloon payment (if so, the buyer must be warned that it may be difficult to obtain refinancing to cover the balloon payment); and
4. employment, income, and credit information about the buyer, or else a statement that the arranger of credit has made no representation regarding the buyer's creditworthiness.

An example of a disclosure form that could be used to comply with the Purchase Money Loan Disclosure Law is shown in Figure 9.8.

Mortgage Loan Broker Law

Real estate agents often help buyers obtain financing. This assistance may go beyond simply helping the buyer apply to one institutional lender. In some cases, it's necessary to get loans from two or more lenders to raise enough cash to close the transaction.

California's **Mortgage Loan Broker Law** (also known as the Necessitous Borrower Act or the Real Property Loan Law) regulates real estate agents who act as loan brokers. The law requires a loan broker to give the borrower a disclosure statement. And for loans secured by residential property, the law restricts the size of the fees and commissions paid by the borrower or received by the loan broker. The following is only a brief overview of a few of the law's key provisions.

Disclosure Statement. The disclosure statement required by the Mortgage Loan Broker Law must be on a form approved by the Real Estate Commissioner (an example is shown in Figure 9.9). It discloses all the costs involved in obtaining the loan,

Fig.9.8 Purchase money loan disclosure statement

CALIFORNIA ASSOCIATION OF REALTORS

SELLER FINANCING DISCLOSURE STATEMENT
(California Civil Code 2956-2967)
CALIFORNIA ASSOCIATION OF REALTORS® (C.A.R.) STANDARD FORM

This two page disclosure statement from the Purchaser (Buyer) and Vendor (Seller) is prepared by an arranger of credit [defined in Civil Code 2957 (a)] and provided to both the Purchaser (Buyer) and Vendor (Seller) in a residential real estate transaction involving four or fewer units whenever the Seller has agreed to extend credit to the Buyer as part of the purchase price.

Buyer: _____
Seller: _____
Arranger of Credit: _____
Real Property: _____

A. Credit Documents: This extension of credit by the Seller is evidenced by ☐ note and deed of trust. ☐ all-inclusive note and deed of trust. ☐ installment land sale contract. ☐ lease/option (when parties intend transfer of equitable title). ☐ other (specify) _____

B. Credit Terms:
1. ☐ See attached copy of credit documents referred to in Section A above for description of credit terms; or
2. ☐ The terms of the credit documents referred to in Section A above are: Principal amount $_____ interest at _____% per annum payable at $_____ per _____ (month/year/etc.) with the entire unpaid principal and accrued interest of approximately $_____ due _____ 19___ (maturity date).

Late Charge: If any payment is not made within _____ days after it is due, a late charge of $_____ or _____% of the installment due may be charged to the Buyer.
Prepayment: If all or part of this loan is paid early, the Buyer ☐ will, ☐ will not, have to pay a prepayment penalty as follows: _____

Due on Sale: If any interest in the property securing this obligation is sold or otherwise transferred, the Seller ☐ has, ☐ does not have, the option to require immediate payment of the entire unpaid balance and accrued interest.
Other Terms: _____

C. Available information on loans/encumbrances * that will be **senior** to the Seller's extension of credit:

	1st	2nd	3rd
1. Original Balance	$_____	$_____	$_____
2. Current Balance	$_____	$_____	$_____
3. Periodic Payment (e.g. $100/month)	$_____ / _____	$_____ / _____	$_____ / _____
4. Amt. of Balloon Payment	$_____	$_____	$_____
5. Date of Balloon Payment			
6. Maturity Date			
7. Due On Sale ('Yes' or 'No')			
8. Interest Rate (per annum)	_____%	_____%	_____%
9. Fixed or Variable Rate: If Variable Rate:	☐ a copy of note attached ☐ variable provisions are explained on attached separate sheet	☐ a copy of note attached ☐ variable provisions are explained on attached separate sheet	☐ a copy of note attached ☐ variable provisions are explained on attached separate sheet
10. Is Payment Current?			

☐ SEPARATE SHEET WITH INFORMATION REGARDING OTHER SENIOR LOANS/ENCUMBRANCES IS ATTACHED.
*IMPORTANT NOTE: Asterisk (*) denotes an estimate.
D. Caution: If any of the obligations secured by the property calls for a balloon payment, then Seller and Buyer are aware that refinancing of the balloon payment at maturity may be difficult or impossible depending on the conditions in the mortgage marketplace at that time. There are no assurances that new financing or a loan extension will be available when the balloon payment is due.
E. Deferred Interest:
"Deferred interest" results when the Buyer's periodic payments are less than the amount of interest earned on the obligation, or when the obligation does not require periodic payments. This accrued interest will have to be paid by the Buyer at a later time and may result in the Buyer owing more on the obligation than at origination.
☐ The credit being extended to the Buyer by the Seller does **not** provide for "deferred interest." or
☐ The credit being extended to the Buyer by the Seller does provide for "deferred interest."
The credit documents provide the following regarding deferred interest:
☐ All deferred interest shall be due and payable along with the principal at maturity (simple interest); or
☐ The deferred interest shall be added to the principal _____ (e.g., annually, monthly, etc.) and thereafter shall bear interest at the rate specified in the credit documents (compound interest); or
☐ Other (specify) _____

F. All-Inclusive Deed of Trust or Installment Land Sale Contract:
☐ This transaction does not involve the use of an all-inclusive (or wraparound) deed of trust or an installment land sale contract; or
☐ This transaction does involve the use of either an all-inclusive (or wraparound) deed of trust or an installment land sale contract which provides as follows:
1) In the event of an acceleration of any senior encumbrance, the responsibility for payment or for legal defense is:
☐ Not specified in the credit or security documents; or
☐ Specified in the credit or security documents as follows:
_____

Buyer and Seller acknowledge receipt of copy of this page, which constitutes Page 1 of _____ Pages.
Buyer's Initials (_____) (_____)   Seller's Initials (_____) (_____)

THIS STANDARDIZED DOCUMENT HAS BEEN APPROVED BY THE CALIFORNIA ASSOCIATION OF REALTORS® (C.A.R.) IN FORM ONLY. NO REPRESENTATION IS MADE AS TO THE APPROVAL OF THE FORM OR OF ANY SUPPLEMENTS NOT CURRENTLY PUBLISHED BY C.A.R. OR THE LEGAL VALIDITY OR ADEQUACY OF ANY PROVISION IN ANY SPECIFIC TRANSACTION. IT SHOULD NOT BE USED WITH EXTENSIVE RIDERS OR ADDITIONS.
A REAL ESTATE BROKER IS THE PERSON QUALIFIED TO ADVISE ON REAL ESTATE TRANSACTIONS. IF YOU DESIRE LEGAL OR TAX ADVICE, CONSULT AN APPROPRIATE PROFESSIONAL.
The copyright laws of the United States (17 U.S. Code) forbid the unauthorized reproduction of this form by any means including facsimile or computerized formats.
Copyright 1989 CALIFORNIA ASSOCIATION OF REALTORS.
525 South Virgil Avenue, Los Angeles, California 90020

OFFICE USE ONLY
Reviewed by Broker or Designee _____
Date _____

M-R AUG. 94

Reprinted with permission, California Association of REALTORS®. Endorsement not implied.

2) In the event of the prepayment of a senior encumbrance, the responsibilities and rights of Seller and Buyer regarding refinancing, prepayment penalties, and any prepayment discounts are:
☐ **Not** specified in the credit or security documents; **or**
☐ Specified in the credit or security documents as follows:

_____
_____

3) The financing provided that the Buyer will make periodic payments to _____
[e.g., a collection agent (such as a bank or savings and loan); Seller; etc.] and that _____
will be responsible for disbursing payments to the payee(s) on the senior encumbrance(s) and to the Seller.

CAUTION: The parties are advised to consider designating a neutral third party as the collection agent for receiving Buyer's payments and disbursing them to the payee(s) on the senior encumbrance(s) and to the Seller.

G. Buyer's Creditworthiness: Section 580(b) of the California Code of Civil Procedure generally limits a Seller's rights in the event of a default by the Buyer in the financing extended by the Seller, to a foreclosure of the property.
☐ No disclosure concerning the Buyer's creditworthiness has been made to the Seller; **or**
☐ The following representations concerning the Buyer's creditworthiness have been made by the Buyer(s) to the Seller:

1. Occupation: _____	1. Occupation: _____
2. Employer: _____	2. Employer: _____
3. Length of Employment: _____	3. Length of Employment: _____
4. Monthly Gross Income: _____	4. Monthly Gross Income: _____
5. Buyer ☐ has, ☐ has **not**, provided Seller a current credit report issued by: _____	5. Buyer ☐ has, ☐ has **not**, provided Seller a current credit report issued by: _____
6. Buyer ☐ has, ☐ has **not**, provided Seller a completed loan application.	6. Buyer ☐ has, ☐ has **not**, provided Seller a completed loan application.
7. Other (specify): _____	7. Other (specify): _____

H. Insurance:
☐ The parties' escrow holder or insurance carrier has been or will be directed to add a loss payee clause to the property insurance protecting the Seller; **or**
☐ No provision has been made for adding a loss payee clause to the property insurance protecting the Seller. Seller is advised to secure such clauses or acquire a separate insurance policy.

I. Request for Notice:
☐ A Request for Notice of Default under Section 2924(b) of the California Civil Code has been or will be recorded; **or**
☐ No provision for recording a Request for Notice of Default has been made. Seller is advised to consider recording a Request for Notice of Default.

J. Title Insurance:
☐ Title insurance coverage will be provided to **both** Seller and Buyer insuring their respective interests in the property; **or**
☐ No provision for title insurance coverage of **both** Seller and Buyer has been made. Seller and Buyer are advised to consider securing such title insurance coverage.

K. Tax Service:
☐ A tax service has been arranged to report to Seller whether property taxes have been paid on the property. _____ (e.g., Seller, Buyer, etc.) will be responsible for the continued retention and payment of such tax service; **or**
☐ No provision has been made for a tax service. Seller should consider retaining a tax service or otherwise determine that the property taxes are paid.

L. Recording:
☐ The security documents (e.g., deed of trust, installment land contract, etc.) will be recorded with the county recorder where the property is located; **or**
☐ The security documents will **not** be recorded with the county recorder. Seller and Buyer are advised that their respective interests in the property may be jeopardized by intervening liens, judgments or subsequent transfers which are recorded.

M. Proceeds to Buyer:
☐ Buyer will **NOT** receive any cash proceeds at the close of the sale transaction; **or**
☐ Buyer will receive approximately $_____ from _____ (indicate source from the sale transaction proceeds of such funds). Buyer represents that the purpose of such disbursement is as follows: _____
_____

N. Notice of Delinquency:
☐ A Request for Notice of Delinquency under Section 2924(e) of the California Civil Code has been or will be made to the Senior lienholder(s); **or**
☐ No provision for making a Request for Notice of Delinquency has been made. Seller should consider making a Request for Notice of Delinquency.

The above information has been provided to: (a) the Buyer, by the arranger of credit and the Seller (with respect to information within the knowledge of the Seller); (b) the Seller, by the arranger of credit and the Buyer (with respect to information within the knowledge of the Buyer).

Arranger of Credit _____

Date _____, 19____   By _____

Buyer and Seller acknowledge that the information each has provided to the arranger of credit for inclusion in this disclosure form is accurate to the best of their knowledge.

Buyer and Seller hereby acknowledge receipt of a completed copy of this disclosure form.

Date _____, 19____   Date _____, 19____

Buyer _____   Seller _____

Buyer _____   Seller _____

OFFICE USE ONLY
Reviewed by Broker or Designee _____
Date _____

M-R AUG. 94

and the actual amount the borrower will receive after all the costs and fees are deducted from the loan. The borrower must receive the statement before signing the note and security instrument, or within three days of the lender's receipt of the borrower's loan application, whichever is earlier.

A disclosure statement is required whenever a real estate agent negotiates a loan or performs services for borrowers or lenders in connection with a loan. It is required for loans secured by commercial property as well as for residential loans.

Commissions, Costs, and Terms. The Mortgage Loan Broker Law limits the commissions and costs that a real estate agent may charge the borrower for arranging a loan secured by residential property with one to four units. But these restrictions only apply when the security instrument is:

- a first deed of trust for less than $30,000, or
- a junior deed of trust for less than $20,000.

For these loans, the maximum commissions the loan broker can charge are:

- for a first deed of trust,
  - 5% of the principal if the loan term is less than three years, and
  - 10% of the principal if the loan term is three years or more.

- for a junior deed of trust,
  - 5% of the principal if the term is less than two years,
  - 10% of the principal if the term is at least two years, but less than three years, and
  - 15% of the principal if the term is three years or more.

The costs of making these loans (such as the appraisal and escrow fees) cannot exceed 5% of the loan amount, or $390, whichever is greater. But the costs charged to the borrower must never exceed $700, and must not exceed the actual costs.

Balloon Payments. The Mortgage Loan Broker Law also prohibits balloon payments in certain residential loans secured by first deeds of trust for less than $30,000 or junior deeds of trust for less than $20,000. Balloon payments are prohibited in these loans if the loan is to be paid off in less than three years. And if the security property is an owner-occupied home, balloon payments are prohibited when the loan term is less than six years. (These rules don't apply to seller financing, however.) For the purposes of this law, a balloon payment is one that is more than twice as large as the smallest payment required by the loan agreement.

Fig.9.9 Mortgage loan broker disclosure statement

MORTGAGE LOAN DISCLOSURE STATEMENT (BORROWER)
CALIFORNIA ASSOCIATION OF REALTORS® (C.A.R.) STANDARD FORM
(As required by the Business and Professions Code Section 10240 and Title 10, California Administrative Code, Section 2840)

_____
(Name of Broker/Arranger of Credit)

_____
(Business Address of Broker)

I. SUMMARY OF LOAN TERMS
  A. PRINCIPAL AMOUNT OF LOAN $ _____
  B. ESTIMATED DEDUCTIONS FROM PRINCIPAL AMOUNT
      1. Costs and Expenses (See Paragraph III-A) $ _____
    • 2. Commission/Loan Origination Fee (See Paragraph III-B) $ _____
      3. Liens and Other Amounts to be Paid on Authorization of Borrower
          (See Paragraph III-C) $ _____
  C. ESTIMATED CASH PAYABLE TO BORROWER (A less B)   . . . . $ _____

II. GENERAL INFORMATION ABOUT LOAN
  A. If this loan is made, you will be required to pay the principal and interest at _____ % per year, payable as
      follows: _____ _____ payments of $_____
                 (number of payments)   (monthly/quarterly/annually)
      and a FINAL/BALLOON payment of $_____ to pay off the loan in full.

      **NOTICE TO BORROWER: If you do not have the funds to pay the balloon payment when it comes due, you may
      have to obtain a new loan against your property to make the balloon payment. In that case, you may again have
      to pay commissions, fees, and expenses for the arranging of the new loan. In addition, if you are unable to
      make the monthly payments or the balloon payment, you may lose the property and all of your equity through
      foreclosure. Keep this in mind in deciding upon the amount and terms of this loan.**

  B. This loan will be evidenced by a promissory note and secured by a deed of trust in favor of lender/creditor on property located at
      (street address or legal description): _____
      _____

  C. 1. Liens presently against this property (do not include loan being applied for):

Nature of Lien	Priority	Lienholder's Name	Amount Owing

      2. Liens that will remain against this property after the loan being applied for is made or arranged (include loan being applied for):

Nature of Lien	Priority	Lienholder's Name	Amount Owing

          NOTICE TO BORROWER: Be sure that the amount of all liens is stated as accurately as possible. If you contract with the broker
          for this loan, but it cannot be made or arranged because you did not state these lien amounts correctly, you may be liable to
          pay commissions, fees, and expenses even though you did not obtain the loan.

  D. If you wish to pay more than the scheduled payment at any time before it is due, you may have to pay a PREPAYMENT PENALTY
      computed as follows: _____
      _____
      _____

  E. The purchase of credit life or credit disability insurance is not required of the borrower as a condition of making this loan.
  F. The real property which will secure the requested loan is an "owner-occupied dwelling."   YES _____   NO _____
                                                                                          (Borrower initial opposite YES or NO)

      "For purposes of restrictions on scheduled balloon payments and unequal payments, an "owner-occupied dwelling" means a single
      dwelling unit in a condominium or cooperative or a residential building of less than three separate dwelling units, one of which will
      be owned and occupied by a signatory to the mortgage or deed of trust for this loan within 90 days of the signing of the mortgage
      or deed of trust. For certain other purposes relating to this loan, "dwelling" means a single dwelling unit in a condominium or
      cooperative, or any parcel containing only residential buildings if the total number of units on the parcel is four or less, which is
      owned by a signatory to the mortgage or deed of trust."

      Borrower hereby acknowledges the receipt of a copy of this page, which constitutes page 1 of 2 pages.
      Borrower's Initials (_____) (_____)

OFFICE USE ONLY
Reviewed by Broker or Designee _____
Date _____

Reprinted with permission, California Association of REALTORS®. Endorsement not implied.

III. DEDUCTIONS FROM LOAN PROCEEDS

  A. ESTIMATED MAXIMUM COSTS AND EXPENSES to be paid by borrower out of the principal amount of the loan are:

	PAYABLE TO	
	Broker	Others
1. Appraisal	_____	_____
2. Credit investigation	_____	_____
3. Delivery	_____	_____
4. Drawing/Document preparation	_____	_____
5. Escrow	_____	_____
6. Notary	_____	_____
7. Notice of delinquency	_____	_____
8. Processing	_____	_____
9. Recording	_____	_____
10. Tax service	_____	_____
11. Title insurance	_____	_____
12. Other costs and expenses:	_____	_____

TOTAL COSTS AND EXPENSES .... $ _____

*B. LOAN BROKERAGE COMMISSION/LOAN ORIGINATION FEE .... $ _____

  C. LIENS AND OTHER AMOUNTS to be paid out of the principal amount of the loan on authorization of the borrower are estimated as follows:

	PAYABLE TO	
	Broker	Others
1. Fire or other hazard insurance premiums	_____	_____
2. Credit life or disability insurance premium (see Paragraph II-E)	_____	_____
3. Beneficiary statement and payoff demand fees	_____	_____
4. Reconveyance and similar fees	_____	_____
5. Discharge of existing liens against property:	_____	_____
6. Other:	_____	_____

TOTAL TO BE PAID ON AUTHORIZATION OF BORROWER $ _____

If the loan to which this disclosure statement applies is a loan secured by a first deed of trust in a principal amount of less than $30,000 or a loan secured by a junior lien in a principal amount of less than $20,000, the undersigned licensee certifies that the loan will be made in compliance with Article 7 of Chapter 3 of the Real Estate Law.

*This loan ☐ may / ☐ will / ☐ will NOT (check one) be made wholly or in part from broker-controlled funds as defined in Section 10241(j) of the Business and Professions Code.

*NOTICE TO BORROWER: This disclosure statement may be used if the broker is acting as an agent in arranging the loan by a third person or if the loan will be made with funds owned or controlled by the broker. If the broker indicates in the above statement that the loan "may" be made out of broker-controlled funds, the broker must notify the borrower prior to the close of escrow if the funds to be received by the borrower are in fact broker-controlled funds.

_____   _____
(Name of Broker)   (Name of Designated Representative)

_____   _____
(License Number)   (License Number)

_____ OR _____
(Signature of Broker)   (Signature of Designated Representative)

NOTICE TO BORROWER: DO NOT SIGN THIS STATEMENT UNTIL YOU HAVE READ AND UNDERSTOOD ALL OF THE INFORMATION IN IT. ALL PARTS OF THE FORM MUST BE COMPLETED BEFORE YOU SIGN.

Borrower hereby acknowledges the receipt of a copy of this page which constitutes page 2 of 2 pages.

DATE: _____   _____
(Borrower)

_____
(Borrower)

D.R.E. MLDS 514 121191   MR OCT 94

MORTGAGE LOAN DISCLOSURE STATEMENT (BORROWER) (MS-14 PAGE 2 OF 2)

Chapter Summary

1. The federal government influences real estate finance directly and indirectly through fiscal and monetary policy. The federal deficit may affect the availability of investment funds. The Federal Reserve Board uses reserve requirements, the discount rate, and open market operations to implement monetary policy, influencing the pace of economic growth and market interest rates.

2. The primary market is the local finance market, in which lenders make mortgage loans to borrowers. In the secondary market, mortgages are bought and sold by investors. The federal government created the major secondary market agencies, Fannie Mae, Freddie Mac, and Ginnie Mae, to help moderate local real estate cycles.

3. Real estate lenders in the primary market include savings and loan associations, commercial banks, savings banks, mortgage companies, credit unions, and private lenders.

4. A promissory note is a written promise to repay a debt. For a real estate loan, the borrower is required to sign a negotiable promissory note along with a security instrument, which makes the borrower's property collateral for the loan.

5. The two main types of security instruments are mortgages and deeds of trust. The central difference between the two is that a deed of trust includes a power of sale clause, which allows the trustee to foreclose nonjudicially in the event of default.

6. Most security instruments include an acceleration clause and an alienation clause; some also have a prepayment provision or a subordination clause. If the loan documents do not have an alienation clause, the loan can be assumed without the lender's consent.

7. A mortgage is foreclosed judicially. The borrower has an equitable right of redemption before the sheriff's sale and a statutory right of redemption for a certain period afterwards. The lender may be entitled to a deficiency judgment.

8. A deed of trust can be foreclosed nonjudicially by the trustee, which is usually much faster and less expensive than judicial foreclosure. Before the trustee's sale, the borrower has the right to cure the default and reinstate the loan. After the sale, the borrower has no right of redemption. The lender cannot obtain a deficiency judgment.

9. There are many different types of mortgage loans, including purchase money, budget, blanket, package, open-end, participation, wraparound, and construction mortgages.

10. The Truth in Lending Act applies to any consumer loan that is secured by real property. It requires lenders and credit arrangers to give loan applicants a disclosure statement about loan costs. It also regulates how financing information is presented in advertising. In California, the Purchase Money Loan Disclosure Law and the Mortgage Loan Broker Law also require disclosure statements to be prepared in certain transactions.

⚷ Key Terms

Federal Reserve Board—The body that regulates commercial banks and sets and implements the federal government's monetary policy; commonly called "the Fed."

Reserve requirements—The percentages of deposits commercial banks must keep on reserve with a Federal Reserve Bank.

Discount rate—The interest rate the Fed charges on loans to member banks.

Open market operations—The Fed's activities in buying and selling government securities.

Primary market—The local finance market, where individuals obtain loans (from mutual savings banks, savings and loans, etc.).

Secondary market—The national finance market, where mortgages are bought and sold as investments.

Mortgage company—A company that acts as an intermediary between lender and borrower, arranging loans and servicing them, or selling them to investors.

Promissory note—A written promise to repay a debt.

Mortgage—A two-party security instrument that gives the lender (mortgagee) the right to foreclose on the security property by judicial process if the borrower (mortgagor) defaults.

Deed of trust—A three-party security instrument that includes a power of sale clause, allowing the trustee to foreclose nonjudicially if the borrower (trustor) fails to pay the lender (beneficiary) or otherwise defaults.

Acceleration clause—A provision that gives the lender the right to declare the whole debt immediately due and payable if the borrower defaults.

Alienation clause—A provision that gives the lender the right to accelerate the loan if the borrower transfers the property; also called a due-on-sale clause.

Assumption—When a borrower sells the security property to a buyer who agrees to take on personal liability for repayment of the existing mortgage or deed of trust.

Defeasance clause—A provision giving the borrower the right to regain title to the security property when the debt is repaid.

Land contract—A contract between a seller (vendor) and a buyer (vendee) of real estate, in which the seller retains legal title to the property while the buyer pays off the purchase price in installments.

Truth in Lending Act (TILA)—A federal consumer protection law that requires disclosure of financing costs and terms to consumer loan applicants and in advertising.

Regulation Z—The Federal Reserve Board's regulation that implements the Truth in Lending Act.

APR—Annual percentage rate; the relationship of the total finance charge to the loan amount, expressed as an annual percentage.

Chapter 9—Quiz
Real Estate Finance: Principles

1. In a tight money market, when business is slow, lowering of interest rates would be expected to cause:

   a) an increase in real estate sales
   b) more bank lending activity
   c) increased business activity
   d) All of the above

2. Which of the following actions by the Federal Reserve Board would tend to increase the money supply?

   a) Selling government securities on the open market
   b) Buying government securities on the open market
   c) Increasing the federal discount rate
   d) Increasing reserve requirements

3. Funds for single-family mortgage loans are supplied by:

   a) Fannie Mae
   b) savings and loan associations
   c) Both a) and b)
   d) Neither a) nor b)

4. With an installment note, the periodic payments:

   a) include both principal and interest
   b) are interest only
   c) are principal only
   d) are called balloon payments

5. A clause in a mortgage that permits the lender to declare the entire loan balance due upon default by the borrower is:

   a) an acceleration clause
   b) an escalator clause
   c) a forfeiture clause
   d) a subordination clause

6. A clause in a mortgage that permits the lender to declare the entire loan balance due if the property is sold is:

   a) an escalator clause
   b) a subordination clause
   c) an alienation clause
   d) a prepayment provision

7. After a mortgage foreclosure sale, the mortgagor has a limited period in which to redeem the property. This period is called:

   a) the lien period
   b) the equitable redemption period
   c) the statutory redemption period
   d) the homestead period

8. After a sheriff's sale, if there are any sale proceeds left over after paying off liens and foreclosure expenses, the money belongs to the:

   a) sheriff
   b) county auditor
   c) mortgagee
   d) mortgagor

9. The Shimuras are borrowing money from a lending institution; the loan will be secured by a mortgage against their house. The Truth in Lending Act applies to this transaction only if:

    a) the loan amount is over $25,000
    b) the loan amount is $25,000 or less
    c) the house is a single-family residence
    d) the Shimuras are using the loan for personal, family, or household purposes

10. The Truth in Lending Act and Regulation Z:

    a) place restrictions on how much a lender can charge for a consumer loan
    b) require lenders to give loan applicants a disclosure statement concerning loan costs
    c) prohibit lenders from advertising specific financing terms
    d) All of the above

11. A loan's APR expresses the relationship between:

    a) the total finance charge and the loan amount
    b) the interest rate on the loan and the discount rate
    c) the downpayment and the total finance charge
    d) the monthly payment and the interest rate

12. A budget mortgage:

    a) is a loan made to a low-income borrower
    b) is a construction loan with a fixed disbursement plan
    c) is secured by personal property as well as real property
    d) has monthly payments that include taxes and insurance as well as principal and interest

13. The owner of five parcels of real property wants a loan. She offers all five parcels as security. She will be required to execute:

    a) a soft money mortgage
    b) a participation mortgage
    c) a package mortgage
    d) a blanket mortgage

14. Van Dyke is borrowing money to buy some land, and he plans to build a home on the property later on. In order to make sure he will be able to get a construction loan when the time comes, Van Dyke should make sure the mortgage he executes for the land loan includes:

    a) a lien waiver
    b) a subordination clause
    c) an acceleration clause
    d) a wraparound clause

15. Under a fixed disbursement plan for a construction loan, the contractor is entitled to his or her final draw when:

    a) the project has been satisfactorily completed
    b) 80% of the work has been completed
    c) the building department issues a certificate of occupancy
    d) the period for claiming construction liens expires

Answer Key

1.d) The Fed lowers interest rates in times of economic downturn in an attempt to stimulate the economy.

2.b) When the Fed buys government securities, it puts more money into circulation, which tends to increase the money supply.

3.c) Mortgage money comes from the primary market (in the form of savings deposits) and from the secondary market (when investors like Fannie Mae buy mortgages).

4.a) An installment note involves periodic payments that include some of the principal as well as interest.

5.a) An acceleration clause gives the lender the right to declare the entire debt immediately due and payable if the borrower defaults.

6.c) An alienation clause allows the lender to accelerate the loan if the borrower transfers the security property without the lender's approval.

7.c) The statutory redemption period is the period of time after the sheriff's sale in which the borrower has the right to redeem the property by paying off the entire debt, plus costs.

8.d) Any excess proceeds from a foreclosure sale belong to the borrower—that is, to the mortgagor (or in the case of a deed of trust, to the trustor).

9.d) Any consumer loan secured by real property is covered by the Truth in Lending Act, regardless of the loan amount. A consumer loan is defined as a loan used for personal, family, or household purposes.

10.b) TILA and Regulation Z require lenders to disclose loan costs to loan applicants, but they do not restrict how much a lender can charge in connection with a loan. And while these laws regulate how financing terms are presented in advertising, they do not prohibit advertisement of financing terms.

11.a) The APR is the annual percentage rate, which indicates the relationship between the total finance charge and the loan amount.

12.d) A budget mortgage payment includes a share of the property taxes and hazard insurance as well as principal and interest.

13.d) A blanket mortgage has more than one parcel of property as collateral.

14.b) A subordination clause in the mortgage for the land loan would give it a lower priority than a mortgage executed later on for a construction loan. Lenders generally require first lien position for construction loans, because they are considered especially risky.

15.d) Construction lenders usually delay the final disbursement until no more construction liens can be filed.

Chapter 10

Real Estate Finance: Loan Underwriting

 Outline

I. Income
  A. Quantity
  B. Quality
  C. Durability
  D. Acceptable types of income
  E. Unacceptable types of income
  F. Calculating stable monthly income
  G. Income ratios
II. Net Worth
  A. Assets
  B. Liabilities
  C. Gift letter
III. Credit History
  A. Credit reports
  B. Explaining derogatory credit information

 Chapter Overview

An institutional lender will finance a real estate transaction only if the buyer qualifies for the proposed loan. This chapter explains how a lender evaluates a buyer's financial situation in deciding whether or not to approve a loan. The process includes analysis of the buyer's income, calculation of the buyer's net worth, and a review of the buyer's credit history.

Introduction

Before agreeing to make a real estate loan, a lender evaluates both the buyer and the property to determine whether they qualify for the loan—whether they meet the lender's minimum standards. This evaluation process is called **loan underwriting.** The person who conducts the evaluation is called a loan underwriter or credit underwriter.

The primary purpose of the evaluation is to determine the degree of risk that the loan would involve. This determination hinges on the answers to two fundamental questions:

1. Does the buyer's overall financial situation indicate that he or she can reasonably be expected to make the proposed monthly loan payments on time?

2. Is there sufficient value in the property pledged as collateral to assure recovery of the loan amount in the event of default?

Because the lender wants to avoid default, the underwriter tries to make sure the buyer is someone who can afford the loan and who is unlikely to default. But since default always remains a possibility, the underwriter also tries to make sure that the property is worth enough so that the proceeds of a foreclosure sale would cover the loan amount. The underwriter's evaluation of the property is based on an appraisal; the appraisal process is discussed in Chapter 12. This chapter focuses on how the underwriter qualifies the buyer.

In theory, a lender is free to set its own underwriting standards, taking virtually any risks it likes. In practice, however, nearly every lender applies standards set by the major secondary market agencies, or by the FHA or VA. Each of these three sets of underwriting standards (Fannie Mae/Freddie Mac, FHA, and VA) is different. The specific rules used for each type of loan will be explained in Chapter 11. But the underwriting process is basically the same no matter what type of loan the buyer has applied for.

In evaluating a loan applicant's financial situation, an underwriter must consider many factors. These factors fall into three main groups:

1. income,
2. net worth, and
3. credit history.

Income

From an underwriter's point of view, income has three dimensions:

1. quantity,
2. quality, and
3. durability.

Quantity

A primary consideration for the underwriter is whether the loan applicant's monthly income is enough to cover the proposed monthly mortgage payment in addition to all of the applicant's other expenses. So the underwriter looks into how much income the applicant has. Not all income is equal in an underwriter's eyes, however. Only income that meets the tests of quality and durability will be taken into account in deciding whether the applicant has enough income to qualify for the loan.

Quality (Dependability)

To evaluate the quality of a loan applicant's income, the underwriter looks at the sources from which it is derived. The income sources should be reasonably dependable, such as an established employer, a government agency, or an interest-yielding investment account. The less dependable the source (a brand new company or a high-risk investment, for example), the lower the quality of the income.

Durability (Probability of Continuance)

Income is considered durable if it can be expected to continue for a sustained period. Wages from permanent employment, disability benefits, and interest on established investments are all examples of durable income.

Acceptable Types of Income

Income that meets the tests of quality and durability is generally referred to as the loan applicant's **stable monthly income**. Typically, stable monthly income is made up of earnings from one primary income source, such as a full-time job, plus earnings from acceptable secondary sources. Secondary income sources can take many forms, such as bonuses, commissions (over and above a base salary), social security payments, military disability and retirement payments, interest on savings or other investments, and so on.

The following are among the types of income that generally meet the tests of quality and durability, so that lenders are willing to count them as part of the loan applicant's stable monthly income.

Permanent Employment. When evaluating income from permanent employment, the underwriter analyzes the loan applicant's employment pattern. An applicant with a history of steady, full-time employment will be given more favorable consideration than one who has changed employers frequently, unless there were good reasons for the changes. If the applicant changed jobs to advance in the same line of work, the underwriter is likely to view the change favorably. On the other hand, persistent job-hopping without advancement often signifies a problem of some kind, and the underwriter will probably regard the applicant's earnings as unstable.

As a general rule, a loan applicant should have continuous employment for at least **two years** in the same field. Occasionally, in special circumstances, loan approval may be warranted even without an established two-year work history; for example, the applicant may have recently left the armed services or finished college. Training or education that has

Fig.10.1 Underwriting: income evaluation

Income

• Quantity, quality, and durability

• Stable monthly income

• Income ratios
   • Debt to income ratio
   • Housing expense to income ratio

prepared the loan applicant for a specific kind of work can strengthen the application.

Bonuses, Commissions, Overtime, Part-time. These forms of income are considered durable if they can be shown to have been a consistent part of the loan applicant's overall earnings pattern for at least one but preferably two years.

Verifying Employment Income. Traditionally, lenders verified employment income by sending an income verification form directly to the loan applicant's employer. The employer filled out the form and then sent it directly back to the lender. The applicant was not allowed to have any contact with the verification forms.

That method of verifying employment income is still in use, but now there is also an alternative method. The loan applicant can provide the lender with W-2 forms for the previous two years and payroll stubs or vouchers for the previous 30-day period. The pay stubs must identify the applicant, the employer, and the applicant's gross earnings for both the current pay period and the year to date. The lender then confirms the employment and earnings information with a phone call to the employer.

Self-employment Income. Self-employed loan applicants should be prepared to provide audited profit and loss statements, balance sheets, and federal income tax returns for the two years prior to the loan application.

If an applicant has been self-employed for less than two years, the underwriter will hesitate to approve the loan. Lenders are wary of new businesses and generally insist that the self-employed borrower have operated his or her business profitably for at least two years.

Retirement Income. Pension and social security payments received by retired persons are usually dependable and durable, so underwriters ordinarily will include them in stable monthly income.

The Equal Credit Opportunity Act, a federal anti-discrimination law, prohibits age discrimination in lending. Nonetheless, it is not illegal for an underwriter to consider the loan applicant's life expectancy when deciding whether or not to approve a loan.

Alimony, Spousal Maintenance, Child Support. These types of income are considered part of stable monthly income only if it appears that the payments will be made reliably. That determination depends on whether the payments are required by a court decree, how long the loan applicant has been receiving the payments, the overall financial and credit status of the payor, and the applicant's ability to compel payment if necessary.

A copy of the court decree must be submitted to the lender, and unless payments are made through the court, proof of receipt of payments is required. The underwriter will examine the record of payment. If some payments were missed or were significantly late, the underwriter will probably exclude the alimony, maintenance, or child support from the applicant's stable monthly income.

An ex-spouse's obligation to pay child support ordinarily ends when the child turns 18. As a result, whether an underwriter will include child support payments in a loan applicant's stable monthly income depends on the age of the applicant's child. The closer a child gets to age 18, the less durable child support becomes. If the child is 16 or older, it is very unlikely that the underwriter will count the child support payments as stable monthly income. For some loan programs the official cutoff age is even younger.

Public Assistance. The Equal Credit Opportunity Act prohibits lenders from discriminating against loan applicants because all or part of their income is derived from a public assistance program (such as welfare, Aid to Families with Dependent Children, or food stamps). Public assistance payments will be counted as part of a loan applicant's stable monthly income as long as they meet the test of durability. If the applicant's eligibility for the assistance program will terminate in the near future, the underwriter will not take the payments into account.

Investment Income. Dividends or interest on investments may be counted as part of stable monthly income. Of course, if the loan applicant is going to cash in an investment to raise the funds needed for closing (see below), then the underwriter will not regard that investment as a durable source of income.

Rental Income. Income from rental properties can be counted as stable monthly income if a stable pattern of rental income can be verified. Authenticated copies of the owner's books showing gross earnings and operating expenses for the previous two years should be submitted, along with the applicant's income tax returns.

There are many unpredictable factors connected with rental income, such as emergency repairs, vacancies, and tenants who don't pay. To leave a margin of error, the underwriter may include only a certain percentage (for example, 75%) of the verified rental income in the loan applicant's stable monthly income.

Co-mortgagors. Frequently a co-mortgagor is used to help a primary borrower qualify for a loan. Parents often lend their established income and financial status to their children who otherwise would be unable to purchase a home. A co-mortgagor is simply a co-borrower, someone who (along with the primary borrower) accepts responsibility for repayment of the loan by signing the promissory note and mortgage. Like the primary borrower, the co-mortgagor must have income, assets, and a credit history that are acceptable to the underwriter.

Keep in mind that a co-mortgagor must be able to support both his or her own housing expense and a proportionate share, if not all, of the proposed housing expense. Marginal co-mortgagors should not be relied on; they may do more harm than good to the loan application.

Unacceptable Types of Income

The following are some types of income that underwriters usually exclude from a loan applicant's stable monthly income.

Temporary Employment Income. Income from any job (full- or part-time) that the employer classifies as temporary ordinarily does not count as stable monthly income, even if there is no definite termination date. In some cases, however, when the loan applicant has supported him or herself through a particular type of temporary work for years, that income can be presented to the lender as income from self-employment.

Unemployment. Unemployment compensation is rarely treated as stable monthly income, because eligibility usually lasts for only 26 weeks.

Income from Other Family Members. An underwriter will ordinarily consider only the earnings of the head(s) of the household—the loan applicant(s)—when calculating stable monthly income. Contributions from teenage children or other family members could stop without notice, so they are not regarded as durable.

Calculating Stable Monthly Income

After deciding which of the loan applicant's forms of income meet the tests of quality and durability, the underwriter returns to the question of quantity. He or she adds up the income from all the acceptable sources to determine the applicant's stable monthly income.

Many types of income are paid to the recipient once a month, but others are paid weekly, every two weeks, quarterly, or annually. Since what matters for the purposes of underwriting is stable monthly income, all payments are converted to monthly figures.

To convert hourly wages to monthly earnings, multiply the hourly wage by 40 (hours in a work week), then multiply by 52 (weeks in a year) and divide by 12 (months in a year).

> **Example:**
> Hourly Wage: $9.50
> Weekly Income: $9.50 × 40 = $380
> Annual Income: $380 × 52 = $19,760
> Monthly Income: $19,760 ÷ 12 = $1,647

Also, notice that being paid every two weeks (26 payments per year) is not the same as being paid twice a month (24 payments per year). If a buyer is paid every two weeks, multiply the payment amount by 26 to get the annual total, then divide that by 12 to get the monthly figure.

Income Ratios

Once the underwriter has calculated the loan applicant's stable monthly income, the next step is to measure the adequacy of that income: Is the applicant's stable monthly income enough so that he or she can afford the proposed monthly mortgage payment? To measure adequacy, underwriters use income ratios. The rationale behind the ratios is that if a borrower's expenses exceed a certain percentage of his or her monthly income, the borrower may have a difficult time making the payments on the loan.

There are two types of income ratios:

- A **debt to income ratio** measures the monthly mortgage payment plus any other regular installment debt payments against the stable monthly income. (This ratio is also called a **total debt service ratio**.)
- A **housing expense to income ratio** measures the monthly mortgage payment alone against the stable monthly income.

For these calculations, the monthly mortgage payment includes principal, interest, taxes, and insurance (often abbreviated PITI). Each ratio is expressed as a percentage; for example, a loan applicant's housing expense to income ratio would be 29% if her proposed mortgage payment represented 29% of her stable monthly income. Whether that ratio would be considered too high would depend on the type of loan she was applying for. The specific income ratio limits used in each financing program—conventional, FHA, and VA—will be discussed in Chapter 11.

Net Worth

An individual's net worth is determined by subtracting personal liabilities from total personal assets. According to Fannie Mae, "accumulation of net worth is a strong indication of creditworthiness." A loan applicant who has built up a significant net worth from earnings, savings, and other investments clearly has the ability to manage financial affairs.

Getting an idea of the loan applicant's financial skills is not the only reason for investigating his or her net worth, however. The underwriter also needs to make sure the applicant has sufficient liquid assets for the purchase. Liquid assets include cash and any other assets that can be quickly converted to cash, such as stock. The applicant must have enough liquid assets to cover the downpayment, the closing costs, and other expenses incidental to the purchase of the property.

In addition, a loan applicant is often required to have reserves left over after making the downpayment and paying the closing costs. The reserves generally must include enough cash on deposit—or enough other liquid assets—to cover two or three months' mortgage payments. (The specific requirement depends on the loan program.) This provides some assurance that the applicant would be able to handle financial emergencies, such as unexpected bills or a temporary interruption of income, without defaulting on the mortgage.

Every loan application includes a section for listing the applicant's assets and liabilities. The

Fig.10.2 Underwriting: net worth evaluation

Net Worth

Assets - Liabilities = Net Worth

- Indication of financial management skills
- Liquid assets for purchase

underwriter will take whatever steps are necessary to verify the information provided. But when a loan applicant's assets are substantial and diverse, an audited financial statement is the best way to present his or her net worth to the underwriter. A financial statement is a summary of facts showing the individual's financial condition; it includes a detailed list of assets and liabilities. An audited statement is one that has been checked by a certified public accountant.

Assets

Any assets held by the buyer can help the loan application—real estate, automobiles, furniture, jewelry, stocks, bonds, or cash value in a life insurance policy. Liquid assets tend to be more helpful than non-liquid ones, and the asset that underwriters usually regard most favorably is the most liquid one of all: money in the bank.

Bank Accounts. An underwriter will use a "Request for Verification of Deposit" form to confirm that the loan applicant has the funds needed for the transaction in his or her bank account(s). This form is sent directly to the bank and returned to the underwriter without passing through the applicant's hands. When the underwriter receives the completed verification of deposit, he or she will look for four things:

1. Does the verified information conform to the statements in the loan application?
2. Does the applicant have enough money in the bank to meet the expenses of purchase?
3. Has the bank account been opened only recently (within the last couple of months)?
4. Is the present balance notably higher than the average balance?

Recently opened accounts or higher-than-normal balances must be explained, as these are strong indications that the applicant has resorted to borrowed funds to pay the downpayment and closing costs. Borrowing from a relative, a friend, or any other source to come up with either the funds needed for closing or the reserves is impermissible, because it would defeat the purpose of the lender's requirements. The buyer would have an additional debt instead of an investment in the property.

An alternative method of verifying deposits is acceptable to some lenders: the loan applicant may submit bank statements for the previous three months to show that there is sufficient cash for closing.

Real Estate for Sale. If a loan applicant is selling another property to raise cash for the current purchase, the net equity in the property that is for sale can be counted as a liquid asset—available to be applied to the downpayment, closing costs, and required reserves. The net equity is the difference between the market value of the property and the sum of the liens against the property plus the selling expenses. In other words, the loan applicant's net equity is the amount of money he or she can expect to receive from the sale of the property.

> **Example:** The Cortinas put their home up for sale a month ago, and now they've found the home they want to buy. They've signed a purchase agreement for the new home that is contingent on the sale of the old home and also on their ability to obtain financing. When they apply for a loan to finance the purchase of their new home, the underwriter will count their net equity in the old home as a liquid asset.

$189,000	market value of old home
− 133,000	first mortgage (to be paid off)
− 10,000	home improvement loan (to be paid off)
46,000	gross equity
− 19,000	estimated cost of selling old home
$27,000	net equity
$27,000	net equity in old home
+ 13,000	cash in savings account
$40,000	available for purchase of new home

The underwriter's calculation of net equity begins either with the appraised value of the old home or, if the loan applicant has already found a buyer for the old home, with the price that buyer has agreed to pay. Estimated selling costs vary from one area of the country to another, but a figure between 10% and 13% of the sales price is generally used.

Other Real Estate. Often a loan applicant owns real estate that he or she is not planning to sell. Whether the real estate is income-producing (e.g., rental property) or not (e.g., vacant land), it is an asset and should be considered in connection with the loan application.

Bear in mind, though, that it is the equity, not the value of the property, that contributes to net worth. Only the equity can be converted into cash in the event of need. When a loan applicant owns real estate with little or no equity in it, its impact as a liability (see below) cancels out its value as an asset.

Liabilities

All of the loan applicant's personal liabilities are subtracted from the total value of his or her assets to calculate net worth. The balances owing on credit cards, charge accounts, student loans, car loans, and other installment debts are subtracted; so are any other debts, such as income taxes that are currently payable. If the applicant owns real estate, the remaining principal balance on the mortgage will be subtracted, along with the amounts of any other liens against the property.

Gift Letter

If a loan applicant lacks some of the funds needed to close a transaction, his or her relatives may be willing to make up the deficit. The underwriter will usually accept this arrangement, as long as the money is a gift to the applicant rather than a loan. The gift should be confirmed by means of a "gift letter" signed by the donor. The letter should clearly state that the money is a gift and does not have to be repaid. Most lenders have forms for gift letters, and some require that their form be used.

Since gift funds have to be verified, the donor should actually give them (not just promise them) to the loan applicant as soon as possible. The applicant should deposit the gift funds in the bank so that they can be verified along with the rest of the money in his or her account.

The underwriter will also verify the information that the donor provides about the source of the funds: Did the donor actually have the money in savings, as he or she claims, or did the donor borrow it from someone else?

Credit History

In addition to evaluating the loan applicant's income and net worth, the underwriter also analyzes the applicant's credit history, using a credit report obtained from a credit rating bureau. If the report reveals derogatory information, the underwriter may turn down the loan application for that reason alone.

Credit Reports

A personal credit report (a report on an individual rather than a business) generally includes information about debts and repayment for the preceding seven years. The report primarily covers credit cards and loans; other bills, such as utility bills, usually aren't listed unless they were turned over to a collection agency. Here are the most common types of negative information on personal credit reports.

Slow payment. If the loan applicant is chronically late in paying his or her bills, that will be indicated on the credit report. The underwriter will interpret that as an inability or unwillingness to pay on time, a signal that the applicant tends to be financially overextended or fails to take debt repayment seriously (or both).

Bill consolidation, refinancing. In some cases, an individual's credit pattern is one of continually increasing liabilities and periodic "bailouts" through refinancing and debt consolidation. Because the pattern suggests a tendency to live beyond a prudent level, the individual may be classified as a marginal risk. This is a subjective consideration, likely to influence the underwriter's decision if the loan applicant is weak in other critical areas, such as income or assets.

Collections. After several attempts to get a debtor to pay a bill, a frustrated creditor may decide to turn the bill over to a collection agency. Collections remain on the debtor's credit report for seven years after the bill is turned over to the collection agency.

Repossessions. If a creditor sells personal property on credit and the debtor doesn't make the payments, the creditor may have the right to repossess the property. Repossessions stay on the debtor's credit report for seven years after they take place.

Foreclosures. A real estate foreclosure appears on the debtor's credit report for seven years after it is completed.

Judgments. If someone has successfully sued the loan applicant in the recent past, that will show up on the credit report. A judgment is listed on a credit report for seven years after it is entered in the public record.

Bankruptcies. There are three different types of bankruptcy: Chapter 7 (request for a total discharge of debts), Chapter 11 (reorganization of a business), and Chapter 13 (reorganization of personal finances). All three types of bankruptcies stay on the debtor's personal credit report for ten years.

Explaining Derogatory Credit Information

In some cases, a negative credit report does not prevent a buyer from obtaining a loan. Credit problems can often be explained. If the underwriter is convinced that the past problems don't reflect the loan applicant's overall attitude toward credit and that the circumstances leading to the problems were temporary and are unlikely to recur, the loan application may well be approved. It's a good idea for buyers to obtain a copy of their credit report before applying for a loan, so that they will be prepared to discuss any problems with the lender.

Most people try to meet their credit obligations on time; when they don't, there is usually a reason. The loss of a job, hospitalization, prolonged illness, a death in the family, or a divorce can create extraordinary financial pressures and adversely affect bill paying habits. If two or three derogatory items show up on a credit report, it may be possible to show that the problems occurred during a specific period of time for an understandable reason, and that prior and subsequent credit ratings have been good.

When explaining credit difficulties to a lender, it is a mistake to blame the problems on misunderstandings or on the creditors. Underwriters hear too many explanations from loan applicants who refuse to accept responsibility for their own acts, insisting instead that the blame lies elsewhere. The reaction to these explanations is very predictable: skepticism, disbelief, and rejection. Underwriters reason that an applicant's reluctance to take responsibility for past credit problems is an indication of what can be expected from him or her in the future.

If a loan applicant's credit report is laced with derogatory ratings over a period of years, there is probably little hope for loan approval. Perpetual credit problems are more likely to reflect an attitude than a circumstance, and it is reasonable to assume that the pattern will continue in the future.

All credit problems can be resolved with time, however. When buyers indicate they have had some credit problems in the past, it would be a mistake to leap to the conclusion that they cannot qualify for a loan. Refer them to a lender and get an expert's opinion.

A buyer's ability to qualify for a real estate loan depends on his or her overall financial situation. Each element (income, net worth, and credit history) is treated as part of the whole picture. Although a problem with any one of these factors may lead the underwriter to reject the loan application, that will not necessarily happen. For instance, a buyer with a marginal income may still qualify for a loan if the net worth is substantial enough to indicate an unusual ability to manage financial affairs. Or strong earnings and substantial assets may be enough to offset the damage caused by a poor credit rating.

Finally, keep in mind that in addition to evaluating the buyer, the underwriter is going to evaluate the property being offered as security for the loan. If the buyer wants to purchase a good property and plans to make a large downpayment, that can offset a marginal income or credit rating. A borrower with a significant amount of money invested in the property is less likely to default than one with little or no equity.

Chapter Summary

1. In qualifying a buyer for a real estate loan, an underwriter examines the buyer's income, net worth, and credit history to determine if he or she can be expected to make the proposed monthly mortgage payments.

2. An underwriter evaluates the quantity, quality, and durability of the loan applicant's income. Income that meets the tests of quality and durability is counted as part of the stable monthly income. Income ratios measure the adequacy of the stable monthly income—whether the applicant can afford the proposed mortgage payment.

3. Net worth is determined by subtracting liabilities from assets. The underwriter looks at net worth as evidence of the loan applicant's ability to manage his or her finances. Also, the applicant must have enough liquid assets to cover the downpayment, closing costs, and required reserves.

4. A loan applicant's credit report is analyzed to see what it reveals about his or her attitude toward credit. A personal credit report shows the applicant's credit history for the past seven years and any bankruptcies for the past ten years.

Key Terms

Loan underwriting—Evaluating the creditworthiness of the buyer and the value of the property to determine if a loan should be approved.

Stable monthly income—Income that satisfies the lender's standards of quality and durability.

Income ratios—Ratios used to determine whether the borrower's stable monthly income is enough to meet the proposed mortgage payments, as well as other monthly obligations.

Debt to income ratio—Measures the monthly mortgage payment plus any other monthly debt obligations against the stable monthly income. Also called the total debt service to income ratio.

Housing expense to income ratio—Measures only the monthly mortgage payment against the stable monthly income.

Net worth—Total personal assets less total personal liabilities.

Liquid assets—Cash and any other assets that can be quickly converted to cash.

Assets—Items of value owned by the borrower.

Gift funds—Money given to a loan applicant by a relative to be used for the downpayment or closing costs.

Gift letter—A letter that clearly states that gift funds do not have to be repaid.

Chapter 10—Quiz
Real Estate Finance: Loan Underwriting

1. To evaluate the quality of a loan applicant's income, an underwriter considers whether the income:

   a) is derived from a dependable source
   b) is taxable
   c) can be expected to continue for a sustained period
   d) can be treated as a liquid asset

2. As a general rule, a loan applicant should have been continuously employed in the same field for at least:

   a) one year
   b) two years
   c) three years
   d) five years

3. The loan applicant receives child support from her ex-husband. Her child is now 17 years old. Will the child support payments be counted as part of the applicant's stable monthly income?

   a) Yes
   b) Only if the ex-husband has made the payments reliably
   c) Only if the applicant can provide proof of receipt
   d) No

4. The Hendersons have applied for a mortgage loan. Which of these is the underwriter most likely to treat as part of their stable monthly income?

   a) Wages the Hendersons' teenage daughter earns at a part-time job
   b) Unemployment compensation the husband is collecting
   c) Overtime the wife has been earning at her permanent job
   d) Money the husband has earned through occasional free-lance work

5. After determining the quantity of the loan applicant's stable monthly income, the underwriter measures the adequacy of the income using:

   a) the consumer price index
   b) income ratios
   c) gross multipliers
   d) federal income tax tables

6. One reason an underwriter looks at a loan applicant's net worth is to see how well the applicant manages his or her financial affairs. Another reason is to:

   a) determine if the applicant has enough liquid assets to cover the costs of purchase and the required reserves
   b) find out if the new mortgage will have first lien position
   c) verify the accuracy of the applicant's credit rating
   d) prevent the applicant from resorting to gift funds for part of the closing costs

7. The Stanleys are selling their old home, and they plan to use the sale proceeds as a down-payment in buying a new home. In adding up the Stanleys' liquid assets, an underwriter would be willing to include:

   a) the sales price of the old home
   b) the Stanleys' net equity in the old home
   c) the Stanleys' gross equity in the old home
   d) None of the above

8. Steinhof doesn't have enough money for closing, so his parents are going to give him $2,500. The underwriter will:

   a) require the parents to sign a gift letter
   b) verify that the gift funds have been deposited into Steinhof's bank account
   c) verify the source of the gift funds
   d) All of the above

9. As a general rule, a personal credit report includes information about an individual's debts and payment history for the preceding:

   a) fifteen years
   b) ten years
   c) seven years
   d) five years

10. Nguyen, who is applying for a mortgage loan, is self-employed. As a result, the underwriter will:

    a) require her to submit income tax returns and other special documentation to verify her income
    b) require her to use a co-mortgagor
    c) require her to have a net worth of $20,000 or more
    d) reject her loan application

11. The Bergerhoffs are applying for a home loan. James Bergerhoff is receiving unemployment benefits, and the family also receives public assistance in the form of welfare. A lender will probably:

    a) take into account both the unemployment and the welfare income
    b) take into account the unemployment income but not the welfare income
    c) take into account the welfare income but not the unemployment income
    d) refuse to take into account either source of income

12. Mary Callard is applying for a home loan. She has a rental property that generates $700 a month in rent. She pays $500 a month in expenses on the rental property, including a mortgage payment. She will probably be able to include in her stable monthly income:

    a) $200 a month
    b) $150 a month
    c) $100 a month
    d) Nothing, as rental income is never acceptable

13. Harris makes $2,500 a month as a takeout cook. His wife, Marie, makes $1,000 at a part-time bookkeeping job. Their daughter, Susan, makes about $200 a month cleaning houses and baby-sitting. Their son, Timothy, makes $500 a month working part-time for a local mill. The family's stable monthly income is:

    a) $2,500 a month
    b) $3,500 a month
    c) $3,700 a month
    d) $4,200 a month

14. Susan Martinez works full-time (40 hours a week). She earns $13.75 an hour. Her monthly income is:

    a) $2,200
    b) $2,152
    c) $2,383
    d) $2,476

15. Net equity in real estate that is for sale can be applied towards a downpayment. Net equity is:

    a) market value minus the liens and the selling expenses
    b) market value plus the selling expenses, minus the liens
    c) the liens plus the selling expenses, minus the market value
    d) market value plus the liens, minus the selling expenses

Answer Key

1.a) Quality of income is measured by the dependability of its source.

2.b) Underwriters like to see loan applicants who have worked in their current field for at least two years.

3.d) Because the child is so near the age of majority, it is unlikely that the child support payments will be counted as stable monthly income.

4.c) Overtime will be considered stable monthly income if it has been a consistent part of the loan applicant's earnings.

5.b) Income ratios determine the adequacy of stable monthly income.

6.a) Net worth is calculated to determine whether the loan applicant can afford to close the transaction.

7.b) Net equity in a home being sold can be counted as a liquid asset.

8.d) Underwriters are very careful to make sure that gift funds are in fact a gift and not a loan.

9.c) Although bankruptcies are listed on a credit report for ten years, the majority of the information covers the borrower's credit history for the past seven years.

10.a) A self-employed loan applicant is required to provide extra documentation for income verification.

11.c) Welfare is usually considered acceptable income, unemployment is usually not.

12.b) 75% of net rental income may generally be considered stable monthly income.

13.b) The income of the applicant and the applicant's spouse may be considered stable monthly income. The income of children may not.

14.c) $13.75 \times 40 \times 52 \div 12 = \$2,383$.

15.a) Net equity is market value minus the liens and the selling expenses.

Chapter 11

Real Estate Finance: Financing Programs

 Outline

 Chapter Overview

The various residential financing programs offered by institutional lenders can be divided into two main groups: conventional loan programs and government-sponsored loan programs. Each program has its own underwriting standards, and its own rules concerning everything from downpayments to interest rates to secondary financing. In this chapter, we will look first at conventional loans; then at the most important types of home loans sponsored by the federal government: FHA-insured loans and VA-guaranteed loans; and then at the state-sponsored Cal-Vet loans.

Conventional Loans

A conventional loan is simply any institutional loan that is not insured or guaranteed by a government agency. For example, FHA-insured and VA-guaranteed loans are not conventional loans, because they are backed by a government agency.

The details of the conventional loan programs presented in this chapter reflect the criteria established by the secondary market agencies that purchase conventional loans, Fannie Mae and Freddie Mac (see Chapter 9). When a loan does not meet secondary market criteria, it is considered **nonconforming** and cannot be sold to the major secondary market agencies. Today, most lenders want to be able to sell their loans on the secondary market, so they consistently tailor their standards for conventional loans to match those set by Fannie Mae or Freddie Mac.

In this section, we will describe the most important characteristics of conventional loans. We will also explain certain basic financing concepts that apply to virtually any type of real estate loan, such as amortization and loan-to-value ratios.

Amortization

Almost all conventional loans are **fully amortized**. A fully amortized loan is repaid within a certain period of time by means of regular payments that include a portion for principal and a portion for interest. As each payment is made, the appropriate amount of principal is deducted from the debt and the remainder of the payment, which represents the interest, is retained by the lender as

earnings or profit. With each payment, the amount of the debt is reduced and the interest due with the next payment is recalculated based on the lower balance. The total payment can remain the same throughout the term of the loan, but every month the interest portion of the payment is reduced and the principal portion is increased. (See Figure 11.1.) The final payment pays off the loan completely; the principal balance is zero and no further interest is owed.

> **Example:** A $90,000 loan at 10.25% interest can be fully amortized over a 30-year term with monthly principal and interest payments of $806.49. If the borrower pays $806.49 each month, the loan will be fully repaid (with interest) after 30 years.

There are two alternatives to the fully amortized loan. A **partially amortized** loan requires regular payments of both interest and principal, but those payments are not enough to repay all of the principal; the borrower must make a large balloon payment (the remaining principal balance) at the end of the term.

Fig.11.1 Loan amortization

Example: $90,000 loan @ 10.25%, 30-year term, monthly payments

Payment No.	Beginning Balance	Total Payment	Interest Portion	Principal Portion	Ending Balance
1	$90,000.00	$806.49	$768.75	$37.74	$89,962.26
2	$89,962.26	$806.49	$768.43	$38.06	$89,924.20
3	$89,924.20	$806.49	$768.10	$38.39	$89,885.81
4	$89,885.81	$806.49	$767.77	$38.72	$89,847.09
5	$89,847.09	$806.49	$767.44	$39.05	$89,808.04

Example: Betty takes back a $90,000 mortgage at 10.25% interest on the sale of her home to Bob. The mortgage calls for regular monthly payments of $806.49 for principal and interest, with a loan term of five years. Because the monthly payments are more than enough to cover the interest on the loan, some of the principal will be repaid during the five-year term. But since it would take 30 years to fully repay the loan at this rate, a substantial amount of principal ($87,060) will still be unpaid after only five years. This amount will be due as a balloon payment, which Bob will have to either refinance or pay in cash.

With an **interest-only** loan, the borrower pays only the interest during the loan term, and all of the principal—the entire amount originally borrowed— is due at the end of the term.

Example: Suppose Betty (from the previous example) had given Bob an interest-only loan for $90,000 at 10.25% interest. In that case, the monthly payments would be only $768.75, the amount needed to cover the monthly interest on the loan. At the expiration of the five-year term, Bob would owe the full $90,000 of principal to Betty.

Partial amortization and interest-only loans are fairly common in seller financing arrangements, but institutional lenders do not use them for residential mortgage loans very often.

Repayment Periods

The loan term (the repayment period) has a significant impact on both the monthly mortgage payment and the total amount of interest paid over the life of the loan. The longer the term, the lower the monthly payment, and the more interest paid.

Since the 1930s, the standard term for a mortgage loan has been 30 years. This long repayment period makes the monthly payments affordable, which reduces the risk of default.

Although 30-year loans continue to predominate, in the last decade 15-year loans have gained popularity. A 15-year loan has higher monthly payments than a comparable 30-year loan, but the 15-year loan offers substantial savings for the borrower in the long run. Lenders frequently offer lower interest rates on 15-year loans, because the shorter term means less risk for the lender. And the borrower will save thousands of dollars in total interest charges

Fig.11.2 A 15-year loan offers substantial savings over a 30-year loan

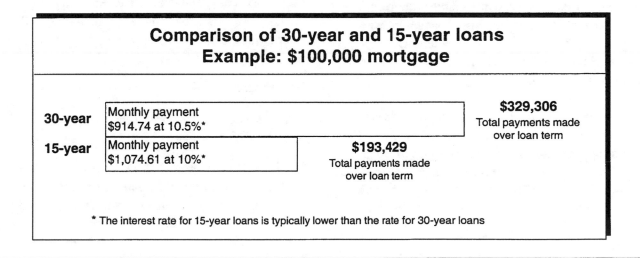

Comparison of 30-year and 15-year loans
Example: $100,000 mortgage

30-year	Monthly payment $914.74 at 10.5%*	**$329,306** Total payments made over loan term
15-year	Monthly payment $1,074.61 at 10%*	**$193,429** Total payments made over loan term

* The interest rate for 15-year loans is typically lower than the rate for 30-year loans over the life of the loan (see Figure 11.2). A 15-year loan also offers free and clear home ownership in half the time.

However, the monthly payments are significantly higher for a 15-year loan, and in some cases a larger downpayment is necessary to reduce the monthly payments to a level the borrower can afford.

> **Example:** Bob has a choice between a 30-year loan at 10.5% and a 15-year loan at 10%. Based on his stable monthly income, he can afford to make monthly principal and interest payments of $1,000. This is enough to amortize a $109,000 loan at 10.5% over 30 years, but will only amortize $93,000 at 10% over 15 years. Bob could qualify for a $109,000 loan under the 30-year plan, but will qualify for only $93,000 if he chooses the 15-year option. The difference would have to be made up in the form of a larger downpayment.

Fixed and Adjustable Interest Rates

A fixed-rate loan is repaid over its term at an unchanging rate of interest. For example, the interest rate is set at 10% when the loan is made, and the borrower pays 10% interest on the unpaid principal throughout the loan term.

Until the late 1970s, most real estate loans were fixed-rate loans. But when market interest rates are high and volatile (as they were in the 1980s) neither borrowers nor lenders feel comfortable with fixed-rate loans. When interest rates are high, many borrowers are priced out of the market. And when market interest rates are fluctuating rapidly, lenders prefer not to tie up their funds for long periods of time at a set interest rate.

A type of loan that addresses both of these issues is the **adjustable-rate mortgage (ARM)**. An ARM permits the lender to periodically adjust the loan's interest rate so that it accurately reflects changes in the cost of money. With an ARM, it is the borrower who is affected by interest rate fluctuations. If rates climb, the borrower's monthly payment goes up; if

they decline, the payment goes down. Because the ARM shifts this risk to the borrower, lenders usually charge a lower rate for an ARM than for a fixed-rate loan.

ARMs became very popular during the 1980s. Now that market interest rates are low again, fixed-rate loans are back in favor, but many borrowers continue to choose ARMs. They appear to have found a permanent niche in the residential financing market.

How an ARM Works. With an ARM, the borrower's interest rate is determined initially by the cost of money at the time the loan is made. Once the rate has been set, it is tied to one of several widely recognized indexes, and future interest adjustments are based on the upward and downward movements of the index.

Index and Margin. An **index** is a published statistical rate that is a reliable indicator of changes in the cost of money. Examples include the one-year Treasury bill index and the Eleventh District cost of funds index. At the time a loan is made, the lender selects the index it prefers, and thereafter the loan interest rate will rise and fall with the rates reported for the index.

Since the index is a reflection of the lender's cost of money, it is necessary to add a **margin** to the index to ensure sufficient income for administrative expenses and profit. The lender's margin is usually 2% or 3%, or somewhere in between. The index plus the margin equals the interest rate charged to the borrower.

> **Example:**
>
> | | |
> |---|---|
> | 6.75% | current index value |
> | + 2.00% | margin |
> | 8.75% | borrower's interest rate |

It is the index that fluctuates during the loan term and causes the borrower's interest rate to increase and decrease; the lender's margin remains constant.

Adjustment Periods. The borrower's interest rate is not adjusted every time the index changes. Each ARM has a **rate adjustment period**, which determines how often its interest rate is adjusted. It may be adjusted every six months, once a year, or every three years. A rate adjustment period of one year is the most common, and ARMs with one-year rate adjustment periods are referred to as one-year ARMs.

An ARM also has a **payment adjustment period**. This is the interval at which the borrower's monthly mortgage payment is increased or decreased (reflecting changes in the interest rate). It is most common for the payment to be adjusted each time the interest rate is adjusted, but some ARMs have a payment adjustment period that is longer than the rate adjustment period. For example, a loan agreement could call for interest rate adjustments once a year, but payment adjustments only once every three years.

Caps. One problem associated with ARMs is a phenomenon known as "payment shock." If market interest rates begin to rise rapidly, so will an ARM's index, which could lead to a sharp increase in the interest rate the lender charges the borrower. Of course, a higher interest rate translates into a higher monthly payment. If the payment increases so dramatically that the borrower can no longer afford it, it's called payment shock.

To protect borrowers from payment shock and themselves from default, lenders impose caps on their ARMs. An **interest rate cap** limits how much the lender can raise the interest rate on the loan, even if the index goes way up. By limiting interest rate increases, the cap prevents the monthly payment from increasing too much. Typical interest rate caps are 2% per year and 5% for the life of the loan.

A second way of limiting payment increases is with a **mortgage payment cap**. A payment cap limits how much the lender can raise the monthly mortgage payment. A typical payment cap limits payment increases to 7.5% annually.

Negative Amortization. When an adjustable-rate mortgage has certain features, such as a mortgage payment cap, payment increases may not keep up with increases in the loan's interest rate, so that the monthly payments do not cover all the interest owed. The lender usually handles this by adding the unpaid interest to the loan's principal balance; this is called **negative amortization**. Ordinarily, a loan's principal balance declines steadily, although gradually. But negative amortization causes the principal balance to go up instead of down. The borrower may owe the lender more money than he or she originally borrowed.

Today, lenders generally structure their ARMs to avoid negative amortization. But when negative amortization is a possibility, the loan usually has a negative amortization cap: a limit on the amount of unpaid interest that can be added to the principal balance. When the negative amortization cap is reached, the loan is reamortized so that the entire principal amount will be paid off by the end of the loan term.

Conversion Option. Some ARM borrowers find they feel uncomfortable with the risk of rate and payment increases their loans involve. Most ARMs made today have a provision that allows the borrower to convert the ARM into a fixed-rate mortgage at a certain point during the loan term.

Example: The Morleys have an ARM with a 7.75% rate. The current fixed rate is 9%. The Morleys fear that rates are going to increase dramatically in the next few years, so they convert their 7.75% ARM into a 9% fixed-rate loan.

Loan-to-Value Ratios

The loan-to-value ratio (LTV) for a particular transaction expresses the relationship between the loan amount and the value of the property offered as security. The lower the LTV, the smaller the loan amount and the bigger the downpayment.

Example: If a lender makes an $80,000 loan secured by a home appraised at $100,000, the loan-to-value ratio is 80%. The loan amount is

80% of the property's value, and the buyer makes a 20% downpayment. If the lender loaned $75,000 secured by the same property, the LTV would be 75%, and the downpayment would be 25%.

The loan-to-value ratio affects the degree of risk involved in the loan—both the risk of default and the risk of loss in the event of default. A borrower who has a substantial investment in the property will try harder to avoid foreclosure; and when foreclosure is necessary, the lender is more likely to recover the entire debt if the LTV is relatively low.

The higher the LTV, the greater the lender's risk. So lenders use loan-to-value ratios to set maximum loan amounts.

Example: If a lender's maximum LTV for a particular type of loan was 75%, and the property's appraised value was $100,000, then $75,000 would be the maximum loan amount.

Lenders actually base the maximum loan amount on the sales price or the appraised value, whichever is less. Thus, if the $100,000 property in the example above was selling for $95,000, the maximum loan amount would be $71,250 (75% of $95,000).

80%, 90%, and 95% Loans. For many years now, the standard conventional loan-to-value ratio (LTV) has been 80% of the appraised value or sales price of the home, whichever is less. Lenders feel confident that a borrower who makes a 20% downpayment with his or her own funds is unlikely to default; the borrower has too much to lose. And even if the borrower were to default, a foreclosure sale is likely to generate at least 80% of the purchase price.

While 80% is the standard LTV for a conventional loan, it is not the maximum. Lenders make conventional loans with loan-to-value ratios up to 95%. The loans are classified as 80%, 90%, or 95% loans, and different rules apply to each category. A loan is classified as an 80% loan if the LTV is 80% or less, as a 90% loan if the LTV is over 80% but not more than 90%, and as a 95% loan if the LTV is over 90% but not more than 95%.

Example: A home has been appraised at $100,000, which is also the sales price. The buyers have $18,000 to use as a downpayment, and the lender has agreed to loan them $82,000, the balance of the price. The LTV for this loan is 82%. Since the LTV is over 80% but not more than 90%, the loan will be treated as a 90% loan.

Because the lender's risk is greater when the borrower's downpayment is smaller, lenders require borrowers to obtain private mortgage insurance for 90% and 95% loans, although it is not required for 80% loans. (Private mortgage insurance is discussed below.) Some lenders also charge higher interest rates and larger loan fees for 90% or 95% loans than for 80% loans.

The rules for 95% loans tend to be especially strict. Most lenders require a 95% loan to have a fixed interest rate, because there's a greater risk of default with an adjustable-rate mortgage. And as you will see later in this chapter, the underwriting standards for 95% loans are more stringent, so that it's harder for a buyer to qualify for a loan with such a low downpayment.

Owner-Occupancy. Unless the borrower is making an unusually large downpayment—well over the standard 20%—owner-occupancy is usually required for a conventional loan. That is, the borrower must intend to occupy the home purchased with the loan, as opposed to renting it out to tenants. Owner-occupants are considered less likely to default than non-occupant borrowers. For an 80% loan, the home may be the borrower's secondary residence (e.g., a vacation home), but if the LTV is over 80%, the home must be the borrower's primary residence.

Private Mortgage Insurance

Private mortgage insurance (PMI) is designed to protect lenders from the greater risk of high LTV loans; PMI makes up for the reduced borrower equity. Both Fannie Mae and Freddie Mac require PMI on home loans with downpayments of less than 20%.

When insuring a loan, the mortgage insurance company actually assumes only a portion of the risk of default. The insurer does not insure the entire loan amount, but rather the upper portion of the loan. The amount of coverage varies; typically it is 20% to 25% of the loan amount.

Example: 20% coverage

$100,000	sales price
× 90%	LTV
$90,000	90% loan
× 20%	amount of coverage
$18,000	amount of policy

In the event of default and foreclosure, the lender, at the insurer's option, will either sell the property and make a claim for reimbursement of actual losses (if any) up to the amount of the policy, or relinquish the property to the insurer and make a claim for actual losses up to the policy amount. Losses incurred by the lender take the form of unpaid interest, property taxes and hazard insurance, attorney's fees, and the cost of preserving the property during the period of foreclosure and resale, as well as the expense of selling the property itself.

Points

Of course, lenders don't loan money free of charge. For mortgage loans, lenders not only charge borrowers interest on the principal, they also charge points. The term "point" is short for "percentage point." A point is one percentage point (one percent) of the loan amount. For example, on a $90,000 loan, one point would be $900; six points would be $5,400.

There are two different types of points: origination fees and discount points.

Origination Fees. A loan origination fee is designed to pay administrative costs the lender incurs in processing a loan; it is sometimes called a service fee, an administrative charge, or simply a loan fee. An origination fee is charged in virtually every residential loan transaction. It is a closing cost, paid when the transaction closes, and it is usually paid by the buyer.

> **Example:** The buyer is borrowing $100,000, and the lender is charging 1.5 points (1.5% of the loan amount) as an origination fee. The buyer will pay this $1,500 fee to the lender at closing.

Discount Points. The second type of point is a discount point. Discount points are used to increase the lender's yield, or profit, on the loan. By charging discount points, the lender not only gets interest throughout the loan term, it collects an additional sum of money up front, when the loan is funded. As a result, the lender is willing to "discount" the loan—that is, make the loan at a lower interest rate than it would have without the discount points. In effect, the lender is paid a lump sum at closing so the borrower can avoid paying more interest later. A lower interest rate also translates into a lower monthly payment.

Discount points are not charged in all loan transactions, but they have become increasingly common. The number of discount points charged usually depends on how the loan's interest rate compares to market interest rates; typically, a lender that offers an especially low rate charges more points to make up for it.

As a rule of thumb, it generally takes about six discount points to increase the lender's yield on a 30-year loan by 1%; so a lender offering an interest rate 1% below market might charge six points to make up the difference. This rule of thumb gives only a rough estimate, however.

Buydowns. In some cases, the seller is willing to pay the discount points on the buyer's loan in order to help the buyer qualify for financing. Even when the lender is not charging discount points, the seller may offer to pay points to make the loan more affordable. This type of arrangement is called a **buydown**: the seller pays the lender points to "buy down" the interest rate on the buyer's loan.

> **Example:** Buyer and Seller have signed a purchase agreement that is contingent on whether Buyer is able to obtain financing. A real estate lender is charging 13% interest, which is the current market rate. Buyer cannot afford such high interest. Seller offers to buy the interest rate down to 12%, which will make the loan affordable. The lender agrees to make the loan at this lower rate if Seller pays six points (6% of the loan amount).

Buydowns are especially common when market interest rates are high, as in the example.

There are two advantages to a buydown plan:

1. The buyer's monthly payment is lower than it would have been without the buydown.
2. The lender often evaluates the buyer on the basis of the reduced payment, making it easier to qualify for the loan.

A buydown can be permanent or temporary. With a permanent buydown, the borrower pays the lower interest rate (and a lower payment) for the entire loan term. With a temporary buydown, the interest rate and monthly payment are reduced only during the first few years of the term. Temporary buydowns appeal to those buyers who feel they can grow into a larger payment, but need time to get established.

There are two types of temporary buydown plans: level payment and graduated payment. A level payment plan calls for an interest reduction that stays the same throughout the buydown period. A graduated payment buydown calls for the largest rate and

payment reduction in the first year, with progressively smaller reductions in each of the remaining years of the buydown period.

Secondary Financing with Conventional Loans

Sometimes a buyer obtains two mortgage loans at once: a primary loan to pay for most of the purchase price, and a second loan to pay part of the downpayment or closing costs required for the first loan. This supplementary second loan is called secondary financing. **Secondary financing** may come from an institutional lender, the seller, or a private third party.

Lenders generally allow secondary financing, whatever the source, in conjunction with a conventional primary loan. However, they typically impose the following requirements on the arrangement:

1. The borrower must make a 10% downpayment out of his or her own funds; the total of the first and second loans cannot exceed 90% of the appraised value or sales price, whichever is less.
2. The LTV of the first loan may not exceed 75%.
3. The term of the second loan may not exceed 30 years or be less than five years.
4. The second loan must be payable at any time without a prepayment penalty.
5. The second loan must have payments scheduled on a regular basis.
6. The payments on the second loan must at least cover the interest; no negative amortization is allowed.
7. The buyer must be able to qualify for the combined payment for both the first and the second loan.

Conventional Qualifying Standards

In Chapter 10, we explained the general process of loan underwriting. Now we will discuss the specific standards that are used in qualifying a buyer for a conventional loan. As you already know, lenders base their standards for conventional loans on the criteria set by Fannie Mae and Freddie Mac, to ensure that the loans can be sold in the secondary market.

Income Analysis. Stable monthly income is income that meets the lender's tests of quality and durability, as explained in Chapter 10. Once the lender determines what a loan applicant's stable monthly income is, it must determine if that income is adequate to cover the proposed monthly mortgage payments. This is where the income ratios come into play.

Total Debt Service Ratio. Lenders consider a borrower's income adequate for a conventional loan if the proposed total housing expense (including principal, interest, taxes, and insurance) plus any other recurring liabilities does not exceed **36%** of his or her stable monthly income. This is called the total debt service ratio. In calculating this ratio, an installment debt such as a car loan or a student loan will be included if more than ten payments remain to be made.

Housing Expense to Income Ratio. The second ratio lenders use is the housing expense to income ratio. For a conventional loan, the proposed housing expense (principal, interest, taxes, and insurance) should not exceed **28%** of the borrower's stable monthly income.

The total debt service ratio is considered a more realistic measure of the borrower's ability to support the mortgage payments, because it takes into account the borrower's other recurring financial obligations.

Using these two ratios, it is a simple matter to determine the maximum mortgage payment a borrower will qualify for. Take the borrower's stable monthly income and multiply that by the maximum total debt service ratio (36%). The borrower's total monthly payments on all long-term obligations (including the proposed mortgage) must not exceed this amount. Take this figure and subtract the borrower's total monthly payments on long-term obligations other than the mortgage; the result is the largest mortgage payment allowed under the total debt service ratio. Next, multiply the stable monthly income by the maximum housing expense to income ratio (28%). This answer is the maximum mortgage payment allowed under the second ratio.

Example:

$4,100	stable monthly income
425	car payment (18 installments remain)
+ 250	child support
$675	monthly obligations
$4,100	stable monthly income
× 36%	maximum total debt service ratio
$1,476	
− 675	monthly obligations
$801	maximum monthly mortgage payment under the total debt service ratio
$4,100	stable monthly income
× 28%	maximum housing expense to income ratio
$1,148	maximum monthly mortgage payment under the housing expense to income ratio

As in the example, the mortgage payment determined by the total debt service ratio is likely to be smaller than the housing expense to income figure. This is because most borrowers have significant recurring obligations besides the proposed mortgage payment. Since the borrower must qualify under both ratios, the smaller of the two is the maximum allowable mortgage payment.

Ratios for 95% Loans. For conventional loans with loan-to-value ratios over 90%, some lenders will not accept a total debt service ratio over **33%**. (The housing expense to income ratio remains 28%.) The lower total debt service ratio makes up for the greater risk of high LTV loans; the loan payment the borrower can qualify for is smaller.

Analysis for ARMs. Because the monthly payments on some ARMs can increase substantially, lenders scrutinize ARM borrowers especially closely. Fannie Mae and Freddie Mac generally accept ARMs underwritten using the standard 36% and 28% ratios, but they expect the lender to consider whether the loan applicant will be able to handle payment increases. An ARM borrower should either have strong potential for increased earnings, significant liquid assets (beyond the standard required reserves), or a demonstrated ability to manage finances and apply a greater portion of income to housing expenses.

Credit History and Net Worth. The general underwriting guidelines for credit history and net worth discussed in Chapter 10 apply to conventional loans. And one important requirement mentioned in that chapter applies only to conventional loans. Fannie Mae and Freddie Mac require all borrowers to have the equivalent of two months' mortgage payments in reserve after making the downpayment and paying all their closing costs. For 95% loans, some lenders require three months' mortgage payments in reserve.

Fannie Mae and Freddie Mac also have requirements regarding the use of gift funds for the downpayment. An individual donor must be related to the borrower, and as a general rule, the borrower is required to make a downpayment of at least 5% of the sales price out of his or her own resources.

FHA-Insured Loans

Now we will look at two types of institutional loans that are backed by the federal government: FHA-insured loans and VA-guaranteed loans. We'll discuss FHA loans first.

The Federal Housing Administration (FHA) was created by Congress in 1934 as part of the National Housing Act. The purpose of the act, and of the FHA, was to generate new jobs through increased construction activity, to exert a stabilizing influence on the mortgage market, and to promote the financing, repair, improvement, and sale of real estate nationwide.

Today the FHA is part of the Department of Housing and Urban Development (HUD). Its primary function is insuring mortgage loans; the FHA compensates lenders who make loans through its programs for any losses that result from borrower default. The FHA does not build homes or make loans.

In effect, the FHA is a giant mortgage insurance agency. Its insurance program, known as the Mutual Mortgage Insurance Plan, is funded with premiums paid by FHA borrowers.

Under the plan, lenders who have been approved by the FHA to make insured loans either submit applications from prospective borrowers to the local FHA office for approval or, if authorized by the FHA to do so, perform the underwriting functions themselves. (Note that prospective borrowers always apply to an FHA-approved lender, not to the FHA itself.) Lenders who are authorized to underwrite their own FHA loan applications are called direct endorsers.

As the insurer, the FHA is liable to the lender for the full amount of any losses resulting from default and foreclosure. In exchange for insuring a loan, the FHA regulates many of the terms and conditions on which the loan is made.

Characteristics of FHA Loans

The typical FHA loan has a 30-year term, although the borrower usually has the option of a shorter term (as short as 15 years). The FHA used to set a maximum interest rate, but now the rate is freely negotiable between the borrower and the lender. As a result, interest rates for FHA loans are determined by market forces.

A lender will charge a 1% origination fee on an FHA loan, and may also charge discount points. The points can be paid by either the borrower or the seller.

FHA loans have a number of features that distinguish them from conventional loans. Here are the most significant differences:

1. **Less stringent qualifying standards.** It is easier to qualify for an FHA loan than for a conventional loan.
2. **Low downpayments.** The downpayment required for an FHA loan (called the minimum cash investment) is often considerably less than it would be for a comparable conventional loan.
3. **No secondary financing for the downpayment.** The borrower may not use secondary financing from the seller or a lender to make up any part of the required minimum cash investment.
4. **Borrower may finance the closing costs.** An FHA borrower can finance certain closing costs along with the sales price. That is not ordinarily permitted with a conventional loan.
5. **Mortgage insurance is required on all loans.** Regardless of the size of the downpayment, mortgage insurance is required on all FHA loans.
6. **No prepayment charges.** FHA loans may be paid off at any time without additional charges.
7. **The property must be an owner-occupied primary residence.** FHA borrowers must intend to occupy the properties they're buying. The properties generally must be used as the borrowers' primary residences, not as second homes.

Almost every new FHA-insured loan has the characteristics listed above. Other features of the loan are determined by the particular FHA program through which it is insured. There are many different FHA programs, each designed to meet specific needs.

The 203(b) program is the standard program, the one used by most FHA borrowers; it accounts for more than two-thirds of all FHA-insured loans. The property purchased with a 203(b) loan can have no more than four units, and the borrower must occupy one of the units.

FHA Loan Amounts

FHA programs are primarily intended to help low- and middle-income homebuyers. So HUD sets maximum loan amounts, limiting the size of loans that can be insured under a particular program. Maximum loan amounts vary from one place to another, because they are based on median housing costs in each area. An area where housing is expensive has a higher maximum loan amount than a low-cost area.

The loan amount for a particular transaction, called the **base loan amount**, is determined by applying a loan-to-value formula to the appraised value or the sales price, whichever is less. The FHA loan-to-value rules are more complicated than conventional LTV ratios (80%, 90%, 95%). Different formulas are applied depending on the value of the home, and the calculations also take closing costs into account. The base loan in some FHA transactions is more than 97% of the appraised value of the property. With such a high LTV, and with financed closing costs, the amount of cash an FHA borrower needs at closing can be much less than he or she would need with a conventional loan.

FHA Insurance Premiums

Mortgage insurance premiums for FHA loans are commonly referred to as the **MIP**. For most programs, an FHA borrower pays both a one-time premium and annual premiums.

The **one-time premium** is also called the upfront premium. The premium is 2.25% of the loan amount for a 30-year loan. It can be paid in cash at closing (by the borrower, the seller, or a third party), or it may be financed and paid off over the loan term.

When the one-time MIP is financed, it is added to the base loan amount to find the total amount financed. Monthly payments are then calculated to pay off the loan amount and the one-time MIP by the end of the loan term. When applying the maximum loan amount rules to a transaction, the financed one-time MIP is not considered part of the loan amount. The borrower can borrow the maximum loan amount allowed in the community plus the full amount of the one-time MIP.

The **annual premium** for a 30-year FHA loan is 0.5% of the loan balance (not including the financed one-time MIP). It is paid in monthly installments: one-twelfth of the annual premium is added to each month's loan payment. The annual premium is not necessarily charged throughout the loan term. The number of years in which it must be paid depends on the loan-to-value ratio. The higher the LTV, the greater the risk of default, and therefore the longer the annual premium must be paid.

Secondary Financing with FHA Loans

As mentioned earlier, an FHA borrower cannot resort to secondary financing to pay the required minimum cash investment. However, it is permissible to combine a first and second mortgage to make up the base loan amount. For this type of secondary financing arrangement, the following conditions usually must be met:

1. The first and second mortgages together may not exceed the base loan amount for the transaction (calculated as if there were no secondary financing involved).
2. The combined total of the payments under the FHA-insured first mortgage and the non-FHA second mortgage may not exceed the borrower's ability to pay. In other words, the borrower is qualified based on the total of both payments.
3. The payments on the second mortgage must be collected on a monthly basis, and each payment must be substantially the same amount as the others.
4. The second mortgage may not have a balloon payment due sooner than ten years after closing.

5. The second mortgage may not impose a prepayment penalty.

Assumption of FHA Loans

An FHA loan closed before December 15, 1989 can be assumed by any buyer. The buyer does not have to occupy the property. The buyer does not have to be approved by the lender or the FHA, unless the original borrower wants to be released from liability.

FHA loans closed on or after December 15, 1989 can only be assumed by buyers who will occupy the property and who meet the FHA's credit standards. And if the loan was closed on or after January 27, 1991, the property must be the buyer's primary residence (not a second home).

FHA Qualifying Standards

As for any institutional loan, the underwriting for an FHA-insured loan involves the analysis of the applicant's income, net worth, and credit history. But the FHA's underwriting standards are not as strict as the Fannie Mae/Freddie Mac standards used for conventional loans. The FHA standards make it easier for low- and middle-income homebuyers to qualify for a mortgage.

Income. When evaluating an application for an FHA-insured loan, an underwriter must determine the applicant's monthly **effective income**. Effective income is the applicant's gross income from all sources that can be expected to continue for the first three years of the loan term.

As with a conventional loan, the FHA underwriter will apply two ratios to determine the adequacy of the applicant's effective income: the fixed payment to income ratio and the housing expense to income ratio. As a general rule, an FHA borrower's fixed payment to income ratio may not exceed **41%**. In addition, the housing expense to income ratio may not exceed **29%**. The applicant must qualify under both tests.

Fixed payments include the proposed monthly housing expense plus all recurring charges (those debts that have ten or more payments remaining). The housing expense includes principal and interest (based on the total amount financed), property taxes, hazard insurance, one-twelfth of the annual mortgage insurance premium, and any dues owed to a homeowners association or condominium association.

Assets for Closing. At closing an FHA borrower must have enough cash to cover the minimum cash investment, any discount points he or she has agreed to pay, and certain other closing costs. Ordinarily, no reserves are required.

Although secondary financing cannot be used for the minimum cash investment, gift funds may be used for part or even all of it.

VA-Guaranteed Loans

The VA home loan program was established to help veterans finance the purchase of their homes with affordable loans. VA financing offers many advantages over conventional financing and has few disadvantages. In this section, we will discuss the eligibility requirements, characteristics of VA financing, and the underwriting standards used to qualify VA loan applicants.

Eligibility for VA Loans

Eligibility is based on the length of active duty service in the U.S. armed forces. The minimum requirement varies from **90 days** to **24 months**, depending on when the veteran served. (Longer periods are required for peacetime service.) Those who received a dishonorable discharge are not eligible.

A veteran's surviving spouse may be eligible for a VA loan if he or she has not remarried and the veteran was killed in action or died of service-related injuries. A veteran's spouse may also be eligible if the veteran is listed as missing in action or is a prisoner of war.

Characteristics of VA Loans

VA-guaranteed loans are made by institutional lenders, just like conventional loans. However, when the loan is approved by the lender, it is guaranteed by the Veterans Administration. The loan guaranty works like mortgage insurance—it protects the lender against a large loss if the borrower fails to repay the loan.

A VA loan can be used to finance the purchase or construction of a single-family residence or a multi-family residence containing up to four units. The VA does not guarantee investor loans, so the veteran must intend to occupy the home. In the case of a multi-family property, the veteran must occupy one of the units.

Traditionally, the interest rate for VA loans was set by the Veterans Administration. In addition, VA borrowers were not permitted to pay discount points; if the lender charged points, they had to be paid by the seller or a third party. In 1992, the rules were changed to allow the interest rate for each loan to be negotiated between the borrower and the lender. The new rules also allow the borrower to pay discount points.

VA-guaranteed loans are attractive to borrowers for several reasons:

- Unlike most loans, a typical VA loan does not require a downpayment. The VA loan amount can be as large as the sales price or appraised value, whichever is less.
- There is no maximum loan amount, nor are there income restrictions. (VA loans are not limited to low- or middle-income buyers.)

- VA loans are usually 30-year fixed-rate loans, and they contain no prepayment penalties.
- VA underwriting standards are less stringent than either conventional or FHA qualifying standards.
- VA loans do not require any mortgage insurance. However, while VA borrowers do not have to pay a mortgage insurance premium, the VA charges a **funding fee** of 2% of the loan amount. (If the borrower makes a downpayment, the funding fee is reduced.)
- VA loans can be assumed; the assumptor (the buyer who is assuming the loan) does not have to be a veteran. To assume any loan made on or after March 1, 1988, the assumptor must pass a complete credit check.

VA Guaranty

One of the most important characteristics of VA loans is that they are guaranteed by the U.S. government. Because the government guarantees part of the loan amount, the lender's risk of loss in the case of default is lessened considerably. Without the guaranty, lenders would be very reluctant to make a no-downpayment loan.

Fig.11.3 VA loan guaranty amounts

VA Guaranty Amounts

Loan Amount	Guaranty Amount
up to $45,000	50% of loan amount
$45,000 - $56,250	$22,500
$56,251 - $90,000	40% of loan amount
$90,001 - $144,000	$36,000
over $144,000	$36,000 plus 25% of amount above $144,000, up to a maximum of $50,750

Like private mortgage insurance, the VA guaranty does not cover the entire loan amount. Only a portion of the loan amount is guaranteed, currently up to a maximum of $50,750. (See Figure 11.3.) The amount of the guaranty is sometimes called the vet's "entitlement."

Reinstatement. If the veteran sells the property financed by the VA loan, and is able to repay the loan in full from the proceeds of the sale, full guaranty entitlement is restored. However, because of the owner-occupancy requirement, the vet generally must demonstrate a need for new housing in order to obtain a new VA loan.

Substitution of Entitlement. If the property is sold and the loan is assumed instead of repaid, the veteran's entitlement can be restored under certain circumstances. The buyer who assumes the loan must be an eligible veteran and must agree to substitute his or her entitlement for the seller's. The loan payments must also be current, and the assumptor must be an acceptable credit risk. If these conditions are met, the vet can formally request a substitution of entitlement from the VA.

VA Loan Amounts

There is no maximum VA loan amount, except for the requirement that the loan may not exceed the appraised value of the property or the sales price, whichever is less. The only other restrictions on loan amount come from the lender. Most lenders require the guaranty entitlement to equal at least 25% of the appraised value or sales price, whichever is less. With the current maximum guaranty amount of $50,750, most lenders will not lend more than $203,000 without a downpayment.

$50,750	maximum guaranty amount
÷ 25%	percentage of value or sales price
$203,000	maximum loan amount

If the vet wants a larger loan, he or she can make a downpayment. The lender then takes the amount of the downpayment plus the guaranty and divides that by 25% to determine the maximum loan amount.

Example: Alice Janowitz wants to buy a $214,000 home. She has a full entitlement of $50,750, but her lender will not make a loan for more than $203,000 unless Janowitz makes a downpayment.

$214,000	desired loan amount
× 25%	ratio of guaranty + downpayment to price
$53,500	25% of loan amount
− 50,750	maximum guaranty
$2,750	required downpayment

$214,000	sales price
− 2,750	downpayment
$211,250	loan amount

Secondary Financing. If the vet does not have enough cash for the required downpayment, he or she can finance part or all of it if the following conditions are met:

1. the total financing does not exceed the appraised value of the property;
2. the buyer has enough income to qualify based on the payments required for both loans;
3. the interest rate on the second loan does not exceed the rate on the VA loan; and,
4. there are no more stringent conditions connected with the second loan than apply to the VA first loan (such as a prepayment penalty).

Qualifying Standards

Lenders use the guidelines established by the Veterans Administration when analyzing a veteran's creditworthiness. Many of the net worth and credit guidelines are identical to the general qualifying principles discussed in Chapter 10. However, the guidelines for analyzing a vet's income are quite different from those used for conventional or FHA loans.

A veteran's income is analyzed by using two different methods: the income ratio method and the

---

Fig.11.4 Minimum residual income requirements for VA loan applicants

Loan Amount $69,999 or Less				
Family Size	North-east	Mid-west	South	West
1	$375	$367	$367	$409
2	$629	$616	$616	$686
3	$758	$742	$742	$826
4	$854	$835	$835	$930
5	$886	$867	$867	$965
For families with more than five members, add $75 for each additional member up to a family of seven.				

Loan Amount $70,000 or More				
Family Size	North-east	Mid-west	South	West
1	$433	$424	$424	$472
2	$726	$710	$710	$791
3	$874	$855	$855	$952
4	$986	$964	$964	$1,074
5	$1,021	$999	$999	$1,113
For families with more than five members, add $80 for each additional member up to a family of seven.				

cash flow method. The vet must qualify under both methods. This means that in underwriting a VA-guaranteed loan it is necessary to go through two separate computations: one to determine the borrower's **income ratio**, and one to determine the borrower's **residual income**.

Income Ratio Analysis. As with conventional and FHA loans, underwriting for VA loans involves an income ratio method of analysis. But instead of using both a housing expense to income ratio and a total debt to income ratio, the VA uses only a total debt to income ratio, which it calls the **total obligations to income ratio**. As a general rule, the vet's total obligations to income ratio should not exceed **41%**.

> **Example:** Roger Young makes $3,000 a month. His monthly obligations, not including the proposed housing expense, add up to $450.
>
> | | |
> |---|---|
> | $3,000 | monthly income |
> | × 41% | maximum total obligations to income ratio |
> | $1,230 | |
> | – 450 | monthly recurring obligations |
> | $780 | maximum housing expense (PITI) |

Cash Flow Analysis. The second method used in qualifying a VA borrower is the cash flow analysis. For this analysis, the proposed housing expense, all other recurring obligations, and certain taxes are subtracted from the veteran's gross monthly income to determine his or her residual income. (The taxes include federal income tax, state or local income tax, social security, medicare, and any other taxes deducted from the veteran's paycheck.) The veteran's residual income must meet the VA's minimum requirements, which are shown in the charts in Figure 11.4. The requirement varies based on the region of the country where the veteran lives, family size, and the size of the proposed loan.

Other Factors Considered. The VA emphasizes that these underwriting standards are merely guide-lines, and failure to meet them should not automatically result in rejection of the loan application. In addition to the income ratio and residual income, a variety of other factors will be considered, such as the likelihood that the borrower's income will increase in the future.

Overall, the VA's rules are much more liberal than the Fannie Mae/Freddie Mac rules. A buyer who would be considered marginal for a conventional loan might easily qualify for a VA loan—as long as he or she is an eligible veteran.

Cal-Vet Loans

The State of California also offers attractive loans to eligible veterans. Its program is called the California Veterans Farm and Home Purchase Program. The loans are commonly called Cal-Vet loans. A Cal-Vet loan may be used to purchase either a farm or a single-family home (including a mobile home or a condominium unit). The state Department of Veterans Affairs processes, originates, and services the loans until they are paid in full.

The Cal-Vet program works very differently from the VA-guaranty program. Under the Cal-Vet program, the state actually purchases and takes title to the homes desired by veteran applicants. The state then sells the properties to the applicants under land contracts. The state retains title throughout the contract term. During this period the veteran has an equitable interest in the property.

Eligibility

To be eligible for Cal-Vet financing, a veteran must have served at least 90 days of active duty, a portion of which was during a wartime period. The veteran must have received an honorable discharge or have been released under honorable conditions. California veterans discharged before 90 days because of a service-connected disability are still eligible. In

Fig.11.5 Summary of qualifying standards for conventional, FHA, and VA loans

Income and Expense Standards for Conventional, FHA, and VA Loans			
Conventiona Loans	**Total Debt Service Ratio**	**Housing Expense to Income Ratio**	**Compensating Factors**
	Housing expense plus debts with more than 10 payments remaining	PITI: Principal, interest, property taxes, hazard insurance, private mortgage insurance	
LTV 90% or less	Generally should not exceed 36%	Generally should not exceed 28%	Ratios may exceed 36% or 28% if there are compensating factors that justify loan approval
LTV over 90%	Generally should not exceed 36% or 33%, depending on lender's policy	Generally should not exceed 28%	Ratios should not exceed 36% or 28% unless there are exceptionally strong compensating factors Lenders that apply 33% ratio may allow ratio up to 36% if there are compensating factors
FHA-Insured Loans	**Fixed Payment to Income Ratio**	**Housing Expense to Income Ratio**	**Compensating Factors**
	Housing expense plus debts with 10 or more payments remaining	PITI: Principal, interest, property taxes, hazard insurance, annual MIP	
	Generally should not exceed 41%	Generally should not exceed 29%	Ratios may exceed 41% or 29% if there are compensating factors
VA-Guarante Loans	**Total Obligations to Income Ratio**	**Cash Flow Analysis**	**Compensating Factors**
	Housing expense plus debts with more than 6 payments remaining		
			Ratio may exceed 41% with compensating factors

lieu of wartime service, a veteran can have served in certain U.S. military campaigns or expeditions.

An eligible veteran must apply for Cal-Vet financing within 30 years after discharge from active duty, unless the veteran was wounded in action, was a prisoner of war, or is a disabled veteran.

Characteristics of Cal-Vet Loans

Cal-Vet loans have many characteristics that make them attractive to borrowers, including low downpayment requirements and inexpensive fees.

Maximum Loan Amounts. Cal-Vet loans cannot exceed the maximum loan amounts set by the state. The maximum loan amounts vary by county; current ranges are shown in Figure 11.6.

Loan-to-Value Ratios. While a downpayment is required for Cal-Vet loans (unlike VA-guaranteed loans), the downpayment requirements are minimal. The maximum Cal-Vet loan-to-value ratio is 97% for home loans based on purchase prices of $35,000 or less, and 95% for home loans based on purchase prices of more than $35,000. For farm properties, the loan amount cannot exceed 95% of the farm's appraised value.

Origination Fee. The vet must pay a loan origination fee of $425, $25 of which must be paid at the time of application.

Interest Rates. The interest rate on most new Cal-Vet loans is 8% (the interest rate on loans for mobile homes in mobile home parks is 9%). The interest rate may vary over the loan term.

Loan Term. The normal contract term for homes and farms is 30 years, although occasionally repayment periods are for as long as 40 years. For the purchase of mobile homes, the loan term is usually 15 to 20 years, depending on the age and condition

Fig.11.6 Range of maximum loan amounts for Cal-Vet loans

Cal-Vet Maximum Loan Amounts

Single-family homes . . . . $170,000–$242,000
(includes a condo unit
or a mobile home on a
lot owned by the vet)

Mobile homes $70,000
in approved parks

Farms . . . . 160% of the county
maximum for single-
family homes

of the unit. The maximum mobile home contract term is 25 years.

Prepayment. If the contract is prepaid in whole or in part within the first five years, the borrower must pay an amount equal to six months' interest on the amount prepaid in excess of 20% of the loan amount.

Secondary Financing. Secondary financing at the time of purchase is allowed, provided the sum of the Cal-Vet loan amount and the secondary loan amount does not exceed 90% of the appraised value (as determined by the Department of Veterans Affairs).

Occupancy. Approved veterans or their immediate families must occupy their properties within 60 days after signing a Cal-Vet contract. Transferring, encumbering, or leasing the property is prohibited without the written permission of the Department of Veterans Affairs. Temporary permission to lease the property will be granted if the need to do so is compelling, but the maximum rental term is four years.

Chapter Summary

1. Traditionally, conventional loans have been 30-year, fixed-rate, fully amortized loans. Today a considerable number have 15-year terms, and many have adjustable interest rates. The interest rate on an adjustable-rate mortgage is tied to an index, and it is adjusted at specified intervals to reflect changes in the index.

2. A conventional loan is classified as an 80%, 90%, or 95% loan, depending on the loan-to-value ratio; owner-occupancy is generally required. Private mortgage insurance is required for loans with LTVs over 80%.

3. Lenders charge an origination fee to cover their administrative costs, and sometimes charge discount points to increase the yield on the loan. A seller may pay for a buydown to help the buyer qualify for financing.

4. A conventional borrower's total debt service ratio generally should not exceed 36%, and the housing expense ratio should not exceed 28%. The borrower should have two months' mortgage payments in reserve after closing.

5. FHA loans are distinguished from conventional loans by less stringent qualifying standards, lower downpayments, and financed closing costs. A home purchased with an FHA loan must be an owner-occupied primary residence.

6. Mortgage insurance is required on all FHA loans. Most FHA programs require a one-time premium (which may be financed) and annual premiums.

7. Secondary financing can be used in conjunction with an FHA loan only if the two loans do not add up to more than the maximum base loan amount for the transaction.

8. A new FHA loan can be assumed only by a buyer who will occupy the home as a primary residence and who passes the creditworthiness review.

9. An FHA borrower's fixed payment to income ratio should not be over 41%, and the housing expense to income ratio should not exceed 29%.

10. The advantages of a VA loan include: no downpayment required; lenient qualifying rules; no mortgage insurance.

11. The VA guarantees up to $50,750 of the loan amount. There is no maximum VA loan amount, but most lenders require the guaranty amount plus any downpayment made to equal at least 25% of the loan amount.

12. A VA loan can be assumed by any buyer who meets the VA's standards of creditworthiness, but the seller's VA entitlement can be restored only if the assumptor is an eligible veteran who agrees to a substitution of entitlement.

13. A VA borrower is generally required to have a total obligations to income ratio of 41% or less, and residual income that meets VA standards.

14. Advantages of the Cal-Vet loan program include low downpayment requirements, loan fees, and interest rates.

O—⚷ Key Terms

Conventional loan—Any institutional loan that is not insured or guaranteed by a government agency.

Nonconforming loan—A loan that does not meet the underwriting standards of the major secondary market agencies.

Fully amortized loan—A loan that is repaid by the end of its term by means of regular principal and interest payments.

Fixed-rate loan—A loan repaid over its term at an unchanging rate of interest.

Adjustable-rate loan—A loan that allows the lender to periodically adjust the loan's interest rate to reflect changes in the cost of money.

Index—A published statistical report that is used as an indicator of the current cost of money.

Margin—The difference between the index value on an ARM and the interest rate the borrower is charged.

Negative amortization—When unpaid interest is added to the loan balance.

Loan-to-value ratio—The relationship between the loan amount and the property's appraised value or sales price, whichever is less.

PMI—Private mortgage insurance; insurance designed to protect lenders from the greater risks of high-LTV conventional loans.

Point—One percent of the loan amount.

Origination fee—A fee that a lender charges to cover the administrative costs of processing a loan.

Discount points—A fee that a lender may charge to increase the yield on the loan above the interest rate.

Buydown—A lump sum paid to the lender (usually by the seller) to reduce the interest rate charged on the loan.

Secondary financing—A second loan to help pay the downpayment or closing costs.

MIP—The mortgage insurance premiums required for FHA-insured loans.

Cash flow analysis—A method of analysis used in qualifying a borrower for a VA loan, which involves calculating the borrower's residual income.

Residual income—The amount of monthly income a VA borrower has left over after deducting monthly expenses and taxes.

Chapter 11—Quiz
Real Estate Finance:
Financing Programs

1. A buydown plan:

   a) helps lower the buyer's initial monthly mortgage payments
   b) helps the buyer qualify for the loan
   c) is a plan in which a party pays a lump sum to the lender up front to reduce the loan's interest rate
   d) All of the above

2. Unpaid interest added to the loan balance is referred to as:

   a) payment shock
   b) teaser shock
   c) negative amortization
   d) amortization

3. A limit placed on the amount an ARM's interest rate can increase in any given year is:

   a) a payment adjustment cap
   b) an amortization cap
   c) a conversion cap
   d) an interest rate cap

4. Fifteen-year mortgages often have all of the following disadvantages, EXCEPT:

   a) a higher interest rate
   b) higher monthly payments
   c) a larger downpayment
   d) All of the above are disadvantages of a 15-year mortgage

5. For conventional loans, private mortgage insurance is required when the loan-to-value ratio is:

   a) 75% or higher
   b) 90% or higher
   c) over 95%
   d) over 80%

6. For an 80% conventional loan, the loan applicant's total debt service ratio should not exceed:

   a) 25%
   b) 28%
   c) 36%
   d) 33%

7. Gene Smith is applying for a 90% conventional loan. His stable monthly income is $2,950. His recurring monthly obligations total $375. What is the maximum monthly mortgage payment he is likely to qualify for?

   a) $826
   b) $687
   c) $725
   d) $712

8. An ARM with a conversion option:

   a) has graduated payments
   b) may be changed to a fixed-rate loan
   c) may be converted into a fully amortized loan
   d) has a negative amortization feature

9. The FHA:

   a) makes loans
   b) insures loans
   c) buys and sells loans
   d) All of the above

10. Barbara Zelinski is buying a duplex. She can finance the transaction with an FHA loan if she intends to:

    a) occupy one of the units as her primary residence
    b) occupy one of the units as a secondary residence
    c) rent out both of the units
    d) Any of the above

11. All of the following statements about FHA loans are true EXCEPT:

    a) Points may not be paid by the borrower
    b) Secondary financing for the minimum cash investment is not allowed
    c) Mortgage insurance is required on all loans
    d) The government no longer sets a maximum interest rate

12. Secondary financing is allowed in conjunction with an FHA loan:

    a) as long as the borrower is making at least a 1% downpayment out of his or her own resources
    b) only if the second loan is from an institutional lender (not from the seller or another private party)
    c) only if the two loans do not add up to more than the FHA base loan amount for the transaction
    d) under no circumstances

13. A VA loan can be assumed:

    a) only by an eligible veteran
    b) only by an eligible veteran who agrees to a substitution of entitlement
    c) by any buyer who passes the credit check
    d) by any buyer, without regard to creditworthiness

14. A veteran may obtain a VA-guaranteed loan on:

    a) a single-family residence only
    b) a four-plex, as long as all units are rented out
    c) a residence with up to two units, as long as the veteran occupies one unit
    d) a one- to four-unit residence, as long as the veteran occupies one unit

15. To qualify for a VA loan, the veteran's total obligations to income ratio generally should not exceed:

    a) 36%
    b) 33%
    c) 41%
    d) 53%

Answer Key

1.d) All three of these statements about buydowns are true.

2.c) Negative amortization is unpaid interest that is added to the loan balance.

3.d) An interest rate cap limits the amount the interest rate can increase in any given year (or over the life of the loan).

4.a) Fifteen-year mortgages usually have lower interest rates than 30-year mortgages.

5.d) When the LTV of a conventional loan is more than 80%, PMI is required.

6.c) The maximum total debt service ratio for conventional loans with LTVs up to 90% is ordinarily 36%.

7.b) Smith can qualify for a $687 mortgage payment. First multiply his stable monthly income by the maximum total debt service ratio for a 90% loan: $2,950 × 36% = $1,062. Next, subtract his other monthly obligations: $1,062 − $375 = $687. Calculate the maximum housing expense to income ratio: $2,950 × 28% = $826. Since $687 is less than $826, Smith's maximum mortgage payment is $687.

8.b) A conversion option allows the borrower to convert the ARM into a fixed-rate loan.

9.b) The FHA only insures loans made by institutional lenders. It does not make loans itself, nor does it buy and sell loans on the secondary market.

10.a) The FHA requires owner-occupancy, and the home must be the borrower's primary residence.

11.a) An FHA borrower is allowed to pay discount points.

12.c) The total of the first and second loans cannot exceed the base loan amount for the transaction.

13.c) A VA loan can be assumed by any buyer, whether or not he or she is an eligible veteran. The buyer is required to pass a credit check, however.

14.d) An eligible veteran can get a VA loan on a one- to four-unit residence, as long as he or she occupies one of the units.

15.c) The veteran's total obligations to income ratio generally should not exceed 41%.

Chapter 12

Real Estate Appraisal

 Outline

 Chapter Overview

The foundation of each real estate transaction is the value placed on the property in question. The value of a home affects its selling price, its financing terms, its rental rate, its income tax consequences, its property tax assessment, and its insurance coverage. It is important to know what the property is worth, aside from any emotional or subjective values placed on it by the buyer or seller. An estimate or opinion of value is called an appraisal. This chapter examines what is meant by the term "value," and explains the various methods appraisers use to estimate value.

Introduction

An appraisal is an estimate or an opinion of value. The term "appraisal" also refers to the act of estimating value. An appraisal usually takes the form of a written statement, called an **appraisal report**, setting forth the appraiser's opinion of the value of a piece of property as of a given date. A synonym for appraisal is **valuation**.

An appraiser may be asked to help a seller decide on a fair asking price, or a buyer may seek an opinion as to how much to pay for the property.

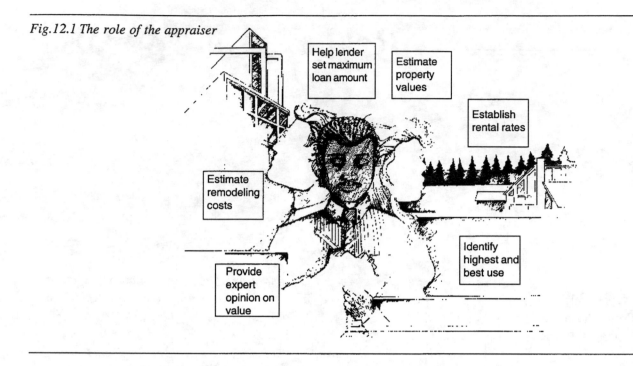

Fig.12.1 The role of the appraiser

Help lender set maximum loan amount

Estimate property values

Establish rental rates

Estimate remodeling costs

Identify highest and best use

Provide expert opinion on value

Most often, an appraisal is requested by a lender, when a buyer has applied for a loan. The lender uses the appraisal to decide whether the property is suitable security for a loan, and if so, what the maximum loan amount should be.

Whoever employs the appraiser is the client. The appraiser is the client's agent. A principal/agent relationship exists and the laws of agency apply, and the appraiser must fulfill all agency duties. (See Chapter 5.) For example, the appraiser must maintain confidentiality—he or she should only discuss the appraisal report with his or her client. Also, if an appraiser is asked to appraise corporate property and the appraiser owns stock in that corporation, he or she must disclose the ownership interest in the appraisal report.

In addition to helping determine a fair price or a maximum loan amount, an appraiser's services are regularly required for any one of the following reasons:

* to estimate the relative values of properties being exchanged;

* to provide an expert opinion of value for properties involved in the liquidation of estates, corporate mergers and acquisitions, or bankruptcies;
* to establish rental rates;
* to determine the amount of hazard insurance coverage necessary;
* to estimate remodeling costs or their contribution to value;
* to identify raw land's highest and best use;
* to estimate value for purposes of taxation;
* to help establish value in a condemnation proceeding.

The State of California licenses and certifies appraisers. Although the state does not require all appraisers to be certified, under federal law only appraisals prepared by state-licensed or certified appraisers in accordance with the Uniform Standards of Professional Appraisal Practice can be used in "federally related" loan transactions. The Uniform Standards are guidelines adopted by the Appraisal Foundation, a nonprofit organization. The majority of real estate loans are federally related, since the category includes loans made by any bank or savings and loan association that is regulated or insured by the federal government. Transactions for $250,000 or less are exempt from this requirement, however.

Value

Value is a term with many meanings. One common definition is "the present worth of future benefits." Value is usually measured in terms of money. For appraisal purposes, value falls into two general classifications: **value in use** and **value in exchange**. Value in use is the subjective value placed on a property by a particular person, while value in exchange is the objective value of a property as viewed by the average person. Value in use and value in exchange may be quite different, depending on the circumstances.

Example: A large, expensive, one-bedroom home, designed, built, and occupied by its owner, would undoubtedly be worth more to the owner than to the average buyer. Most buyers would look at the property objectively and expect more than one bedroom for the price.

Market Value

Exchange value, more commonly called market value, is the more significant of the two types of value. Estimating a property's market value is the purpose of most appraisals.

Here is the most widely accepted definition of market value, taken from the Uniform Standards of Professional Appraisal Practice:

The most probable price which a property should bring in a competitive and open market under all conditions requisite to a fair sale, the buyer and seller each acting prudently and knowledgeably, and assuming the price is not affected by undue stimulus.

Notice that according to this definition, market value is the *most probable* price (not "the highest price") that the property *should bring* (not "will bring"). Appraisal is a matter of estimation and likelihood, not certainty.

The Federal Housing Administration offers this succinct explanation of market value: "The price which typical buyers would be warranted in paying for the property for long-term use or investment, if they were well informed and acted intelligently, voluntarily, and without necessity."

Market Value vs. Market Price. There is an important distinction between market value and market price. Market price is the price actually paid for a property, regardless of whether the parties to the transaction were informed and acting free of unusual pressure. Market value is what should be paid if a property is purchased and sold under all the conditions requisite to a fair sale. A sale made under those conditions is called an **arm's length transaction**.

Principles of Value

Of the major forces that influence our attitudes and behavior, three interact to create, support, or erode property values:

- social ideals and standards,
- economic fluctuations, and
- government regulations.

A change in attitudes regarding family size and the emergence of the two-car family are examples of social forces that affect the value of homes with too many bedrooms or one-car garages. Economic forces include employment levels, interest rates, and any other factors that affect the community's purchasing power. Government regulations such as zoning ordinances serve to promote, stabilize, or discourage the demand for property.

Over the years, appraisers have developed a reliable body of principles, referred to as the **prin-**

Fig.12.2 Principle of highest and best use

Highest and Best Use (Alternative Use Considerations)		
	Annual Income	**Estimated Value**
Present Use: Warehouse	$19,280 (actual)	$175,000
Alternative Use 1: Parking lot	$16,800 (estimated)	$151,000
Alternative Use 2: Service station	$20,500 (estimated)	$184,000
Alternative Use 3: Tri-plex	$14,300 (estimated)	$132,000

ciples of value, that take these many factors into account and guide appraisers in making decisions in the valuation process.

Principle of Highest and Best Use. Highest and best use refers to the most profitable use of a piece of property: the use that will provide the greatest net return over a period of time. Net return usually refers to net income, but it cannot always be measured in terms of money. With residential properties, for example, net return might manifest itself in the form of amenities—the pleasure and satisfaction derived from living on the property.

Determining the highest and best use may be a simple matter of confirming that deed restrictions or an existing zoning ordinance limit the property to its present use. Often the present use of a property is its highest and best use. But change is constant, and a warehouse site that was once profitable might now generate a greater net return as a parking lot.

Principle of Change. The principle of change holds that real estate values are constantly in flux, moving up and down in response to changes in the various forces that affect value. A property that was worth $100,000 last year may be worth $120,000 today, and its value is likely to change in the coming year as well. Because value is always subject to change, an estimate of value must be tied to a specific point in time, called the **effective date** of the appraisal.

Related to the principle of change is the theory that property has a four-phase life cycle: **integration, equilibrium, disintegration,** and **rejuvenation.** Integration (also called development) is the early stage, when the property is being developed. Equilibrium is a period of stability, when the property undergoes little, if any, change. Disintegration is a period of decline, when the property's economic usefulness is near an end and constant upkeep is necessary. And rejuvenation (also known as revitalization) is a period of renewal, when the property is reborn, usually with a different highest and best use.

Every property has both a physical and an economic life cycle. It is invariably the economic life—the period when the land and its improvements are profitable—that ends first. The appraiser must recognize and take into account which stage of the life cycle a property is in when estimating its present worth.

Principle of Anticipation. It is the future, not the past, that is important to appraisers. Knowing that property values change, an appraiser asks: What is happening to this property? What is its future? How do prospective buyers view its potential? The appraiser must be aware of the social, economic, and governmental factors that will affect the future value of the property.

Value is created by the anticipated future benefits of owning a property. It is future benefits, not past benefits, that arouse a desire to own.

Anticipation can help or hurt value, depending on what informed buyers and sellers expect to happen to the property in the future. They usually expect property values to increase, but in certain situations they anticipate that values will decline, as when the community is experiencing a severe recession.

Principle of Supply and Demand. The principle of supply and demand affects almost every commodity, including real estate. Values tend to rise as demand increases and supply decreases, and diminish when the reverse is true. It is not so much the demand for or supply of real estate in general that affects values, but the demand for or supply of a particular type of property. For instance, a generally depressed community may have one or two very attractive, sought-after neighborhoods. The value of these homes remains high, no matter what the general trend is for the rest of the community.

Principle of Substitution. This principle states that no one will pay more for a piece of property than they would have to pay for an equally desirable substitute property, provided that there would be no unreasonable delay in acquiring that substitute property. Explained another way, the principle of substitution holds that if two properties for sale are alike in every respect, the least expensive will be in greater demand.

Principle of Conformity. The maximum value of land is achieved when there is an acceptable degree

Fig.12.3 Principle of conformity
The undesirable property will have a regressive effect on the more appealing property alongside it.

of social and economic conformity in the area. Conformity should be reasonable, not carried to an extreme.

In a residential appraisal, one aspect of conformity the appraiser considers is similarity in the size, age, and quality of the homes in the neighborhood. Nonconformity can work to the benefit or detriment of the nonconforming home. A home of noticeably lower quality than those around it will have a regressive effect on the value of those homes; this is the **principle of regression**. Conversely, its association with the higher quality homes will have a progressive effect on its own value; this is the **principle of progression**.

> **Example:** A small, unkempt home in a neighborhood of large, attractive homes will bring down the value of the surrounding homes. However, it will be worth more in this neighborhood than if it were situated in a neighborhood of other small homes in poor condition.

Principle of Contribution. Contribution refers to the value an improvement adds to the overall value of the property. Some improvements will add more value than they cost to make; others will cost more than they contribute to value.

A remodeled basement ordinarily will not contribute its cost to the value of the home. On the other hand, the addition of a second bathroom may increase a home's value by more than the cost of installing it.

Principle of Competition. Competition may have a dramatic impact on the value of property, especially income property. For example, if one convenience store in a neighborhood is extremely profitable, its success is likely to bring a competing convenience store into the area. This competition will probably mean lower profits for the first store, as its customers also begin doing business with the second store, and lower profits will reduce the property's value.

The Appraisal Process

Properly done, the appraisal process is orderly and systematic. While there is no official procedure, appraisers generally carry out the appraisal process in the following manner.

1. **Define the problem.** Each client wants an appraiser to solve a specific problem: to estimate the value of a particular property as of a particular date and for a particular purpose. The first step in the appraisal process is to define the problem to be solved. This involves identifying the subject property—what property and which aspect(s) of it are to be appraised—and establishing the function of the appraisal and how the client intends to use it.
2. **Determine what data is needed and where it can be found.** The data that the value estimate will be based on is divided into two categories: general and specific.

   General data concerns matters outside the subject property that affect its value. It includes population trends, prevailing economic circumstances, zoning, and proximity of amenities (such as shopping, schools, and public transportation), as well as the condition and quality of the neighbor-

hood. Specific data concerns the subject property itself. The appraiser will gather information about the title, the buildings, and the site.
3. **Gather and verify the general data.**
4. **Gather and verify the specific data.**
5. **Select and apply the valuation method(s).** In many cases, the appraiser will approach the problem of estimating value three different ways: with the sales comparison approach, the cost approach, and the income approach. In other cases, he or she will use only the method that seems most appropriate for the problem to be solved. Whether one, two, or three approaches are used is a matter of judgment.

   Sometimes a particular method cannot be used. Raw land, for example, cannot be appraised by the cost approach. A public library, on the other hand, must be appraised by the cost method because it does not generate income and no market exists for it.
6. **Reconcile value indicators for final value estimate.** The figures yielded by each of the three approaches are called value indicators; they give indications of what the property is worth, but are not final estimates themselves.

Fig.12.4 The appraisal process

Steps in the Appraisal Process

1. Define the problem
2. Determine data needed
3. Gather and verify data
4. Apply three approaches
   - Sales comparison
   - Cost
   - Income
5. Reconciliation
6. Final estimate
7. Issue appraisal report

The appraiser will take into consideration the purpose of the appraisal, the type of property being appraised, and the reliability of the data gathered for each of the three approaches. He or she will place the greatest emphasis on the approach that seems to be the most reliable indication of value.

7. **Issue appraisal report.** The formal presentation of the value estimate and an explanation of what went into its determination are made in the form of an appraisal report.

Gathering Data

Once the appraiser knows what property he or she is to appraise and what the purpose of the appraisal is, the appraiser begins to gather the necessary data. As mentioned above, data is broken down into general data (about the neighborhood and other external influences) and specific data (about the subject property itself).

General Data

General data includes both general economic data about the community and information about the subject property's neighborhood.

Economic Trends. The appraiser examines economic trends for hints as to the direction the property's value might take in the future. Economic trends can take shape at the local, regional, national, or international level. Generally, prosperous conditions tend to have a positive effect on property values; economic declines have the opposite effect.

Economic forces include population growth shifts, employment and wage levels (purchasing power), price levels, building cycles, personal tax and property tax rates, building costs, and interest rates.

Neighborhood Analysis. A property's value is inevitably tied to its surrounding neighborhood. A neighborhood is a residential, commercial, industrial, or agricultural area that contains similar types of properties. Its boundaries are determined by physical boundaries (such as highways and bodies of water), land use patterns, the age or value of homes or other buildings, and the economic status of the residents.

Neighborhoods are continually changing and, like the individual properties that give them form, they have a four-phase life cycle of integration, equilibrium, disintegration, and rejuvenation. When evaluating the future of a neighborhood, the appraiser must consider its physical, social, and economic characteristics, and also governmental influences.

Here are some of the specific factors appraisers look at when gathering data about a residential neighborhood:

1. **Percentage of homeownership.** Is there a high degree of owner-occupancy, or do rental properties predominate? Owner-occupied neighborhoods are generally better maintained and less susceptible to deterioration.
2. **Vacant homes and lots.** An unusual number of vacant homes or lots suggests a low level of interest in the area, which has a negative effect on property values. On the other hand, significant construction activity in a neighborhood signals strong interest in the area.
3. **Conformity.** The homes in a neighborhood should be reasonably similar to one another in style, age, size, and quality. Strictly enforced zoning and private restrictions promote conformity and protect property values.
4. **Changing land use.** Is the neighborhood in the midst of a transition from residential use to some other type of use? If so, the properties may be losing their value.
5. **Contour of the land.** Mildly rolling topography is preferred to terrain that is either monotonously flat or excessively hilly.
6. **Streets.** Wide, gently curving streets are more appealing than narrow or straight streets. Streets should be hard surfaced and well maintained.

Fig.12.5 Neighborhood data form

NEIGHBORHOOD DATA FORM

Property adjacent to:
NORTH _____ *Plum Boulevard, garden apartments*
SOUTH _____ *Cherry Boulevard, single-family residences*
EAST _____ *14th Avenue, single-family residences*
WEST _____ *12th Avenue, single-family residences*

Population: ☐ increasing ☐ decreasing ☑ stable

Stage of Life Cycle: ☐ integration ☑ equilibrium ☐ disintegration ☐ rebirth

Tax Rate: ☐ higher ☐ lower ☑ same as competing areas

Services: ☑ police ☑ fire ☑ garbage ☐ other

Average family size: ___*3.5*___
Predominant occupations: _____ *white collar, skilled tradesman*

_____

Distance from:
Commercial areas _____ *3 miles*
Primary schools _____ *6 blocks*
Secondary schools _____ *1 mile*
Recreational areas _____ *2 miles*
Cultural areas _____ *3 miles*
Places of worship _____ *Methodist, Catholic, Baptist*
Public transportation _____ *Bus stops nearby, excellent service*
Freeways/highways _____ *10 blocks*

Typical Properties	%	Age	Price Range	% Owner-Occupied
vacant lots	0			
single-family residences	80%	10 years	$80,000-95,000	93%
2- to 4-unit apartments	15%	15 years		
over 4-unit apartments	5%	5 years		
non-residential	0			

Nuisances in neighborhood (odors, noise, etc.) _____ *none*
Hazards in neighborhood (chemical storage, pollution, etc.) _____ *none*

Fig.12.6 Site data form

SITE DATA FORM

Address: _____10157 - 13th Avenue_____

Legal Description: _see attached description_

Size _50' x 200'_   Shape _Rectangular_

Square Feet _10,000_   Street Paving _Asphalt_

Landscaping _professional_   Topsoil _good_

Drainage _good_   Frontage _good_
                                     ☐ corner lot   ☑ inside lot

Utilities: ☑ water ☑ telephone   **Improvements:** ☑ sidewalks
☑ gas ☑ sewers ☑ electricity   ☑ curb ☑ alleys ☑ driveway
☑ storm drains

---

7. **Utilities.** Is the neighborhood adequately serviced by electricity, water, gas, sewers, telephones, and cable T.V.?

8. **Nuisances.** Nuisances in or near a neighborhood (odors, eyesores, industrial noises or pollutants, or exposure to unusual winds, smog, or fog) hurt property values.

9. **Prestige.** Is the neighborhood considered prestigious, in comparison to others in the community? If so, that will increase property values.

10. **Proximity.** How far is it to traffic arterials and to important points such as downtown, employment centers, and shopping centers?

11. **Schools.** What schools serve the neighborhood? Are they highly regarded? Are they within walking distance? The quality of a school or school district can make a major difference in property values in a residential neighborhood.

12. **Public services.** Is the neighborhood properly serviced by public transportation, police, and fire units?

13. **Pedestrian access.** The ease of pedestrian access is important for commercial properties. Is there plenty of nearby parking or access to public transportation? Do sidewalks and crosswalks allow easy access?

14. **Government influences.** Does zoning in and around the neighborhood promote residential use and insulate the property owner from nuisances? How do the property tax rates compare with those of other neighborhoods nearby?

Specific Data

Specific data has to do with the property itself. Often the appraiser will evaluate the site (the land and utilities) and the improvements to the site separately. For example, where properties are being assessed for tax purposes, most states require the assessments to show the distribution of value between land and its improvements. Another reason for appraising the land separately is to see if it is worth too much or too little compared to the value of the improvements. Where an imbalance exists, the land is not serving its highest and best use. The primary purpose of site analysis is to determine highest and best use.

Site Analysis. A thorough site analysis calls for accumulation of a good deal of data concerning the physical characteristics of the property, as well as factors affecting its use or the title. A site's physical characteristics include all of the following:

1. **Width.** This refers to the lot's measurements from one side boundary to the other. Width can vary from front to back, as in the case of a pie-shaped lot on a cul-de-sac.
2. **Frontage.** Frontage is the length of the front boundary of the lot, the boundary that abuts a street or a body of water. The amount of frontage is often a more important consideration than width, because it measures the property's accessibility, or its access to something desirable.
3. **Area.** Area is the size of the site, usually measured in square feet or acres. Comparisons between lots often focus on the features of frontage and area.

   Commercial land is usually valued in terms of frontage; that is, it is worth a certain number of dollars per front foot. Commercial land may also be valued in acres; a commercial acre is one acre minus the area allocated to streets, sidewalks, curbs, and alleys. Industrial land tends to be valued in terms of square feet or acreage. Residential lots are measured both ways: in square feet or by acreage in most instances, but by front foot when the property abuts a lake or river, or some other desirable feature.
4. **Depth.** Depth is the distance between the site's front boundary and its rear boundary. Greater depth (more than the norm) can mean greater value, but it doesn't always. For example, suppose Lot 1 and Lot 2 are the same, except that Lot 2 is deeper; Lot 2 is not necessarily more valuable than Lot 1. Each situation must be analyzed individually to determine whether more depth translates into greater value.

   Under certain circumstances, combining two or more adjoining lots to achieve greater width, depth, or area will make the larger parcel more valuable than the sum of the values of its component parcels. The increment of value that results when two or more lots are combined to produce

greater value is called **plottage**. The process of assembling lots to increase their value is most frequently part of industrial or commercial land development.

5. **Shape.** Lots with uniform width and depth (such as rectangular lots) are almost always more useful than irregularly shaped lots. This is true for any kind of lot—residential, commercial, or industrial.
6. **Topography.** A site is generally more valuable if it is aesthetically appealing. Rolling terrain is preferable to flat, monotonous land. On the other hand, if the site is costly to develop because it sits well above or below the street or is excessively hilly, that lessens its value.
7. **Soil.** The character of soil affects construction costs and the growth of vegetation. Soil is characterized as alkaline, sandy, adobe, or expansive.
8. **Utilities.** Site analysis includes an investigation into the availability and cost of utility connections. Remote parcels lose value because the cost of bringing utility lines to the site is high, or even prohibitive.
9. **Site in relation to area.** How a lot is situated in relation to the surrounding area influences its value. For instance, a retail store is often worth more if it is located on a corner, because it enjoys more exposure and its customers have access from two different streets. The effect the corner location has on the value of a business site is called **corner influence**.

Building Analysis. The improvements to the site must also be analyzed. Here are some of the primary considerations in a residential appraisal:

1. **Construction quality.** Is the quality of the materials and workmanship good, average, or poor?
2. **Orientation.** Orientation refers to the placement of the house on the site in relation to sun, wind, neighbors, and view. Orientation has a significant impact on value. For example, homes that offer privacy from neighbors or shelter

Fig.12.7 Building data form

BUILDING DATA FORM

Address: _____ *10157 - 13th Avenue* _____

Age: ___ *7 yrs.* ___   Square feet: _____ *1,350* ___

Number of rooms: ___ *7* ___ Quality of construction: ___ *excellent* ___

Style: ___ *ranch* ___

	Good	Bad	Fair
Exterior (general condition)	✔		
Foundation(slab/bsmt./(crawl sp.))	✔		
Exterior (brick/(frame)/veneer/stucco/aluminum)	✔		
Garage((attached)/detached/single/double)	✔		
(Patio)/porch/shed/other	✔		
Interior (general condition)	✔		
Walls ((drywall)/wood/plaster)	✔		
Ceilings	✔		
Floor (wood/tile/(carpet)/concrete)	✔		
Electrical wiring	✔		
Heating ((electrical)/gas/oil/other)	✔		
Air conditioning	✔		
Fireplace(s) *one*	✔		
Kitchen	✔		
Bathroom(s) *two*	✔		
Bedroom(s) *three*	✔		

Additional amenities _____ *none* _____

Design advantages _____ *convenient, sunny kitchen* _____

Design flaws _____ *none* _____

Energy efficiency _____ *insulation, weather-stripping, storm windows, heat pump*

	Living Rm.	Dining Rm.	Ktchn.	Bdrm.	Bath	Family Rm.
Basement						
1st Floor	✔	✔	✔	✔	✔	
2nd Floor						
Attic						

Depreciation:

  Deferred Maintenance _____ *normal wear* _____

  Functional Obsolescence _____ *none* _____

  External Obsolescence _____ *none* _____

from strong winds are more valuable than houses that do not.

3. **Age/condition.** How old is the home? Is its overall condition good, average, or poor?

4. **Size of house (square footage).** This includes the improved living area, excluding the garage, basement, and porches.

5. **Basement.** A functional basement, especially a finished basement, contributes to value. (As we mentioned earlier, however, the amount a finished basement contributes to value is often not enough to recover the cost of the finish work.)

6. **Interior layout.** Is the floor plan functional and convenient? It should not be necessary to pass through a public room (such as the living room) to reach other rooms, or to pass through one of the bedrooms to reach another.

7. **Number of rooms.** The appraiser will add up the total number of rooms in the house, excluding bathrooms and (usually) basement rooms.

8. **Number of bedrooms.** The number of bedrooms has a major impact on value. For instance, if all else is equal, a two-bedroom home is worth considerably less than a three-bedroom home.

9. **Number of bathrooms.** A full bath is a lavatory (wash basin), toilet, and bathtub, with or without a shower; a ¾ bath is a lavatory, toilet, and shower (no tub); a ½ bath is a lavatory and toilet only. The number of bathrooms can have a noticeable effect on value.

10. **Air conditioning.** The presence or absence of an air conditioning system is important in hot regions.

11. **Energy efficiency.** With spiraling energy costs, an energy-efficient home is more valuable than a comparable one that is not. Energy-efficient features such as double-paned windows, good insulation, and weather stripping increase value.

12. **Garage/carport.** An enclosed garage is generally better than a carport. How many cars can it accommodate? Is there work or storage space in addition to parking space? Is it possible to enter the home directly from the garage or carport, protected from the weather?

Methods of Appraisal

Once the appraiser has accumulated the necessary general and specific data, he or she will begin applying one or more of the three methods of appraising property:

- the sales comparison approach,
- the cost approach, and
- the income approach.

Different types of properties lend themselves to different appraisal methods. For example, appraisers usually rely most on the sales comparison method in valuing older residential properties. Government buildings, such as libraries or courthouses, are not sold on the open market, nor do they generate income, so the cost approach is invariably used. On the other hand, the most reliable method for appraising an apartment complex is likely to be the income approach.

Sales Comparison Approach to Value

The sales comparison approach (also known as the market data approach) is commonly used to appraise residential property. It involves comparing the subject property to similar properties that have recently sold, referred to as **comparable sales** or **comparables**. The appraiser gathers pertinent information about comparables and makes feature-by-feature comparisons with the subject property. The appraiser then translates his or her findings into an estimate of the market value of the subject property. Appraisers use this method whenever possible, because the sales prices of comparables—which reflect the actions of informed buyers and sellers in the marketplace—are excellent indicators of market value.

An appraiser needs at least three reliable comparable sales to have enough data to evaluate a residential property. It is usually possible to find three good comparables, but when it is not, the appraiser will turn to the alternative appraisal methods—the cost approach and the income approach.

Elements of Comparison. To determine whether a particular sale can legitimately be used as a comparable, the appraiser checks the following aspects of the transaction, which are known as the primary elements of comparison.

Date of Comparable Sale. The sale should be recent, within the past six months if possible. Recent sales give a more accurate indication of what is happening in the marketplace today. If the market has been inactive and there are not three legitimate comparable sales from the past six months, the appraiser can go back further. (Comparable sales over one year old are generally not acceptable, however.) When using a comparable more than six months old, it is necessary to make adjustments for the time factor, allowing for inflationary or deflationary trends or any other forces that have affected prices in the area.

> **Example:** A comparable residential property sold ten months ago for $127,000. In general, local property values have risen by 5% over the past ten months. The comparable property, then, should be worth approximately 5% more than it was ten months ago.
>
> | $127,000 | value ten months ago |
> | × 105% | inflation factor |
> | $133,350 | approximate present value |

Location of Comparable Sale. Whenever possible, comparables should be selected from the neighborhood where the subject property is located. In the absence of any legitimate comparables in the neighborhood, the appraiser can look elsewhere, but the properties selected should at least come from comparable neighborhoods.

If a comparable selected from an inferior neighborhood is structurally identical to the subject property, it is probably less valuable; conversely, a structurally identical comparable in a superior neighborhood is probably more valuable than the subject property. It is generally conceded that location contributes more to the value of real estate than any other characteristic. A high-quality property cannot overcome the adverse effects on value that a low-quality neighborhood causes. On the other hand, the value of a relatively weak property is enhanced by a stable and desirable neighborhood.

Physical Characteristics. To qualify as a comparable, a property should have physical characteristics (construction quality, design, amenities, etc.) that are similar to those of the subject property. When a comparable has a feature that the subject property lacks, or lacks a feature that the subject property has, the appraiser will adjust the comparable's price.

> **Example:** One of the comparables the appraiser is using is quite similar to the subject property overall, but there are several significant differences. The subject property has a two-car garage, while the comparable has only a one-car garage. Based on experience, the appraiser estimates that space for a second car adds approximately $2,000 to the value of a home in this area. The comparable actually sold for $122,500. The appraiser will add $2,000 to that price, to estimate what the comparable would have been worth with a two-car garage.
>
> On the other hand, the comparable has a fireplace and the subject property does not. The appraiser estimates a fireplace adds approximately $800 to the value of a home. She will subtract $800 from the comparable's price, to estimate what the comparable would have sold for without a fireplace.
>
> After adjusting the comparable's price up or down for each difference in this way, the appraiser can identify what the comparable would have sold for if it had been identical to the subject property. When the appraiser repeats this process for each comparable, the value of the subject property becomes evident.

Terms of Sale. The terms of sale can affect the price a buyer will pay for a property. Attractive financing concessions (such as seller-paid discount points or seller financing with an especially low interest rate) can make a buyer willing to pay a higher price than he or she would otherwise be willing to pay.

An appraiser has to take into account the influence the terms of sale may have had on the price paid for a comparable property. If the seller offered the property on very favorable terms, there is an excellent chance the sales price did not represent the true market value of the comparable.

Under the Uniform Standards of Professional Appraisal Practice, an appraiser giving an estimate of market value must state whether it is the most probable price:

1. in terms of cash;
2. in terms of financial arrangements equivalent to cash; or
3. in other precisely defined terms.

If the estimate is based on financing with special conditions or incentives, those terms must be clearly set forth, and the appraiser must estimate their effect on the property's value. Market data supporting the value estimate (comparable sales) must be explained in the same way.

Arm's Length Transaction. Finally, a comparable sale can only be relied on as an indication of what the subject property is worth if it was an arm's length transaction. That is, both the buyer and seller were informed of the property's attributes and deficiencies; both were acting free of unusual pressure; and the property was offered for sale on the open market for a reasonable length of time.

Thus, the appraiser must investigate the circumstances of each comparable sale to determine whether the price paid was influenced by a condition that would render it unreliable as an indication of value. For example, if the property sold only days before a scheduled foreclosure sale, the sales price may have reflected the pressure under which the seller was acting. Or if the buyer and seller were relatives, it's possible that the price was less than it would have been between two strangers. Or if the home sold the same day it was listed, it may have been underpriced. In each of these cases, there is reason to suspect that the sales price did not reflect the property's true value, so the appraiser would not use the transaction as a comparable sale.

Comparing Properties and Making Adjustments. A proper comparison between the subject property and each comparable is essential to an accurate estimate of value. The more similar the properties, the easier the comparison. A comparable property that is the same design and in the same condition as the subject property, on a very similar site in the same neighborhood, which sold under typical financing terms the previous month, will give an excellent indication of the market value of the subject property. However, except perhaps in a new subdivision where the houses are nearly identical, the appraiser usually cannot find such ideal comparables. There are likely to be at least some significant differences between the comparables and the subject property. So, as you've seen, the appraiser has to make adjustments, taking into account differences in time, location, physical characteristics, and terms of sale.

It stands to reason that the more adjustments an appraiser has to make, the less reliable the resulting estimate of value will be. These adjustments are an inevitable part of the sales comparison approach, but appraisers try to keep them to a minimum by selecting the best comparables available.

The appraiser bases his or her estimate of the subject's value on the adjusted prices of the comparables, but the value estimate is never merely an average of those prices; careful analysis is required.

Use of Listings. When comparable sales are scarce (as when the market is just emerging from a dormant period), the appraiser may compare the subject property to properties that are presently listed for sale. The appraiser must keep in mind, however, that listing prices tend to be high and frequently

Fig.12.8 Comparable sales comparison chart

Comparable Sales Comparison Chart					
	Subject Property	Comparables			
		1	2	3	4
Sales price		$91,750	$96,500	$87,000	$88,500
Location	quiet street				
Age	7 yrs.				
Lot size	50'x200'				
Construction	frame			+6,000	
Style	ranch				
Number of Rooms	7		-5,000		
Number of Bedrooms	3				
Number of Baths	2	+3,500		+3,500	+3,500
Square feet	1,350				
Exterior	good				
Interior	good				
Garage	1 car attached				
Other improvements		-4,000			
Financing					
Date of sale		-3,000	-3,000		
Net Adjustments		-3,500	-8,000	+9,500	+3,500
Adjusted Price		$88,250	$88,500	$96,500	$92,000

represent the ceiling of the market value range. The appraiser might also use prices offered by buyers, though these can be difficult to confirm, since records of offers aren't always kept. Offers are usually at the low end of the market value range. Actual market value is typically somewhere between offers and listing prices.

Cost Approach to Value

The cost approach is based on the premise that the value of a property is limited by the cost of replacing it. (This is the principle of substitution: if the asking price for a home was more than it would cost to build a new one just like it, no one would buy it.)

This approach involves estimating how much it would cost to replace the subject property's existing buildings, then adding to that the estimated value of the site on which they rest. Because the cost approach involves estimating the value of land and buildings separately, then adding the estimates together, it is sometimes called the **summation method**.

There are three steps to the cost approach:

1. Estimate the cost of replacing the improvements.
2. Estimate and deduct any accrued depreciation.
3. Add the value of the lot to the depreciated value of the improvements.

It is important to distinguish between replacement cost and reproduction cost. **Reproduction cost** is the cost of constructing an exact duplicate—a replica—of the subject building, at current prices. **Replacement cost**, on the other hand, is the current cost of constructing a building with the same utility as the subject—that is, a building that can be used in the same way. Reproduction cost and replacement cost may be the same if the subject property is a new home. But if the structure is older, and was built with the detailed workmanship and expensive materials of earlier times, then the reproduction cost and the replacement cost will be quite different. So the appraiser must base his or her estimate of value on the replacement cost. The reproduction cost would be prohibitive, and it would not represent the current market value of the improvements.

Estimating Replacement Cost. The replacement cost of a building can be estimated in three different ways:

1. the square foot method,
2. the unit-in-place method, and
3. the quantity survey method.

Square Foot. The simplest way to estimate replacement cost is the square foot method (also known as the comparative cost method). By analyzing the average cost per square foot of construction for recently built comparable homes, the appraiser can calculate what the square foot cost of replacing the subject home would be. The number of square feet in a home is determined by measuring the outside dimensions of each floor of the structure.

To calculate the cost of replacing the subject property's improvements, the appraiser multiplies the estimated cost per square foot by the number of square feet in the subject.

Example: The subject property is a ranch-style house with a wooden exterior, containing 1,600 square feet. Based on an analysis of the construction costs of three recently built homes of comparable size and quality, the appraiser estimates that it would cost $59.38 per square foot to replace the home.

Fig.12.9 Method of calculating value using cost approach

Cost Approach

Replacement cost of improvements
− depreciation
+ value of land
_____
Value of subject property

```
 1,600    square feet
× 59.38    cost per square foot
$95,008    estimated cost of replacing improvements
```

Of course, a comparable structure (or "benchmark" building) is unlikely to be exactly the same as the subject property. Variations in design, shape, and grade of construction will affect the square foot cost—moderately or substantially. When recently built comparable homes are not available, the appraiser relies on current cost manuals to estimate the basic construction costs.

Unit-in-Place. The unit-in-place method involves estimating the cost of replacing specific components of the building, such as the floors, roof, plumbing, and foundation. For example, one of the estimates might be a certain number of dollars per one hundred square feet of roofing. Another component estimate would be a certain amount per cubic yard of concrete for an installed foundation. Then the appraiser adds all the estimates together to determine the replacement cost of the structure itself.

Quantity Survey. This method involves a detailed estimate of the quantities and prices of construction materials and labor, which are added to the indirect costs (building permit, survey, etc.) for what is generally regarded as the most accurate replacement cost estimate. Because it is complex and time consuming, this method is generally used only by experienced contractors and price estimators.

Estimating Depreciation. When the home being appraised is a used home, the presumption is that it is not as valuable as a comparable new home; it has depreciated in value. So, after estimating replacement cost—which indicates what the improvements would be worth if they were new—the appraiser's next step is to estimate the depreciation.

Depreciation is a loss in value due to any cause. Value can be lost as a result of physical wear and tear (**deferred maintenance**); functional inadequacies, often caused by age or poor design (**functional obsolescence**); and factors outside the property, such as a deteriorating neighborhood or poor access to important areas like downtown and employment centers (**external obsolescence**).

Deferred Maintenance. This includes any type of physical deterioration (wear and tear, decay, cracks, etc.) and structural defects. Deferred maintenance is measured in terms of how much it would cost to correct it. It is the easiest form of depreciation to spot, and also the easiest to estimate.

Functional Obsolescence. This is a loss in value due to functional inadequacies such as a poor floor plan, unappealing design, outdated fixtures, or too few bathrooms in relation to the number of bedrooms.

Deferred maintenance and functional obsolescence may be either **curable** or **incurable**. Depreciation is considered curable if the cost of correcting it could be recovered when the property was sold. Depreciation is incurable if it is impossible to correct, or if it would cost so much to correct that it would be impractical to do so.

External Obsolescence. External obsolescence (also called economic obsolescence) is caused by conditions outside the property itself, such as zoning changes, neighborhood deterioration, traffic problems, or exposure to nuisances, like noise from airport flight patterns. Since external obsolescence is beyond a property owner's control, it is virtually always incurable.

Fig.12.10 A house with four bedrooms and just one bath loses value due to functional obsolescence

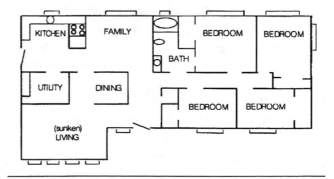

Estimating depreciation accurately is the most difficult phase of the replacement cost method of appraisal. In many cases, depreciation estimates are highly subjective, and they are never any more reliable than the judgment and skill of the appraiser who is making them.

Adding Land Value. The last step in the replacement cost process is to add the value of the land to the depreciated value of the improvements. The value of the land is estimated by the sales comparison method. Prices recently paid for lots similar to the subject lot are compared and used as indications of what the subject lot is worth.

Income Approach to Value

The income method of appraisal (also known as the capitalization method) is based on the idea that there is a relationship between the income a property generates and its market value to an investor.

Gross Income. When using the income method, the appraiser tries to find the property's gross income. He or she does this by estimating the rent the property would bring if it were presently available for lease on the open market. What it would earn on the open market is called the **economic rent**, as distinguished from what it is actually earning now, which is called the **contract rent** or **historical rent**. Contract rent can be used to gauge the property's earnings potential. Steady rent increases or decreases are strong indications of whether the contract rent is above or below the economic rent.

The economic rent is the property's **potential gross income**, what it could earn if it were fully occupied and all rents owed were collected. But it is unrealistic to expect a rental property to be fully occupied throughout its productive life; vacancies must be expected. Also, there are going to be tenants who do not pay their rent. So the appraiser must make a deduction from potential gross income to allow for occasional vacancies and unpaid rents. Called a **bad debt/vacancy factor**, this deduction is expressed as a percentage of the potential gross income. For example, the appraiser might deduct 5% from potential gross income as a bad debt/vacancy factor. Once the bad debt/vacancy factor is deducted, the appraiser is left with a more reliable income figure, called **effective gross income**.

Net Income. From the effective gross income, the appraiser deducts the expenses connected with operating the building. They fall into three classifications: fixed expenses, maintenance expenses, and reserves for replacement.

- **Fixed expenses:** real estate taxes and hazard insurance.
- **Maintenance expenses:** services for tenants, utilities, supplies, cleaning, administration costs, building employee wages, and repairs.
- **Reserves for replacement:** regular allowances set aside to replace structures and equipment that are expected to wear out, such as roofs, heating equipment, air conditioners, and (in a residential building) kitchen ranges.

The income that is left when operating expenses are deducted from effective gross income is called **net income**. It is net income that is capitalized to determine the property's value.

Some expenses related to the property, such as the owner's income taxes, depreciation reserves, and mortgage payments (called **debt service**), are not deducted from the effective gross income to arrive at the net income. These are not considered operating expenses from an appraisal standpoint.

Capitalization. The process of converting net income into a meaningful value is called capitalization. The mathematical procedure is expressed as follows:

Annual Net Income ÷ Capitalization Rate = Value

Example: The property's net income is $25,700 and the capitalization rate is 11%.

$$\frac{\$25,700}{0.11} = \$233,636 \text{ value}$$

The capitalization rate is the rate of return an investor (a potential purchaser) would want to receive on the money he or she invests into the property (the purchase price). When the investor chooses the rate of return, it is plugged into the equation shown above. By dividing the net income by the desired rate of return, the investor can determine how much he or she can pay for the property and still realize that desired return.

Example:

> Property's annual net income: $10,000
> Investor's desired return: 12%
>
> $10,000 ÷ 12% = $83,333

The investor can pay up to $83,333 for a property earning $10,000 net income and realize her desired yield of 12%.

Selecting a Capitalization Rate. To appraise property using the income approach, the appraiser must be familiar with the rate of return that investors generally demand for similar properties.

There are a number of ways the appraiser can determine a property's capitalization rate. For instance, he or she can analyze recent sales of comparable properties and assume the subject property would have a capitalization rate similar to theirs. This is called the **direct comparison method**. Regardless of the method used for selecting the capitalization rate, two very important considerations are the quality and durability of the investment property's income. Quality (how reliable the tenants are) and durability (how long the income can be expected to last) influence the risk factor. The greater the risk, the higher the capitalization rate and the lower the property's value. On the other hand, the smaller the risk, the lower the capitalization rate and the higher the value.

Gross Multipliers. Residences generally are not regarded as income-producing properties, so traditional income analysis techniques do not apply. If a residential appraiser uses an income method at all, he or she will use the **gross rent multiplier method** (also called the gross income multiplier method). As a rule, it is applied only when appraising residential rental properties.

In the gross rent multiplier method, the appraiser looks at the relationship between a rental property's income and the price paid for the property.

Example:

Sales price:	$126,000
Monthly rent:	$835
Conclusion:	Monthly rent is equal to 0.66% of the sales price; the sales price is approximately 150 times the monthly rent.

Monthly rents may run about 1% of selling prices in one market, and more or less in another. A market exists where specific rental properties compete with each other for tenants. For competitive reasons, rents charged for similar properties tend to be much alike within the same market. As a result, if one rental property has a monthly income that is 1% of its sales price, comparable properties will have similar income-to-price ratios.

A monthly multiplier (called the gross rent multiplier or GRM) is established by dividing the sales price by the monthly rental income. An annual multiplier (called the gross income multiplier or GIM) is calculated by dividing the sales price by the annual rental income.

Example:

Sales Price		Monthly Rent		Gross Rent Multiplier
$126,000	÷	$835	=	150.90

Sales Price		Annual Rent		Gross Income Multiplier
$126,000	÷	$10,020	=	12.57

After locating at least four comparable residential rental properties, the appraiser can determine their gross rent or gross income multipliers (either is acceptable—it's a matter of the appraiser's preference) by dividing the rents into their respective selling prices. In this example, we will use gross rent multipliers, the monthly figure.

Example:

Comp No.	Sales Price	Monthly Rent	Gross Rent Multiplier
1	$117,500	$800	146.88
2	$125,000	$825	151.52
3	$132,600	$895	148.16
4	$137,800	$950	145.05

The appraiser uses the multipliers of the comparables to determine an appropriate multiplier for the subject property, taking into account the similarities and differences between the properties. Then the appraiser multiplies the rent that the subject property is generating by the chosen gross rent multiplier, for a rough estimate of its value as income-producing property.

The principal weakness of the gross multiplier method is that it is based on gross income figures and does not take into account vacancies or operating expenses. If two rental homes have the same rental income, the gross multiplier method would indicate they are worth the same amount; but if one is older and has higher maintenance costs, the net return to the owner would be less, and so would the value of the property.

If possible, the appraiser should use the subject property's economic rent as opposed to the contract rent (the rent the owner is actually receiving) in calculating the gross multiplier.

Example: The owner leased the home two years ago for $850 a month, and the lease contract has another year to go. Market rents have risen sharply over the past two years, so that the property could now command a much higher rent—probably about $1,075 a month. If the appraiser were to use the $850 contract rent in the gross rent multiplier method, it would distort the estimate of value.

Reconciliation and Final Estimate of Value

Throughout the appraisal process, the appraiser is gathering facts on which he or she will base the ultimate conclusion, the final estimate of the property's value. In many cases, the facts require nothing beyond simple verification; their meaning is self-evident. In other instances, they require expert interpretation. Appraisers refer to assembly and interpretation of all the facts that influence a property's value as **reconciliation**. Nowhere in the appraisal process does the appraiser's experience and judgment play a more critical role.

The final value estimate is not simply the average of the results yielded by the three appraisal methods—sales comparison, cost, and income. Rather, it is the figure that represents the appraiser's expert opinion of the subject property's value after all the data have been assembled and analyzed.

Once the appraiser has determined the final estimate of value, he or she presents it to the client in an appraisal report. The two most common types of reports are the narrative report and the form report.

Narrative Report. A narrative report is a thorough, detailed, written presentation of the facts and reasoning behind the appraiser's estimate of value.

Form Report. A form report is a brief, standard form used by government agencies (e.g., the FHA and the VA) and lending institutions, presenting only the key data and the appraiser's conclusions. This is the most common type of appraisal report; a copy of the most commonly used form report, the Uniform Residential Appraisal Report, is shown in Figure 12.11.

Fig.12.11 Uniform Residential Appraisal Report form

UNIFORM RESIDENTIAL APPRAISAL REPORT   File No.

Property Description [X][X]

SUBJECT

Property Address	City · State · Zip Code
Legal Description	County
Assessor's Parcel No.	Tax Year · R.E. Taxes $ · Special Assessments $
Borrower	Current Owner · Occupant [ ]Owner [ ]Tenant [ ]Vacant
Property rights appraised [ ]Fee Simple [ ]Leasehold	Project Type [ ]PUD [ ]Condominium (HUD/VA only) · HOA$ /Mo.
Neighborhood or Project Name	Map Reference · Census Tract
Sales Price $ · Date of Sale	Description and $ amount of loan charges/concessions to be paid by seller
Lender/Client	Address
Appraiser	Address

NEIGHBORHOOD

Location	[ ]Urban	[ ]Suburban	[ ]Rural
Built up	[ ]Over 75%	[ ]25-75%	[ ]Under 25%
Growth rate	[ ]Rapid	[ ]Stable	[ ]Slow
Property values	[ ]Increasing	[ ]Stable	[ ]Declining
Demand/supply	[ ]Shortage	[ ]In balance	[ ]Over supply
Marketing time	[ ]Under 3 mos.	[ ]3-6 mos.	[ ]Over 6 mos.

Predominant occupancy: [ ]Owner [ ]Tenant [ ]Vacant (0-5%) [ ]Vacant (over 5%)

Single family housing: PRICE $(000) Low / High / Predominant ; AGE (yrs)

Present land use %: One family / 2-4 family / Multi-family / Commercial / ( )

Land use change: [ ]Not likely [ ]Likely [ ]In process To:

Note: Race and the racial composition of the neighborhood are not appraisal factors.

Neighborhood boundaries and characteristics:

Factors that affect the marketability of the properties in the neighborhood (proximity to employment and amenities, employment stability, appeal to market, etc.):

Market conditions in the subject neighborhood (including support for the above conclusions related to the trend of property values, demand/supply, and marketing time such as data on competitive properties for sale in the neighborhood, description of the prevalence of sales and financing concessions, etc.):

PUD

Project Information for PUDs (if applicable) - - Is the developer/builder in control of the Home Owners' Association (HOA)? [ ]Yes [ ]No
Approximate total number of units in the subject project _____. Approximate total number of units for sale in the subject project _____
Describe common elements and recreational facilities:

SITE

Dimensions	Topography
Site area	Size
Specific zoning classification and description	Shape
Zoning compliance [ ]Legal [ ]Legal nonconforming (Grandfathered use) [ ]Illegal [ ]No zoning	Drainage
Highest & best use as improved [ ]Present use [ ]Other use (explain)	View

Corner Lot [ ]Yes [ ]No

Utilities	Public	Other		Off-site Improvements	Type	Public	Private
Electricity				Street			
Gas				Curb/gutter			
Water				Sidewalk			
Sanitary sewer				Street lights			
Storm sewer				Alley			

Landscaping / Driveway Surface / Apparent easements
FEMA Special Flood Hazard Area [ ]Yes [ ]No
FEMA Zone ___ Map Date ___ / FEMA Map No.

Comments (apparent adverse easements, encroachments, special assessments, slide areas, illegal or legal nonconforming zoning use, etc.):

DESCRIPTION OF IMPROVEMENTS

GENERAL DESCRIPTION	EXTERIOR DESCRIPTION	FOUNDATION	BASEMENT	INSULATION
No. of Units	Foundation	Slab	Area Sq. Ft.	Roof
No. of Stories	Exterior Walls	Crawl Space	% Finished	Ceiling
Type (Det./Att.)	Roof Surface	Basement	Ceiling	Walls
Design (Style)	Gutters & Dwnspts.	Sump Pump	Walls	Floor
Existing/Proposed	Window Type	Dampness	Floor	None
Age (Yrs.)	Storm/Screens	Settlement	Outside Entry	Unknown
Effective Age (Yrs.)	Manufactured House	Infestation		

ROOMS	Foyer	Living	Dining	Kitchen	Den	Family Rm.	Rec. Rm.	Bedrooms	# Baths	Laundry	Other	Area Sq. Ft.
Basement												
Level 1												
Level 2												

Finished area above grade contains: ___ Rooms; ___ Bedroom(s); ___ Bath(s); ___ Square Feet of Gross Living Area

INTERIOR	Materials/Condition	HEATING	KITCHEN EQUIP.	ATTIC	AMENITIES	CAR STORAGE:
Floors		Type	Refrigerator	None	Fireplace(s) #	None
Walls		Fuel	Range/Oven	Stairs	Patio	Garage # of cars
Trim/Finish		Condition	Disposal	Drop Stair	Deck	Attached
Bath Floor		COOLING	Dishwasher	Scuttle	Porch	Detached
Bath Wainscot		Central	Fan/Hood	Floor	Fence	Built-in
Doors		Other	Microwave	Heated	Pool	Carport
		Condition	Washer/Dryer	Finished		Driveway

COMMENTS

Additional features (special energy efficient items, etc.):

Condition of the improvements, depreciation (physical, functional, and external), repairs needed, quality of construction, remodeling/additions, etc.:

Adverse environmental conditions (such as, but not limited to, hazardous wastes, toxic substances, etc.) present in the improvements, on the site, or in the immediate vicinity of the subject property:

Freddie Mac Form 70 6-93   10 CH.   PAGE 1 OF 2   Fannie Mae Form 1004 6-93

UNIFORM RESIDENTIAL APPRAISAL REPORT   File No.

Valuation Section

COST APPROACH

ESTIMATED SITE VALUE .... = $ _____
ESTIMATED REPRODUCTION COST-NEW OF IMPROVEMENTS:
Dwelling _____ Sq. Ft @ $ _____ = $ _____
_____ Sq. Ft @ $ _____ = _____
_____ = _____
Garage/Carport _____ Sq. Ft @ $ _____ = _____
Total Estimated Cost-New .... = $ _____
Less   Physical | Functional | External
Depreciation _____ = $ _____
Depreciated Value of Improvements .... = $ _____
"As-is" Value of Site Improvements .... = $ _____
INDICATED VALUE BY COST APPROACH .... = $ _____

Comments on Cost Approach (such as, source of cost estimate, site value, square foot calculation and, for HUD, VA and FmHA, the estimated remaining economic life of the property): _____

SALES COMPARISON ANALYSIS

ITEM	SUBJECT	COMPARABLE NO. 1		COMPARABLE NO. 2		COMPARABLE NO. 3	
Address							
Proximity to Subject							
Sales Price	$		$		$		$
Price/Gross Liv. Area	$	$		$		$	
Data and/or Verification Sources							
VALUE ADJUSTMENTS	DESCRIPTION	DESCRIPTION	+ (-) $ Adjustment	DESCRIPTION	+ (-) $ Adjustment	DESCRIPTION	+ (-) $ Adjustment
Sales or Financing Concessions							
Date of Sale/Time							
Location							
Leasehold/Fee Simple							
Site							
View							
Design and Appeal							
Quality of Construction							
Age							
Condition							
Above Grade Room Count	Total Bdrms Baths	Total Bdrms Baths		Total Bdrms Baths		Total Bdrms Baths	
Gross Living Area	Sq. Ft.	Sq. Ft.		Sq. Ft.		Sq. Ft.	
Basement & Finished Rooms Below Grade							
Functional Utility							
Heating/Cooling							
Energy Efficient Items							
Garage/Carport							
Porch, Patio, Deck, Fireplace(s), etc.							
Fence, Pool, etc.							
Net Adj. (total)		+ - $		+ - $		+ - $	
Adjusted Sales Price of Comparable			$		$		$

Comments on Sales Comparison (including the subject property's compatibility to the neighborhood, etc.): _____

ITEM	SUBJECT	COMPARABLE NO. 1	COMPARABLE NO. 2	COMPARABLE NO. 3
Date, Price and Data Source for prior sales within year of appraisal				

Analysis of any current agreement of sale, option, or listing of the subject property and analysis of any prior sales of subject and comparables within one year of the date of appraisal:

RECONCILIATION

INDICATED VALUE BY SALES COMPARISON APPROACH .... $ _____
INDICATED VALUE BY INCOME APPROACH (If Applicable) Estimated Market Rent $ _____ /Mo. x Gross Rent Multiplier _____ = $ _____
This appraisal is made ☐ "as is" ☐ subject to the repairs, alterations, inspections, or conditions listed below ☐ subject to completion per plans and specifications.
Conditions of Appraisal: _____
Final Reconciliation: _____

The purpose of this appraisal is to estimate the market value of the real property that is the subject of this report, based on the above conditions and the certification, contingent and limiting conditions, and market value definition that are stated in the attached Freddie Mac Form 439/Fannie Mae Form 1004B (Revised _____).
I (WE) ESTIMATE THE MARKET VALUE, AS DEFINED, OF THE REAL PROPERTY THAT IS THE SUBJECT OF THIS REPORT, AS OF _____
(WHICH IS THE DATE OF INSPECTION AND THE EFFECTIVE DATE OF THIS REPORT) TO BE $ _____.
APPRAISER: SUPERVISORY APPRAISER (ONLY IF REQUIRED):
Signature _____   Signature _____   ☐ Did ☐ Did Not
Name _____   Name _____   Inspect Property
Date Report Signed _____   Date Report Signed _____
State Certification # _____ State   State Certification # _____ State
Or State License # _____ State   Or State License # _____ State

Freddie Mac Form 70 6-93   10 CH.   PAGE 2 OF 2   Fannie Mae Form 1004 6-93

Chapter Summary

1. An appraisal is an estimate or an opinion of value. Most real estate appraisals concern a property's market value, the price it is likely to bring on the open market in an arm's length transaction.

2. Appraisers have developed many "principles of value" that guide them in the valuation process. These include the principles of highest and best use, change, supply and demand, substitution, conformity, contribution, anticipation, and competition.

3. The steps in the appraisal process include defining the problem, determining what data is needed and where it can be found, gathering and verifying general and specific data, selecting and applying the valuation methods, reconciling the value indicators, and issuing the appraisal report.

4. General data concerns factors outside the subject property itself that influence the property's value; the appraiser gathers general data by evaluating economic and social trends and by performing a neighborhood analysis. Specific data (about the subject property itself) is gathered through site analysis and building analysis.

5. In the sales comparison approach to value (which is the most important method of appraisal for residential properties), the appraiser compares the subject property to comparable properties that were sold recently, and uses the sales prices of the comparables to estimate the value of the subject property.

6. In the cost approach, the appraiser estimates the cost of replacing the improvements, deducts any depreciation, and adds the estimated value of the land to arrive at an estimate of the value of the whole property. Depreciation takes the form of deferred maintenance, functional obsolescence, and external obsolescence.

7. In the income approach to value, the appraiser divides the property's net income by a capitalization rate to estimate its value to an investor. The appraiser first estimates the property's potential gross income (economic rent), then deducts a bad debt/vacancy factor to determine the effective gross income, then deducts operating expenses to determine net income. The gross multiplier method is a simplified version of the income approach that is sometimes used in appraising residential rental properties.

O⟀ Key Terms

Market value—The most probable price that a property should bring in a competitive and open market under all conditions requisite to a fair sale, the buyer and seller each acting prudently and knowledgeably, and assuming the price is not affected by undue stimulus.

Arm's length transaction—A transaction in which both parties have full knowledge of the property's merits and shortcomings, neither party is acting under unusual pressure, and the property has been exposed on the open market for a reasonable length of time.

Highest and best use—The most profitable use of the property; the one that provides the greatest net return over time.

Principle of change—Property is in a constant state of change—integration, equilibrium, disintegration, and rejuvenation.

Principle of substitution—No one will pay more for a piece of property than they would have to pay for an equally desirable substitute.

Sales comparison approach—The method of appraisal in which the appraiser compares the subject property to recently sold comparable properties.

Cost approach—The method of appraisal in which the appraiser estimates the replacement cost of the building, deducts depreciation, and adds the estimated value of the site.

Depreciation—Loss in value due to any cause.

Deferred maintenance—Depreciation caused by wear and tear; physical deterioration.

Functional obsolescence—Depreciation caused by functional inadequacies or outmoded design.

External obsolescence—Depreciation caused by forces outside the property, such as neighborhood decline or proximity to nuisances; also called economic obsolescence.

Income approach—The method of appraising property in which net income is converted into value by use of a capitalization rate.

Potential gross income—The income a property would generate if it were fully occupied at all times and all rents owed were collected.

Effective gross income—Potential gross income less a bad debt/vacancy factor.

Net income—Effective gross income less operating expenses.

Capitalization rate—The rate of return an investor wants on his or her investment in the property.

Chapter 12—Quiz
Real Estate Appraisal

1. An appraisal is:

   a) a scientific determination of a property's value

   b) a property's average value, as indicated by general and specific data

   c) an estimate of a property's value as of a specific date

   d) a mathematical analysis of a property's value

2. The focus of most appraisals is the subject property's:

   a) market value

   b) market price

   c) sales price

   d) value in use

3. A property's highest and best use is:

   a) the use that will generate the greatest net return

   b) the best use it could be put to if there were no zoning or other restrictions

   c) the use that best promotes the public health, safety, and welfare

   d) the use that is best suited to the present owner's plans

4. The earliest phase of a property's life cycle, when it is being developed, is called:

   a) substitution

   b) regression

   c) integration

   d) disintegration

5. Developers have announced plans to build a multi-million dollar shopping center next door to a vacant commercial lot you own. Property values in the area will tend to increase as a result of this announcement. This is an example of the principle of:

   a) highest and best use

   b) supply and demand

   c) substitution

   d) anticipation

6. The owner of an apartment building has asked an appraiser to determine if it would make financial sense to put in a swimming pool for the tenants' use. The appraiser will be most concerned with the principle of:

   a) regression

   b) substitution

   c) conformity

   d) contribution

7. If someone were to build a high-quality home costing $250,000 in a neighborhood where all the other homes were valued at around $90,000, the expensive home would suffer a loss in value. This illustrates the principle of:

   a) regression

   b) supply and demand

   c) progression

   d) aversion

8. An appraiser gathers general data in:

   a) a site analysis

   b) a building analysis

   c) a neighborhood analysis

   d) None of the above

9. The sales comparison approach would almost certainly be much more important than the other two methods (the cost approach and the income approach) in the appraisal of:

   a) a six-unit apartment building
   b) an industrial building
   c) a shopping center
   d) a single-family home

10. A residential appraiser looking for good comparables is most likely to consider homes that:

    a) have not changed hands within the past three years
    b) are currently listed for sale
    c) were sold within the past six months
    d) were listed for less than they eventually sold for

11. In which of the following situations would the sales comparison method of appraisal be least reliable?

    a) When all the comparables are in the same price range
    b) In an inactive real estate market
    c) When some of the comparables are located in another neighborhood
    d) When the subject property is in better condition than the comparables

12. When applying the sales comparison method to appraise a single-family home, an appraiser would never use as a comparable a similar home that:

    a) sold over six months age
    b) sold recently but is located in another neighborhood
    c) was sold by owners who were forced to sell because of financial difficulties
    d) is situated on a corner lot

13. When using the replacement cost approach, which of the following would be least important?

    a) Current construction cost per square foot
    b) Rental rate per square foot
    c) Depreciation
    d) Estimated land value

14. An appraiser is applying the cost approach in valuing an elegant building that was built in 1894. Which of the following is most likely to be true?

    a) The building's replacement cost is the same as its reproduction cost
    b) The building's replacement cost is a better indicator of its market value than its reproduction cost
    c) The building's reproduction cost is a better indicator of its market value than its replacement cost
    d) The building's replacement cost is much greater than its reproduction cost

15. In the income approach to value, which of the following is not considered to be one of the property's operating expenses?

    a) General real estate taxes
    b) Maintenance expenses
    c) Reserves for replacement
    d) Mortgage payments

Answer Key

1.c)   An appraisal is only an estimate or opinion of value, and it is only valid in regard to a specified date.

2.a)   An appraiser is usually asked to determine the subject property's market value (or value in exchange).

3.a)   The highest and best use is the use that would produce the greatest net return over time, given the current zoning and other restrictions on use.

4.c)   Integration is the period during which the property is being developed.

5.d)   This is an example of the principle of anticipation, which holds that value is created by the expectation of future benefits to be derived from owning a property.

6.d)   The appraiser will be concerned with the principle of contribution. Will the proposed improvement—the swimming pool—contribute enough to the property's value (in the form of higher rents from tenants, and, ultimately, net income to the owner) to justify the expense of installing it?

7.a)   The principle of regression holds that association with properties of much lower quality reduces a property's value.

8.c)   General data is data concerning factors outside the subject property itself that affect the property's value. A neighborhood analysis involves collection of general data, whereas site and building analysis involve collection of specific data—that is, data about the subject property itself.

9.d)   In the appraisal of single-family homes, the sales comparison approach is given the most weight.

10.c)   A sales comparison appraisal of residential property is usually based on the sales prices of homes that sold within the past six months.

11.b)   There is little data available in an inactive market. (However, the appraiser can use comparable sales that took place up to one year earlier, if he or she determines the rate of appreciation or depreciation and adjusts the prices accordingly.)

12.c)   Forced sales are never used as comparables for appraisal purposes. Comparable sales must be arm's length transactions, where neither party was acting under unusual pressure.

13.b)   The cost method involves estimating the current cost of construction, subtracting the amount of accrued depreciation, then adding back in the estimated value of the land. How much the property rents for is irrelevant to the cost approach.

14.b)   The cost of producing a replica of an old building at current prices (reproduction cost) is invariably much higher than the cost of constructing a building with the same utility using modern materials (replacement cost). Reproduction cost is not a good indicator of an old building's market value.

15.d)   The mortgage payments—referred to as the property's debt service—are not considered operating expenses for the purposes of the income approach.

Chapter 13

Escrow and Settlement Statements

 Outline

I. Escrow
   A. Purpose of escrow
   B. Escrow agents
II. Closing Costs and Settlement Statements
   A. Preparing a settlement statement
   B. Guide to settlement statements
      1. settlement charges
      2. prorations
      3. cash at closing
III. Income Tax Aspects of Closing
   A. 1099 reporting
   B. FIRPTA
IV. Real Estate Settlement Procedures Act
   A. Transactions covered by RESPA
   B. RESPA requirements
   C. Uniform Settlement Statement

 Chapter Overview

The real estate agent's job doesn't end when the parties sign the purchase and sale agreement. Many matters must be taken care of before the sale can be finalized, and the service provided by the real estate agent during the closing process is just as important as the agent's marketing efforts before the sale. Guiding the parties through closing prevents unnecessary delays and earns the agent a reputation for professionalism. Every real estate agent should be familiar with escrow procedures and the allocation of closing costs. This chapter explains the purpose of escrow and the steps involved in closing a transaction. It also covers how settlement statements work, how closing costs are allocated and prorated, and the requirements of the Real Estate Settlement Procedures Act.

Introduction

Once a purchase and sale agreement has been signed and all the contingencies (such as arranging financing) have been satisfied, preparations are made to finalize the transaction. Finalizing a real estate transaction is called **closing** or **settlement**.

The closing process varies considerably from one state to another. In some states, all the parties get together to sign and exchange documents and transfer funds. In many other states (including California), the closing process is handled by a neutral third party, through the creation of an escrow.

Escrow

Escrow is an arrangement in which money and documents are held by a neutral third party (the **escrow agent**) on behalf of the buyer and the seller. The parties usually give the escrow agent written **escrow instructions**, which determine under what conditions and at what time the agent will distribute the money and documents to the proper parties.

The purpose of escrow is to ensure that the seller receives the purchase price, the buyer receives clear title to the property, and the lender's security interest in the property is perfected. Escrow protects each party from the other's change of mind. For example, if the seller suddenly doesn't want to sell the property as agreed, he or she can't just refuse to deliver the deed to the buyer. Once a deed has been given to an escrow agent, if the buyer fulfills all the conditions specified in the escrow instructions and deposits the purchase price into escrow, the escrow agent is required to deliver the deed to the buyer. An added advantage of escrow is convenience: the parties do not have to be present to close the transaction.

Escrow agents perform a wide variety of services to prepare a transaction for closing. Most escrow closings involve all of the following steps:

- gathering the information necessary to prepare escrow instructions;
- obtaining a preliminary title report from the title insurance company;
- paying off existing loans secured by the property;
- preparing documents, such as the deed;
- depositing funds from the buyer (and seller if necessary);
- prorating expenses and allocating closing costs;
- preparing a Uniform Settlement Statement;
- obtaining title insurance policies;
- recording documents; and
- disbursing funds and delivering documents.

Escrow Agents

Title companies are the most common escrow agents in northern California. In the southern part of the state, independent escrow companies also close a large number of transactions. Many institutional lenders have their own escrow departments, to close their own loan transactions.

California's Escrow Law requires all escrow companies to be licensed by the state Department of Corporations. Only corporations may be licensed as escrow companies; individuals are not eligible. Banks, savings and loans, insurance companies, attorneys, and real estate brokers are exempt from this licensing requirement, because they are regulated by other agencies.

Note that real estate brokers are only exempt from the escrow licensing requirement while performing acts that require a real estate license and that are in the course of a real estate transaction in which the broker is an agent or a party. This exemption allows brokers to provide escrow services to their clients without becoming subject to regulation by another agency. It does not permit brokers to operate as escrow agents for transactions in which they have no bona fide interest other than that of providing escrow services.

Closing Costs and Settlement Statements

Most real estate transactions involve a wide variety of costs in addition to the purchase price: inspection fees, title insurance charges, loan fees, and so on. These are known as **closing costs**. Some of these closing costs are paid by the buyer, and some are paid by the seller. Some are paid by one party to the other; for example, the buyer may have to reimburse the seller for property taxes the seller already paid. Other closing costs are paid by one of the parties to a third party; the seller may be required to pay a pest inspector's fee, for instance.

There are also other payments to be made in connection with closing. For example, the seller often has to pay off an existing mortgage or other liens. Who is required to pay how much to whom at closing can become a complicated matter.

So for each transaction, the escrow agent prepares a **settlement statement**. A settlement statement (also known as a closing statement) sets forth all the financial aspects of the transaction in detail. It shows exactly how much the buyer will have to pay at closing, and exactly how much the seller will take away from closing. A simple example of a settlement statement is shown in Figure 13.1.

Preparing a Settlement Statement

The items listed on the settlement statement are either debits or credits. A debit is a charge payable by a particular party; the purchase price is a debit to the buyer, for example, and the sales commission is a debit to the seller. Credits are items payable to a party; the buyer is credited for his or her new loan, and the seller for the purchase price.

Preparing a settlement statement involves little more than determining what charges and credits apply to a given transaction and making sure that each one is allocated to the right party. When allocating expenses, the escrow agent is generally guided by the terms of the purchase and sale agreement or the escrow instructions. The allocation can also be influenced by custom (local or general), provided the custom does not conflict with the terms of the parties' contract. For example, in most communities the buyer usually pays the cost of an appraisal, so that cost would ordinarily be charged to the buyer at

closing. But if the seller agreed in the purchase and sale agreement to pay the appraisal fee, custom would be disregarded and the expense would be a debit to the seller at closing.

Of course, neither custom nor the agreement between the parties can run contrary to local, state, or federal law.

Although a real estate agent may not necessarily be called upon to prepare a formal settlement statement, every agent should know what closing costs are likely to be involved in a transaction and how they are customarily allocated. The buyer and the seller may want to negotiate about the allocation of particular costs, and in any case they are entitled to know the full extent of their costs before signing a contract. A real estate agent should be able to prepare a good estimate of closing costs for each party.

Guide to Settlement Statements

The double entry accounting method is used for settlement statements, so each party has a credit column and a debit column. The sum of the buyer's credits must equal the sum of his or her debits. This is also true of the seller's credits and debits. Think of the settlement statement as a check register for a bank account. Debits are like checks written against the account, and credits are the equivalent of deposits into the account. When the transaction closes, the balance in each party's account should be zero.

When an item is payable by one party to the other, it will appear on the settlement statement as a debit to the paying party and as a credit to the party paid. An obvious example is the purchase price, which is debited to the buyer and credited to the seller.

If an item is paid by one of the parties to a third party, it appears on the settlement statement in the paying party's debit column, and it does not appear in the other party's columns at all. For example, the seller is customarily charged for the state excise tax, which is paid to the county treasurer. The tax is a debit to the seller, but it is not a credit to the buyer.

Fig.13.1
Simplified
settlement
statement

	BUYER		SELLER	
	Debits	**Credits**	**Debits**	**Credits**
Purchase price	181,000.00			181,000.00
Earnest money deposit		7,250.00		
Documentary transfer tax			199.10	
Sales commission			12,670.00	
New loan		162,900.00		
Assumption of seller's loan				
Seller financing				
Payoff of seller's loan			115,300.00	
Owner's title insurance			256.00	
Lender's title insurance	392.00			
Origination/assumption fee	2,443.50			
Discount points	4,887.00			
Property taxes: in arrears				
Property taxes: paid in advance	260.52			260.52
Hazard insurance: refund to seller				
Hazard insurance: assumption	289.95			53.95
Hazard insurance: new policy				
Interest: payoff of seller's loan			312.75	
Interest: assumption				
Prepaid interest (new loan)	843.57			
Impound account: refund to seller				
Impound account: new loan				
Credit report	45.00			
Appraisal	250.00			
Survey				
Personal property				
Recording fees	22.00		13.00	
Escrow fee	180.00		180.00	
Attorney's fees				
Balance due from buyer		20,463.54		
Balance due to seller			52,383.62	
TOTALS	190,613.54	190,613.54	181,314.47	181,314.47

Certain items are shown as a credit to one party, but not as a debit to the other. The seller's reserve balance is a case in point. If the sale calls for the payoff of the seller's existing mortgage, any property tax and insurance reserves held by the seller's lender are refunded. They are a credit to the seller, but not a debit to the buyer.

Settlement Charges. Here is a list of the items that appear on the settlement statements for most standard transactions.

Purchase Price. Paid by the buyer to the seller, it is listed as a debit to the buyer and a credit to the seller.

Deposit. In most transactions, the buyer gives the seller a deposit—called an earnest money deposit or good faith deposit—when the purchase and sale agreement is signed. Since the buyer has already paid the earnest money, it appears on the settlement statement as a credit to the buyer. And since the full purchase price has already been debited to the buyer and credited to the seller, no entry is made on the seller's side of the statement.

Sales Commission. The real estate broker's commission is normally paid by the seller, so it is entered as a debit to the seller.

New Loan. If the buyer secures a new loan to finance part or all of the sale, the loan amount is listed as a credit to the buyer. Like the deposit, the buyer's loan is part of the purchase price already credited to the seller, so no entry is made on the seller's side of the statement.

Assumed Loan. If the buyer assumes the seller's existing loan, it is part of the money used to finance the transaction, so (like a new loan) it is credited to the buyer. The assumed loan balance is a debit to the seller.

Seller Financing. If the seller accepts a mortgage or deed of trust from the buyer for part of the purchase price, that shows up in the buyer's credit column, just like an institutional loan. At the same time, a seller financing arrangement reduces the amount of cash the seller will receive at closing, so it is listed as a debit to the seller.

Land Contract. If the property is sold under a land contract, the contract price (less the downpayment) is credit extended by the seller. It reduces the seller's net at closing and is used by the buyer to finance the purchase, so it is a debit to the seller and a credit to the buyer.

Payoff of Existing Mortgage. If the seller pays off an existing loan, his or her net is reduced by that amount. The payoff is a debit to the seller. No entry is made on the buyer's side of the statement.

Prepayment Penalty. This is a charge the seller's lender may impose on the seller for paying the loan off before the end of its term (not allowed for FHA or VA loans). It would be a debit to the seller on the settlement statement.

Reserve Account. As was mentioned earlier, the seller often has reserves on deposit with his or her lender to cover property taxes and hazard insurance premiums. When the seller's loan is paid off, the unused balance in the reserve account is refunded to the seller. It appears as a credit on the seller's side of the settlement statement. If the buyer is assuming the loan and the reserve account, the reserves would appear as a credit to the seller and a debit to the buyer.

Appraisal Fee. The appraisal is usually required by the buyer's lender, so the fee is ordinarily a debit to the buyer.

Credit Report. The buyer's lender charges the buyer for the credit investigation, so this is also a debit to the buyer.

Survey. Sometimes a lender requires a survey as a condition for making the loan. Unless otherwise agreed, the cost of the survey is a debit to the buyer.

Origination Fee. This is the lender's one-time charge to the borrower for setting up the loan (see Chapter 11). It's a debit to the buyer.

Discount Points. The discount points are a debit to the buyer, unless the seller has agreed to pay for a buydown (see Chapter 11). In that case, the points are a debit to the seller.

Assumption Fee. This is a fee the lender charges the buyer when the seller's existing loan is assumed. It is a debit to the buyer.

Owner's Title Insurance Premium. In northern California, the buyer usually pays the premium for the owner's title insurance policy (which protects the buyer); in southern California, the seller usually pays it.

Lender's Title Insurance Premium. The lender requires the buyer to provide an extended coverage policy to protect the lender's lien priority. The premium for this policy is a debit to the buyer, unless otherwise agreed.

Title Search Fee. In some cases, there is a separate charge for the title search, in addition to the title insurance premiums. This is usually a debit to the buyer.

Sale of Personal Property. If the seller is selling the buyer some personal property along with the real property, the price of these items should be credited to the seller and debited to the buyer. (The seller should sign a bill of sale to be delivered to the buyer at closing along with the deed.)

Inspection Fees. The cost of an inspection is allocated by agreement between the parties. For example, the buyer might agree to pay for the cost of a pest inspection, while the seller agrees to pay for repairs if the inspection shows any are necessary.

Hazard Insurance Policy. The lender generally requires the buyer to pay for one to three years of hazard insurance coverage in advance. This is a debit to the buyer.

Excise Tax. This is a tax imposed on every sale of real property in California (see Chapter 4). It is sometimes called the **documentary transfer tax**. It is customarily paid by the seller, so it would usually be listed in the seller's debit column.

Attorney's Fees. A buyer or seller who is represented by an attorney in the transaction is responsible for his or her own attorney's fees. On the settlement statement, the fees will show up as a debit to the appropriate party.

Recording Fees. The fees for recording the various documents involved in the transaction are usually charged to the party who benefits from the recording. For example, the fees for recording the deed and the new mortgage or deed of trust are debits to the buyer; the fee for recording a certificate of discharge for the old mortgage is a debit to the seller.

Escrow Fee. Also called a settlement fee or closing fee, this is the escrow agent's charge for his or her services. The buyer and the seller commonly agree to split the escrow fee; in that case, half the fee will be debited to each party.

Prorations. There are, of course, certain recurring expenses connected with ownership of real estate, including property taxes, hazard insurance premiums, and mortgage interest payments. As a general rule, the seller is responsible for these expenses during his or her period of ownership, but not beyond. In preparing a settlement statement, the escrow agent checks to see whether the seller will be current, in arrears, or paid in advance with respect to these expenses on the closing date. The escrow agent then **prorates** the expenses, determining what share of them the seller is responsible for. To prorate an expense is to divide and allocate it proportionately, according to time, interest, or benefit.

If, in regard to a particular expense, the seller will be in arrears on the closing date, the amount he or she owes is entered as a debit on the settlement statement. If the seller has paid in advance, he or she is entitled to a partial refund, which appears as a credit on the statement. If the expense is one that will continue after closing (as in the case of property taxes), the buyer is responsible for it once his or her period of ownership begins. That will show up on the buyer's side of the settlement statement as a credit (if the seller is in arrears) or a debit (if the seller has paid in advance).

The first step in prorating an expense is to divide it by the number of days it covers to determine the **per diem** (daily) rate. So an annual expense would be divided by 365 days (366 in a leap year); the per diem rate would be $1/365$ of the annual amount. A monthly expense would be divided by the number of days in the month in question (28, 29, 30, or 31).*

The next step is to determine the number of days during which a particular party is responsible for the expense. The final step is to multiply that number of days by the per diem rate, to arrive at the share of the expense that party is responsible for. Examples appear below. (See Chapter 17 for further discussion of proration calculations.)

Property Taxes. The seller is responsible for property taxes up to the day of closing; the buyer is responsible for them on the day of closing and thereafter. If the seller has already paid the property taxes for the year, he or she is entitled to a prorated refund at closing. On the settlement statement, this will appear as a credit to the seller and a debit to the buyer. (Note: In California, the property tax year runs from July 1 to June 30.)

> **Example**: Brown sold her house to Madra. The sale closed on January 2. The property taxes for the year are $1,095. The per diem rate is $3.00 ($1,095.00 ÷ 365 = $3.00). Brown is responsible for paying the taxes through January 1, or 185 days. The buyer, Madra, is responsible for the taxes from January 2 through the end of the fiscal year, the remaining 180 days.
>
> Brown has already paid the full year's taxes, so at closing she will be entitled to a credit for the share that is Madra's responsibility. The escrow agent multiplies the number of days for which Madra is responsible by the per diem rate to determine the amount Madra will owe Brown at closing.
>
> $$\$3.00 \times 180 = \$540$$
>
> This $540 will appear as a credit on the seller's side of the settlement statement, and as a debit on the buyer's side of the statement.

Hazard Insurance. Hazard insurance is usually paid for well in advance. At closing, the seller is entitled to a refund for the unused portion of the policy. For example, if the seller has paid the premium for the year, and there are three months left in the year, the seller is entitled to a refund of one-fourth of the premium. This would show up as a credit to the seller on the settlement statement. If the buyer is going to assume the policy, the seller will be credited and the buyer will be debited for the appropriate amount.

Interest on Seller's Loan. Interest on a real estate loan is almost always paid in arrears. In other words, the interest that accrues during a given month is paid at the end of that month. For instance, a loan payment that is due on September 1 includes the interest that accrued during August. If a transaction closes in the middle of the payment period, the seller owes his or her lender some interest.

> **Example:** The closing date is August 15. Although the seller made a mortgage payment on her loan on August 1, that payment did not include any of the interest that is accruing during August. The seller owes the lender interest for the period from August 1 through August 14. The escrow agent prorates the interest, charging the seller only for those days, rather than the whole month's interest. The prorated amount is entered on the settlement statement as a debit to the seller.
>
> If the buyer assumes the loan, his first payment will be due September 1, and it will pay all of the interest for August. The seller will be debited for the interest owed through August 14, and the buyer will be credited for the same amount.

Note that some loan programs—such as FHA loan programs—do not allow proration of interest when a loan is paid off in the middle of a payment

---

* It was once a common practice to simplify proration calculations by using a 360-day year and 30-day months (regardless of how many days there actually were in a particular month or year). But now that calculators are so widely available, most closing agents use the exact number of days in the year or month in question.

period. The seller must pay for a full month's interest, regardless of the closing date.

Prepaid Interest on Buyer's Loan. Another expense that the escrow agent prorates (one that does not concern the seller) is the interest on the buyer's new mortgage loan. As a general rule, the first payment date for a new loan is not the first day of the month immediately following closing, but rather the first day of the next month after that.

Example: The buyer is financing the purchase with a new institutional loan. Closing takes place on January 23. The buyer is not required to make a payment on the new loan on February 1. Instead, the first payment is not due until March 1.

Even though the first payment isn't due for an extra month, interest begins accruing on the loan on the closing date. As was explained above, the first regular payment will cover the interest for the preceding month. So if the transaction closes on January 23, the first payment will be due on March 1, and that payment will cover the interest accrued in February. However, it will not cover the interest accrued between January 23 and January 31. Instead, the lender requires the buyer to pay the interest for those nine days in January at closing. This is called **prepaid interest** or **interim interest**. It will appear as a debit to the buyer on the settlement statement.

Example: The buyer is borrowing $73,000 at 10% interest to finance the purchase. The annual interest on the loan during the first year will be $7,300 ($73,000 × 10% = $7,300). The escrow agent divides that annual figure by 365 to determine the per diem interest rate. $7,300 ÷ 365 = $20.00 per diem.

There are nine days between the closing date (January 23) and the first day of the following month, so the lender will expect the buyer to prepay nine days' worth of interest at closing.

$20.00 × 9 days = $180.00 prepaid interest

The escrow agent will enter $180.00 as a debit to the buyer on the settlement statement.

Rent. So far we've only discussed prorated expenses. In some transactions, there is also income to be prorated at closing. If the property generates rental income and the tenants have paid for some period beyond the closing date, the seller is debited and the buyer credited for the rent paid in advance. If the rent is paid in arrears, the seller will be credited for the amount due up to closing, and the buyer will be debited for the same amount.

Cash at Closing. As we said earlier, on a settlement statement the sum of one party's credits should equal the sum of that party's debits, so that the final balance in each party's "account" is zero. In order for the statement to work this way, it must list the amount of cash that the buyer will have to bring to closing, and also the amount of cash the seller will take away from closing.

Balance Due from Buyer. Add up all of the buyer's credits and all of the buyer's debits. Then subtract the buyer's credits from the buyer's debits to find the balance due, which is the amount of cash the buyer will be required to pay at closing. Enter this amount as a credit for the buyer. (Now the buyer's credits should add up to exactly the same amount as the buyer's debits.)

Balance Due to Seller. Add up all of the seller's credits and all of the seller's debits. Then subtract the seller's debits from the seller's credits. The result is the amount of cash the seller will receive at closing (if any). Enter this amount as a debit if credits exceed debits, but enter it as a credit if debits exceed credits. (Now the seller's credits should add up to exactly the same amount as the seller's debits.)

Income Tax Aspects of Closing

All real estate transactions have tax implications for the parties (see Chapter 14) and, naturally, the parties are expected to fulfill their individual tax obligations. However, escrow agents also must meet certain reporting requirements. Real estate agents

Fig.13.2 Settlement statement guide

	BUYER		SELLER	
	Debits	**Credits**	**Debits**	**Credits**
Purchase price	X			X
Earnest money deposit		X		
Documentary transfer tax			X	
Sales commission			X	
New loan		X		
Assumption of seller's loan		X	X	
Seller financing		X	X	
Payoff of seller's loan			X	
Owner's title insurance	*Varies according to local custom*			
Lender's title insurance	X			
Origination/assumption fee	X			
Discount points	*By agreement*			
Property taxes: in arrears		X	X	
Property taxes: paid in advance	X			X
Hazard insurance: refund to seller				X
Hazard insurance: assumption	X			X
Hazard insurance: new policy	X			
Interest: payoff of seller's loan			X	
Interest: assumption		X	X	
Prepaid interest (new loan)	X			
Impound account: refund to seller				X
Impound account: new loan	X			
Credit report	X			
Appraisal	X			
Survey	*By agreement*			
Personal property	X			X
Recording fees	X		X	
Escrow fee	*By agreement*			
Attorney's fees	X		X	
Balance due from buyer		X		
Balance due to seller			X	
TOTALS	X	X	X	X

need to be familiar with these requirements because, if the escrow agent fails to comply with them, the real estate agents involved in the transaction may be liable.

1099 Reporting

Escrow agents must report every sale of real property to the Internal Revenue Service. Form 1099-S is used to report the seller's name and social security number and the gross proceeds from the sale. The escrow agent may not charge an extra fee for filling out the 1099-S.

If the escrow agent fails to report the sale to the IRS, the mortgage lender is required to do so. If the mortgage lender also fails to report the sale, it becomes the real estate broker's responsibility to do so.

FIRPTA

The Foreign Investment in Real Property Tax Act (FIRPTA) was passed in 1980 to help prevent foreign investors from evading their tax liability on income generated from the sale of real estate. FIRPTA requires escrow agents to determine whether the property seller is a U.S. citizen. If the seller is not a citizen, the escrow agent must withhold 10% of the net proceeds of the sale and forward that amount to the IRS. Payment must be made within ten days after the transfer date. (Many residential transactions are exempt from FIRPTA.)

Most standard purchase and sale agreements provide for FIRPTA compliance. If the escrow agent fails to comply with FIRPTA requirements, anybody involved in the sale, including the real estate agents, can be required to pay the money to the IRS.

Real Estate Settlement Procedures Act

The Real Estate Settlement Procedures Act (RESPA), a federal law, was passed in 1974. It affects how closing is handled in most residential transactions financed with institutional loans. The law has two main goals:

1. to provide borrowers with information about their closing costs; and
2. to eliminate kickbacks and referral fees that unnecessarily increase the costs of settlement.

Transactions Covered by RESPA

RESPA applies to "federally related" loan transactions. A loan is federally related if:

1. it will be used to finance the purchase of real property;
2. it will be secured by a first or second mortgage or deed of trust against:
   - property on which there is (or on which the loan proceeds will be used to build) a dwelling with four or fewer units;
   - a condominium unit or a cooperative apartment;
   - a lot with (or on which the loan proceeds will be used to place) a mobile home; and
3. the lender is federally regulated, has federally insured accounts, is assisted by the federal government, makes loans in connection with a federal program, sells loans to Fannie Mae, Ginnie Mae, or Freddie Mac, or makes real estate loans totaling more than one million dollars per year.

In short, the act applies to almost all institutional lenders and to most residential purchase loans.

Exemptions. RESPA does not apply to the following loan transactions:

1. a loan used to purchase 25 acres or more;
2. any loan that does not have first or second lien position;
3. a loan used to purchase vacant land, unless there will be a one- to four-unit dwelling built on it or a mobile home placed on it;
4. a construction loan when the borrower already owns the lot;

Fig.13.3 Good faith estimate of closing costs

GOOD FAITH ESTIMATE OF SETTLEMENT CHARGES AND ITEMIZATION OF AMOUNT FINANCED

Listed below is the Good Faith Estimate of Settlement Charges made pursuant to the requirements of the Real Estate Settlement Procedures Act (RESPA). Loan types: ☐ CONV ☐ Fixed Rate ☐ ARM ☐ GEM ☐ FHA ☐ VA ☐ Assumption ☐ Substitution of Liability.

This Good Faith Estimate is provided, based upon your application for a loan of $ ________ for ______ years, with a requested interest rate of ______ %. (______ % of Loan to Value). This Loan has a ______ year call option.

Branch ________ Number ______ Purchaser ________
Prepared by ________ Date ______
Application # ________ Prop. Address ________
Mailing Address ________

ESTIMATED SETTLEMENT CHARGES*

Estimate Closing Date ______

		Loan Amount	$
Amount Paid to You Directly	$	Prepaid Finance Charges	
Amount Paid to Your Account	$	Loan Fee	$
Amount Paid to Others on Your Behalf		Loan Discount (Paid by Borrower)	$
Credit Reporting Agency	$	Buy Down Fee (Paid by Borrower)	$
Appraisal	$	Tax registration	$
Title Company	$	Private Mtge. Insur. Prem.	$
Reconveyance	$	Insurance Reserve PMI/FHA	$
Public Officials	$	Interim Interest $ ____ per Day	$ ____ ++
Settlement Fee to Lender	$	Review Fee	$
Inspection Fee	$		
Attorney Review Fee	$	Total Prepaid Finance Charges	$ ____ (2)
Real Estate Taxes	$		
Real Estate Tax Reserve to Lender	$	Total Amount Financed (Loan Amount-Prepaid Finance Charges)	$
Hazard Insurance Reserve to Lender	$		
	$		
	$		
	$		
	$		
	$		
Total Amount Paid to Others	$ ____ (1)		

This is a notice to you as required by the Right to Financial Privacy Act of 1978 that the Veterans Administration Loan Guaranty Service or Division/Federal Housing Administration has right of access to financial records held by a financial institution in connection with the consideration or administration of assistance to you. Financial records involving your transaction will be available to the Veterans Administration Loan Guaranty Service or Division/Federal Housing Administration without further notice or authorization but will not be disclosed or released to another Government agency or department without your consent except as required or permitted by law.

"THIS FORM DOES NOT COVER ALL ITEMS YOU WILL BE REQUIRED TO PAY IN CASH AT SETTLEMENT. FOR EXAMPLE, DEPOSIT IN ESCROW FOR REAL ESTATE TAXES AND INSURANCE. YOU MAY WISH TO INQUIRE AS TO THE AMOUNTS OF SUCH OTHER ITEMS. YOU MAY BE REQUIRED TO PAY OTHER ADDITIONAL AMOUNTS AT SETTLEMENT," (FOR FURTHER EXPLANATION OF THESE CHARGES CONSULT YOUR BOOKLET ON SETTLEMENT COSTS.)

++This interest calculation represents the greatest amount of interest you could be required to pay at settlement. The actual amount will be determined by the day of the month on which your settlement is concluded.

Principal & Interest	$ ____ **	Purchase Price	$	Total to Close	$
Mtg. Ins. Prem.	$	Less Loan Amount	$	Less Monies Paid	$
1/12 Annual R/E Taxes	$	Down Payment	$	Est. Funds to CLOSE	$
1/12 Hazard Ins.	$	Plus:	$	Source of Funds to CLOSE:	
Homeowner's Dues	$	C/C Etc. (1&2 Above)	$		
Other	$				
EST. MONTHLY PMT.	$				

**Principal and Interest Amounts for GPM's, GEM's and Buydown (years) 1st $ ____ 2nd $ ____ 3rd $ ____
Annual percentage increase in payment ____ %. 4th $ ____ 5th $ ____ 6th $ ____
7th $ ____ 8th $ ____ 9th $ ____
10th $ ____ 11th $ ____ 12th $ ____

☐ Adjustable Rate Mortgage: Payment Rate ____ % Index ____ Chg. Rate: Pmt. ____ mos. Int. ____ mos.

The undersigned hereby acknowledges receipt of a photocopy of this page and a HUD Guide to Settlement Costs booklet.

________ (Borrower) ________ (Co-Borrower)

RL-040 6-89

5. an assumption or a purchase subject to an existing mortgage loan.

RESPA Requirements

RESPA has four basic requirements:

1. The lender must give all loan applicants a copy of a **booklet about settlement procedures** within three days after receiving a written loan application. This booklet, prepared by HUD, explains RESPA, closing costs, and the settlement statement.
2. The lender must also give all applicants a **good faith estimate of closing costs** within three days after receiving the loan application. (An example of the type of form lenders use for this is shown below.) If the lender requires the use of a particular provider of settlement services (such as a particular title insurance company or escrow agent), the good faith estimate must include the costs of those services and give information about the provider.
3. The closing agent (whoever handles closing, whether it is an employee of the lender, an escrow agent, a real estate broker, a lawyer, etc.) must itemize all loan settlement charges on a **Uniform Settlement Statement** form, which will be given to all parties at closing. The closing agent must allow the borrower to inspect the Uniform Settlement Statement one business day before closing, if the borrower asks to do so.
4. The lender may not pay kickbacks or referral fees to anyone for referring customers for any transaction involving a federally related loan.

Uniform Settlement Statement

A copy of the Uniform Settlement Statement form is shown on the following pages. It does not have the same format as the simplified settlement statement shown earlier in this chapter (with buyer's credit and debit columns and seller's credit and debit columns side by side), but it presents the same information.

On the Uniform Settlement Statement, each party's closing costs are itemized on the back of the form (that is, on the second page shown here), with the buyer's costs in the left column and the seller's costs in the right column. Each column is added up, and the two totals are transferred to the front of the form. The buyer's total costs are entered on line 103, and the seller's total costs are entered on line 502.

On the front of the Uniform Settlement Statement form, lines 101 through 120 correspond to the "Buyer's Debits" column on the simplified version. Lines 201 through 301 correspond to the "Buyer's Credits" column. Lines 401 through 420 are the equivalent of the "Seller's Credits" column, and lines 501 through 601 represent the "Seller's Debits" column. The amount of cash the buyer must bring to closing is shown on line 303, and the amount of cash the seller will receive at closing is shown on line 603.

Fig.13.4 Uniform Settlement Statement

A. **Settlement Statement**

U.S. Department of Housing
and Urban Development

OMB Approval No. 2502-0265

B. Type of Loan

1. ☐ FHA 2. ☐ FmHA 3. ☐ Conv. Unins.
4. ☐ VA 5. ☐ Conv. Ins.

6. File Number	7. Loan Number	8. Mortgage Insurance Case Number

C. **Note:** This form is furnished to give you a statement of actual settlement costs. Amounts paid to and by the settlement agent are shown. Items marked "(p.o.c.)" were paid outside the closing; they are shown here for informational purposes and are not included in the totals.

D. Name and Address of Borrower	E. Name and Address of Seller	F. Name and Address of Lender

G. Property Location	H. Settlement Agent
	Place of Settlement
	I. Settlement Date

J. Summary of Borrower's Transaction		K. Summary of Seller's Transaction	
100. Gross Amount Due From Borrower		**400. Gross Amount Due To Seller**	
101. Contract sales price		401. Contract sales price	
102. Personal property		402. Personal property	
103. Settlement charges to borrower (line 1400)		403.	
104.		404.	
105.		405.	
Adjustments for items paid by seller in advance		*Adjustments for items paid by seller in advance*	
106. City/town taxes to		406. City/town taxes to	
107. County taxes to		407. County taxes to	
108. Assessments to		408. Assessments to	
109.		409.	
110.		410.	
111.		411.	
112.		412.	
120. Gross Amount Due From Borrower		**420. Gross Amount Due To Seller**	
200. Amounts Paid By Or In Behalf Of Borrower		**500. Reductions In Amount Due To Seller**	
201. Deposit or earnest money		501. Excess deposit (see instructions)	
202. Principal amount of new loan(s)		502. Settlement charges to seller (line 1400)	
203. Existing loan(s) taken subject to		503. Existing loan(s) taken subject to	
204.		504. Payoff of first mortgage loan	
205.		505. Payoff of second mortgage loan	
206.		506.	
207.		507.	
208.		508.	
209.		509.	
Adjustments for items unpaid by seller		*Adjustments for items unpaid by seller*	
210. City/town taxes to		510. City/town taxes to	
211. County taxes to		511. County taxes to	
212. Assessments to		512. Assessments to	
213.		513.	
214.		514.	
215.		515.	
216.		516.	
217.		517.	
218.		518.	
219.		519.	
220. Total Paid By/For Borrower		**520. Total Reduction Amount Due Seller**	
300. Cash At Settlement From/To Borrower		**600. Cash At Settlement To/From Seller**	
301. Gross Amount due from borrower (line 120)		601. Gross amount due to seller (line 420)	
302. Less amounts paid by/for borrower (line 220)	( )	602. Less reductions in amt. due seller (line 520)	( )
303. Cash ☐ From ☐ To Borrower		603. Cash ☐ To ☐ From Seller	

Previous Edition Is Obsolete

HUD-1 (3-86)
RESPA, HB 4305.2

L. Settlement Charges

	Paid From Borrowers Funds at Settlement	Paid From Seller's Funds at Settlement
700. Total Sales/Broker's Commission based on price $ @ % =		
Division of Commission (line 700) as follows:		
701. $ to		
702. $ to		
703. Commission paid at Settlement		
704.		
800. Items Payable In Connection With Loan		
801. Loan Origination Fee %		
802. Loan Discount %		
803. Appraisal Fee to		
804. Credit Report to		
805. Lender's Inspection Fee		
806. Mortgage Insurance Application Fee to		
807. Assumption Fee		
808.		
809.		
810.		
811.		
900. Items Required By Lender To Be Paid In Advance		
901. Interest from to @$ /day		
902. Mortgage Insurance Premium for months to		
903. Hazard Insurance Premium for years to		
904. years to		
905.		
1000. Reserves Deposited With Lender		
1001. Hazard insurance months@$ per month		
1002. Mortgage insurance months@$ per month		
1003. City property taxes months@$ per month		
1004. County property taxes months@$ per month		
1005. Annual assessments months@$ per month		
1006. months@$ per month		
1007. months@$ per month		
1008. months@$ per month		
1100. Title Charges		
1101. Settlement or closing fee to		
1102. Abstract or title search to		
1103. Title examination to		
1104. Title insurance binder to		
1105. Document preparation to		
1106. Notary fees to		
1107. Attorney's fees to		
(includes above items numbers:)		
1108. Title insurance to		
(includes above items numbers:)		
1109. Lender's coverage $		
1110. Owner's coverage $		
1111.		
1112.		
1113.		
1200. Government Recording and Transfer Charges		
1201. Recording fees: Deed $; Mortgage $; Releases $		
1202. City/county tax/stamps: Deed $; Mortgage $		
1203. State tax/stamps: Deed $; Mortgage $		
1204.		
1205.		
1300. Additional Settlement Charges		
1301. Survey to		
1302. Pest inspection to		
1303.		
1304.		
1305.		
1400. Total Settlement Charges (enter on lines 103, Section J and 502, Section K)		

Chapter Summary

1. After a purchase and sale agreement has been signed, the next stage of the transaction is the closing process. Closing is often handled through escrow, an arrangement in which money and documents are held by a neutral third party (the escrow agent) on behalf of the buyer and the seller, and distributed when all of the conditions in the escrow instructions have been fulfilled.

2. The escrow agent prepares a settlement statement, detailing all the charges payable by (debits) and to (credits) each of the parties at closing. Who pays which closing costs may be determined by agreement or by local custom. Certain expenses must be prorated as of the closing date.

3. Real estate agents must be aware of the closing agent's obligation to comply with 1099 reporting and FIRPTA requirements. If the closing agent does not fulfill those requirements, the real estate agent may be liable.

4. RESPA applies to almost all residential purchase loan transactions involving institutional lenders. It requires a lender to give a loan applicant a good faith estimate of closing costs within three days after a written loan application is submitted. RESPA also requires the lender to complete a Uniform Settlement Statement and have it available to the borrower one day before closing, if the borrower asks to see it in advance.

Key Terms

Closing—The final stage of a real estate transaction, in which documents are signed and delivered and funds are transferred.

Escrow—An arrangement in which money and documents are held by a neutral third party on behalf of the buyer and the seller.

Escrow agent—A neutral third party who holds money and documents in trust and carries out the closing process.

Escrow instructions—A written document that tells the escrow agent how to proceed and states the conditions each party must fulfill before the transaction can close.

Settlement statement—A statement that sets forth all the financial aspects of a real estate transaction in detail and indicates how much cash each party will be required to pay or will receive at closing.

Debit—A charge payable by a party.

Credit—A charge payable to a party.

Reserve account—Funds on deposit with a lender to pay the property taxes and insurance premiums when due.

Prorate—To divide and allocate an expense proportionately, according to time, interest, or benefit, determining what share of it a particular party is responsible for.

Prepaid interest—Interest on the buyer's new mortgage loan that the lender requires to be paid at closing, covering the period from the closing date through the last day of the month.

Uniform Settlement Statement—The settlement statement form closing agents are required to use in transactions covered by the Real Estate Settlement Procedures Act.

Chapter 13—Quiz
Escrow and Settlement Statements

1. Every debit on the buyer's side of the settlement statement is a charge that:

   a) will be paid to the buyer at closing
   b) must be paid by the buyer at closing
   c) the buyer must pay to the seller at closing
   d) the seller must pay to the buyer at closing

2. On a settlement statement, the purchase price will be listed as:

   a) a debit to the buyer
   b) a debit to the seller
   c) Both of the above
   d) Neither of the above

3. The transaction is closing on September 16. The seller has already paid the annual premium for hazard insurance, and the buyer will not be assuming the policy. On the settlement statement, part of the insurance premium will be listed as:

   a) a debit to the buyer and a credit to the seller
   b) a debit to the seller and a credit to the buyer
   c) a credit to the buyer
   d) a credit to the seller

4. How does the buyer's earnest money deposit show up on a settlement statement?

   a) It is listed as a debit on the buyer's side of the statement, and as a credit on the seller's side of the statement
   b) It is listed as a credit on the buyer's side of the statement, but it is not listed on the seller's side because it is included in the purchase price
   c) It is listed as a credit on the seller's side of the statement, but it is not listed on the buyer's side because it will be refunded at closing
   d) It is listed as a debit on both the buyer's side and the seller's side of the statement

5. When a buyer assumes a mortgage, how does the mortgage balance appear on the settlement statement?

   a) Only as a credit to the seller
   b) Only as a debit on the seller's side of the statement
   c) As a credit to the buyer and a debit to the seller
   d) As a credit to the seller and a debit to buyer

6. Which of the following is ordinarily one of the seller's closing costs?

   a) Sales commission
   b) Credit report fee
   c) Appraisal fee
   d) Origination fee

7. Which of the following is ordinarily one of the buyer's closing costs?

   a) Sales commission
   b) Lender's title insurance premium
   c) Excise tax
   d) None of the above

8. On a settlement statement, prepaid interest would usually appear as a:

   a) seller's debit
   b) buyer's credit
   c) seller's credit
   d) buyer's debit

9. The Matsons are selling their home. They are current on their mortgage payments, having made their most recent payment on May 1. They will be paying off their mortgage when the sale closes on May 17. At closing, the Matsons will probably be:

    a) entitled to a refund of the mortgage interest accruing in May
    b) required to pay the mortgage interest accruing in May
    c) entitled to a refund of the prepayment penalty
    d) required to pay part of the mortgage interest that accrued in April

10. A settlement statement:

    a) is given only to the buyer
    b) sets out the items to be paid by each party
    c) is given only to the lender
    d) None of the above

11. When an item is prorated it means that:

    a) it is deleted from the cost of the sale
    b) it is calculated on the basis of a particular time period
    c) it is not paid until closing
    d) the escrow agent must pay the fee

12. Under RESPA, a loan is considered federally related if:

    a) it will be used to finance the purchase of real property
    b) it is secured by a first or second mortgage
    c) the lender is federally regulated
    d) All of the above

13. Under FIRPTA:

    a) a foreign investor can never buy or sell property without special authorization
    b) if a seller is not a U.S. citizen, the escrow agent will have to deduct 10% of the sale proceeds and send it to the IRS
    c) escrow agents must notify the real estate broker if the buyer is a foreigner investor
    d) a foreign investor purchasing property in the U.S. must pay an additional 10% over and above the purchase price and submit it to the IRS

Answer Key

1.b) A debit on the buyer's side of the statement is a charge that the buyer must pay. In some cases, it is a charge that the buyer must pay to the seller (a refund for taxes paid in advance, for example), but in other cases the buyer owes it to a third party (the loan fee paid to the lender, for example).

2.a) The purchase price is a debit to the buyer and a credit to the seller.

3.d) The seller is entitled to a refund for the insurance he or she paid in advance, and this will show up as a credit on the seller's side of the settlement statement. Since the buyer is not assuming the policy, the seller's insurance is not listed on the buyer's side of the statement.

4.b) The earnest money deposit is a credit to the buyer, since it has already been paid. It does not appear on the seller's side of the statement, because the full purchase price is listed as a credit to the seller, and the deposit is included in the price.

5.c) A loan the buyer uses to finance the transaction is listed as a credit to the buyer, whatever its source. When the financing comes through the seller—either through an assumption of the seller's loan, or through seller financing—it is a debit to the seller as well as a credit to the buyer.

6.a) The seller almost always pays the real estate broker's commission. The other expenses listed relate to the buyer's loan, and they are ordinarily paid by the buyer.

7.b) The buyer is usually required to pay the premium for the lender's extended coverage title insurance policy.

8.d) Prepaid interest—interest on a new loan to cover the period from the closing date through the last day of the month—is one of the buyer's debits.

9.b) Because mortgage interest is paid in arrears—the month after it accrues—at closing the sellers will be required to pay the interest that has accrued during May. (Their May 1 mortgage payment included the interest that accrued in April.)

10.b) A settlement statement sets forth the charges that must be paid by each party.

11.b) Prorating an expense is calculating it on the basis of a particular time period, such as a certain number of days.

12.d) All of these are elements of a federally related loan under RESPA.

13.b) FIRPTA requires the escrow agent to deduct 10% of the sales price and send it to the IRS when the seller is a foreign investor.

Settlement Statement Problem

Settlement Statement Problem

Fill in the settlement statement form on the next page using the information provided below. For your prorations, use a 365-day year, with the buyer responsible for charges beginning with the day of closing. This problem is self-contained: do not add, delete, or change expenses or costs based on the actual practices in your community. Leave blank any lines on the form that do not pertain to the transaction described below.

On September 27, Consuela Zelaya of Superior Realty listed a house for $131,500. The sellers agreed to pay a 7% commission.

Zelaya found a buyer for the home, who signed a deposit receipt with the sellers on October 24. The closing date is set for December 28. The buyer made an earnest money deposit of $6,500. The contract calls for a sales price of $129,750, contingent on the buyer's obtaining an 80% conventional loan at an interest rate of 9.25%. The buyer is to pay all costs associated with the loan application and approval. The buyer's first mortgage payment will be due February 1. The sellers will pay off their outstanding loan at closing, and they have agreed to pay the premium for the owner's policy of title insurance (standard coverage). The escrow fee is to be split equally between the parties.

The closing costs and other payments to be listed on the settlement statement (prorated, if necessary) include:

- appraisal fee: $200
- credit report: $55
- loan origination fee: 1% of the loan amount
- outstanding balance on the sellers' loan: $79,500 (the interest rate is 10% and the loan is current—the last payment was made December 1)
- annual property taxes: $1,026 (they have been paid for the fiscal year)
- buyer's three-year hazard insurance policy premium: $480 (the buyer must prepay the first year)
- sellers' one-year hazard insurance policy: $190 (it has been paid through the end of next June)
- owner's title insurance policy: $218
- lender's title insurance policy: $382
- documentary transfer tax: $143
- escrow fee: $240
- attorney's fees: $115 for buyer, $90 for sellers
- recording fees: $20 for buyer, $12 for sellers
- sellers' impound account to be refunded: $285.50

	BUYER		SELLER	
	Debits	*Credits*	*Debits*	*Credits*
Purchase price				
Earnest money deposit				
Documentary transfer tax				
Sales commission				
New loan				
Assumption of seller's loan				
Seller financing				
Payoff of seller's loan				
Owner's title insurance				
Lender's title insurance				
Origination/assumption fee				
Discount points				
Property taxes: in arrears				
Property taxes: paid in advance				
Hazard insurance: refund to seller				
Hazard insurance: assumption				
Hazard insurance: new policy				
Interest: payoff of seller's loan				
Interest: assumption				
Prepaid interest (new loan)				
Impound account: refund to seller				
Impound account: new loan				
Credit report				
Appraisal				
Survey				
Personal property				
Recording fees				
Escrow fee				
Attorney's fees				
Balance due from buyer				
Balance due to seller				
TOTALS				

Calculations for Settlement Statement Problem

Sales commission: $129,750 x 7% = $9,082.50

New loan: $129,750 × 80% = $103,800

Origination fee: $103,800 × 1% = $1,038

Property taxes

> $1,026 ÷ 365 = $2.81 per diem
> $2.81 × 185 days = $520.03 (buyer's prorated share)
> (The period from December 28 through June 30 is 185 days.)

Hazard insurance

> Seller's refund: $190 ÷ 365 = 0.52 per diem × 185 days = $96.30
> Buyer's premium: $480 ÷ 3 years = $160 annual premium

Interest

> Interest accruing on seller's loan from Dec. 1 to Dec. 27:
> $79,500 × 10% = $7,950 ÷ 365 = $21.78 per diem × 27 days = $588.08
> Prepaid interest that will accrue on buyer's loan from Dec. 28 to Dec. 31:
> $103,800 × 9.25% = $9,601.50 ÷ 365 = $26.31 × 4 days = $105.24

Escrow fee: $240 ÷ 2 = $120

Balance due from Buyer:

> $132,465.25
> −110,300.00
> $22,165.25

Balance due to Seller:

> $130,651.83
> − 89,753.58
> $40,898.25

	BUYER		SELLER	
	Debits	**Credits**	**Debits**	**Credits**
Purchase price	129,750.00			129,750.00
Earnest money deposit		6,500.00		
Documentary transfer tax			143.00	
Sales commission			9,082.50	
New loan		103,800.00		
Assumption of seller's loan				
Seller financing				
Payoff of seller's loan			79,500.00	
Owner's title insurance			218.00	
Lender's title insurance	382.00			
Origination/assumption fee	1,038.00			
Discount points				
Property taxes: in arrears				
Property taxes: paid in advance	520.03			520.03
Hazard insurance: refund to seller				96.30
Hazard insurance: assumption				
Hazard insurance: new policy	160.00			
Interest: payoff of seller's loan			588.08	
Interest: assumption				
Prepaid interest (new loan)	105.24			
Impound account: refund to seller				285.50
Impound account: new loan				
Credit report	55.00			
Appraisal	200.00			
Survey				
Personal property				
Recording fees	20.00		12.00	
Escrow fee	120.00		120.00	
Attorney's fees	115.00		90.00	
Balance due from buyer		22,165.27		
Balance due to seller			40,898.25	
TOTALS	132,465.27	132,465.27	130,651.83	130,651.83

Chapter 14

Income Taxation and Real Estate

 Outline

 Chapter Overview

Almost every business transaction has tax consequences, and real estate transactions are no exception. Not only are there taxes that arise at the time of sale (such as the documentary transfer tax discussed in Chapter 4), there are also income tax ramifications for the parties involved. This chapter provides an overview of how federal and state income taxation affects the transfer and ownership of real estate. It explains some income tax terminology, discusses certain types of transactions that receive special treatment (such as "tax-free" exchanges), and also covers tax deductions available to real estate owners.

Basic Taxation Concepts

As you almost certainly know, in the United States the federal government taxes the income of individuals and businesses on an annual basis. Before discussing how the transfer or acquisition of real estate can affect the federal income taxes a seller or buyer is required to pay, we need to explain some basic terms and concepts.

Progressive Tax

A tax may be "proportional," "regressive," or "progressive," depending on how its burden is distributed among taxpayers. A tax is proportional if the same tax rate is applied to all levels of income. A tax is regressive if the rate applied to higher levels of income is lower than the rate applied to lower levels. Our federal income tax is a **progressive** tax. This means that the more a taxpayer earns in a given tax year, the higher his or her tax rate will be. In other words, someone who earns a large income is generally required not just to pay more taxes than someone who earns a small income, but to pay a greater percentage of his or her income in taxes.

Tax rates increase in uneven steps called **tax brackets**. An additional dollar earned by a given taxpayer may be taxed at a higher rate than the dollar earned just before it, because it crosses the line into a higher bracket. But the additional dollar earned will not increase the tax the taxpayer is required to pay on dollars previously earned.

Income

When asked about their income, many people tend to think only in terms of the wages or salary they earn at a job. The Internal Revenue Service (IRS) takes a much broader view of income, however. It regards any economic benefit realized by a taxpayer as part of his or her income, unless it is a type of benefit specifically excluded from income by the tax code. (The concept of realization is discussed below.)

Deductions and Tax Credits

The tax code authorizes certain expenses to be deducted from income. For example, if a business loses money in a particular tax year, the owner may be allowed to deduct the loss. A taxpayer who is entitled to a deduction can subtract a specified amount from his or her income before it is taxed. By reducing the amount of income that is taxed, the deduction also reduces the amount of tax the taxpayer owes.

In contrast to deductions, tax credits are subtracted directly from the amount of tax owed. The taxpayer's income is added up, the tax rate is applied, and then any applicable tax credits are subtracted to determine how much the taxpayer will actually have to pay.

The government often uses deductions and tax credits to implement social and economic policy. For example, allowing homeowners to deduct mortgage interest from their taxable income helps make homeownership more affordable. (The mortgage interest deduction is explained later in this chapter.)

Gains and Losses

The sale or exchange of an asset (such as real estate) nearly always results in either a gain or a loss. Gains are treated as income, so any gain is taxable unless the tax code specifically says otherwise. On the other hand, a loss may be deducted from income only if the deduction is specifically authorized by the tax code. Most deductible losses are losses incurred in a trade or business or in transactions entered into for profit. A business entity (such as a corporation) can deduct all of its losses. An individual taxpayer can deduct a loss only if it was incurred in connection with:

1. the taxpayer's trade or business,
2. a transaction entered into for profit, or
3. a casualty loss or theft of the taxpayer's property.

No deduction is allowed for a loss suffered on the sale of the taxpayer's principal residence or other real property owned for personal use.

A gain or loss on the sale of an asset held for personal use or as an investment is considered a **capital gain** or a **capital loss**. Capital gains and losses are netted against each other. If there is a net gain, it is taxed; the maximum tax rate applied to capital gains is 28% (as opposed to 39.6% for other income). If there is a net loss, up to $3,000 may be deducted from income. Individuals may deduct no more than $3,000 in capital losses in one year. (And as stated above, losses in connection with personal use property are generally not deductible at all.) Any losses in excess of the $3,000 limit may be carried forward to be deducted in future years.

A long-term capital gain is a gain on the sale of an asset held longer than one year. Up until 1987, only 40% of a long-term capital gain was taxable. The Tax Reform Act of 1986 eliminated that special treatment for long-term capital gains.

Basis

For income tax purposes, a property owner's **basis** in the property is his or her investment in it. If a taxpayer sells an asset, the basis is the maximum amount that he or she can receive in payment for the asset without realizing a gain. To determine gains and losses, it is necessary to know the taxpayer's basis in the property in question.

In most cases, a taxpayer's initial basis is equal to the actual amount of his or her investment—that is, how much it cost to acquire the property. A person who paid $120,000 for a house plus $7,000 in closing costs has an initial basis of $127,000 in the property. He or she could turn around and sell the house for $127,000 without having to report a gain to the IRS.

Adjusted Basis

The initial basis may be increased or decreased to arrive at an **adjusted basis**, which reflects capital expenditures and any allowable depreciation or cost recovery deductions. **Capital expenditures** are expenditures made to improve the property, such as

money a homeowner spends on adding a new room or remodeling the kitchen. Capital expenditures increase the value of the property or significantly extend its useful life. They are added to the initial basis in calculating the adjusted basis.

> **Example:** Greene buys a home for $135,000 plus $5,000 in closing costs. Four years later, she spends $30,000 on improvements to the property, adding a third bedroom and remodeling both bathrooms. Her adjusted basis in the property is now $170,000.

Maintenance expenses, such as repainting or replacing a broken window, are not capital expenditures. Maintenance expenses do not affect basis.

For certain types of property, a taxpayer's initial basis is also adjusted to take into account depreciation or cost recovery deductions, which will be discussed later in this chapter. These deductions are subtracted from the initial basis in calculating the adjusted basis.

```
  Initial basis
+ Capital expenditures
- Depreciation/Cost recovery deductions
  Adjusted basis
```

Realization

Not every gain is immediately taxable. A gain is not considered taxable income until it is **realized**. Ownership of an asset involves gain if the asset is appreciating in value. But for tax purposes, a gain is realized only when a sale or exchange occurs; the gain is then separated from the asset.

> **Example:** Referring back to the example given above, suppose that during Greene's four years of ownership property values have been increasing steadily. Her improved house (which she bought for $140,000 and invested another $30,000 in) now has a market value of $205,000. She has enjoyed an economic gain or benefit: she now owns

property that is worth $35,000 more than what she put into it. However, that $35,000 is not realized—and therefore is not treated as income subject to taxation—until she sells the house.

The gain or loss realized on a transaction is the difference between the net sales price (referred to as the **amount realized**) and the adjusted basis of the property:

    Amount realized (net sales price)
− Adjusted basis
    Gain or Loss

In calculating the amount realized, the sales price includes money or other property received in exchange for the property, plus the amount of any mortgage debt that is eliminated. This means that if the buyer takes the property subject to the seller's mortgage or assumes it, the amount of that debt is treated as part of the sales price for tax purposes.

The sales price is reduced by selling expenses (such as the brokerage commission and the seller's other closing costs) to arrive at the amount realized.

    Money received
+ Market value of other property received
+ Mortgage debt disposed of
− Selling expenses
    Amount realized (net sales price)

Recognition and Deferral

A gain is said to be **recognized** in the year it is taxed. A gain will be recognized in the year it is realized, unless there is a specific exception in the tax code that allows the taxpayer to defer payment of taxes on the gain until a later tax year or a later transaction. For example, the tax code permits an individual selling his or her principal residence to defer taxation of the gain if the sale proceeds are used within two years to buy another residence.

The tax code provisions that allow recognition of a gain to be deferred are called "nonrecognition provisions." The nonrecognition provisions that apply to real estate transactions (including the rule just mentioned concerning sale of a principal residence) are discussed in detail later in this chapter.

Classifications of Real Property

Whether a particular type of real estate transaction qualifies for special tax treatment depends on the type of property involved. The tax code divides real property into the following classes:

1. principal residence property,
2. personal use property,
3. unimproved investment property,
4. property held for the production of income,
5. property used in a trade or business, and
6. dealer property.

Principal Residence Property. This is the home the taxpayer owns and occupies as his or her primary dwelling. It may be a single-family home, a duplex, a condominium unit, a cooperative apartment, or a mobile home. If the taxpayer owns two homes and lives in both of them, the one in which he or she lives most of the time is the principal residence. A taxpayer cannot have two principal residences at the same time.

Personal Use Property. Real property that a taxpayer owns for personal use, other than the principal residence, is classified as personal use property. A second home or a vacation cabin would belong in this category.

Unimproved Investment Property. Unimproved investment property is vacant land that produces no rental income. The land is held simply as an investment, in the expectation that it will appreciate in value.

Fig.14.1 IRS property classifications

Principal Residence

Personal Use Property

Property held for the Production of Income

Unimproved Investment Property

Property used in a Trade or Business

Dealer Property

Property Held for Production of Income. Property held for the production of income includes residential, commercial, and industrial property that is used to generate rental income for the owner.

Property Used in a Trade or Business. This category includes land and buildings that the taxpayer owns and uses in his or her trade or business, such as a factory owned by the manufacturer, or a small building the owner uses for his or her own retail business.

Dealer Property. This is property held primarily for sale to customers rather than for long-term investment. If a developer subdivides land for sale to the public, the lots will usually be included in this classification until they are sold.

Nonrecognition Transactions

As was explained earlier, when a nonrecognition provision in the tax code applies to a particular transaction, the taxpayer is not required to pay taxes on a gain in the year it is realized. The real estate transactions that are covered by nonrecognition provisions include all of the following:

- installment sales,
- the sale of a principal residence,
- involuntary conversions,
- sales of low-income housing, and
- "tax-free" exchanges.

Keep in mind that nonrecognition provisions do not completely exclude the gain from taxation, but merely defer the tax consequences to a later tax year. These are not really "tax-free" transactions. The realized gain is simply recognized and taxed in a subsequent year.

Fig.14.2 Eligibility for installment sale reporting

Installment Sale Reporting

1. Less than 100% of sales price received in year of sale

2. All classifications of real property eligible except dealer property

Installment Sales

The tax code considers a sale to be an installment sale if less than 100% of the sales price is received in the year of sale. Nearly all seller-financed transactions are installment sales. Installment sale reporting allows the taxpayer/seller to defer recognition of part of the gain to the year(s) in which it is actually received. In effect, taxes are paid only on the portion of the profit received each year. Installment sale reporting is permitted for all classes of property, except that dealer property is eligible only under special conditions.

In installment sales, the gain recognized in any given year is calculated based on the ratio of gross profit to the contract price. The gross profit is the difference between the sales price and the adjusted basis.

To calculate the gross profit, take the seller's adjusted basis at the time of sale, add the amount of the commission and other selling expenses, and subtract this sum from the sales price.

Example: Once again, we'll use Greene as an example. Her basis in her house was $170,000.

She sold the property for $205,000. She had to pay a $10,250 commission and $2,200 in other selling expenses.

$205,000	sales price

$170,000	seller's basis
+ 12,450	commission and selling expenses
$182,450	adjusted basis

$205,000	sales price
−182,450	adjusted basis
$22,550	gross profit

The next step is to compare the gross profit to the contract price to arrive at the gross profit ratio. The contract price is the total amount of all principal payments the buyer will pay the seller. In most cases, unless the buyer assumes an existing loan, the contract price is the same as the sales price.

Example:

Gross Profit	÷	Contract Price	=	Gross Profit Ratio
$22,550	÷	$205,000	=	11%

The gross profit ratio is applied to the principal payments received in each year to determine how much of the principal is gain to be taxed that year. Note that the gross profit ratio is not applied to the interest the buyer pays the seller; all of the interest payments are treated as taxable income in the year received.

If the seller in the example above received a $20,500 downpayment, $1,250 in principal installment payments, and $16,500 in interest the first year, the taxable income would be calculated as follows:

$20,500	downpayment
+ 1,250	installment principal payments
$21,750	total principal payments

$21,750	
× 11%	
$2,392	recognized gain
+ 16,500	interest income
$18,892	total taxable income

If the buyer assumes or takes subject to a mortgage that is larger than the seller's basis in the property, the excess is treated as payment received from the buyer. If the property is subject to recapture provisions because of depreciation or cost recovery deductions (discussed later in this chapter), the amount recaptured is also treated as a payment received in the year of sale.

Sale of a Principal Residence

A taxpayer who sells his or her principal residence and replaces it within two years (by purchasing or building another one) is allowed to defer recognition of the gain. This is sometimes called a **rollover**.

Recognition is deferred only to the extent that the gain from the sale of the old home is reinvested in the replacement home. It isn't necessary for all of the cash the owner receives from the sale to actually be invested in the new home. It's the relationship between the cost of the new home and the amount realized on the sale of the old home that is important. This means that if the acquisition cost of the new home is as much as or greater than the amount realized on the sale of the old home, then the entire gain is deferred.

Example:

$90,000	amount realized (after selling costs)
− 80,000	seller's basis in old home
$10,000	gain realized

A year and a half after selling the old home, the seller buys a replacement home for $92,000. Recognition of the entire $10,000 gain will be deferred.

If the acquisition cost of the new home is less than the amount realized on the sale of the old home, the taxpayer is only entitled to defer recognition of the part of the gain that was reinvested.

Example: Referring back to the example above, suppose the seller's replacement home cost only $83,000 instead of $92,000. In that case, only $3,000 of the $10,000 gain has been reinvested. The seller will be allowed to defer recognition of that $3,000, but the $7,000 that was not reinvested will be taxed.

After a rollover, the taxpayer's basis in the replacement home is reduced by the amount of the deferred gain. In the first example above (where the replacement home cost $92,000 and the entire $10,000 gain was deferred), the taxpayer's basis in the replacement home would be $82,000. In the second example (with an $83,000 replacement home and a $3,000 deferred gain), the basis would be $80,000.

A taxpayer who intends to take advantage of the rollover rules must report the sale of the old residence to the IRS in the year of the sale. If the residence isn't replaced within two years, the entire gain will be taxed at that time.

Sale of Residence by Taxpayer Over 55. Anytime a taxpayer sells a principal residence and replaces it within two years, he or she is entitled to the deferral of gain discussed above. In addition, once in a lifetime, a taxpayer is entitled to an exclusion of gain of up to $125,000 on the sale of a principal residence. (For a married taxpayer filing separately, the maximum exclusion is $62,500.) This is more than a deferral; when the taxpayer chooses to use this exclusion, the gain is never included in his or her income—not in the year of sale, and not later on. This is one of the few provisions of the tax code that allows a taxpayer to realize a gain that will never be taxed.

To qualify for this exclusion, the taxpayer must be at least 55 years old (for a married couple, only one spouse must be 55). The property sold must have been used as the taxpayer's principal residence for at least three of the last five years. It is not necessary to reinvest the excluded gain in a new residence.

Involuntary Conversions

An involuntary conversion occurs when an asset is turned into cash without the voluntary action of the owner, as when an asset is condemned, destroyed, stolen, or lost, and the owner receives a condemnation award or insurance proceeds. Since the award or proceeds usually represent the property's replacement cost or market value, the owner often realizes a gain on an involuntary conversion.

However, recognition of a gain on an involuntary conversion can be deferred if the taxpayer uses the money received to replace the property within the replacement period set by the IRS. Generally, the replacement period lasts for two years after the end of the tax year in which the gain was realized; for business or income property, the period is three years. Recognition of the gain is deferred only to the extent that the condemnation award or insurance proceeds are reinvested in the replacement property.

Sales of Low-Income Housing

A taxpayer who owns certain qualified low-income housing may sell it and reinvest the proceeds in similar housing within one year without recognizing a gain on the sale. Gain that is not reinvested in similar property is recognized in the year of the sale.

"Tax-Free" Exchanges

A "tax-free" exchange is really just a tax-deferred exchange. If investment property, income

Fig.14.3 Eligibility for "tax-free" exchanges

"Tax-Free" Exchanges

1. Only property held for production of income, for use in trade or business, or for investment is eligible.
2. Must be exchanged for like-kind property.
3. Any boot is taxed in the year it is received.

---

property, or property used in a trade or business is exchanged for **like-kind** property, recognition of any realized gain will be deferred. A principal residence, personal use property, and dealer property are not eligible for this type of deferral.

"Tax-free" exchanges are used to reduce or eliminate current tax expenses. And a taxpayer may be able to acquire property in an exchange that it would have been impossible to buy with the after-tax proceeds from the sale of the old property.

The property the taxpayer receives in the exchange must be like-kind—that is, the same kind as the property given. This requirement refers to the general nature of the properties rather than their quality. Most real estate is considered to be of like kind for the purposes of the exchange deferral, without regard to whether it is improved, unimproved, residential, commercial, or industrial. For example, if a taxpayer exchanges a strip shopping center for an apartment complex, the transaction can qualify as a "tax-free" exchange.

If nothing other than like-kind property is received in the exchange, no gain or loss is recognized in the year of the exchange. However, anything other than like-kind property that the taxpayer re-

ceives is called **boot** and recognized in the year of the exchange. In a real estate exchange, boot might be cash, stock, other types of personal property, or the difference between mortgage balances.

> **Example:** A taxpayer trades a property with a mortgage debt of $50,000 for a property with a mortgage debt of $30,000. The taxpayer has received $20,000 in boot because of the reduction in debt (regardless of whether or not there has been a formal assumption of the loan). The taxpayer will have to pay taxes on a gain of $20,000, just as if he or she had received $20,000 in cash along with the real property.

The taxpayer's basis in the property exchanged is transferred to the property he or she receives. If nothing other than like-kind property is exchanged, no adjustments are necessary. But if the exchange involved boot, the basis must be adjusted for any boot that was paid or received, and for any gain or loss that was recognized because of the boot.

Deductions Available to Property Owners

As was explained earlier, a deduction is subtracted from a taxpayer's income before the tax rate is applied. The income tax deductions allowed to real property owners are a significant benefit of ownership. Although some deductions were restricted or eliminated by the Tax Reform Act of 1986, there still are deductions for:

- depreciation and cost recovery,
- repairs,
- real property taxes,
- mortgage interest, and
- passive losses.

Depreciation and Cost Recovery Deductions

What used to be called depreciation deductions in the tax code are now called cost recovery deductions, but they are essentially the same thing. They permit a taxpayer to recover the cost of an asset used for the production of income or used in a trade or business. They cannot be taken in connection with a principal residence, personal use property, unimproved investment property, or dealer property.

Depreciable Property. In general, only property that wears out and will eventually have to be replaced is **depreciable**—that is, eligible for depreciation or cost recovery deductions. For example, apartment buildings, business or factory equipment, and commercial fruit orchards all have to be replaced, so they are depreciable. But land does not wear out, so it is not depreciable.

Time Frame. The entire expense of acquiring an asset cannot be deducted in the year it is incurred (although that is permitted with many other business expenses, such as wages, supplies, and utilities). However, the expense can be deducted over a number of years; for most real estate, the recovery period is between 15 and 31½ years. The length of the recovery period is a reflection of legislative policy and has little, if any, relationship to the actual length of time that the property will be economically useful. The whole field of depreciation and cost recovery deductions has been subject to frequent modification by Congress.

Effect on Basis. As we said in the discussion of basis at the beginning of the chapter, any allowable depreciation or cost recovery deductions reduce the taxpayer's adjusted basis in the property. Note that this reduction occurs whether or not the taxpayer actually takes the deduction. If the deduction was allowable—that is, the taxpayer was entitled to take

it—the basis will be reduced. By reducing the basis, these deductions affect the taxpayer's eventual gain or loss on resale of the property.

Repair Deductions

For most real estate other than principal residences and personal use property, expenditures for repairs are deductible in the year paid. A repair expense is one incurred to keep the property in ordinary, efficient, operating condition.

Repair expenses should not be confused with capital expenditures. As explained earlier, capital expenditures add to the value of the property and frequently prolong its economic life. Capital expenditures are not deductible in the year made, but rather are added to the taxpayer's basis. The resulting increase in the basis will affect the gain or loss on the eventual sale of the property. It will also increase the allowable depreciation or cost recovery deductions if the property is eligible for those.

Property Tax Deductions

General real estate taxes are deductible. Special assessments for repairs or maintenance are deductible, but those for improvements (such as new sidewalks) are not.

Mortgage Interest Deductions

For most property, interest paid on a mortgage or deed of trust is usually completely deductible. However, the Tax Reform Act of 1986 and subsequent amendments placed some limitations on interest deductions for personal residences (which are now the only allowable consumer interest deductions).

A taxpayer may deduct interest payments on mortgage debt of up to $1,000,000 used to buy, build, or improve a first or second residence. In addition, interest on a home equity loan of up to

Fig.14.4 Tax-deferred transactions

Eligibility for Favorable Income Tax Treatment			
	Installment Sale	"Tax-Free" Exchange	Recovery Deductions
Principal Residence	Yes	No	No
Personal Use	Yes	No	No
Unimproved Investment	Yes	No	No
Trade or Business	Yes	Yes	Yes
Income	Yes	Yes	Yes
Dealer	No	No	No

$100,000 can be deducted without regard to the purpose of the loan. When the loan amount exceeds these limits, the interest on the excess is not deductible.

Because **points** are considered prepaid interest, they can also be deducted. The points paid on a loan to purchase or improve a principal residence can be deducted in the year they are paid if the following requirements are met:

1. the loan is secured by the principal residence;
2. the charging of points is an established business practice in the taxpayer's geographical area;
3. the number of points charged did not exceed the norm for the area;
4. the amount of the fee was computed as a percentage of the loan amount and was specifically called "points," "loan origination fee," or "loan discount" in the closing statement; and
5. the points were paid directly to the lender.

Points that are paid on refinancing can be deducted over the life of the loan. If the loan is paid off early, the remaining balance of the discount points may be deducted in the year the loan terminates. Note that points charged for administrative expenses (such as many loan origination fees) can never be deducted. Instead, these charges are added to the taxpayer's basis.

Deduction of Passive Losses

The tax code treats income generated by income property (such as an apartment building) as **passive income**. A loss from income property is considered a **passive loss**. Under the Tax Reform Act of 1986, passive losses can only be offset against passive income. They can no longer be offset against income from wages, salaries, interest, dividends, or royalties. However, an undeducted passive loss can be carried forward and used in a year when the taxpayer does have passive income.

Example: If a taxpayer had $30,000 salary income and owned one rental property, which had a net loss of $2,000 for the year, the $2,000 net loss could not be deducted from the $30,000 salary income. But if the rental property generates net income next year, the taxpayer could deduct this year's passive loss from that passive income.

There is one exception to these rules concerning passive loss deductions, in favor of individuals who actively participate in managing their rental property and whose adjusted gross income does not exceed $100,000. For these taxpayers, up to $25,000 in losses from the rental property can be offset against their non-passive income.

The requirement for "active participation" is met if the owner actually exercises some control over the management of the rental property—for example, by selecting tenants, setting rental terms, or authorizing repairs and maintenance work. This exception is only available to individuals; thus, it could not be used by an investor in a limited partnership that owns a rental property. The exception is also not available to a taxpayer who owns less than a 10% interest in the property.

If the taxpayer's adjusted gross income is more than $100,000, the maximum $25,000 passive loss deduction is reduced by fifty cents for every dollar of income over the $100,000 limit. So a taxpayer whose adjusted gross income exceeds $150,000 would not be able to take any advantage of this limited exception. He or she could offset passive losses only against passive income.

California Income Tax

In addition to the federal income tax, there is a California state income tax. California income tax laws are substantially the same as the provisions of the Internal Revenue Code. For example, with limited exceptions, the California statutes simply refer to the federal law for such items as the definitions of gross income, adjusted gross income, itemized deductions, and taxable income. There is a different standard deduction under state law for those who do not itemize and, of course, the tax rates on taxable income are different. As with federal law, the state income tax is a progressive tax with higher rates imposed on higher income levels. Income tax brackets and the standard deduction are adjusted for inflation by the California Franchise Tax Board each year based on the California Consumer Price Index.

Chapter Summary

1. Any economic benefit realized by a taxpayer is treated as part of his or her income, unless there is a specific provision of the tax code that excludes it from income. The tax code provides for certain deductions from income before the tax rate is applied, and also for tax credits, which are subtracted from the amount of tax owed.

2. A gain or a loss is realized when an asset is sold. A gain is recognized (taxed) in the year it is realized, unless a nonrecognition provision in the tax code applies.

3. A taxpayer's initial basis in property is the amount he or she originally invested in it. To determine the adjusted basis, capital expenditures are added to the initial basis, and allowable cost recovery deductions are subtracted from it. The taxpayer's gain or loss is the difference between the amount realized and the adjusted basis.

4. In the tax code, real property is classified as principal residence property, personal use property, unimproved investment property, property held for the production of income, property used in a trade or business, or dealer property.

5. The tax code's nonrecognition provisions for real property transactions allow taxation of gain to be deferred in installment sales, the sale of a principal residence, involuntary conversions, sales of certain low-income housing, and "tax-free" exchanges. There is also a once-in-a-lifetime exclusion of gain allowed on the sale of a principal residence by a taxpayer over 55.

6. The tax deductions available to property owners include cost recovery deductions (only for income property and property used in a trade or business); repair deductions (not for principal residences or personal use property); deduction of property taxes; and deduction of mortgage interest. There are some limits on the mortgage interest deduction for personal residences, and on deduction of losses incurred in connection with income property (passive losses).

Key Terms

Income—Any economic benefit realized by a taxpayer that is not excluded from income by the tax code.

Deduction—An expense that can be used to reduce taxable income.

Initial basis—The amount of the taxpayer's original investment in the property; what it cost to acquire the property.

Adjusted basis—The initial basis plus capital expenditures and minus allowable depreciation or cost recovery deductions.

Realization—A gain or a loss is realized when it is separated from the asset; this separation generally occurs when the asset is sold.

Recognition—A gain is said to be recognized when it is taxable; it is recognized in the year it is realized unless recognition is deferred by the tax code.

Installment sale—A sale in which less than 100% of the sales price is received in the year of sale.

Rollover—When a taxpayer sells his or her principal residence and replaces it within two years, allowing taxation of the gain to be deferred.

Involuntary conversion—When property is converted to cash without the voluntary action of the owner, as when it is condemned, destroyed, stolen, or lost.

Cost recovery deductions—Deductions from the taxpayer's income to allow the cost of an asset to be recovered; allowed only for depreciable property that is held for the production of income or used in a trade or business. Also called depreciation deductions.

Repair expenses—Money spent on repairs to keep property in ordinary, efficient operating condition.

Capital expenditures—Money spent on improvements to property, which add to its value or prolong its economic life.

"Tax-free" exchange—When like-kind property is exchanged, allowing taxation of the gain to be deferred.

Like-kind property—In a tax-free exchange, property received that is of the same kind as the property transferred; any two pieces of real estate are considered to be of like kind.

Boot—Something given or received in a "tax-free" exchange that is not like-kind property, such as cash.

Chapter 14—Quiz
Income Taxation and
Real Estate

1. A homeowner's basis would be adjusted to reflect:

   a) cost recovery deductions
   b) expenses incurred to keep the property in good repair
   c) mortgage interest paid
   d) the cost of installing a deck

2. A married couple bought a home for $150,000. After living in the home for three years, they sold it for only $146,000. How much of this loss can they deduct on their federal income tax return?

   a) The full $4,000 loss
   b) Only $3,000
   c) Only $2,000
   d) None of it

3. Which of the following could the owner of unimproved investment property deduct on his or her federal income tax return?

   a) A loss on the sale of the property
   b) The depreciation of the land
   c) Cost recovery deductions
   d) Any of the above

4. Which of the following exchanges could not qualify as a "tax-free" exchange?

   a) An office building for a hotel
   b) An apartment house for a warehouse
   c) Timber land for farm equipment
   d) A city lot for a ranch

5. Under the federal income tax code, income is always taxed in the year it is:

   a) realized
   b) recognized
   c) recovered
   d) deferred

6. Munson just sold his principal residence. After deducting his selling costs, the amount realized was $163,000. He is planning to buy a replacement residence immediately. Munson will be allowed to defer taxation of the entire gain on the sale of his old home only if:

   a) he is 55 or older
   b) he has never claimed this deferral before, since it can only be used once in a lifetime
   c) the gain is $125,000 or less
   d) the acquisition cost of the new home is at least $163,000

7. Torino owns a small apartment building. She paid $450,000 for it, including her closing costs. The allowable cost recovery deductions for the property have amounted to $20,000, Torino has spent $50,000 on capital improvements, and the market value of the property has risen by 15%. What is Torino's adjusted basis?

   a) $537,500
   b) $500,000
   c) $480,000
   d) $430,000

8. Gillespie is buying a home that will be his principal residence. He is financing the purchase with a $200,000 mortgage loan. How much of the interest that he pays on the loan can he deduct from his income?

   a) All of it
   b) Up to $100,000 in interest
   c) 50%
   d) None of it

9. The Louies are selling some property on a five-year contract. Their gross profit ratio on the sale is 15%. This year, they will receive $4,775 in interest and $1,675 in principal. With installment sale reporting, approximately how much of that will be recognized and included in the Louies' taxable income for this year?

   a) $251
   b) $967
   c) $2,391
   d) $5,026

10. Sherrick is selling some property for $72,000. Her adjusted basis in the property is $56,000. In addition to the 6% commission she'll be paying her real estate broker, she will also have to pay $2,500 in closing costs. For federal income tax purposes, what is the gain Sherrick will realize in this transaction?

    a) $6,820
    b) $9,180
    c) $16,000
    d) $22,820

Answer Key

1.d) The cost of installing a deck is a capital expenditure, which would be added to the taxpayer's basis. Remember that personal residences do not qualify for depreciation or cost recovery deductions.

2.d) A loss on the sale of a personal residence is never deductible.

3.a) If the owner loses money on the sale of the property, he or she may be able to deduct that loss. Depreciation and cost recovery deductions are not allowed for unimproved investment property, because land is not depreciable.

4.c) The like-kind property requirement means that real estate must be exchanged for other real estate.

5.b) Income is taxed when it is recognized. It is often recognized in the same year it is realized, but that is not true if a nonrecognition provision applies.

6.d) The acquisition cost of the new home must equal or exceed the amount realized on the sale of the old home if the entire amount of the gain is to be deferred. (All of the other answer options listed reflect requirements for the *exclusion* of a gain on the sale of a principal residence; they are not requirements for deferral.)

7.c) The initial basis, plus the capital expenditures, less the allowable cost recovery deductions, equals an adjusted basis of $480,000.

$450,000 + $50,000 − $20,000 = $480,000

(Ignore the increase in market value; it does not affect the taxpayer's basis.)

8.a) A taxpayer can deduct all of the interest paid on a loan of up to $1,000,000 used to purchase a first or second personal residence.

9.d) Multiply the principal payments by the gross profit ratio to determine the amount of principal that will be recognized this year. Then add that to the entire amount of interest received (all of the interest is taxable).

$1,675 × 15\% = $251.25 + $4,775 = $5,026.25

10.b) Sherrick will realize a $9,180 gain in the transaction. First subtract her selling expenses (the commission and closing costs) from the sales price to determine the amount realized; then subtract her adjusted basis from the amount realized to determine the gain.

$72,000 × 6\% = $4,320 commission

$4,320 + $2,500 costs = $6,820

$72,000 − $6,820 = $65,180 (amount realized)

$65,180 − $56,000 = $9,180 (gain realized)

Chapter 15

Civil Rights and Fair Housing

 Outline

 Chapter Overview

Unfair discrimination is prohibited in almost all real estate transactions by federal and state law. With limited exceptions, it is illegal for either property owners or real estate professionals to discriminate. In this chapter, we will cover several federal antidiscrimination laws, including the Civil Rights Act of 1866, the Federal Fair Housing Act, and the Americans with Disabilities Act. We will also discuss various state laws that prohibit discrimination in housing as well as in other real estate transactions.

Introduction

Over the years, various civil rights laws have been enacted to achieve one major goal: the freedom of choice. In the context of real estate, freedom of choice means that all types of people with similar financial resources should have equal access to the same types of housing. Anyone with the requisite income, net worth, and credit history should be able to choose a home or apartment in any affordable neighborhood, regardless of race, national origin, gender, or other similar characteristics.

Today, civil rights laws are an integral part of the real estate profession. The importance of the right to equal housing is well established, and real estate professionals must become familiar with both federal and state laws that prohibit discrimination.

The Civil Rights Act of 1866

This law states that "all citizens of the United States shall have the same right, in every state and territory as is enjoyed by white citizens thereof to inherit, purchase, lease, sell, hold and convey real and personal property." The act prohibits any discrimination based on race or ancestry.

Enacted immediately after the Civil War, the act was largely ignored for almost a century. In the 1960s, during the civil rights movement, the act was challenged as an unconstitutional interference with private property rights. But the U.S. Supreme Court upheld the act in the landmark case of *Jones v. Mayer*, decided in 1968. The court ruled that the 1866 Act "prohibits all racial discrimination, private or public, in the sale and rental of property," and that it is constitutional based on the 13th Amendment to the U.S. Constitution, which prohibits slavery.

Someone who has been discriminated against in violation of the Civil Rights Act of 1866 can sue in federal court. The court could issue an injunction ordering the defendant to stop discriminating. The court could also order the defendant to pay the plaintiff both compensatory damages (to compensate for losses and suffering caused by the discrimination) and punitive damages (an additional sum to punish the defendant for wrongdoing).

The Civil Rights Act of 1964

The Civil Rights Act of 1964 was one of the first attempts made by the federal government to implement fair housing ideals. The act prohibited discrimination based on race, color, religion, or national origin in many programs and activities for which the federal government offered financial assistance. Unfortunately, the effect of the act was extremely limited, because most FHA and VA loans were not covered. In fact, it is estimated that only about 0.5% of all houses purchased were covered by the act. It was not until the Civil Rights Act of 1968 that major progress was made towards fair housing.

The Federal Fair Housing Act

Contained in Title VIII of the Civil Rights Act of 1968, this law goes much farther than either the 1866 Act or the 1964 Act, making it illegal to discriminate on the basis of **race, color, religion, sex, national origin, handicap**, or **familial status** in the sale or lease of residential property, or in the sale or lease of vacant land for the construction of residential buildings. The law also prohibits discrimination in advertising, lending, real estate brokerage, and other services in connection with residential real estate transactions. However, unlike the 1866 Act, the Fair Housing Act does not apply to nonresidential transactions.

Prohibited Acts

The Fair Housing Act prohibits any of the following acts if they are done on the basis of race, color, religion, sex, national origin, handicap, or familial status:

- refusing to rent or sell residential property after receiving a bona fide offer;
- refusing to negotiate for the sale or rental of residential property, or otherwise making it unavailable;
- changing the terms of sale or lease for different potential buyers or tenants;

- using advertising that indicates a preference or intent to discriminate;
- representing that property is not available for inspection, sale, or rent when it is in fact available;
- discrimination by a commercial lender in making a housing loan;
- limiting participation in a multiple listing service or similar service;
- coercing, intimidating, threatening, or interfering with anyone on account of his or her enjoyment, attempt to enjoy, or encouragement or assistance to others in enjoying the rights granted by the Fair Housing Act.

Also prohibited are the discriminatory practices known as blockbusting, steering, and redlining.

- **Blockbusting** occurs when someone tries to induce homeowners to list or sell their properties by predicting that members of another race (or handicapped people, people of a particular ethnic background, etc.) will be moving into the neighborhood, and that this will have undesirable consequences such as lower property values. The blockbuster then profits by purchasing the homes at reduced prices or (in the case of a real estate agent) by collecting commissions on the induced sales. Blockbusting is also known as **panic selling**.

Example: An African-American family recently moved into an all-white neighborhood. Aryan Realty immediately began calling all the other homeowners in the neighborhood. Aryan's salespeople warned the homeowners of the following: several African-American families were planning on moving into the neighborhood; city police predicted a significant increase in crime in the neighborhood; property values would drop dramatically; and within months homeowners would find it difficult to sell their properties to anyone at any price. Because of these "facts" made up by

Aryan agents, several homeowners immediately listed their homes with Aryan Realty. Aryan Realty is guilty of blockbusting.

- **Steering** refers to channeling prospective buyers or tenants toward or away from specific neighborhoods based on their race (or religion, national origin, etc.) in order to maintain or change the character of those neighborhoods.

Example: Upright Realty has 17 white salespeople and three Hispanic salespeople. All Hispanic buyers are directed to Hispanic salespeople, who are "encouraged" to show them properties in minority neighborhoods only. This is done on the principle that Hispanic buyers would be more "comfortable" living in minority neighborhoods. Upright Realty is guilty of steering.

- **Redlining** is the refusal to make a loan because of the racial or ethnic composition of the neighborhood in which the security property is located.

Example: Buyer Jones applies to Community Savings for a loan to purchase a home located in the Cherrywood neighborhood. Cherrywood is a predominantly minority neighborhood. Community Savings rejects the loan application, because it fears that property values in Cherrywood may suffer in the future because of possible racial tension. Community Savings is guilty of redlining.

The prohibition against redlining is enforced by the **Home Mortgage Disclosure Act of 1975**, which requires large institutional lenders to file an annual report of all mortgage loans made. The loans are categorized according to the locations of the security properties, which makes it easier to discover cases of redlining. The Home Mortgage Disclosure Act is discussed in more detail later in this chapter.

Exemptions. The following residential transactions are exempt from the provisions of the Fair Housing Act.

Fig.15.1 Fair housing poster

U.S. Department of Housing and Urban Development

EQUAL HOUSING OPPORTUNITY

We Do Business in Accordance With the Federal Fair Housing Law

(The Fair Housing Amendments Act of 1988)

It Is Illegal To Discriminate Against Any Person Because of Race, Color, Religion, Sex, Handicap, Familial Status, or National Origin

- In the sale or rental of housing or residential lots
- In advertising the sale or rental of housing
- In the financing of housing

- In the provision of real estate brokerage services
- In the appraisal of housing
- Blockbusting is also illegal

Anyone who feels he or she has been discriminated against may file a complaint of housing discrimination with the:

U.S. Department of Housing and Urban Development
Assistant Secretary for Fair Housing and Equal Opportunity
Washington, D.C. 20410

Previous editions are obsolete

form HUD-928.1 (3-89)

1. The law does not apply to the sale or rental of a single-family home by its owner, provided that:
   - the owner does not own more than three such homes;
   - no real estate broker or agent is employed in the transaction; and
   - no discriminatory advertising is used.

   If the owner isn't the most recent occupant of the home, he or she may use this exemption only once every 24 months.

2. The law does not apply to the rental of a unit or a room in a dwelling with up to four units, provided that:
   - the owner occupies one of the units as his or her residence;
   - no real estate broker or agent is employed; and
   - no discriminatory advertising is used.

   (This is sometimes called the "**Mrs. Murphy exemption**.")

3. In dealing with their own property in noncommercial transactions, religious organizations or societies or affiliated nonprofit organizations may limit occupancy to or give preference to their own members, provided that membership isn't restricted on the basis of race, color, or national origin.

4. Private clubs with lodgings that aren't open to the public and that aren't operated for a commercial purpose may limit occupancy to or give preference to their own members.

These limited exemptions apply very rarely. Remember, the 1866 Civil Rights Act prohibits discrimination based on race or ancestry in any property transaction, regardless of any exemptions available under the Fair Housing Act. In addition, there is no exemption for any transaction involving a real estate licensee.

Familial Status and Handicap. The Federal Fair Housing Act originally did not prohibit discrimination based on familial status or handicap; these classifications were added to the law in 1988.

Familial Status. Discrimination on the basis of familial status refers to discrimination against a person because he or she has a child (under 18 years old) living with him or her. Parents, legal guardians, pregnant women, and those in the process of obtaining custody of a child are protected against discrimination on the basis of their familial status.

While the Federal Fair Housing Act does not override local laws limiting the number of occupants permitted in a dwelling, it is unlawful for anyone to discriminate in selling, renting, or lending money to buy residential property because the applicant is pregnant or lives with a child. "Adults only" apartment or condominium complexes are forbidden, and so are complexes divided into "adult" and "family" areas.

However, the law includes an exemption for properties that qualify as "housing for older persons." Children can be excluded from properties that fit into one of the following categories:

1. properties developed under a government program to assist the elderly;
2. properties intended for and solely occupied by persons 62 years old or older; or
3. properties intended for older persons and designed to meet their physical and social needs, if at least 80% of the units are occupied by at least one person who is 55 years old or older.

Handicap. Under the Fair Housing Act, it is illegal to discriminate against someone because he or she has a physical disability or mental impairment that substantially limits one or more major life activities. This includes people suffering from chronic alcoholism, mental illness, or AIDS. But the act does not protect those who are a direct threat to the health or safety of others, or who are currently using controlled substances.

A residential landlord must allow a handicapped tenant to make reasonable modifications to the property at the tenant's expense. (The landlord can require the tenant to restore the premises to their original condition at the end of the tenancy, however.) Landlords must also make reasonable exceptions to their rules to accommodate handicapped tenants. For example, even if they do not allow pets, they cannot refuse to rent to someone with a guide dog.

There are special wheelchair accessibility rules that apply to new residential construction (first occupied after March of 1991) with four units or more.

Enforcement. The Fair Housing Act is enforced by the Department of Housing and Urban Development (HUD), through its Office of Fair Housing and Equal Opportunity. An aggrieved person may file a complaint with HUD, or file a lawsuit in federal or state court. If a complaint is filed with HUD, the agency will investigate the complaint and attempt to confer with the parties in order to reconcile their differences and persuade them to abide by the law.

If the dispute is not resolved by this process, an administrative hearing will be held, unless either party chooses at this point to have the case decided in federal court instead. In an administrative hearing, HUD attorneys litigate the case on behalf of the complainant. If the case goes from HUD to federal court, the U.S. Attorney General's office litigates for the complainant.

When someone is held to have violated the Fair Housing Act, the administrative law judge or the court may issue an injunction ordering the violator to stop certain discriminatory conduct. The violator may also be ordered to pay compensatory damages and attorneys' fees to the complainant. A federal court can order the violator to pay punitive damages to the complainant. An administrative law judge cannot award punitive damages, but can impose a civil penalty (ranging from a maximum of $10,000

for a first offense, to $50,000 for the third offense within seven years), which the violator is required to pay to the government.

In states such as California, where the state fair housing laws are very similar to the federal laws, HUD may refer complaints to the equivalent state agency (e.g., the California Department of Fair Employment and Housing).

Fair Lending Laws

Real estate agents and sellers are not the only ones who must avoid discriminatory activities. There are federal laws and regulations designed to eliminate discrimination in lending. They include:

- the Federal Fair Housing Act (discussed above),
- the Equal Credit Opportunity Act,
- the Home Mortgage Disclosure Act, and
- regulations to implement and explain these statutes.

The Fair Housing Act prohibits discrimination in home loans and other aspects of residential financing. It does not apply to any other credit transactions.

The **Equal Credit Opportunity Act (ECOA)** applies to all consumer credit, including residential real estate loans. Consumer credit is credit that is extended to an individual (not a corporation or business) for personal, family, or household purposes. The act prohibits lenders from discriminating based on race, color, religion, national origin, sex, marital status, or age (as long as the applicant is of legal age), or because the applicant's income is derived partly or wholly from public assistance.

The **Home Mortgage Disclosure Act** is a way of learning whether lenders are fulfilling their obligation to serve the housing needs of the communities where they are located. The act facilitates the enforcement of federal laws against redlining.

Under the Home Mortgage Disclosure Act, institutional lenders in metropolitan areas with assets of over $10 million must make annual reports on residential mortgage loans (both purchase and improvement loans) that were originated or purchased during the fiscal year. The information is categorized as to number and dollar amount, type of loan (FHA, VA, FmHA, other), and geographic location by census tract or county (for small counties with no established census tracts). The reports disclose areas where few or no home loans have been made and alert investigators to potential redlining.

Equal Access to Facilities

The **Americans with Disabilities Act (ADA)**, which became effective in January of 1992, is a federal law that was passed to ensure that disabled persons have equal access to public facilities. The ADA requires any business or other facility open to the public to be accessible to the disabled.

Under the ADA, no one can be discriminated against on the basis of disability in any place of public accommodation. A **public accommodation** is defined as any private entity with facilities open to the public, as long as the operation of the facility affects commerce. A **disability** is defined as any physical or mental impairment that substantially limits one or more of the individual's major life activities.

Real estate offices are considered to be public accommodations, along with hotels, restaurants, retail stores, shopping centers, banks, and the offices of attorneys, accountants, and doctors.

To ensure accessibility to public accommodations, the ADA requires each of the following to be accomplished, as long as it is "readily achievable":

- both architectural and communication barriers must be removed so that goods and services are accessible to the disabled;

- auxiliary aids and services must be provided so that no disabled person is excluded, denied services, segregated, or otherwise treated differently than other individuals; and
- new commercial construction must be accessible to the disabled, unless structurally impractical.

For example, the owner of a commercial building with no elevator may have to install automatic entry doors and a buzzer at street level so that customers of a second-floor business can ask for assistance. A commercial building owner might also be required to alter the height of a pay phone to make it accessible to someone in a wheelchair, add grab bars to restroom stalls, and take a variety of other steps to make the building's facilities accessible.

California Civil Rights and Fair Housing Laws

In California, the Unruh Civil Rights Act, the Fair Employment and Housing Act, and the Housing Financial Discrimination Act all include provisions designed to promote fair housing within the state.

Unruh Civil Rights Act

California's Unruh Civil Rights Act states that all persons are entitled to the full use of any services provided by a business establishment, regardless of race, color, religion, ancestry, sex, national origin, blindness, physical disability, or age. The act prohibits a broker from discriminating in the performance of his or her work, since a brokerage firm is a business establishment. A broker cannot refuse a listing or turn away a prospective buyer for discriminatory reasons.

Apartment houses, condominium owners' associations, and other real estate developments are considered business establishments under the Unruh Act. Thus, the Act makes it unlawful for most condominium or apartment complexes to have a "no children" rule. However, "senior citizen" developments may require at least one member of each household to be at least 62 or older, and may exclude those younger than 45. Remember that this state law must be interpreted in conjunction with the federal rules concerning housing for older persons, discussed above. The state law may be applied to give more protection against age discrimination than federal law, but it may not be applied to give less protection.

Fair Employment and Housing Act

This act generally prohibits all housing discrimination in California based on race, color, religion, sex, marital status, national origin, disability, or ancestry.

It is unlawful for any owner, lessor, assignee, managing agent, real estate broker or salesperson, or any business establishment to discriminate in selling or leasing any housing accommodation. The law specifically prohibits a seller or lessor from asking about the race, color, religion, sex, marital status, national origin, disability, or ancestry of any prospective buyer or tenant.

The act also prohibits discrimination in the financing of housing. Under the act, it is unlawful for any person, bank, mortgage company, or other financial institution to discriminate against any person because of his or her race, color, religion, sex, marital status, national origin, disability, or ancestry.

Housing discrimination complaints are submitted to the Department of Fair Employment and Housing. The complaints are investigated by the Department's staff. If the Department determines a violation has occurred, it first tries to persuade the violator to correct the violation and then, if persuasion fails, it may file a court action.

The act doesn't apply to the rental of a portion of a single-family owner-occupied home to one boarder, or to accommodations operated by nonprofit religious, fraternal, or charitable organizations.

Fig.15.2 Antidiscrimination legislation

Legislation	Prohibits Discrimination
Civil Rights Act of 1866	Based on race or ancestry, in any property transaction
Civil Rights Act of 1964	In limited federal programs
Federal Fair Housing Act	In the sale, lease, or financing of housing
Americans with Disabilities Act	In public accommodations
Unruh Civil Rights Act	By any business entity
Fair Employment and Housing Act	By owners, lessors, agents, lenders in residential transactions
Housing Financial Discrimination Act	By lenders in residential transactions

Housing Financial Discrimination Act

This law requires a lender to make lending decisions based on the merits of the borrower and the security property, rather than on the fact that the property is in a particular neighborhood. A lender cannot refuse to lend money simply because the borrower wishes to purchase a home in an Asian or Hispanic neighborhood, for example.

The California Housing Financial Discrimination Act (which is sometimes called the **Holden Act**) states that it is against California's public policy to deny mortgage loans or to impose stricter terms on loans because of neighborhood characteristics unrelated to the creditworthiness of the borrower or the value of the real property. Under this act, financial institutions may not:

- discriminate in the provision of financial assistance to purchase, construct, rehabilitate, improve, or refinance housing on the basis of the characteristics of the neighborhood surrounding the property, unless the lender can demonstrate that such consideration is necessary to avoid an unsound business practice;
- discriminate in the provision of financial assistance for housing on the basis of race, color, religion, sex, marital status, national origin, or ancestry; or
- consider the racial, ethnic, religious, or national origin composition of the neighborhood surrounding the property.

Real Estate License Law and Regulations

Both the real estate license law and the Commissioner's Rules and Regulations prohibit discriminatory behavior by licensees. Licensees who engage in discriminatory behavior are subject to disciplinary action, and may have their licenses suspended or revoked. (See Chapter 18.)

Brokers have the duty to supervise their affiliated licensees and take reasonable steps to make sure they are familiar with the requirements of both federal and state laws prohibiting discrimination.

Chapter Summary

1. Discrimination in real estate transactions is prohibited by the Civil Rights Act of 1866, the Federal Fair Housing Act, and California antidiscrimination statutes.

2. The Civil Rights Act of 1866 prohibits all discrimination based on race or ancestry in the sale and rental of property. The Civil Rights Act of 1964 prohibited discrimination in programs and services for which the federal government provided financial assistance.

3. The Federal Fair Housing Act goes farther than the Civil Rights Acts of 1866 and 1964 by prohibiting discrimination based on race, color, religion, sex, national origin, handicap, or familial status. However, it applies only to transactions involving residential property.

4. Three specifically prohibited acts under the Federal Fair Housing Act are blockbusting, steering, and redlining. Blockbusting is attempting to obtain listings or arrange sales by predicting the entry of minorities into the neighborhood and implying that this will cause a decline in the neighborhood. Steering is the channeling of buyers or renters to specific neighborhoods based on race or other protected characteristics. Redlining is the refusal to make loans on properties located in particular areas for discriminatory reasons.

5. Federal laws and regulations that prohibit discrimination in credit transactions include the Federal Fair Housing Act, the Equal Credit Opportunity Act, and the Home Mortgage Disclosure Act.

6. The Americans with Disabilities Act guarantees equal access to facilities regardless of physical or mental disability.

7. California state law prohibits discrimination not just in housing, but also in employment, credit transactions, and other types of business activities. There are only limited exemptions.

O—⚷ Key Terms

Blockbusting—Attempting to induce homeowners to list or sell their homes by predicting that members of another race or ethnic group, or people suffering from some disability, will be moving into the neighborhood.

Steering—Channeling prospective buyers or tenants toward or away from particular neighborhoods based on their race, religion, or national origin, in order to maintain or change the character of the neighborhoods.

Redlining—Refusing to make a loan because of the racial or ethnic composition of the neighborhood in which the security property is located.

Familial status—A category including persons who have children (under 18 years old) living with them. It also includes someone who is pregnant or is in the process of securing custody of a child.

Disability—A physical disability or mental impairment that substantially limits one or more major life activities.

Quiz: Chapter 15
Civil Rights and Fair Housing

1. When a real estate agent channels prospective buyers away from a particular neighborhood because of their race, it is called:

   a) blockbusting
   b) steering
   c) redlining
   d) clipping

2. Rental of a room in an owner-occupied dwelling is exempt from the Federal Fair Housing Act if the dwelling contains:

   a) two or more units
   b) three units or less
   c) fewer than five units
   d) six units or more

3. Yolanda Murray, a real estate broker, is helping the Jacksons sell their single-family home. Can this transaction be exempt from the Federal Fair Housing Act?

   a) Yes, as long as the Jacksons own no more than three single-family homes
   b) Yes, as long as no discriminatory advertising is used
   c) No, because a real estate agent is involved
   d) No, the act applies to all residential sales transactions, without exception

4. The Gardenia Village condominium has a "no kids" rule. This is not a violation of the Federal Fair Housing Act:

   a) if the condo qualifies as "housing for older persons" under the terms of the law
   b) if no discriminatory advertising is used
   c) because age discrimination is not prohibited by the law
   d) because condominiums aren't covered by the law

5. Title VIII of the Civil Rights Act of 1968 precludes:

   a) discrimination in housing
   b) discrimination in lending
   c) Both a) and b)
   d) Neither a) nor b)

6. Blockbusting is an acceptable practice:

   a) only under the supervision of real estate licensees
   b) only when approved by either HUD or the Justice Department
   c) under no circumstances
   d) only if the seller and buyer mutually agree

7. A deed restriction created in 1920 that prohibits the sale of property to a non-Caucasian person until after 2005 is:

   a) valid until all the property owners agree to eliminate the restriction
   b) enforceable
   c) unenforceable
   d) covered by title insurance

8. The Home Mortgage Disclosure Act helps to enforce the prohibition against:

   a) redlining
   b) steering
   c) blockbusting
   d) None of the above

9. A landlord who is subject to the provisions of the Federal Fair Housing Act must:

   a) permit a handicapped tenant to make reasonable modifications to the property at the tenant's expense
   b) make reasonable exceptions to the landlord's rules to accommodate handicapped tenants; for example, by allowing a guide dog when pets are not normally allowed
   c) Both a) and b)
   d) Neither a) nor b)

10. Where property is subject to deed restrictions prohibiting it from being conveyed to a black person, a deed naming a black person as grantee of said property would be:

    a) void
    b) valid
    c) the restriction would prevail and the property could not be conveyed
    d) the restriction is unenforceable and the deed is consequently void

11. The Unruh Civil Rights Act prohibits discriminatory activities by:

    a) lenders only
    b) real estate agents only
    c) all real estate–related businesses
    d) any business entity

12. Under California law, it would be permissible for a landlord to refuse to rent to a prospective tenant because the tenant:

    a) has a child
    b) is blind
    c) cannot afford the rent
    d) All of the above

13. A developer who intended to rent housing in a particular development only to persons 45 years of age or over would be in violation of the:

    a) Civil Rights Act of 1866
    b) Civil Rights Act of 1964
    c) Federal Fair Housing Act
    d) Americans with Disabilities Act

14. Under the Americans with Disabilities Act:

    a) real estate firms are exempt
    b) real estate firms must not discriminate against the disabled when taking listings
    c) real estate firms must be accessible to the disabled
    d) only individual real estate agents are prohibited from discriminating against the disabled

15. The California Housing Financial Discrimination Act prohibits:

    a) redlining
    b) steering
    c) blockbusting
    d) panic selling

Answer Key

1.b) Channeling prospective buyers or tenants away from (or toward) certain neighborhoods based on their race, religion, or national origin is called steering. It is a violation of the Federal Fair Housing Act and California's Fair Employment and Housing Act.

2.c) The Fair Housing Act exemption for rentals applies to owner-occupied dwellings with up to four units.

3.c) No residential transaction in which a real estate agent is employed is exempt from the Federal Fair Housing Act.

4.a) The Federal Fair Housing Act does not allow apartment houses and condominiums to discriminate on the basis of familial status unless the complex qualifies as "housing for older persons."

5.c) Title VIII of the 1968 Civil Rights Act is the Federal Fair Housing Act. It prohibits discriminatory practices when selling, renting, advertising, or financing housing.

6.c) Blockbusting is a discriminatory practice prohibited by the Federal Fair Housing Act.

7.c) A deed containing such a provision is valid, but the restriction is unenforceable.

8.a) The Home Mortgage Disclosure Act helps to enforce the prohibition against redlining by requiring large institutional lenders to file an annual report of all mortgage loans made during that year. Loans are categorized according to location, alerting investigators to areas of possible redlining.

9.c) The Fair Housing Act requires a residential landlord to allow a handicapped tenant to make reasonable modifications. It also requires a residential landlord to make reasonable exceptions to the rules to accommodate handicapped tenants. However, at the end of the lease, the landlord can require a tenant who has made modifications to restore the premises to their original condition.

10.b) The deed would be valid and title would be conveyed. The restriction in the deed relating to discrimination would be unenforceable.

11.d) The Unruh Civil Rights Act prohibits discriminatory activities by business entities.

12.c) It is permissible for a landlord to reject an applicant because he or she cannot afford the rent.

13.c) This would violate the Federal Fair Housing Act. Senior housing is legal, but 45 is not the cutoff age.

14.c) Under the provisions of the ADA, real estate firms must take reasonable actions necessary to make their accommodations accessible to the disabled.

15.a) This California law (also known as the Holden Act) prohibits redlining.

Chapter 16

Residential Real Estate

 Outline

I. Construction
   A. Building codes and regulations
   B. The architect
   C. Architectural styles
   D. Plans and specifications
   E. Wood frame construction
   F. Glossary of construction terms
II. To Rent or to Buy?
   A. Advantages of renting
   B. Advantages of buying
   C. Buying versus renting
III. Factors to Consider When Choosing a Home
IV. Investing in Real Estate
   A. Advantages and disadvantages
   B. Choices when investing in real estate

 Chapter Overview

In bringing a buyer and seller together, the real estate agent must be a "jack of all trades." Not only must he or she be familiar with property values, contracts, and financing, the agent must also be familiar with the rudiments of residential construction, the advantages of buying a home, the elements to look for in a home, and the benefits of investing in real estate. This chapter briefly describes some aspects of residential construction, focusing on wood frame construction. Then the chapter goes on to discuss the relative merits of renting or buying a home, and the factors to consider when choosing a home— either as a residence or as an investment.

Construction

A real estate agent is not a home inspector or an architect, nor should he or she give that impression to clients and customers. However, California law does impose a duty on all licensees to visually inspect the homes they sell. Furthermore, most homebuyers rely on their real estate agents for some advice on the structural quality of a particular home. Thus, agents must be able to evaluate the basic soundness of a home's construction. This preliminary evaluation should be supplemented, whenever necessary, with the opinions of professional inspectors, especially with respect to structural integrity and the safety and suitability of the plumbing and electrical components of the building.

In order to evaluate the basic soundness of a home, real estate agents should be familiar with the following aspects of residential construction:

- local building codes and regulations,
- architectural styles,
- plans and specifications, and
- construction methods and terminology.

Building Codes and Regulations

Local building codes prescribe the types of materials that must be used in residential construction, the acceptable methods of construction, and the number and placement of such items as electrical outlets, plumbing fixtures, and windows. The size and placement of a building on its lot are also governed by building codes and other local regulations.

These codes and regulations promote some degree of uniformity in construction. The construction guidelines assure a homebuyer that the home's quality meets at least minimum requirements. This is especially important in regard to safety issues. For example, a home's ability to resist fire or earthquake damage is of vital importance to both the homeowner and the surrounding community. (See Chapter 4 for a discussion of the local government's authority to enact and enforce building codes.)

Key sources of information regarding local regulations are local planning and building departments, architects, and construction contractors.

The Architect

The architect is the construction industry professional the real estate agent is most likely to meet. Most people think of an architect as a person who designs buildings, but a good architect will also provide a range of other services throughout the construction process.

Under a standard contract, an architect will first work with the owner to develop a design that fulfills the owner's needs. Next, the architect will prepare more detailed drawings, describing all the components of the building, along with an estimate of the probable cost of construction. When the design has been approved by the owner, the architect will draw up the official plans and specifications and will help the owner get bids from contractors and permits from government agencies.

Finally, the architect acts as the owner's representative throughout the actual construction phase, visiting the site to inspect the work, approving periodic payments to the contractor, and interpreting the plans and specifications.

Architectural Styles

Homes come in a variety of architectural styles. The quality of a home's construction is not determined by its style (although the style may affect the cost of constructing the home). No one style is inherently more desirable than another. The value of each particular style depends on the personal preference of the homebuyer.

Several common architectural styles are illustrated in Figure 16.1. Of course, many homes have their own unique style, or are combinations of two or more styles. Split-level, Spanish, California ranch, and modern (sometimes called contemporary) are popular architectural styles in California.

Fig.16.1 Architectural styles

Split-level homes have visually attractive designs and make effective use of hilly terrains. Spanish-style homes are one- or two-story homes with white or pastel stucco exteriors and red tile roofs. Spanish-style homes look cool and comfortable in southern California's heat. Modern-style homes usually incorporate large windows and glass doors, and are designed with an open interior. Because of the flexibility of modern home designs, they are well suited for building on hillsides or other difficult sites. California ranch type homes are one-story homes with low-pitched or flat roofs. The exterior may be wood, masonry, or stucco.

A one-story ranch home is the simplest to construct and maintain. However, it requires more land in relation to living space than a two-story or split-level home. Thus, a one-story home may be uneconomical where land is at a premium. Split-level construction is more expensive, but it is popular because it effectively utilizes land with varying topography. Two-story construction is the most economical per square foot of living space, since twice as much living space is provided with one foundation, one roof, and the same amount of land. The inconvenience of stairs and exterior maintenance on the upper story are the primary drawbacks of two-story homes.

Plans and Specifications

Plans and specifications are the drawings and accompanying text that explain in detail how a building is constructed. Plans are drawings of the vertical and horizontal cross-sections of the building. They show the placement of foundations, floors, walls, roofs, doors, windows, fixtures, and wiring. Specifications are the text that accompanies the plans. This text prescribes the type of materials to be used and the required quality of workmanship. Plans and specifications are usually prepared by an architect, in the form of blueprints.

Wood Frame Construction

The most common type of home construction is the wood frame building. It is popular because of its low cost, ease and speed of construction, and flexibility of design. One-story, two-story, and split-level homes can all be wood frame homes.

The construction of a wood frame building is illustrated in the following diagrams, and a glossary of construction terms is provided for use in conjunction with these diagrams.

Elements of Wood Frame Construction. It is easier to judge the quality of a home with some knowledge of the basic elements of construction. The materials required for each element are usually specified by local building codes. Because wood frame buildings are so common, this is the type of construction we will focus on here. The following are some basic elements of residential wood frame construction.

Foundation. Virtually all modern building foundations are made with reinforced concrete. Concrete has the advantages of low cost, plasticity, and high compressive strength. When concrete is reinforced by steel bars or mesh, it also has good tensile strength (resistance to bending or cracking).

Framing. The framing is usually constructed of wooden boards and dimensional lumber, although the use of metal framing is becoming more common in some areas. The size and length of framing members varies, depending upon their particular application as girders, joists, studs, rafters, etc. Lumber is classified as either "green" or "dry," depending on its moisture content. Dry lumber is considered superior to green lumber for framing because it is less prone to warpage—the deformity in shape caused by uneven shrinking.

Exterior Sheathing and Siding. Exterior sheathing is the covering applied to the outside of the frame. The most common form of exterior sheathing is plywood panels that are four feet wide by eight

Fig.16.2 Construction details

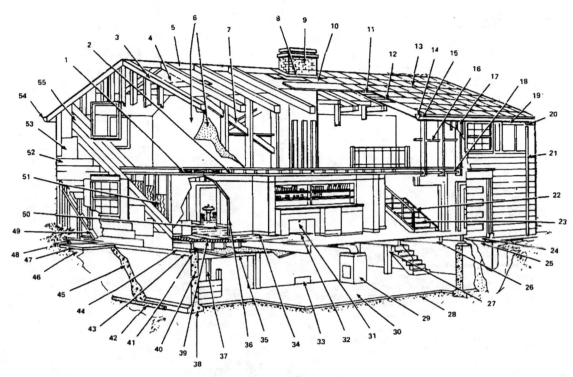

CONSTRUCTION DETAILS

1. CROSS BRIDGING
2. SECOND FLOOR JOISTS
3. ROOF RAFTERS
4. COLLAR BEAM
5. RIDGE BOARD
6. PLASTER BASE,LATH AND PLASTER WALLS
7. CROSS BRACING
8. FLASHING AND COUNTER FLASHING
9. BRICK CHIMNEY
10. TIGHT ROOF SHEATHING (ALL OTHER COVERINGS)
11. SPACED 1" x 4" SHEATHING (WOOD SHINGLES)
12. ROOFING FELT
13. FINISH ROOFING (SHINGLE)
14. SOFFIT OR CORNICE
15. FACIA OF CORNICE
16. FIRE STOPS
17. VERTICAL BOARD AND BATTEN SIDING

18. RIBBON PLATE
19. FACIA BOARD
20. LEADER HEAD OR CONDUCTOR HEAD
21. LEADER, DOWNSPOUT OR CONDUCTOR
22. STAIR STRINGER
23. MAIN STAIR TREADS AND RISERS
24. ENTRANCE DOOR SILL
25. CONCRETE STOOP
26. FIRST FLOOR JOISTS
27. BASEMENT POST
28. CINDERFILL
29. BOILER OR FURNACE
30. BASEMENT CONCRETE FLOOR
31. DAMPER CONTROL
32. ASH DUMP
33. CLEANOUT DOOR
34. BASEBOARDS
35. GIRDER

36. FRAME PARTITION
37. POST
38. FOOTING
39. SUB-FLOORING, DIAGONAL
40. FOUNDATION WALL
41. PLATE ANCHOR BOLT
42. DRAIN TILE
43. TERMITE SHIELD
44. SILL PLATE
45. GRAVEL FILL
46. GRADE LINE
47. BASEMENT AREAWAY
48. SOLE PLATE
49. CORNER BRACING
50. FINISH FLOOR
51. INSULATION, BATTS
52. WALL SIDING
53. WALL BUILDING PAPER
54. GUTTER
55. WALL SHEATHING, DIAGONAL

Fig.16.3 Methods of roof framing

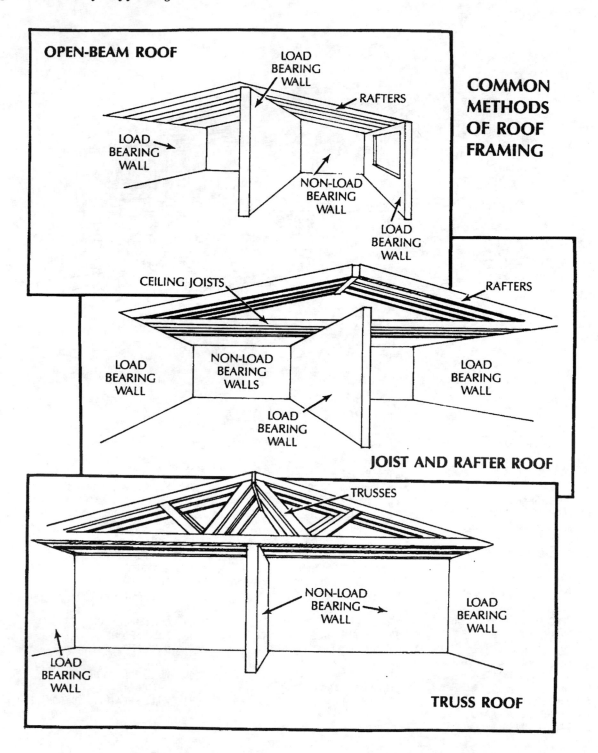

Fig.16.4 Roof styles

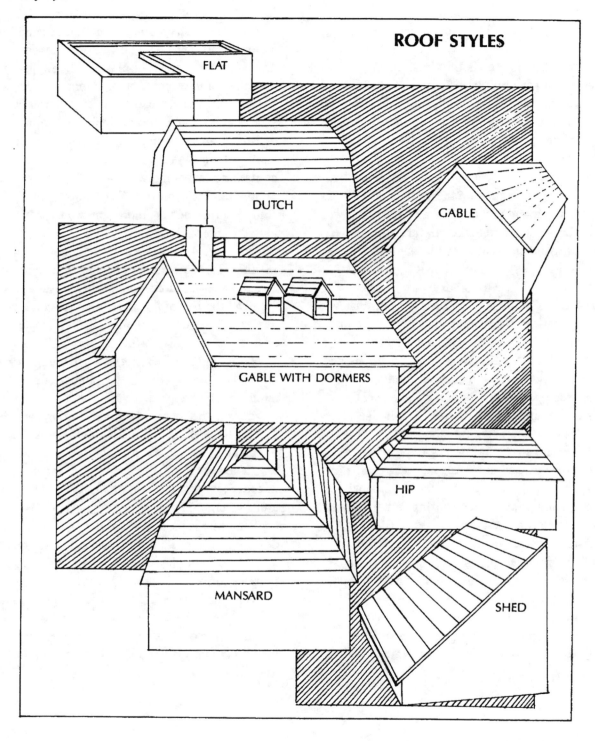

feet long. Plywood serves an additional function by adding shear strength to the walls. Shear strength is the capacity of a wall to resist a sideways racking force, and it is normally provided by corner bracing in the frame.

Exterior siding is the visible finish layer applied to the outside of the building. It may be plywood, boards, aluminum siding, shingles, or other materials. The two most important characteristics of siding are its resistance to weathering and its aesthetic appeal.

Interior Sheathing. This is the covering applied to the inside of the frame, on the walls and ceilings. In the past, the most common form of sheathing was lath and plaster, a cement-like mixture applied over a matrix of wood strips attached to the frame. Modern buildings use drywall construction for interior sheathing. The term "drywall" is used because there is no need to add water to the material before application. Drywall products usually come in large sheets (like plywood) and are fastened to the frame with glue, nails, or screws. Sheetrock and wallboard are two common drywall products. The joints between panels are hidden by covering them with a strip of tape imbedded in a plaster-like filler. This process is called "taping" the joints.

Roofing. The structural part of the roof is composed of plywood or boards laid perpendicular to the rafters. This sheathing is then covered with a tar-impregnated paper called roofing felt. The final layer of roofing may be wood shingles, tiles, or composition roofing (tar-like shingles or rolls of material). Sometimes hot tar is simply interspersed with more layers of felt; this is called a "built-up" roof.

Floor Covering. The strength of the floor is provided by tongue-and-groove floor boards or plywood attached to the floor joists, which is called the subflooring. The subflooring is then covered with finished flooring, which may be carpet, tile, linoleum, hardwood strips, or other material.

Plumbing. The plumbing includes drain pipes, supply pipes, and fixtures. The drain pipes are made of cast iron, concrete, or plastic. The supply pipes are made of galvanized steel, copper, or plastic. Plumbing fixtures are either cast iron or pressed steel that is coated with enamel or fiberglass.

Electrical. Most modern wiring is in the form of cable, which is an insulated cord-like material containing two or more strands of copper or aluminum wire. The cable runs in circuits from a supply source (a fuse box or, more commonly, a breaker panel) to the various outlets for plugs or light fixtures. Breaker panels are a series of circuit breakers that automatically shut off the current in a circuit under overload conditions. Most outlets supply 110 volts of power, except for certain outlets designed for major appliances (ranges, water heaters, dryers, etc.), which supply 220 volts.

Heating, Ventilating, and Air Conditioning (HVAC). These systems are composed of heating and/or cooling appliances that serve warm, cool, or fresh air to the rooms of a house through a series of galvanized sheet metal tubes called ducts. The ducts open at various places in the building called registers. The registers may be closed off independently in order to direct the heat or air conditioning to areas where it is needed.

Insulation is used to make HVAC systems less costly to run. Insulation is material that is resistant to the transfer of heat, and comes in batts, rolls, or in loose form. It is inserted between wall studs and between the joists of floors and ceilings. Insulation also comes in the form of sheets that are secured to the sheathing of the structure. The effectiveness of insulating materials is gauged by an "R-value." The

Glossary of Construction Terms

Anchor bolts—bolts embedded in concrete, used to hold structural members in place.

Areaway—an open space around a basement window or doorway that provides light, ventilation, and access.

Beam—a principal structural member used between posts, columns, or walls.

Bearing wall or partition—a wall or partition that supports a vertical load in addition to its own weight.

Board—lumber that is less than two inches thick.

Bridging—pieces fitted in pairs from the bottom of one floor joist to the top of adjacent joists, and crossed to distribute the floor load.

BTU—British Thermal Unit; a measure of heating capacity.

Built-up roof—a roof composed of several layers of rag felt, saturated with pitch or asphalt.

Cased opening—an interior opening without a door that is finished with jambs and trim.

Caulk—to seal cracks and joints to make them waterproof.

Collar beam—a beam connecting rafters at a point considerably above the wall plate.

Column—an upright supporting member, circular or rectangular in shape.

Conduit—a pipe or tube, usually metal, in which wiring is installed.

Corner braces—diagonal braces set into studs to reinforce corners of frame structures.

Counterflashing—flashing used on chimneys at the roof line to cover shingle flashing and prevent the entry of moisture.

Crawl space—a space between the ground and the first floor that is used for access.

Dimensional lumber—lumber that is two to five inches thick and up to twelve inches wide.

Dormer—a projecting structure built out from a sloping roof.

Drywall—materials used for wall covering that do not need to be mixed with water before application (e.g., sheetrock).

Eaves—the margin or lower part of a roof that projects over an exterior wall.

Fascia—a wooden member nailed to the ends of projecting rafters.

Fire stop—a block or stop used in a wall between studs to prevent the spread of fire and smoke.

Flashing—sheet metal or other material used in roof and wall construction to prevent rain or other water from entering.

Flue—the space in a chimney through which smoke, gas, or fumes rise.

Footing—the spreading course at the base of a foundation wall, pier, or column.

Framing—the timber structure of a building that gives it shape and strength; it includes the wall, floors, ceilings, and roof.

Gable—that portion of a wall contained between the slopes of a roof.

Glazing—the process of installing glass into sashes and doors.

Gutter—a wooden or metal trough attached to the edge of a roof to collect and conduct water from rain and melting snow.

Header—a horizontal structural member that supports the load over an opening, such as a window or door.

Hip roof—a roof that rises from all four sides of the building.

Interior trim—a general term for all the molding, casing, baseboards, and other trim items applied inside the building.

Insulation—any material high in resistance to heat transmission that is used to reduce the rate of heat flow.

Jamb—the top and two sides of a door or window frame that contact the door or sash.

Joist—one of a series of parallel framing members used to support floor and ceiling loads.

Lath—material fastened to the frame of a building to act as a base for plaster.

Molding—a narrow strip of wood used to conceal surface or angle joints, or as an ornamentation.

Partition—an interior wall that subdivides space within a building.

Pier—a column of masonry used to support other structural members.

Pilaster—a part of a wall that projects not more than one-half of its own width beyond the outside or inside face of a wall.

Pitch—inclination or slope.

Plan—a drawing representing any one of the cross-sections of a building.

Plaster—a mixture of lime, cement, and sand used to cover inside or outside wall surfaces.

Plate—the horizontal member of a wall frame to which the studs are attached.

Rafter—one of a series of structural members of a roof.

Reinforced concrete—concrete poured around steel bars or steel meshwork, in such a manner that the two materials act together to resist force.

Riser—the vertical stair member between two consecutive stair treads.

R-value—a measure of resistance to heat transfer.

Sheathing—structural covering; boards or prefabricated panels that are attached to the exterior studding or rafters.

Siding—the finish covering of the outside walls of a frame building.

Sill—the lowest member of the frame of a structure, usually horizontal, resting on the foundation. Also, the lower member of a window or exterior door frame.

Specifications—a written document stipulating the quality of materials and workmanship required for a job.

Stud—one of a series of vertical wood or metal structural members in walls and partitions. In most modern frame buildings, the studs are set 16 inches apart.

Subfloor—boards or panels laid directly on floor joists, over which a finished floor will be laid.

Timber—a piece of lumber five inches or larger in its least dimension.

Trim—the finish materials in a building (moldings, etc.).

Trimmer—the stud into which a header is framed; it adds strength to the side of the opening.

Truss—a structural unit, usually triangular in shape, which provides rigid support over wide spans.

Weephole—a small hole in the foundation wall to drain water to the outside.

higher the R-value, the more resistant the material is to the transfer of heat, and the better it is for insulation purposes. Local building codes require insulation with a minimum R-value to be used in all new construction.

Termite Problems. One major problem with wood frame buildings is their susceptibility to damage by wood-eating insects, especially termites. Several techniques are used to minimize the possibility of termite damage:

- the ground under and around the building may be treated with a chemical that keeps termites away from the foundation;
- lumber that is in contact with the soil or the foundation, such as sills or beams, may be treated with a chemical to prevent termites from gaining access to the frame of the building; and
- metal shields may be inserted between the foundation and the superstructure to physically prevent termites from reaching the wood.

It is always a good idea to have a licensed termite inspector examine a home before the sale closes (lenders often require such a report). The termite inspector will provide a complete report on the structural soundness of the building, listing any defects caused by moisture and fungus or by insects. Real estate agents should make sure the buyer gets a copy of any termite or other structural pest report.

To Rent or to Buy?

Real estate agents are often asked to discuss the relative advantages and disadvantages of renting versus buying a place to live. Some considerations are primarily emotional, such as security, pride of ownership, and the freedom to have pets or to remodel according to personal preference. These types of considerations cannot be evaluated objectively by a third party—their importance can be measured only by the prospective homebuyer.

However, other elements of comparison are largely financial, and a real estate agent can help a prospective homebuyer evaluate these elements objectively.

Advantages of Renting

The advantages of renting over buying can be briefly summarized:

- renting requires less financial commitment and risk;
- renting gives the tenant greater mobility; and
- renting carries with it fewer responsibilities.

Financial Commitment. Compared to the funds necessary to buy a home, the initial cash outlay to rent a home or apartment is quite modest. In most cases, a security deposit and one or two months of prepaid rent is sufficient. Even in conjunction with low-downpayment financing, the cash required to purchase a home (including the downpayment, loan fees, and closing costs) normally far exceeds the cost of moving into an apartment or rental home. Furthermore, at least for the first few years, the monthly rental payment is likely to be substantially less than a monthly mortgage payment.

Financial Risk. Renters have little financial investment in their rented premises and the neighborhood in which they live. Therefore, there is little financial risk in renting. If the property values in a neighborhood decline and the neighborhood becomes run down or otherwise undesirable, renters can simply give the required notice—or wait until the lease expires—and move away. A homeowner in the same neighborhood runs the risk of losing some or all of his or her investment in the property.

Mobility. It is faster, easier, and cheaper for a renter to move than for a homeowner to move. A renter only has to give the required notice or wait until the lease expires before he or she can move out. Even if a renter has to leave abruptly, any deposit or prepaid rent that may be forfeited is almost sure to be less than the cost of selling one home and buying another. Selling a home is a lengthy and expensive process, taking at least a few months and costing up to 10% of the home's value.

Maintenance and Repairs. An owner is responsible for maintaining the property and making any needed repairs. For a renter, the cost of maintenance and repair is simply included in the rent. The renter usually has no direct responsibility for doing maintenance work and making repairs. Also, a renter does not face the burden of sudden large expenditures for unexpected repairs.

Amenities. In many cases, renters enjoy the use of recreational facilities, such as swimming pools and tennis courts, that are beyond the financial reach of most homeowners.

Advantages of Buying

For many people, buying instead of renting affords both the subjective advantages of security and personal satisfaction, and the financial advantages of equity appreciation and tax deductions.

Security. A homeowner enjoys a certain amount of security in knowing that he or she can continue to live in the home as long as the mortgage payments are made. A renter has no real security beyond the term of the lease. When the lease expires, or when the landlord gives the required notice, a renter will have to find another place to live.

Privacy and Freedom from Restrictions. In most cases, a homeowner enjoys greater privacy than a renter, and has greater freedom to use the property. An owner can redecorate or remodel a home to suit his or her own taste, and can keep pets or engage in other activities prohibited by many rental agreements.

Monthly Payments. A homeowner's monthly mortgage payment usually starts out higher than the rental payment for equivalent lodging. However, over time, rents usually rise at a faster rate than mortgage payments. This is especially true if the mortgage interest rate is fixed. In that case, payments usually increase slowly as the property tax and insurance portions of the mortgage payments increase. If the mortgage loan has an adjustable interest rate, payments may increase rapidly if interest rates rise, but they will decrease if interest rates go down. Thus, it is quite possible for a monthly rental payment to eventually exceed a monthly mortgage payment.

Investment Appreciation. Although it is impossible to predict whether or how much a particular home will appreciate in value, over the last several decades average home values have increased at a rate that is higher than the average inflation rate. Typically, a homeowner enjoys an increase in home equity—and thus an increase in net worth—as his or her home appreciates in value. For a renter, the appreciation of property values is likely to mean only a rent increase.

Tax Advantages. For the homeowner, federal income tax laws allow tax deductions for property taxes and the interest paid on a home loan. The interest on a personal residence loan is the only type of consumer interest that is still eligible for federal income tax deduction following the 1986 Tax Reform Act. Also, at least part of the gain realized on the sale of a principal residence by taxpayers over 55 years of age is never taxed at all. An equivalent tax benefit is simply not available to those who rent their principal residence. (See Chapter 14 for a more complete discussion of income taxes.)

Comparison of Renting and Buying

Many real estate agents use worksheets to compare the net costs of renting and buying. Worksheet forms take into account not only the monthly mortgage or rental payments, but also the homeowner's increases in equity and the benefit of income tax deductions. These worksheets demonstrate to prospective buyers that the overall cost of buying a home may well be less than the cost of renting.

A simplified example of such a worksheet form is shown in Figure 16.5, on the following page. This worksheet has been filled in with data for a proposed purchase of a $100,000 home, with the buyer making a 10% downpayment and obtaining a $90,000 loan at a fixed annual interest rate of 8%. (These figures were chosen to keep the example simple; the $100,000 price is too low to be realistic in many California communities.) Closing costs bring the total cash requirement for the purchase up to $13,000. Taxes, homeowners' insurance, the annual appreciation rate for local property values, and the buyers' income tax bracket have all been estimated. The total estimated monthly payment, including principal and interest, property taxes, homeowners' insurance, and the monthly renewal premium for private mortgage insurance (estimated at .35% of the outstanding loan balance per year) is approximately $819.

The monthly cost of buying the home on these terms is compared with the cost of renting comparable housing at a monthly rent of $700. At first glance, a comparison of the monthly mortgage payment of $819 to the monthly rental payment of $700 would seem to give the advantage to renting, especially considering the substantial amount of cash required for the purchase. However, an analysis of all the economic benefits of homeownership results in a lower net cost for the home purchase, even when taking into account the interest lost on the money spent for the downpayment and closing costs.

To begin with, part of the monthly payment goes to amortize the loan. These payments to principal are typically recovered when the home is sold. For a $90,000 loan with a 30-year term, the average monthly amortization would be $250 ($90,000 ÷ 360 months = $250). Of course, in the early years a much smaller portion of each payment would go to principal, and in the later years a larger portion of the monthly payment would go to principal.

Next, some portions of the payment, the interest and the property taxes, are tax deductible. In this case, the average monthly interest is $410 (again, in the early years a larger portion would go to interest, and in the later years a smaller portion would go to interest), and the monthly property tax payment is $100, for a total of $510 in tax-deductible items. If the buyer is in the 28% income tax bracket, that would represent a tax savings of about $143 per month ($510 × .28 = $142.80).

Finally, the home is likely to appreciate in value and give the purchaser a return on his or her investment as well as a place to live. Even at the modest rate of appreciation used in this example, 3% per year, the appreciation return is substantial. On $100,000, it would be $3,000 per year, or about $250 per month.

After taking into account all the economic benefits of purchasing, the net effective cost of buying is only $176 per month.

The monthly rental is $700, with no federal income tax deductions and no benefits to the renter if the property appreciates in value. The renter would be able to obtain some interest or other investment yield on the $13,000 not used for a downpayment and closing costs. In this example, a yield of 4% is used, giving the renter a monthly benefit of $43 and a net effective cost of renting of $657 per month.

Fig.16.5 Comparison of renting and buying

Comparison of Estimated Net Cost of Renting and Buying

Buying

Purchase price	$100,000
Cash required (downpayment and closing costs)	$13,000
Loan amount	$90,000
Loan term	30 yrs
Interest rate	8%
Property taxes (estimated)	$1,200
Homeowner's insurance premium (estimated)	$400
Property appreciation rate (estimated)	3%
Income tax bracket (estimated)	28%

Out of pocket costs:
Monthly payment

principal and interest		$660
property taxes		100
homeowner's insurance		33
other monthly expenses (PMI)		+ 26
Total monthly payment		$819

less:

Average monthly principal amortization		− 250
Tax benefits		
interest portion of payment	$410	
property tax portion of payment	100	
other	+ 0	
total deductible items	$510	
Monthly value of tax deduction		− 143
Effective monthly cost of ownership		$426

less:

Average monthly appreciation	− 250
Monthly Net Cost of Buying	**$176**

Renting

Out-of-pocket costs:

Monthly rent	$700

less:

Interest from savings not used for purchase ($13,000 @ 4%)	− 43
Monthly Net Cost of Renting	**$657**

It should be emphasized that this example is based on estimates and assumptions that are subject to change. A change in interest rates, property tax rates, or the tax law would significantly alter the income tax benefits of buying. Also, the average monthly principal and interest portions would be different for a buyer who intended to own the home for less than the full 30-year amortization term. Perhaps most importantly, a change in the rate of appreciation would have a great impact on the final net cost of homeownership. However, worksheets of this type serve a useful purpose in displaying the benefits of homeownership that can offset what first appears to be the higher cost of buying a home.

Factors to Consider When Choosing a Home

When a real estate agent shows a home to a buyer, both the buyer and the seller often rely on the agent to point out the positive features of that home. So it is important that real estate agents understand what considerations are important to most homeowners. Note that many of these features are examined by appraisers during the appraisal process. These features have an impact on both the property's subjective attractiveness to a homebuyer and the property's objective value as estimated by an appraiser. (Appraisal is discussed in Chapter 12.)

Neighborhood Considerations

Since the surrounding neighborhood greatly influences the overall desirability of a home and also has a great impact on value, careful consideration should be given to neighborhood characteristics.

Percentage of Homeownership. Are most of the homes owner-occupied, or is there a large percentage of rental properties? Neighborhoods that are predominantly owner-occupied are generally better

maintained, less susceptible to loss in value, and more likely to appreciate in value.

Conformity. Values are protected if there is a reasonable degree of homogeneity in the neighborhood. This includes homogeneity of styles, ages, prices, sizes, and quality of structures. Strictly enforced zoning ordinances and land use restrictions promote conformity.

Changing Land Use. Does the neighborhood land use appear stable, or are there indications of a transition from residential to some other type of land use?

Street Pattern. Do the neighborhood streets have good access to traffic arteries? If a property does not front on a publicly dedicated and maintained street, the buyer should ask whether there is an enforceable road maintenance agreement signed by the property owners.

Availability of Utilities. Are the home and neighborhood adequately serviced by water, electricity, gas, sewers, telephones, and other desirable services, such as television cable?

Prestige. Is there a prestige factor that makes the neighborhood more desirable than another?

School District. In what primary and secondary school districts is the neighborhood located? How far away are the schools? Are they within walking distance? The quality of the local schools or school district can make a major difference in value and can be an extremely important basis of decision for many buyers with school-age children.

Public Services. Is the neighborhood adequately served by public transportation, police, and fire protection?

Taxes and Other Government Influences. How do property taxes and special assessments compare with the levels in other neighborhoods? How is the neighborhood and surrounding area zoned? Does the zoning promote residential use and insulate the homeowner from nuisances, such as unpleasant sights, sounds, and odors from industrial use areas?

Social Services. Are there places of worship, hospitals or health care facilities, and other social services nearby?

Overall Neighborhood Values. Does it appear that the overall condition and values in the neighborhood are stable, increasing, or decreasing?

The Home

A home's size, condition, and amenities should be evaluated.

Site/View. What is the size and shape of the lot? Rectangular lots are usually more desirable than odd or irregularly shaped parcels. Is the lot on the corner? Is it level, gently sloping, or steep? Unusually steep lots present a danger of soil instability. Does it appear that water runoff and drainage are good? What is the quality and extent of the landscaping? In a new home, has any landscaping (such as the lawn, shrubbery, and trees) already been done, or will the buyer have to do it all? The cost of new landscaping can be quite a bit more than many homebuyers realize.

Is there a view? In many areas, a view can increase value substantially and add greatly to the property's appeal.

Street and Sidewalks. What is the condition of the driveway, street, and sidewalks? Are there street lights and fire hydrants on the block? Are there telephone and power line poles or is there underground wiring? Are there any easements across the property that might interfere with or diminish the buyer's use and enjoyment of the property?

Sewer/Septic. If the property is served by sanitary and/or storm sewers, have they already been paid for, or is there a special assessment against the property? If the property is served by a septic tank and drain field, when was the last time it was cleaned or inspected? Has the system always functioned properly?

Exterior Appearance. How old is the roof, and when was the house last painted? What is the condition of the roof and flashing, gutters, downspouts, paint, siding, windows, doors, and weather stripping? Thin or curled shingles, cracked, blistered, or peeling paint, and rusted or sagging gutters and downspouts are indications that costly repairs may soon be needed. Does the foundation appear to be in good order, or are there cracks or other evidence of settling? If there is no basement, are the vents and crawlspace adequate?

Overall Interior Layout. Is the floor plan convenient and efficient? Is it necessary to pass through the living room to reach other rooms, or through one of the bedrooms to reach another?

Does the home have bedrooms, closets, and bathrooms in sufficient number and size for the family's needs? Is there a separate dining room, or is the dining area part of the kitchen or living room? Is there a separate family room, children's playroom, or other recreational area needed by the family? Is there sufficient work space in the kitchen and laundry room, and is there storage space for cleaning and gardening tools? What is the condition of the paint or wallpaper?

Are there enough windows and natural light, especially in the kitchen and other work or recreational spaces?

Living Room/Family Room. How large are the living room and the family or recreation room (if any)? Is the shape of each room and the available wall space adequate for the furniture that will be placed in it?

Dining Room or Dining Area. Is the dining area convenient to the kitchen and large enough (in relation to the size of the home, as well as for the number of people who will be eating there)?

Kitchen. Is the kitchen convenient to an outside entrance and to the garage or carport? Is there adequate counter and cabinet space? What is the quality and condition of the kitchen cabinets? What is the type, quality, and condition of the kitchen floor? Are any of the appliances to be included in the sale? If so, are they large enough, of good quality, and in good repair?

Bedrooms. Is the number of bedrooms and their size adequate for the family? The size of the master bedroom is especially important. Are the closets large enough? It is better for the bedrooms to be located apart from the family room, living room, kitchen, and other work or recreational spaces.

Bathrooms. There should be at least two bathrooms if the home has more than two bedrooms. In many areas, particularly in newer homes, it is standard for there to be a private bathroom off the master bedroom. What is the type and condition of the tile or other wall and floor coverings? Are there windows or ceiling fans to provide adequate ventilation?

Design Deficiencies. Here is a brief list of some of the most common design deficiencies that homebuyers should watch out for:

- the front door opens directly into the living room;
- there is no front hall closet;
- the back door is difficult to reach from the kitchen, or from the driveway or garage;
- there is no comfortable area in or near the kitchen where the family can eat;
- the dining room is not easily accessible from the kitchen;
- the stairway is off of a room rather than in a hallway or foyer;

- bedrooms and baths are visible from the living room or foyer;
- the family room (or rec room) is not visible from the kitchen;
- there is no access to the basement from outside the house;
- the bedrooms are not separated by a bathroom or closet wall (for soundproofing); and
- outdoor living areas are not accessible from the kitchen.

Plumbing and Electrical Systems. If it is not a new home, what is the age of the plumbing and electrical systems? Is the plumbing copper, plastic, or some combination of materials? Is the water pressure adequate? Do the electrical service panel and existing outlets indicate there is sufficient electrical service to the home? Do the electrical and plumbing systems, or as much of them as can be seen, appear to be in good condition?

Heating, Ventilating, Air Conditioning. What type of heating system does the home have: electric, gas, or oil; forced air, floor furnaces, baseboard heaters? What is the type and size of the water heater? If there is air conditioning, is it a central system or window units? If it is not a new home, what is the age and apparent condition of the heating, hot water, and air conditioning systems? Is the present owner aware of any problems, inadequacies, or defects?

Garage/Carport. Generally, a garage is better than a carport. What is the size of the garage or carport—single, double, or triple? Is there work or storage space in addition to space for parking? Is there an entrance, protected from the weather, directly from the garage or carport into the home?

Attic/Basement. Is there a basement or attic? If so, what type of access is there from the rest of the home? Is there room for storage or work space? Would it be possible to convert all or part of the basement into additional bedrooms or living area?

Energy-Efficient Features. Escalating energy costs have created an increased demand for energy-efficient homes. Examples of energy-efficient features include clock-controlled thermostats, insulation-wrapped water heaters, insulated ducts and pipes in unheated areas, adequate insulation for floors, walls, and attic, and weather stripping for doors and windows. In some areas, solar water and space heating equipment is popular.

Investing in Real Estate

After buying a home, many people become interested in purchasing real estate as an investment. They realize that while the value of real estate fluctuates, property that is in good condition and that is located in a good neighborhood will usually increase in value in the long run. (A word of caution: real estate agents should not act as investment counselors; they should always refer clients to an accountant, attorney, or investment specialist for investment advice.)

An investment is an asset that is expected to generate a **return** (a profit). A return on an investment can take various forms, including interest, dividends, or appreciation in value. Assets appreciate in value because of inflation, and because of a rising demand for the asset. For example, a parcel of prime vacant land appreciates in value as developable land become increasingly scarce. Investment income (such as interest, dividends, or rent) is often distinguished from earned income (salaries, wages, or self-employment income) for tax purposes.

Investments can be divided into two general categories: ownership investments and debt invest-

ments. With some investments, the investor takes an ownership interest in the asset. Real estate and stocks are examples of ownership investments. The return on these types of investments usually takes the form of dividends or appreciation (or both, in some cases). Debt investments are essentially loans that the investor makes to an entity. For example, a bond is a debt owed by a government entity or corporation. The investor lends the borrower money for a set period of time, and in return the borrower promises to repay the money at a specific date (the maturity date), along with a certain amount of interest.

Investors often choose to diversify their investments—that is, they choose to invest in a variety of different types of investments. The mix of investments owned by an individual or company is referred to as a **portfolio**.

Every investment offers three potential advantages: liquidity, safety, and total return on the investment (sometimes called **yield**). These three characteristics are interrelated. For example, liquidity and safety generally go together. On the other hand, for a high return, an investor often sacrifices safety or liquidity (or both).

Liquidity is the ability to convert an asset into cash quickly. Money in a bank account is extremely liquid: to convert it into cash, the investor need only present the bank with a withdrawal slip or check. Mutual funds, stocks, and bonds are less liquid—they take a little longer (perhaps a week or so) to convert to cash. Other items, such as coin collections, are not considered to be liquid assets at all. The investor may have to wait months to exchange the asset for cash. Real estate, like a coin collection, is not considered a liquid asset.

Liquid investments do not offer very high returns. In general, the more liquid the asset, the lower the return. For example, the money in your wallet is the most liquid asset you can have, but it earns no return (interest) at all. Money in a savings account is a little less liquid—you have to go to the bank in order to withdraw it—but offers a modest return in the form of a low rate of interest. On the other hand, real estate can offer a very high rate of return, but is not at all liquid.

The most liquid investments are generally considered the safest. With liquid assets, there is little risk of losing the asset itself. Money in the bank is both liquid and safe. Since your deposit is insured by the federal government (up to $100,000), there is little chance of losing your investment. Other, less liquid types of investments, such as gold or real estate, are not as safe. For example, if an investor who owns property must sell when real estate values are low, the investor may lose a good portion of his or her original investment in the property.

Investments that are both safe and liquid offer the lowest returns. In a sense, investors "pay" for safety and liquidity with a low return. Savings accounts and certificates of deposit, both safe investments, offer relatively low returns. Mutual funds, gold, or real estate can generate high returns, but at a considerable risk to the investor. For some types of assets, such as real estate, the safety of the investment will increase if the investor can afford to keep the investment for a long period of time. For example, if an investor does not need to cash out his or her investment in real estate for ten or fifteen years, chances are good that the investor will reap a high return. This is true because the investor will have more control over when to sell the asset, and will therefore be able to take full advantage of healthy market conditions.

> **Example:** Jones and Harris both invest $25,000 in rental homes in the same year. One year later, Jones desperately needs some cash and is forced to sell the rental home at a loss. He ends up with only $17,000 of his original $25,000 investment. Harris, on the other hand, keeps her rental home for 12 years. She is in no hurry to sell the

Fig.16.6 Four advantages of investing in real estate

```
Advantages of
Real Estate Investment

• Appreciation
• Leverage
• Cash flow
• Tax benefits
```

property, so she can wait for optimal market conditions. She sells at the peak of a real estate cycle, when property values are high. Because she can afford to choose when she sells the property, she is able to walk away from the transaction with $60,000, a healthy return on her original $25,000 investment.

Advantages and Disadvantages

There are both advantages and disadvantages to investing in real estate.

Advantages. The advantages of investing in real estate can be broken down into four general categories:

- appreciation,
- leverage,
- cash flow, and
- tax benefits.

Appreciation. Although real estate values fluctuate, over a period of several years real estate usually increases in value at a rate equal to or higher than the rate of inflation. Thus, real estate is often an effective hedge against inflation. Furthermore, as buildable property becomes more scarce, properties in prime locations increase in value at a rate higher than the inflation rate.

Appreciation causes a property owner's equity to increase. **Equity** is the difference between the value of the property and the liens against it, so an increase in the property's value will increase the owner's equity in the property. Also, each monthly mortgage payment increases the owner's equity, in proportion to the reduction of the principal amount of the loan. Equity adds to the investor's net worth and can also be used to secure a home equity loan. So even though real estate is not considered a liquid asset, equity in real estate can be used to generate cash funds.

Leverage. Real estate investors can take advantage of leverage. **Leverage** is defined as using borrowed money to invest in an asset. If the asset appreciates, the investor earns money on the money borrowed as well as the money invested.

Example: Martinez purchases a rental home for $115,000. He makes a $30,000 downpayment and borrows the rest of the purchase price. The rent generated by the property covers all the expenses of operating the property, plus the mortgage payment and income taxes. The property appreciates at 3% per year for five years. At the end of the five years, he sells the property for $133,000. He made an $18,000 profit over five years on his $30,000 investment. This averages out to a 9.86% return. The property appreciated at 3% per year, but because he only invested 25% of the purchase price, he was able to generate a 9.86% return on his investment.

Cash Flow. Real estate investments may generate a positive cash flow, as well as appreciate in value. **Cash flow** is defined as spendable income—the amount of money left after all the property's expenses have been paid, including operating costs, mortgage payments, and taxes. When a real estate investment generates a positive cash flow, the investor's monthly income increases. Thus, a real estate investment can increase both the investor's net worth (through appreciation) and his or her income (through positive cash flow).

Tax Benefits. The tax benefits of real estate investment include reducing taxes with deductions for depreciation, mortgage interest, and operating expenses, and deferring taxes with tax-free exchanges and installment sales. The income tax implications of real estate ownership are discussed in Chapter 14.

Disadvantages of Investing in Real Estate. Of course, real estate investments can be a mixed blessing. There are some disadvantages to real estate investments that must be considered carefully.

First of all, expert advice is often required to invest in real estate. Investing in real estate is a lot more complicated than putting money in a savings account or mutual fund. It is also more time-consuming. Not only does the initial purchase take time and effort, but the property must be managed after it is purchased. Rental rates must be set, tenants found, rents collected, and maintenance and repairs completed. Even if the investor decides to hire a property manager to manage the property, there are many decisions that must be made by the investor.

As we discussed earlier, real estate investments are not liquid. Time is required to convert real estate into cash. Furthermore, there are substantial risks involved in investing in real estate. There is no guarantee that the investor will not lose some or all of his or her downpayment. For instance, there is always the chance that the property's value may decline because of a local economic trend.

Example: On a national scale, property values are keeping pace with inflation. However, Lumbertown relies solely on the timber industry and the local lumber mill for employment. The local mill shuts down and the town is economically crippled. Even though real estate is usually a good investment, property values in that town will decline rapidly.

Also, the income generated by a property may not be enough to cover the expenses of operating the property. A negative cash flow may force the investor to sell the property quickly, for less than was paid for it.

Choices When Investing in Real Estate

There are two different ways to invest in real estate. One way is to purchase the property as an individual investor. The other way is to invest in real estate indirectly, through real estate investment syndicates, real estate investment trusts, real estate mortgage investment conduits, or mortgage-backed securities.

A **real estate investment syndicate** is created when people or companies form a business entity (syndicate) in order to purchase and develop a piece of real estate. The syndicate may take the form of a partnership, a corporation, a trust, or a limited liability company.

A **real estate investment trust** (REIT) is an investment company that takes the form of a trust. If the requirements set forth in the tax code are met, an REIT can take advantage of special tax benefits. (REITs are discussed in Chapter 2.)

A **real estate mortgage investment conduit** (REMIC) is a special business entity that is formed for tax purposes. To qualify for special tax treatment, a substantial amount of a REMIC's investments must be in qualified mortgage loans. Like an REIT, a REMIC is subject to complicated legal restrictions.

Investors may also purchase **mortgage-backed securities** issued by one of the secondary market agencies, such as Fannie Mae or Freddie Mac. The secondary market is discussed in detail in Chapter 9.

Types of Properties. If an investor decides to purchase real property directly, the investor must first decide what type of property to invest in, and then which particular piece of property to purchase.

An investor has many types of real estate to choose from. There are residential properties (including single-family homes, duplexes, tri-plexes, four-plexes, and apartment buildings), office properties, retail properties, and industrial parks. Of course, an investor can always choose to purchase vacant land and develop it, or simply hold onto it to reap the benefits of appreciation.

Most real estate investors start out by purchasing residential property. The first choice is often a single-family home or duplex.

There are many advantages to investing in a rental house. Rental houses are more affordable for the beginning investor than other types of income property. Rental houses are scarce in many communities, so they are often easier to rent. Single-family homes often attract stable tenants, such as single professionals or young families. Rental houses are usually easier to sell, should the investor need to liquidate. Also, single-family homes can be managed easily by the owner. Two- to four-unit residential properties have many of these same advantages. In addition, the investor may choose to live in one of the units of a duplex, tri-plex, or four-plex, thus increasing its manageability.

Qualities to Look For. Purchasing rental properties is often easier than purchasing a home—it is a business decision rather than an emotional decision. When a family purchases a home, it looks for a house that fits its lifestyle and satisfies its emotional needs. On the other hand, a rental home usually has to meet only a few requirements: it should be in good condition, it should be located in a good neighborhood, it should contain enough square footage to satisfy the average tenant, and the design should not be so unconventional as to alienate the average tenant.

The location of a rental property should appeal to its potential tenants, which include blue collar workers, singles, career persons, seniors, and small families. The neighborhood should have easy access to employment centers, transportation, shopping, and schools. A rental home will have extra appeal if it is located near a college, hospital, or shopping center.

The structural components of the property should be in good condition. This will attract better tenants and eliminate the need for costly upkeep and repairs. Foundations are critical—are there any cracks, breaks, bulges, or shifts? The age and condition of the heating, wiring and plumbing systems should be examined. Are they expensive to maintain or repair? What about the insulation? Will the tenant be faced with large electricity or gas bills?

Once an investor has found a suitable house in a good location, he or she will be ready to begin managing that property (perhaps with the help of a professional property manager) and learning first hand about how real estate investments work.

Chapter Summary

accurately assess the value of a home, a real estate agent needs to be able to judge the quality of the construction. It is important to be familiar with common construction techniques and materials, and to have some understanding of the technical systems (plumbing, wiring, heating, and cooling). Knowing how to read plans and specifications can be very useful, especially when dealing with new construction.

2. A real estate agent is often asked to compare buying a home to renting one. The advantages of renting include less financial commitment and risk, fewer maintenance responsibilities, greater mobility, and facilities a homeowner often could not afford. The advantages of buying include security, satisfaction in ownership, privacy, and freedom from restrictions. Although a mortgage payment is typically much larger than a rental payment, property appreciation, equity, and tax deductions make buying far less expensive than renting in the long run.

3. In addition to judging construction quality, a real estate agent helping a customer choose a home should evaluate the neighborhood, the site, and the exterior and interior design.

4. After purchasing a home, many decide to venture into real estate investments. The advantages of real estate investment include appreciation, leverage, cash flow, and tax benefits. The disadvantages include the time required to choose and manage property, the fact that real estate investments are not liquid, and the risk of losing the investment.

Key Terms

Investment—An asset that is expected to generate a return (a profit).

Portfolio—The mix of investments owned by an individual or company.

Liquidity—The ability to convert an asset into cash quickly.

Appreciation—When an asset increases in value; generally due either to inflation or to an increasing scarcity of or demand for the asset.

Equity—The difference between the value of the property and the liens against it.

Leverage—Using borrowed money to invest in an asset. If the asset appreciates, the investor earns money on the money borrowed as well as the money invested.

Cash flow—Spendable income; the amount of money left after all the property's expenses have been paid, including operating costs, mortgage payments, and taxes.

Real estate investment syndicate—A group of people or companies who join together to purchase and develop a piece of real estate.

Real estate investment trust—A trust that invests exclusively in real estate and real estate mortgages.

Real estate mortgage investment conduit—A special business entity that must invest a substantial amount of its funds in qualified mortgage loans to qualify for special tax treatment.

Chapter 16—Quiz
Residential Real Estate

1. In building construction, standards of construction quality are assured through:

   a) the planning commission
   b) zoning ordinances
   c) building codes
   d) None of the above

2. All of the following are likely to go up eventually; which of them will probably increase the most gradually?

   a) A rental payment
   b) A fixed-rate mortgage payment
   c) An adjustable-rate mortgage payment
   d) All of the above will increase at the same rate

3. All of the following lots contain the same area. Which would generally be considered the most desirable?

   a) A rectangular lot with a gentle slope
   b) A triangular lot with a steep slope
   c) A triangular lot with a gentle slope
   d) A level T-shaped lot

4. Which of the following is considered a drawback in a floor plan?

   a) A door leads directly from the kitchen to the garage
   b) The front door leads directly into the living room
   c) The separate dining room is right next to the kitchen
   d) The bedrooms are isolated from the kitchen and family room

5. The value of a home is enhanced if:

   a) there are rental properties in the neighborhood as well as owner-occupied homes
   b) there are retail businesses as well as homes on the block
   c) strict zoning laws made the lots and houses in the neighborhood similar to one another
   d) All of the above

6. When comparing a mortgage payment to a rental payment, all of the following should be taken into account except:

   a) the landlord's equity in the rental property
   b) appreciation of the homeowner's property
   c) the federal tax deduction for mortgage interest
   d) whether the mortgage interest rate is fixed or adjustable

7. A house with many horizontal projections and vertical lines, with large areas of glass, is classified as:

   a) contemporary
   b) ranch
   c) colonial
   d) Spanish

8. Which of the following is an advantage of renting, as opposed to owning, a home?

   a) Security and stability
   b) Appreciation
   c) Federal tax deduction
   d) Mobility

9. Which of the following is not drywall material?

   a) Wallboard
   b) Plywood
   c) Sheetrock
   d) Plaster

10. R-value is a term used in reference to:

    a) a type of loan
    b) a zoning classification
    c) a government agency
    d) insulation

11. The mix of investments owned by an individual or company is known as:

    a) a portfolio
    b) leverage
    c) yield
    d) equity

12. Martinson's investments consist of $10,000 in a money market account, $5,000 in a savings account, and $12,000 in certificates of deposit. Martinson's main investment concern is probably:

    a) a high return
    b) liquidity
    c) safety
    d) Both b) and c)

13. A major disadvantage to investing in real estate is:

    a) the use of leverage to increase returns
    b) lack of liquidity
    c) uniformly low returns
    d) that a constantly increasing supply decreases values

14. Stocks, real estate, and investment in an REIT all have what in common?

    a) They are all considered liquid investments
    b) They are all very safe investments
    c) They all provide safe, but low, returns
    d) They are all ownership investments

15. The difference between the value of real property and the liens against it is the definition of:

    a) equity
    b) leverage
    c) portfolio
    d) cash flow

Answer Key

1.c) Building codes are local ordinances that set standards for construction quality.

2.b) A fixed-rate mortgage payment will increase very gradually, as property taxes and mortgage insurance premiums go up.

3.a) Rectangular lots are preferred to odd-shaped lots because more of the area can be used efficiently. Steeply sloping lots are often difficult to build on and are unstable, so level land or a gentle slope is preferable.

4.b) It is a disadvantage to have the front door open directly into the living room (rather than into an entry hall), since it is then necessary to pass through the living room to get to the rest of the house. All of the other design features listed are considered advantages.

5.c) While few people would like all the houses on their street to be identical, a reasonable degree of conformity is considered desirable and enhances the value of the homes.

6.a) The landlord's equity in the rental property is not likely to have much effect on the rental payment. However, appreciation, mortgage rates, and federal and state income tax deductions do affect how mortgage payments compare to rental payments.

7.a) The house described is contemporary, or modern, in design. One of the main features of contemporary houses is many large windows.

8.d) It is much easier and less expensive to move out of a rental than to sell a home and buy a new one. All of the other answers are advantages of owning a home.

9.d) Drywall material (unlike plaster) does not require the addition of water during construction.

10.d) R-value is a measure of insulating capacity.

11.a) A portfolio is the mixture of investments owned by a person or entity.

12.d) All of these types of investments are both relatively liquid and relatively safe.

13.b) The lack of liquidity is a serious disadvantage of investing in real estate. The use of leverage is one of the benefits of investing in real estate.

14.d) Stocks and real estate (either owned directly or through a real estate investment trust) are both considered ownership investments.

15.a) Equity is the difference between the value of real estate and the liens against it (such as a mortgage loan).

Chapter 17

Real Estate Math

 Outline

 Chapter Overview

Real estate agents use math constantly: to calculate their commissions, to determine the square footage of homes they are listing or selling, to prorate closing costs, and so on. Electronic calculators make all of these tasks much easier than they once were, but it is still necessary to have a basic grasp of the math involved. This chapter provides step-by-step instructions for solving a wide variety of real estate math problems.

Approach to Solving Math Problems

We are going to begin our discussion of real estate math with a simple approach to solving math problems. Master this four-step process, and the solution to most math problems you are likely to encounter as a real estate agent will be within your grasp.

1. Read the question

The most important step is to thoroughly read and understand the question. You must know what you are looking for before you can successfully work any math problem. Once you know what you want to find out (for example, the area, the commission amount, or the total profit) you will know which formula to use.

2. Write down the formula

Write down the correct formula for the problem you need to solve. For example, the area formula is *Area = Base × Height*, which is abbreviated $A = B \times H$. Formulas for each type of problem are presented throughout this chapter, and there is a complete list at the end of the chapter.

3. Substitute

Substitute the relevant numbers from the problem into the formula. Sometimes there are numbers in the problem that you will not use. It is not unusual for a math problem to contain unnecessary information, which is why it is very important to read the question first and determine what you are looking for. Then the formula will help you decide what information is necessary.

In some problems you will be able to substitute numbers into the formula without any additional steps, but in other problems you will have to take one or more preliminary steps first. For instance, you may have to convert fractions to decimals.

4. Calculate

Once you have substituted the numbers into the formula, you are ready to perform the calculations to find the unknown—the element in the formula that was not given in the problem. Most of the formulas have the same basic form: $A = B \times C$. The problem will give you two of the three numbers (or information to enable you to find two of the numbers) and then you will either have to divide or multiply to find the third number, which is the solution to the problem.

Whether you will need to multiply or divide is determined by which element in the formula you are trying to discover. For example, the formula $A = B \times C$ may be converted into two other formulas. All three formulas are equivalent, but they are put into different forms depending on the element to be discovered.

If the quantity A is unknown, then the following formula is used:

$$A = B \times C$$

The number B is **multiplied** by C. The product of B multiplied by C is A.

If the quantity B is unknown, the following formula is used:

$$B = A \div C$$

The number A is **divided** by C. The quotient of A divided by C is B.

If the quantity C is unknown, the following formula is used:

$$C = A \div B$$

The number A is **divided** by B. The quotient of A divided by B is C.

Thus, the formula $A = B \times C$ may be used three different ways depending on which quantity is unknown.

$$A = B \times C$$

or

$$B = A \div C$$

or

$$C = A \div B$$

Now let's try an example. Suppose a room is 10 feet wide and 15 feet long. How many square feet does it contain? Remember to use the four-step approach to solve the problem.

1. **Read the question.** This problem asks you to find the area of a room. You will need the area formula.

$$Area = Base \times Height$$

$$A = B \times H$$

2. **Write down the formula.** $A = B \times H$

3. **Substitute.** Substitute the numbers given in the problem into the formula. $A = 10 \times 15$

4. **Calculate.** Multiply B and H to get the answer. $10 \times 15 = 150$. Thus, $A = 150$. The room has 150 square feet.

Suppose the problem had given you different pieces of information. Suppose you knew that the area of the room was 150 square feet and that one side was 10 feet long. You were asked to discover the length of the remaining side.

Let's use the four-step approach again.

1. **Read the question.** This problem asks you to find the length of one side of a room. You will need the area formula.

$$Area = Base \times Height$$

$$A = B \times H$$

2. **Write down the formula.** $A = B \times H$

3. **Substitute.** Substitute the numbers given in the problem into the formula.

$$150 = 10 \times H$$

4. **Calculate.** The height, or the remaining side, is what the problem asks for. Thus, the basic formula would be converted into a division problem to find the quantity H.

$$H = A \div B$$

$$H = 150 \div 10$$

The quantity A (the area) is divided by B (the base).

$$150 \div 10 = 15$$

The quotient of 150 divided by 10 is 15. The remaining side, the height, is therefore 15 feet.

Converting Fractions to Decimals

Most people find it much easier to work with decimal numbers than with fractions. Also, hand calculators can multiply and divide by decimals. Therefore, in most instances you should change fractions into decimals. To do so, divide the top number of the fraction (called the numerator) by the bottom number of the fraction (called the denominator).

Example: To change ¾ into a decimal, divide the top number, 3, by the bottom number, 4.

$$3 \div 4 = .75$$

Example: To convert ⅔ into a decimal, divide the top number, 2, by the bottom number, 3.

$$2 \div 3 = .66667$$

If you are using a hand calculator, it will make the conversion for you. Divide 2 by 3 and your calculator will give you the answer with the decimal point in the correct place.

To add or subtract decimals, put the numbers in a column with their decimal points lined up.

Example: To add 3.75, 14.62, 1.245, 679, 1,412.8, and 1.9, put the numbers in a column with the decimal points lined up as shown below, then add them together.

$$
\begin{array}{r}
3.75 \\
14.62 \\
1.245 \\
679.00 \\
1,412.8 \\
+\ 1.9 \\
\hline
2,113.315
\end{array}
$$

To multiply decimal numbers, first do the multiplication without worrying about the decimal points. Then put a decimal point into the answer in the correct place. (A hand calculator will do this automatically.) The answer should have as many decimal places (that is, numbers to the right of its decimal point) as the total number of decimal places in the numbers that were multiplied.

Example: Multiply 24.625 times 16.15. The two numbers contain a total of five decimal places (three in 24.625 and two in 16.15).

$$
\begin{array}{r}
24.625 \\
\times\ 16.15 \\
\hline
397.69375
\end{array}
$$

Just count the decimal places in the numbers you are multiplying and put the decimal point the same number of places to the left in the answer. In some cases, it will be necessary to include one or more zeros in the answer to have the correct number of decimal places.

Example: Multiply .2 × .4. There is a total of two decimal places.

$$
\begin{array}{r}
.2 \\
\times\ .4 \\
\hline
.08
\end{array}
$$

A zero has to be included in the answer in order to move the decimal point two places left.

To divide by a decimal number, move the decimal point in the outside number (the denominator) all the way to the right, and then move the decimal point in the inside number (the numerator) the same number of places to the right. (In some cases it will be necessary to add one or more zeros to the inside number in order to move the decimal point the correct number of places.)

Example: Divide 26.145 by 1.5.

$$26.145 \div 1.5$$

Move the decimal point in 1.5 all the way to the right (in this case, that is only one place) and move the decimal in 26.145 the same number of places to the right.

$$26.145 \div 1.5 \ becomes \ 261.45 \div 15$$

Now divide.

$$261.45 \div 15 = 17.43$$

Just as with addition, subtraction, and multiplication, these steps are unnecessary if you use a hand calculator. If the numbers are punched in correctly, the calculator will automatically give you an answer with the decimal in the correct place.

Area Problems

A real estate agent often needs to calculate the area of a lot, a building, or a room. The formula used depends on the shape of the area in question.

Squares, Rectangles, and Parallelograms

The formula for finding the area of squares, rectangles, and parallelograms is:

$$Area = Base \times Height$$

$$A = B \times H$$

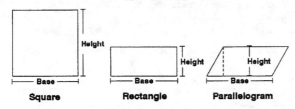

Example: If a rectangular room measures 15 feet along one wall and 12 feet along the adjoining wall, how many square feet of carpet would be required to cover the floor?

1. Read the question.

2. Write down the formula. $A = B \times H$

3. Substitute. $A = 15 \times 12$

4. Calculate. Since the quantity *A* is unknown, multiply *B* times *H* for the answer.

$$B \times H = A$$

$$15 \times 12 = 180$$

It would require 180 square feet of carpet to cover the floor.

Example: If carpet is on sale for $12 per square yard, how much would it cost to carpet the room in the example above?

1. Read the question. In this problem, you must first determine how many square feet there are in a square yard and then determine how many square yards there are in 180 square feet. A square yard is a square that measures one yard on each side. There are three feet in a yard.

2. Write down the formula. $A = B \times H$

3. Substitute. $A = 3 \times 3$

4. Calculate. The quantity *A* is the unknown; thus, multiply *B* times *H*.

$$B \times H = A$$

$$3 \times 3 = 9$$

So there are 9 square feet in a square yard. Now divide 9 into 180 to see how many square yards there are in 180 square feet.

$$180 \ sq. \ ft. \ \div \ 9 = 20 \ square \ yards$$

There are 20 square yards in the room. If carpet is selling for $12 per square yard, it will cost $12 × 20, or $240, to carpet the room.

Triangles

The formula for finding the area of a triangle is:

$$Area = \tfrac{1}{2} Base \times Height$$

$$A = \tfrac{1}{2} B \times H$$

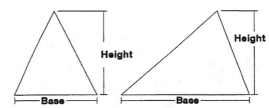

Example: If commercial building lots in a certain neighborhood are selling for approximately $5 per square foot, approximately how much should the lot pictured below sell for?

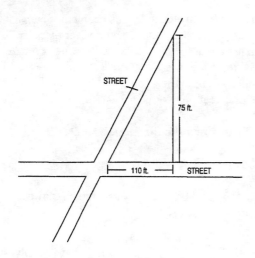

1. Write down the formula. *A = ½ B × H*

2. Substitute. *A = ½ × 110 × 75*

3. Calculate. The quantity *A* is unknown; thus, multiply *½ B × H* or, with the substitution, *½ × 110 × 75.*

The order of multiplication is not important. You can multiply 110 times 75 and then multiply that product by ½, or you can multiply ½ times 75 and then multiply the product by 110. The answer will be the same. (To make the multiplication easier, convert ½ to a decimal number: *½ = 0.5.*)

a) *110 × 75 = 8,250*
    .5 × 8,250 = 4,125

b) *.5 × 110 = 55*
    55 × 75 = 4,125

c) *.5 × 75 = 37.5*
    37.5 × 110 = 4,125

The lot contains 4,125 square feet. If similar lots are selling for about $5 per square foot, this lot should sell for about $20,625: $5 × 4,125 = $20,625.

Odd Shapes

The best approach to finding the area of an odd-shaped figure is to divide it up into squares, rectangles, and triangles. Find the areas of those figures and add them all up to arrive at the area of the odd-shaped lot, room, or building in question.

Example: If the lot pictured below is leased on a 66-year lease for $3 per square foot per year, with rental payments made monthly, how much would the monthly rent be?

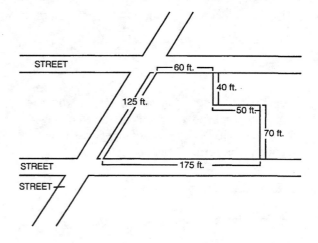

First, divide the lot up into rectangles and triangles.

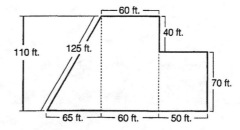

The next step in the problem is to find the areas of the following figures and add them together.

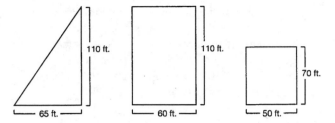

Triangle:
1. **Write down the formula.** $A = \frac{1}{2} B \times H$
2. **Substitute.** $A = .5 \times 65 \times 110$
3. **Calculate.** $.5 \times 65 \times 110 = 3,575$

Rectangle:
1. **Write down the formula.** $A = B \times H$
2. **Substitute.** $A = 110 \times 60$
3. **Calculate.** $110 \times 60 = 6,600$

Rectangle:
1. **Write down the formula.** $A = B \times H$
2. **Substitute.** $A = 50 \times 70$
3. **Calculate.** $50 \times 70 = 3,500$

Add the three areas:

$$\begin{array}{r} 3,575 \\ 6,600 \\ +\ 3,500 \\ \hline 13,675 \end{array}$$

The lot contains 13,675 square feet. The annual rent at $3 per square foot per year would be $41,025:

$$\$3 \times 13,675 = \$41,025 \; per \; year$$

The monthly rental payment would be one-twelfth of the annual rent:

$$\$41,025 \div 12 = \$3,418.75$$

Thus, the monthly rental payment for this odd-shaped lot is $3,418.75.

Percentage Problems

It is necessary to convert percentages to decimal numbers and vice versa, so that the arithmetic in a percentage problem can be done in decimals, then translated back into a percentage.

To convert a percentage to a decimal, remove the percent sign and move the decimal point two places to the left. This may require adding zeros.

Example: *98% becomes .98*
5% becomes .05
32.5% becomes .325
17.5% becomes .175

To convert a decimal into a percentage, do just the opposite. Move the decimal point two places to the right and add a percent sign.

Example: *.15 becomes 15%*
.08 becomes 8%
.095 becomes 9.5%

The conversion of percentages to and from decimals is necessary to work a wide variety of real estate math problems, including commission, interest, capitalization, and profit and loss problems. The percent key on a calculator performs the conversion of a percentage to a decimal number automatically.

In a math problem, whenever something is expressed as a percentage "of" another number, that's an indication that you should multiply the percentage by that other number.

Example: What is 75% *of* $40,000?

First convert the percentage to a decimal: 75% becomes .75. The phrase "of $40,000" means you should multiply by $40,000.

$$.75 \times \$40,000 = \$30,000$$

Thus, 75% of $40,000 is $30,000.

Percentage problems are usually of the type shown in the example above. You have to find a part of something or a percentage of the total.

A general formula might be: *A percentage of the total equals the part.* This can be written:

$$Percentage \times Total = Part, \text{ or}$$

$$\% \times T = P, \text{ or}$$

$$P = \% \times T$$

Example: A house is listed for sale with a broker at a price of $72,000, with an agreement to pay a commission of 6% of the sales price. It sells for $70,000. How much is the commission?

1. Write down the formula. $P = \% \times T$

2. Substitute. Change the percentage to a decimal.

$$6\% \text{ becomes } .06$$

$$P = \% \times T$$

$$P = .06 \times \$70,000$$

3. Calculate. The unknown quantity is *P*, the part; thus, the total is multiplied by the percentage.

$$.06 \times \$70,000 = \$4,200$$

The commission is $4,200.

Commission Problems

Like the example above, most commission problems can be solved with the general percentage formula:

$$Part = Percentage \times Total$$

$$P = \% \times T$$

The percentage is the commission rate and the total is the amount that the commission is based on.

This is most often the sales price of a piece of property, but it could be lease payments instead. The part is the amount of the commission.

Example: A listing agreement provides for a commission of 7% of the sales price to be paid to the broker. If the broker and the salesperson agreed that the salesperson is entitled to ⅔ of the commission, how much should the salesperson receive if the property sells for $65,000?

1. Write down the formula. $P = \% \times T$

2. Substitute. Change the percentage to a decimal number.

$$7\% \text{ becomes } .07$$

$$P = .07 \times \$65,000$$

3. Calculate. The part is the unknown quantity; thus, the percentage is multiplied by the total.

$$.07 \times \$65,000 = \$4,550$$

The commission is $4,550. The salesperson is entitled to ⅔ of that amount. Convert the fraction to a decimal, and then convert the decimal to a percentage:

$$⅔ = .6667 \qquad .6667 = 66.67\%$$

The salesperson is entitled to approximately 67% of the total commission.

1. Write down the formula. $P = \% \times T$

2. Substitute. Change the percentage back to a decimal.

$$66.67\% \text{ becomes } .6667$$

$$P = .6667 \times \$4,550$$

3. Calculate.

$$.6667 \times \$4,550 = \$3,033$$

The salesperson is entitled to approximately $3,033.

Example: A listing agreement provided for a commission of 7% of the first $100,000 and 5% of any amount over $100,000. If the commission was $8,250, what was the sales price?

1. Write down the formula. $P = \% \times T$

First find out how much of the commission is attributable to the first $100,000.

2. Substitute. $P = .07 \times \$100,000$

3. Calculate. $P = \$7,000$

So $7,000 of the commission is from the first $100,000.

Next, determine how much commission remains:

$$
\begin{array}{ll}
\$8,250 & \textit{total commission} \\
-\ 7,000 & \textit{commission for first \$100,000} \\
\hline
\$1,250 &
\end{array}
$$

Therefore, $1,250 is attributable to the part of the sales price in excess of $100,000.

1. Write down the formula. $P = \% \times T$

2. Substitute. $\$1,250 = .05 \times T$

3. Calculate. The quantity T is unknown. The basic formula should be converted to isolate the unknown, T.

$$T = P \div \%$$

$$T = \$1,250 \div .05$$

$$\$1,250 \div .05 = \$25,000$$

The sales price in excess of $100,000 is $25,000; thus, the total sales price is $100,000 plus $25,000, or $125,000.

Interest Problems

Interest problems are worked in basically the same manner as percentage problems. The formula is:

$$Interest = Principal \times Rate \times Time$$

$$I = P \times R \times T$$

Although there is an additional element, this is quite similar to the general percentage formula, *Part = Percentage × Total*.

Here, the interest is the part, the interest rate is the rate (or percentage), and the principal (the loan amount or sales price) is the total. Interest rates are expressed as annual rates, that is, as a certain percentage per year. It is therefore necessary to account for the time in years or parts of years.

Example: If a $2,000 note bears interest at the rate of 13% per annum and matures in one year, how much interest will be paid each year?

1. Write down the formula. $I = P \times R \times T$

2. Substitute. $I = \$2,000 \times .13 \times 1$

3. Calculate. $I = \$260$

The annual interest will amount to $260.

Example: If $450 in interest at the annual rate of 12½% accrues on a loan in six months, how much is the loan amount?

1. Write down the formula. $I = P \times R \times T$

2. Substitute. $\$450 = P \times .125 \times {}^{6}\!/_{12}$

The time is expressed as a fraction of a year. It will be more convenient to convert the fraction to a decimal.

$$\$450 = P \times .125 \times .5$$

3. Calculate. Isolate the unknown quantity, *P*.

$$P = \frac{I}{R \times T}$$

$$P = \frac{\$450}{.125 \times .5}$$

First multiply the two bottom numbers together and then divide that product into the top number.

$$P = \frac{\$450}{.0625}$$

$$\$450 \div .0625 = \$7,200$$

The principal, or the loan amount, is $7,200.

Example: A home loan has monthly payments of $625, which include principal and 9% interest (paid in arrears) and $47.50 per month for tax and insurance reserves. If $27.75 of the June 1 payment was applied to the principal, what was the outstanding principal balance during the month of May?

1. Write down the formula. $I = P \times R \times T$

2. Substitute. $I = P \times .09 \times \frac{1}{12}$

The interest portion of the payment can be found by deducting the portions of the payment allocated to reserves and principal.

$625.00	*total payment*
− 47.50	*reserves*
$577.50	
− 27.75	*principal payment*
$549.75	*interest portion of June payment*

$$\$549.75 = P \times .09 \times \frac{1}{12}$$

Convert the fraction to a decimal: $1 \div 12 = .0833$

3. Calculate.

$$P = \frac{I}{R \times T}$$

$$P = \frac{\$549.75}{.09 \times .0833}$$

$$P = \frac{\$549.75}{.0075}$$

$$\$549.75 \div .0075 = \$73,300$$

The outstanding principal balance is $73,300.

Profit and Loss Problems

Profit and loss problems can be solved in the same way as percentage problems. The formula for profit and loss problems is another variation on the percentage formula.

Value After = % × Value Before

$$VA = \% \times VB$$

The value after is the value of the property after the profit or loss is taken. The value before is the value of the property before the profit or loss is taken. The percentage is 100% plus the percentage of profit or minus the percentage of loss. The idea is to express the value of the property after a profit or loss as a percentage of the property's value before the profit or loss. If there is no profit or loss, the value after is exactly 100% of the value before, because the value has not changed. If there is a profit, the value after will be greater than 100% of the value before, since the value has increased. If there is a loss, the value after the loss is less than the value before the loss, so the value after will be less than 100% of the value before. Remember, a percentage "of" a number means you should multiply the percentage by that number.

Example: Brown bought a house five years ago for $50,000 and sold it this year for 30% more than she paid for it. What did she sell it for?

1. Write down the formula. $VA = \% \times VB$

2. Substitute. To get the percentage you must add the percentage of profit to or subtract the percentage of loss from 100%. In this case there is a profit, so you add 30% to 100% and convert it to a decimal number.

$$100\% + 30\% = 130\% = 1.30$$

$$VA = 1.30 \times \$50,000$$

3. Calculate.

$$VA = 1.30 \times \$50,000$$

$$VA = \$65,000$$

Brown sold the house for $65,000.

Example: Panza sold his house this year for $40,000. He paid $60,000 for it two years ago. What was the percentage of loss?

1. Write down the formula. $VA = \% \times VB$

2. Substitute. $\$40,000 = \% \times \$60,000$

3. Calculate. The percentage is the unknown quantity; thus, the value after is divided by the value before: $\% = VA \div VB$

$$\% = VA \div VB$$

$$\% = \$40,000 \div \$60,000$$

$$\$40,000 \div \$60,000 = .67 = 67\%$$

The value after the sale is approximately 67% of the value before. Subtract 67% from 100% to find the percentage of loss:

$$
\begin{array}{r}
1.00 \\
-.67 \\
\hline
.33 \quad loss
\end{array}
$$

There was a 33% loss.

Example: A house sold for 18% more than the owner paid for it. The owner received $62,000 from escrow after paying a commission of 7% of the sales price and other closing costs totaling $589. What did the owner originally pay for the house?

1. Write down the formula. $VA = \% \times VB$

2. Substitute. $VA = 1.18\,(100\% + 18\%) \times VB$

A separate calculation must be performed here in order to determine the value after. The value after is the total of the seller's net ($62,000), plus the closing costs ($589), plus the broker's commission (7% of the total). In mathematical form, it looks like this:

$$T\,(total) = \$62,000 + \$589 + (7\% \times T), \text{ or}$$

$$T - (7\% \times T) = \$62,000 + \$589$$

Since T is equal to 100% of the total, we can rewrite the equation as:

$$(100\% \times T) - (7\% \times T) = \$62,000 + \$589$$

or

$$(100\% - 7\%) \times T = \$62,589$$

$$93\% \times T = \$62,589$$

$$.93 \times T = \$62,589$$

$$T = \$62,589 \div .93$$

$$\$62,589 \div .93 = \$67,300$$

The sales price is $67,300, which can now be substituted into the profit and loss formula as the value after.

$$VA = 1.18 \times VB$$

$$\$67,300 = 1.18 \times VB$$

3. Calculate. Isolate the unknown.

$$VB = \$67,300 \div 1.18$$

$$\$67,300 \div 1.18 = \$57,033.90$$

The owner paid $57,034 for the house.

Capitalization Problems

Capitalization problems involve the capitalization approach to value, a method of real estate appraisal that is discussed in detail in Chapter 12.

Capitalization problems are another form of percentage problem. The formula is:

$$Income = Rate \times Value$$

$$I = R \times V$$

The income in this case is the annual net income produced by the investment property. Depending on the problem, it may be necessary to deduct a bad debt/vacancy factor and operating expenses from gross income to arrive at the net income. The rate is the capitalization rate, the percentage of return the investor desires on the investment. The rate of return varies according to many factors. A higher desired rate of return will mean a higher capitalization rate and a lower value for the same income. The value is the property's value, or the purchase price the investor should be willing to pay for the property in order to obtain the specified rate of return.

Again, this formula is very similar to the basic percentage formula, *Part = % × Total*.

Example: A property produces an annual net income of $26,000. If an investor desires an 11% rate of return, what should he pay for the property?

1. **Write down the formula.** $I = R \times V$

2. **Substitute.** $\$26,000 = .11 \times V$

3. **Calculate.** Isolate the unknown quantity:
$V = \$26,000 \div .11$

$$\$26,000 \div .11 = \$236,363.64$$

The investor should be willing to pay approximately $236,363 for the property.

Example: If a property is valued at $100,000 using an 8% capitalization rate, what would its value be using a 10% capitalization rate?

1. **Write down the formula.** $I = R \times V$

2. **Substitute.** $I = .10 \times V$

Here it is necessary to work a preliminary problem to find the income. Use the same formula and the value at an 8% capitalization rate:

$$I = R \times V$$

$$I = .08 \times \$100,000$$

$$I = \$8,000$$

The net income is $8,000 annually. Now substitute that figure into the formula to find the value at a 10% capitalization rate.

$$I = R \times V$$

$$\$8,000 = .10 \times V$$

3. **Calculate.** Isolate the unknown quantity:
$V = \$8,000 \div .10$

Divide the top number by the bottom number.

$$\$8,000 \div .10 = \$80,000$$

The value of the same property using a 10% capitalization rate is $80,000. This problem demonstrates that a higher capitalization rate applied to the same net income will result in a lower value for the property.

Example: A ten-unit apartment building has six units that rent for $300 per month and four units that rent for $350 per month. Allow 5% for vacancies and uncollected rent. Operating expenses include annual property taxes of $4,800, monthly utilities of $475, and maintenance expenses of approximately $1,600 per year. The owner has an outstanding mortgage balance of $21,000 at 8%

interest, with monthly payments of $312. If an investor requires a 13% rate of return, how much should she offer for the property?

1. Write down the formula. $I = R \times V$

2. Substitute. It is necessary to calculate the annual net income before substituting. First, calculate the annual gross income.

$300 × 12 months = $3,600/year × 6 units = $21,600
$350 × 12 months = $4,200/year × 4 units = $16,800
                                           $38,400

The gross income is $38,400 per year.

Next, find the bad debt/vacancy factor and deduct it from the gross income to find the effective gross income. The bad debt/vacancy factor is 5% of the gross income.

Bad debts & vacancies = .05 × $38,400

Bad debts & vacancies = $1,920

The loss to be expected from uncollected rents and vacancies is $1,920 per year.

$38,400	*gross income*
– 1,920	*bad debts and vacancies*
$36,480	*effective gross income*

Next, deduct the operating expenses from the effective gross income to arrive at the net income. Remember, since you are trying to find annual net income, all the expenses must be annual also. The operating expenses add up as follows:

Property taxes $4,800 per year	*$4,800*
Utilities $475 per month × 12	*5,700*
Maintenance $1,600 per year	*+ 1,600*
	$12,100

The annual operating expenses are $12,100. (The mortgage payments are not treated as operating expenses. See Chapter 12.)

$36,480	*effective gross income*
– 12,100	*annual expenses*
$24,380	*annual net income*

Now, substitute the net income and the rate into the formula $I = R \times V$:

$$\$24,380 = .13 \times V$$

3. Calculate. Isolate the unknown quantity.

$$V = \frac{\$24,380}{.13}$$

Divide the top number by the bottom number to find the unknown quantity, the value.

$$\$24,380 \div .13 = \$187,538.46$$

The investor should be willing to pay approximately $187,538 for the property.

Example: Assume a property with the same income and expenses as the one in the preceding problem. If an investor paid $250,000 for the apartment house, what capitalization rate was used?

1. Write down the formula. $I = R \times V$

2. Substitute. We already know the net income from working the preceding problem.

$$\$24,380 = R \times \$250,000$$

3. Calculate. Isolate the unknown quantity.

$$R = \frac{\$24,380}{\$250,000}$$

Divide the top number by the bottom number.

$$\$24,380 \div \$250,000 = .0975$$

The investor used a capitalization rate of approximately 9.75%.

Prorations

Proration is the allocation of one expense between two or more parties. As was explained in Chapter 13, prorations are usually required in real estate closings, where the cost of such items as taxes and insurance are prorated based on the closing date.

The formula for proration is:

Share = daily Rate × number of Days

$$S = R \times D$$

To work a proration problem:

1. Find the annual or monthly expense.
2. Then calculate the per diem (daily) rate of the expense. To find the per diem rate of an annual expense, divide the amount of the expense by 365 (or 366 in a leap year). To find the per diem rate of a monthly expense, divide the amount of the expense by the number of days in that particular month (28, 29, 30, or 31). (Per diem rates should be calculated to an accuracy of at least four decimal places for monthly expenses, and five decimal places for annual expenses.)
3. Next, determine the number of days for which the person is responsible for the expense.
4. Finally, substitute the per diem rate and the number of days into the formula and calculate.

Example: The buyer is required to pay prepaid interest (interim interest) as part of her closing costs. This is the amount of interest that will accrue from the date of closing to the end of the month. The loan has a principal amount of $122,000. The interest rate is 10%. The transaction closes on June 22.

1. Write down the formula. $S = R \times D$

a) Find the annual or monthly interest expense. For this problem, use the interest formula to calculate the amount of the expense.

$$I = P \times R \times T$$
$$I = \$122,000 \times .10 \times 1$$
$$I = \$12,200$$

The interest is $12,200 per year.

b) Then find the per diem rate of the expense. Divide the annual rate by 365.

$$\$12,200 \div 365 = \$33.42466$$

The daily rate is $33.42466.

c) Next, find the number of days the buyer is responsible for. On interest and tax prorations, the buyer pays for the day of closing. There are nine days: June 22, 23, 24, 25, 26, 27, 28, 29, and 30.

d) Finally, substitute the daily rate and number of days into the formula and calculate.

2. Substitute. $S = \$33.42466 \times 9$

3. Calculate. $\$33.42466 \times 9 = \$300.82$

The buyer's interest charge would be $300.82.

Example: A real estate sale closes on August 10. The annual property taxes of $1,440 have not yet been paid. How much does the seller owe the buyer at closing?

The seller owes the buyer taxes for the period from July 1 through August 9 (the period of time the seller owned and occupied the house). The buyer is responsible for the taxes from August 10 onward.

1. Write down the formula. $S = R \times D$

a) First, find the annual or monthly expense. Here, the annual expense is given to you: $1,440.

b) Next, find the daily rate.

$$\$1,440 \div 365 = \$3.94521$$

c) Determine the number of days the seller is responsible for.

July	*31 days*
August	*9 days*
	40 days

d) Multiply the daily rate by the number of days.

2. Substitute. *S = $3.94521 × 40*

3. Calculate. *$3.94521 × 40 = $157.81*

The seller will owe the buyer $157.81 for taxes at closing.

Formulas

Converting fractions to decimals:

Divide numerator (top number) by denominator (bottom number).

Converting decimals to percentages:

Move decimal point two places to the right and add a percent sign.

Converting percentages to decimals:

Move decimal point two places to the left and drop the percent sign.

Area formula for squares, rectangles, and parallelograms:

Area = Base × Height
$A = B \times H$

Area formula for triangles:

Area = ½ Base × Height
$A = ½ B \times H$

Percentage formula:

Part = Percentage × Total
$P = \% \times T$

Interest formula:

Interest = Principal × Rate × Time
$I = P \times R \times T$

Value After formula:

Value After = % × Value Before
$VA = \% \times VB$

Capitalization formula:

Income = Rate × Value
$I = R \times V$

Proration formula:

Share = daily Rate × number of Days
$S = R \times D$

1. *Find annual or monthly amount;*
2. *Find daily rate;*
3. *Determine number of days; and*
4. *Substitute and calculate.*

☑ Quiz: Chapter 17
Real Estate Math

1. Christine Baxter and Tom Erickson bought a house one year ago for $68,500. If property values in their neighborhood are increasing at an annual rate of 7%, what is the current market value of their house?

   a) $73,295
   b) $74,270
   c) $75,980
   d) $76,893

2. A home just sold for $83,500. The listing broker charged the seller a 6½% commission. The broker will pay 30% of that amount to the listing salesperson, Lindquist, and 25% to the selling salesperson, Shimura. How much will Lindquist's share of the commission be?

   a) $895.54
   b) $1,221.19
   c) $1,356.88
   d) $1,628.25

3. A rectangular lot with a 45-foot frontage that contains 1,080 square yards has a depth of:

   a) 63 feet
   b) 216 feet
   c) 188 feet
   d) 97 feet

4. An acre contains 43,560 square feet. What is the maximum number of lots measuring 50 feet by 100 feet that can be created from a one-acre parcel?

   a) Six
   b) Seven
   c) Eight
   d) Nine

5. Firenza sold a client's building for $80,000 and received a commission of $5,600. What was his commission rate?

   a) 6.5%
   b) 7%
   c) 7.5%
   d) 8%

6. The Jorgensens bought a lot for $5,000 and later sold it for $8,000. What was their percentage of profit?

   a) 60%
   b) 75%
   c) 80%
   d) 85%

7. Driscoll wants to purchase an income property that has an annual net income of $16,000. If she wants at least an 8% return on her investment, what is the most she should pay for the property?

   a) $150,000
   b) $175,000
   c) $195,000
   d) $200,000

8. Garvey purchases a building for $85,000. The building shows an annual net income of $5,100. What is his rate of return?

   a) 5.5%
   b) 6%
   c) 6.5%
   d) 7%

9. How many square yards are there in a rectangle that measures 75 × 30 feet?

   a) 6,750
   b) 2,250
   c) 750
   d) 250

10. Miro is purchasing an apartment building. The closing date is September 15, and the seller has already collected the monthly rents in the amount of $13,960 for September. At closing, the seller will have to pay Miro a prorated share of the September rents, which will amount to approximately:

   a) $612
   b) $931
   c) $7,445
   d) $9,035

11. A triangular lot has a 40-foot base and a 30-foot height. What is the area of the lot?

   a) 500 square feet
   b) 600 square feet
   c) 750 square feet
   d) 650 square feet

12. What is the decimal equivalent of ⁵/₈?

   a) .625
   b) .0825
   c) 1.58
   d) 1.60

13. Kohler has obtained a $112,000 loan at 8.5% interest to finance the purchase of a home. At closing, the lender will require him to prepay interest for April 26 through April 30. Assuming that the closing agent uses a 365-day year for the proration, how much will that prepaid interest amount to?

    a) $64.35
    b) $104.32
    c) $130.41
    d) $1,403.84

14. The Binghams are selling their house and paying off the mortgage at closing. The remaining principal balance on the mortgage at closing will be $168,301.50. They will also have to pay interest that accrued over the 7-day period between their last mortgage payment and the closing date. If the annual interest rate on the Binghams' mortgage was 10%, how much will they have to pay in interest at closing? (Use a 365-day year for the proration.)

    a) $85.21
    b) $322.77
    c) $409.86
    d) $694.41

15. Crowe has just paid $460,000 for a building that will bring her a 9.75% return on her investment. What is the building's annual net income?

    a) $34,965
    b) $36,750
    c) $41,220
    d) $44,850

Answer Key

1. a)   The current market value of Baxter and Erickson's house is approximately $73,295. The question asks you to determine the "value after" of the house, so the applicable formula is Value After = Percentage × Value Before, VA = % × VB. Here, the value has increased by 7%, so the appropriate percentage is 107% (100% + 7%), or 1.07 (as a decimal). 1.07 × $68,500 = $73,295.

2. d)   Lindquist, the listing salesperson, will get $1,628.25. This is a percentage question with two parts. First multiply the sales price by the broker's commission rate to determine the full commission. $83,500 × .065 = $5,427.50. Then multiply that number by 30% to determine Lindquist's share. $5,427.50 × .30 = $1,628.25.

3. b)   The depth of the lot is 216 feet. The question asks you to determine the length of one of the sides of a rectangle, so the applicable formula is Area = Base × Height, A = B × H. First convert the area from square yards to square feet, so that it is in the same unit of measurement as the frontage. A square yard is a square that measures 3 feet on each side, or 9 square feet (3 × 3 = 9). Thus, 1,080 square yards is 9,720 square feet (1,080 × 9 = 9,720). Now substitute the numbers you have into the formula. 9,720 = 45 × H. Isolate the unknown quantity, H, by changing to another version of the same formula.

   H = 9,720 ÷ 45

Divide the area, 9,720 square feet, by the length of the base, 45 feet, to determine the height of the rectangle. 9,720 ÷ 45 = 216 feet.

4. c)   There are eight 50' × 100' lots in an acre, with one somewhat smaller lot left over. Use the area formula to determine the area of a 50' × 100' lot. A = 50 × 100 = 5,000 square feet. Thus, each lot will have an area of 5,000 square feet. Now divide the total number of square feet in the acre by the area of each lot: 43,560 ÷ 5,000 = 8.71.

5. b)   Firenza's commission rate was 7%. Use the percentage formula, Part = Percentage × Total, P = % × T. You know the part ($5,600) and the total ($80,000), so switch the formula to isolate the percentage, then substitute.

   P ÷ T = %
   $5,600 ÷ $80,000 = %

   Now calculate. $5,600 ÷ $80,000 = .07. Thus, the commission rate was 7%.

6. a)   The Jorgensens' profit on the sale of the lot was 60%. The question asks you to determine what percentage of the original price (the value before) the sales price (the value after) represents. So use the value after formula, VA = % × VB, switching it around to isolate the unknown quantity, the percentage:

   VA ÷ VB = %
   $8,000 ÷ $5,000 = 1.60 = 160%

The value after is 160% of the value before—in other words, 60% more than the value before. Thus, their profit on the sale was 60%.

7. d) Driscoll could pay $200,000 for the property and get an 8% return on that investment. This is a capitalization problem, so use the capitalization formula, Income = Rate × Value, I = R × V. You know the net income ($16,000) and the capitalization rate (8%), so switch the formula to isolate the unknown quantity, V:

I ÷ R = V
$16,000 ÷ .08 = $200,000

8. b) Garvey has a 6% return on his investment. This problem calls for the capitalization formula again, but this time it's the rate that is unknown. Switch the formula to isolate the rate, R:

I ÷ V = R
$5,100 ÷ $85,000 = .06 = 6%

9. d) There are 250 square yards in a 75' × 30' rectangle. The area formula, A = B × H, will give you the area in square feet: 75 × 30 = 2,250 square feet. Then you must convert that figure to square yards. There are 9 square feet in a square yard, so divide 2,250 by 9. 2,250 ÷ 9 = 250 square yards.

10. c) Miro, the buyer, is entitled to approximately $7,445 in rent for the period from the closing date through September 30. The proration formula is Share = daily Rate × number of Days, S = R × D. First determine the per diem rate for the rents by dividing the total amount by the number of days in the month: $13,960 ÷ 30 = $465.3333. Next, determine the number of days for which the buyer is entitled to the rent: September 15 through 30 is 16 days. Finally, multiply the rate by the number of days to find the buyer's share: $465.3333 × 16 = $7,445.

11. b) The area of the lot is 600 square feet. Since the lot is triangular, the appropriate area formula is Area = ½ Base × Height, A = ½ B × H. Here, the base is 40 feet, so ½ the base is 20 feet. 20 feet × 30 feet = 600 square feet.

12. a) The decimal equivalent of ⁵/₈ is .625. To determine this, divide the denominator of the fraction (the bottom number, 8) into the numerator (the top number, 5). 5 ÷ 8 = .625.

13. c) The prepaid interest will be $130.41. First determine the annual interest, using the interest formula. Interest = Principal × Rate × Time, I = P × R × T. The principal is $112,000, the rate is 8.5%, and the time is 1 (for one year).

$112,000 \times .085 \times 1 = \$9,520$.

Next, divide the annual interest by 365 to determine the per diem rate.

$\$9,520 \div 365 = \$26.08219$.

Multiply the per diem rate by the number of days for which Kohler is responsible for this expense—five days.

$\$26.08219 \times 5 = \$130.41$.

14.b) They will have to pay $322.77 in interest at closing. To find the annual interest amount, use the interest rate formula, Interest = Principal × Rate × Time, I = P × R × T. $168,301.50 × .10 × 1 year = $16,830.15. Divide that figure by 365 to determine the per diem rate. $16,830.15 ÷ 365 = $46.11. Finally, multiply the per diem rate by the number of days. $46.11 × 7 days = $322.77.

15.d) The building's annual net income is $44,850. Use the capitalization formula, Income = Rate × Value. .0975 × $460,000 = $44,850.

Chapter 18

California Real Estate License Law

 Outline

I. Administration
   A. Real Estate Commissioner
   B. Advisory Commission
   C. Attorney General
II. Real Estate Licenses
   A. When a license is required
   B. When a license is not required
   C. License qualifications
   D. License application and term
   E. Miscellaneous license provisions
   F. Special licenses
III. Disciplinary Action
   A. Disciplinary procedures
   B. Grounds for disciplinary action
   C. Real Estate Fund
IV. Trust Funds
   A. Definition of trust funds
   B. Handling trust funds
   C. Trust accounts
   D. Trust fund records
V. Documentation Requirements
   A. Copies given to signators
   B. Broker's review of documentation
   C. Broker/salesperson agreements

 Chapter Overview

*In California, the real estate profession is closely regulated by the state government. In part, this regulation takes the form of the **Real Estate Law**. This law was passed to protect the public from the abuses of unethical, dishonest, or incompetent real estate agents. Both real estate licensing requirements and the day-to-day responsibilities of real estate agents are set forth in the Real Estate Law. This chapter discusses the various requirements of the Real Estate Law and how the law is administered.*

Administration

The Real Estate Law is administered by the **Department of Real Estate**, a division of the California Business and Transportation Agency. The Real Estate Law is enforced by the chief officer of the Department of Real Estate, the **Real Estate Commissioner**.

Real Estate Commissioner

The Real Estate Commissioner's job is to implement and enforce the provisions of the Real Estate Law so as to give the maximum protection possible to those who deal with real estate licensees. The

Commissioner is given many broad powers to accomplish this end.

Authority. The Commissioner has the power to adopt, amend, or repeal regulations necessary to enforce the Real Estate Law. These regulations have the force and effect of law.

The Commissioner also has the authority to:

- investigate non-licensees alleged to be performing activities for which a license is required;
- screen and qualify applicants for a license;
- investigate complaints against licensees; and
- regulate some aspects of the sale of subdivisions, franchises, and real property securities.

Furthermore, the Commissioner may:

- hold formal hearings to determine issues involving a licensee, license applicant, or a subdivider and, after such a hearing, suspend, revoke, or deny a license or stop sales in a subdivision;
- bring actions for injunctions and claims for restitution on behalf of those injured by licensees who violate the Real Estate Law; and
- bring actions to stop trust fund violations.

Qualifications. The Real Estate Commissioner is appointed by the Governor and serves at his or her pleasure. To qualify for the position of Commissioner, a person must have been a real estate broker, actively engaged in business for five years in California, or must have related experience associated with real estate activity in California for five of the previous ten years. The Commissioner (as well as any of his or her employees) is prohibited from engaging in professional real estate activities, and from having an interest in any real estate firm.

Advisory Commission

The Commissioner is not without assistance. A **Real Estate Advisory Commission** meets with the Commissioner and offers suggestions on the policies and functions of the Real Estate Department.

The Advisory Commission is comprised of ten members—six real estate brokers and four public members—who are appointed by the Commissioner. The Commissioner must call at least four meetings of the Advisory Commission per year. The Commissioner must also solicit the opinions of all real estate licensees and the public at these Commission meetings.

Attorney General

The Real Estate Commissioner is advised on legal matters by the state Attorney General. However, it is the duty of the district attorney of each county to prosecute those who violate the Real Estate Law within that county.

Real Estate Licenses

A common way of regulating an industry or profession is to require its members to be licensed. The state can try to control a licensed person's competence and professional activities by requiring education, testing, and recordkeeping, and by enforcing ethical codes.

When a License is Required

The Real Estate Law requires certain people to be licensed before they can engage in real estate activities: anyone who is acting, advertising, or assuming to act as a real estate broker or real estate salesperson must have a real estate license.

Definition of Real Estate Broker. A real estate broker is a person who does or negotiates to do certain acts on behalf of another, for compensation or in the expectation of compensation. These acts include:

1. selling, buying, leasing, collecting rents from, and buying, selling, or exchanging leases on

real property or business opportunities. (**Exception:** a resident apartment manager, who manages the apartment complex in which he or she lives);

2. filing applications for the purchase or lease of federal land;

3. soliciting borrowers or lenders, negotiating loans, performing services in connection with loans, or buying, selling, or exchanging obligations secured by real property;

4. listing, advertising, or offering real property or business opportunities for sale, lease, or exchange or financing;

5. engaging as a principal in the business of buying, selling, or exchanging eight or more real property securities (e.g., sales contracts or promissory notes) within one year; and

6. collecting an advance fee to promote the sale or lease of real property or business opportunities by advertising, listing with a broker's association, or otherwise.

Definition of Salesperson. A real estate salesperson is someone who is employed by a broker to do one or more of the acts listed above. It should be noted that a salesperson's license permits real estate activity only while in the employ of and under the control and supervision of a broker. A real estate salesperson cannot act directly for a principal in a real estate transaction. (Note: If a broker chooses to work for another broker instead of operating his or her own brokerage, that broker has the same rights and duties as a salesperson. This type of broker is referred to as an **associate broker**.)

Penalties for Unlicensed Activities. The penalty for doing any of the acts listed above without a real estate broker's or salesperson's license is a fine of up to $10,000 and/or six months' imprisonment for an individual, or a fine of up to $50,000 for a corporation.

Note that it is unlawful for a broker to employ or compensate any unlicensed person for performing a

Fig.18.1 Types of licensees

Broker

- Individual, corporation, or partnership
- Authorized to operate brokerage and represent clients

Affiliated Licensees

- Work with and represent broker
- Cannot represent principal directly

---

salesperson's acts. If a broker does so, he or she could be subject to disciplinary action and could be charged a fine of up to $10,000.

When a License is Not Required

There are several important exceptions to the licensing requirements. These exceptions are meant to exclude those who are acting on their own behalf, those who are regulated by another agency (such as licensed securities brokers), and those who are merely performing clerical functions. These exceptions include:

1. those acting on their own behalf with respect to their own property, or a corporate officer acting on behalf of the corporation with respect to corporate property;

2. a person acting under a duly recorded power of attorney from the owner of the property;

3. attorneys in the performance of their duties;

4. persons acting under court order (e.g., a receiver in bankruptcy or a trustee);

5. a trustee under a deed of trust;

6. an appraiser making an appraisal;

7. with respect to real property securities transactions:

a. employees of banks, savings and loan associations, insurance companies, or credit unions;

b. licensed personal property brokers (e.g., finance companies);

8. with respect to business opportunity transactions, a licensed securities broker or dealer;

9. any cemetery authority that is authorized to do business in California, or its authorized agent;

10. persons performing clerical functions and not discussing the price, terms, or conditions of the property;

11. the manager of a hotel, motel, or trailer park; and

12. persons who negotiate for the use of property for photographic purposes.

License Qualifications

Several qualifications must be met before a person can obtain a real estate license. By imposing these qualifications, particularly the education requirements, the state tries to ensure the minimum competency of all real estate professionals.

Salesperson's Qualifications. To obtain a salesperson's license, an applicant must:

1. be at least eighteen years old;
2. be honest and truthful;
3. pass the qualifying exam;
4. apply on the prescribed form;
5. pay the license fee;
6. be fingerprinted;
7. complete nine semester units of education:
   a. one course, real estate principles, must be completed prior to taking the examination;
   b. two more courses must be completed either before the original license is issued, or within 18 months of licensure. These two courses must be chosen from the following: real estate practice, appraisal, accounting, legal aspects of real estate, real estate financing, real estate economics, property management, real

estate office management, escrow, or business law. (NOTE: If the required education is not completed within 18 months of licensure, the license is automatically suspended.)

Broker's Qualifications. To obtain a broker's license, an applicant must:

1. have two years' experience as a real estate licensee, or equivalent real estate experience;
2. be at least eighteen years old;
3. be honest and truthful;
4. pass the qualifying exam;
5. apply on the prescribed form;
6. pay the license fee;
7. be fingerprinted;
8. complete 24 semester units (eight courses) of education:
   a. the following five courses must be completed: real estate practice, appraisal, economics or accounting, legal aspects of real estate, and financing;
   b. the remaining three courses may be chosen from the following: advanced legal aspects of real estate, advanced appraisal, advanced financing, real estate principles, property management, escrow, or business law.

License Application and Term

License applicants must apply for their licenses within one year of passing the exam. Brokers' and salespersons' licenses must be renewed every four years.

License Renewals. Licenses are renewed by completing the continuing education requirements (discussed below), applying to the Department of Real Estate, and paying the appropriate fees. The licensee does not have to be reexamined. The renewal application must be postmarked prior to midnight of the expiration date to prevent the license from expiring. However, the renewal application may not be filed earlier than 60 days before the expiration date.

Late Renewal. A license that has expired within the previous two years may be renewed without examination, at the Commissioner's discretion. The licensee must file a renewal application at least 30 days prior to the expiration of the two-year grace period, and pay a late renewal fee. If the license is not renewed within the two-year grace period, all license rights are lost. This means that in order to be licensed again, the former licensee must meet all the requirements for original license applicants, including passing the qualifying exam.

Continuing Education. A real estate license cannot be renewed unless the licensee fulfills the continuing education requirement: 45 hours of approved courses within the four-year period preceding license renewal. A special form that confirms attendance must accompany the renewal application.

There are new requirements for continuing education, effective as of January 1, 1996. The first time that a licensee renews his or her license on or after January 1, 1996, he or she must have taken the following courses:

1. a three-hour course in ethics;
2. a three-hour course in agency;
3. a three-hour course in trust fund handling;
4. a three-hour course in fair housing; and
5. no less than 18 hours of courses designated as consumer protection courses.
6. The remaining hours are to consist of courses designated as consumer service courses (offerings generally related to business skills that enable the licensee to competently serve customers).

Fig.18.2 Summary of continuing education requirements

Type of License	CE Requirements for Renewal Dates		
	Initial Renewal on or after 1/1/96	Second Renewal on or after 1/1/96	All Subsequent Renewals
All licensees (brokers and salespersons) except as provided below	45 hours, including agency, ethics, fair housing, and trust fund handling, plus at least 18 hours of consumer protection courses and up to 15 hours of consumer service courses	45 total hours, including 18 hours of consumer protection courses and ...	45 total hours, including 18 hours of consumer protection courses and ....
Salespersons renewing for the first time	Agency, ethics, fair housing, and trust fund handling courses	any two of the four mandated courses (agency, ethics, fair housing, and trust fund handling), or a four-hour survey course covering the four mandatory subjects	if two of the four mandated courses were taken for the previous renewal, the two courses not previously taken, or a four-hour survey course; or if the survey course was used in the previous renewal period, another survey course, or two of the four mandated courses
Note: Licenses that expire on December 31 of any year have a license renewal date of January 1 of the following year.			

The next time that the licensee renews his or her license, he or she must complete as part of the standard 45 hours of continuing education:

1. either a four-hour survey course covering the four mandatory subjects (ethics, agency, trust fund handling, and fair housing), or
2. separate three-hour courses in any two of the four mandatory subjects.

Then, for all subsequent renewals, the licensee must complete the following as part of the 45 hours:

1. either a four-hour survey course covering the four mandatory subjects (ethics, agency, trust fund handling, and fair housing), or
2. the two mandatory courses that were not taken for the previous renewal.

Example: When Martina Lopez was preparing to renew her license in 2000, she chose to take a three-hour course in agency and a three-hour course in fair housing. When she's preparing to renew her license again in 2004, she can choose to take the four-hour survey course, or a three-hour course in ethics and a three-hour course in trust fund handling.

Salesperson's Initial Renewal. There's an exception to the general continuing education requirements for a salesperson who is renewing his or her license for the first time. For this initial renewal, the salesperson is only required to complete four three-hour courses in ethics, agency, trust fund handling, and fair housing (instead of the 45 hours normally required).

Miscellaneous License Provisions

The Real Estate License Law has some miscellaneous provisions pertaining to licenses that all licensees should be aware of.

Location of Licenses. Brokers are required to keep the licenses of all the salespersons they employ. All real estate licenses (including the broker's) must remain in the broker's main office.

Transfer of Salesperson's License. If a salesperson is transferring employment, both the former employing broker and the new employing broker must notify the Commissioner of this fact in writing.

Cancellation of Broker's License. If a broker dies or has his or her license suspended or revoked, all of his or her salespersons' licenses are automatically canceled. The salesperson may then transfer his or her license to another broker. The license of a salesperson who quits or is discharged is also canceled, and the broker must notify the Commissioner immediately.

Discharge for Disciplinary Cause. If a salesperson is discharged for conduct that is grounds for disciplinary action, the employing broker must file a certified written statement of facts with the Commissioner. If the employing broker fails to file the certified written statement, his or her own license could be suspended or revoked.

Change of Name or Address. When a broker changes his or her office name or address, the broker must forward written notice to the Department within one business day. When the license change occurs, the certificate can be corrected by the licensee. To cancel or add a branch office, the broker must file a special form. Each branch office requires a separate license.

Change of Status. A broker who wishes to change his or her status and work as a salesperson may relinquish his or her broker's license and apply for a salesperson's license, which is issued without examination.

Fictitious Names. A real estate broker may obtain a license under his or her fictitious business name, unless the name:

1. is misleading or would constitute false advertising;
2. implies a partnership or corporation that does not exist;
3. includes the name of a real estate salesperson;
4. violates provisions of the law; or
5. is the name formerly used by a licensee whose license has since been revoked.

Special Licenses

Special real estate licenses are available for particular kinds of license applicants or in special circumstances.

Corporate Licenses. A real estate license can be issued to a corporation. At least one corporate officer must be designated to act as the broker under the corporate brokerage license. That officer must also be individually licensed as a broker, and can only act as a broker with respect to the corporate brokerage.

Partnerships. While there is no "partnership license," a partnership may perform acts for which a broker's license is required, provided that every partner through whom the partnership acts is a licensed real estate broker.

Restricted Licenses. The Commissioner will sometimes issue a restricted license to replace a license that has been suspended or revoked. The restricted license is, in effect, a probationary license, and it may have a limited term, restrict the licensee to certain types of activities, require employment by a particular broker or the filing of a surety bond, or impose other limitations.

Mineral, Oil, and Gas Licenses. Brokers are no longer required to have a special mineral, oil, and gas license or permit. Only a real estate license is required for transactions involving mineral, oil, or gas rights.

Real Property Securities Dealers. A real property securities dealer is a person engaged in the business of selling or reinvesting funds in real property securities. A real property securities dealer must have a broker's license and a special permit from the Department of Real Estate.

Disciplinary Action

Any law designed to regulate an industry will fail if its provisions are ignored by those who are supposed to be regulated. So the Real Estate Commissioner is empowered to enforce the Real Estate Law by investigating and disciplining licensees who violate its provisions.

Disciplinary Procedures

The Commissioner is required to investigate the actions of a licensee when someone makes a written complaint. The Commissioner may also investigate a licensee on his or her own motion, even when no formal complaint has been made. The investigation usually consists of getting statements from witnesses and the licensee; checking bank records, title company records, and public records; and perhaps calling an informal meeting of all concerned.

If it appears that a violation of the law has occurred, an **accusation** is filed. An accusation is a written statement of the charges against the accused licensee. The accusation must be filed within three years of the allegedly unlawful act, unless the act involved fraud, misrepresentation, or a false promise. In that case, an accusation must be filed within one year after discovery by the injured party or within three years after the act (whichever is later), but in no case can it be filed more than ten years after the act.

The licensee is served with the accusation. A date is set for an **administrative hearing**; an administrative law judge will hear the case. The accused licensee is also given an explanation of his or her rights at the hearing.

The licensee may appear at the hearing with or without an attorney. Testimony is taken under oath, and a record is made of the proceedings. The administrative judge then makes a proposed decision based on his or her findings. The Commissioner may accept or reject the proposed decision in making his or her own formal decision. If the evidence at the hearing substantiates the charges against the licensee, his or her license will be suspended or revoked, and he or she may not apply for reinstatement for one year. The licensee may petition for reconsideration, and has the right to appeal the formal decision to superior court.

If it is in the public interest, the Commissioner may impose a fine rather than suspend or revoke a license. The amount of the monetary penalty cannot exceed $250 for each day the license would have been suspended, up to $10,000.

If a person obtains a license through fraud, misrepresentation, deceit, or material misstatements of fact, the license can be suspended without a hearing. This power of the Commissioner expires 90 days after the license is issued, and the suspension is only effective until a hearing is held and the Commissioner makes a formal decision.

Grounds for Disciplinary Action

The grounds for suspending, revoking, or denying a license are set forth in the Real Estate Law; the main list can be found in Sections 10176 and 10177 of the Business and Professions Code. While the licensing and license renewal requirements discussed in the first part of this chapter attempt to ensure the licensee's minimum competence, it is this list of acts or omissions that sets the standard for the licensee's day-to-day behavior.

The grounds for disciplinary action include the following:

1. Making a substantial misrepresentation—deliberately or negligently making a false statement of fact, or failing to disclose a material fact to a principal.

2. Making a false promise that is likely to persuade someone to do or refrain from doing something.

3. Embarking on a continued and flagrant course of misrepresentation or false promises.

4. Acting as a dual agent without the knowledge or consent of all the parties involved.

5. Commingling your own money or property with money or property you received or are holding on behalf of a client or customer (trust funds).

6. Failing to put a definite termination date in an exclusive listing agreement.

7. Making an undisclosed amount of compensation on a transaction (a secret profit).

8. If you have a listing agreement that includes an option to purchase the listed property, exercising the option without revealing to the principal in writing the amount of profit to be made and obtaining the principal's written consent.

9. Acting in any way, whether specifically prohibited by statute or not, that constitutes fraud or dishonest dealing.

10. Getting a purchaser's written agreement to buy property and to pay a commission, without first obtaining the written authorization of the property owner (a listing agreement).

11. Acquiring or renewing a license by fraud, misrepresentation, or deceit.

12. Being convicted of a felony or a misdemeanor involving moral turpitude.

13. False advertising.

14. Willfully using the term "Realtor" or any trade name of a real estate organization that you are not actually a member of.

15. Having a real estate license denied, revoked, or suspended in another state for actions that would be grounds for denial, revocation, or suspension in California.

16. Performing license activities negligently or incompetently.

17. As a broker, failing to exercise reasonable supervision over the activities of your salespersons.

18. Using government employment to gain access to private records, and improperly disclosing their confidential contents.

19. Violating the terms of a restricted license.

20. Using "blockbusting" tactics: soliciting business on the basis of statements regarding race, color, religion, sex, handicap, marital status, ancestry, or national origin.

21. Violating the Corporations Code or the Franchise Investment Law.

22. When selling property in which you have a direct or indirect ownership interest, failing to disclose the nature and extent of that interest to a buyer.

23. Having a final judgment entered against you in a civil suit for fraud, misrepresentation, or deceit in regard to a real estate transaction.

24. As a broker, failing to notify the Commissioner in writing of the discharge of any salesperson based on his or her violation of the license law or regulations.

25. Committing fraud in an application for the registration of a mobile home, failing to provide for the delivery of a properly endorsed certificate of ownership of a mobile home from the seller to the buyer, or participating in the sale or disposal of a stolen mobile home.

26. Failing to include a licensee designation and your employing broker's name in advertisements (placing "blind ads").

27. As a broker, failing to notify the buyer and the seller in writing of the property's selling price within one month after the sale closes, unless escrow issues a closing statement.

28. Employing or compensating an unlicensed person for any act that requires a license.

29. Failing to give a copy of any contract to the person signing it at the time of signing.

30. Accepting compensation for referring a customer to any of the following types of companies: escrow, pest control, home warranty, or title insurer.

31. Discriminating against the physically handicapped.

Ethical Standards

The Real Estate Commissioner has also adopted a **code of ethics,** to protect the public and to enhance the professionalism of the real estate industry. A code of ethics is a system of moral principles and rules that set standards of conduct for the members of a profession in their dealings with the public, clients, and other members of the profession.

Some of the Commissioner's ethical standards are mandatory: violating these standards is considered a violation of the license law and can be grounds for disciplinary action. Other standards (those in the "suggested conduct" section) are encouraged but not required; they are not grounds for disciplinary action.

The code of ethics, found in Section 2785 of the Commissioner's Regulations, is reprinted here in full.

California Code of Ethics and Professional Conduct

Unlawful Conduct

A. Unlawful Conduct in Sale, Lease and Exchange Transactions. Licensees when performing acts within the meaning of Section 10131(a) of the Business and Professions Code shall not engage in conduct which would subject the licensee to adverse action, penalty or discipline under Sections 10176 and 10177 of the Business and Professions Code including, but not limited to, the following acts and omissions:

1. Knowingly making a substantial misrepresentation of the likely value of real property to:

   a) Its owner either for the purpose of securing a listing or for the purpose of acquiring an interest in the property for the licensee's own account.

   b) A prospective buyer for the purpose of inducing the buyer to make an offer to purchase the real property.

2. Representing to an owner of real property when seeking a listing that the licensee has obtained a bona fide written offer to purchase the property, unless at the time of the representation the licensee has possession of a bona fide written offer to purchase.

3. Stating or implying to an owner of real property during listing negotiations that the licensee is precluded by law, by regulation, or by the rules of any organization, other than the broker firm seeking the listing, from charging less than the commission or fee quoted to the owner by the licensee.

4. Knowingly making substantial misrepresentations regarding the licensee's relationship with an individual broker, corporate broker, or franchised brokerage company or that entity's/person's responsibility for the licensee's activities.

5. Knowingly underestimating the probable closing costs in a communication to the prospective buyer or seller of real property in order to induce that person to make or to accept an offer to purchase the property.

6. Knowingly making a false or misleading representation to the seller of real property as to the form, amount and/or treatment of a deposit toward the purchase of the property made by an offeror.

7. Knowingly making a false or misleading representation to a seller of real property, who has agreed to finance all or part of a purchase price by carrying back a loan, about a buyer's ability to repay the loan in accordance with its terms and conditions.

8. Making an addition to or modification of the terms of an instrument previously signed or initialed by a party to a transaction without the knowledge and consent of the party.

9. A representation made as a principal or agent to a prospective purchaser of a promissory note secured by real property about the market value of the securing property without a reasonable basis for believing the truth and accuracy of the representation.

10. Knowingly making a false or misleading representation or representing, without a reasonable basis for believing its truth, the nature and/or condition of the interior or

exterior features of a property when soliciting an offer.

11. Knowingly making a false or misleading representation or representing, without a reasonable basis for believing its truth, the size of a parcel, square footage of improvements or the location of the boundary lines of real property being offered for sale, lease or exchange.

12. Knowingly making a false or misleading representation or representing to a prospective buyer or lessee of real property, without a reasonable basis to believe its truth, that the property can be used for certain purposes with the intent of inducing the prospective buyer or lessee to acquire an interest in the real property.

13. When acting in the capacity of an agent in a transaction for the sale, lease or exchange of real property, failing to disclose to a prospective purchaser or lessee facts known to the licensee materially affecting the value or desirability of the property, when the licensee has reason to believe that such facts are not known to nor readily observable by a prospective purchaser or lessee.

14. Willfully failing, when acting as a listing agent, to present or cause to be presented to the owner of the property any written offer to purchase received prior to the closing of a sale, unless expressly instructed by the owner not to present such an offer, or unless the offer is patently frivolous.

15. When acting as the listing agent, presenting competing written offers to purchase real property to the owner in such a manner as to induce the owner to accept the offer which will provide the greatest compensation to the listing broker without regard to the benefits, advantages and/or disadvantages to the owner.

16. Failing to explain to the parties or prospective parties to a real estate transaction for whom the licensee is acting as an agent the meaning and probable significance of a contingency in an offer or contract that the licensee knows or reasonably believes may affect the vacating of the property by the seller or its occupancy by the buyer.

17. Failing to disclose to the seller of real property in a transaction in which the licensee is an agent for the seller the nature and extent of any direct or indirect interest that the licensee expects to acquire as a result of the sale. The prospective purchase of the property by a person related to the licensee by blood or marriage, purchase by an entity in which the licensee has an ownership interest, or purchase by any other person with whom the licensee occupies a special relationship where there is a reasonable probability that the licensee could be indirectly acquiring an interest in the property shall be disclosed to the seller.

18. Failing to disclose to the buyer of real property in a transaction in which the licensee is an agent for the buyer the nature and extent of a licensee's direct or indirect ownership interest in such real property. The direct or indirect ownership interest in the property by a person related to the licensee by blood or marriage, by an entity in which the licensee has an ownership interest, or by any other person with whom the licensee occupies a special relationship shall be disclosed to the buyer.

19. Failing to disclose to a principal for whom the licensee is acting as an agent any significant interest the licensee has in a particular entity when the licensee recommends the use of the services or products of such entity.

20. The refunding by a licensee, when acting as an agent for the seller, of all or part of an offer-

or's purchase money deposit in a real estate sales transaction after the seller has accepted the offer to purchase, unless the licensee has the express permission of the seller to make the refund.

B. Unlawful Conduct When Soliciting, Negotiating or Arranging a Loan Secured by Real Property or the Sale of a Promissory Note Secured by Real Property. Licensees when performing acts within the meaning of subdivision (d) or (e) of Section 10131 of the Business and Professions Code shall not violate any of the applicable provisions of subdivision (a), or act in a manner which would subject the licensee to adverse action, penalty or discipline under Sections 10176 and 10177 of the Business and Professions Code including, but not limited to, the following acts and omissions:

1. Knowingly misrepresenting to a prospective borrower of a loan to be secured by real property or to an assignor/endorser of a promissory note secured by real property that there is an existing lender willing to make the loan or that there is a purchaser for the note, for the purpose of inducing the borrower or assignor/endorser to utilize the services of the licensee.

2. (a) Knowingly making a false or misleading representation to a prospective lender or purchaser of a loan secured directly or collaterally by real property about a borrower's ability to repay the loan in accordance with its terms and conditions;

   (b) Failing to disclose to a prospective lender or note purchaser information about the prospective borrower's identity, occupation, employment, income and credit data as represented to the broker by the prospective borrower;

   (c) Failing to disclose information known to the broker relative to the ability of the borrower to meet his or her potential or existing contractual obligations under the note or contract including information known about the borrower's payment history on an existing note, whether the note is in default or the borrower in bankruptcy.

3. Knowingly underestimating the probable closing costs in a communication to a prospective borrower or lender of a loan to be secured by a lien on real property for the purpose of inducing the borrower or lender to enter into the loan transaction.

4. When soliciting a prospective lender to make a loan to be secured by real property, falsely representing or representing without a reasonable basis to believe its truth, the priority of the security, as a lien against the real property securing the loan, i.e., a first, second or third deed of trust.

5. Knowingly misrepresenting in any transaction that a specific service is free when the licensee knows or has a reasonable basis to know that it is covered by a fee to be charged as part of the transaction.

6. Knowingly making a false or misleading representation to a lender or assignee/endorsee of a lender of a loan secured directly or collaterally by a lien on real property about the amount and treatment of loan payments, including loan payoffs, and the failure to account to the lender or assignee/endorsee of a lender as to the disposition of such payments.

7. When acting as a licensee in a transaction for the purpose of obtaining a loan, and in receipt of an "advance fee" from the borrower for this purpose, the failure to account to the borrower for the disposition of the "advance fee."

8. Knowingly making a false or misleading representation about the terms and conditions of a loan to be secured by a lien on real

property when soliciting a borrower or negotiating the loan.

9. Knowingly making a false or misleading representation or representing, without a reasonable basis for believing its truth, when soliciting a lender or negotiating a loan to be secured by a lien on real property about the market value of the securing real property, the nature and/or condition of the interior or exterior features of the securing real property, its size or the square footage of any improvement on the securing real property.

Suggestions for Professional Conduct

A. Suggestions for Professional Conduct in Sale, Lease and Exchange Transactions. In order to maintain a high level of ethics and professionalism in their business practices, real estate licensees are encouraged to adhere to the following suggestions in conducting their business activities:

1. Aspire to give a high level of competent, ethical and quality service to buyers and sellers in real estate transactions.

2. Stay in close communication with clients or customers to ensure that questions are promptly answered and all significant events or problems in a transaction are conveyed in a timely manner.

3. Cooperate with the California Department of Real Estate's enforcement of, and report to that Department evident violations of, the Real Estate Law.

4. Use care in the preparation of any advertisement to present an accurate picture or message to the reader, viewer or listener.

5. Submit all written offers in a prompt and timely manner.

6. Keep oneself informed and current on factors affecting the real estate market in which the licensee operates as an agent.

7. Make a full, open and sincere effort to cooperate with other licensees, unless the principal has instructed the licensee to the contrary.

8. Attempt to settle disputes with other licensees through mediation or arbitration.

9. Advertise or claim to be an expert in an area of specialization in real estate brokerage activity, e.g., appraisal, property management, industrial siting, mortgage loan, etc., only if the licensee has had special training, preparation or experience in such area.

10. Strive to provide equal opportunity for quality housing and a high level of service to all persons regardless of race, color, sex, religion, ancestry, physical handicap, marital status or national origin.

11. Base opinions of value, whether for the purpose of advertising or promoting real estate brokerage business, upon documented objective data.

12. Make every attempt to comply with these Suggestions for Professional Conduct and the Code of Ethics of any organized real estate industry group of which the licensee is a member.

B. Suggestions for Professional Conduct When Negotiating or Arranging Loans Secured by Real Property or Sale of a Promissory Note Secured by Real Property. In order to maintain a high level of ethics and professionalism in their business practices when performing acts within the meaning of subdivisions (d) and (e) of Section 10131 and Sections 10131.1 and 10131.2 of the Business and Professions Code, real estate licensees are encouraged to adhere to the following suggestions, in addition to any applicable provisions of subdivision (A), in conducting their business activities:

1. Aspire to give a high level of competent, ethical and quality service to borrowers and lenders in loan transactions secured by real estate.

2. Stay in close communication with borrowers and lenders to ensure that reasonable questions are promptly answered and all significant events or problems in a loan transaction are conveyed in a timely manner.

3. Keep oneself informed and current on factors affecting the real estate loan market in which the licensee acts as an agent.

4. Advertise or claim to be an expert in an area of specialization in real estate mortgage loan transactions only if the licensee has had special training, preparation, or experience in such area.

5. Strive to provide equal opportunity for quality mortgage loan services and a high level of service to all borrowers or lenders regardless of race, color, sex, religion, ancestry, physical handicap, marital status or national origin.

6. Base opinions of value in a loan transaction, whether for the purpose of advertising or promoting real estate mortgage loan brokerage business, on documented objective data.

7. Respond to reasonable inquiries of a principal as to the status or extent of efforts to negotiate the sale of an existing loan.

8. Respond to reasonable inquiries of a borrower regarding the net proceeds available from a loan arranged by the licensee.

9. Make every attempt to comply with the standards of professional conduct and the code of ethics of any organized mortgage loan industry group of which the licensee is a member.

As you can see, there are many grounds for disciplinary action in California. These provisions are the state's attempt to prevent unscrupulous behavior by real estate licensees. However, suspending a real estate license after the fact does not help someone who lost money because of a licensee's unlawful actions. Of course, the injured party has a right to sue the licensee in a civil court, but what if the licensee has no money or other assets? In that case, a civil judgment would be worthless. Under those circumstances, the state has provided an additional means of redress, through the Real Estate Fund.

The Real Estate Fund

All license fees go to the State Treasury and are then credited to a fund called the **Real Estate Fund**. The money in the Real Estate Fund is then disbursed to other accounts. For example, eight percent of the money is credited to an **Education and Research Account**, and is then used to advance real estate education and research projects. Twelve percent of the money in the Real Estate Fund is credited to the **Recovery Account**. The purpose of the Recovery Account is to reimburse those injured by real estate licensees.

When an injured party gets a civil judgment (or arbitration award) against a licensee based on the licensee's fraud, misrepresentation, deceit, or conversion of trust funds, he or she can apply to the Recovery Account for payment of the judgment. The injured party must be able to show that the licensee has no funds or assets that could be seized to pay the judgment.

The Recovery Account will pay up to $20,000 for any one transaction and up to $100,000 for any one licensee. Once a payment is made from the Recovery Account on behalf of a licensee, his or her license is automatically suspended as of the day of payment. The license cannot be reinstated until the amount disbursed from the Recovery Account is fully repaid, with interest. Even bankruptcy does not release the licensee from this obligation.

Trust Funds

The most common cause of disciplinary action is the mishandling of trust funds. This is largely due to confusion as to what trust funds are and what is to be done with them. However, California law is very specific about how trust funds are to be handled, and it is imperative that all licensees be thoroughly acquainted with the rules and regulations governing trust funds.

Definition of Trust Funds

The first step toward properly handling trust funds is learning to recognize them. Simply stated, trust funds are money or other valuables in the possession of a licensee that belong to someone else. Trust funds can be cash, a check, a promissory note, or any other item of personal property. The licensee merely holds the money or property on behalf of another party (usually a client or customer) while a real estate transaction is in progress. Here is a more complete definition of trust funds:

> *Money or other things of value received by a broker or salesperson on behalf of a principal or any other person, and which are held for the benefit of others in the performance of any acts for which a real estate license is required.*

The most common example of trust funds is the good faith deposit that a buyer gives to the broker along with the buyer's offer to purchase real property. The broker holds the deposit "in trust" while the seller decides whether or not to accept the buyer's offer.

Other types of funds, such as real estate commissions, general operating funds, or rent from a broker's own real estate, are not trust funds because the broker is not holding them on behalf of someone else.

Handling Trust Funds

Because trust funds belong to someone else, licensees must manage them very carefully. Licensees violate not only the license law, but also their fiduciary duties as agents, if they fail to handle trust funds properly.

When a broker accepts trust funds from a client or customer, he or she must deposit them immediately into:

1. a neutral escrow account,
2. the hands of the principal, or
3. a trust account maintained by the broker in a bank or other recognized depository.

"Immediately" means no later than the next business day following the receipt of the funds.

If trust funds are given to a salesperson instead of directly to the broker, that salesperson must immediately deliver those funds to the broker, or, if so directed by the broker, to one of the three places listed above.

There is one exception to this rule. When a broker receives a deposit check from a buyer, the broker can hold the check uncashed before the buyer's offer is accepted, if:

1. the check is not negotiable by the licensee, or the buyer has given written instructions that the check is not to be deposited or cashed until the offer is accepted; and
2. the seller is informed (before or when the offer is presented) that the check is being held.

Once the offer is accepted, the broker can continue to hold the uncashed check only if he or she receives written authorization from the seller to do so.

Trust funds must stay in the trust account until their owner directs otherwise. While the owner of the trust funds is usually easy to identify, it should be noted that the ownership of trust funds may change as the real estate transaction progresses. For example, the ownership of an earnest money deposit varies depending on whether or not the buyer's offer has been accepted. Before acceptance, the funds belong to the buyer and must be handled according to his or her instructions. After accep-

Fig.18.3 Rules for handling trust funds

Handling Trust Funds

- Must be deposited no later than next business day following receipt

- Salesperson must deliver funds to broker or deposit in trust account

- Check for good faith deposit can be held uncashed before buyer's acceptance under certain circumstances

- Broker must not commingle his or her own funds with trust funds

---

tance, however, ownership is not so clear-cut, and the funds must be handled as follows:

- A check held uncashed by the broker before acceptance of the offer may continue to be held uncashed only on written authorization from the seller.
- The check may be given to the seller only if both parties so provide in writing.
- No part of the deposit money can be refunded without the express written permission of the seller.

Trust Accounts

The primary reason for maintaining a separate account for trust funds is to avoid **commingling**. Commingling means mixing trust funds with personal funds. A broker must never put trust funds into his or her general account. Likewise, the broker must never put his or her own funds into a trust account. This is true even if careful records are kept of the deposits and withdrawals.

The prohibition against commingling makes it more difficult for a broker to "borrow" trust funds.

It also protects trust funds from any legal action that might be taken against the broker.

> **Example:** Suppose a broker dies, or is sued by a client. The broker's general account could very well be frozen during the course of the probate or lawsuit. If trust funds were kept in the broker's general account, they would be unavailable to the client until the probate was completed or the lawsuit concluded.

Shortages or Overages. The total amount of funds in the trust account must always equal the broker's aggregate trust fund liability. In other words, the total trust fund balance must equal all the balances due to individual clients and customers.

If the trust account balance is less than the total liability, a **trust fund shortage** results. Such a shortage is a violation of the Real Estate Commissioner's regulations. If the trust account balance is greater than the total liability, there is a **trust fund overage**, which is also a violation of the regulations, since non-trust funds cannot be commingled with trust funds.

Brokers should always make sure that a check deposited into the trust account clears before disbursing any funds against the check. If funds are disbursed and the check has not cleared, or the check bounces, a trust fund shortage will occur.

Exceptions to Commingling Rule. There are two exceptions to the rule against commingling.

1. The broker must pay the service charges on the trust account out of his or her general funds. The broker can have up to $100 of personal funds in a trust account for this purpose. However, it is better to have the bank deduct the trust account service fees directly from the broker's general account.
2. Sometimes a broker is entitled to deduct his or her commission from trust funds. In this case, the broker should promptly transfer the commission out of the trust account into his or her

general account. However, if it is not practical to transfer the commission immediately, it can stay in the trust account for up to 30 days.

The broker should never pay personal obligations out of the trust account, even if the payments are a draw against the broker's commission. The earned commission must be transferred to the broker's general account before it can be used to pay personal obligations.

Account Requirements. The trust account must be set up with the broker as the trustee, and the financial institution cannot require prior written notice before allowing withdrawals from the account. The trust account cannot be an interest-bearing account, with one exception: at the request of the trust fund owner, the broker can deposit the trust funds into a separate interest-bearing trust account, as long as the broker discloses how the interest is calculated, who pays the service charges, and how the interest is to be paid. The broker may not receive any of the interest.

Withdrawals. Withdrawals from a trust account can only be made with the signature of the broker or an authorized person. The broker may authorize any of the following to withdraw trust funds:

1. a salesperson or associate broker employed by the broker;
2. the designated corporate officer of a corporation licensed as a broker; and
3. any unlicensed employee, provided that he or she is covered by a fiduciary bond equal to the total amount held in trust.

While the broker can authorize other people to withdraw trust funds, he or she cannot delegate responsibility for the funds. The broker is always accountable for any trust fund violation, even if the violation was caused by the negligence or irresponsibility of an employee.

Trust Fund Records

It is very important to keep proper records of all trust funds, including trust fund checks that are held uncashed, trust funds that are sent to escrow, and trust funds that have been released to the owner. Thorough trust fund records enable the broker to prepare accurate accountings for clients, to calculate the amounts owed to clients at any given time, and to see if there is an imbalance in the trust account.

A broker can use one of two types of accounting systems to keep track of trust funds: a simple columnar system or a system that complies with general accounting practices. Regardless of which method is used, the accounting system must show the following:

1. all trust fund receipts and disbursements with pertinent details in chronological order;
2. the balance of each trust account based on all recorded transactions;
3. all receipts and disbursements affecting each client or customer's account in chronological order; and
4. the balance owing to each beneficiary based on recorded transactions.

Columnar System. If a broker chooses to use the columnar recordkeeping system, there are three types of records he or she must keep:

1. **A record of all trust funds received and disbursed.** This record is used to list all trust funds deposited to and disbursed from the trust account. It must include the following information:
   a. the date the funds were received;
   b. from whom they were received;
   c. the amount received;
   d. the date of deposit;
   e. the amount paid out;
   f. the check number and date; and
   g. the daily balance of the bank account.

2. **A record for each client/customer or transaction.** This record lists the funds received from or for each client or customer, and must include the following information:

   a. the date of the deposit;
   b. the amount of the deposit;
   c. the name of the payee or the payor;
   d. the check number, date, and amount; and
   e. the daily balance of the individual account.

3. **A record of trust funds received but not deposited to the trust account.** This record must show:

   a. the date the funds were received;
   b. the form of the payment;
   c. the amount received;
   d. the description of any property received in lieu of funds;
   e. where the funds were forwarded to; and
   f. the date of disposition.

General Accounting Practices System. If a broker uses a system that complies with generally accepted accounting practices, that system must include a journal, a cash ledger, and beneficiary records for each trust account.

1. **Journals.** These are daily chronological records of trust fund receipts and disbursements that show:

   a. all trust fund transactions in chronological order;
   b. enough information to identify the transaction (e.g., date, amount received, name of payee, etc.); and
   c. the total receipts and total disbursements at least once a month.

2. **Cash ledger.** This shows, usually in summary form, the increases and decreases in the trust account and the resulting account balance.

3. **Beneficiary ledger.** A beneficiary ledger must be maintained for each client or customer or for each transaction or series of transactions. It shows, in chronological order, the details of all receipts and disbursements relating to that individual's account, and the resulting account balance.

All trust fund records are subject to inspection by the Commissioner. The broker must keep copies of all the trust records (including canceled checks) for each transaction for three years. The three-year period begins on the date the transaction closes, or on the date of the listing if the transaction does not close.

Documentation Requirements

In addition to trust fund records, the Department of Real Estate also requires brokers to keep all the documents connected with a real estate transaction. These documents include:

- listings;
- purchase and sale agreements;
- rent collection receipts;
- bank deposit slips;
- canceled checks;
- supporting papers for checks, such as invoices, escrow statements, or receipts;
- agency disclosure statements;
- transfer disclosure statements; and
- property management agreements.

These documents must be kept for at least three years and must be available for inspection by the Commissioner. If there is sufficient cause, these records may be audited.

A broker must keep mortgage loan disclosure statements (discussed in Chapter 9) and real property security statements for four years.

Copies Given to Signators

Whenever a broker or salesperson prepares a document for signature, he or she must deliver a copy of the document to the person signing it when the signature is obtained. These documents include listing agreements, purchase and sale agreements, contract addendums, and property management agreements.

Broker's Review of Documentation

Brokers are responsible for supervising their salespersons, and failure to do so is grounds for disciplinary action. These supervisory duties are very specific in the area of documentation. Whenever a salesperson prepares or signs any document in connection with a real estate transaction, the broker must review, initial, and date the document within five working days, or before the close of escrow, whichever occurs first.

It is possible for a broker to delegate this specific supervisory responsibility, in writing, to:

1. any licensed broker, or
2. any salesperson in the broker's employ who has two years of full-time experience as a salesperson during the preceding five-year period.

Broker-Salesperson Agreements

Whenever a broker hires a real estate salesperson, there must be a written agreement that documents their relationship. The broker must keep the agreement on file at the broker's office, and then retain the agreement for at least three years after the relationship is terminated.

Chapter Summary

1. The California Real Estate Law requires those engaging in real estate activities to be licensed, and then regulates the actions of those licensees. The purpose of the Real Estate Law is to protect members of the public who deal with real estate agents.

2. The Real Estate Commissioner enforces the provisions of the Real Estate Law by enacting regulations, investigating the activities of licensees, and taking disciplinary action against those who violate the Real Estate Law. The Commissioner is advised by the Real Estate Advisory Commission and the state Attorney General.

3. The Real Estate Law determines who is required to have a real estate license and sets forth the licensing requirements for brokers and salespersons.

4. The Real Estate Law and related regulations also specify the grounds for disciplinary action and set forth recommended standards of professional behavior. Licensees should become very familiar with these standards, both those that are mandatory and those that are suggested.

5. It is essential for a licensee to know the rules concerning trust funds. Trust funds generally must be deposited into a trust account or a neutral escrow, or delivered to the principal, within one business day after they are received.

6. Brokers are required to keep trust account and transaction records for at least three years.

Key Terms

Real Estate Law—A California statute that governs the licensing and business practices of real estate agents.

Department of Real Estate—The government agency that administers the Real Estate Law.

Real estate broker—A person who is licensed to represent others for compensation in real estate transactions.

Real estate salesperson—A person who is licensed to work for and represent a broker in real estate transactions.

Real Estate Fund—A special account into which all license fees are placed.

Recovery Account—An account funded by license fees, used to reimburse those injured by the unlawful acts of real estate licensees.

Trust funds—Funds held by a broker on behalf of clients or customers.

Commingling—The mingling of trust funds with a broker's personal or business funds.

Trust account—A bank account held in a broker's name and specially designated for trust funds; it is used to keep trust funds segregated from the broker's personal or business funds.

Quiz: Chapter 18
California Real Estate
License Law

1. Someone applying to renew his or her real estate license usually must have completed _____ hours of approved courses within the four-year period preceding license renewal.

   a) 15
   b) 20
   c) 45
   d) 90

2. A corporation may engage in the real estate brokerage business if the officer acting for the corporation:

   a) is a licensed salesperson
   b) is given the proper authority from the Corporations Commissioner
   c) is a licensed broker
   d) is the president of the corporation

3. Commingling is:

   a) the same as embezzlement
   b) mixing personal funds with trust funds
   c) any dishonest behavior related to trust funds
   d) paying a commission to a non-licensed person

4. Brokers must retain copies of all listings, purchase and sale agreements, and trust records for:

   a) one year
   b) two years
   c) three years
   d) four years

5. Withdrawals cannot be made from a broker's trust account by:

   a) a salesperson in the broker's employ who has been authorized by the broker
   b) the broker's secretary, who has been authorized by the broker and is covered by a fiduciary bond
   c) any corporate officer of a corporation licensed as a broker
   d) the unlicensed, unbonded spouse of a broker who has been authorized by the broker

6. The Recovery Account will pay a maximum of _____ per transaction.

   a) $20,000
   b) $40,000
   c) $100,000
   d) There is no limit

7. The California Real Estate Advisory Commission consists of:

   a) seven members
   b) ten members
   c) twelve members
   d) thirteen members

8. A broker's trust account records:

   a) can be kept by a columnar method
   b) must be kept in a safe deposit box at a financial institution in California
   c) can be kept by the principal
   d) should be discarded one year after the transaction closes

9. A broker may keep an earned commission in a trust account for no more than:

    a) one day
    b) seven days
    c) thirty days
    d) sixty days

10. It is legal for a broker to place a good faith deposit:

    a) in a trust account
    b) in a neutral escrow
    c) in the hands of the broker's principal
    d) Any of the above

11. The maximum amount of a broker's own funds allowed in his or her trust account is:

    a) none
    b) $50
    c) $100
    d) $250

12. The commission rate a listing broker can charge on a sale is determined by:

    a) the Real Estate Commissioner
    b) the seller and the broker
    c) the multiple listing service
    d) the buyer and the seller

13. A broker's license:

    a) must be carried by the broker at all times
    b) should be kept in a safe place, such as a home safe or a safe deposit box at a bank
    c) must be kept in the broker's main office
    d) is kept in the field office of the Department of Real Estate nearest the broker's main office

14. A salesperson's license is valid for:

    a) two years
    b) three years
    c) four years
    d) five years

15. The funds that support the Recovery Account come from:

    a) interest accruing on trust accounts
    b) a surcharge on fines from real estate criminal convictions
    c) private donations
    d) real estate license fees

16. Trust funds must be deposited into the broker's trust account:

    a) by the next business day following receipt of the funds
    b) within 30 days of receipt of the funds
    c) by the broker's certified public accountant
    d) within three days after the transaction closes

17. All applicants for a broker's license must have:

    a) three years' experience as a real estate licensee
    b) 24 semester units of real estate education
    c) a sponsoring broker willing to testify to the applicant's honesty
    d) All of the above

18. A resident apartment manager who manages the apartment complex he or she lives in:

    a) must have a real estate salesperson's license

    b) need not have a real estate license

    c) must be supervised by a real estate licensee

    d) must register with the Department of Real Estate

19. All of the following are grounds for disciplinary action except:

    a) commingling

    b) failing to put a termination date in an exclusive listing

    c) negotiating with a seller to establish the commission rate

    d) a broker failing to supervise his or her salesperson

20. Trust funds:

    a) are always money, never items of personal property

    b) may be put into the broker's general account, as long as scrupulous records are kept of the deposits and withdrawals

    c) can be given to the Real Estate Commissioner for deposit

    d) must never be deposited into the broker's general account

☑ Answer Key

1.c) License renewal applicants must have completed 45 hours of continuing education during the four years prior to renewal, except for salespersons renewing their licenses for the first time

2.c) Under a corporate license, any officer designated to represent the corporation must also be licensed as a broker.

3.b) Mixing personal funds with trust funds is called commingling.

4.c) Most records must be kept for three years.

5.d) Withdrawals may not be made without the signature of the broker or of an authorized licensee, corporate officer, or bonded employee.

6.a) The Recovery Account will pay up to $20,000 per transaction to satisfy an unpaid judgment against a licensee.

7.b) The Real Estate Advisory Commission consists of six brokers and four public members.

8.a) The broker's trust fund records can be kept by a columnar method.

9.c) Earned commissions should be withdrawn as soon as possible, but may remain in the trust account for up to thirty days if necessary.

10.d) A good faith deposit may be placed in a trust account or in a neutral escrow, or be given to the principal.

11.c) A broker may keep up to $100 in a trust account to cover service charges.

12.b) Commissions are negotiated between the broker and the client/seller.

13.c) A broker's license must be displayed at the broker's main office.

14.c) A salesperson's license must be renewed every four years.

15.d) Twelve percent of all real estate license fees go into the Recovery Account.

16.a) Trust funds must be deposited in a trust account by the next business day after receipt of the funds.

17.b) Broker applicants must complete 24 semester units (eight courses) of real estate education.

18.b) A resident apartment manager need not be licensed.

19.c) Brokers are free to negotiate their commissions with sellers. (In fact, it is grounds for disciplinary action to lead a seller to believe the rate of commission is set by regulation.)

20.d) Trust funds must never be deposited into the broker's general account. This would be commingling, which is grounds for disciplinary action.

Glossary

The definitions given here explain how the listed terms are used in the real estate field. Some of the terms have additional meanings, which can be found in a standard dictionary.

AAA Tenant—A nationally known tenant with the highest credit rating, whose name would lend prestige to the property.

Abandonment—Failure to occupy and use property, which may result in a loss of rights.

Abrogate—To repeal, annul, nullify, abolish, or otherwise bring to an end by official or formal action.

Absolute Fee—*See*: Fee Simple.

Abstract of Judgment—A document summarizing the essential provisions of a court judgment which, when recorded, creates a lien on the judgment debtor's real property.

Abstract of Title—*See*: Title, Abstract of.

Abut—To touch, border on, be adjacent to, or share a common boundary with.

Acceleration Clause—A provision in a promissory note or security instrument allowing the lender to declare the entire debt due immediately if the borrower breaches one or more provisions of the loan agreement. Also referred to as a call provision.

Acceptance—1. Agreeing to the terms of an offer to enter into a contract, thereby creating a binding contract. 2. Taking delivery of a deed from the grantor.

Acceptance, Qualified—*See*: Counteroffer.

Accession—The acquisition of title to additional property by its annexation to real estate already owned. This can be the result of human actions (as in the case of fixtures) or natural processes (such as accretion and reliction).

Accord and Satisfaction—An agreement to accept something different than (and usually less than) what the contract originally called for.

Accretion—A gradual addition to dry land by the forces of nature, as when waterborne sediment is deposited on waterfront property.

Accrued Items of Expense—Expenses that have been incurred but are not yet due or payable; in a settlement statement, the seller's accrued expenses are credited to the buyer.

Acknowledgment—When a person who has signed a document formally declares to an authorized official (usually a notary public) that he or she signed voluntarily. The official can then attest that the signature is voluntary and genuine.

Acquisition Cost—The amount of money a buyer was required to expend in order to acquire title to a piece of property; in addition to the purchase price, this might include closing costs, legal fees, and other expenses.

Acre—An area of land equal to 43,560 square feet, or 4,840 square yards, or 160 square rods.

Actual Age—*See*: Age, Actual.

Actual Authority—*See*: Authority, Actual.

Actual Eviction—*See*: Eviction, Actual.

Actual Notice—*See*: Notice, Actual.

Adjacent—Nearby, next to, bordering, or neighboring; may or may not be in actual contact.

Adjustable-Rate Mortgage—*See*: Mortgage, Adjustable-Rate.

Administrative Agency—A government agency (federal, state, or local) that administers a complex area of law and policy, adopting and enforcing detailed regulations that have the force of law. For example, the California Department of Real Estate is the administrative agency charged with regulating the real estate profession.

Administrative Law Judge—An official appointed to decide cases in which an individual is in conflict with the rules and regulations of an administrative agency. For example, a disciplinary hearing against a real estate agent accused of violating the Real Estate Law would ordinarily be conducted by an administrative law judge.

Administrator—A person appointed by the probate court to manage and distribute the estate of a deceased person, when no executor is named in the will or there is no will.

Ad Valorem—A Latin phrase that means "according to value," used to refer to taxes that are assessed on the value of property.

Adverse Possession—Acquiring title to real property that belongs to someone else by taking possession of it without permission, in the manner and for the length of time prescribed by statute.

Affiant—One who makes an affidavit.

Affidavit—A sworn statement made before a notary public (or other official authorized to administer an oath) that has been written down and acknowledged.

Affirm—1. To confirm or ratify. 2. To make a solemn declaration that is not under oath.

After-Acquired Title—*See*: Title, After-Acquired.

Age, Actual—The age of a structure from a chronological standpoint (as opposed to its effective age); how many years it has actually been in existence.

Age, Effective—The age of a structure indicated by its condition and remaining usefulness (as opposed to its actual age). Good maintenance may increase a building's effective age, and poor maintenance may decrease it; for example, a 50-year-old home that has been well maintained might have an effective age of 15 years, meaning that its remaining usefulness is equivalent to that of a 15-year-old home.

Agency—A relationship of trust created when one person (the principal) grants another (the agent) authority to represent the principal in dealings with third parties.

Agency, Apparent—When third parties are given the impression that someone who has not been authorized to represent another is that person's agent, or else given the impression that an agent has been authorized to perform acts which are in fact beyond the scope of his or her authority. Also called ostensible agency.

Agency, Dual—When an agent represents both parties to a transaction, as when a broker represents both the buyer and the seller.

Agency, Exclusive—*See*: Listing, Exclusive.

Agency, Ostensible—*See*: Agency, Apparent.

Agency Confirmation Statement—A written statement that indicates which party a real estate agent is representing. It must be signed by both the buyer and the seller before they enter into a residential transaction.

Agency Disclosure Form—A form that explains the duties of a seller's agent, a buyer's agent, and a dual agent. It must be signed by both the buyer and the seller before they enter into a residential transaction.

Agency Law—The body of legal rules that govern the relationship between agent and principal, imposing fiduciary duties on the agent and also imposing liability for the agent's actions on the principal.

Agent—A person authorized to represent another (the principal) in dealings with third parties.

Agent, Closing—The person who handles the closing process on behalf of the parties to a real estate transaction. It may be an independent escrow agent, an employee of the lender or the title company, the real estate broker, or a lawyer.

Agent, Dual—*See*: Agency, Dual.

Agent, Escrow—A neutral third party who holds funds, documents, or other valuables on behalf of the parties to a transaction, releasing these items to the parties only when certain conditions in the escrow instructions have been fulfilled.

Agent, General—An agent authorized to handle all of the principal's affairs in one area or in specified areas.

Agent, Gratuitous—An agent who does not have a legal right to claim compensation for his or her services (such as a broker who does not have a written employment contract with the seller).

Agent, Listing—A broker who has a listing agreement with a seller, or a salesperson representing the listing broker. The listing agent may or may not turn out to also be the selling agent, the one who negotiates an acceptable offer from the buyer.

Agent, Selling—The real estate agent who writes and presents the offer to purchase that the seller accepts. The selling agent may or may not also be the listing agent, but is considered to be an agent of the seller unless otherwise agreed.

Agent, Special—An agent with limited authority to do a specific thing or conduct a specific transaction.

Agent, Universal—An agent authorized to do everything that can be lawfully delegated to a representative.

Agents in Production—The elements necessary to generate income and establish a value in real estate: labor, coordination, capital, and land.

Agreement—*See*: Contract.

Air Lot—A parcel of property above the surface of the earth, not containing any land; for example, a condominium unit on the third floor.

Air Rights—The right to undisturbed use and control of the airspace over a parcel of land; may be transferred separately from the land.

Alienation—The transfer of ownership or an interest in property from one person to another, by any means.

Alienation, Involuntary—Transfer of an interest in property against the will of the owner, or without action by the owner, occurring through operation of law, natural processes, or adverse possession.

Alienation, Voluntary—When an owner voluntarily transfers an interest to someone else.

Alienation Clause—A provision in a security instrument that gives the lender the right to declare the entire loan balance due immediately if the borrower sells or otherwise transfers the security property. Also called a due-on-sale clause.

All-Inclusive Trust Deed—*See*: Mortgage, Wraparound.

Allodial System—A system of individual ownership of land (as opposed to the feudal system, in which the sovereign owned all the land).

Alluvion—The solid material deposited along a riverbank or shore by accretion. Also called alluvium.

Alquist-Priolo Special Studies Zone Act—A California law that requires geologic reports when residences are built in certain areas of the state.

ALTA—American Land Title Association, a nationwide organization of title insurance companies. An extended coverage title policy is sometimes referred to as an ALTA policy.

Amendment—A supplementary agreement changing one or more terms of a contract, which must be signed by all of the parties to the original contract. Also called a contract modification.

Amenities—Features of a property that contribute to the pleasure or convenience of owning it, such as a fireplace, a beautiful view, or its proximity to a good school.

Amortization, Negative—The addition of unpaid interest to the principal balance of a loan, thereby increasing the amount owed.

Amortize—To gradually pay off a debt with installment payments that include both principal and interest. *See also*: Loan, Amortized.

Annexation—Attaching personal property to real property, so that it becomes part of the real property (a fixture) in the eyes of the law.

Annexation, Actual—The physical attachment of personal property to real property, so that it becomes part of the real property.

Annexation, Constructive—The association of personal property with real property in such a way that the law treats it as a fixture, even though it is not physically attached; for example, a house key is constructively annexed to the house.

Annual Percentage Rate (APR)—All of the charges that a borrower will pay for the loan (including the interest, loan fee, discount points, and mortgage insurance costs), expressed as an annual percentage of the loan amount.

Annuity—A sum of money received in a series of payments at regular intervals (often annually) over a period of time.

Anticipation, Principle of—An appraisal principle which holds that value is created by the expectation of benefits to be received in the future.

Anticipatory Repudiation—Action taken by one party to a contract to inform the other party, before the time set for performance, that he or she does not intend to fulfill the contract.

Anti-deficiency Rules—Laws that prohibit a secured lender from suing the borrower for a deficiency judgment in certain circumstances (for example, after nonjudicial foreclosure of a deed of trust).

Appeal—When one of the parties to a lawsuit asks a higher court to review the judgment or verdict reached in a lower court.

Appellant—The party who files an appeal because he or she is dissatisfied with the lower court's decision. Also called the petitioner.

Appellee—In an appeal, the party who did not file the appeal. Also called the respondent.

Apportionment—A division of property (as among tenants in common when the property is sold or partitioned) or liability (as when responsibility for closing costs is allocated between the buyer and seller) into proportionate, but not necessarily equal, parts.

Appraisal—An estimate or opinion of the value of a piece of property as of a particular date. Also called valuation.

Appraiser—One who estimates the value of property, especially an expert qualified to do so by training and experience.

Appreciation—An increase in value; the opposite of depreciation.

Appropriation—Taking property or reducing it to personal possession, to the exclusion of others.

Appropriation, Prior—A system of allocating water rights, under which a person who wants to use water from a certain lake or river is required to apply for a permit; a permit has priority over other permits that are issued later. *Compare*: Riparian Rights.

Appropriative Rights—The water rights of a person who holds a prior appropriation permit.

Appurtenances—Rights that go along with ownership of a particular piece of property, such as air rights or mineral rights; they are ordinarily transferred with the property, but may, in some cases, be sold separately.

Appurtenances, Intangible—Rights that go with ownership of a piece of property that do not involve physical objects or substances; for example, an access easement (as opposed to mineral rights).

Appurtenant Easement—*See*: Easement Appurtenant.

APR—*See*: Annual Percentage Rate.

Area—1. Locale or region. 2. The size of a surface, usually in square units of measure, such as square feet or square miles.

ARM—*See*: Mortgage, Adjustable-Rate.

Arm's Length Transaction—1. A transaction in which both parties are informed of the property's merits and shortcomings, neither is acting under unusual pressure, and the property has been exposed on the open market for a reasonable length of time. 2. A transaction in which there is no pre-existing family or business relationship between the parties.

Artificial Person—A legal entity, such as a corporation, that the law treats as an individual with legal rights and responsibilities; as distinguished from a natural person, a human being. Sometimes called a legal person.

Assemblage—Combining two or more adjoining properties into one tract.

Assessment—The valuation of property for purposes of taxation.

Assessor—An official who determines the value of property for taxation.

Asset—Anything of value that a person owns.

Assets, Capital—Assets held by a taxpayer other than: (1) property held for sale to customers; and (2) depreciable property or real property used in the taxpayer's trade or business. Thus, real property is a capital asset if it is used for personal use or for profit.

Assets, Liquid—Cash and other assets that can be readily turned into cash (liquidated), such as stock.

Assets, Section 1231—Properties used in a trade or business or held for the production of income (a reference to Section 1231 in the federal income tax code).

Assign—To transfer rights (especially contract rights) or interests to another.

Assignee—One to whom rights or interests have been assigned.

Assignment—1. A transfer of contract rights from one person to another. 2. In the case of a lease, the transfer by the original tenant of his or her entire leasehold estate to another. *Compare*: Sublease.

Assignment of Contract and Deed—The instrument used to substitute a new vendor for the original vendor in a land contract.

Assignor—One who has assigned his or her rights or interest to another.

Assumption—Action by a buyer to take on personal liability for paying off the seller's existing mortgage or deed of trust.

Assumption Fee—A fee paid to the lender, usually by the buyer, when a mortgage or deed of trust is assumed.

Attachment—Court-ordered seizure of property belonging to a defendant in a lawsuit, so that it will be available to satisfy a judgment if the plaintiff wins. In the case of real property, attachment creates a lien.

Attachments, Man-Made—*See*: Fixture.

Attachments, Natural—Plants growing on a piece of land, such as trees, shrubs, or crops. *See*: Emblements; Fructus Industriales; Fructus Naturales.

Attestation—The act of witnessing the execution of an instrument, such as a deed or will.

Attorney in Fact—Any person authorized to represent another by a power of attorney; not necessarily a lawyer (an attorney at law).

Auditing—Verification and examination of records, particularly the financial accounts of a business or other organization.

Authority, Actual—Authority actually given to an agent by the principal, either expressly or by implication.

Authority, Apparent—Authority to represent another that someone appears to have and that the principal is estopped from denying, although no actual authority has been granted.

Authority, Express—Actual authority that the principal has expressly given to his or her agent, either orally or in writing.

Authority, Implied—An agent's authority to do everything reasonably necessary to carry out the principal's express orders.

Avulsion—1. A sudden (not gradual) tearing away of land by the action of water. 2. A sudden shift in a watercourse.

Bad Debt/Vacancy Factor—A percentage deducted from a property's potential gross income to determine the effective gross income, estimating the income that will probably be lost because of vacancies and tenants who don't pay.

Balance, Principle of—An appraisal principle which holds that the maximum value of real estate is achieved when the agents in production (labor, coordination, capital, and land) are in proper balance with each other.

Balance Sheet—*See*: Financial Statement.